W9-BZP-895

Footprint

Argentina

The travel guide

Handbook

Charlie Nurse

'There are many Argentinas and they all exist within the idea of the richness of the land.'

VS Naipaul, *The Return of Eva Perón*

Argentina Handbook
Second edition
© Footprint Handbooks Ltd 2000

Published by Footprint Handbooks
6 Riverside Court
Lower Bristol Road
Bath BA2 3DZ. England
T +44 (0)1225 469141
F +44 (0)1225 469461
Email discover@footprintbooks.com
Web www.footprintbooks.com

ISBN 1 900949 67 9
CIP DATA: A catalogue record for this
book is available from the British Library

In USA, published by
NTC/Contemporary Publishing Group
4255 West Touhy Avenue, Lincolnwood
(Chicago), Illinois 60712-1975, USA
T 847 679 5500 F 847 679 2494
Email NTCPUB2@AOL.COM

ISBN 0-658-01082-4
Library of Congress Catalog Card
Number 00-132903

Credits

Series editors
Patrick Dawson and Rachel Fielding

Editorial
Editor: Stephanie Lambe
Maps: Sarah Sorensen

Production
Typesetting: Richard Ponsford, Leona
Bailey and Alasdair Dawson
Maps: Robert Lunn, Claire Benison and
Angus Dawson and Maxine Foster
Colour maps: Kevin Feeney
Cover: Camilla Ford

Design
Mytton Williams

Photography and drawings
Front cover: Axiom
Back cover: Impact Photos
Inside colour section: Travel Ink, Eye
Ubiquitous, Impact Photos, gettyone
Stone, John Wright, Robert Harding and
South American Pictures
Illustrations: Gustavo R Carrizo and
Claire Benison

Print
Manufactured in Italy by LEGOPRINT

Every effort has been made to ensure
that the facts in this Handbook are
accurate. However, travellers should still
obtain advice from consulates, airlines
etc about current travel and visa
requirements before travelling. The
authors and publishers cannot accept
responsibility for any loss, injury or
inconvenience however caused.

Argentina

Contents

Left: the bright lights of Buenos Aires, De Julio by night.

Right: let's dance, put on your red dress... dancing the tango in a café in Buenos Aires.

A foot in the door

6

Next page: nice and icy, glacial waters in the fore of the Perito Moreno Glacier, Patagonia.
Right: trekker taking in the peaks of Fitzroy and Cerro Poincenot at Laguna de los Tres.
Below: contact on planet earth, green machines on Florida Street, Buenos Aires

Above: get on your hoss and herd some sheep on the vast open plains, the pampas.
Right: unable to make up their minds on a colour scheme, the residents of La Boca decided not to.

Highlights

Argentina is geared up to thrill – from nights tangoing in the chic quarter of Buenos Aires to gaucho riding in the grasslands of the Pampas. It is also a merry-go-round of incongruity: traditional cream teas in the Welsh community of the Chubut valley, the birthplace of the Marxist revolutionary Che Guevara, stomping ground of Maradona, source of Evita worship, museums of meteorites, huge numbers of dinosaur fossils, celebrity spotting on the ski slopes of Bariloche, and home to the most southerly city in the world.

City slicking

Dynamic and bustling, a city which seems never to sleep, Buenos Aires is one of the most exciting cities in Latin America. Tango was born here, restaurants serve an all manner of world cuisine, bars play the latest music, cafés spill on to the streets and nightclubs allow dancing throughout the night. Cultural capital of a society which traces its roots to European immigration, it is famous throughout South America for its theatres, museums and galleries. Gucci, Armani, Prada, to name a few, line the boulevards catering for the fashion conscious *porteños*, their offerings as stylish as anything found in the cities in Europe or North America.

Grasslands & gauchos

West of the throbbing capital is another Argentina, the pampas, a great open plain home to cattle and sheep farmed on the vast *estancias* (ranches). Some of the most popular images of Argentina are drawn from these plains: the galloping gaucho on horseback, poncho on shoulders and cowboy hat on head; the drinking of yerba maté, the bitter herbal tea drunk from a gourd through a metal straw, a ritual dating back to the precolumbian Indian days; and the *asado*, an event loosely translated as a barbeque, where an outstanding amount of all varieties of meat are consumed. Although estancias are usually seen as typical of the pampas, they can be found throughout rural Argentina.

On a high

Far west of Buenos Aires lie the Andes separating Argentina from Chile. The Andean provinces offer some of the most spectacular and varied scenery in the country, ranging from the high plateaus and steep and isolated valleys of the northwest to the lakes and forests of the Lake District and the glaciers of the far south. Some of these regions are popular with travellers and offer as wide a range of adventure activities as anywhere else in South America; others are little visited and provide great opportunities for those who prefer not to share their wilderness with others. Popular attractions include the unforgettable *Tren a las Nubes* (Train to the Clouds) from Salta up the gorge of the Río Toro to San Antonio de las Cobres and, much further south, the Parque Nacional los Glaciares (see below).

Desert delight

Away from the rich agricultural land of the pampas, much of Argentina is covered by deserts: these range from the burnt landscapes of the Chaco, and the classic cacti-strewn expanses of the west and northwest to the great steppes which cover most of Patagonia, where high winds, low rainfall and low temperatures have combined to deter human settlement. For the traveller all of these have their interest: parts of the Chaco are one of the best bird habitats in Argentina; oasis towns such as Cafayate in the northwest are famous for their wines, olives and other products; the vast wastes of Patagonia attract travellers perhaps as much for their remoteness as for the Welsh influences of the Chubut valley and the glaciers of the far south.

Things can only get wetter

King of the cascades Large areas of western Argentina may be hot, dry and barren but other parts of the country are equally as wet. The gargantuan Iguazú Falls, situated in the extreme northeast on the frontier with Brazil and near the border with Paraguay, is one of the natural wonders of the continent. There are no fewer than 275 separate falls but the most spectacular of these is the appropriately named Garganta del Diablo (Devils Throat), which alone makes the journey worthwhile. Away from the bustle around the falls, the warm climate and heavy rainfall support a diverse range of tropical wildlife, including over 400 species of birds and more than 100 species of butterfly. South of Iguazú in the province of Corrientes are the Esteros de Iberá, extensive areas of marshland (similar to the better known Brazilian Pantanal) which are a birdwatchers paradise, as yet little visited by travellers.

Peaches of beaches Argentina's Atlantic coastline stretches south from Buenos Aires to Tierra del Fuego and offers further variety. The stretch just south of the capital is lined with beach resorts, the most famous of which is Mar del Plata, seen by Argentines as 'the Biarritz of Argentina'. Far away from the beach-towels and seaside entertainment of "Mardel", the southern Argentine beaches are occupied by penguins and sea lions. Their breeding seasons are a big attraction, especially on the Valdés Peninsula, near Puerto Madryn in northern Patagonia, where whales, penguins and other sea mammals and birds can be seen. If you prefer your wildlife away from the distractions of other travellers, there are lots of less well known sites further south along the Patagonian coast and in Tierra del Fuego, where boat trips are offered along the Beagle Channel to see colonies of sea lions and fur seals.

Land of the lakes Southwest of the pampas are the great lakes of the Argentine Lake District. Surrounded by natural forest and with the Andean peaks towering above, they are protected by a string of national parks. The main centre for visiting this area is Bariloche, situated on the shores of the beautiful Lago Nahuel Huapi; nearby are chocolate box scenes of rolling hills and wooden Alpine style houses. Bariloche is also the departure point for the most famous route across the Andes, to Puerto Montt by boat across three lakes with bus connections between them. Away from the bustle of the main streets of Bariloche you can escape to lesser known lakes, stay in small towns and kill time walking in stunning scenery, climbing and fishing. Even if you are not a railway enthusiast you will want to ride the 'Old Patagonian Express' (made famous by Paul Therroux) on its regular run from Esquel, south of Bariloche.

Glacial glory Far to the south is another park, the Parque Nacional Los Glaciares, which covers parts of two more great lakes as well as 47 glaciers, most of which break off the giant Campo de Hielo Sur, the third largest ice-cap on earth. One of these glaciers, the Perito Moreno, made a name for itself by pushing across and blocking one of the fiords of Lago Argentino, the great lake which it feeds, until the waters trapped behind it rose and broke through sending giant icebergs downstream. Though the glacier no longer performs this party-piece, it still pulls in the crowds who come to gaze at the blue-tinged ice which creaks and sighs as it breaks up and sheds icebergs. If visiting the Perito Moreno whets your appetite for glaciers, there are boat trips to some of the others in the park.

Left: a view of the lakes from Cerro Campinario, near Bariloche.
Below: the magnificent Iguazú Falls.

Above: don't fly for me Argentina, king penguins walking their walk in file.
Left: parasol paradise, Mar del Plata, Argentina's most popular beach.
Next page: leggy locals, San Telmo, Buenos Aires.

*Right: a Carlos Gardel wannabe in San Telmo, Buenos Aires. **Below**: livin' la vida boca.*

__Above__: gauchos bareback in a rodeo in San Andres de Giles, the pampas.
*__Right__: it takes two to tango. **Next page**: it's a seals life at Punta Norte.*

Thrills, spills and hills

Argentina offers great opportunities for adventure travel. Climbers will want to head for the Andes. Aconcagua, the highest mountain in the Americas, and Fitzroy, which challenges even the best climbers, are well known but there are many other peaks, especially in the northwestern provinces of Catamarca and La Rioja, little visited by travellers, which include some of the highest peaks in the Andean range. In season (usually July/August) skiing is popular in Bariloche and at the international resort of Las Leñas, but there are lesser known resorts where you may hire equipment and try out the *pistes*. From El Chaltén, at the base of Fitzroy, skiing expeditions are offered on the ice-fields of the *Campo de Hielo Sur*. Good trekking country can be found in the Andean foothills and especially, once again, around El Chaltén. If you get bored with the walks there, it is a short trip from El Chaltén across the frontier to the spectacular Parque Nacional Torres del Paine in Chile where there are even better opportunities. Horseriding is an Argentine passion; horses are widely available and riding is part of any *estancia* trip. As for watersports surfing, windsurfing and waterskiing are practiced along the Atlantic coast and rafting and other sports are offered particularly in the Lake District, and further north around Mendoza and in the Sierras de Córdoba. Aerial sports such as parapenting and ballooning are also increasing in popularity.

Take a walk on the wide side

Wherever you go in Argentina there are other ways of entertaining yourself. Football is an Argentine passion. They are boca crazy. Watching the Buenos Aires rivals Boca Juniors and River Plate is an unforgettable experience and most other major cities have their own teams and excited supporters. If you don't go near a game you can experience some of the enthusiasm simply by sitting in a bar since football is shown on TV most evenings. Fans of most other sports will find something of interest including, around Buenos Aires, rugby, polo and even cricket.

On the run

Tango is special to Buenos Aires but other parts of the country have their own musical traditions. Good opportunities to hear these are often provided by the colourful local fiestas. Carnival is celebrated with great enthusiasm and colour especially in Corrientes and elsewhere in the northeast. Other cities have their own celebrations; Mendoza, for instance, at the heart of the wine-producing region, has a great party to celebrate the grape-harvest. In Salta the locals party to celebrate the city's delivery from a series of earthquakes. In the far northwestern valleys very different traditions are celebrated: there are festivities to the Andean earth deity *Pachamama* and in the little Andean village of Casabindo you can witness *El Toreo de la Vincha*, a bull fight with a difference.

Crazy about Carnival

Though Argentina is an immigrant society, not everything is modern and bustling and the Andean regions are littered with remnants of the period before the Spanish arrived. In the northwest is the sacred valley of Tafí, often swathed in mysterious mists; nearby there are pre-hispanic ruins at Quilmes, now the name of Argentina's largest brewery but once the home of the most ferocious enemies of the Spanish. In southern Patagonia the cave paintings at the Cueva de las Manos are further evidence of the artistic character of ancient peoples. Not far from the Lake District, in Neuquén, there are even reminders of Argentina's more ancient inhabitants: enough dinosaur fossils have been discovered here for this to be justifiably labelled a dinosaur graveyard.

Blast into the past

Essentials

2

Essentials

Planning your trip

Where to go

Tastes in travel, as in everything else, differ and Argentina's attractions are so varied that the country has something to offer most visitors. Several destinations, however, stand out for their popularity with travellers.

Buenos Aires, home of the tango, is one of the great cities of South America. With its European-inspired architecture and atmosphere of *fin de siecle* decadence, it should be on the itinerary of all but the most hardened city-hater. It should be said that although other large Argentine cities lack the capital's cultural attractions they are often much friendlier and offer the traveller greater insight into the lifestyle of ordinary Argentines. Escaping from the city's bustle is easy: the most popular excursion is to Tigre and the delta of the Río Paraná, but day-trips can also be made to *estancias* and the Uruguayan city of **Colonia del Sacramento**, a Portuguese colonial gem, is a short boat trip away on the eastern bank of the Río de la Plata. West of Buenos Aires are the **Pampas**, extensive flat plains which form the agricultural heartland of the country. Unless you are particularly interested in visiting *estancias* you will probably head straight across the pampas by plane, bus or car. South of Buenos Aires the eastern edge of the Pampas, however, is formed by the Atlantic Ocean; along this coastline are Argentina's most popular beach resorts, the most famous of which is **Mar del Plata**.

Buenos Aires & around

The large colonial city of **Salta** is, for many travellers, a base for visiting the northwest. The most famous excursion is the **Tren a las Nubes**, a spectacular rail journey up the gorge of the Rio Toro to the mining town of San Antonio de las Cobres, but there are many other options including **Cafayate**, an oasis town which produces some of the best wine in Argentina and which is reached through the **Quebrada de Cafayate**, a beautiful gorge with rock-features of diverse colours and shapes. North of Salta is **Jujuy,** an unattractive city at the southern end of the **Quebrada de Humahuaca**, another gorge which offers some of the most stunning landscapes in Argentina including, near Purmamarca, a hill with rock strata in seven contrasting colours.

The west & northwest

Visitors with more time at their disposal will find that the area around the Quebrada de Humahuaca offers much more including vibrant Amerindian communities (very rare in Argentina) and bleak highland landscapes, known as the *puna* which are more akin to Bolivia. Not all of the northwest is, however, at a high altitude. The mountains fall away steeply to the east; Argentina's three cloudforest parks, **El Rey**, **Calilegua** and **Baritú**, are situated on these slopes. South of Salta **Tucumán** provides further contrasts; the largest and most dynamic city in the north, it lies at the heart of a sub-tropical zone and surrounded by sugar estates. From Salta and Tucumán buses cross the inhospitable Chaco Desert to reach the northeast.

While the northwest is one of the most popular destinations for travellers, those with more than two or three weeks in the country may care to visit a number of other centres. These include: the **Central Sierras**, easily accessible from Córdoba, Argentina's second city; **Mendoza**, at the heart of the wine-producing region and a good stepping-off point for skiing or climbing Aconcagua and other Andean peaks; **San Juan** and **La Rioja**, both smaller and of less interest than Mendoza but both centres for exploring the Andes and for visiting the lunar landscapes of the **Parque Provincial Ischigualasto** and the **Parque Nacional Talampaya**.

The major attraction in the northeast is **Iguazú**, the spectacular falls on the frontier with Brazil; travellers should award these at least two days of their lives. From here side-trips can easily be made into Brazil and Paraguay. Southwest of Iguazú is **San**

The northeast

Ignacio Mini, the best-preserved of the former Jesuit missions which were once common in this part of the country and nearby areas of Brazil and Paraguay. Travellers in a hurry tend to pass through or over the rest of the northeast, but for those with more time there are further attractions, including the **Esteros del Iberá**, an expanse of marshland, the home to diverse species of birds and mammals, and the **Chaco**, which is also good for viewing birds. The cities attract few travellers, but there are several good options for two-day stopovers, notably **Santa Fe** and the neighbouring city of of **Paraná**.

The south   Situated southwest of Buenos Aires and west of the Pampas, the **Lake District** is one of the country's major tourist destinations, offering attractive lake scenery, mountains and a wide range of outdoor activities, including skiing, hiking and watersports. **Bariloche**, situated on the lakeshore of Lago Nahuel Huapi, is the main base for boat trips and excursions as well as skiing. Travellers with more than two or three days to spare in this region may consider visiting smaller centres such as **San Martín de los Andes** and **Junín de los Andes**, both of which are bases for exploring the **Parque Nacional Lanín**. South of Bariloche is more lake scenery as well the town of **Esquel**, which is famous as the southern terminal of **La Trochita**, the train which achieved fame as the *Old Patagonian Express*.

    Argentine Patagonia, which stretches south from the Río Colorado, consists mainly of vast steppeland, with very few inhabitants except in the coastal cities. One of the main destinations for visitors is the **Valdés Peninsula**, easily reached from Puerto Madryn, which offers Argentina's best views of Atlantic marine mammals and birds. Much further south is the **Parque Nacional los Glaciares**, one of the largest national parks in Argentina, which includes the famous **Perito Moreno Glacier**, one of the country's most popular attractions the area at the base of **Mount Fitzroy**, in the north of the park, is one of Argentina's best areas for trekking and climbing. The small town of Calafate is the centre for visiting the Perito Moreno glacier; those with little time at their disposal usually spend two or three nights here before leaving this region but it is well worth delaying a few days in Chaltén, the base for exploring the Fitzroy region. From Calafate it is a relatively short distance across the frontier to Puerto Natales in Chile, from where you can visit the truly spectacular **Parque Nacional Torres del Paine.** With its glacial lakes of differing colours, its glaciers and mountain and its solitude, this is one of the great attractions of Chile.

    South of Patagonia, across the Straits of Magellan, lies the large island of **Tierra del Fuego**, divided between Argentina and Chile. The main centre is Ushuaia, from where more superb mountain scenery can be visited and voyages can be made down the Beagle Channel.

Suggested itineraries

See also page 56 for special interest travel & adventure tourism

The three main factors which determine possible itineraries in Argentina are the time at your disposal, the time of year (see page 21), and how and where you enter the country (see page 33). It goes without saying that if you have the luxury of unlimited time you can visit all parts of the country at leisure. The following suggestions are intended merely to give a rough idea of how long you could spend in a particular region. They do not allow for the detailed exploration which some travellers will prefer.

Buenos Aires and the Río de la Plata   From a few days to two weeks allowing for excursions to nearby areas including Colonia de Sacramento and depending on how much you enjoy the city's nightlife and other cultural offerings.

The pampas   A few days unless you are particularly fond of the coastal resorts (warmer months only) or *estancias*.

The Central Sierras Córdoba can be seen in one to two days while the nearby Sierras can be visited as day trips from Córdoba and San Luis or on longer visits.

The west Allow two days for Mendoza with its vineyards. The cities of San Juan and La Rioja can be explored in half a day but visits to the more distant valleys in these provinces will probably require more than a day trip. To these add as many days as required for skiing, climbing and other activities especially around Malargüe.

The northwest The city of Salta can be explored in a day but add several days for excursions. Careful planning and advance booking are advised if you wish to travel on the Tren a las Nubes. Those with more time could spend up to 10 days exploring the remote parts of Jujuy or a few days in Catamarca.

The northeast Suggesting time schedules becomes more difficult here. Travellers should award the Iguazú Falls at least two days. San Ignacio Miní is a good base for a few relaxing days walking. Further south in this region, the cities attract few travellers, but there are several good options for two day stopovers, including Santa Fe and the neighbouring city of Paraná. Day trips and longer excursions to the Chaco can be arranged form Resistencia and Formosa.

The Lake District Bariloche is the main centre for excursions and boat trips and many travellers pass two or three days here. Those with more time may wish to base themselves elsewhere, perhaps on one of the smaller lakes, especially if camping.

Patagonia Planning a trip in Patagonia requires careful planning as distances are large and transport needs to be booked in advance especially in high summer. The main attractions are Puerto Madryn, with Valdés Peninsula (allow two days) and the great Parque Nacional Los Glaciares. The Perito Moreno glacier in the park is usually visited on a day trip from Calafate and, although there is little else to do in Calafate a further three or four days could be added for exploring the Fitz Roy region at the southern end of the park.

Chilean Patagonia The Parque Nacional Torres del Paine is a must. This requires at least an overnight stay, but to make the most of hiking opportunities in this stunning region allow five to six days. A further two days could be added for visiting Punta Arenas.

Tierra del Fuego Due to heavy demand in the high season journeys to and from Tierra del Fuego require careful planning and advance booking. The main centre is Ushuaia. With excursions and boat trips allow two to three days.

When to go

As Argentina is in the southern hemisphere, the seasons are the reverse of those in the northern hemisphere. Spring is from September to November, summer is between December and February, autumn is from March to May and winter from June to August.

The northeast is best visited in winter when it is cooler and drier. Winter is also a good time to visit the northwest but routes to Chile across the Andes may be closed by snow at this time. Spring and autumn are better if crossing the border. The summer rains, especially in Jujuy, can make roads impassable. Spring and autumn are best for Buenos Aires. Summer is unpleasantly hot and humid and in late December and early January the city is half-closed as many people escape on holiday. Spring and autumn are the best seasons for visiting the Lake District, as many services are closed off season. Ideally Patagonia should be visited in December or February/March, avoiding the winter months when the weather is cold and many services are closed. January is

Essentials

 Tourist offices overseas

For tourism enquiries in Australia, Canada, New Zealand and United Kingdom contact the Consulate or Embassy addresses given below.

Australia *Argentine Consulate, 1 Alfred Street, 13th floor, Circular Quay, (2000) Sydney. T92513402/3, F92513405, conargen@ram.net.au, www.consarsydney.org.au*

Brazil *Ruben Eduardo Ali, Argentine Embassy, Avenida Paulista 1106, piso 9, São Paulo, T5511-2511223, F5511-2511016.*

Canada *Argentine Consulate, 1 First Canadian Place, Suite 5840, Toronto, (M5X-1K2) Ontario. T4169559075, F4169550868, fctoro@mrecic.gov.ar*

Germany *Eduardo Piva, Penthouse 1, Suite F, Building AmeriFirst, Adenauerallee 52, 5300 Bonn, T49228-228011, F49228-214809.*

Italy *Luis Ruzzi, Piazza dell'Esquilino 2, 00185 Rome, T3906-47823788, F3906-47823796.*

New Zealand *Argentine Embassy, 142 Lambton Quay, 14th floor, Wellington. PO Box 5430, T44728330, F44728331, enzel@arg.org.nz, www.arg.org.nz*

United Kingdom *Argentine Consulate, 27 Three Kings Yard, London W1Y 1FL, T0207-3181340, F3181349.*

United States *López Lecube, 12 West 56th Street, New York, NY10019, T1212-6030433, F1212-3155545.*

best avoided if you can as this is the Argentine summer holiday period and some destinations, notably in Patagonia, are very crowded. There are also school holidays in July and some facilities such as youth hostels may be heavily booked in this period. Bariloche is a very popular destination for school groups in July and December to early January so avoid if you don't want to share your holidays with young hordes.

Tours and tour operators

Austral Tours, 20 Upper Tachbrook St, London SW1V 1SH, T0207-2335384, F2335385, www.latinamerica.co.uk *Cox & Kings Travel* St James Court, 45 Buckingham Gate, London, T0207-8735001, F6306038, cox.kings.sprint.com *Destination South America* 51 Castle Street, Cirencester, Gloustershire, GL7 1QD, T01285-885333, www.destinationsouthamerica.co.uk *Encounter Overland* 267 Old Brompton Rd, London, SW5 9JA, T0207-3706845, wwwencounter.co.uk *Exodus Travels* 9 Wier Road, London, SW12 0LT, T0208-7723822, www.exodus.co.uk *Hayes & Jarvis* 152 King St, London, W6 0QU, T0208-2227844. *Journey Latin America* 12-13 Healthfield Terrace, Chiswick, London, W4 4JE, T0208-7478315, and 28-30 Barton Arcade, Deansgate, Manchester, M3 2BH, T0161-8321441, www.journeylatinamerica.co.uk Long established company running escorted tours throughout the region. They also offer a wide range of flight options. *Ladatco Tours*, 2220 Coral Way, Miami, Florida 33145, USA, T800-327-6162, F850504, www.ladatco.com *Last Frontiers*, Fleet Marston Farm, Aylesbury, Buckinghamshire, HP18 0QT, T01296-658650, www.lastfrontiers.co.uk *Passage to South America* Fovant Mews, 12 Noyna Rd, London, SW17 7PH, T0208-7678989. *South American Experience* 47 Causton St, Pimlico, London, SW1P 4AT, T0207-9765511, F9766908, www.sax.mcmail.com Small efficient company offering range of escorted tours, flights, hotel bookings and other services. *Southtrip*, Sarmiento 347, 4th floor of 19, Buenos Aires, Argentina, T5411-43287075, www.southtrip.com *STA Travel Priory House*, 6 Wrights Lane, London, W8 6TA, T0207-3616166, www.statravel.co.uk *Trailfinders* 194 Kensington High St, London, W8 7RG, T0207-9383939.

Language

No amount of dictionaires, phrase books or word lists will provide the same enjoyment as being able to communicate directly with the people of the country you are visiting. Learning Spanish is an important part of the preparation for any trip to Argentina and you are encouraged to make an effort to grasp the basics before you go. As you travel you will pick up more of the language and the more you know, the more you will benefit from your stay.

See page 555 for a list of useful words & phrases

Spanish, with variant words and pronunciation, is the first language although some people speak English, particularly in tourist areas, and French and Italian. Information in hotels is frequently posted in English and restaurant menus may be available in English but this does not mean that English is spoken (or understood). *AmeriSpan Unlimited*, PO Box 40007, Philadelphia, PA 19106-0007, T (worldwide) 215-7511100, F 215-7511986, (USA, Canada) T 1-800-8796640, www.amerispan.com, offers Spanish immersion programs, educational tours, volunteer and internship positions throughout Latin America including Buenos Aires.

Essentials

√

Before you travel

Getting in

Passports are not required by citizens of neighbouring countries who hold identity cards issued by their own governments. Other visitors should carry passports at all times; backpackers are particular targets for thorough searches. It is illegal not to have identification. When crossing land frontiers, remember that though the migration and

Documents

● ●

☞ *Embassies and consulates*

Australia *100 Miller Street, Suite 6, Level 30, North Sydney, New South Wales 2060, T2-9227272, F9231798.*

Belgium *225 Avenue Louise B.3, 1050 Brussels, T2-6477812, F4679319.*

Canada *90 Sparks Street, Suite 620, Ottawa KIP 5B4, T613-2362351, F2352659.*

France *Rue Cimarosa 75116 Paris, T1-45533300, F455344633.*

Germany *Wiesenhuettenplatz 26, 8th Floor, 6000 Frankfurt, T496-9231050, F9236842.*

Netherlands *Herengracht 94 1015 BS, Amsterdam, T2-023-2723/6242, F06267344.*

New Zealand *11 Floor, Harbour View Building, 52 Quay Street, PO Box 2320, Auckland, T9-391757, F3735386.*

Spain *Paseo de la Castellana 53, Madrid 1, Madrid, T1-4424500, F4423559.*

United Kingdom *27 Three Kings Yard, London W1Y 1FL, T0207-3181340, F3181349.*

United States *12 West 56th Street, New York 10019, T212-6030400, F3973523.*

● ●

customs officials are generally friendly, helpful and efficient, the police at the control posts a little further into Argentina tend to be extremely bureaucratic.

If you are staying for several weeks, it may be worth while registering at your embassy or consulate; if your passport is stolen, the process of replacing it is simplified and speeded up.

Visas are not necessary for US citizens, British citizens and nationals of other Western European countries, Canada, Bolivia, Brazil, Chile, Panama, Paraguay, Uruguay, Venezuela, Mexico, El Salvador, Guatemala, Nicaragua, Honduras, Costa Rica, Colombia, Ecuador, Peru, Dominican Republic, Haiti, Barbados, Jamaica, Malaysia, Israel, Czech Republic, Slovak Republic, Hungary, Poland, Turkey, Croatia, Yugoslavia, South Africa, Australia, New Zealand, Singapore and Japan, who are given a tourist card on entry and may stay for three months, a period which can be renewed for another three months (fee US$100) at the National Directorate of Migration. For all others there are three forms of visa: a business 'temporary' visa (US$25, valid one year), a tourist visa (US$20 approximately, fees change monthly), and a transit visa. Tourist visas are usually valid for three months and multiple entry. If leaving Argentina on a short trip, check on re-entry that border officials look at the correct expiry date on your visa, otherwise they will give only 30 days. Renewing a visa is difficult and can only be done for 30-day periods.

At **land borders** 90 days permission to stay is usually given without proof of transportation out of Argentina. Make sure you are given a tourist card, otherwise you will have to obtain one before leaving the country. If you need a 90-day extension for your stay in Argentina, leave the country, at Iguazú or to Uruguay, and 90 further days will be given on return. Visa extensions may also be obtained from Antártida Argentina 1325, edificio 3, Buenos Aires, T43128661/9, ask for `Prorrogas de Permanencia': fee US$100. No renewals are given after the expiration date. To authorize an exit stamp if your visa or tourtist stamp has expired, go to Yrigoyen 952 where a 10-day authorization will be given for US$50. Alternatively, you can forego all the paperwork by paying a US$50 fine at a border immigration post (queues are shorter than in Buenos Aires, but still allow 30 minutes). At Argentine/Uruguayan borders one immigration official will stamp passports for both countries. Argentine immigration and customs officials wear civilian dress. The border patrol, *gendarmería*, in green combat fatigues, operate some borders. It is your responsibility to ensure that your passport is stamped in and out when you cross frontiers. The absence of entry and exit stamps can cause serious difficulties: seek out the proper migration offices if the stamping process is not carried out as you cross. Do not lose your entry card; replacing one causes a lot of trouble, and possibly expense. Citizens of countries which oblige visitors to have a visa can expect more delays and problems at border crossings.

Many European and US motoring organizations have reciprocal arrangements with the *Automóvil Club Argentino* (ACA) (see below); if you can show your membership you are entitled to use of ACA facilities and discounts off hotel charges, car rentals, maps, towing charges, etc. Business people should carry a good supply of visiting cards, which are essential for good business relations in Latin America. Identity, membership or business cards in Spanish (or a translation) and an official letter of introduction in Spanish are also useful.

Membership cards

If you are in full-time education you will be entitled to an *International Student Identity Card* (ISIC), which is distributed by student travel offices and travel agencies in 77 countries and which ISIC gives you special prices on all forms of transport (air, sea, rail et cetera), and access to a variety of other concessions and services. If you need to find the location of your nearest ISIC office contact: The ISIC Association, Box 9048, 1000 Copenhagen, Denmark T+45-33-939303. All student cards must carry a photograph if they are to be of any use for discounts.

No vaccinations are required for entry.

Vaccinations

Duty free allowance   No duties are charged on clothing, personal effects, toiletries, etc. Cameras, typewriters, binoculars, radios and other things which a tourist normally carries are duty-free if they have been used and only one of each article is carried. This is also true of scientific and professional instruments for personal use. Travellers may only bring in new personal goods up to a value of US$200 (US$100 from neighbouring countries); the amount of duty and tax payable amounts to 50% of the item's cost. At airport customs, you press a button for the red or green channel. Baggage claim tags are inspected at the exit from the customs inspection area.

Customs
You can buy duty-free goods on arrival at Ezeiza airport

Two litres of alcoholic drinks, 400 cigarettes and 50 cigars are also allowed in duty-free. For tourists originating from neighbouring countries the quantities allowed are one litre of alcoholic drinks, 200 cigarettes and 20 cigars.

If you have packages sent to Argentina, do not use the green customs label unless the contents are of real value and you expect to pay duty. For such things as books or samples use the white label if available. A heavy tax is imposed on packages sent to Argentina by courier.

What to take

Here is a list of items that you might find useful: an inflatable travel pillow for neck support, comfortable strong shoes, a first-aid kit, waterproof clothing, earplugs and an airline-type eye mask, a sheet sleeping-bag, a sarong (which can be used as a towel, a bedsheet, beach towel, makeshift curtain and wrap), a hat, a nailbrush, a universal bath plug, string, strong tape, velcro, a Swiss Army knife, an alarm clock or watch, a candle, a torch, a padlock (combination lock is best), photocopies of essential documents, (including your flight ticket), and some additional passport-sized photographs. See also page 59 for a list of trekking equipment.

Always take more money & less clothes than you think you'll need

For a full medical checklist see page 60, but to add to that is lipsalve with sun protection and pre-moistened wipes. Toilet paper is also useful especially on long distance bus trips. Contact lens wearers will find a wide selection of products for the care of lenses sold in a chemist/pharmacy rather than an optician's.

Remember not to throw away spent batteries containing mercury or cadmium; take them home to be disposed of, or recycled properly.

Money

Cost of living

Income levels in Argentina are more unequal than in most of Western Europe. Although the average monthly income for Argentina as a whole in 1999 was US$940, this figure is of limited value. Unemployment is high (over 15% of the labour force in 1999) and official figures on unemployment (and incomes) do not take into account the large number of people who are underemployed (and who eke out a living in part-time employment or selling goods and services). Moreover there are enormous differences in incomes in different parts of the country; in 1999 the highest average monthly incomes were recorded in the Federal District of Buenos Aires (US$1,250), Tierra del Fuego (US$1,240), Santa Cruz (US$1,070), Neuquén and Chubut (both US$1,000). Averages for the northeast were much lower: Formosa (US$620), Chaco (US$630), Misiones (US$650), Corrientes (US$660) and Entre Ríos (US$670). Perhaps an easier way to think about how much Argentines earn is to look at what different groups of workers earn. The following figures are for the city of Buenos Aires where it is estimated that US$1,000 is the minimum monthly income necessary to enable a family with 2 children (and no savings) to live decently. The lowest pension is about US$200 a month, fast food assistants earn US$200-300, supermarket assistants US$300, state primary school teachers US$400, shop assistants US$500, waiters US$600-800, bank clerks US$700 and local bus drivers US$800. Some people earn much more than this, of course, among them the President whose monthly salary is US$6,000.

Cost of travelling

In 2000 Argentina was very expensive for the foreign visitor. In Buenos Aires cheap accommodation costs at least US$15-20 per person and an evening meal in an ordinary restaurant will cost US$10 or more without drinks. Travellers on less restricted budgets will find that they can easily spend as much on accommodation and food as in Western Europe or North America. Away from the capital (except in Patagonia and Tierra del Fuego) food and accommodation are generally cheaper but not much. Travellers on low budgets should expect to pay at least US$15 for a double room. Snacks in bars are often not much cheaper than a meal in restaurant. In most cities, a cheaper option for eating is in or around the market. Some bus terminals also have stalls selling cheap snacks, but these are becoming less common (and less cheap) as the old terminals are rebuilt and/or relocated. The high cost of transporting goods and the large distances involved as well as the short tourist season make Patagonia and Tierra del Fuego more expensive than the rest of the country; Calafate and Ushuaia are particularly expensive, though dormitory accommodation can be obtained for US$10-12 per person (double rooms start at US$30-40). Long distance bus travel on major routes, especially to and from Buenos Aires, is often very cheap, depending on how much competition there is between companies. Internal air travel is a good option, though more expensive. In Patagonia travelling by bus is often no cheaper than flying.

Currency

When crossing a land frontier into Argentina make sure you have some Argentine currency: normally there are no facilities at the border

The peso, which is at par with the dollar, is divided into 100 centavos. Peso notes in circulation are 2, 5, 10, 20, 50 and 100. Coins in circulation are 1, 5, 10, 25 and 50 centavos and 1 peso. Most major towns have exchange shops (*casas de cambio*). Exchange rates are quoted in major newspapers daily. Money remitted to Argentina from abroad is normally paid out in local currency. The three main ways of keeping in funds while travelling are with US$ cash, US$ travellers' cheques, or plastic.

It is best to take US$ cash rather than sterling and other currencies. Dollar bills are widely accepted, but take only utterly unblemished notes, as dirty or torn notes are usually refused. Many forged bills are in circulation. Take and accept only new-style dollars with centre thread, microprinting and watermarks. Though the risk of loss is greater than with travellers' cheques, better rates and lower commissions can usually be obtained for them. If you are travelling on the cheap watch weekends and public holidays carefully and never run out of local currency, especially away from major cities.

Cash

These are convenient but attract thieves (though refunds can of course be arranged). Denominations of US$50 and US$100 are preferable to larger values, but it is a good idea to take some US$20 cheques. Travellers' cheques are generally difficult to change, especially in smaller towns and at weekends. They are often scrutinized very closely any variation between signatures can lead to their being refused. A passport is essential and you may have to show proof of purchase. Transactions can take a long time and there are often many forms. There is a 3% tax and banks generally charge about 4% commission though can be as high as 10%. Commission can be avoided if you go to a branch of the issuing bank, especially if changing small amounts. Hotels will normally change travellers' cheques for their guests (often at a rather poor rate).

    American Express, Visa or Thomas Cook US$ travellers' cheques are better known by hotels and other establishments than *Citibank* or *Bank of America* travellers' cheques. American Express travellers' cheques, which can be changed at the American Express bank in Buenos Aires, are hard to change in northern Argentina although the Amex card is widely accepted. Emergency cash from Amex is available only in Buenos Aires and Bariloche. Amex emergency number is T43121661, Buenos Aires. *Citibank* travellers' cheques have been recommended; no commission is charged at their own branches around the country. Thomas Cook Visa TC refund assistance is T000811-7840553, F44-1733-502370.

Travellers' cheques

American Express, Diners Club, Visa and Mastercard cards are all widely accepted in the major cities and provincial capitals, though less so outside these. There is a high surcharge on credit card transactions in many establishments; many hotels offer reductions for cash. Credit cards are readily accepted in all main towns, even in the south, but outside main towns their use is limited. Many service stations accept credit cards (ACA stations only take cards from members; YPF accepts Visa). All shops, hotels and places showing Argencard (head office, Peru 143, Buenos Aires, T43312088) signs will accept Eurocard and Access, but you must state that these cards are affiliated to Mastercard. Argencard will not permit cash advances on these cards in outlying regions, and is itself very slow in advancing cash. Mastercard emergency number is T0800- 5550507 and Visa is T0800-32222.

    Make sure you know the correct procedure if your cards are lost or stolen. For security, insist that imprints are made in your presence and that any imprints incorrectly completed should be torn into tiny pieces. Also destroy the carbon papers after the form is completed (signatures can be copied from them).

Credit cards

Automatic Telling Machines (ATMs), known as *Cajeros Automáticos*, are available in Buenos Aires and a few other major cities. It is straightforward to withdraw cash against a credit card and, in the text, we give the names of banks which do so. There are two international ATM acceptance systems, Plus and Cirrus. Many issuers of debit and credit cards are linked to one, or both (for example Visa is Plus, Mastercard is Cirrus). Visa can be used at *Banelco* ATMs. Cirrus card can be used at ATMs with Link sign, for example *Banco Nacional de Lavoro*. Look for the relevant symbol on an ATM and draw cash using your PIN. See the inside front cover for what ATM coverage there is and what international 'functionality' your card has. Check if your bank or credit card company imposes handling charges. Obviously you must ensure that the account to

Frequently, the rates of exchange on ATM withdrawals are the best available

which your debit card refers contains sufficient funds. With a credit card, obtain a credit limit sufficient for your needs, or pay money in to put the account in credit. If travelling for a long time, consider a direct debit to clear your account regularly. Do not rely on one card, in case of loss. If you do lose a card, immediately contact the 24-hour helpline of the issuer in your home country (keep this number in a safe place).

Transfers Money can be transferred between banks. A recommended method is, before leaving, to find out which local bank is correspondent to your bank at home, then when you need funds, ask your bank to send the money to the local bank (confirming by fax or email). Give the exact information to your bank of the routing number of the receiving bank. Allow 2-3 days; cash is usually paid in pesos and is be subject to tax. For Western Union, T11-4322-7774. If staying for a long time in Argentina and especially Buenos Aires, it may be a good idea to transfer money into a local bank, opening an account in pesos or dollars. Paperwork is not complicated and your money is safe and gaining interest. Check with your bank before leaving.

Getting there

Air

From Europe There are flights to Buenos Aires from London, Amsterdam, Barcelona, Madrid, Frankfurt, Paris, Milan, Rome, Zurich with *Aerolíneas Argentinas* (AR) and/or European carriers.

From North America & Canada *Aerolíneas Argentinas* and/or other South American and North American airlines fly from Miami, New York, Los Angeles, San Francisco, Atlanta, New Orleans, Dallas and Chicago. *Canadian Air International* fly from Toronto.

From Australasia & South Africa *Aerolíneas Argentinas* and *Qantas* fly from Sydney, Australia, via Auckland, New Zealand, twice a week. On the outward flight from Argentina, *Aerolíneas Argentinas* stop at Río Gallegos, but it is difficult to board there in high season. *Malaysia Airlines* and *Aerolíneas Argentinas* fly twice a week from Johannesburg via Cape Town, originating in Kuala Lumpur. *South African Airways* fly twice a week from Johannesburg.

From Latin America *Aerolíneas Argentinas* and other national carriers fly between Buenos Aires and all the South American capitals, plus Santa Cruz and Cochabamba in Bolivia and Guayaquil in Ecuador. Several flights between Buenos Aires and Rio de Janeiro and São Paulo stop over in Porto Alegre, Florianópolis and Curitiba. There are also flights from Belo Horizonte, Salvador, Recife and Fortaleza. See under Brazil for the Mercosur Air Pass. There are also flights from Havana, Mexico City and Cancún. Note that

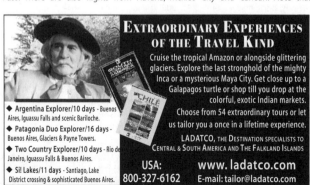

Discount flight agents in Australia and New Zealand

Flight Centres, 82 Elizabeth St, Sydney, T13-1600; 205 Queen St, Auckland, T09-309 6171. Also branches in other towns and cities.
STA Travel, T1300-360960, www.statravelaus.com.au; 702 Harris St,

Ultimo, Sydney, and 256 Flinders St, Melbourne. In NZ: 10 High St, Auckland, T09-366 6673. Also in major towns and university campuses.
Travel.com.au, 80 Clarence St, Sydney, T02-929 01500, www.travel.com.au

commercial flights between Argentina and the Falklands/Malvinas resumed in October 1999 when LanChile's service Santiago-Puerto Montt-Punta Arenas stopped over in Río Gallegos before continuing to Mount Pleasant airport.

Airlines will only allow a certain weight of luggage without a surcharge; this is normally 30 kg for first class and 20 kg for business and economy classes, but these limits are often not strictly enforced when it is known that the plane is not going to be full. On some flights from the UK special outbound concessions are offered (by *Iberia*, *Air France*, *Avianca*) of a two-piece allowance up to 32 kg, but you may need to request this. Passengers seeking a larger baggage allowance can route via USA, but with certain exceptions, the fares are slightly higher using this route. On the other hand, weight limits for internal flights are often lower; best to enquire beforehand. **General tips**

■ It is generally cheaper to fly to Latin American destinations from London rather than a point in continental Europe. Travellers starting their journey in continental Europe should make local enquiries about charters and agencies offering the best **Prices & discounts**

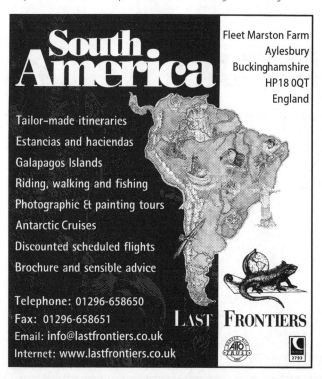
Essentials

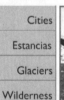
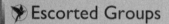
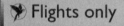

Discount flight agents in the UK and Ireland

Council Travel, 28a Poland St, London, W1V 3DB, T020-74377767, www.destinations-group.com
STA Travel, 86 Old Brompton Rd, London, SW7 3LH, T020-74376262, www. statravel.co.uk They have other branches in London, as well as in Brighton, Bristol, Cambridge, Leeds, Manchester, Newcastle-Upon-Tyne and Oxford and on many university campuses. Specialists in low-cost student/youth flights and tours,

also good for student IDs and insurance.
Trailfinders, 194 Kensington High Street, London, W8 7RG, T020-79383939.
Usit Campus, 52 Grosvenor Gardens, London, SW1 0AG, T0870 240 1010, www.usitcampus.co.uk Student/youth travel specialists with branches also in Belfast, Brighton, Bristol, Cambridge, Manchester and Oxford. The main Ireland branch is at 19 Aston Quay, Dublin 2, T01-602 1777.

deals. Fares vary from airline to airline, destination to destination and according to time of year. Check with an agency for the best deal for when you wish to travel.

■ Most airlines offer discounted fares of one sort or another on scheduled flights. These are not offered by the airlines direct to the public but through agencies who specialize in this type of fare. See the boxes.

■ The very busy seasons are 7 December to 15 January and 10 July to 10 September. If you intend travelling during those times, book as far ahead as possible. Between February to May and September to November special offers may be available.

Other fares fall into three groups, and are all on scheduled services:
Excursion (return) fares With restricted validity for example 5-90 days. Carriers are introducing flexibility into these tickets, permitting a change of dates on payment of a fee.
Yearly fares These may be bought on a one-way or return basis. Some airlines require a specified return date, changeable upon payment of a fee. To leave the return completely open is possible for an extra fee. You must fix the route (some of the cheapest flexible fares now have six months validity).
Student (or under 26) fares Some airlines are flexible on the age limit, others strict. One way and returns available, or 'Open Jaws' (see below). Do not assume that student tickets are the cheapest; though they are often very flexible, they are usually more expensive than Excursion or Yearly fares. On the other hand, there is a wider range of cheap one-way student fares originating in Latin America than can be bought outside the continent. If you foresee returning home at a busy time (for example Christmas-beginning of January, August), a booking is advisable on any type of open-return ticket.

■ 'Open Jaws' fares are for those people intending to travel a linear route and return from a different point from that which they entered available on student, yearly, or excursion fares. Many of these fares require a change of plane at an intermediate point, and a stopover may be permitted, or even obligatory, depending on schedules. Simply because a flight stops at a given airport it does not mean you can break your journey there – the airline must have traffic rights to pick up or set down passengers between points A and B before it will be permitted. This is where dealing with a specialized agency (like *Journey Latin America!*) will really pay dividends. There are dozens of agencies that offer the simple returns to Rio or Lima at roughly the same (discounted) fare but on multi-stop itineraries, the specialized agencies can often save clients hundreds of pounds.

Essentials

☞ *Discount flight agents in North America*

Air Brokers International, 323 Geary St, Suite 411, San Francisco, CA94102, T01-800-883 3273, www.airbrokers.com Consolidator and specialist on RTW and Circle Pacific tickets.

Council Travel, 205 E 42nd St, New York, NY 10017, T1-888-COUNCIL, www. counciltravel.com Student/budget agency with branches in many other US cities.

Discount Airfares Worldwide On-Line, www.etn.nl/discount.htm A hub of consolidator and discount agent links.

International Travel Network/Airlines of the Web, www.itn.net/airlines Online

air travel information and reservations. **STA Travel**, 5900 Wilshire Blvd, Suite 2110, Los Angeles, CA 90036, T1-800-777 0112, www.sta-travel.com Also branches in New York, San Francisco, Boston, Miami, Chicago, Seattle and Washington DC.

Travel CUTS, 187 College St, Toronto, ON, M5T 1P7, T1-800-667 2887, www.travelcuts.com Specialist in student discount fares, Ids and other travel services. Branches in other Canadian cities.

Travelocity, www.travelocity.com Online consolidator.

■ Although it's a little more complicated, it's possible to sell tickets in London for travel originating in Latin America at substantially cheaper fares than those available locally. This is useful for the traveller who doesn't know where he will end up, or who plans to travel for more than a year. Because of high local taxes (see below) a one-way ticket from Latin America is more expensive than a one-way in the other direction, so it's always best to buy a return (but see **Student fares**, above). Taxes are calculated as a percentage of the full IATA fare; on a discounted fare the tax can therefore make up as much as 30-50% of the price.

■ If you buy discounted air tickets always check the reservation with the airline concerned to make sure the flight still exists. Also remember that *IATA* airlines' schedules change in March and October each year, so if you're going to be away a long time it's best to leave return flight coupons open (but see **Student fares**, above). In addition, check whether you are entitled to any refund or re-issued ticket if you lose, or have stolen, a discounted air ticket. Some airlines require the repurchase of a ticket before you can apply for a refund, which will not be given until after the validity of the original ticket has expired. The Iberia group and Air France, for example, operate this costly system. Travel insurance in some cases covers lost tickets.

■ Some South American carriers change departure times of short-haul or domestic flights at short notice and, in some instances, schedules shown in the computers of transatlantic carriers differ from those actually flown by smaller, local carriers. If you book, and reconfirm, both your transatlantic and onward sectors through your transatlantic carrier you may find that your travel plans have been based on out of date information. The surest solution is to reconfirm your outward flight in an office of the onward carrier itself.

■ If travelling the cheap way in Latin America pay for all transport as you go along, and not in advance. This advice does not apply to people on a tight schedule, paying as you go along may save money, but it is likely to waste your time somewhat. The one exception to this general principle is in transatlantic flights; here money is saved by booking as far as possible in one operation. International air tickets are very expensive if purchased in Latin America. If buying airline tickets routed through the USA, check that US taxes are included in the price.

The *Mercosur Airpass* which applies to Argentina, Brazil, Chile, Uruguay and Paraguay (1998), using nine local carriers, is available to any passenger with a return ticket from South America to a Mercosur country. It must be bought in conjunction with an international flight; minimum stay is seven days, maximum one month; at least two countries must be visited. Maximum number of coupons is eight. Fares are calculated on a mileage basis and range from US$225 to US$870. See below for the *Aerolíneas Argentinas* 'Visit Argentina' airpass and the *LAPA* airpass. **Airpasses**

Road

There are many entry points from the neighbouring tates: Bolivia, Brazil, Chile, Paraguay and Uruguay. If your entry point is Buenos Aires, there are two obvious routes – north or south. In summer the northeast is very hot and humid and in the northwest it is the rainy season which may make unpaved roads impassable. In winter the southern areas are cold and the further south you go, the greater the chance that transport will not operate or will be disrupted and that hotels, tours and sights will be closed. There are many other entry points from neighbouring Bolivia, Chile and Paraguay. The main ones are as follows: in the west by road or air from Santiago (Chile) to Mendoza; in the northwest by road from Villazón (Bolivia) to Jujuy and Salta; in the northeast by road from Asunción (Paraguay) to Resistencia, from Encarnación (Paraguay) to Posadas and from Foz do Iguazú (Brazil) to Puerto Iguazú; in the Lake District by boat and bus from Puerto Montt (Chile) to Bariloche; in Patagonia by road from Puerto Natales (Chile) to Calafate or by road and ferry crossings from Tierra del Fuego to Río Gallegos and Calafate. There are also three road crossings from Uruguay via bridges over the Río Uruguay as well several ferry crossings, the most important of which are from Montevideo and Colonia de Sacramento to Buenos Aires. Entering via any of these will affect your choice of routes within the country.

There are no passenger rail services into Argentina

The **Amerbuspass** covers the whole of Latin America, from Mexico City to Ushuaia, and entitles the holder to 15-20% discounts on tickets with participating operators; bookable in all Latin American capitals, Europe, Asia, Africa, Oceania, it is valid for 9,999 miles, up to 180 days. Unlimited stopovers, travel with either a confirmed or open itinerary. Contact TISA Internacional, B Irigoyen 1370, Oficina 25/26, 1138 Buenos Aires, Argentina, T307-1956, F300-5591, PO Box 40 Suc 1 (B), 1401 Buenos Aires.

Sea

Voyages on passenger-carrying cargo vessels between South America and Europe, the USA, or elsewhere, are listed here: the **Grimaldi Line** sails from Tilbury to Brazil (Vitória, Santos, Paranaguá, Rio) and Buenos Aires via Hamburg, Amsterdam and Antwerp, Le Havre, round trip about 51 days, US$3,040-5,400, also from Genoa to Paranaguá, Santos and Rio for US$1,100-1,400 (round trip or south-bound only, no north-bound only passages).

A number of German container ships sail the year round to the east coast of South America: Felixstowe, Hamburg, Antwerp, Bilbao or Algeciras, Santos, Buenos Aires, Montevideo, Rio Grande do Sul, Itajaí, Santos, Rio de Janeiro, Rotterdam, Felixstowe (about 45 days, US$3,100-3,500 per person round trip). There are also German sailings from Genoa or Livorno (Italy), or Spain to the east coast of South America.

Polish Ocean Line's services include Gdynia to Buenos Aires, Montevideo and Santos (2-2½ months, US$2,700 per person double, US$2,900 single).

From the USA, **Ivaran Lines** serve East Coast USA, Brazilian ports, Montevideo and Buenos Aires; the *Americana* container ship carries 80 passengers in luxury accommodation (New Orleans, Houston, Puerto Cabello, La Guaira, Rio, Santos, Buenos Aires, Montevideo, Rio Grande do Sul, Itajaí, Paranaguá, Santos, Salvador, Fortaleza, Bridgetown, San Juan, Veracruz, Tampico, New Orleans, US$6,645-11,340 per person round trip, fares depend on season, one-way north or south possible). Ivaran also have the *San Antonio*, carrying 12 passengers on the route Port Elizabeth (New Jersey), Baltimore, Norfolk, Savannah, Miami, Puerto Cabello, La Guaira, Rio, Santos, Buenos Aires, Montevideo, Rio Grande do Sul, Itajaí, Santos, Rio (possibly Salvador and Fortaleza), Port Elizabeth; 44-day round trip US$4,085-4,825 per person, one-way subject to availability.

Enquiries regarding passages should be made through agencies in your own country, or through John Alton of *Strand Cruise and Travel Centre*, Charing Cross Shopping Concourse, The Strand, London WC2N 4HZ, T020-7836 6363, F020-7497 0078. They are booking agents for all the above. Elsewhere in Europe, contact *Wagner Frachtschiffreisen*, Stadlerstrasse 48, CH-8404, Winterthur, Switzerland, T052-242-1442, F242-1487. In the USA, contact *Freighter World Cruises*, 180 South Lake Ave, Pasadena, CA 91101, T818-449-3106, or *Traveltips Cruise* and *Freighter Travel Association*, 163-07 Depot Road, PO Box 188, Flushing, NY 11358, T800-872-8584. Do not try to get a passage on a non-passenger carrying cargo ship to South America from a European port; it is not possible.

Touching down

Airport information

Unless flying from a neighbouring country, all visitors arriving by air generally arrive at **Ezeiza international Airport** (officially known as Ministro Pistarini), situated 35 km southwest of Buenos Aires (for detailed information including transport to Buenos Aires, see page 75). All internal flights as well as some flights to/from neighbouring countries are handled from **Jorge Newbery Airport** (usually known as Aeroparque),

Touching down

Hours of business *Banks, government offices, insurance offices and business houses are not open on Saturday.*

Government offices: 1230-1930 in the winter and 0730-1300 in summer.

Banks: generally 1000-1600 but time varies according to the city and sometimes according to the season. (See under names of cities in text.)

Post offices: stamps on sale during working days 0800-2000 but 0800-1400 on Saturday.

Shops: from about 0900 to 1900, though many close at midday on Saturday. Outside the main cities many close for the daily afternoon siesta, reopening at about 1700. 24-hour opening is allowed except on Monday; this applies mainly to restaurants, foodshops, barbers, newspaper shops, art, book and record stores.

Dance halls open at 2300 but don't fill up till after midnight; nightclubs open after midnight. In city centres, cafés and restaurants are busy till after midnight and many evening events, such as lectures, may not start before 2200.

Official time *3 hours behind GMT.*

Voltage *220 volts (and 110 too in some hotels), 50 cycles, AC, European Continental-type plugs in old buildings, Australian 3-pin flat-type in the new. Adaptors can be purchased locally for either type (ie from new 3-pin to old 2-pin and vice-versa).*

Weights and measures *The metric system is used.*

Essentials

situated 4 km north of the centre of Buenos Aires on the bank of the Río de la Plata (see page 77 for details). Most provincial airports have tourist offices (though these may be closed even when flights arrive), banking facilities and a *confitería* (cafeteria) as well as car hire. There are usually minibus services into the city and taxis are available. Do not send unaccompanied luggage to Argentina; it can take up to three days of form- filling to retrieve it from the airport. Paying an extra baggage allowance, though expensive, saves time.

Fee US$15 for all international flights, except to Montevideo from Aeroparque, which is subject to US$5 tax; US$3-6, payable only in pesos also for internal flights (Calafate and Ushuaia US$13). When in transit from one international flight to another, you may be obliged to pass through immigration and customs, have your passport stamped and be made to pay an airport tax on departure. There is a 5% tax on the purchase of air tickets. Airport tax can be prepaid. **Airport tax**

Tourist information

There are tourist information offices in provincial capitals and in major tourist destinations. In some cases there are also offices in bus terminals. Most offices supply maps and some provide lists of accommodation with prices. English is spoken in offices in tourist destinations (and sometimes French, German, Italian) and the staff in most offices are helpful. Offices are often open for long hours (typically 0800-2000 in summer) but usually close at weekends. Most bus terminals have an office (often signed *Informes*) which provides bus information only. All Argentina provinces and some major tourist destinations have offices in Buenos Aires. The address of the national tourist office in Buenos Aires is Santa Fe 883. Addresses of tourist offices around the country are given in the text. **Tourist offices**

Essentials

☞ *Eco travelling: a few tips*

■ *Where possible choose a destination, tour operator or hotel with a proven ethical and environmental commitment, and if in doubt ask.*

■ *Spend money on locally produced (rather than imported) goods and services and use common sense when bargaining – your few dollars saved may be a week's salary to others.*

■ *Use water and electricity carefully – travellers may receive preferential supply while the needs of local communities are overlooked.*

■ *Don't give money or sweets to children – it encourages begging – instead give to a recognized project, charity or school.*

■ *Learn about local etiquette and culture – consider local norms and behaviour – and dress appropriately for local cultures and situations.*

■ *Protect wildlife and other natural resources – don't buy souvenirs or goods made from wildlife unless they are clearly sustainably produced and are not protected under CITES legislation.*

■ *Always ask before taking photographs or videos of people.*

■ *Consider staying in local, rather than foreign owned, accommodation – the economic benefits for host communities are far greater – and there are far greater opportunities to learn about local culture.*

Travelling with children People contemplating overland travel in South America with children should remember that a lot of time can be spent waiting for buses, trains, and especially for aeroplanes. On bus journeys, if the children are good at amusing themselves, or can readily sleep while travelling, the problems can be considerably lessened. If your child is of an early reading age, take reading material with you as it is difficult, and expensive to find. Travel on trains, while not as fast or at times as comfortable as buses, allows more scope for moving about. Some trains provide tables between seats, so that games can be played.

Food can be a problem if the children are not adaptable. It is easier to take biscuits, drinks, bread etc with you on longer trips than to rely on meal stops where the food may not be to taste. Avocados are safe, easy to eat and nutritious; they can be fed to babies as young as 6 months and most older children like them.

On all long-distance buses you pay a **fare** for each seat, and there are no half-fares if the children occupy a seat each. For shorter trips it is cheaper, if less comfortable, to seat small children on your knee. In city and local excursion buses, small children generally do not pay a fare, but are not entitled to a seat when paying customers are standing. On sightseeing tours you should always bargain for a family rate – often children can go free. In trains, reductions for children are general, but not universal. All civil airlines charge half for children under 12, but some military services don't have half-fares, or have younger age limits. Children's fares on *Lloyd Aéreo Boliviano* are considerably more than half, and there is only a 7 kilos baggage allowance. LAB checks children's ages on passports. Note that a child travelling free on a long excursion is not always covered by the operator's travel insurance; it is adviseable to pay a small premium to arrange cover.

In all **hotels**, try to negotiate family rates. If charges are per person, always insist that two children will occupy one bed only, therefore counting as one tariff. If rates are per bed, the same applies. In either case you can almost always get a reduced rate at cheaper hotels. Occasionally when travelling with a child you will be refused a room in a hotel that is 'unsuitable'. On river boat trips, unless you have very large hammocks, it may be more comfortable and cost effective to hire a 2-berth cabin for 2 adults and a child. In **restaurants**, you can normally buy children's helpings, or divide one full-size helping between two children.

Travel with children can bring you into closer contact with Latin American families and, generally, presents no special problems – in fact the path is often smoother for family groups. Officials tend to be more amenable where children are concerned and they are pleased if your child knows a little Spanish or Portuguese. Moreover, even thieves and pickpockets seem to have some of the traditional respect for families, and may leave you alone because of it!

The main opportunities for English-speakers is teaching English. Most teaching posts are in the Buenos Aires area. Further details of opportunities in English teaching are given in the Buenos Aires section. It is possible to get jobs in some countries of South America, *Jobs Abroad* will arrange work permits, visas and immigration, send 2 x 27p stamps for information to Worldwide House, Broad Street, Port Ramsgate, Kent, CT11 8NQ.

Working in Argentina

Essentials

Rules, customs and etiquette

Remember that politeness – even a little ceremoniousness – is much appreciated. In this connection professional or business cards are useful. Men should always remove any headgear and say 'con permiso' when entering offices, and be prepared to shake hands (this is much commoner in Latin America than in Europe or North America); always say 'Buenos días' (until midday) or 'Buenas tardes' and wait for a reply before proceeding further. The traveller from abroad has usually enjoyed greater advantages in life than most Argentine minor officials, and should be friendly and courteous in consequence. Politeness should also be extended to street traders saying 'No, gracias' with a smile rather than an arrogant dismissal. Never be impatient and do not criticize situations in public: the officials may know more English than you think and they can certainly interpret gestures and facial expressions. Be judicious about discussing politics with strangers. Politeness can be a liability, however, in some situations; most Latin Americans are disorderly queuers. In commercial transactions (buying a meal, goods in a shop, et cetera) politeness should be accompanied by firmness, and you should always ask the price first.

Politeness & courtesy
Always ask permission before photographing people

Whether you give money to beggars is a personal matter, but your decision should be influenced by whether a person is begging out of need or trying to cash in on the tourist trail. In the former case, local people giving may provide an indication. Giving money to children is a separate issue, upon which most agree: don't do it. There are occasions where giving food in a restaurant may be appropriate, but first inform yourself of local practice.

Begging

There is a natural prejudice in all countries against travellers who ignore personal hygiene and have a generally dirty and unkempt appearance. Most Argentines, if they can afford it, devote great care to their clothes and appearance; it is appreciated if visitors do likewise. How you dress is mostly how people will judge you. Buying clothing locally can help you to look less like a tourist. It may be advantageous to carry a letter from someone in an official position testifying to one's good character, on official-looking notepaper. Shorts are worn in Buenos Aires and residential suburbs in spring, summer and autumn, but their use is not common outside the capital. In general, dress tends to be formal (unless casual wear is specified on an invitation) in Buenos Aires and for evening outings to shows, etc. Men wearing earrings can expect comments, even hostility, in the provinces.

Appearance

Safety

Argentina is one of the safest countries in South America. The following tips are meant to forewarn but not alarm you. They mainly apply to major cities.

Protecting money, documents & valuables

In Buenos Aires be particularly careful when boarding buses & near the Retiro train & bus stations & beware of bag snatching gangs in parks & markets

Keep all documents secure. Hide your main cash supply in different places or under your clothes: extra pockets sewn inside shirts and trousers, pockets closed with a zip or safety pin, moneybelts (best worn below the waist rather than outside or around the neck). Keep your camera in a bag (preferably with a chain or wire in the strap to defeat the slasher). Don't wear wrist-watches or jewellery. If you wear a shoulder-bag in a market, carry it in front of you. Backpacks are vulnerable to slashers - try not to stand still for too long. Use a pack which is lockable at its base.

It is best, if you can trust your hotel, to leave any valuables you don't need in safe-deposit there, when sightseeing locally. Always keep an inventory of what you have deposited. If you don't trust the hotel, lock everything in your pack and secure that in your room. If you lose valuables, always report to the police and note details of the report – for insurance purposes.

When you have all your luggage with you at a bus or railway station, be especially careful: don't get into arguments with any locals if you can help it, and lock all the items together with a chain or cable if you are waiting for some time. Take a taxi between airport/bus station/railway station and hotel, if you can afford it. Keep your bags with you in the taxi and pay only when you and your luggage are safely out of the vehicle. Make sure the taxi has inner door handles, in case a quick exit is needed. Avoid night buses, never arrive at night and watch your belongings being stowed inside. Major bus lines often issue a luggage ticket when bags are stored in the hold of the bus. When getting on a bus, keep your ticket handy; someone sitting in your seat may be a distraction for an accomplice to rob you while you are sorting out the problem. Finally, never accept food, drink, sweets or cigarettes from unknown fellow-travellers on buses or trains. They may be drugged, and you would wake up hours later without your belongings. In this connection, never accept a bar drink from an opened bottle (unless you can see that that bottle is in general use): always have it uncapped in front of you.

Tricksters

In Buenos Aires and other major cities beware of the common trick of spraying mustard, ketchup or some other substance on you and then getting an accomplice to clean you off (and remove your wallet). If you are sprayed, walk straight on. Ignore also strangers' remarks like 'what's that on your shoulder?' or 'have you seen that dirt on your shoe?'. Furthermore, don't bend over to pick up money or other items in the street. These are all ruses intended to distract your attention and make you easy for an accomplice to steal from. If someone follows you when you're in the street, let him catch up with you and 'give him the eye'. While you should take local advice about being out at night, do not assume that daytime is safer than nighttime. If walking after dark in dangerous parts of big cities, walk in the road, not on the pavement/sidewalk.

Be wary of 'plainclothes policemen'; insist on seeing identification and on going to the police station by main roads. Do not hand over your identification (or money – which he should not need to see anyway) until you are at the station. On no account take them directly back to your lodgings. Be even more suspicious if he seeks confirmation of his status from a passer-by. If someone tries to bribe you, insist on a receipt. If attacked, remember your assailants may well be armed, and try not to resist.

Rape

This can happen anywhere in the world. If you are the victim of a sexual assault, you are advised in the first instance to contact a doctor (this can be your home doctor if you prefer). You will need tests to determine whether you have contracted any sexually-transmitted diseases; you may also need advice on post-coital contraception. You should also contact your embassy, where consular staff are very willing to help in cases of assault.

Drugs

Users of drugs, even of soft ones, without medical prescription should be particularly careful, as some countries impose heavy penalties – up to 10 years' imprisonment –

for even the simple possession of such substances. In this connection, the planting of drugs on travellers, by traffickers or the police, is not unknown. If offered drugs on the street, make no response at all and keep walking. Note that people who roll their own cigarettes are often suspected of carrying drugs and subjected to intensive searches. It is advisable to stick to commercial brands of cigarettes.

Many points of security, dress and language have been covered already. First time **Travelling alone** exposure to countries where sections of the population live in extreme poverty or squalor can cause odd psychological reactions in visitors. So can the exceptional curiosity extended to visitors, especially women. Simply be prepared for this and try not to over-react. These additional hints have mainly been supplied by women, but most apply to any single traveller. When you set out, err on the side of caution until your instincts have adjusted to the customs of a new culture. If, as a single woman, you can befriend a local woman, you will learn much more about the country you are visiting. Unless actively avoiding foreigners like yourself, don't go too far from the beaten track; there is a very definite 'gringo trail' which you can join, or follow, if seeking company. This can be helpful when looking for safe accommodation, especially if arriving after dark (which is best avoided). Remember that for a single woman a taxi at night can be as dangerous as wandering around on her own. At borders dress as smartly as possible. Travelling by train is a good way to meet locals, but buses are much easier for a person alone; on major routes your seat is often reserved and your luggage can usually be locked in the hold. It is easier for men to take the friendliness of locals at face value; women may be subject to much unwanted attention. To help minimize this, do not wear revealing clothing and do not flirt. By wearing a wedding ring, carrying a photograph of your 'husband' and 'children', and saying that your 'husband' is close at hand, you may dissuade an aspiring suitor. If politeness fails, do not feel bad about showing offence and departing. When accepting a social invitation, make sure that someone knows the address and the time you left. Ask if you can bring a friend (even if you do not intend to do so). A good rule is always to act with confidence, as though you know where you are going, even if you do not. Someone who looks lost is more likely to attract unwanted attention. Do not disclose to strangers where you are staying.

Whereas in Europe and North America we are accustomed to law enforcement on a **Police** systematic basis, enforcement in Argentina, as in other parts of Latin America, is often achieved by periodic campaigns. The most typical is a round-up of criminals in the cities just before Christmas. In December, therefore, you may be asked for identification, and if you cannot produce it, you will be jailed. If a visitor is jailed his/her friends should provide food every day. This is especially important for people on a diet, such as diabetics. In the event of a vehicle accident in which anyone is injured, all drivers involved are automatically detained until responsibility has been established, and this does not usually take less than two weeks.

Never offer a bribe: wait until an official makes the suggestion, or offer money in some form which is apparently not bribery, for example 'In our country we have a system of on-the-spot fines (*multas de inmediato*). Is there a similar system here?'. Do not assume that an official who accepts a bribe is prepared to do anything else that is illegal. You bribe him to persuade him to do his job, or to persuade him not to do it, or to do it more quickly, or more slowly. You do not bribe him to do something which is against the law. The mere suggestion would make him very upset. If an official suggests that a bribe must be paid before you can proceed on your way, be patient (assuming you have the time) and he may relent.

Where to stay

Hotels, residenciales & hospedajes
During public holidays or high season it may be advisable to book ahead

There are often great seasonal variations in hotel prices especially in resorts. In the beach and inland resorts where there are many good hotels, *residenciales* and *hospedajes* (names are not always given in the text). *Residenciales* and *hospedajes* are usually cheaper than hotels. In many cities they are found near bus terminals. Good value hotels can also be found near truckers' stops/service stations; they are usually secure. In the text 'with bath' means with private bathroom which usually means 'with shower and toilet', not 'with bath tub'. Remember, cheaper hotels don't always supply soap, towels and toilet paper. In any class, hotel rooms facing the street may be noisy, especially in big cities, but interior rooms may not have windows; always ask for the best, quietest room. To avoid price hikes for foreigners, ask if there is a cheaper room or a discount. The electric showers used in innumerable hotels should be checked for obvious flaws in the wiring; try not to touch the head while it is producing hot water.

Youth hostels

Hostelling International Argentina, or *Red Argentina de Alojamiento para Jóvenes (RAAJ),* Florida 835, 3rd floor of 319b, Buenos Aires, T45118712, F43120089, www.hostels.org.ar, offers 10% discount to card-holders at their hostels throughout Argentina. *The Danmark Organization,* Junín 1616, p 3, Buenos Aires, T54-11- 48033700, has a network of clean, cheap youth hostels throughout Argentina (no age limit, but card needed): in Bariloche, El Bolsón, Pinamar, Calafate and the Tigre Delta. There are few other youth hostels (many open only February to March), but some towns offer free accommodation to young travellers in the holiday season, on floors of schools or church halls; some fire stations will let you sleep on the floor for free (sometimes men only).

Cockroaches

These are unpleasant, but not dangerous. Take some insecticide powder if staying in cheap hotels; *Baygon* (Bayer) has been recommended. Stuff toilet paper in any holes in walls that you may suspect of being parts of cockroach runs.

Toilets

Many hotels, restaurants and bars have inadequate water supplies. In most places used toilet paper should **not** be flushed down the pan, but placed in the receptacle provided. This applies even in quite expensive hotels. Failing to observe this custom will block the pan or drain, a considerable health risk. It is quite common for people to stand on the toilet seat (facing the wall – easier to balance).

Camping

Organized campsites are referred to in the text immediately below hotel lists, under each town. Camping is very popular in Argentina (except in Buenos Aires) and there are sites with services, both municipal, free, and paying private campsites in most

Hotel prices and facilities

LL *(over US$151) and* **L** *(US$101-150)*
Hotels in these categories can be found in
most of the large cities but especially where
there is a strong concentration of business
travellers. They should offer pool, sauna, gym,
jacuzzi, all business facilities (including
email), restaurants and bars. A safe box is
usually provided in each room. Credit cards
are generally accepted.

AL *(US$81-100) and* **A** *(US$61-80) Hotels in*
this category should provide more than the
standard facilities and a fair degree of
comfort. Many include a good breakfast and
offer extras such as a TV, minibar, air
conditioning and a swimming pool. They
may also provide tourist information and
their own transport for airport pickups.
Service is generally good and most accept
credit cards although a lower rate for cash is
often offered.

AB *(US$46-60),* **B** *(US$31-45) and* **C**
(US$21-30) Hotels in these categories
range from very comfortable to functional
and there are some real bargains to be
had. You should expect your own
bathroom, constant hot water, a towel,
soap and toilet paper. There is sometimes
a restaurant and a communal sitting area.
In tropical regions rooms are usually
equipped with air conditioning although
this may be rather old. Hotels used to
catering for foreign tourists and
backpackers often have luggage storage,
money exchange and kitchen facilities.

D *(US$12-20),* **E** *(US$7-11),* **F** *(US$4-6) and*
G *(up to US$3) Hotels in these categories*
are often extremely simple with bedside or
ceiling fans, shared bathrooms and little in
the way of furniture. Standards of
cleanliness may not be high and rooms
may also be rented to couples by the hour.

Essentials

tourist centres. Most are very noisy and many are closed off-season. In Patagonia strong winds can make camping very difficult. Prices have increased in recent years, though the quality of service is variable. Campers should always make sure they carry insect repellent. Camping is allowed at the side of major highways and in all national parks (except at Iguazú Falls). Many ACA and YPF service stations have a site where one can camp (usually free) and in general service station owners are very friendly to campers, but ask first. Service stations usually have hot showers. A list of camping sites is available from ACA (labelled for members, but should be easily available) and from the national tourist information office in Buenos Aires, which has a free booklet, *1ra Guía Argentina de Campamentos*; see also Autoclub magazine. ACA campsites offer discounts to members, and to holders of the International Driving Licence; European automobile clubs' members are allowed to use ACA sites.

'Wild' camping is possible in deserted area. Obey the following rules: (1) arrive in daylight and pitch your tent as it gets dark; (2) ask permission to camp from the parish priest, or the fire chief, or the police, or a farmer regarding his own property; (3) never ask a group of people – especially young people; (4) never camp on a beach (because of sandflies and thieves). If you can't get information from anyone, camp in a spot where you can't be seen from the nearest inhabited place, or road, and make sure no one saw you go there. Camping wild may be preferable to those organized sites which are treated as discotheques with only the afternoon reserved for sleeping.

Equipment If taking a cooker, the most frequent recommendation is a multifuel stove which will burn unleaded petrol or, if that is not available, kerosene, *benzina blanca*, et cetera. Alcohol-burning stoves are simple, reliable, but slow and you have to carry a lot of fuel. Fuel can usually be found in chemists/pharmacies. Gas cylinders and bottles are usually exchangeable, but if not can be recharged; specify whether you use butane or propane. Gas canisters are not always available. Regular (blue bottle)

Camping Gaz International is available in Buenos Aires, at an electrical goods store on Avenida 9 de Julio, near Teatro Colón, and *Suntime*, Lima 225, Guatemala 5908 (Palermo), Juramento 2452 (Belgrano) and *América Pesca*, Alfredo Pollini Alvear 1461. White gas (*bencina blanca*) is readily available in hardware shops (*ferreterías*). *Camping Center*, Acoyte 1622, Buenos Aires, T855-0619, rents camping, fishing and backpacking equipment, 5% discount for ISIC holders.

Getting around

Be careful when asking directions. Women probably know more about the neighbourhood; men about more distant locations. Policemen are often helpful. However people may sometimes give you the wrong answer rather than admit they do not know.

Air

Even though sometimes offices in various towns may tell you the flights are full, it is usually worth a try out at the airport

Internal air services are run by *Aerolíneas Argentinas* (AR), *Austral*, *Lapa* (reliable, cheaper than main airlines, 15 kilos baggage allowance), *Transporte Aéreo Neuquén* (TAN) in the south (book tickets through Austral), *Dinar* (based in Salta, serving the capital, Mar del Plata and the north, cheap fares), *Tapsa* (serving Patagonia, Neuquén), *LAER* (Entre Ríos, Mesopotamia), *Andesmar*, *Southern Winds* (both in the north and west) and the army airline *LADE* (in Patagonia), which provides a good extended schedule with new Fokker F-28 jets. *LADE* will not accept IATA MCOs. Deregulation and privatization has permitted the introduction of discounts by the major carriers. Ask at a travel agency. Some airlines operate during the high season, or are air taxis on a semi-regular schedule. *AR* and *Austral* offer discounted, *banda negativa* fares on a limited number of seats on many flights, but reserve well in advance. *Lapa* and *Dinar* maintain low fares as long as a flight is not fully booked. All airlines operate standby systems, at half regular price, buy ticket two to three hours before flight. It is only worth doing this off season. *Plan familiar* tickets allow couples to travel with a 25% discount for the spouse. Children under three travel free. *LADE* also operates discount spouse (65) and children (35) tickets. If travelling by *AR* or *Austral* a long linear distance, eg Río Gallegos-Buenos Aires, but wishing to stop en route, it is cheaper to buy the long flight and pay extra (about US$2) for stopovers.

Tips All local flights are fully booked way in advance for travel in December. Don't lose your baggage ticket; you won't be able to collect your bags without it. Some travellers have recommended checking in two hours before flight to avoid being

'bumped off' from overbooking. Meals are rarely served on internal flights. There is a US$3 airport tax on internal flights and a 5% tax on airline tickets. Timetables are given in *Guía Argentina de Tráfico Aéreo* and *Guía Internacional de Tráfico*. It is unwise to set up too tight a schedule because of delays which may be caused by bad weather. Flights between Buenos Aires and Río Gallegos are often fully booked two to three weeks ahead, and there may be similar difficulties on the routes to Bariloche and Iguazú. If you are 'wait-listed' they cannot ensure a seat. Reconfirmation at least 72 hours ahead of a flight is important and it is essential to make it at the point of departure. It can be difficult to obtain cash refunds for internal airline tickets if you change your plans: better to change your ticket for a different one.

Aerolíneas Argentinas sells an Argentina airpass, three flight coupons US$299, **Airpasses** US$105 for each extra coupon up to a maximum of eight. It is valid for 60 days and must be purchased outside Argentina and in conjunction with an international flight ticket on *Aerolíneas Argentinas* or *British Airways*. Note that for children under two years airpass costs 10 of the above rates and that normally very young children travel free. Routing must be booked when the coupons are issued though dates may be left open: one change of date and of destination is free (but subsequent changes cost US$50). One stop only is permitted per town; this includes making a connection (as many flights radiate from Buenos Aires, journeys to and from the capital count as legs on the airpass, so a four-coupon pass might not get you very far). If you start your journey outside Buenos Aires on a Sunday, when *Aerolíneas Argentinas* offices are closed, you may have difficulty getting vouchers issued at the airport. If you wish to visit Tierra del Fuego and Calafate it is better fly on the Airpass to Río Grande or Ushuaia and travel around by bus or LADE from there than to stop off in Río Gallegos, fly to Ushuaia and thence back to Buenos Aires, which will use three coupons.

LAPA offer a similar airpass, valid for 60 days, which may only be bought in conjuction with an international ticket to Argentina bought outside the country on any airline, US$339 for three coupons, US$100 for each additional coupon up to a maximum of eight.

Bus

Fares are charged at about US$4.50 per 100 km. Sleeper services from the capital to Mendoza, Córdoba and Bariloche cost US$7 per 100 km. There are also 'ómnibus truchos' (fake buses), which do not start or end services at bus stations and which have less reliable equipment or time-keeping; they charge less than US$4 per 100 km (ask at travel agents or hotels). Bus companies may give a 20% student discount if you show an international student card; a Hostelling International card is also useful. The same discount may also be given to foreign, as well as Argentine, teachers and university professors but you must carry documentary proof of your employment. It can be difficult to get reductions between December and March. Express buses between cities are dearer than the *comunes*, but well worth the extra money for the fewer stops. When buying tickets at a bus office, don't assume you've been automatically allotted a seat: make sure you have one. Buses have strong air conditioning, even more so in summer; take a sweater for night journeys. Note that luggage is only insured up to a maximum of 15 kilos per traveller. Luggage is handled by *maleteros*, who expect payment (theoretically US$1, but in practice you can offer less) though many Argentines refuse to pay.

Car

Most main roads are paved, if rather narrow (road maps are a good indication of quality), and roadside services are good. Road surface conditions vary once you leave the main towns. Many minor roads are gravel (*ripio*); on these and on the dirt roads a guard for the windscreen is essential. Most main roads now have private tolls, ranging from US$2 to US$10; tolls are spaced about every 100 km. Secondary roads (which have not been privatized) are generally in poor condition. Sometimes you may not be allowed to reach a border if you do not intend to cross it, stopping for example 20 km from the border.

All motorists are required to carry two warning triangles, a fire-extinguisher, a rigid tow bar, a first aid kit, full car documentation together with international driving licence (for non-residents, but see **Car hire** below), and the handbrake must be fully operative. Safety belts must be worn if fitted. Although few checks are made in most of the country, with the notable exceptions of roads into Rosario and Buenos Aires, checks have been reported on cars entering the country. Police checks around Buenos Aires can be very officious, even to the point of charges being invented and huge 'fines' demanded. You may not export fuel from Argentina, so use up fuel in spare jerry cans while you are in the country. Always fill up when you can in less developed areas like Chaco and Formosa and in parts of Patagonia as filling stations are infrequent. Diesel fuel 'gas-oil' prices are US$0.27 per litre. Octane rating for gasoline ('*nafta*') is as follows: regular gasoline 83 (US$0.65 per litre); super 93 (US$0.78 per litre). Fuel prices are much lower in Patagonia than in the rest of the country as no tax is levied. Unleaded fuel is not widely available but its use is increasing (it is called Ultra SP and costs a little more than super). *ACA* sells petrol vouchers (*vales de nafta*) for use in *ACA* stations. *Shell* and *Esso* stations are slightly more expensive.

To obtain documents for a resident (holder of resident visa, staying at least six months in the country) to take a car out of Argentina, you can go to *ACA* in Buenos Aires, which may take up to four working days, or you can ask for a list of other *ACA* offices that can undertake the work; take forms with you from Buenos Aires, and papers may be ready in 24 hours. You will need at least one passport-size photo, which you can have taken at *ACA* at a fair cost. If the car is not your own (or is hired), you require a special form signed by the owner and witnessed by a notary public. Non-residents may buy a car in Argentina but are in no circumstances allowed to take it out of the country; it must be resold in Argentina, preferably in the province where it was purchased. Non-residents who take cars into Argentina are not allowed to sell them and will encounter problems trying to leave the country without the vehicle. Third party insurance is obligatory; best obtained from the *ACA*, for members only.

Automóvil Club Argentino (ACA) The office in Buenos Aires can be found at Av Libertador Gen San Martín 1850, 1st floor, touring department on 3rd floor, 1425 Buenos Aires, T48026061/9, www.aca.org.ar (take *colectivo* 130 from LN Alem and Corrientes down Alem, Libertador and F Alcorta, alight opposite ACA and walk one block through park; to return take the 130 from corner of Libertador on left as you leave building). It opens at 1000 to 1800. The office in Oficina Plaza San Martín, Santa Fe 887, has a travel document service, complete car service facilities, insurance facilities, road information, road charts (*hojas de ruta*-about US$2.35 each to members, if available) and maps (has a road map of whole country, with service stations and *hosterías* shown, US$4 to members, US$9.50 to non-members and of each province), a hotel list, camping information, and a tourist guide book sold at a discount to its members and members of other recognized, foreign automobile clubs upon presentation of a membership card. Members of other recognized automobile clubs are advised to check if their club has reciprocity with ACA, thus allowing use of ACA facilities and benefit from discounts. The club has service stations, some with parking garages, all over the

Route 40

Route 40 is to Argentina what the Trans-Alaskan Highway is to North America or the (now largely disused) Trans-Amazon Highway to Brazil. Route 40 is a trunk road which runs along the eastern edge of the Andes, virtually from the frontier with Bolivia in the north almost to Tierra del Fuego in the south.

Almost 5,000 km long, one third paved, the rest ripio or dirt, it runs through practically every type of climate from boiling hot to freezing cold and through all kinds of surroundings, ancient and modern, indigenous societies and modern cities. At the Abra del Acay (4,895 m) it even climbs to an altitude higher than Mont Blanc. And, on top of this, it provides access to several national parks and other wonders such as Mount Aconcagua and the great glaciers of the southern lakes.

In recent years the idea of driving along this magnificent route has become a great attraction to Argentines. Now an increasing number of foreigners is beginning to head towards it, whether by ordinary car or by a vehicle with four wheel drive, for which Route 40 is ideal. The 5,000 km, which becomes 10,000 if you add on the distance to get there at each end, obviously demands adequate time.

country. If you are not a member of *ACA* you will not get any help when in trouble. *ACA* membership, US$20 per month, permits you to pay with Eurocard (Argencard) for fuel at their service stations, gives 20% discount on hotel rooms and maps, and discounts at associated hotels, campsites, and 10% discount on meals.

ACA accommodation comes in four types: *motel*, *hostería*, *hotel*, and *unidad turística*, and they also organize campsites. A *motel* may have as few as three rooms, and only one night's stay is permitted. *Hosterías* have very attractive buildings and are very friendly. *Hotels* are smarter and more impersonal. All have meal facilities of some kind. Anyone, motorist or not, can get in touch with the organization to find out about accommodation or road conditions.

Their office is at Esmeralda 605 and Tucumán 781, third floor, T392-6742. This club has similar travel services but no service stations.

Touring Club Argentino

What kind of motoring you do will depend on what kind of car you set out with. Four-wheel drive is not necessary, but it does give you greater flexibility in mountain terrain and unmade roads off the beaten track. In Patagonia, main roads are gravel rather than paved: perfectly passable without four-wheel drive, just rough and dusty. Consider fitting wire guards for headlamps, and for windscreens too, if you don't mind peering out through a grill like a caged chimpanzee. Wherever you travel you should expect from time to time to find roads that are badly maintained, damaged or closed during the wet season, and delays because of floods, landslides and huge potholes.

The machine

Diesel cars are much cheaper to run than petrol ones, and the fuel is easily available. Most towns can supply a mechanic of sorts, and probably parts for Bosch fuel injection equipment. Watch the mechanics like a hawk, since there's always a brisk market in spares, and some of yours may be highly desirable. That apart, they enjoy a challenge, and can fix most things, eventually.

Argentina is very expensive for maintenance of any make of car so obviously any part that is not in first class condition should be replaced. It's well worth installing extra heavy-duty shock-absorbers before starting out, because a long trip on rough roads in a heavily laden car will give heavy wear. Fit tubes on 'tubeless' tyres, since air plugs for tubeless tyres are hard to find, and if you bend the rim on a pothole, the tyre will not hold air. Take spare tubes and an extra spare tyre. Also take spare plugs, fan-belts, radiator hoses and headlamp bulbs; even though local equivalents can easily be

Essentials

found in cities, it is wise to take spares for those occasions late at night or in remote areas when you might need them. You can also change the fanbelt after a stretch of long, hot driving to prevent wear (for example after 15,000 km per 10,000 miles). Dirty fuel is a frequent problem, so be prepared to change filters more often than you would at home: in a diesel car you will need to check the sediment bowl often, too. An extra in-line fuel filter is a good idea if feasible (although harder to find, metal canister type is preferable to plastic), and for travel on dusty roads an oil bath air filter is best for a diesel car. It is wise to carry a spade, jumper cables, tow rope and an air pump. Fit tow hooks to both sides of the vehicle frame. A 12 volt neon light for camping and repairs will be invaluable. Spare fuel containers should be steel and not plastic, and a siphon pipe is essential for those places where fuel is sold out of the drum. Take a 10 litre water container for self and vehicle.

Security Apart from the mechanical aspects, spare no ingenuity in making your car secure. Your model should be the Brink's armoured van: anything less secure can be broken into by the determined and skilled thief. Use heavy chain and padlocks to chain doors shut, fit security catches on windows, remove interior window winders (so that a hand reaching in from a forced vent cannot open the window). All these will help, but none is foolproof. Anything on the outside – wing mirrors, spot lamps, motifs et cetera – is likely to be stolen too. So are wheels if not secured by locking nuts. Try never to leave the car unattended except in a locked garage or guarded parking space. Remove all belongings and leave the empty glove compartment open when the car is unattended. Also lock the clutch or accelerator to the steering wheel with a heavy, obvious chain or lock. Street children will generally protect your car fiercely in exchange for a tip. Be sure to note down key numbers and carry spares of the most important ones (but don't keep all spares inside the vehicle).

Documents In general, motorists in South America seem to fare better with a *libreta* or *carnet de passages* than without it. The *libreta*, a 10-page book of three-part passes for customs, costs about US$350, but is more for those who are not members of automobile clubs; about a third of the cost is refundable. The *carnet de passages* is issued only in the country where the vehicle is registered (in the UK it costs US$65 for 25 pages, US$55 for 10 pages, valid 12 months, either bank indemnity or insurance indemnity, half of the premium refundable value of the vehicle and countries to be visited required), available from the *RAC* or the *AA*. In the USA the *AAA* does not issue the *carnet*, although the HQ in Washington DC may give advice. It is available from the *Canadian Automobile Association*, 1775 Courtwood Crescent, Ottawa, K2C 3JZ, T613-2267631, F2257383, for Canadian and US citizens and costs C$400. Full details are obtainable from the *CAA*. Thanks to Paul Gowen, RAC Touring Information Manager, Binka Le Breton and other motorists for this information.

Land entry procedures are simple though time-consuming, as the car has to be checked by customs, police and agriculture officials. All you need is the registration document in the name of the driver, or, in the case of a car registered in someone else's name, a notarized letter of authorization. Officially you are required to give a written undertaking that the car will be exported after a given period, either of the *carnets*, or the *libreta* (in practice, nothing is asked for beyond the title document, except at remote border crossings which may demand a *libreta*). Of course, you should be very careful to keep **all** the papers you are given when you enter, to produce when you leave. If the car is stolen or written off you will be required to pay very high import duty on its value.

Car hire The main international car hire companies operate in Argentina, but they tend to be very expensive, reflecting the high costs and accident rates. Hotels and tourist agencies will tell you where to find cheaper rates, but you will need to check that you have such basics as spare wheel, toolkit and functioning lights et cetera. You'll probably have more fun if you drive yourself, although it's always possible to hire a car with driver. If you plan to do a lot of driving and will have time at the end to dispose of it, investigate the possibility of buying a second hand car locally: since hiring is so expensive it may well work out cheaper and will probably do you just as well.

To rent a small car (for four plus luggage) costs from US$75 to US$145 a day, with 150 km free, not including insurance and tax (20%); highest prices are in Patagonia. Discounts are available for several days', or weekly rental. Minimum age for renting is 25 (private arrangements may be possible). A credit card is useful. You must ensure that the renting agency gives you ownership papers of the vehicle, which have to be shown at police and military checks. At tourist centres such as Salta, Posadas, Bariloche or Mendoza it may be more economical to hire a taxi with driver, which includes the guide, the fuel, the insurance and the mechanic. Avis offers a good and efficient service with the possibility of complete insurance and unlimited mileage for rentals of seven days or more, but you should prebook from abroad; no one-way fee if returned to another Avis office, but the car may not be taken out of the country. Localiza, a Brazilian company, accepts drivers aged at least 21 (according to Brazilian rules, but higher insurance). They also offer four-wheel drive vehicles, though only from Buenos Aires. Taking a rented car out of Argentina is difficult with any company. Other companies are given in the text.

If you do not have an international driver's licence, you can get a three-month licence from Dirección de Transportes de la Municipalidad, Avenida Roca 5225, Buenos Aires, T602-6925, Monday-Friday 0800-1300; bring documentation from home.

Insurance Check exactly what the hirer's insurance policy covers. In many cases it will only protect you against minor bumps and scrapes, not major accidents, nor 'natural' damage (for example flooding). Ask if extra cover is available. Also find out, if using a credit card, whether the card automatically includes insurance. Beware of being billed for scratches which were on the vehicle before you hired it.

You can ship a vehicle from Europe to Argentina. Recommended as good value are **Shipping a** *Polish Ocean Lines*, 10 Lutego, Gdynia, Poland. *Carnet* is necessary; *POL* agent deals with **vehicle** customs. Departure dates are not scheduled in advance. Vehicles can also be shipped from the USA. Anything left inside the car while it is being shipped will be stolen. As long as your vehicle is not over 2.28 m high, it can go in a container, but permission must be obtained for any belongings to remain in the car, and separate insurance for effects purchased. If the car is going ro-ro (drive on), it should be empty of all belongings, unless they are thoroughly secured.

Two books containing much practical information on South American motoring conditions and requirements are *Driving to Heaven*, by Derek Stansfield (available from the author, Ropley, Broad Oak, Sturminster Newton, Dorset DT10 2HG, T/F01258-472534, US$8.85 plus postage, if outside the UK), and the more recent *Central and South America by Road*, Pam Ascanio (Bradt Publications 1996).

Motorbike

People are generally very amicable to motorcyclists and you can make many friends by returning friendship to those who show an interest in you.

It should be off road capable: for example the BMW R80/100/GS for its rugged and **The machine** simple design and reliable shaft drive, but a Kawasaki KLR 650s, Honda Transalp/Dominator, or the ubiquitous Yamaha XT600 Tenere would also be suitable. A road bike can go most places an off road bike can go at the cost of greater effort.

Essentials

Preparations Many roads in Argentina are rough. Fit heavy duty front fork springs and the best quality rebuildable shock absorber you can afford (Ohlins, White Power). Fit lockable luggage such as Krausers (reinforce luggage frames) or make some detachable aluminium panniers. Fit a tank bag and tank panniers for better weight distribution. A large capacity fuel tank (Acerbis), +300 mile/480 km range is essential if going off the beaten track. A washable air filter is a good idea (K&N), also fuel filters, fueltap rubber seals and smaller jets for high altitude Andean motoring. A good set of trails-type tyres as well as a high mudguard are useful. Get to know the bike before you go, ask the dealers in your country what goes wrong with it and arrange a link whereby you can get parts flown out to you. If riding a chain driven bike, a fully enclosed chaincase is useful. A hefty bash plate/sump guard is invaluable.

Spares Reduce service intervals by half if driving in severe conditions. A spare rear tyre is useful but you can buy modern tyres in most cities. Take oil filters, fork and shock seals, tubes, a good manual, spare cables (taped into position), a plug cap and spare plug lead. A spare electronic ignition is a good idea, try and buy a second hand one and make arrangements to have parts sent out to you. A first class tool kit is a must and if riding a bike with a chain then a spare set of sprockets and an 'o' ring chain should be carried. Spare brake and clutch levers should also be taken as these break easily in a fall. Parts are few and far between, but mechanics are skilled at making do and can usually repair things. Castrol oil can be bought everywhere and relied upon.

Take a puncture repair kit and tyre levers. Find out about any weak spots on the bike and improve them. Get the book for international dealer coverage from your manufacturer, but don't rely on it. They frequently have few or no parts for modern, large machinery.

Clothes & equipment A tough waterproof jacket, comfortable strong boots, gloves and a helmet with which you can use glass goggles (Halycon) which will not scratch and wear out like a plastic visor. The best quality tent and camping gear that you can afford and a petrol stove which runs on bike fuel is helpful.

Security Not a problem generally. Try not to leave a fully laden bike on its own. An *Abus D* or chain will keep it secure and a cheap alarm gives you peace of mind if you leave the bike outside a hotel at night. Most hotels will allow you to bring the bike inside. Look for hotels that have a courtyard or more secure parking.

Documents Passport, International Driving Licence, bike registration document are necessary. Riders fare much better with a *carnet de passages* than without it.

Bicycle

At first glance a bicycle may not appear to be the most obvious vehicle for a major journey, but given ample time and reasonable energy it most certainly is the best. It can be ridden, carried by almost every form of transport from an aeroplane to a canoe, and can even be lifted across one's shoulders over short distances. Cyclists can be the envy of travellers using more orthodox transport, since they can travel at their own pace, explore more remote regions and meet people who are not normally in contact with tourists.

The machine The choice of bicycle depends on the type and length of expedition being undertaken and on the terrain and road surfaces likely to be encountered. Unless you are planning a journey almost exclusively on paved roads – when a high quality touring bike such as a Dawes Super Galaxy would probably suffice – a mountain bike is strongly recommended. The good quality ones (and the cast iron rule is never to skimp on quality) are incredibly tough and rugged, with low gear ratios for difficult terrain, wide tyres with plenty of tread for good road-holding, cantilever brakes, and a low centre of gravity for improved stability. Although touring bikes, and to a lesser extent mountain bikes, and spares are available in the larger cities, remember that locally manufactured goods are shoddy and rarely last. Buy everything you possibly can before you leave home.

A small but comprehensive tool kit (to include chain rivet and crank removers, a spoke **Equipment** key and possibly a block remover), a spare tyre and inner tubes, a puncture repair kit with plenty of extra patches and glue, a set of brake blocks, brake and gear cables and all types of nuts and bolts, at least 12 spokes (best taped to the chain stay), a light oil for the chain (for example Finish-Line Teflon Dry-Lube), tube of waterproof grease, a pump secured by a pump lock, a Blackburn parking block (a most invaluable accessory, cheap and virtually weightless), a cyclometer, a loud bell, and a secure lock and chain. *Richard's Bicycle Book* makes useful reading for even the most mechanically minded.

Strong and waterproof front and back panniers are a must. When packed these are likely to be heavy and should be carried on the strongest racks available. Poor quality racks have ruined many a journey for they take incredible strain on unpaved roads. A top bag cum rucksack (for example Carradice) makes a good addition for use on and off the bike. A Cannondale front bag is good for maps, camera, compass, altimeter, notebook and small tape-recorder. (Other recommended panniers are Ortlieb – front and back – which is watproof and almost 'sandproof', Mac-Pac, Madden and Karimoor). 'Gaffa' tape is excellent for protecting vulnerable parts of panniers and for carrying out all manner of repairs.

All equipment and clothes should be packed in plastic bags to give extra protection against dust and rain. Also protect all documents, et cetera carried close to the body from sweat. Always take the minimum clothing. It's better to buy extra items *en route* when you find you need them. Naturally the choice will depend on whether you are planning a journey through tropical lowlands, deserts, high mountains or a combination, and whether rain is to be expected. Generally it is best to carry several layers of thin light clothes than fewer heavy, bulky ones. Always keep one set of dry clothes, including long trousers, to put on at the end of the day. The incredibly light, strong, waterproof and wind resistant goretex jacket and overtrousers are invaluable. Training shoes can be used for both cycling and walking.

Wind, not hills is the enemy of the cyclist. Try to make the best use of the times of day **Useful tips** when there is little; mornings tend to be best but there is no steadfast rule. In parts of Patagonia there can be gusting winds of 80 kph around the clock at some times of year, whereas in other areas there can be none. Take care to avoid dehydration by drinking regularly. In hot, dry areas with limited supplies of water, be sure to carry an ample supply. For food, carry the staples (sugar, salt, dried milk, tea, coffee, porridge oats, raisins, dried soups, et cetera) and supplemented these with whatever local foods can be found in the markets. Give your bicycle a thorough daily check for loose nuts or bolts or bearings. See that all parts run smoothly. A good chain should last 2,000 miles, 3,200 km or more but be sure to keep it as clean as possible – an old toothbrush is good for this – and to oil it lightly from time to time. Always camp out of sight of a road. Remember that thieves are attracted to towns and cities, so when sight-seeing, try to leave your bicycle with someone such as a café owner or a priest. However, don't take unnecessary risks; always see that your bicycle is secure (most hotels will allow bikes to be kept in rooms). In more remote regions dogs can be vicious; carry a stick or some small stones to frighten them off. Most towns have a bicycle shop of some description, but it is best to do your own repairs and adjustments whenever possible. In an emergency it is amazing how one can improvise with wire, string, dental floss, nuts and bolts, odd pieces of tin or 'Gaffa' tape!

Most cyclists agree that the main danger comes from other traffic, especially on major roads. A rearview mirror has been frequently recommended to forewarn you of vehicles which are too close behind. You also need to watch out for oncoming, overtaking vehicles, unstable loads on trucks, protruding loads et cetera. Make yourself conspicuous by wearing bright clothing and a helmet.

The *Expedition Advisory Centre*, administered by the Royal Geographical Society, 1 Kensington Gore, London SW7 2AR has published a useful monograph entitled *Bicycle Expeditions*, Paul Vickers (March 1990). It is available direct from the Centre, price US$6.50 (postage extra if outside the UK). In the UK there is also the *Cyclist's Touring Club*, CTC, Cotterell House, 69 Meadrow, Godalming, Surrey, GU7 3HS, T01483-417217, cycling@ctc. org.uk, for touring, and technical information.

Hitchhiking

Argentina seems to be getting increasingly difficult for this. Ask at petrol stations. Traffic can be sparse especially at distances from the main towns and in Patagonia, which is popular with Argentine hitchhikers. Though they tend to be more reserved in manner than most Latin Americans, Argentines are generally friendly and helpful, especially to foreigners.

Train

On 10 March 1994, the government withdrew its funding for Ferrocarriles Argentinos, handing responsibility for all services to the provinces through which the lines run. Few provinces accepted the responsibility, because of lack of resources. As a result trains now run on only 22,000 of the original 42,000 km of track and most of its is used only by freight services. Surviving passenger services are run either by provincial governments or by the private sector. There are few passenger services outside the Buenos Aires area.

Keeping in touch

Internet   Communications on the internet are getting easier. *Telefónica Argentina* and *Telecom* offices in many cities have email services, US$5 per hour. Some *locutorios* have compatible equipment but static on the lines makes data transmission difficult and you are charged regardless.

Post   Letters from Argentina take 10-14 days to get to the UK and the USA. Rates for letters up to 20 g: US$0.75 Mercosur, US$1 rest of Latin America, US$1.25 rest of world (add US$2 for *certificado*); up to 150 g, US$1.50, US$2.25, US$3 respectively. For assured delivery, register everything.

Small parcels of up to 1 kilo can be sent from all post offices. Larger parcels must be sent from *Encomiendas Internacionales*, Centro Postal Internacional, Av Comodoro Py y Antártida Argentina, near Retiro Station, Buenos Aires, and in main provincial cities. *Encomiendas vía superficie* (by sea) costs from US$15 for 1 kilo, US$26 for three, up to US$108 for 28 kilos. *Encomiendas vía aérea* costs double. Larger parcels must first be examined before final packing by customs and then wrapped (up to 2 kilos in brown paper; over 2 kilos sewn in linen cloth), then sealed by customs and taken to Encomiendas Internacionales for posting. Cheap packing services are available. Customs usually open in the morning only. Having parcels sent to Argentina incurs a customs tax of US$5.75 per package and all incoming packages are opened by customs. *Poste restante* is available in every town's main post office, fee US$1.

Two private companies operate telephone services, *Telecom* in the north and *Telefónica Argentina* in the south. Buenos Aires Federal District and the country as a whole are split roughly in two halves. For the user there is no difference and the two companies' phone cards are interchangeable. For domestic calls public phones operate on *cospeles* (tokens) which can be purchased at news stands (different tokens for local and inland calls). Domestic phone calls are priced at three rates: normal 0800-1000, 1300-2200, Saturday 0800-1300; peak 1000-1300, Monday-Friday; night rate 2200-0800, Saturday 1300-0800 and all day Sunday and holidays. Peak is most expensive; night rate is cheapest and at this time also international calls are reduced by 20%. International calls are: rates per minute Uruguay US$0.82; USA, Canada, Brazil, Chile, Paraguay, Bolivia US$1.13 (0.85 each subsequent minute); France, Germany, UK, Spain, Italy US$1.90 (1.43); Japan, Australia, New Zealand US$4.66 (3.50). In main cities there are also privately-run phone offices (*locutorios*), offering a good telephone and fax service. International public phones display the DDI sign (Discado Directo Internacional); DDN (Discado Directo Nacional) is for phone calls within Argentina. Provide yourself with enough tokens or phone cards in Buenos Aires because, in the regions, phone booths exist, but the tokens and cards are not on sale. Most telephone company offices in principal cities have a phone for USA Direct; if they do not, they can direct you to one. BT Chargecard can be used to the UK via the operator (T0800-54401). American Express in Buenos Aires allows card holders to receive faxes at US$1 per sheet and to send them at US$8 per sheet (to Europe). *Telefónica* and *Telecom* send faxes abroad for US$1.23 per page, plus cost of the call, and US$1.82 per page to receive. You get charged for sending the fax even if it does not get through. There is frequently a high mark-up on calls made from hotels. No reverse-charge calls to South Africa. The operators speak English.

Telephone
There are few phone booths in Patagonia

Newspapers Buenos Aires dailies are *La Nación* (www.lanacion.com.ar), *La Prensa*, *Clarín* (www.clarin.com.ar), *La Razón*. Evening papers are *Crónica*, an English language daily and *Buenos Aires Herald*, www.buenosairesherald.com Magazines include *Noticias, Gente, Redacción, Mercado, El Gráfico* (sports). The daily, *Página Doce*, is very popular among students and intellectuals. *La Maga* is a weekly cultural review, Wednesday, US$5. English language magazines are *The Review of the River Plate*, commercial, agricultural, political and economic comment and *The Southern Cross* about the Irish community. A German-language weekly, *Argentinisches Tageblatt*, is available everywhere and is very informative. There is a weekly international edition of *La Nación*, priced in Europe at US$1.30. Write for further information to: La Nación, Edición Internacional, Bouchard 557, 1106 Buenos Aires.

Media

Radio English language radio broadcasts can be heard daily on short wave: 0100-0130 on 6060 KHz 49m, 0230-0300 on 11710 KHz 25m, 0430-0500 and 2230-2300 on 15345 KHz 19m; **BBC World Service** in Buenos Aires: 97.1Mhz from 1200 noon to 0500. **Radiodifusión Argentina al Exterior,** Casilla de Correo 555, 1000, Buenos Aires. This is a government station and broadcasts also in Japanese, Arabic, German, French, Italian and Portuguese. Broadcasts by foreign radio stations (including the BBC) are receivable on short wave.

Food and drink

Argentine cuisine, strictly speaking, does not exist. What is eaten in Argentina is, by and large, an inherited culture – an adaptation of Spanish, Italian, Arabic (Middle Eastern anyway) and other European influences. Lately a smattering of Oriental – Chinese, Japanese and Korean basically restaurants have sprung up in Buenos Aires and a few cities of the interior – Mar del Plata in particular – giving local cuisine a slightly more cosmopolitan touch. What should be the basis of Argentina cooking – the authentic and truly native dishes – is almost non-existent except in isolated pockets and regions of the country.

Dining out
Lunch is usually eaten between 1300-1430 & evening meal after 2200

Many restaurants serve a set price meal at lunchtime; often this is very good value. Eating out in the evening is usually much more expensive with no set price options. In major cities some large modern supermarkets have self-service cafétérias, which offer good quality food at good prices. Vegetables (other than chips) are not included in menu prices, but in cheaper restaurants outside Buenos Aires you can sometimes ask for a salad instead of chips and fill up on bread if you are hungry. In cheaper restaurants you will usually be offered corn oil with a salad, but it is always worth asking whether olive oil is available. Vegetarians should be able to list all the foods they cannot eat as saying 'Soy vegetariano/a' (I'm a vegetarian) or 'no como carne' (I don't eat meat) is often not enough.

Meat
Argentina is basically beef eating country. South of the Rio Colorado, where Patagonia officially commences, beef gives way to sheep, Argentina being one of the world's major producers of wool, lamb and mutton. However, only recently have Argentines come to appreciate what one lamb lover and expert, Iranian restaurateur Fereydoun Kia, calls "the best lamb in the world". The trouble is that local cooks have still to learn how to cook and present lamb, and Argentina housewives still have to throw off the idea that mutton (and lamb by inference) is solely the dogs – as it was until quite recently.

Parrilla
Beef is consumed in a variety of ways. The most traditional is, of course, the *parrilla* or *parrillada*, the local version of the American barbecue. Barbecue is a derivative of the Inca word *barbacoa* – their method of cooking meat over hot coals impaled on green branches taken from nearby bushes and trees. Parrilla refers to the roasting method: on a grill over hot coals; parrillada is a sum of different meats and cuts – including variety meats and offal – served together. Sausages, blood sausages, sweet-breads, thin intestines, rib roast cut in strips and tenderloin are but some of the many possibilities, which also include chicken but hardly ever lamb, pork or kid. It is usual to order one parrillada for two and menus frequently specify how many people can normally eat from one order.

Al asador
Lamb, pork and kid are generally roasted on a spit stuck into the ground and slightly leaning over the hot coals. This method is called *al asador*. One can also find an *asador al spiedo*, a mechanical spit which turns in front of an electric or gas heater. Nowadays it is usually used to roast chickens. All roasts are cooked with a touch of salt and nothing else. With the meat will be served a series of local condiments, *chimichurri* being very typical and usually quite spicy. It is a mixture of dried herbs, garlic, oil and (sometimes) vinegar.

American influences
Pasta is also very widespread and along with hamburgers, hot dogs, and pizza these represent the most visible evidence of the foreign influence. Argentine pizza, at least that which is found in Buenos Aires, is considered one of the finest and most varied in the world. New Yorkers, who claim the pizza championship, frequently admit that they have found a worthy rival in Buenos Aires.

Vegetables
Argentines are not great vegetable eaters, and their choices seldom go much beyond potatoes, tomato, lettuce, onion and garlic. The classic *ensalada mixta* (mixed salad) however, has aquired a name for itself amongst visitors from abroad. A simple combination of crisp lettuce, sliced tomato, sliced onion, oil and vinegar (lemon juice is also popular) it owes its popularity to the fact that local vegetables still maintain all the flavour and characteristics which hothouse vegetables lack. Argentina still relies

Yerba Maté

Originally drunk by precolombian Indians and known in the colonial period as 'Jesuit tea', yerba maté *is a stimulating herbal tea made from the leaves of* ilex paraguaiensis, *a bush similar to holly. The Jesuit Missions encouraged its consumption as an alternative to alcohol and produced some of the best quality yerba maté; finding that Buenos Aires traders offered low prices, they set up their own marketing system. It became popular among the gauchos but today it is consumed widely in Argentina, Uruguay, Paraguay and southern Brazil. The main producing areas in Argentina are the provinces of Misiones and Corrientes.*

Traditionally it was served in a gourd, called a maté, used because it preserved the temperature and flavour of the brew; alternatives to the gourd are now common, among them palo santo (a very hard wood), cowhorn and, less interestingly, aluminium. The container is filled to above half-capacity with leaves and hot water is added; the liquid is drunk through a bombilla, *a metal straw with a filter at the base, with extra water and leaves being added as required. It is normally consumed without sugar, though milk is sometimes added instead of water. In summer it is drunk as* tereré, *cold with a little lemon.*

Drinking maté is a great ritual and most maté-drinkers adopt their own techniques which they argue gives the best brew. It is an exceptionally social drink: maté is usually drunk in company and passed around the group, with one person being responsible for adding more water. It can be considered an insult to refuse when offered. If you develop a liking for it, remember that saying 'thank you' after drinking maté indicates that you do not want any more.

on nature rather than technology for its food supplies. This explains the particular quality of local beef, Argentine steers being range bred and fed the year round.

Eating in Buenos Aires and environs is quite different to the cuisine which is found in the rest of the country. Buenos Aires is modern and relatively sophisticated; the rest of the country, including such important cities as Rosario, Córdoba, Mendoza and Mar del Plata are another story altogether. Mendoza is a particularly curious case. Capital of Argentina's wine country and industry – one of the world's largest – it has no local cuisine to boast of and its restaurants are very poor indeed. Only Bariloche, centre of Argentina's spectacular Andean tourist country, has something resembling a regional cuisine, largely based on German, Austrian and Central European influences.

Geographical variations

In spite of being one of the worlds last great fishery reserves, fish and seafood occupies a very small role in local eating habits. Like lamb, fish is an almost unknown quantity in Argentina and local cooks tend to overcook their dishes mercilessly. Even in Mar del Plata, centre of the fishing industry, it is hard to obtain a really good seafood meal. *Centolla* (king crab) in Ushuaia, Tierra del Fuego, is one of Argentina's most interesting sea products, while from rivers and lakes can be fished the *pejerrey* (Brasilichthys argentinensis), a unique and extremely fine and delicate fish indeed.

Fish & seafood

Essentials

☞ *Dining out*

waiter	mozo	ham	jamón
waitress	señorita	bacon	panceta
the menu	la carta	pork chop	costillita de cerdo
today's specialities	el menu del día	suckling pig	lechón
the bill	la cuenta	eggs	huevos
tip	propina		
starter	entrada	**Fish**	**pescado**
main course	plato principal	hake	merluza
dessert	postre	trout	trucha
		tuna	atún

Drinks	**bebidas**		
beer	cerveza	**Seafood**	**mariscos**
coffee	café	shrimps	camarones
white coffee	café cortado	lobster	langosta
milk	leche	octopus	pulpo
mineral water	agua mineral	squid	calamares
still	sin gas		
sparkling	con gas	**Vegetables**	**verduras**
tea	té	lettuce	lechuga
white wine	vino blanco	potatoes	papas
red wine	vino tinto	(chips)	papas fritas)
orange juice	jugo de naranja	(mashed potatoes	puré de papas)
		tomato	tomate
Meat	**carne**	salad	ensalada
beef	bife, carne de	carrot	zanahoria
	vaca/carne vacuna	onion	cebolla
chicken	pollo	beans	porotos
pork	carne de cerdo		
lamb	cordero	**Fruit**	**fruta**
veal	ternera	apple	manzana
kid	chivito	banana	plátano
kidney	riñón	orange	naranja
entrails	chinchulines	grapefruit	pomelo
sweetbread	molleja	lemon	limón
blood sausage	morcilla	pear	pera
sausage	chorizo or	plum	ciruela
	salchicha	peach	durazno
barbecue	asado	grapes	uvas
flank	vacío		
flank steak	matambre	**Other food**	**Otra comida**
rumpsteak	bife de chorizo	bread	pan
Tenderloin	bife de lomo	butter	manteca
rib or t-bone steak	bife de costilla	jam	mermelada
beef stew	estofado	honey	miel
rib strip	asado de tira	cheese	queso
round rump	peceto	empanada	pasty
steak in breadcrumbs	milanesa	rice	arroz
veal cutlet in	milanesa	ice cream	helado
breadcrumbs	deternera		

Essentials

Noquis on the Payroll

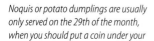

Noquis or potato dumplings are usually only served on the 29th of the month, when you should put a coin under your plate for luck. The term is, however, also used for employees who turn up for work once a month to collect their salary.

One has to go to the northwestern corner of Argentina (and to a lesser extent the northeast) to discover traces of the old, authentic cuisine. A number of foods based on maize, such as the humitas and the tamales are quite common, and tasty and filling stews such as *carbonada* and *locro* should not be passed up if one has the chance to taste them. And I have said nothing about the traditional *puchero* which knows no particular region or recipe. A local version of a French *pot-au-feu*, similar to stew, it can be made with whatever meat and vegetable there is to hand. Tradition has it however, that to be a true puchero it must have some sort of beef, chickpeas and corn on the cob, amongst the ingredients. **Authentic cuisine**

Argentines have a sweet tooth but are not very imaginative as to desserts. The local flan has nothing to do with the English version; it is a baked custard served with a caramel sauce and can also be garnished with a little whipped cream or dulce de leche. This extremely sweet and delicious confection can best be described as milk jam. It is milk boiled with plenty of sugar until it turns thick and caramel colour. Quince or sweet potato preserve with cheese (queso y dulce) is very popular, as is a true Argentine creation: *panqueque de manzana* (apple pancake, which is made by cooking thinly sliced apple in batter and caramel on both sides. Pastries and cakes are European in style and jams are faithful copies of what can be found the world over. Fresh fruit is bountiful and varied. Local apples and pears are especially fine (most are exported) and citrus fruits are abundant. For local recipes (in Spanish) *Las Comidas de Mi Pueblo*, by Margarita Palacios, is recommended. **Desserts**

The local beers, mainly lager-type, are quite acceptable. Hard liquor is relatively cheap, except for imported whisky. Argentine wines are very good. The ordinary *vinos de la casa*, or *comunes* are wholesome and relatively cheap; reds are better than the whites. In restaurants wines have become more expensive (up to US$20 per bottle for a good quality wine). It is usual to drink soda or mineral water at restaurants, and many Argentines mix it with their cheaper wine, with ice, as a refreshing drink in summer. *Clericó* is a white-wine *sangría* also drunk in summer. It is best not to drink the tap water; in the main cities it is often heavily chlorinated. **Drink**
See page 520 for information on Argentine wine

Shopping

In Buenos Aires the best bargains are local leather goods. Leather from the *carpincho* is from the capybara and is illegal and so should not be purchased. Other good buys are a gourd for drinking *yerba maté* and the silver *bombilla* which goes with it (see box on page 53) and perhaps a pair of *gaucho* trousers, the *bombachas*. Ponchos (red and black for men, all colours for women), articles of onyx, (especially in Salta), silver handicrafts and knitted woollens (especially in Bariloche and Mar del Plata) are also worth looking at. **Best buys**

Film is expensive in Argentina. Pre-paid Kodak slide film cannot be developed anywhere in South America; it is also very hard to find. Kodachrome is almost impossible to buy. Some travellers (but not all) have advised against mailing exposed films home; either take them with you, or have them developed, but not printed, once you have checked **Photography**
Keeping your camera & exposed film in a plastic bag may reduce the effects of humidity

the laboratory's quality. Postal authorities may use less sensitive equipment for X-ray screening than the airports do. Modern controlled X-ray machines are supposed to be safe for any speed of film, but it is worth trying to avoid X-ray as the doses are cumulative. Many airport officials will allow film to be passed outside X-ray arches; they may also hand-check a suitcase with a large quantity of film if asked politely.

Holidays and festivals

The main holiday period is January to March, though some areas, such as Tierra del Fuego, begin to fill up in November and December. Winter school holidays, in which travelling and hotels may be difficult, are the middle two weeks of July. Work must cease on the national holidays (1 January, Good Friday, 1 May, 25 May, 10 June, 20 June, 9 July, 17 August, 12 October and 25 December) except where specifically established by law. There are limited bus services on 25 and 31 December. On Holy Thursday and 8 December employers are left free to decide whether their employees should work, but banks and public offices are closed. Banks are also closed on 31 December. There are *gaucho* parades throughout Argentina, with traditional music, on the days leading up to the Día de la Tradición, 10 November. On 30 December (not 31 because so many offices in centre are closed) there is a ticker-tape tradition in downtown Buenos Aires: it snows paper and the crowds stuff passing cars and buses with long streamers.

Sport and special interest travel

See also page 540 Argentina's climatic and geographical diversity is so great that most tourist activities are available somewhere in the country. Most outdoor activities are covered in detail below. Travellers interested in the arts will find much to attract them in the cultural life of Buenos Aires. For wine lovers Mendoza provides opportunities to visit vineyards and bodegas; similar tours are also available elswhere in the Andean foothills, notably in San Juan and Cafayate. Those interested in wildlife will be attracted by Argentina's network of national parks.

Although Argentina is no longer cheap to visit, many of these types of tourism can be enjoyed by budget travellers, especially if they avoid the most popular destinations and travel off-season.

Estancia
tourism
The word *estancia* has a wide range of meanings, covering cattle ranches, farms, plantations, villas or country houses. In recent years many estancias have opened their gates to guests. Although in most cases this is merely a way of earning extra income, on some estancias it is fast becoming their main activity; some have added swimming pools, tennis courts and large restaurants. Many estancias offer full day and/or half day programmes without accomodation; these are know as *dia del campo*. Visiting an estancia, whether for an afternoon or for several days, offers not only the opportunity to relax in the countryside, but also insights into important aspects of the culture and economy of Argentina.

Though estancias are found throughout rural Argentina, they vary enormously in climate, landscape and activities. In the province of Buenos Aires you will find estancias covering thousands of hectares of flat grassland with large herds of cattle and windpumps to extract water; in Patagonia there are giant sheep estancias overlooking glaciers, mountains and lakes; in Mendoza, San Juan and La Rioja estancias have vineyards and in the northeast, in the swamps between the Ríos Uruguay and Paran, you will find estancias where the horses readily swim through the swamps, with or without a rider. Many estancias concentrate more on arable farming, growing cereals, rice, fruit and other crops.

The estancia itself, the owner's house with its surrounding buildings, also varies in style: many older estancias are built in so-called 'colonial style', introduced by settlers from Europe in the late 19th century. Some of the larger ones have their own little school for the workers' children and a chapel for mass and local weddings. Some, especially in Patagonia, have their own landing strip for small planes, reducing the isolation of estancias which may be well over 100 km apart.

Argentine landowners used to live in the large cities, especially in Buenos Aires, leaving a *capataz* (foreman) to oversee their estancia, which they visited for holidays or at weekends or to entertain friends. Nowadays many *dueños* (owners) live on the estancia, doing the job of the capataz, while their wives stay in town for much of the year to look after the children's education. Perhaps one of the most interesting features of a stay at an estancia is eating with the dueño and listening to his stories of daily life.

Estancia workers, usually referred to as *gauchos*, can still be seen on horseback, whether on the estancia itself or along the roads and in neighbouring villages. Typical gaucho clothing today includes *bombachas* (baggy trousers which are very comfortable for spending hours on horseback), a wide leather belt with silver clasps and a knife, a poncho, a *pañuelo* or neckerchief, a beret and on the feet *alpargatas* (espadrilles). Regional variations include the flat-topped felt hat worn on sunny days.

Not surprisingly a visit to an estancia offers great opportunities for riding horses. Argentines have their own style of horseriding, quite distinct from the European style which is known as estilo inglés. Using one hand only, the rider is meant to be as comfortable as possible for the long distances involved. The other activities available on estancias vary, often depending on the season: birdwatching, canoeing, fishing and walking are very common, while an *asado* (barbeque) is part of any visit. Often there are also opportunities to watch the work of the estancia.

essentials

Combining a visit to an estancia with some of the other highlights of Argentina is not difficult. The Estancia Mercedes, situated in the subtropical forests of Misiones, for example, can be visited fairly easily by travellers to the Iguazú falls. At the other extreme is the Estancia Monte Dinero, south of Río Gallegos, which can be combined with a trip to see the colony of Magellanic penguins at Cabo Vírgenes. Further details of these, and other estancias can be found in the text. Accommodation prices given are usually full board per person in a shared room. Some estancias do not have private bathrooms. Advanced booking is strongly advised, either by contacting the estancia itself or through travel agencies which specialize in this area. See the book *Guía de turismo en Estarcios y Hosterías*, published by *Tierra Buena*, US$12, www.tierrabuena.com.ar

Fishing The three main areas for fishing are the Northern Zone, around Junín de los Andes, extending south to Bariloche, the Central Zone around Esquel and the Southern Zone around Río Gallegos in Patagonia and Río Grande in Tierra del Fuego. The first two of these areas are in the Lake District. In the Northern Zone some of the best fishing can be found in the lakes of the Parque Nacional Lanín, notably Meliquina, Falkner, Villarino, Nuevo, Lacar, Lolog, Curruhu, Chico, Huechulafquen, Paimún, Epulafquen and Tromen. The Río Limay has good trout fishing, as do the rivers further north, the Quilquihue, Malle, Chimehuín, Collón-Cur , Hermoso, Meliquina and Caleufú. All these rivers are 'catch and release'. The Central Zone includes Lagos Gutiérrez, Mascardi and Lago Futalaufquen in the Parque Nacional Los Alerces. In the far south Lago Argentino is good for trout and salmon and there is good sea trout fishing along the southern Patagonian coast.

Fishing can also be found in other parts of the country and is offered by many estancias. Pejerrey, corvina and pescadilla can be found in large quantities along the coast of Buenos Aires province. Many of the reservoirs of the Central Sierras, the West and Northwest are well stocked.

The season runs from early November to the end of March, but the best time is at the beginning of the season. To fish anywhere in Argentina you need a permit, which costs US$10 per day, US$30 per week, US$100 per year. In the Northern Zone forestry commission inspectors are very diligent.

Birdwatching An increasing number of foreign visitors are birdwatchers. At least 980 of the 2,926 species of birds registered in South America exist in Argentina, in places, with easy access. Enthusiasts head for Península Valdés, Patagonia, the subtropical forests in the northwest, or the Chaco savannah in the northeast. Specialist tours led by expert guides can be arranged. For further details contact the Asociación Ornitológica del Plata (address under Buenos Aires).

Adventure tourism

Though Argentina may lag behind Chile in this respect, adventure tourism is growing rapidly and an increasing number of agencies specialize in this area. The main adventure tourism regions are well away from the capital and include Mendoza, Salta and the Lake District, as well as the Fitz Roy Area in Patagonia. In the Lake District San Martín de los Andes is rapidly growing as an adventure tourism centre, while the small town of Malargüe in southern Mendoza, which somewhat grandly styles itself the 'national capital of adventure tourism', is a fairly good base, though there are surprisingly few agencies.

Climbing The Andes offer great climbing opportunities. Among the most popular peaks are Aconcagua, in Mendoza province (see page 193), Pissis in Catamarca (see page 240) and Lanín and Tronador (see pages 368 and 388). The northern part of the Parque Nacional Los Glaciares around Fitz Roy (see page 451) offers some very difficult climbing. There are climbing clubs (known as *Clubs Andino*) in Bariloche, Esquel, Junín de los Andes, Mendoza, Ushuaia and a number of other cities. Further details and equipment hire are given in the text.

Surfing, windsurfing and waterskiing are practised along the Atlantic coast south of Buenos Aires. White water rafting and other watersports are growing in popularity. Rafting is found in Mendoza province, both near the provincial capital and further south near San Rafael and Malargüe, as well as in the Lanín, Nahuel Huapi and Los Alerces National Parks in the Lake District.

Watersports

The skiing season runs from May to the end of October, but dates vary between resorts. Las Leñas, south of Mendoza, is a major international ski resort with varied accommodation. There are three other major resorts, all of them in the Lake District, Cerro Catedral and Cerro Otto, both near Bariloche, and Chapelco near San Martín de los Andes. Smaller resorts include Los Penitentes, Vallecitos and Manantiales, all near Mendoza, and Caviahue, Cerro Bayo and La Hoya, all in the Lake District. In the far south there are small resorts near Río Turbio in Patagonia and near Ushuaia in Tierra del Fuego. Smaller resorts are cheaper but have fewer facilities. Details of all of these resorts are given in the text.

Skiing

The best areas for trekking are in the west of the country around Mendoza and further south near Malargüe as well further north around San Juan and La Rioja. The Lake District in the Lanín, Nahuel Huapi and Los Alerces National Parks offers good trekking as do the valleys around Salta in the northwest and in the Fitz Roy area of the Glaciares National Park in Patagonia .

Trekking

When planning treks in the Andes you should be aware of the effects and dangers of acute mountain sickness, and cerebral and pulmonary oedema (see page 65). These can be avoided by spending a few days acclimatizing to the altitude before starting your walk, and by climbing slowly. Otherwise there are fewer dangers than in most cities. However in mountain areas, where the weather can deteriorate rapidly, trekkers should consider taking the following equipment:

Clothing: a warm hat (wool or man-made fibre), thermal underwear, T-shirts/shirts, trousers (quick-drying and preferably windproof, never jeans), warm (wool or fleece) jumper/jacket (preferably two), gloves, waterproof jacket and over trousers (preferably Gore-Tex), shorts, walking boots and socks, change of footwear or flip-flops. **Camping gear**: tent (capable of withstanding high winds), sleeping mat (closed cell – Karrimat – or inflatable – Thermarest), sleeping bag (three-season minimum rating), sleeping bag liner, stove and spare parts, fuel, matches and lighter, cooking and eating utensils, pan scrubber, survival bag. **Food**: very much personal preference but at least two days more supplies than you plan to use; tea, coffee, sugar, dried milk; porridge, dried fruit, honey; soup, pasta, rice, soya (TVP); fresh fruit and vegetables; bread, cheese, crackers; biscuits, chocolate; salt, pepper, other herbs and spices, cooking oil. **Miscellaneous**: map and compass, torch and spare batteries, pen and notebook, Swiss army knife, sunglasses, sun cream, lip salve and insect repellent, first aid kit, water bottle, toiletries and towel.

Some but not all of these things are available locally

Hikers have little to fear from the animal kingdom apart from insects (although it's best to avoid actually stepping on a snake), and robbery and assault are very rare. You are much more of a threat to the environment than vice versa. Leave no evidence of your passing; don't litter and don't give gratuitous presents of sweets or money to rural people. Respect their system of reciprocity; if they give you hospitality or food, then is the time to reciprocate with presents.

Essentials

Offroading Large areas of Argentina are ideal for off-roading. Across wide expanses of flat land or gently rolling hills there are no woods to obstruct you, nor snow or ice; the vegetation is sparse and there are few animals and hardly any people. Patagonia in particular, with its endless steppes interrupted only by rivers, gorges and gullies, is recommended but some of the Andean valleys of the West and Northwest are worth exploring in this way. Three of the rougher roads in the Andes are especially recommended: the route from San Antonio de los Andes to Catamarca via Antofagasta de la Sierra; the route from Catamarca to Chile via Paso San Francisco and the Laguna Brava area in La Rioja.

Though four wheel drive vehicles are difficult to hire in Buenos Aires, they can be hired from hire companies such as *Localiza* and *Hertz* in some major cities of the interior, notably Mendoza, Tucumán, Bariloche and Ushuaia, as well as from Marina Servicios in Salta. Prices are high, from US$2,000 for 15 days, US$3,500 for 1 month, plus fuel, but if you divide this between 4 adults it becomes more reasonable. Buy road maps in advance from the *Automóvil Club Argentino* (ACA) in Buenos Aires. Before setting out you should obtain as much information as possible; employees in the provincial tourist information offices are unlikely to be able to answer your questions, so it is more important to ask them for names of local guides (baqueanos). It is important to avoid the coldest and the wettest months of the year; spring (October and November) and autumn (April and May) are the best seasons.

Health

Before travelling

Take out medical insurance. Make sure it covers all eventualities especially evacuation to your home country by a medically equipped plane. You should have a dental check up, obtain a spare glasses prescription, a spare oral contraceptive prescription (or enough pills to last) and, if you suffer from a chronic illness (such as diabetes, high blood pressure, ear or sinus troubles, cardio-pulmonary disease or nervous disorder) arrange for a check up with your doctor, who can at the same time provide you with a letter explaining the details of your disability in English and if possible Spanish. Check the current practice in countries you are visiting for malaria prophylaxis (prevention). If you are on regular medication, make sure you have enough to cover the period of your travel.

What to take Many drugs and medicines are manufactured under licence from American or European companies, so the trade names may be familiar to you. This means you do not have to carry a whole chest of medicines with you, but remember that the shelf life of some items, especially vaccines and antibiotics, is markedly reduced in hot conditions. Buy your supplies at the better outlets where there are refrigerators, even though they are more expensive and check the expiry date of all preparations you buy. Immigration officials occasionally confiscate scheduled drugs (Lomotil is an example) if they are not accompanied by a doctor's prescription.

Self-medication may be forced on you by circumstances so the following text contains the names of drugs and medicines which you may find useful in an emergency or in out-of-the-way places. You may like to take some of the following items with you from home:

Sunglasses (designed for intense sunlight); earplugs (for travel and noisy hotels); high protection suntan cream; insect repellent; lightweight mosquito net (permethrin-impregnated); travel sickness tablets; tampons; condoms; contraceptives; water sterilising tablets; antimalarial tablets; anti-infective ointment eg Cetrimide; dusting powder for feet containing fungicide; antacid tablets for indigestion; sachets of rehydration salts and anti-diarrhoea preparations; painkillers; antibiotics for diarrhoea etc; first aid kit containing a few sterile syringes and needles and disposable gloves.

The following are recommended: **Typhoid** A disease spread by the insanitary preparation of food. A number of new vaccines against this condition are now available; the older TAB and monovalent typhoid vaccines are being phased out. The newer, eg Typhim Vi, cause less side effects, but are more expensive. For those who do not like injections, there are now oral vaccines.

Poliomyelitis Despite its decline in the world this remains a serious disease if caught and is easy to protect against. There are live oral vaccines and in some countries injected vaccines. Whichever one you choose it is a good idea to have booster every 3-5 years if visiting developing countries regularly.

Tetanus One dose should be given with a booster at 6 weeks and another at 6 months and ten yearly boosters thereafter are recommended. Children should already be properly protected against diphtheria, poliomyelitis and pertussis (whooping cough), measles and HIB.

Infectious hepatitis Is less of a problem for travellers than it used to be because of the development of two extremely effective vaccines against the A and B form of the disease. A combined hepatitis A & B vaccine is now licensed and available – one jab covers both diseases.

Yellow fever Yellow fever vaccination is not required for Argentina, but is required for neighbouring countries such as Brazil and Paraguay. This is a live vaccination not to be given to children under 9 months of age or persons allergic to eggs. Immunity lasts for 10 years, an International Certificate of Yellow Fever Vaccination will be given and should be kept.

Other vaccinations might be considered in the case of epidemics eg meningitis. There is an effective vaccination against rabies which should be considered by all travellers, especially those going through remote areas or if there is a particular occupational risk, eg for zoologists or veterinarians.

Further information on health risks abroad may be available from a local travel clinic. If you wish to take specific drugs with you such as antibiotics these are best prescribed by your own doctor. Beware, however, that not all doctors can be experts on the health problems of other countries. More detailed or more up-to-date information than local doctors can provide are available from various sources.

There are additional computerized databases which can be accessed for destination-specific up-to-the-minute information. In the UK there is MASTA (Medical Advisory Service to Travellers Abroad), T0207-8375540, F0113-2387575, www.masta.org and *Travax* (Glasgow, T0141-9467120 ext 247). Other information on medical problems overseas can be obtained from the book by Dawood, Richard (Editor) (1992) *Travellers' Health: How to stay healthy abroad*, Oxford University Press, fourth edition 2000, US$15. General advice is also available in the UK in *Health Information for Overseas Travel* published by the Department of Health and available from HMSO, and *International Travel and Health* published by WHO, Geneva.

On the road

The main symptoms are pains in the stomach, lack of appetite, lassitude and yellowness of the eyes and skin. Medically speaking there are two main types. The less serious, but more common is Hepatitis A for which the best protection is the careful preparation of food, the avoidance of contaminated drinking water and scrupulous attention to toilet hygiene. The other, more serious, version is Hepatitis B which is acquired usually as a sexually transmitted disease or by blood transfusions. It can less commonly be transmitted by injections with unclean needles and possibly by insect

Sidebar:

Vaccination & immunizations

Essentials

Further information

Infectious hepatitis (jaundice)

bites. The symptoms are the same as for Hepatitis A. The incubation period is much longer (up to 6 months compared with 6 weeks) and there are more likely to be complications.

Hepatitis A can be protected against with gamma globulin. It should be obtained from a reputable source and is certainly useful for travellers who intend to live rough. You should have a shot before leaving and have it repeated every 6 months. The dose of gamma globulin depends on the concentration of the particular preparation used, so the manufacturer's advice should be taken. The injection should be given as close as possible to your departure and as the dose depends on the likely time you are to spend in potentially affected areas, the manufacturer's instructions should be followed. Gamma globulin has really been superseded now by a proper vaccination against Hepatitis A (Havrix) which gives immunity lasting up to 10 years. After that boosters are required. Havrix monodose is now widely available as is Junior Havrix. The vaccination has negligible side effects and is extremely effective. Gamma globulin injections can be a bit painful, but it is much cheaper than Havrix and may be more available in some places.

Hepatitis B can be effectively prevented by a specific vaccine (Engerix) – three shots over 6 months before travelling. If you have had jaundice in the past it would be worthwhile having a blood test to see if you are immune to either of these two types, because this might avoid the necessity and costs of vaccination or gamma globulin. There are other kinds of viral hepatitis (C, E etc) which are fairly similar to A and B, but vaccines are not available as yet.

AIDS AIDS, known as ASSIDA in Argentina, is not wholly confined to the well known high risk sections of the population, ie homosexual men, intravenous drug abusers and children of infected mothers. Heterosexual transmission is now the dominant mode and so the main risk to travellers is from casual sex. The same precautions should be taken as with any sexually transmitted disease. The AIDS virus (HIV) can be passed by unsterilized needles which have been previously used to inject an HIV positive patient, but the risk of this is negligible. It would, however, be sensible to check that needles have been properly sterilized or disposable needles have been used. If you wish to take your own disposable needles, be prepared to explain what they are for. The risk of receiving a blood transfusion with blood infected with the HIV virus is greater than from dirty needles because of the amount of fluid exchanged. Supplies of blood for transfusion should now be screened for HIV in all reputable hospitals, so again the risk is very small indeed. Catching the AIDS virus does not always produce an illness in itself (although it may do). The only way to be sure if you feel you have been put at risk is to have a blood test for HIV antibodies on your return to a place where there are reliable laboratory facilities. The test does not become positive for some weeks.

Typhus Can still occur carried by ticks. There is usually a reaction at the site of the bite and a fever. Seek medical advice.

Leptospirosis Various forms of leptospirosis are transmitted by a bacterium which is excreted in rodent urine. Fresh water and moist soil harbour the organisms which enter the body through cuts and scratches. If you suffer from any form of prolonged fever consult a doctor.

Leishmaniasis Leishmaniasis is carried by sandflies, which tend to bite at dawn and dusk, through all forested areas. It causes a persistent crusty sore or ulcer on the skin, sometimes followed by destructive lesions in the nose, mouth or throat (Espundia). Protect against sandfly bites by wearing impregnated long trousers and long sleeved shirt, and DET on exposed skin. Sleep under an inpregnated bed net. Seek advice for any persistent skin lesion or nasal symptom. Treatment is daily injections for three weeks.

This is a chronic disease, almost endemic in rural parts of Argentina, and difficult to treat. It is, however, very rarely caught by travellers. It is transmitted by the simultaneous biting and excreting of the Reduvid bug, also known as the Vinchuca or Barbeiro. Somewhat resembling a small cockroach, this nocturnal bug lives in poor adobe houses with dirt floors often frequented by opossums. If you cannot avoid such accommodation, sleep off the floor with a candle lit, use a mosquito net, keep as much of your skin covered as possible, use DET repellent or a spray insecticide. If you are bitten overnight (the bites are painless) do not scratch them, but wash thoroughly with soap and water.

Chagas' disease (South American trypano- somiasis)

Rabies is endemic in Latin America, so avoid dogs that are behaving strangely and cover your toes at night from the vampire bats, which also carry the disease. If you are bitten by a domestic or wild animal, do not leave things to chance: scrub the wound with soap and water and/or disinfectant, try to have the animal captured (within limits) or at least determine its ownership, where possible, and seek medical assistance at once. The course of treatment depends on whether you have already been satisfactorily vaccinated against rabies. If you have then some further doses of vaccine are all that is required. Human diploid vaccine is the best, but expensive. Other, older kinds of vaccine, such as that derived from duck embryos may be the only types available. These are effective, much cheaper and interchangeable generally with the human derived types. If not already vaccinated then anti rabies serum (immunoglobulin) may be required in addition. It is important to finish the course of treatment whether the animal survives or not.

Rabies

This is a very rare event indeed for travellers. If you are unlucky (or careless) enough to be bitten by a venomous snake, spider, scorpion or sea creature, try to identify the creature, but do not put yourself in further danger. Snake bites in particular are very frightening, but in fact rarely poisonous – even venomous snakes bite without injecting venom. What you might expect if bitten are fright, swelling, pain and bruising around the bite and soreness of the regional lymph glands, perhaps nausea, vomiting and a fever. Signs of serious poisoning would be the following symptoms: numbness and tingling of the face, muscular spasms, convulsions, shortness of breath and bleeding. Victims should be got to a hospital or a doctor without delay. It is best to rely on local practice in these cases, because the particular creatures will be known about locally and appropriate treatment can be given.

Snake bite

    Reassure and comfort the victim frequently. Immobilize the limb by a bandage or a splint or by getting the person to lie still. Do not slash the bite area and try to suck out the poison because this sort of heroism does more harm than good. If you know how to use a tourniquet in these circumstances you will not need this advice. If you are not experienced do not apply a tourniquet.

    To prevent being bitten: avoid walking in snake territory in bare feet or sandals and wear proper shoes or boots. If you encounter a snake stay put until it slithers away, and do not investigate a wounded snake.

Apart from mosquitos the most dangerous animals are men, be they bandits or behind steering wheels. Think carefully about violent confrontations and wear a seat belt if you are lucky enough to have one available to you.

Other dangerous animals

Travellers' diarrhoea and vomiting is usually caused by eating food which has been contaminated by food poisoning germs, often passed on by the insanitary habits of food handlers. As a general rule Argentine restaurants are clean and intestinal upsets are unlikely. Drinking water is rarely the culprit. Sea water or river water is more likely to be contaminated by sewage and so swimming in such dilute effluent can also be a cause.

Intestinal upsets

Infection with various organisms can give rise to travellers' diarrhoea. They may be viruses, bacteria, eg Escherichia coli (probably the most common cause worldwide), protozoal (such as amoebas and giardia), salmonella and cholera. The diarrhoea may come on suddenly or rather slowly. It may or may not be accompanied by vomiting or by severe abdominal pain and the passage of blood or mucus when it is called dysentery.

Foods to avoid: uncooked, undercooked, partially cooked or reheated meat, fish, eggs, raw vegetables and salads, especially when they have been left out exposed to flies. Shellfish eaten raw are risky and at certain times of the year some fish and shellfish concentrate toxins from their environment and cause various kinds of food poisoning. The local authorities notify the public not to eat these foods. Do not ignore the warning. Tap water is safe in the urban areas but less so in rural areas, especially in the rainy season. Bottled mineral water is readily available. If your hotel has a central hot water supply this water is safe to drink after cooling. Wash and dry your hands before eating.

How do you know which type you have caught and how to treat it? If you can time the onset of the diarrhoea to the minute ('acute') then it is probably due to a virus or a bacterium and/or the onset of dysentery. The treatment in addition to rehydration is Ciprofloxacin 500 milligrams every 12 hours; the drug is now widely available and there are many similar ones. If the diarrhoea comes on slowly or intermittently ('sub-acute') then it is more likely to be protozoal, ie caused by an amoeba or giardia. Antibiotics such a Ciprofloxacin will have little effect. These cases are best treated by a doctor as is any outbreak of diarrhoea continuing for more than 3 days. Sometimes blood is passed in ameobic dysentery and for this you should certainly seek medical help. If this is not available then the best treatment is probably Tinidazole (Fasigyn) one tablet four times a day for 3 days. If there are severe stomach cramps, the following drugs may help but are not very useful in the management of acute diarrhoea: Loperamide (Imodium) and Diphenoxylate with Atropine (Lomotil). They should not be given to children. Any kind of diarrhoea, whether or not accompanied by vomiting, responds well to the replacement of water and salts, taken as frequent small sips, of some kind of rehydration solution. There are proprietary preparations consisting of sachets of powder which you dissolve in boiled water or you can make your own by adding half a teaspoonful of salt (3.5 g) and four tablespoonsful of sugar (40 g) to a litre of boiled water.

Thus the linchpins of treatment for diarrhoea are rest, fluid and salt replacement, antibiotics such as Ciprofloxacin for the bacterial types and special diagnostic tests and medical treatment for the amoeba and giardia infections. Salmonella infections and cholera, although rare, can be devastating diseases and it would be wise to get to a hospital as soon as possible if these were suspected. Fasting, peculiar diets and the consumption of large quantities of yoghurt have not been found useful in calming travellers' diarrhoea or in rehabilitating inflamed bowels. Oral rehydration has on the other hand, especially in children, been a life saving technique and should always be practised, whatever other treatment you use. As there is some evidence that alcohol and milk might prolong diarrhoea they should be avoided during and immediately after an attack.

Diarrhoea occurring day after day for long periods of time (chronic diarrhoea) is notoriously resistent to amateur attempts at treatment and again warrants proper diagnostic tests (most towns with reasonable sized hospitals have laboratories for stool samples). There are ways of preventing travellers' diarrhoea for short periods of time by taking antibiotics, but this is not a foolproof technique and should not be used other than in exceptional circumstances. Doxycycline is possibly the best drug. Some preventatives such as Enterovioform can have serious side effects if taken for long periods.

Paradoxically constipation is also common, probably induced by dietary change, inadequate fluid intake in hot places and long bus journeys. Simple laxatives are useful in the short-term and bulky foods such as maize, beans and plenty of fruit are also useful.

Travelling to high altitudes can cause medical problems, though these can be **High altitude**
prevented if care is taken. On reaching heights above about 3,000m, heart pounding
and shortness of breath, especially on exertion are a normal response to the lack of
oxygen in the air. A condition called acute mountain sickness (*soroche* in Argentina)
can also affect visitors. It is more likely to affect those who ascend rapidly, eg by plane
and those who over-exert themselves (teenagers for example). *Soroche* takes a few
hours or days to come on and presents with a bad headache, extreme tiredness,
sometimes dizziness, loss of appetite and frequently nausea and vomiting. Insomnia is
common and is often associated with a suffocating feeling when lying in bed. Keen
observers may note their breathing tends to wax and wane at night and their face
tends to be puffy in the mornings – this is all part of the syndrome. Anyone can get this
condition and past experience is not always a good guide.

The treatment of acute mountain sickness is simple – rest, painkillers (preferably
not aspirin based) for the headache and anti-sickness pills for vomiting. Oxygen is not
much help except at very high altitude. Various local panaceas – Coramina glucosada,
Effortil, Micoren are popular in Latin America and *mate de coca* (an infusion of coca
leaves available in the northwest and legal) will alleviate some of the symptoms.

To prevent the condition: on arrival at places over 3,000 m have a few hours rest in a
chair and avoid alcohol, cigarettes and heavy food. If the symptoms are severe and
prolonged, it is best to descend to a lower altitude and to reascend slowly or in stages.
If this is impossible because of shortage of time or if you are going so high that acute
mountain sickness is very likely, then the drug Acetazolamide (Diamox) can be used as
a preventative and continued during the ascent. There is good evidence of the value
of this drug in the prevention of *soroche*, but some people do experience peculiar side
effects. The usual dose is 500 mg of the slow release preparation each night, starting
the night before ascending above 3,000m.

Watch out for **sunburn** at high altitude. The ultraviolet rays are extremely powerful.
The air is also excessively dry at high altitude and you might find that your skin dries
out and the inside of your nose becomes crusted. Use a moisturiser for the skin and
some vaseline wiped into the nostrils. Some people find contact lenses irritate
because of the dry air. It is unwise to ascend to high altitude if you are pregnant,
especially in the first 3 months, or if you have a history of heart, lung or blood disease,
including sickle cell.

A more unusual condition can affect mountaineers who ascend rapidly to high
altitude – acute pulmonary oedema. Residents at altitude sometimes experience this
when returning to the mountains from time spent at the coast. This condition is often
preceded by acute mountain sickness and comes on quite rapidly with severe
breathlessness, noisy breathing, cough, blueness of the lips and frothing at the mouth.
Anybody who develops this must be brought down as soon as possible, given oxygen
and taken to hospital.

A rapid descent from high places will make sinus problems and middle ear
infections worse and might make your teeth ache. Lastly, don't fly to altitude within 24
hours of scuba diving. You might suffer from 'the bends'.

Full acclimatization to high temperatures takes about 2 weeks. During this period it is **Heat & cold**
normal to feel a bit apathetic, especially if the relative humidity is high. Drink plenty of
water, use salt on your food and avoid extreme exertion. Tepid showers are more
cooling than hot or cold ones. Large hats do not cool you down, but do prevent
sunburn. Remember that, especially in the highlands, there can be a large and sudden
drop in temperature between sun and shade and between night and day, so dress
accordingly. Warm jackets or woollens are essential after dark at high altitude. Loose
cotton remains the best material when the weather is hot.

Insects These are mostly more of a nuisance than a serious hazard and if you try, you can prevent yourself entirely from being bitten. Some, such as mosquitos are, of course, carriers of potentially serious diseases, so it is sensible to avoid being bitten as much as possible. Sleep off the ground and use a mosquito net or some kind of insecticide. Preparations containing Pyrethrum or synthetic pyrethroids are safe. They are available as aerosols or pumps and the best way to use these is to spray the room thoroughly in all areas (follow the instructions rather than the insects) and then shut the door for a while, re-entering when the smell has dispersed. Mosquito coils release insecticide as they burn slowly. They are widely available and useful out of doors. Tablets of insecticide which are placed on a heated mat plugged into a wall socket are probably the most effective. They fill the room with insecticidal fumes in the same way as aerosols or coils.

You can also use insect repellents, most of which are effective against a wide range of pests. The most common and effective is diethyl metatoluamide (DET). DET liquid is best for arms and face (care around eyes and with spectacles – DET dissolves plastic). Aerosol spray is good for clothes and ankles and liquid DET can be dissolved in water and used to impregnate cotton clothes and mosquito nets. Some repellents now contain DET and Permethrin, insecticide. Impregnated wrist and ankle bands can also be useful.

If you are bitten or stung, itching may be relieved by cool baths, antihistamine tablets (care with alcohol or driving) or mild corticosteroid creams, eg hydrocortisone (great care: never use if any hint of infection). Careful scratching of all your bites once a day can be surprisingly effective. Calamine lotion and cream have limited effectiveness and antihistamine creams are not recommended – they can cause allergies themselves. Bites which become infected should be treated with a local antiseptic or antibiotic cream such as Cetrimide, as should any infected sores or scratches.

When living rough, skin infestations with body lice (crabs) and scabies are easy to pick up. Use whatever local commercial preparation is recommended for lice and scabies. Crotamiton cream (Eurax) alleviates itching and also kills a number of skin parasites. Malathion lotion 5 (Prioderm) kills lice effectively, but avoid the use of the toxic agricultural preparation of Malathion, more often used to commit suicide.

Other afflictions **Ticks** They attach themselves usually to the lower parts of the body often after walking in areas where cattle have grazed. They take a while to attach themselves strongly, but swell up as they start to suck blood. The important thing is to remove them gently, so that they do not leave their head parts in your skin because this can cause a nasty allergic reaction some days later. Do not use petrol, vaseline, lighted cigarettes etc to remove the tick, but, with a pair of tweezers remove the beast gently by gripping it at the attached (head) end and rock it out in very much the same way that a tooth is extracted. **Sunburn** The burning power of the sun, especially at high altitude, is phenomenal. Always wear a wide brimmed hat and use some form of suncream lotion on untanned skin. Use high factor suntan lotions. **Prickly heat** A very common intensely itchy rash is avoided by frequent washing and by wearing loose clothing. Cured by allowing skin to dry off through use of powder and spending two nights in an air-conditioned hotel! **Athletes foot** This and other fungal skin infections are best treated with Tolnaftate or Clotrimazole.

Children Perhaps a little more care should be taken when travelling to remote areas where health services are primitive. This is because children can be become more rapidly ill than adults (on the other hand they often recover more quickly). Diarrhoea and vomiting are the most common problems, so take the usual precautions, but more intensively. Breastfeeding is best and most convenient for babies, but powdered milk is generally available and so are baby foods in most countries. Papaya, bananas and avocados are all nutritious and can be cleanly prepared. The treatment of diarrhoea is the same for adults, except that it should start earlier and be continued with more persistence. Children get dehydrated very quickly in hot countries and can become drowsy and uncooperative unless cajoled to drink water or juice plus salts. Upper respiratory infections, such as colds, catarrh and middle ear infections are also common and if your child suffers from these normally take some antibiotics against the possibility. Outer ear infections after swimming are also common and antibiotic eardrops will help. Wet wipes are always useful and sometimes difficult to find in South America, as, in some places are disposable nappies.

When you get home

If you have had attacks of diarrhoea it is worth having a stool specimen tested in case you have picked up amoebas. If you have been living rough, blood tests may be worthwhile to detect worms and other parasites. If you have been exposed to bilharzia (schistosomiasis) by swimming in lakes etc, check by means of a blood test when you get home, but leave it for 6 weeks because the test is slow to become positive. Report any untoward symptoms to your doctor and tell the doctor exactly where you have been and, if you know, what the likelihood of disease is to which you were exposed.

The above information has been compiled for us by Dr David Snashall, who is presently Senior Lecturer in Occupational Health at the United Medical Schools of Guy's and St Thomas' Hospitals in London and Chief Medical Adviser to the British Foreign and Commonwealth Office. He has travelled extensively in Central and South America, worked in Peru and in East Africa and keeps in close touch with developments in preventative and tropical medicine. Dr Anthony Bryceson, Emeritus Professor of Tropical Medicine at the London School of Hygiene and Tropical Medicine has also contributed to this section. He has worked in Laos, Nigeria, Kenya and Ethiopia and at the Hospital for Tropical Diseases. He has also undertaken research trips to Peru, Mexico, India and the Middle East.

Further reading

Literature Bethell, Leslie, ed, *The Cambridge History of Latin America, Volume X* (1995), Cambridge. **Boldy, S**, *The Novels of Julio Cortázar* (1977), Cambridge. **Collier, S**, *The Life, Music and Times of Carlos Gardel* (1986), University of Pittsberg Press. **King, J**, ed, *Modern Latin American Fiction: A Survey* (1987) London. **J King**, *Sur: an Analysis of the Argentine Literary Journal and its Role in the Development of a Culture* (1985) Cambridge; **Gerald Martin**, *Journeys Through the Labyrinth* (1989) London and New York; **Sarlo, Beatriz**, *Jorge Luis Borges: A Writer on the Edge* (1993) London and New York; **Shumway, Nicolas**, *The Invention of Argentina* (1991) Berkeley; **Smith, Verity**, ed, *The Encyclopaedia of Latin American Literature* (1997) London.

Travel literature Early writing on Argentina includes **Bridges, Lucas**, *Uttermost Part of the Earth* (1987) Century. This is the classic account of growing up among the indigenous peoples of Tierra del Fuego, first published 1948. **Cunninghame Graham, R B**, *A Vanished Arcadia* (1988) Century. A somewhat romantic view of the Jesuit missions, first published 1901. **Musters, George**, *At Home with the Patagonians*, (1871/1973), London. A history of 19th-century life of Patagonian Indians. Among the works of **Hudson, W H**, are *Far Away and Long Ago* (1985) and *Idle Days in Patagonia* (1984), Everyman. Both books deal with his early life in the countryside. The most famous recent travel book on Argentina is probably **Chatwin, Bruce**, *In Patagonia*, Picador. A wonderful mixture of fact and fantasy. **France, Miranda**, *Bad Times in Buenos Aires*, (Phoenix 1999). Perceptive, thought-provoking and sometimes humorous account of life in Buenos

Essentials

W H Hudson, 1841-1922

The son of immigrants from New England, Hudson was brought up in what was then an isolated spot on the pampas. In Far Way and Long Ago (1918), written in old age after serious illness, he described the adventures of a childhood spent wandering the pampas on his pony. His early education at the hands of a series of private tutors was sporadic but he would spend hours alone watching birds and snakes. His life was altered when he caught typhus fever at the age of 15 after a short holiday in Buenos Aires and his health was permanently affected.

In 1869 Hudson sailed for England, never to return because, he later claimed,

he believed that large-scale immigration, especially by Italians, had destroyed the birdlife of the pampas. In London he lived in poverty, marrying Emily Wingrave, who was 15 years his elder and who kept boarding houses in Leinster Square and Bayswater. His novels, in the style of utopian romances, achieved little success, but he was soon recognized as a great naturalist, becoming famous for The Naturalist In La Plata *(1892) and his later works on the English countryside, among them* A Shepherd's Life *(1910). In 1925 a statue was erected in his memory in Hyde Park, London.*

Aires through the eyes of a British journalist. **Pilkington, John,** *An Englishman in Patagonia* (1991) Century. Offers a critical commentary on Chatwin. *The Motorcycle Diaries* by **Che Guevara (1995)** Verso offer an illuminating, and at times humorous, account of the young Che's trip through Argentina and Chile in 1952. **Shipton, Eric,** *Tierra del Fuego: The Fatal Lodestone* (1973) Charles Knight, is also worth reading.

History

Most general histories of Latin America have extensive sections on Argentina

Among those which can be recommended is **Williamson, Edwin,** *The Penguin History of Latin America* (1992) Penguin. **Rock, David,** *Argentina 1516-1987* (1987) IB Taurus. Though heavy going, perhaps the best single volume history of Argentina. **Crawley, Eduardo,** *A House Divided: Argentina 1880-1980* (1984) Hurst. More accessible for the modern period. **Falcoff, M** and **Dolkart, R H,** *Prologue to Peron: Argentina in Depression and War* (University of California Press, 1975). Deals with cultural, social and political aspects of the 1930s. On Perón see **Crassweller, R,** *Perón and the Enigmas of Argentina* (Norton, 1987). Offers a fine portrait of its subject, but is poor on the historical context. **Page, Joseph,** *Perón: A Biography* (1983). An alternative. On Evita see **Navarro, Marysa,** *Evita* (1980). Covers the military dictatorship of 1976-1983 and the Dirty War. **Anderson, ME,** *Dossier Secreto* (1993) Westview. Argues that the 'threat' of guerrilla insurgency was deliberately exaggerated by the armed forces themselves. **Graham-Youll, Andrew,** *A State of Fear* (1986) Eland. A chilling first-hand account by a 'Buenos Aires Herald' journalist. The Falklands/Malvinas War 1982 has produced a flood of books: a good introduction which examines the Argentine background is by **Burns, Jimmy,** a 'Financial Times' journalist who was in Buenos Aires at the time, *The Land Which Lost Its Heroes,* (1987) IB Taurus.

On other aspects of Argentine history in **Wilson, James,** *Buenos Aires* (1999), Latin America Bureau/Signal Books. Explores the events, people and writing which have shaped the development of the capital. **Martínez Sarasola, Carlos,** *Nuestros Paisanos Los Indios.* An excellent compendium on the history and present of Argentine Indian communities, recommended. The British connection with Argentina is examined in **Graham-Youll, Andrew,** *The Forgotten Colony* (1981) and in **Hennessy, Alastair** and **King, John** (ed) *The Land That England Lost* (1992), IB Taurus. **Williams, Glyn,** *The Desert and the Dream: The History of Welsh Colonisation of the Chubut* (1975) University of Wales Press. Looks at the Welsh community of Patagonia. **Andrews, GR,** *The Afro-Argentines of Buenos Aires 1800-1900* (University of Wisconsin Press, 1980).

Explores a forgotten aspect of the city's history. **Meadows, Ann,** *Digging Up Butch and Sundance* (1996) Bison Books. The fate of Butch Cassidy and the Sundance Kid is examined. **Pickford, Nigel,** *The Atlas of Shipwreck and Treasure* (1994) Dorling Kindersley. Further details are offered of shipwrecks off the Argentine coast. On Che Guevara see **Anderson, Jon** *Che Guevara: A Revolutionary Life* (1997) Bantam and **Castañeda, Jorge***Compañero: The Life and Death of Che Guevara* (1997) Bloomsbury.

King, J, *Magical Reels: A History of Cinema in Latin America* (1990) London and New York; **Barnard, Tim** and **Rist, Peter,** eds, *South American Cinema: A Critical Filmography, 1915-1994* (1996) New York and London; **Barnard, Tim,** *Argentine Cinema* (1986) Toronto; **Chanan, Michael** (ed), *Twenty five Years of the New Latin American Cinema* (1983) London; **Burton, Julianne,** ed, *The Social Documentary in Latin America* (1990) Pittsburgh and **M Pick, Zuzana,** *The New Latin American Cinema: A Continental Project* (1993) Austin.

Cinema
See further page 525

The Latin American Travel Advisor is a quarterly news bulletin with up-to-date detailed and reliable information on countries throughout South and Central America. The publication focuses on public safety, health, weather and natural phenomena, travel costs, economics and politics in each country. Annual airmail subscriptions cost US$39, a single current issue US$15, electronically transmitted information (fax or email), US$10 per country. Payment by US$ cheque, MasterCard or VISA (no money orders, credit card payments by mail or fax with card number, expiry date, cardholder's name and signature). Free sample available. Contact PO Box 17-17-908, Quito, Ecuador, international F593-2-562566, USA and Canada toll free F888-2159511, LATA@pi.pro.ec, www. amerispan. com/latc/

Magazines

Federico Kirbus has probably written the widest range of books for travellers in Argentina. These include his excellent *Guía Ilustrada de las Regiones Turísticas Argentinas,* (1995) El Ateneo. Four volumes (US$18-21 each), northwest, northeast, centre, south. About 300 black and white photos, colour pictures and colour plates on flora and fauna. Among his other works are the highly informative *Guía de Aventuras y Turismo de la Argentina* (with comprehensive English index – 1989), obtainable at El Ateneo or from the author at Casilla de Correo 5210, 1000, Buenos Aires; *La Argentina, país de Maravillas,* Manrique Zago ediciones (1993), a beautiful book of photographs with text in Spanish and English; *Patagonia* (with Jorge Schulte) and *Ruta Cuarenta,* both fine photographic records with text (both Capuz Varela, 1996); *Las Mil Maravillas de la Argentina* (1989) which focusses on archaeological and geological sites; *La Primera De Las Tres Buenos Aires* (1990) which examines the first founding of the capital city; *Arqueológia Argentina* (El Ateneo, 1994) and *El Fascinante Tren a Las Nubes* (1993) El Ateneo. Recounts the building of many of the most famous railway lines in South America. The **Fundación Vida Silvestre** (conservation organization and bookshop), Defensa 245/251, has information and books on Argentine flora and fauna. A new series on flora and fauna is being written by **de la Vega, Santiago G,** *Iguazú. Las leyes de la selva* (Contacto Silvestre, Buenos Aires, 1999). English translation, US$8, fully illustrated. *Las leyes del bosque,* 1999. English translation due in 2000, as are *Patagonia, Las leyes entre las costas y el mar,* and *Antártida.* Birdwatchers should consult the field guide to Argentine birds: *Guía para la identificación de las aves de Argentina y Uruguay* by **Narosky, T** and **Yzurieta, D,** with drawings and colour. Available in USA: *Birds of Isla Grande* (Tierra del Fuego) by **Humphrey, Philip S,** and *A Guide to the Birds of South America,* by **Meyer de Schauensee, Rodolphe.** For fishing try *Argentine Trout Fishing: A Fly Fisherman's Guide to Patagonia* by **C Leitch, William.** A useful guide to estancias in Argentina is *Guía de Turismo en Estancias y Hosterías,* published by Tierra Buena www.tierrabuena.com.ar, US$12, Spanish, Portuguese and English editions available.

Guide books

Maps   Several series of road maps are available including those of the Automóvil Club Argentino (ACA) and the *Automapas* published by Línea Azul. The former are available from ACA offices around the country, though usually they will only stock local maps. These are half-price to ACA members and to members of national motoring associations with reciprocity. Topographical maps are issued by the Instituto Geográfico Militar, Cabildo 301, Casilla 1426, Buenos Aires, one block from Ministro Carranza *Subte* station (Line D), or take bus 152 from Retiro. 1:500,000 sheets cost US$3 each and are 'years old'; better coverage of 1:100,000 and 1:250,000, but no general physical maps of the whole country or city plans. Helpful staff, sales office accessible from street, no passport required, map series indices on counter, open Monday-Friday, 0800-1300.

Argentina on the web

Although there are many websites on Argentina many are of limited use to the traveller; many are outdated while others are in Spanish only. The following brief list includes some of the more helpful sites:

For accommodation two sites are particularly useful: **www.hostels.com.ar** gives details of all the hostels in the Red Argentino de Albergues Juveniles and **www.hotelnet.com.ar** lists some of the more expensive hotels. For information on *estancias* go to **www.argentina-ranches.com** National parks in Patagonia are covered in **www.gorp.com** while **www.patadv.com** has details of fly fishing and other outdoor activities in Patagonia. Most provincial tourist boards have their own websites though these vary in quality: among useful sites on provinces and cities are **www.directorio.bariloche.com.ar**, **www.tourismosalta.com.ar** and **www.tierradel fuego.org.ar**

Buenos Aires and the Río de la Plata

3

Buenos Aires and the Río de la Plata

Buenos Aires is usually seen as more like Paris, Milan or Barcelona than South America. In the centre are fine boulevards, parks, museums, theatres, public buildings, shopping centres and a lively and incredibly varied nightlife. Here you can eat in the finest restaurants in the country, find music and entertainment to suit most tastes including, of course, the tango which the city claims as its own musical creation. Perhaps more striking than any of these, though, are its fashionable shops and fashion-conscious people, its cafés and street life. The contrast between this city and the outlying parts of Argentina is stark; if you want to understand Argentina, you will need to visit Buenos Aires. Situated on the west bank of the Río de la Plata, a broad estuary which separates Argentina from Uruguay, Buenos Aires sprawls inland, far beyond the official city limits; together with the surrounding areas, the city has a population of over ten million people, almost a third of the total population of the country.

Just north of the city is the Tigre Delta, a network of rivers and canals weaving between small islands where there are bars and restaurants. South of Buenos Aires is the city of La Plata, a modern city inspired by European city planners in the late nineteenth century. A world away, on the eastern bank of the Río de la Plata, is the Uruguayan city of Colonia del Sacramento, a Portuguese colonial gem easily reached by boat from Buenos Aires and well worth the trip.

Background

Geography

Phone code: 011
Colour map 4, grid B5
Population: Federal
District: 2,988,006; Gran
Buenos Aires 13,333,670
Total area: 4,326sq km

The Río de la Plata (literally 'silver river') is neither silver nor a river. It is a large estuary produced by the confluence of the Paraná and Uruguay rivers. These two rivers drain an area comprising 100% of Paraguay, 80% of Uruguay, 32% of Argentina, 19% of Bolivia and 17% of Brazil. Some 300 km long, the estuary widens from an initial width of 37 km to 220 km at the point at which it enters the Atlantic. While its northern shore (in Uruguay) is relatively steep, reaching 50 m in some places, its southern (or Argentine) shore is flat and in some areas consists of swampland. The estuary is muddy and shallow and the passage of ocean vessels is only made possible by continuous dredging. The tides are of little importance, for there is only a 1.2 m rise and fall at spring tides. The depth of water is determined by the direction of the wind and the flow of the Ríos Paraná and Uruguay.

Climate
Extreme humidity
& unusual pollen
conditions may affect
asthma sufferers

From mid-December to the end of February the Buenos Aires area can be oppressively hot and humid, with temperatures ranging from 27°C (80°F) to 35°C (95°F) and an average humidity of 70%. Beware of the high pollen count in the pollinating season if you have allergy problems. The winter months of June, July and August are best for business visits, though spring is often very pleasant.

Federal District of Buenos Aires

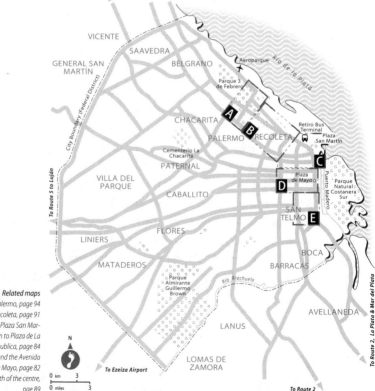

Related maps
A Palermo, page 94
B Recoleta, page 91
C From Plaza San Martin to Plaza de La Republica, page 84
D Around the Avenida de Mayo, page 82
E South of the centre, pge 89

Hooligans in the 1820s?

"The society of the lower class of English at Buenos Aires is very bad, and their constitutions are evidently impaired by drinking, and by the heat of the climate, while their morals and characters are much degraded. Away from the religious and moral example of their own country, and out of sight of their own friends and relations, they sink rapidly into habits of carelessness and dissipation, which are

but too evident to those who come fresh from England; and it is really too true, that all the British emigrants at Buenos Aires are sickly in their appearance, dirty in their dress, and disreputable in their behaviour."

Francis Bond Head, Journeys Across the Pampas and Among the Andes 1825-6 (Southern Illinois University Press, 1967).

History

The first attempt to found a settlement on the Río de la Plata by Pedro de Mendoza in 1536 failed and it was not until 1580 that an expedition under Juan de Garay succeeded in founding the city which he named after the patron saint of sailors, *Santa María del Buen Aire* (Santa María of the good winds). For much of the colonial period the city, though an administrative centre, was of little importance but, by 1776, when it became capital of the Vice-Regency of Río de la Plata, it was a growing city with an economy based on trading (much of it illegal) and servicing the cattle economy of the pampas. By independence its population was some 40,000.

In 1862 following the long struggle between Buenos Aires province and the Argentine interior, the city emerged as capital of the newly united state of Argentina, but shortly afterwards it was split from its province and made into a separate federal district. The massive waves of immigration into Argentina after 1870 transformed the city; between 1869 and 1914 its population grew from 177,000 to over one million and by 1914 half of its residents were foreign-born. By 1914 Buenos Aires was regarded as the most important city in South America. As the city grew and prospered, urban improvements were made. Gas, street lighting and better water supplies were introduced and suburban railway lines and a metro system were built. Many of the city's public buildings and major avenues date from this period, leaving very few older buildings.

During the 20th century the city has continued to grow, expanding across the boundaries of the federal territory into the province of Buenos Aires. Though immigration dropped after 1929, the city's population continued to increase as it absorbed large numbers of migrants from the poorer interior provinces. The connurbation of Gran Buenos Aires is the country's major industrial centre. By the 1980s it accounted for about half of all industrial jobs in Argentina.

Ins and outs

Getting there

Ezeiza (officially Ministro Pistarini), the international airport, is 35 km southwest of the centre by a good dual carriageway, which links with the General Paz circular highway round the city. Facilities include exchange (Banco de la Nación, 1.5% commission) and ATMs (Visa and Mastercard), post office (open 0800-2000) (under the stairs) a left luggage office (US$5 per piece) and a tourist information desk which offers a free

Ezeiza airport
Airport information,
T4806111

Buenos Aires and the Río de la Plata

 Main bus services from Buenos Aires

To Córdoba *US$25, 9 hrs, many companies (10).*
To Mendoza *US$55 c/c, 14 hrs, many companies (7).*
To San Juan *US$50 c/c, 15 hrs, Sendas, TAC, Autotransportes San Juan.*
To Bariloche *US$90 c/c, 22 hrs, TAC, Via Bariloche, Andesmar, Chevallier.*
To Puerto Madryn US$59 s/c, 19 hrs, Quebus, TAC, El Condor, Andesmar, Costa Criolla.
To Río Gallegos *US$92 común, US114 s/c, 36 hrs, Don Otto, El Pingüino, TAC.*
To Neuquén *US$47 s/c, 20 hrs, TAC, Ko Ko, Chevallier.*
To Tucumán *US$52 común, US$73 c/c, 15 hrs, many companies (9).*

To Salta *US$65 común, US$72 c/c, TAC, Panamericana, Brown, Chevallier, La Internacional.*
To Jujuy *US$65 pullman, 23 hrs, TAC, La Estrella, La Internacional, Panameericana.*
To Catamarca *US$71 c/c, 15 hrs, Sierras de Córdoba, Gutierrez, Ysalles, Chevallier.*
To La Rioja *US$62 común, US$68 c/c, 15 hrs, Chevallier, ABLO, Río de la Plata.*
To Puerto Iguazú *US$46 s/c, US$55 c/c, 17 hrs, Expreso Tigre Iguazú, Via Misiones, Crucero del Norte.*
To Resistencia *US$40 común, US$45 s/c, 14 hrs, La Internacional, Giralda, Caraza, Tala.*

c/c coche cama

hotel booking service with a list of competitively-priced hotels. There are no hotels nearby. A display in immigration shows choices and prices of transport into the city.

For departing travellers there is a duty-free shop (expensive) and a desk marked *Devolución IVA* for return of VAT on purchases such as leather goods. Reports of pilfering from luggage; to discourage this have your bags sealed after inspection by Your Packet International SA, US$5-10 per piece (*British Airways* insists on this and pays for it for backpacks).

Transport to & from the centre

Airport bus Two companies run efficient special bus service: *Manuel Tienda León* (office at customs exit), service to the company office at Av Santa Fe 790 (T43143616/ 43155115, F43113722, or airport T/F4800597/0374 – 24 hrs), 0400, 0500, then every 30 mins till 2030, US$14, return US$25, credit cards accepted. Passengers picked up from city centre hotels. City centre office has check-in desk for *Aerolíneas Argentinas* flights; and **San Martín Bus**, office opposite *Air France* and *KLM*, service to company office at Santa Fe 1162, T48167676, F48167679 , Ezeiza 44809464, smbus@fibertel.com.ar, 15 mins past each hr, US$11, 10% ISIC and GO 25% discount (will also collect passengers from hotels in centre for no extra charge, book previous day), recommended.

Only one bag is normally allowed; passengers with backpacks may be charged double fare

Local bus No 86 bus (white and blue, marked 'Fournier') runs to the centre from outside the airport terminal to the right (*servicio diferencial* takes 1½ hrs, US$4, *servicio común* 2½ hrs, US$1, coins only, no change given) between 0500 and 2400. To travel to Ezeiza, catch the bus at Av de Mayo y Perú, one block from Plaza de Mayo – make sure it has '*Aeropuerto*' sign in the window as many 86's stop short of Ezeiza. There are no direct bus services between Ezeiza and the Retiro bus and train stations.

Taxi *Remise* charges fixed fare and can be booked from the Manuel Tienda León counter at Ezeiza, US$35 (including US$2.70 toll) payable in advance. If you take an ordinary taxi, the Policía Aeronáutica on duty notes down the car's licence and time of departure. Avoid unmarked cars no matter how attractive the fare may sound; drivers are adept at separating you from far more money than you can possibly owe them. From the centre to Ezeiza ordinary taxis charge US$30-35 depending on your bargaining skills while *Remises* charge US$18-20. *Remises* will also do return trip for US$18 plus US$6 per hr waiting time and US$3 per hr parking.

Train Local electric trains run between Ezeiza station and Buenos Aires (Constitución station) US$0.80, 40 mins. Ezeiza station is reached from the airport by bus 502, 20 mins, US$0.70.

Transfer to Aeroparque *Manuel Tienda León* operates buses between Ezeiza and Aeroparque airports, stopping in city centre, US$15. *Aerolíneas Argentinas* offer free transfers between the 2 airports to passengers whose incoming and connecting flights are both on: ask at AR desk for a voucher.

Aeroparque (officially known as Jorge Newbery Airport), 4 km north of the centre **Aeroparque** near the river, T47712071, handles all internal flights, services to Punta del Este and **airport** Montevideo and flights from Latin American countries with an intermediate stop in Argentina. The terminal is divided into 3 sections, 1 each for *Aerolíneas Argentinas* and *Austral* and the third, in between, for other airlines. *Aerolíneas Argentinas* section has duty-free facilities, post office, tourist information, *confitería*, car rental, *Manuel Tienda León* office (see below) and luggage deposit (US$3 per piece). There are exchange facilities with *Banco de la Ciudad* (Austral section) and *casa de cambio*, also ATMs. The airport is very expensive with a poor quality restaurant upstairs.

Airport bus *Manuel Tienda León* buses go to and from the centre (see above for address), 0710-2110 every 30 mins, US$5; to Ezeiza US$10. *Ecuador/TAS* buses go to Plaza San Martín US$3; to Ezeiza US$10.

Local bus No 45 runs from outside the airport to the Retiro railway station, then follows Av Alem and Paseo Colón to La Boca. No 37C goes from Plaza del Congreso to Aeroparque but make sure it has '*Aeroparque*' sign, US$0.70. There are no direct services between Aeroparque and the Retiro bus and train stations.

Taxi To Congreso US$7, Plaza de Mayo US$6, Retiro US$5, La Boca US$9. *Remise* are operated by *Universalflet* (office in Austral section, T47722950), Manuel Tienda León, US11-13 to centre, US$35 to Ezeiza, and Ecuador/TAS, US$11 to centre, US$13 to Consitución.

All long-distance buses arrive at the **Retiro bus terminal** at Ramos Mejía y Antártida **Bus terminal** Argentina. The terminal is on three floors. Arrivals and departures are on the middle floor where there are also stalls selling food and gifts and where departures are displayed on large screens. Ticket offices are on the upper floor. At the top of the escalator there is a list of companies and their stall numbers. These are organised by regions of the country (each region is colour coded). There are left-luggage lockers, tokens from kiosks, US$2.50. Large baggage should be left at *depositos* on the lower floor. The service of luggage porters is supposed to be free. Buenos Aires city information is at desk 83 on upper floor. Bus information at the Ramos Mejía entrance on the middle floor: tell them where you want to go and they will give you names of companies and schedules. For information, T3142323. Taxis leave from the lower floor, one level below arrivals. There are no direct bus services to either airport.

Nearby is the **Retiro railway station** and entrance to **Subte Line C**. The passage between the bus station and Retiro is packed with market stalls and is narrow (beware pickpockets), all designed to inconvenience those with luggage (although, as one correspondent points out, this also slows down anyone trying to make a speedy escape with your belongings).

Buenos Aires and the Río de la Plata

Getting around

Bus   *Colectivos* (city buses) cover a very wide radius, and are clean, frequent, efficient and very fast (hang on tight). The basic fare is US$0.70 (shorter trips US$0.65), US$1 to the suburbs. Have coins ready for ticket machine as drivers do not sell tickets. The bus number is not always sufficient indication of destination, as each number has a variety of routes, but bus stops display routes of buses stopping there and little plaques are displayed in the driver's window. *Guía T* and *Lumi* are guides obtainable at news stands that give routes of all buses.

Metro ('Subte')   There are 5 lines, labelled 'A' to 'E' which run under major avenues – 4 of which link the
Map available free   outer parts of the city to the centre. The 5th line 'C' links Plaza Constitución with the
from stations & from   Retiro railway station and provides connections with all the other lines. In the centre 3
tourist office   stations, 9 de Julio (Line 'D'), Diagonal Norte (Line 'C') and Carlos Pellegrini (Line 'B') are linked by pedestrian tunnels.

    The trains are run by *Metrovías*, T45530044. The fare is US$0.70 and covers any direct trip or combination between lines. Tokens (*fichas*) must be bought at the station before boarding. Buy a few in advance to save time (dollars not accepted). The system operates Monday to Saturday 0500-2215 approximately and Sunday 0800-2215 approximately. Backpacks and luggage allowed.

Metro (Subte)

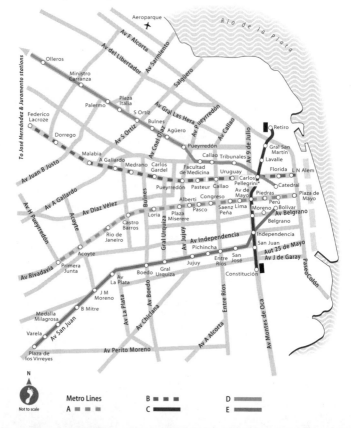

Ups and downs in the Subte

The Buenos Aires metro is the oldest in Latin America and one of the first in the world; only 11 cities had underground railways when the first section of Line A was built in 1913 from Plaza de Mayo to Plaza Once, a distance of 3,970 m. This line still runs many of its original carriages, the oldest operating underground wagons in the world. Line B opened in 1930 with two innovations: turnstiles and the first escalators in the country. Lines C, D and E were completed in 1934, 1937 and 1944 respectively.

A further line, Line F is under construction below Avenida Entre Ríos, Avenida Callao and Avenida Las Heras; it will provide a badly needed connection between Constitución and Plaza Italia.

Many of the stations in the centre especially on Line E have fine tilework murals, the work of Argentine and Spanish artists, which depict typical national landscapes and recount popular Argentine legends.

Today there are over 44 km of track and 65 stations. Each weekday the trains travel some 80,000 km and transport some 800,000 Argentines. Nevertheless the system has been dwarfed in recent decades by the rapid growth of the city. Lacking investment and strained by ever-increasing numbers of passengers, the network was near collapse when privatized in 1991.

Since privatization there have been many changes: the acquisition of 100 used Japanese carriages on Line B may be an unwelcome reminder to some passengers of the encroaching stainless-steel and glass modernity above ground, but it has meant greater travel comfort. Closed circuit television screens in many stations offer distraction, advertising and noise. More litter bins, greater frequency of service during rush hour, a few more benches and better lighting on platforms, have made the system more bearable. Nevertheless when trains break down in dark tunnels, when doors slam on passengers' limbs, when passengers are forced to climb stationary escalators or force their way as civilly as possible into overcrowded carriages during an ever-extending rush `hour', you can hear the now customary Argentine `privatization' groan move down the platform or carriage in waves.

Taxis are painted yellow and black, and carry *Taxi* flags. Fares are shown in pesos. The meter starts at US$1.12 when the flag goes down and US$0.14 is added for each 200 m travelled; make sure it isn't running when you get in. A charge is sometimes made for each piece of hand baggage (ask first). In theory fares double for journeys outside city limits (General Paz circular highway), but you can negotiate over this.

Taxi
Tips are not usual except for Remise

Remise taxis operate all over the city; they are run from an office, have no meter but charge fixed prices and are often much cheaper than yellow-and-black cabs. Some *Remise* companies do not charge extra for journeys outside the city limits. The companies are identified by signs on the pavement. Fares can be verified by phoning the office and items left in the car can easily be reclaimed. One good company is **Le Coq**, T49639391/2, 9638532.

US$2-3 tip expected

Orientation

The city centre is situated just inland from the docks on the south bank of the Río de la Plata. The main public buildings are grouped around the Plaza de Mayo; from here a broad avenue, Av de Mayo leads west 1 km to the Congress building in the Plaza del Congreso. Halfway it crosses the wide Av 9 de Julio. It consists of 3 major carriageways, with heavy traffic, separated in some parts by wide grass borders. In the north the Av 9 de Julio meets the Av del Libertador, the principal way out of the city to the north and west.

Av 9 de Julio is one of the widest avenues in the world

Buenos Aires and the Río de la Plata

Taxis in Buenos Aires

Taxi drivers in Buenos Aires, in common with their counterparts all over the world, are the subject of numerous complaints. Though most drivers are as honest and courteous as anywhere else, there are a number of common tricks:

Taking you on a longer than necessary ride; switching low-denomination notes for higher ones proffered by the passenger (don't back down, demand to go to the police station); grabbing the passenger's baggage and preventing him/her from leaving the taxi (scream for help); quoting `old' prices for new, eg `quince' (15) for

1.50 pesos, `veinte y seis' (26) for 2.60 pesos, etc.

All taxis are licensed: avoid unofficial taxis and unmarked cars. The worst places used to be the two airports and the Retiro bus terminal but when you catch a taxi from these points you are now given a certificate with the cab number and contact phone number. If possible, keep your luggage with you. Make sure you know what the fare should be before the journey. If you think you have been cheated, ask to see the taxi driver's licence. T4343-5001 to complain.

The city's commercial and banking area is located north of the Plaza de Mayo. The traditional shopping centre, Calle Florida runs north from Av de Mayo to Plaza San Martín and is pedestrianized. Another shopping street is Av Santa Fe, which crosses Florida at Plaza San Martín; it has become as touristy and as expensive as Florida. The traditional entertainment centre, Av Corrientes, which runs westwards parallel to Av de Mayo, is a street of theatres, restaurants, cafés and night life. There are cinemas and many good and reasonable restaurants in the nearby streets – though this area is in decline as the city's main entertainment areas move out from the centre, it is still worth a visit. The main hotel areas are around Av de Mayo and north of it towards Plaza San Martín.

East of the centre is the Puerto Madero dock area; its 19th-century warehouses have been renovated and turned into a popular nightspot, with restaurants and bars; it also provides a pleasant area for a stroll. Further east still is a stretch of marshland which forms the Parque Natural Costanera Sur, a wildlife reserve.

The remainder of the city fans out north, south and west from the central area. To the south are some of the older *barrios* (neighbourhoods); 2 of them, San Telmo and La Boca, attract visitors. San Telmo is an artistic centre, with plenty of cafés, antique shops and a pleasant atmosphere; and there is a regular Sunday antiques market at the Plaza Dorrego, with tango demonstrations on Sunday evening. La Boca, further south, has its own distinctive life; formerly run down, it has been renovated and now offers some pleasant riverside walks. It is especially lively when the Boca Juniors football club is playing at home. To the northwest are the wealthier *barrios* of Recoleta and Palermo, both of interest to visitors, the former chiefly for its museums, the latter for its parks.

Streets are organized on a grid pattern. Numbers start from the dock side rising from east to west, but north/south streets are numbered from Av Rivadavia, 1 block north of Av de Mayo rising in both directions. Note that some streets may be referred to by 2 names, notably Calle Juan D Perón which used to be called Cangallo.

Sights

Most historic churches apart from the cathedral are open from 0730-1230 and 1600-2000. State and municipal museums and parks are free on Wednesday. Check opening hours with tourist office; many close in January or February.

24 hours in the city

Early morning, when the city is still quiet, is a good time to visit some of the sights of the centre. Stroll along the Avenida de Mayo at this time and stop off for a typical Argentine breakfast of coffee with croissants (media-lunas) at the Café Tortoni, the most famous café in Buenos Aires. Nearby is the Perú metro station, its architecture unchanged since it was built from 1913. Follow Avenida de Mayo to its eastern end, the Plaza de Mayo, and explore the historic city centre. From here bus 29 or 64 will take you to Caminito, the most colourful barrio in the city, where the gaily coloured houses turn to yellow and blue near the football stadium. Sometimes you can hear refrains of tangos or the drums of a marga. The same buses will take you back to San Telmo. Get off at Calle Brasil to visit the Parque Lezama. The crowded Sunday fair on Plaza Dorrego is famous, but on weekdays these streets enjoy the usual slow pace of any Buenos Aires barrio. Smitten by the stylish old houses, the antique shops and the cobbled old streets you may choose to stay longer and grab something to eat. Bife de chorizo is a good choice in any of the restaurants but don't expect to be

energetic after a helping.

From San Telmo grab a taxi to Plaza San Martín, a good area for shopping. The plaza itself is a splendid oasis, enjoyed by Borges during his regular walks; from here the mansions of the upper classes of the early 20th century will lead you along Avenida Alvear to Recoleta, the most chic area of the city, where porteños like to be seen and show off. Here you can wander around art galleries and museums, or if you prefer, you can join the crowds enjoying a drink outside the cafes.

Two good, and cheap, options for the evening are the superb Teatro Colón (though it is advisable to check in advance) and the tango show at the Almagro club. If not live music, dancing, eating and drinking is Buenos Aires and you won't have any difficulty finding somewhere to party. However Palermo is particularly popular: try the Las Cañitas area (especially around Calle Baéz) or Palermo Viejo, both sides of the railway (off Santa Fe y Av Juan B Justo). The music might just stop by light and then you can fall into the nearest café for another of those Argentine breakfasts.

The city centre

Surrounded by some of the major public buildings, this is the historic heart of the city. On its east side, in front of the famous Casa de Gobierno (Casa Rosada), is a statue to General Belgrano. Further east, behind the Casa de Gobierno, in the semi-circular Parque Colón, is a large statue of Columbus.

Plaza de Mayo

The **Casa Rosada**, the Presidential Palace, lies on the east side. It is notable for its statuary, the rich furnishing of its halls and for its libraries. See box on page 82. ■ *Tours Mon, Tue, Thu, Fri 1000-1800, Sun 1400-1800, T43443804.* On the east side (at the back of the palace) is the entrance to the **Museo de los Presidentes**, containing historical memorabilia of former Presidents. ■ *Tue, Wed, Thu 0900-1400, Fri, Sun 1400-1800.* The museum also provides access to the tunnels and warehouses built in 1854 as part of the *Aduana* (customs house).

The **Antiguo Congreso Nacional** (Old Congress Hall) on the south side of the plaza, built in 1864, was encircled and built over by the Banco Hipotecario: it now functions as a conference centre. ■ *Guided tours Thu, 1500-1700, free.*

The **Cabildo**, or town hall, opposite the Casa Rosada on the west side of the plaza, has been rebuilt several times since the original structure was put up in the 18th century, most recently in 1940. Inside is the **Museo del Cabildo y la Revolución de Mayo**, containing paintings, documents, furniture, arms, medals and maps recording the May 1810 revolution and the 1806 British attack; also Jesuit art. In the patio is La Posta del Cabildo café and stalls selling

The Casa Rosada

Built 1874-1882, the Casa de Gobierno is known as the Casa Rosada because it is coloured pink, the result of a decision made by Sarmiento to symbolize national unity by blending the colours of the rival factions which had fought each other for much of the 19th century: the Federalists (red) and the Unitarians (white).

The palace is particularly well-known for its balcony, used in the film Evita *as the*

location of Eva Perón's speech renouncing public office. Sadly, though the balcony was the scene of other Peronist triumphs, the renunciation did not take place here: Evita was offered, and turned down, the Vice-Presidential nomination on 22 August 1951 at a great rally held on the Avenida Nueve de Julio, which could accommodate larger crowds than the Plaza de Mayo.

handicrafts. ■ *Tue-Fri 1230-1900, Sun 1500-1900. Open till 2000 in summer, US$1. Library, Mon-Fri, 1100-1900. Guided tours 1230-1430 and 1630. T43341782 for tours in English.*

The **cathedral**, on the north side of the plaza, lies on the site of the first church in Buenos Aires. The current structure was built between 1758 and 1807, when funds ran out before the twin towers could be erected: the architectural proportions have suffered as a result. A frieze upon the Greek façade represents Joseph and his brethren. Inside, in the right-hand aisle, is the imposing tomb of General

Around the Avenida de Mayo

■ **Sleeping**

1 Alcazar *C3*	9 Cecil *C3*	la Paix *B3*	24 Micki *A2*
2 Astoria *C3*	10 Chile *C2*	17 La Argentina *C4*	25 Novel *C4*
3 Avenida *C4*	11 City *C5*	18 Liberty *A4*	26 Nuevo Mundial *C2*
4 Avenida Petit *C2*	12 Continental *B4*	19 Lisboa *B2*	27 Orense *B2*
5 Bristol *B3*	13 Eibar *A5*	20 Madrid *C3*	28 Reina *C3*
6 Callao *B1*	14 Europa *B2*	21 Majestic *B3*	29 Ritz *C3*
7 Castelar *C3*	15 Gran Hispano *C4*	22 Marbella *C2*	30 Roma *C2*
8 Ceballos Palace *D1*	16 Gran Hotel de	23 Mediterráneo *B1*	31 Salles *B3*

N
Not to scale

José de San Martín (1880) guarded by soldiers in fancy uniforms. ■ *Masses Mon-Fri 0900,1100,1230, Sat 1730, Sun 1100,1200,1300. Visiting hrs Mon-Fri 0800-1830, Sat 0900-1230, 1700-1930, Sun 0900-1400, 1600-1930.*

The **Banco de la Nación**, just east of the cathedral, is regarded as one of the great works of the architect Alejandro Bustillo. Built in 1939, its central hall is topped by a marble dome 50 m in diameter. It contains the **Museo Numismático e Histórico del Banco Nacion**, entrance at B Mitre 326, piso 1, coins and notes, furniture and historical documents, ■ *Mon-Fri 1000-1500, T43424041, extension 607.*

Just north of the Plaza de Mayo, between 25 de Mayo and the pedestrianized Calle Florida, lies the main banking district known as La City. **La City**

The **Bolsa de Comercio**, 25 de Mayo y Sarmiento, is a handsome building dating from 1916 and housing the stock exchange. Visits not permitted.

Banco Hipotecario (formerly the Bank of London and South America), Reconquista y B Mitre, has a miniature museum on its fifth floor. ■ *Open during banking hours.* The building, designed by SEPRA (Santiago Sánchez Elia, Federico Peralta Ramos, and Alfredo Agostini) and completed in 1963, is worth seeing.

The **Church of La Merced**, Reconquista 207, founded 1604 and rebuilt 1760-1769, was used as a command post in 1807 by Argentine troops resisting the British invasion. One of the altars has an 18th-century wooden figure of Christ, the work of indigenous carvers from Misiones. It has one of the few fine carillons of bells in Buenos Aires.

The **Museo Numismático del Banco Central**, San Martín 216, piso 1, T43948411, fascinating, well kept. ■ *Tue 1000-1400, Wed and Fri tour at 1400, free, overlooks central foyer, ask guard for directions.*

The **Museo y Biblioteca Mitre**, San Martín 336, T43948240, preserves intact the household of President Bartolomé Mitre; has coin and map collection and historical archives. ■ *Mon-Fri 1330-1830, US$1.*

The **Museo de la Policía Federal**, San Martín 353, piso 8 y 9, T43946857. Interesting but extremely gruesome forensic section (for strong stomachs only; no one under 15 admitted). ■ *Tue-Fri 1400-1800.*

Three streets, Balcarce, Defensa and Bolívar, lead south from the Plaza de Mayo towards San Telmo (see below). The church of **San Francisco**, Alsina y Defensa, controlled by the Franciscan Order, was built 1730-1754 and given a new façade in 1911. Note the barroque pulpit and the chapel of San Roque.

South of the Plaza de Mayo
Next door to the museum is a lovely old café, 'La Puerto Rico', built 1887, furnishings from the 1930s

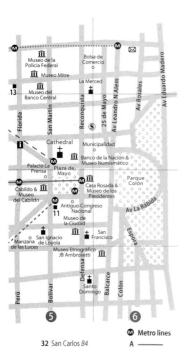

5 **6**

Ⓜ **Metro lines**

A ────────
B ‑ ‑ ‑ ‑ ‑
C ··········
D ─ ─ ─

Buenos Aires and the Río de la Plata

On the opposite corner is the **Museo de la Ciudad**, Alsina 412, T43432123, which includes the *Farmacia La Estrella* and covers social history and popular culture and houses special exhibitions on daily life in Buenos Aires (changed every two months) and a reference library open to the public. ■ *Mon-Fri 1100-1900, Sun 1500-1900, US$1. Free on Wed.*

The **Manzana de las Luces**, one block further west, is celebrated as the centre of learning in early Buenos Aires. The seat of the Jesuits before their expulsion, it was then occupied by the University of Buenos Aires. Occupying the whole block, it includes several buildings, including the National High School, the Procuraduría de las Misiones and a network of 17th-century Jesuit tunnels. ■ *Daily 1700-2000. US$3.50, free Fri. Guided tours (recommended) Sat 1500, Sun 1500, 1600, 1700, arrive 20mins early.* On the Perú y Alsina corner there is a handicrafts market ■ *Mon-Fri 1100-1930.* On the Alsina y Bolívar corner is the former Jesuit church of **San Ignacio de Loyola**, the oldest church in the city. Its two lofty towers date from the 1690s while the nave was rebuilt between 1710 and 1734. ■ *Guided tours Sat/Sun 1700 but open at other hrs.*

From Plaza San Martín to Plaza de la República

■ Sleeping
1 Best Western Comfort *C2*	9 Central Córdoba *B5*	17 Italia Romanelli *C5*
2 Bisonte *B3*	10 Crillón *B4*	18 Kings *D4*
3 Bisonte Palace *B3*	11 Embajador *B3*	19 Lancaster *C5*
4 Bolivia *D3*	12 Goya *B3*	20 Libertador
5 Camino Real *C4*	13 Gran Hotel Buenos Aires *B4*	21 Marriott Plaza *B4*
6 Carlton *B2*	14 Gran King *D5*	22 Panamericano *C3*
7 Carsson *C4*	15 Gran Orly *B5*	23 Principado *B5*
8 Central Argentino *A4*	16 Impala *A2*	

Palo borracho

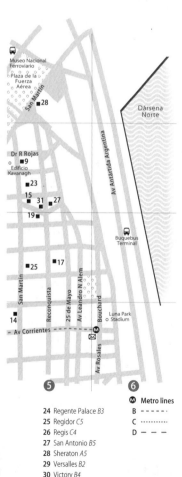

The name palo borracho *(drunken tree) is given to two related species: chorisia insignis and chorisia speciosa. The former, known as yuchán, comes from the Argentine northwest and prefers a drier climate than the latter. Known in North America as the White Floss tree or Silk Floss tree, it has white or yellow flowers and likes a dry climate. It was used by the Indians for making canoes. Chorisia speciosa (samohú) comes from the northeast and has pink, red or purple flowers and can grow to 20 m in height. Good examples of both species can be found in Buenos Aires, some as old as 100 years. Both varieties have palmate leaves and their green trunks turn grey with age.*

The **Museo Etnográfico J B Ambrosetti**, one block south of the San Francisco church at Moreno 350, T43317788, contains anthropological and ethnographic collections from around the world, including Bolivian and Mapuche silverwork. ■ *Mon-Fri 1400-1800 (1900 on Sat/Sun) closed Feb, US$1.*

The church of **Santo Domingo**, one block further south at Defensa y Belgrano, was founded in 1751. During the British attack on Buenos Aires in 1806 some of Whitelocke's soldiers took refuge in the church and it was bombarded by local forces; the British capitulated and their regimental colours were preserved in the church. The damage to one of the towers, supposedly caused by the seige, is a fake, added in the 19th century when the tower was restored. General Belgrano is buried here. There are summer evening concerts in the church; check times.

The **Museo Nacional del Grabado**, Defensa 372, T43455300, contains 15,000 works including some by Picasso, Dalí and Miró. ■ *Sun-Fri 1400-1800.*

Avenida de Mayo Running west from the Plaza de Mayo, this broad avenue was opened up between 1889 and 1894 to link the Presidential Palace to the Congress building then under construction at the other end. Lined with tall buildings, many of them with attractive French and Italian style façades, it is a street of hotels of all categories, restaurants and bars. Among the highlights are:

The **Palacio La Prensa**, No 575, just off the Plaza de Mayo and dating from 1898, formerly the offices of one of the country's most important newspapers.

(sidebar, vertical text) Buenos Aires and the Río de la Plata

Map labels:
Museo Nacional Ferroviario
Plaza de la Fuerza Aérea
San Martín
■28
Dársena Norte
Dr R Rojas
■9
Edificio Kavanagh
■23
15 ■
■31 ■27
19■
Av Antártida Argentina
Buquebus Terminal
■25 ■17
San Martín
Reconquista
25 de Mayo
Av Leandro N Alem
Bouchard
Luna Park Stadium
14
Av Corrientes
Av Rosales

⑤ **⑥**

Ⓜ **Metro lines**

B - - - - -
C ············
D — — —

The Café Tortoni

Founded in 1858 and named after a Parisian café, the Tortoni moved to its present site in 1880, though at that time the entrance was on Avenida Rivadavia. With the opening up of Avenida de Mayo, it gained a new frontage and greater popularity. Its greatest period was between 1926 and 1943 when it was the meeting place of the famous Peña de Tortoni, a group of bohemian artists and writers. The Tortoni's owner, Celestino Curutchet, laid down one of the most important rules of the peña: "here you may talk, drink in moderation and give full expression to your opinions, but only the arts may be discussed". Despite such strictures, Curutchet arranged for the peña to meet in the basement to avoid offending the upper-class clientele upstairs. As the fame of the Tortoni spread, it was frequented by many important Argentine artists and in its heyday poems and tangos were written in its honour.

The **Café Tortoni**, No 825, is the most famous bar in Buenos Aires, closely associated with the history of tango. The walls are decorated with posters and photos of its heyday in the 1930s and earlier. Live music is performed here in the evenings. Next door is the *Academia Nacional del Tango*.

The **Teatro Avenida**, No 1222, which opened in 1908, will take your passport and give you a ticket for your seat and a pink slip to reclaim your passport. You may stay as long as you wish, but must remain seated. ■ *Guided tours (in Spanish and English) can be taken on Mon, Tue and Fri at 1100 and 1700 when Congress is not sitting.*

From Retiro to the Plaza de la República Ten blocks north of the Plaza de Mayo is the **Plaza San Martín**. It lies on a hill overlooking the Retiro railway and bus terminals. In the centre is an equestrian statue to San Martín, first erected in 1862. At the northern end of the plaza is a memorial with an eternal flame to those who fell in the Falklands/Malvinas War, 1982.

Around the plaza are several elegant mansions, among them the **Palacio La Paz**, housing the Circulo Militar (a military club) and the **Museo de Armas**, T43111071, which contains a collection of all kinds of weaponry related to Argentine history, including the Falkands War, plus Oriental weapons ■ *Tue-Fri 1430-1900, Sat/Sun 1400-1800, closed 15 Dec-15 Mar, US$1.* The **Edificio Kavanagh**, east of the plaza, was the tallest building in South America when completed in 1935. Behind it is the **Basilica del Santísimo Sacramento** (1916), the church favoured by wealthy *porteños*. The elegant **Palacio San Martín** (19051909), just west of the plaza, is now occupied by the Ministry of Foreign Affairs. ■ *Free tours Thu 1100, 1200, Fri 1500, 1600, 1700, 1800, last Sat of each month 1100, 1200, 1500, 1600, 1700, 1800; for groups T48198092, F48197309.*

The **Plaza de la Fuerza Aérea**, northeast of Plaza San Martín, was until 1982, called the Plaza Británica; in the centre is a clock tower presented by British and Anglo-Argentine residents in 1916; 'a florid Victorian sentinel, royal crest upon its bosom'. Nearby, opposite the Retiro stations is the Plaza Canadá

Historic trains and trams

One of the most dynamic and enterprising cities in South America in the early years of this century, Buenos Aires was a pioneer in the development of municipal transport. Transport aficionados should not miss the opportunity to travel in the Tren Histórico, a Scottish-built 1888 Neilson steam engine pulling old wooden carriages, which runs from the Federico Lacroze station to Capilla del Señor with lunch or a folkloric show at an estancia (departs Sunday 0900, returns 1900). Prices: return fare US$15, return fare with lunch and show US$30, reductions for children. T4796-3618 or cellular phone

15-578-0738.

Another attraction is the old-fashioned green and white tram (street car) operated by Asociación de los Amigos del Tranvía (T476-0476) which runs (free) from April-November on Saturdays and holidays 1600-1900 and Sunday 1000-1300, 1600-1930 (not Easter Sunday) and from December-March on Saturdays and holidays 1700-2000, Sundays 1000-1300, 1600-1900. The circular route runs along the streets of Caballito district, from Calle Emilio Mitre 500, Subte Primera Junta (Line A) or Emilio Mitre (Line E), no stops en route.

in which there is a Pacific Northwest Indian totem pole, donated by the Canadian government.

The **Retiro** railway station is really three separate termini; the westernmost of these, the **Mitre**, is the finest, dating from 1908; its *confitería* is worth a visit. Behind the station at Avenida del Libertador 405 is the **Museo Nacional Ferroviario**, for railway fans. It contains locomotives, machinery and documents on the history of Argentine railways. The building is in very poor condition. ■ *Mon-Fri, 0900-1800.*

Three blocks west of the Retiro along the Avenida del Libertador is the **Museo de Arte Hispanoamericano Isaac Fernández Blanco**, Suipacha 1422. Housed in a beautiful 1920s neocolonial mansion with Spanish-style gardens, it contains an interesting and valuable collection of colonial art, especially silverware from Alto Peru, Peru and Río de la Plata. ■ *Tue-Sun, 1400-1900, US$2; Thu free, closed Jan. For guided visits in English or French T43270228; guided tours in Spanish Sat, Sun 1600.*

Avenida Santa Fe, one of the city's most expensive streets runs west from Plaza San Martín. It crosses the broad Avenida 9 de Julio, which leads south to the great **Plaza de la República**, in the centre of which is a 67 m obelisk commemorating the 400th anniversary of the city's founding.

Overlooking 9 de Julio, between Calles Viamonte and Tucumán, is the **Teatro Colón**, opened in 1908 on the site of an earlier theatre of the same name. The interior, seating over 4,000 people, is resplendent with red plush and gilt; the stage is huge, and salons, dressing rooms and banquet halls are equally sumptuous. The season runs from April to early December and the theatre also stages concerts, recitals and ballet. ■ *Daily (not Sun), guided tours Mon-Fri hourly 0900-1600, Sat 0900-1200, in Spanish, French and English, US$5 (children US$2), from entrance at Viamonte 1180. Recommended. Closed Jan-Feb, T43826632. Tickets, sold several days before performance, on the Calle Tucumán side of the theatre. The cheapest seat is US$6 (available even on the same day), and there are free performances most days (Tue-Fri) at 1730 in the Salón Dorado – check programme in the visitors' entrance.* In the same building at Tucumán 1161 is the **Museo del Teatro Colón**, T43821430, which displays documents and objects related to the theatre. ■ *Mon-Fri 0900-1600, Sat 0900-1200, closed in Jan.*

One of the world's great opera houses

Buenos Aires and the Río de la Plata

Nearby are two other museums: the **Museo Israelita**, Libertad 773. Housed in a late 19th-century synagogue, this contains scriptures, coins, concentration camp items and objects relating to Jewish presence in Argentina. ■ *Tue/Thu 1600-1830, identification essential for entry.* The **Museo del Teatro Nacional Cervantes**, Córdoba 1155, with displays on the history of the theatre in Argentina. ■ *Mon-Fri 1430-1800, Sat/Sun 1000-1300, T48158881 in advance.*

Four blocks west of the Plaza de la República, at Avenida Corrientes 1530, is the **Centro Cultural San Martín**, an ugly building which houses the **Teatro Municipal San Martín** and a salon of the **Museo Municipal de Arte Moderno**. ■ *US$1, Wed free.*

South of the centre

San Telmo   The *barrio* of San Telmo, south of the Plaza de Mayo, built along the slope which marks the old beach of the Río de la Plata, is one of the oldest parts of the city. Though one of the few areas where buildings remain from the mid-19th century, its network of narrow streets is much older. Formerly one of the wealthiest areas of the city, it was abandoned by the rich after the great outbreak of yellow fever in 1871. It is a recognized artistic centre, with plenty of cafés, antique shops and a pleasant atmosphere.

The *barrio* centres on the **Plaza Dorrego**, a small square 10 blocks south of the Plaza de Mayo. Here on Sundays, 1000-1700 there is one of the best, and most famous, 'antiques' markets.

Nearby on Humerto I is the church of **Nuestra Señora de Belén**. Begun by the Jesuits in 1734, but only finished in 1931, it is best described as eclectic in style. Note for instance the barroque columns and the Spanish style tiles. Next door at Humberto I 378, is the **Museo Penitenciario Argentino Antonio Ballue**, the museum of the penal system, housed in a building which was originally the headquarters of the Jesuits and which later served as slave quarters, hospital and prison. ■ *Tue-Fri 1000-1200, 1400-1700, Sun 1000-1200, 1300-1700, US$1.*

The **Museo Municipal de Arte Moderno**, one block further south in an old tobacco warehouse at San Juan 350, houses international exhibitions and a permanent collection of contemporary Argentine art. ■ *Mon-Fri 1000-2000, Sat and Sun 1200-2000, US$1.50 T43611121. Guided tours Tue-Sun 1700.* The museum also has a salon in the Centro Cultural San Martín, Corrientes 1530.

The **Museo del Cine Pablo Ducros Hicken**, nearby at Defensa 1220, T43612462 (not to be confused with the Museo Municipal de Cine) is dedicated to the development of Argentine cinema from 1896 to the present. There is a film library of over 600 sound films and four decades of newsreels. ■ *Mon-Fri 1300-1900. US$1, free on Wed.*

The **Museo Internacional de Caricatura y Humorismo**, six blocks west of Plaza Dorrego at Lima 1037, houses a collection of original 20th-century cartoons and caricatures, though with a very small international section. ■ *Mon, Tue, Thu, Fri 1700-2000, Sat 1200-1700, US$1.*

The **Parque Lezama**, Defensa y Brasil, was originally one of the most beautiful parks in the city. According to tradition Pedro de Mendoza founded the city on this spot in 1535. There is an imposing statue to him in the centre of the park. It was here that the last defence against the British invasion of the city in 180s took place. On the west side of the park is the **Museo Historico Nacional**, T43074457, containing trophies and mementoes of historical events, divided into halls depicting stages of Argentine history. Here are San Martín's uniforms, a replica of his sabre, and the original furniture and door of the house in which he died at Boulogne. ■ *Tue-Sun 1200-1800. Guided tours Sat/Sun 1500. Free.*

East of the Plaza de Mayo, behind the Casa Rosada, a broad avenue, Paseo **La Boca**
Colón, runs south towards the picturesque old port district known as La Boca,
where the Riachuelo flows into the Plata. An area of heavy Italian immigration,
La Boca has its own distinctive feel. Though parts of it are becoming touristy, the
area, with the adjacent industrial and meat-packing suburb of Avellaneda across
the high Avellaneda bridge, is generally dirty and run down. For a tour of La
Boca, start at Plaza Vuelta de Rocha, near Avenida Pedro de Mendoza, then walk
up Caminito, the little pedestrian street used as a theatre and an art market.

The **Museo de Bellas Artes de la Boca**, Pedro de Mendoza 1835,
T43011080, houses over 1,000 works by Argentine artists, including Beito
Quinquela Martín (1890-1977). ■ *Mon-Fri 0800-1800, Sat/Sun 1000-1700,
free. Guided tours by prior arrangement.*

The **Museo Histórico de Cera**, Valle Iberlucea 1261, T43011497. The only
wax museum in the country, this depicts scenes from the history of southern
Buenos Aires. ■ *Mon-Fri 1000-1800, Sat 1100-1930, Sun 1100-2000. US$3,
children under 8 years, free.*

■ *Getting there: To La Boca from the centre take Bus 152 which runs along
Santa Fe and Alem, or bus 29 from Plaza de Mayo, US$0.60.*

South of the centre

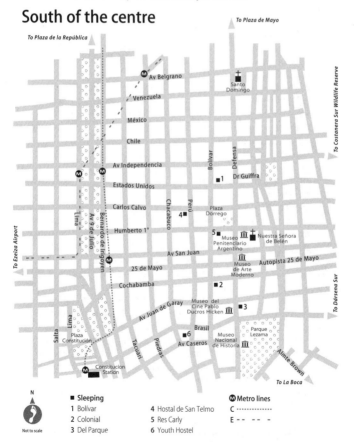

N
Not to scale

The Argentine way of death

The cemeteries of Buenos Aires offer fascinating insights into Argentine society. Two cemeteries are particularly interesting: La Recoleta and La Chacarita.

Although the Argentine elite, the so-called `bovine aristocracy', was perhaps less ostentatious than some of its counterparts, the taste for displaying wealth was fairly strong. Nowhere was this more apparent than after death: an Argentine landowner, industrialist or politician was not really dead if their obituary had not been published in La Prensa, *a newspaper with the prestige of the London Times; neither could they rest in peace if their remains did not lie in the Recoleta cemetery. To be buried here was (and still is) so important that it was said to be the most expensive plot of land in the world. It is so densely occupied that in many of the mausoleums, the caskets are piled up 8 m to 10 m high. In the past (and, maybe still) fictitious funerals took place in which the remains of the dead were taken to their "ultimate" resting place in the Recoleta, only to be removed quietly a few days later to a common cemetery.

La Chacarita to the west of the centre (see below) is much less socially exclusive. Here cost, rather than social acceptability, are the barriers to entry, though families unable to keep up with maintenance payments are told to move their loved ones elsewhere.

To walk through La Recoleta is, therefore, not only to pass through a forest of interesting sculptures, but also a way of revisiting Argentine history, for just as almost everyone who has played an important role in the country's past is remembered through a street or plaza, so they have a space in La Recoleta. Here lie the remains of Sarmiento and Mitre, of Roca and many other names from the past. Also here are their former enemies: Juan Manuel de Rosas; Facundo Quiroga, the caudillo demonized by Sarmiento; and Eva Perón, despised and hated in life by the Argentine elite and now lying among them in death. At least two great 20th-century figures did not qualify for La Recoleta, Juan Perón and Carlos Gardel. Both are buried at La Chacarita.

Along the Costanera Sur

East of San Telmo the spacious Avenida Costanera runs north along the far side of the docks. The Puerto Madero dock area, west of Avenida Costanera, with its 19th-century warehouses has been renovated and turned into a popular nightspot, with restaurants and bars; it also provides a pleasant area for a stroll.

The **Parque Natural Costanera Sur**, east of the costanera, lies on a stretch of marshland claimed from the river by a system similar to the one used in the construction of the Dutch polders. Though drained between 1978 and 1981 to provide a site for a satellite city, the project was abandoned. More than 200 species of birds can be seen including the rare black-headed duck and the curve-billed reed hunter and there are also large numbers of *coypu* (large rodents). There are three trails ranging from 2 km to 6 km long and an 8 km path around the outside. In summer it is very hot with little shade. Excellent maps from the Visitors' Centre. For details, contact *Fundación Vida Silvestre*, Defensa 245, piso 6. ■ *Daily 0800-1900 (Nov-Mar), 0800-1800 (Apr-Oct) but much can be seen from the road (binoculars useful), free, guided tours available at weekends, T43154129. The entrance is near the southern end of the park at Avenida Tristán Achabal Rodríguez 1550 (reached by buses 4 and 2).*

The **Museo de Telecomunicaciones** lies about 1 km further north along the Costanera at Avenida de los Italianos 851 and is housed in a magnificent art-deco building which used to belong to Cervecería Munich. ■ *Tue-Fri 0930-1800, Sat/Sun 1400-1800. T4683112.*

Further north in the docks at the northern end of Puerto Madero are two sailing ships which can be visited. The **Fragata Presidente Sarmiento**, Dock 3, Avenida Dávila y Perón, was the Argentine flagship from 1899 to 1938, after which it served as a naval training ship until 1961. T43349336. ■ *Mon-Fri 0900-2000, Sat/Sun 0900-2200, US$1.* Nearby, in Dock 1, is the **Corbata Uruguay**, T43141090, the sailing ship which rescued Otto Nordenskjold's Antarctic expedition in 1903. ■ *Daily 0800-2000 all year, US$1.*

North of the centre

Situated 1½ km north of Plaza San Martín and built on the site of a Jesuit monastery, the Recoleta district became fashionable when wealthy families moved here from the crowded city centre after the yellow fever outbreak of 1871. An area of parks and museums, at its heart is the **Plaza de la Recoleta**, with expensive *confiterías* and the famous *gran gomero*, a large rubber tree. There is a good craft market here on Saturday and Sunday at 1100 until 1800.

The **Cementerio de la Recoleta**, just off the plaza, is the final resting place of the most famous names in Argentine history. ■ *0700-1800.* With its streets and alleys separating family mausoleums built in every imaginable achitectural style, La Recoleta is frequently compared to a miniature city. Among the famous names from Argentine history is Evita Perón who lies in the Duarte family mausoleum: to find it from the entrance walk straight ahead to the main plaza; turn left and where this avenue meets a main avenue (just past the Turriata tomb, about 13 'blocks'), turn right and take the third passage on the left. On Saturday and Sunday there is a good craft market near the entrance from 1100 to 1800 with street artists and performers.

Recoleta

Buenos Aires and the Río de la Plata

Recoleta

Sleeping
1 Alvear Palace	4 Carlton	7 Hyatt
2 Arenales	5 Embajador	8 Impala
3 Caesar Park	6 Etoile	9 Plaza Francia

10 Recoleta Plaza	
11 Suipacha	Ⓜ Metro lines
	D – – –

Not to scale

The former Jesuit church of **El Pilar**, next to the cemetery, is a jewel of colonial architecture dating from 1732, restored in 1930. See the colonial altarpiece, made in Alto Peru and the fine wooden image of San Pedro de Alcántara, attributed to the famous 17th-century Spanish sculptor Alonso Cano, which is preserved in a side chapel on the left.

The **Centro Cultural Recoleta**, alongside the Recoleta cemetery, occupying the former monastery, specializes in contemporary local art with many free exhibitions by young artists. It includes a section of the **Museo de Arte Plasticas Eduardo Sivori**. ■ *Tue-Sun 1200-1800, US$1, free on Wed*. A passage leads from the centre to the **Buenos Aires Design Centre**, which houses many good restaurants. Nearby there is another square, the **Plaza San Martín de Tours**, with more *gomeros* and a natural amphitheatre as well as the glass-covered **Palais de Glace**, built in the late 19th century and used as an exhibition centre.

The **Museo de Bellas Artes**, Avenida del Libertador 1473, T48013390, lies just north of the Recoleta cemetery. In addition to a fine collection of European works, particularly strong in the 19th-century French school, there are 16th- and 17th-century paintings representing the conquest of Mexico, many good Argentine works including new 19th- and 20th-century exhibits, and wooden carvings from the Argentine hinterland. ■ *Tue-Fri 1230-1930, Sat/Sun 0930-1930. US$1 (Thu free), ISIC holders free. Recommended. Guided tours: 1700 for Argentine art, 1800 for European art, Saturday 1500 for children.*

■ *Getting there: To Recoleta buses: 110, 17; 60 (walk from corner of Las Heras y Junín, two blocks); from downtown, eg Correo Central, 61/62, 93, to Pueyrredón y Av del Libertador, or 130 to Facultad de Derecho.*

North of Recoleta Avenida del Libertador runs north from Recoleta towards Palermo past further parks and squares as well as several museums.

The **Biblioteca Nacional** or National Library, Avenida del Libertador 1600 y Agüero 2502, T48066155, is in a modern thirteen-storey building with an art gallery. Only a fraction of its stock of about 1.8 million volumes and 10,000 manuscripts is available. Cultural events and festivals are held here. ■ *Mon-Sat 0800-2100, Sun 1100-2100. Excellent guided tours (Spanish) Mon-Fri 1530 from main entrance, for tours in other languages contact in advance.*

The **Museo Nacional de Arte Decorativo**, Avenida del Libertador 1902, contains collections of painting, furniture, porcelain, crystal, sculpture; classical music concerts Wednesday and Thursday. ■ *Daily except Tue 1400-1900, T48026606, US$1, half-price to ISIC holders. Guided visits Thu 1700. Walkman in Spanish or English 1500-1830.* Also in the same building is the **Museo Nacional de Arte Oriental**, containing a permanent exhibition of Chinese, Japanese, Hindu and Islamic art. ■ *Mon-Sat 1400-1900, Sun 1500-1900. US$1. Guided tours Mon-Fri 1700. Videos on oriental themes, Tue/Sat 1500, 1630, 1830.*

The **Museo del Instituto Nacional Sanmartiniano**, nearby at Gral Ramón Castillo y Avenida A M de Aguado, is a Replica of San Martín's house in exile in Grand Bourg near Paris. There is also a large library on the Liberator. ■ *Mon-Fri 0900-1700, T48023311 in advance.*

The **Museo de Motivos Populares Argentinos José Hernández**, Avenida Libertador 2373, housing the widest collection of Argentine folkloric art, with rooms dedicated to prehispanic, colonial and Gaucho artefacts; handicraft sale and library. ■ *Wed-Fri 1300-2000, Sat/Sun 1500-2000. T48029967, F48027294, mujose@mujose.edu.ar, for guided visits in English or French. US$1, free on Sun (closed in Feb).*

Charles Thays

The main plazas of most large Argentine cities bear witness to the influence of Charles Thays. A landscape gardener born in France, Thays probably did more to change Argentine city centres in the early 20th century than any single architect. He was responsible for replacing the traditional colonial plazas, bare expanses devoid of greenery, with the gardens which adorn them today. Although his major works in Buenos Aires were the

Plaza San Martín, the Parque Tres de Febrero and the Jardín Botánico, he also designed the Parque San Martín in Mendoza, the Parque Nueve de Julio in Tucumán and the Parque Sarmiento in Córdoba as well as parks in Chile and Uruguay. The Buenos Aires botanical gardens are, though, his greatest legacy: a lover of native Argentine plants, Thays travelled throughout the country in search of specimens for this collection.

Further northwest is Palermo, named after Juan Dominguez Palermo who **Palermo** owned these lands in the 17th century. The site of Rosas's mansion in the early 19th century, its series of great parks, established by Sarmiento and designed by Charles Thays, make it the most popular spot in the city for spending weekends.

The **Parque Tres de Febrero**, the largest park, has lakes, tennis courts, a rose garden ■ *Winter: Mon-Fri 0800-1800, Sat/Sun 0800-2000; Summer 0800-2000 daily*, a Japanese garden with fish to feed ■ *Closed Mon, admission US$2 and an Andalusian Patio*. It also contains the **Planetarium**, at the entrance to which there are several large meteorites from Campo del Cielo (see page 330). ■ *Tue-Fri 1000-1600, Sat/Sun 1500-1900, free.* The **Museo de Arte Moderno Eduardo Sivori**, also in the park, T47749452, specializes in 19th- and 20th-century Argentine engravings, tapestries, sculptures, drawings and paintings. ■ *Tue-Sun 1200-1800, US$1. Guided tours Sat 1200-1500.*

Further north is the **Hipódromo Argentino** (the Palermo race course) with seats for 45,000. Well worth a visit even for non-racegoers, see box. ■ *Sun 1500, US$3, senior citizens free.* Nearby are the Municipal Golf Club, Buenos Aires Lawn Tennis Club, riding clubs and polo field, and the *Club de Gimnasia y Esgrima* (Athletic and Fencing Club).

The **Jardín Zoológico**, Las Heras y Sarmiento, west of the Japanese gardens, covers 18 ha and is home to 89 species of mammals, 49 varieties of reptiles and 175 bird species. ■ *1000-1730, guided visits available, US$7 for adults, children under 13 free.*

The **Municipal Botanical Gardens**, west of the zoo at Santa Fe 2951, contain characteristic specimens of the world's vegetation. The trees native to the different provinces of Argentina are brought together in one section. The gardens contain the **Museo del Jardín Botánico**, T48312951, with a collection of Argentine flora. ■ *Mon-Fri 0700-1600.* The gardens are full of stray cats, fed regularly by local residents. ■ *The gardens close at 1800. Entrance is from Plaza Italia (take Subte, line D).*

North of the zoo are the showgrounds of the **Sociedad Rural Argentina**, where in July the Annual Livestock Exhibition, known as Exposición Rural, is staged. The show provides interesting insights into Argentine society. ■ *Entrance from Plaza Italia.*

The **Museo de la Asociación Evaristo Carriego**, 10 blocks south of the botanical gardens at Honduras 3784, is dedicated to tango and will appeal to *aficionados*. ■ *Mon-Fri 1300-2000.*

North of the parks on the coast is **Aeroparque** (Jorge Newbery Airport), the city's domestic airport. Next to it is the **Museo Nacional de Aeronáutica**, Avenida Costanera Rafael Obligado 4550, housing a collection of civil and military aircraft, plus displays of navigational material, documents, equipment. Mainly of specialist interest. ■ *US$3, Tue-Fri 0830-1630, Sun 1400-1900, T47730665.*

Belgrano
*Lying NW of Palermo,
this suburb is the
location of several
museums*

Museo Histórico Sarmiento, Juramento 2180, T47837555, the National Congress and presidential offices in 1880; documents and personal effects of Sarmiento; library of his work. ■ *Tue-Fri 1500-1900, Sun 1500-1900 only; closed Jan/Feb.*

Museo de Arte Español Enrique Larreta, Juramento 2291, entrance on Avenida Rafael Obligado. The home of the writer Larreta with Andalucían-style gardens, this houses a collection of Spanish art and works spanning the 13th to 20th centuries. ■ *Sat-Sun 1500-1900; Mon, Tue, Fri 1400-1945. Closed Wed, Thu and Jan. US$1. Free on Tue. Guided tours Sun 1600, 1800. T47832640 for guided tour in language other than Spanish.* Also **Biblioteca Alfonso El Sabio**, Monday-Friday, 1300-1930.

Palermo

The **Museo Histórico Saavedra**, northwest of Belgrano at Crisólogo Larralde 6309, T45720746, is housed in the former attractive *estancia* (dating from the 1870s) of Luis Maria Saavedra. It is also known as the Museo Histórico de la Ciudad de Buenos Aires, it should not to be confused with Museo de la Ciudad. Displays on the history of the city from the 18th century, furniture, arms, documents, jewellery, coins and religious art. ■ *Daily guided tours. Tue-Fri, 0900-1800, Sun 1400-1800, US$1, closed Feb.*

Museo Casa Yrurtia, O'Higgins y Blanco Encalada, T/F47810385, US$1. Housing sculptures, paintings and furniture of the artist Rogelio Yrurtia. ■ *Tue-Fri 1500-1900, Sat 1600-1900.*

West of the centre

La Chacarita, Guzman 780, reputedly the largest cemetery in South America, is less socially exclusive than Recoleta. The most-visited tombs here are those of Juan Perón and Carlos Gardel, the tango singer. ■ *Daily 0900-1700. Subte Line B to the Federico Lacroze station.*

The **Museo de Ciencias Naturales Bernardino Rivadavia**, Avenida Angel Gallardo 470, facing Parque Centenario, T49825243. There are palaeontological, zoological, mineralogical, botanical, archaeological and marine sections. Meteorites from the Campo del Cielo are on display. ■ *All year, daily, 1400-1700 (closed holidays), US$1. Library, Mon-Fri, 1100-1700. Guided tours US$2.50.* In the same building is the **Museo de la Dirección Nacional del Antártico**, with specimens of Antarctic flora, fauna and fossils and a library of taped birdsong. ■ *Tue, Thu and Sun, 1400-1800.* The **Museo de Esculturas Luis Perlotti**, Pujol 642, T4312825, in the former workshop of this Argentine sculptor. ■ *Tue-Fri 1100-1900, Sat/Sun 1000-1300, 1400-2000, US$1, Wed free.* ■ *Getting there: Subte Line A to Primera Junta or Buses 25, 26, 55, 76, 84, 86, 92, 96, 99.*

Museo Municipal de Cine, Sarmiento 2573, T49524598, traces the development of Argentine cinema and contains permanent exhibitions on María Luisa Bemberg and Niní Marshall. ■ *Mon-Fri 1000-1830, US$1. Subte A to Plaza Miserere or buses 5, 7, 24, 26, 41, 61.*

Museo Histórico Dr Ernesto 'Che' Guevara, Oroño Nicasio 458, in Caballito, near Rivadavia 6,000, T49033285. ■ *Sat/Sun 1700-2000, free. Buses 26, 36, 86, 132, 141.*

Museo y Biblioteca Ricardo Rojas, Charcas 2837. The famous writer Rojas lived in this beautiful colonial house for several decades. It contains his library, souvenirs of his travels, and many intriguing literary and historical curios. ■ *Tue-Fri 1400-1800.*

Museo del Automovil, Irigoyen 2265, on the far outskirts of the city, T 46413969, www.museodelautomovil.com An eclectic collection of vehicles including the 1929 Hudson which belonged to Borges, the 1937 Dodge Brothers used in the film *Evita* and an 1897 Krieger.

Excursions

The main excursions are northwest to Tigre and Isla Martín García, see page 120, Luján and San Antonio de Areco, see page 140, and the Reserva Nacional Otamendi, see page 305, southeast to La Plata, see page 122, and northeast across the Río de la Plata to the Uruguayan coastal resorts including Colonia del Sacramento, see page 125. For excursions to visit estancias see page 122.

Essentials

Sleeping

All hotels, guest houses, inns and camping sites are graded by the number of beds available and the services supplied. The Dirección de Turismo fixes maximum and minimum rates for 1, 2 and 3-star hotels, guest houses and inns, but the ratings do not provide very useful guidance. Both 4 and 5-star hotels are free to apply any rate they wish.

The following list is only a selection; exclusion does not necessarily imply non-recommendation. Rates given below are generally the minimum rates. Room tax is 15% and is not always included in the price. A/c is a must in high summer. Many of the cheaper hotels in the central area give large reductions on the daily rate for long stays. Hotels with red-green lights or marked *Albergue Transitorio* are hotels for homeless lovers (for stays of 1½-2 hrs).

Expensive **LL** *Alvear Palace*, Alvear 1891, T/F48082100. Older-style, near Recoleta, with roof garden, shopping gallery, elegant, extremely good. **LL** *Caesar Park*, Posadas 1232, T48191296, F48191121. Pool, solarium. **LL** *Camino Real*, Maipú 572, T43223162, F43259756. Pleasant, central. **LL** *Claridge*, Tucumán 535, T43147700, F43148022. Highly recommended, but variable reports about its restaurant. **LL** *Continental*, Sáenz Peña 725, T43261700/7741. With breakfast, comfortable. **LL** *Crillón*, Santa Fe 796, T43128181. Comfortable, good breakfast. **LL** *Etoile*, Ortiz 1835 in Recoleta, T48045272/7703, F48053616. Outstanding location, rooftop pool, rooms with kitchenette. Recommended. **LL** *Libertador Kempinski*, Córdoba 680, T43228800, F43229703, fine views over the city from 22nd floor. **LL** *Park Hyatt*, Posadas 1086, T43211234, F43211235. **LL** *Sheraton*, San Martín 1225, T43189000, F43189150. Good buffet breakfast. **LL** *Reconquista Plaza*, Reconquista 602, T43114600, F43113302, www.reconquistaplaza.com.ar Good location, sauna and gymnasium. **LL** *Regente Palace*, Suipacha 964, T43286600, F43287460. Very good, central, English spoken, buffet breakfast, sports facilities, stores luggage.

L *Aspen Towers*, Paraguay 857, T43131919, F43132662. Small, spacious rooms, good breakfast. **L** *Best Western Confort*, Viamonte 1501, T48144917. With breakfast, English spoken, 50% ISIC discount. **L** *Bisonte*, Paraguay 1207, T43165770, F43939086. A/c, bar, modern, central, good value. **L** *Bisonte Palace*, MT de Alvear 910, T43284751, F43286476. Very good, welcoming. **L** *Deauville*, Talcahuano 1253, T48113629, F48145732. A/c, restaurant, bar, garage, recommended. **L** *Gran King*, Lavalle 560, T43934452. Helpful, English spoken. **L** *Lancaster*, Córdoba 405, T43124061, F43113021. Includes breakfast, expensive laundry service, charming. **L** *Principado*, Paraguay 481, T43133022, F43133952. With breakfast, central, helpful.

AL *Bristol*, Cerrito 286, T43825403, F43823384. Good breakfast. **AL** *Carsson*, Viamonte 650, T43223551, F43323801. Comfortable, quiet except rooms on street (ending in 17). **AL** *Embajador*, Pellegrini 1185, T43265302. Good. **AL** *Gran Hotel Buenos Aires*, M T de Alvear 767, T/F43123003. Rundown but clean. **AL** *Impala*, Libertad 1215, T/F48160430. With breakfast. **AL** *Italia Romanelli*, Reconquista 647, T/F43126361. Comfortable. Recommended. **AL** *Liberty*, Corrientes 632, T/F43250260. With breakfast, English spoken, luggage stored, various sized rooms. **AL** *Salles*, 9 de Julio/Cerrito y J D Perón, 2 blocks from *Obelisco*, T43820091, F43820754. Recommended. **AL** *Savoy*, Callao 181, T43725972, F43259589. Helpful.

Mid-price **A** *Ayacucho Palace*, Ayacucho 1408, T48061815, F48064467. 10 minutes from centre bus 10, helpful, comfortable, English spoken. Recommended. **A** *City*, Bolívar 160,

T43426481, F43426486. Recommended. **A** *Ecuador*, Alsina 2920, near Plaza Once, T49560533, F4979987. Recommended. **A** *Eibar*, Florida 328, T43250969. With breakfast, quiet, helpful, old fashioned. **A** *Regis*, Lavalle 813, T43272605/10, F43272618. Good value, nice atmosphere, quiet at back. **A** *Sarmiento Palace*, Sarmiento 1953, T49533420, F49536247. Comfortable, English spoken. Recommended. **A** *Victory*, Maipú 880, T43145440/8415, F43228415. A/c, modern, heating, TV, comfortable, front rooms noisy, luggage storage unreliable.

AB *Constitución Palace*, Lima 1697, T43059020. With breakfast, 30% ISIC discount. **AB** *Goya*, Suipacha 748, T43229269. A/c, quiet. **AB** *Gran Hotel de la Paix*, Rivadavia 1155, T43818061. Old but good, large rooms. **AB** *Gran Orly*, Paraguay 474, T/F43125344. Old fashioned, good service, good lunches, English spoken, holds mail for guests, a/c, good value. Recommended. **AB** *Nuevo Mundial*, Av de Mayo 1298, T43830011, F43836318, mundialhouse.com.ar Good beds, comfortable. **AB** *Plaza Roma*, Lavalle 110, T/F43140666. With breakfast. Recommended. **AB** *Prince*, Arenales 1627, T/F48118004. Small, quiet. **AB** *Promenade*, M T de Alvear 444, T/F43125681. No charge for credit cards, helpful, stores luggage, recommended. **AB** *Regidor*, Tucumán 451, T43149516, F43117441. A/c, breakfast included, recommended. **AB** *San Antonio*, Paraguay 372, T43125381. Nice atmosphere, garden. Recommended. **AB** *Tres Sargentos*, Tres Sargentos 346, T43126081. Secure, new bathrooms, good value. **AB** *Waldorf*, Paraguay 450, T43122071, F43122079. Comfortable, rooms of varying standards, garage, a/c. Recommended.

Avenida de Mayo **A** *Castelar*, No 1152, T43835000, F43838388. Elegant and attractive 1920s hotel (Federico Garcia Lorca lived here in 1933-1934), good value. **AB** *Gran Hotel Hispano*, No 861, T43452020, F43315266. Without breakfast, attractive, spacious, pleasant patio, stores luggage, helpful. **AB** *Astoria*, No 916, T/F43349061. Without breakfast, pretty patio, nice rooms, poor beds. **AB** *Avenida*, No 623, T4342566. Without breakfast, modernized, bar, clean, pleasant. **AB** *Chile*, No 1297, T/F43837877. With breakfast, also cheaper rooms, clean, friendly, noisy. **AB** *Madrid*, No 1135, T43819021. Without breakfast. **AB** *Marbella*, No 1261, T/F43838566. Modernized, quiet, with breakfast, a/c, English spoken. Highly recommended. **AB** *Vedra*, No 1350, T43830584. Good value, good beds, stores luggage. Recommended.

Near Plaza del Congreso AB *Callao*, Callao y Sarmiento, T4763534. Noisy. **AB** *Majestic*, Libertad 121, T4351949. Good value, with breakfast. **AB** *Orense*, Mitre 1359, T4763173, **C** without bath, with breakfast, fan, laundry and cooking facilities. Recommended.

Avenida de Mayo **B** *Novel*, No 915, T43450507. With breakfast. **B** *Reina*, No 1120, T43810547. Old fashioned with masses of character and large breakfast, 20% ISIC discount. **B** *Ritz*, No 1111, T43839001, clean, breakfast extra. **C** *Alcazar*, No 935, T43450926. Attractive, good value. **C** *Cecil*, No 1239, T43833511, F43837929. Without breakfast. **C** *Hotel La Giralda*, Tacuarí 17, T43453917, F43422142. Student discounts and for long stays. Recommended. **C** *Roma*, No 1413, T43814921. Without breakfast, also rooms without bath, old but clean, good value.

Cheaper
For Youth Hostel associations see useful addresses below

Near Plaza del Congreso B *Ceballos Palace*, Virrey Ceballos 261, T4372763. Safe (next to police HQ). **B** *Europa*, Mitre 1294, T43819629. A/c, 10% ISIC discount. **B** *Lisboa*, Mitre 1282, T43831141. With breakfast, central. **B** *Micki*, Talcahuano 362, T43712376. No a/c, basic, good value. **C** *Sportsman*, Rivadavia 1425, T43818021/2. Old fashioned, without bath, ISIC discount. **D** *Mediterráneo*, Rodríguez Peña 149, T4762852. Basic, central, helpful, safe, stores luggage, laundry facilities. Recommended. **D** *Hosp Esterlina*, Mitre 1266. Old, rambling, dirty.

Buenos Aires and the Río de la Plata

Avenida de Mayo towards Plaza de Mayo **B** *Avenida Petit*, No 1347, T43817831. Without breakfast. **B** *Turista*, No 686, T43312281. Nice rooms, comfortable. **C** *La Argentina*, No 860, T43420078/9. Without breakfast, run down, comedor. **C** *Tandil*, No 890, T43432597. Without breakfast, with bath, also **D** without bath, poor beds, clean.

San Telmo C *La Casita de San Telmo*, Cochabamba 286, T/F43075073, guimbo@pinos.com, colonial style house, minimum stay 1 week, with large kitchen. **C** *Bolívar*, Bolívar 886, T43615105. Good. **D** *Res Carly*, Humberto 1° 464. Without bath, fan, quiet, basic, kitchen facilities, good value. **D** *Colonial*, Bolívar 1357. Hostelling International reduction, also dormitories, good kitchen. **D** *Hotel del Parque*, Defensa 1537. Basic. **E** *Hostal de San Telmo*, Carlos Calvo 614, T43006899, F43009028. Small dormitories, kitchen and laundry facilities, clean, quiet, modern, English spoken. Recommended.

Elsewhere AB *Aguirre*, Aguirre 1041, T47735027. Safe. **AB** *Central Argentino*, Av del Libertador 174, T43126742. Secure, near Retiro stations, noisy, overpriced. **AB** *El Cabildo*, Lavalle 748, T43926745. Without breakfast. **AB** *Kings*, Corrientes 623, T43228161, F43934452. With breakfast, a/c, helpful, top floor rooms have balcony. **AB** *Versalles*, Arenales 1394, T48115214, west of Av 9 de Julio. Basic, no breakfast, fine staircase and mirrors. **B** *Central Córdoba*, San Martín 1021, T/F43128524. Very central, a/c, helpful, quiet, good value. **B** *Hispano Argentino*, Lima 1483, T43045855. Some rooms with bath, quiet, convenient. **B** *Juncal Palace*, Juncal 2282, T48212770. Old fashioned, 20% ISIC discount. **B** *Maipú*, Maipú 735, T43225142. Popular, hot water, basic, stores luggage, laundry facilities. Recommended. **B** *O'Rei*, Lavalle 733, T43937186. **C** without bath, basic, central, dark, ask for a balcony. **B** *Uruguay*, Tacuarí 83, T43343456. Central, good value, no credit cards, recommended. **C** *Bahía*, H Yrigoyen 3062. Hot showers, pleasant, safe, central but noisy. Recommended. **C** *Bolivia*, Corrientes 1212, T43821780. Without bath. **C** *Du Helder*, Rivadavia 857, T43453644. Old fashioned, clean, poor beds. **C** *Frossard*, Tucumán 686, T43221811. Heating. **C** *Metropolitan I*, Corrientes 3973, T48623366 and *Metropolitan II*, Boedo 449, T48623366, F49311133 (Subte Line A to Barros Arana or Line E to Boedo). With breakfast, kitchen and laundry facilities, parking, English spoken, good value. **C** *Sil*, H Yrigoyen 775, T42318273. Nice but no heating. **D** per person *Lion d'Or*, Pacheco de Melo 2019, T48038992. Handy for Recoleta, basic, clean, without bath or breakfast. **E** *Zavalia*, Juan de Garay 474, T43621990, per person, without bath, noisy.

Student residences E *Hosp Encuentro*, Sarmiento 4470, T48655684 (Subte Line B to Gallardo); **E** Dido, Sarmiento 1343, T43735349. Per person. With kitchen, also longer term accommodation; **D** per person [La Porteña], Warnes 87, T48545303. Metro

Angel Gallardo, with breakfast. Entre Ríos 2165, T43066021. With bath, also meals, social areas, reduced rates for longer stay. Longer term accommodation (min 2 weeks) is offered by Juan Carlos Dima, Puan 551 C, T4324898, F4327101. US$450 per month per room, kitchen faciities, English spoken. Also try *Sra Anita*, Corrientes 2989, piso 10, C, T48644132, shared rooms.

Youth hostels D per person *V & S Youth Hostel Backpackers*, Viamonte 887, T43220994/43275131, hostelvsAvsyhbue.com.ar Recently refurbished old building in centre, good double rooms and small dormitories, kitchen and laundry facilities, excellent value. **D** per person *Buenos Aires International Hostel*, Brasil 675 near Constitución station, T43009321, (buses 4,62, 143, 186) **E** with Hostelling International card (ISIC card accepted), with breakfast, sheets provided, hot water 24 hrs, basic, recommended, no cooking facilities, cheap meals, doors closed 1200-1800 and from 0200, women should be aware that they could attract unwelcome attention near Constitución station as prostitutes operate there. *Hostel International Buenos Aires*, Moreno 1273, T43819760, bahostel@hostels.org.ar **E** *Del Aguila*, Espinosa 1628, T45816663. Hot water, cooking and laundry facilities, membership not necessary (buses 24, 105, 106, 109, 146). **D/E** per person *Recoleta Youth Hostel*, Libertad 1218, Recoleta T48124419, F48156622. Dormitories, also double rooms, cooking facilities, quiet, good location. **D** per person *Federacion de las ACFS*, Humberto 1 2360, with kitchen, women only. **E** per person *Hostal Colonial*, Bolivar 1357, without bath.

Apartments contracts are usually for at least 1 year and owners will demand a guarantor or a deposit covering at least 6 months rent (security or cash). One agent is Sr Aguilar, Florida 520, 3°-314, T43224074. An agency which arranges sharing apartments (often with senior citizens) is Martha Baleiron, Esmeralda 1066, 5°F, T43119944. US$50 fee if an apartment is found, US$10 if not. All agencies should provide contracts which should be read carefully. To rent flats on a daily basis try *Edificios Esmeralda*, M T de Alvear 842, T43113929. Includes cleaning, facilities for up to 6 persons. Also *Edificio Suipacha*, Suipacha 1235, T/F43226685, and *Aspen Apartment Hotel*, Esmeralda 933, T43139011. *Edificio Lemonde*, San Martín 839, T43132032. Recommended. *Res Trianon*, Callao 1869, T48123335.

Camping About 15 km out at Lomas de Zamora, US$3 per night, includes swimming pool, 24-hr security, take own drinking water; difficult to find, take bus 141 from Plaza Italia or 28 from Pellegrini to Puente La Noria then No 540 to Villa Albertini which passes the entrance.

Eating

Eating out in Buenos Aires is very good but expensive. Good restaurants charge US$30 and up; more modest places charge US$15-20. Many mid to upper range restaurants offer a menu ejecutivo at lunchtime which is much cheaper than ordering á la carte. Lunch or dinner in a cheap restaurant costs US$10-12 (cutlet, salad, glass of table wine, dessert); a portion at a *comidas para llevar* (take away) place cost US$2.50-3.50. Many cheaper restaurants are *tenedor libre*, eat as much as you like for a fixed price. Several supermarkets have good, cheap restaurants; one which is very central is *Coto*, Viamonte y Paraná, upstairs. Also *Supercoop* stores at Sarmiento 1431, Lavalle 2530, Piedras y Rivadavia and Rivadavia 5708. Good snacks all day and night at Retiro and Constitución railway termini. For fast and very cheap pizzas look out for *Ugi's*, many branches. For quick cheap snacks the markets are recommended. The snack bars in underground stations are also cheap. *DeliCity* bakeries, several branches, very fresh pastries, sweets, breads, authentic American donuts. *Biscuit House*, bakery chain, 20 branches, *media lunas*, *empanadas* and breads.

For restaurants with shows, see page 103, & restaurants with music, see page 104

Buenos Aires and the Río de la Plata

'The Buenos Aires Herald' publishes a handy *Guide to Good Eating in Buenos Aires* (with a guide to local wines) by Dereck Foster. There is also *El Libro de los Restaurantes de Buenos Aires*, published annually, describing the city's major restaurants. The following, for reasons of space not quality, lists only those restaurants easily accessible for people staying in the city centre.

Banking district
Between Av Corrientes & Plaza de Mayo. Mostly closed at weekends.

Expensive *Catalinas*, Reconquista 875. Seafood, very expensive. *Clark's*, Sarmiento 645, in old English outfitter's shop (also at Junín 1777). Well cooked food, very expensive, busy, fish and lamb specialities, set lunch very good value, live show Thu evenings. *London Grill*, Reconquista 455. British, busy, famous for roast beef and turkey curries, open 0800-1700 only. *Sabot*, 25 de Mayo 756. Very good business lunches.

Mid-range *ABC*, Lavalle 545. Traditional, good value. German specialities. *Bolsa de Comercio*, 25 de Mayo 359, downstairs at the Stock Exchange. Good but expensive. Lunches only. *Brizzi*, Reconquista 536. Business lunches, good and worth the price. *Club Inglés*, 25 de Mayo 586. Lunches only. *El Figón de Bonilla*, Alem 673. Rustic style. Good. *El Palacio de la Papa Frita*, Lavalle 735 and 954, Corrientes 1612, Laprida 1339, Maipú 431. 10% discount for ISIC and youth card holders, despite name no chips. *La Pipeta*, San Martín 498. Downstairs, serving for 30 years, good, noisy, closed Sunday. *La Estancia*, Lavalle 941. Popular with business people, excellent grills and service, expensive. *Los Troncos*, Suipacha 732. Good grills, US$18 *menú*.

Cheaper *Banco Nación*, Rivadavia y 25 de Mayo (opposite Casa de Gobierno), the cheapest place in the area and an opportunity to visit this huge building. *El Palacio de la Pizza*, Corrientes 751. *La Casona del Nonno*, Lavalle 827. Popular, *parrilla* and pasta, not cheap. *Las Cuartetas*, Corrientes 838, pizza, try also its unusual dessert *sopa inglesa* (English soup). Good value *parrillas* at *La Posada del Maipú*, Maipú 440. *Los Inmortales*, Lavalle 746. Specializes in pizza, good value, large selection, 10% ISIC discount. There are other locations: some serve *à la carte* dishes which are plentiful, and are open from 1500-2000 when most other restaurants are closed. *Memorabilia*, Maipú 761. Pizzas, bar, music, 20% discount for ISIC cards, *tenedor libre*. *Patio San Ramón*, at the Convento de la Merced, Reconquista 269. Light meals in the most pleasant place in the centre. *Pizzería Roma*, Lavalle 800. Cheap and good quality, delicious spicy *empanadas* and *ñoquis*, good breakfasts.

A few blocks from this district

Expensive *El Aljibe*, at *Sheraton*, smoked salmon, tournedos Rossini, baby beef. *La Chacra*, Córdoba 941. Good *parrilla*, expensive. La Recova, an area on the 1000 block of Posadas, near *Hyatt*, has several moderate to expensive restaurants, eg *El Mirasol de la Recova* and *Piegari*, No 1052, US$40, pastas. **Mid-range** *Club Sueco*, Tacuarí 147, Mon to Fri lunches only, Swedish meals; smorgasbord on Wed, US$35 pp all included, for bookings T.43347813. *El Navegante*, Viamonte y Bouchard. Good meals, dating from the period when the city was an active port. *El Establo*, Paraguay 489, good *parrilla*. *Filo*, San Martín 975. Trendy place, pizza, salads. **Cheaper** *Budapest*, 25 de Mayo 690. *Dora*, Alem 1016. Huge steaks, get there early to beat the queue. *Dansk Mad*, at the *Club Danés*, Alem 1074 12th floor, recommended, Danish meals. *Florentino*, Viamonte 826, good light meals.

Palermo
Cheaper *Rivadavia*, Sanchez de Bustamante 2616, Palermo Chico. Huge portions, good value. *La Cupertina*, Cabrera 5300, Palermo Viejo, small, family run place, good for cheap local dishes and home made desserts.

Recoleta
There are many medium range to expensive restaurants in the **Buenos Aires Design Centre**, next to the Centro Cultural Recoleta. **Expensive** Nearby, 2 blocks from Recoleta towards Av Callao, *Au Bec Fin*, Vicente López 1827, reservations needed,

open 2000-0200 daily. *Harper's*, Junín 1773. Also in La Recova (see above). *Hippopotamus*, Junín 178. Good value executive lunch. Dinners only on Fri and Sat.Turning left on Ortiz: *Lola*, No 1805. Good pasta, lamb and fish but expensive. *Munich Recoleta*, Junín 1871. Good steaks, pleasant atmosphere, no credit cards. **Medium** On the corner of Roberto M Ortiz is *La Biela* (see tea rooms, etc, below). *Rodi Bar*, Vincente López 1900. Excellent *bife*.

Expensive *Calle de Angeles*, Chile 318. Nice setting in an old, covered street, high standards. *El Remanso de San Telmo*, Carlos Calvo 242, T43625473. Excellent, expensive, reserve in advance. *La Casa de Estebán de Luca*, Defensa 1000. Very good, good wines, closed Mon. *La Convención de San Telmo*, Carlos Calvo 375. Good, but expensive. For ice cream, *Sumo*, Independencia y Piedras. **Cheaper** *El Desnivel*, Defensa e Independencia, good *parrilla*. *La Coruña*, olívar y Carlos Calvo, next to the market gates, a low budget option. *Pizzalandia*, on Brasil (near Youth Hostel) serves cheap *empanadas*, *salteñas* and pizzas.

San Telmo area

Expensive Along the river front (far end of Aeroparque) is lined with little eating places (take a taxi, or colectivo 45 from Plaza Constitución, Plaza San Martín or Retiro to Ciudad Universitaria): *Happening*, *Clo Clo*, La Pampa y Costanera Norte, reservation required, T47880488. Typical *parrilla* at *Rodizio*, opposite Balneario Coconor, self-service and waiter service, other branches, eg Callao y Juncal, good value, popular.

Costanera Norte

Expensive *Las Lilas*, No 516. Excellent *parrilla*. *Cholila*, No 102. Chic. *El Mirasol del Puerto*, No 202, and opposite, *Bice*, No 192, mostly Italian, good. Also branches of *Rodizio*, No 838, *tenedor libre* and *Happening*, No 300. **Mid-range** *Caballerizá*, 560, overpriced. *Columbus*, No 292, popular. *Bahía Madero*, No 430. Highly recommended. *Xcaret*, No 164. **Cheaper** South of the Plaza de Mayo, *Y Siga La Vaca*, Alicia Moreau de Justo 1700, *tenedor libre*, Ukranian staff. *Paréntesia*, Alicia Moreau de Justo 1500 (access via Calle Chile), is a university refectory, the cheapest place in Puerto Madero.

Puerto Madero
All situated across the docks north from Plaza de Mayo on Alicia Moreau de Justo

Expensive *Edelweiss*, Libertad 431. Tuna steaks, pasta, grill, expensive and famous. *Gran Bar Danzón*, Libertad 1161, also bar with live music. *Pizza Piola*, Libertad 1078. Good, pricey. *Tomo Uno*, Pellegrini 525 (*Hotel Panamericano*). Expensive, trout, mignon, shrimp, home-made pasta, closed Sun. *9 de Julio*, Pellegrini 587. Very good value. **Cheaper** *El Cuartito*,Talcahuano 937. *Güerrín*, Corrientes 1368. American Club, Viamonte 1133, piso 10.

Near Teatro Colón

Expensive Also near Congress: *Plaza Mayor*, Venezuela 1399. Estancia-style. Opposite is *Campo dei Fiori*. Italian. Recommended. **Mid-range** *Chiquilín*, Montevideo 321. Pasta and meat, good value. *Los Teatros*, Talcahuano 350. Good (live music 2300-0100). *Pepito*, Montevideo 381. Very good. *Pippo*, Montevideo 341. Large pasta house, simple food, very popular, also at Paraná 356. *Quorum*, Combate de los Pozos 61, behind Congress. Popular with politicians. **Cheaper** *La María*, Mexico 1316, good *parrilla* and pasta.

Near Congreso & Av Corrientes

Mid-range *El Obrero*, Caffarena y Pedro de Mendoza, recommended for pasta. **Cheaper** *El Puentecito*, Vieytes 1895, cheap Argentine dishes, good value. *El Candil*, Pi y Margall y Necochea, for *empanadas* and *locro*. *Banchero*, Suárez y Almirante Brown, good pizza and *minutas*, also *fainá* (other branches at Corrientes y Talcahuano and at Pueyrredón y Bartolomé Mitre).

La Boca

Expensive Italian *Broccolino*, Esmeralda 776. Excellent, very popular, try *pechuguitas*. **Spanish** *El Imparcial*, H Yrigoyen 1204. Recommended. **Mid-range Armenian** *Asociación Armenia*, Armenia 1366 piso 1, evening meals

International

Buenos Aires and the Río de la Plata

only. **British** *The Alexandra*, San Martín 774. Curries, fish and seafood, nice bar, closed in evening. **German** *Frank*, Bulnes y Santa Fe. **Italian** *La Spiagge di Napoli*, Av Independencia y Av Boedo. *Prosciutto*, Venezuela 1212. 3 famous *pizzerías* in the centre are on Corrientes: *Banchero*, No 1298; *Las Cuartetas*, No 838, and *Los Inmortales*, No 1369, same chain as above. *Il Gatto*, Corrientes 959. Popular and reasonably priced. **Oriental** *Morizono*, Reconquista 899, Japanese. *Chino Central*, Rivadavia 656. *Casa China*, Viamonte 1476. **Spanish** *El Globo*, H Yrigoyen 1199. Recommended. *El Museo del Jamón*, Cerrito 8, good tapas, fish soup and seafood. **Swedish** *Club Sueco*, Tacuarí 147. A few blocks from the banking district. Open to non-members. **Cheaper Armenian** *Sarkis*, Jufré y Thames. **Oriental** *Tulasi*, Marcelo T Alvear 628. Indian and vegetarian, Mon-Fri 900 to 1900, Sat 1000-1500. *Cantón*, Córdoba 4015. Many cheap but authentic Taiwanese restaurants in Arribeños between Juramento y Mendoza in Belgrano. *Nuevo Oriental*, Maipú near Lavalle, Chinese *tenedor libre*, US$6, good choice. *La China*, J D Perón y Montevideo, *tenedor libre*. *Tsuru*, ground floor of *Sheraton*. Authentic Japanese, small, recommended. *Katmandu*, Córdoba 3547, Palermo, T49631122, Indian. **German** *Hermann*, Santa Fe 3902.

Vegetarian **Cheaper** *Ever Green* is a chain of *tenedor libre* vegetarian restaurants, branches: Paraná 746, Sarmiento 1728 and Cabildo 2979. *Granix*, Florida 126 and 467 *tenedor libre* US$8, bland but filling, lunchtime Mon-Fri. *La Esquina de las Flores*, Córdoba 1599. Excellent value, also good health-food shop. *La Huerta II*, Lavalle 895, piso 2, *tenedor libre*, US$7, reasonable. *Lotos*, Av Córdoba 1577, only for lunches. *Macrobiotica Universal*, Paraguay 858. Highly recommended.

Tea rooms, cafés & bars

Watch whisky prices in bars, much higher than in restaurants. Most cafés serve tea or coffee plus 'facturas' (pastries) for breakfast, US$2.50-3 (bakery shops sell 10 facturas for US$2)

Richmond, Florida 468 between Lavalle and Corrientes, genteel (chess played between 1200-2400). Well-known are the *Confitería Suiza*, Tucumán 753, and the *Florida Garden* Florida y Paraguay. *Confitería Ideal*, Suipacha 384, historic but falling into decadence (part of the Alan Parker film 'Evita' was made here), good service, cakes and snacks. Recommended. Many on Av del Libertador in the Palermo area. *Café Querandí*, Venezuela y Chacabuco. Popular with intellectuals and students, good atmosphere, well known for its Gin Fizz. The more bohemian side of the city's intellectual life is centred on Av Corrientes, between Cerrito and Callao, where there are many bars and coffee shops. *Bar Seddon*, 25 de Mayo, small tango bar, packed from midnight on. *Pub Bar Bar O*, Tres Sargentos 451, good music and prices. *The Shamrock*, Rodriguez Peña 1220, Irish run, Guinness until 0500. *Druid Pub*, Reconquista 1040, Irish bar, 120 whiskeys, 20 beers, happy hour Mon-Fri 1800-2100. *Café 1234*, Santa Fe 1234. Open late when everything else is closed. *Clásica y Moderna*, Callao y Paraguay. Bookshop at back, expensive but very popular, jazz usually on Wed night, open 24 hrs. *Freddo*, Pacheco de Melo y Callao, with another branch at Santa Fe y Callao, 'the city's best ice-cream' (Brad Krupsaw). Next door (Quintana y Recoleta) is café *La Biela*, restaurant and *whiskería*, elegant. Also in Recoleta: *Café Victoria*, Ortiz 1865. Whiskería/sandwichería, popular. *La Vanguardia*, Montevideo 1671. 30% discount for ISIC card. *Buller Brew Pub*, Ortíz 1827, wide range of beers, also food. In Paseo del Pilar *Hard Rock Café*, great salads, and *Café Rix*, both with ISIC and GO 25 discount. *Henry J Bean's*, Junín 1747, ISIC and GO 25 discount. On Lavalle there are *whiskerías* and *cervecerías* where you can have either coffee or exotic drinks. *Barila*, Santa Fe 2375, has excellent confectionery. *Café Tortoni*, Av de Mayo 825-9. Delicious cakes, coffee, a haunt of artists, very elegant, over 100 years old, interesting *peña* evenings of poetry and music. On Saturday at 2315 it becomes a 'Catedral del Jazz', with Fénix Jazz Band, US$15 entrance. *Parakultural New Border*, Chacabuco 1072, mostly avant-garde theatre, popular. A 'bohemian, bizarre' bar is *El Dorado*, H Yrigoyen 971. Good bars in San Telmo around Plaza Dorrego, eg *El Balcón de la Plaza*, and on Humberto I. *Café Remis Paris*, Rodriguez Peña 1032. *Boquitas Pintadas*, Estados Unidos y Santiago del Estero, good bar. *Los 36 Billares*, Av de Mayo 1265, traditional café open till late.

Entertainment

For details see *La Maga*, US$5, published weekly and available from newsstands. On Fridays separate entertainment sections are published in the *Buenos Aires Herald* (called '*Get Out*') and *La Nacion* (entitled '*Via Libre*').

There are trendy places in the Las Cañitas area in Palermo, around Av Luis María Campos y Av Dorrego, including **Voodoo**, Báez 340. **Dada Bistró**, San Martín 941. In Palermo, there are several bars with live music open at night around Honduras y Serrano and around Honduras y Bonpland including **Acabar** and **Espero Infinito**, El Salvador y Carranza, www.esperoinfinito.com.ar Cinema show on Tue, good drinks and light meals. The latest trend (2000) is the 'supper club', a fashionable restaurant serving dinner around 2200, which clears the table at 0100 for all-night dancing, eg **La Morocha**, Dorrego y Libertador, and **El Living**, M T de Alvear 1540, T48156574. **Clubs** include *Le Club*, small and exclusive, Quintana 111. **Morocco**, H Yrigoyen 851, popular, fashionably kitsch décor, reasonable prices, couples and singles, dinner, dance, show, reservations T43435353. **Cemento**, Estados Unidos 1238, disco with live shows, usually hard rock and heavy metal, popular with younger crowds, as is **New York City**, Alvarez Thomas 1391, T45524141, chic. **Pacha**, Costanera Norte y La Pampa, T49782232. **Tobago**, Alvarez Thomas 1368, T45535030. Live music, books and intellectuals. **Mitos Argentinos**, Humberto I 489, near Plaza Dorrego, T43627810, dancing to 'rock national' music, in the daytime has tango and lunch with live music and public participation. **Pacha**, Costanera Norte y La Pampa, T49782232. **El Dorado**, H Yrigoyen y 9 de Julio, interesting, different. **El Nacional**, Reconquista 915, in tunnels formerly used for smuggling; **Cachaça Tropical**, on Brasil (1 block from Plaza Constitución), big disco with Latin American music, good meeting place. **Saturnalia**, San Martín 954, 1st floor, Mon to Sat, live music.

Bars & clubs
Generally it is not worth going to discos before 0230 at weekends. Dress is usually smart. Some discos serve breakfast for additional charge at entry

Gay clubs **Bunker**, Anchorena 1170, Fri-Sun, large, loud. **Enigma**, Suipacha 925, T43139940, Fri-Sat. Most gay discos charge US$10-15 entry on door. Tickets are much cheaper if bought from bars around Santa Fe y Pueyrredón from 0100.

The selection of films is as good as anywhere else in the world and details are listed daily in all main newspapers. Films are shown uncensored and most foreign films are subtitled. Tickets best booked early afternoon to ensure good seats (average price US$6 in 1996, 50% discount Wed and for 1st show Mon-Fri). Tickets are obtainable, sometimes for a cheaper price, from ticket agencies (*carteleras*), such as **Vea Más**, Paseo La Plaza, Corrientes 1600, local 19 (the cheapest), **Cartelera**, Lavalle 742, T4322 9263, **Teatro Lorange**, Corrientes 1372, T43727386, and **Cartelera Baires**, Corrientes 1372, local 25. There is a charge of US$1 for credit card bookings. There are many cinemas on Lavalle, around Santa Fe and Callao and in Belgrano (Av Cabildo and environs). Film club at **Foro Gandhi**, Montevideo 453 on Fri and Sat evenings, showing old, foreign and 'art' films, US$1.50, open to non-members. On Sat nights many central cinemas have *trasnoches*, late shows starting at 0100. There are also *trasnoches* on Wed at the **Recoleta Village**, a large new cinema complex in Recoleta.

Cinemas

Bailantas are music and dance halls where they play popular styles which for years have been despised as 'low class' but which are now fashionable among the upper classes. A popular place is **Metropolis**, Santa Fe at Plaza Italia, rather seedy. **For salsa** **Niceto**, Niceto Vega 5510, salsa, Fri and Sat, bar opens 2000, dancing from 0100, salsa dance class Fri 2100. **El Club**, Yerbal 1572, friendly, for all ages, not trendy, all welcome. **La Salsera**, Yatay 961, highly regarded salsa place. **Salson**, Alvarez Thomas 1166, T45516551. **Saduca**, Pueyrredon y Santa Fe, popular salsa club. On Sarmiento between Callao and Montevideo, there are several clubs with 'tropical' music such as **Maluco**, Sarmiento 1728, T43721737, also live Brazilian music.

Music

Fun times in Buenos Aires

For years it was the classic Avenida Corrientes, followed by Calle Lavalle, but today both of these are considered faded and the most popular parts of town chosen by most Porteños for having a good time are around Palermo. Here both the Paseo de la Infanta and Los Arcos (Mitre y Cáceres), located some 500 m from each other, are lined with fine bars and restaurants which, come midnight, pull in their tables, turn on the dance lights and turn into hopping discos and gathering spots for those who come to see and be seen. Age groups range from 14 to what one Porteño calls `marrying age'. The most popular spots on the lips of late night weekenders include Buenos Aires News, Puente Mitre, Tequila, Bonito Bonito, Coyote, Hanoi, Gitana and Fashion Café.

Equally fashionable but only slightly less popular is the Paseo del Pilar in Recoleta, where a string of restaurants compete along an airy and well-lit promenade. Other attractions are the Hard Rock Café, a couple of gay bars and the Centro Cultural Recoleta, which offers live music and art exhibitions.

The Puerto Madero docks are quickly gaining popularity with pleasant areas for strolling along the river, restaurants bathed in soft light and an ultra-modern cinema complex. Costanera Norte also manages to whip up an active nightlife. Pizza Banana, a dance and mingle spot more for the middle-aged crowd and popular with couples as well as singles, receives good revues, as do Happening, Pacha (disco for 20s and 30s) and El Cielo

(a disco with terrace overlooking the river).

Although traces of the Argentine passion for cinema can still be seen at weekends on Calle Lavalle and Avenida Corrientes, their glory days are long gone. Corrientes is still second to none for theatre, but the most popular cinemas are now around the intersection of Avenida Santa Fe and Avenida Callao, though this has been surpassed by a modern multiplex in Puerto Madero.

For a more unique evening the cantinas along Calle Necochea 1200 block, in La Boca, move to a colourful perhaps more popular rhythm with their Italian tarantellas and local, Brazilian or Caribbean live music. Non-stop noise, dancing and great portions of food mark this traditional Italian neighbourhood as a spot for those with a taste for the slightly crude and bizarre.

During the daytime Porteños flock to the new Tren de la Costa so they can get out and window-shop at the shopping-stations (San Isidro is a favourite) and restaurants. The Costanera Sur Wildlife Reserve attracts crowds for walking, sunbathing and biking (rent a cycle here) along its dirt roads in warmer weather. Tourists and locals alike roam the antique shops and weekend market in San Telmo or mix with the crowds at the Recoleta crafts market. At the rose garden in Palermo you can paddle-boat around the artificial lake or sit on a shady bench with the masses. The zoo is a social event, while the Botanical Gardens next door are that rarest of phenomena in Buenos Aires:

Bars and restaurants in San Telmo district, with live music (usually beginning 2330-2400): *Players*, Humberto I 528 (piano bar). *Samovar de Rasputin*, Iberlucea 1251, Caminito, T43023190. Good blues, dinner and/or show. Cover charges between US$5 and US$20, or more.

Jazz *Oliverio Allways*, in the *Hotel Bauen*, Callao 360, T43726906. Excellent live jazz features the great Fats Fernández, Fri-Sat 2330 and 0100. *Café Tortoni*, Av de Mayo 829, T43424328. Classic tango spot, features the Creole Jazz Band, Fri 2300, 40% ISIC and GO25 discount, also tango concert Fri-Sun 2130. Recommended.

Tango in Buenos Aires

After years of decline, the tango scene is once again enjoying great popularity. Most neighbourhoods of the city have their own tango scene with even the kids dancing a kind of hybrid tango-rock. The best way to enjoy tango is to see it the way the porteños do, away from the tourist spots. In San Telmo there are several famous clubs which any hotel employee or resident will tell you are a 'must' but two of the best places are less well-known.

One of these is the Club del Vino, Cabrera 4347, where the repertoire is a spectacular blend of the traditional and the Piazzola-style modern. Some of the finest shows in the city feature members of the 'guardia vieja' (old guard) who still linger on from the 1940s and 1950s, considered by many to be the best decades of Buenos Aires tango. At the Club del Vino on a Saturday night you can be witness to living tango history. Here Nelly Omar, who came out of the Francisco Canaro orchestra, one of the first so-called 'tipica' groups which were all the rage in the 30s, 40s and 50s, still sings her heart out. Tipica groups were made up of concertina, violin, piano and bass and the Club del Vino still features the eminent concertist Nestor Marconi, who performed in the first orchestra which accompanied the legendary singer Roberto Goyeneche.

Of the better known places in San Telmo, El Viejo Almacén has a show which features the concertist Julian Plaza who used to arrange the famous orchestra of Aníbal 'Pichuco' Troilo, while La Cumparsita shines on Fridays and Saturdays with the excellent singer Roberto Ayala.

If you are looking to dance tango, then another spot off the beaten track is the Club Almagro, Medrano 522, T4774-7454; every evening of the week the dancing starts with a one hour class for US$6; after this warm-up the place starts dancing.

Casablanca, Balcarce 668, T43314621, very touristy, large coach parties, US$40 including drinks. **Michelangelo**, Balcarce 433, T43344321, impressive setting, concert café in an old converted monastery, various types of music including tango and folklore, Tue-Sun, and **La Ventana**, Balcarce 425, dinner at 2000 daily, show at 2230, T43313648/3341314. Very touristy but very good show, US$60 for show, dinner and unlimited wine, US$40 for show and two drinks, book through an agency, 20% discount for ISIC and youth card holders, from Asatej office. **El Viejo Almacén**, Independencia y Balcarce, T43077388. Dinner 2000, show 2130, US$ for show and drinks, US$ dinner, show and drinks. **Querandi**, Peru 302, T43450331. Mon-Sat from 2030, show US$45, dinner and show US$60. Tango shows also at **La Cumparsita**, Chile 302, T43616880. Authentic, US$50 for 2 including wine, daily 2230-0430. **Club del Vino**, Cabrera 4737, T48330050. **Bar Sur**, Estados Unidos 299, San Telmo, T43626086. Daily 2100-0400, US$15 including pizza. **Antigua Tasca de Cuchilleros**, Carlos Calvo 319, San Telmo, T43623811/28. Pleasant surroundings, show US$20, show and dinner, US$32. The best affordable tango bars are in La Boca, but it is difficult to find authentic tango for locals, most are tourist-oriented. Good show also at **La Veda**, Florida 1, T43316442. Average meal with wine and other drinks US$40, Tue-Sat. **Viejo Buzón**, Corrientes y Rodríguez Peña, good tango, no dinner but plenty of dancing, locals and tourists **La Casa de Aníbal Troilo**, Carlos Calvo 2540, good singers and bands, for tourists. **Tango Danza**, J M Moreno 351, Fri, Sat, Sun, from 2200. **Salón La Argentina**, Rodríguez Peña 365, Thu-Sun, 2200, more modern-style tango with bandoneon (report that address changed). Also recommended are **Italia Unita**, Perón 2535. **Galería Tango Argentino**, Boedo 722 y Independencia, T4931829/7527. Wed-Sat, less touristy than others, dinner (usually), show and dancing, has dancers and tango lessons (Mon-Fri, 1800-2100), well-known bands. **Volver**, Corrientes 837, Mon-Fri, 1800-2100. **Caño 14**, Vicente López 2134, T48036170/3636. Mon-Sat dinner-show 2030; show: Mon-Thu 2200, Fri/Sat 2230,

Tango

US$40 show with two drinks. US$75 dinner, show and drinks. *Armenonville*, Alvear 1879, Recoleta, T48041033/4033. Mon-Sat dinner 2030, show 2230, show US$50, dinner and show US$90. *Casablanca*, Balcarce 668, T43314621/43435002. Tango and folklore show, Mon-Fri 2200, Sat 2030 and 2230, US$40 with drinks. *Club del Vino*, Cabrera 4737, T48330055.

Tango lessons *Confitería Ideal*, address above, T43260521. Hours and teachers vary, dinner show Saturday 2200, low price. Also at *Club Almagro*, Medrano 522, T47747454. Classes last 2hrs. *Café Tortoni*, address above, has tourist information on tango Mon-Fri 1400-1800. Some shows (tango or disco) are hugely overpriced and inauthentic; they usually have touts inviting tourists.

Theatre There are about 20 commercial theatres play all year round. Recommended is the *Teatro Liceo*. There are many amateur theatres. You are advised to book as early as possible for a seat at a concert, ballet, or opera. For ticket agencies, see cinemas, above.

Cultural centres

Argentine Association of English Culture, Suipacha 1333 (library for members only). **British Chamber of Commerce**, Corrientes 457. **British Council**, M T de Alvear 590, piso 4, T43119814, F3117747 (open 1000-1200, 1430-1630). **Goethe Institut**, Corrientes 311, German library (open 1300-1900 excluding Wed, and 1000-1400 1st Sat of month) and newspapers, free German films shown, cultural programmes, German language courses. In the same building, upstairs, is the German Club, Corrientes 327. **Alliance Française**, Córdoba 946. **USA Chamber of Commerce**, Diagonal Sáenz Peña 567. **Instituto Cultural Argentino-Norteamericano** (ICANA), Maipú 686, T43223855/4557. Large library, borrowing only for members; **St Andrew's Society**, Perú 352. **Southern Cross**, Riobamba 451, T43721041. Offices of Irish newspaper printed since 1876.

Clubs **American Club**, Viamonte 1133, facing Teatro Colón, temporary membership available; **American Women's Club**, Córdoba 632, piso 11; **English Club**, 25 de Mayo 586, T43119121. Open for lunch only, temporary membership available to British business visitors. The American and English Clubs have reciprocal arrangements with many clubs in USA and UK. **Swedish Club**, Tacuarí 147. **Organización Hebrea Argentina Macabi**, Tucumán 3135, T49620947. Social and sporting club for conservative Jews.

Cultural events *From mid-Dec to end-Feb many, but not all, theatres & concert halls are closed*

The *Luna Park* stadium holds pop/jazz concerts, ballet and musicals, at Bouchard 465, near Correo Central, T43115100. Free parking at Corrientes 161. *Teatro Municipal General San Martín*, Av Corrientes 1530, organizes many cultural activities of which quite a few are free of charge, including concerts Sat and Sun evenings, 50% ISIC and GO 25 discount; the theatre's Sala Leopoldo Lugones shows international classic films, Sat-Sun, US$3. *Teatro Alvear*, Corrientes 1659, T43749470, is a municipal theatre, shows are generally inferior in quality to those in the Teatro Municipal General San Martín. *Tango Week*, leading up to National Tango Day (11 December), has free events all over the city, details posted around the city and at tourist offices. Free concerts at ProMusica music shop, Florida 638. Schedule in window. *Centro Cultural General San Martín*, Sarmiento 1551, and the *Centro Cultural de Recoleta*, Junín 1930, next to the Recoleta cemetery have many free activities: for details see main newspapers and *La Maga*.

Shopping

The main, fashionable shopping streets are Florida and Santa Fe (especially between 1,000 and 2,000 blocks). Visit the branches of *H Stern* for fine jewellery at the *Sheraton* and *Plaza* hotels and at the international airport. *Kelly's*, Paraguay 431, has a very large selection of reasonably priced Argentine handicrafts in wool, leather, wood, etc. *Plata Nativa*, Galería del Sol, Florida 860, local 41, for Latin American folk handicrafts. *Campanera Dalla Fontana*, Reconquista 735, leather factory, fast, efficient and reasonably priced for made-to-measure clothes, ISIC and GO 25 discount. Good quality leather clothes factory at Boyacá 2030, T4582 6909 to arrange time with English speaking owner. *Aida*, Florida 670, can make a leather jacket to measure in 48hrs. *El Guasquero*, Av Santa Fe 3117, traditionally made leather goods. *Galería del Caminante*, Florida 844, has a variety of good shops with leather goods, arts and crafts, souvenirs, etc. *XL*, in Paseo Alcorta, Alto Palermo and Alto Avellaneda shopping malls, for leather goods, ISIC and GO 25% discounts. *Marcelo Loeb*, galería at Maipú 466, for antique postcards from all over the world, not cheap, same galería has several philatelic and numismatic shops. Calle Defensa in San Telmo is good for antique shops. *Pasaje de Defensa*, Defensa 791, is a beautifully restored colonial house containing small shops. *Casa Piscitelli*, San Martín 450, has a large selection of tapes and CDs. *Galerías Broadway*, Florida 575, for cheap electronic goods, CDs, tapes. For cheap fashion clothes try the area round El Once station. *Mega Sports*, Cabildo 1950, for sports clothing, ISIC and GO 25 discounts.

Most shops close lunchtime on Sat

Patio Bullrich, Libertador 750, entrance also on Posadas, has boutiques selling high quality leather goods but very expensive. **Alto Palermo**, Coronel Díaz y Santa Fe, very smart and expensive. **La Plaza Shopping Centre**, at Corrientes 1600, also has a few restaurants. **Paseo Alcorta**, Figueroa Alcorta y Salguero, 4 levels, cinemas, supermarket, stores, many cheap restaurants (take colectivo 130 from Correo Central). **Galerías Pacífico**, on Florida, between Córdoba and Viamonte, is a beautiful mall with fine murals and architecture, many exclusive shops and fast food restaurants in basement. Also good set-price restaurant on second floor and free lunchtime concerts on lower-ground floor (details in the press).

Shopping malls

Try *Yenny*, No 571, for new English classics (also 9 other branches) and *Distal*, No 913. also *Fausto*, No 1316 and 1243. *ABC*, Córdoba 685 and Rawson 2105 in Martínez suburb, good but expensive selection of English and German books, also sells *South American Handbook*. *Joyce Proust y Cía*, Tucumán 1545, piso 1, T403977, paperbacks in English, Portuguese, French, Italian. classics, language texts, etc, good prices. *Librería Rodríguez*, Sarmiento 835, good selection of English books and magazines upstairs, has another branch on Florida, 300 block. French bookshop at Rivadavia 743. *Librería Goethe*, Lavalle 528, good selection of English and German books. Italian books at *Librería Leonardo*, Córdoba 335, also newspapers and magazines. *Liber Arte*, Corrientes 1555, also café, alternative press, good video selection, no English books, 10% ISIC discount. *Promoteo*, Corrientes 1916, rare books, ISIC discount. *La Viscontea*, Libertad 1067. *Asatej Bookshop*, Florida 835, piso 3, Oficina 320, T43151457, and Santa Fe 2450, Loc 93, sells this *Handbook* 'at the best price' with ISIC discount; *El Ateneo*, Florida 340, basement has good selection of English books, other branches including Callao 1380. *Kel Ediciones*, MTde Alvear 1369 and Conde 1990 (Belgrano), good stock of English books and sells *South American Handbook*. *Acme Agency*, Suipacha 245, first floor, for imported English books, also Arenales 885. Prices at *Harrods* on Florida are lower than most. *LOLA*, Viamonte 976, piso 2, T43223920, Mon-Fri 1200-1900, the only specialist in Latin American Natural History, birdwatching, most books in English. *Librería del Turista*, Florida 937, wide range of travel books including *South American Handbook*, ISIC and GO 25% discounts. *Librería de Avila*, Alsina 500, T43433374, new, used and antique books, good selection. For used and rare books *The Antique Bookshop*,

Bookshops

There are many along Av Corrientes, W of Av 9 de Julio, though most have no foreign language sections. Prices are very high for foreign books

Buenos Aires and the Río de la Plata

Libertad 1236, is recommended. *Fernández Blanco*, Tucumán 712. *Casa Figueroa*, Esmeralda 970. and *L'Amateur*, Esmeralda 882. Second-hand English language books from *British and American Benevolent Society*, Catamarca 45 (take train to Acassuso). *Aquilanti*, Rincón 79, esp good on Patagonia; *Juan Carlos Pubill*, Talcahuano 353 (ring bell), and from *Entrelibros*, Cabildo 2280 and Santa Fe 2450, local 7, expensive. Several used book shops in basement at Florida 833.

For **foreign newspapers** try the news stands on Florida, and kiosk at Corrientes y Maipú.

Every April the **Feria del Libro** is held at the Centro De Exposiciones, Figueroa Alcorta y Pueyrredón, Recoleta; exhibitions, shows and books for sale in all languages.

Camping equipment Good camping equipment and fuel from *Fugate* (no sign), Gascón 238 (off Rivadavia 4100 block), T49820203, also repairs equipment. *Outside Mountain Equipment*, Donado 4660, T45412084. *Panamericana y Paraná*, Martínez (Shopping Unicenter, 3rd level). *Imperio Deportes*, Ecuador 696, T/F49619024. Also repairs, very helpful. Good camping stores also at Guatemala 5908 and 5451. Camping gas available at Mitre 1111, *Todo Gas*, Paraná 550, and El Pescador, Paraguay y Libertad. Every kind of battery (including for Petzl climbing lamps) at Callao 373. *Cacique Camping* manufacture camping equipment and clothing, their 2 shops: Juan Justo 3326, and San Lorenzo 4220, Munro, Provincia Buenos Aires, T4762 0261, F756 1392. Also sell the *South American Handbook*.

Markets For souvenirs and antiques, etc, **Plaza Dorrego**, San Telmo, with food, dancers, buskers, Sat and Sun 0900-1700, entertaining, not cheap, an interesting array of 'antiques'. **Feria Hippie**, in Recoleta, near cemetery, big craft and jewellery market, Saturday and Sunday, good street atmosphere, expensive. **Feria Mataderos**, Lisandro de la Torre y Av de los Corrodes, T46875602/43619174. Sun and public holidays 1100. This is a fair of 'Argentine popular handicrafts and traditions': participate in climbing the greasy pole, tug of war and sack races or watch *gauchos* perform their skills with horses. Also many traditional, idigenous and criollo handicrafts, music and dancing and regional meals. Bus 36, 92, 126, 141. **Feria de Las Artes** (Friday, 1000-1700) on Defensa y Alsina. Saturday craft, jewellery, etc market, at **Plaza Belgrano**, near Belgrano Barrancas station on Juramento, between Cuba y Obligado, 1000-2000. Handicraft markets at weekends at Parque Lezama, San Telmo. A secondhand book market is at **Plaza Lavalle** in front of Tribunales, a few English titles (ask around), weekdays only. **Plazoleta Santa Fe**, Santa Fe y Uriarte (Palermo) old books and magazines, Saturday 1200-2000, Sunday 1000-2000; plastic arts in the **Caminito**, Vuelta de Rocha (Boca), 1000-2000 summer, 0900-1900 winter. At **Parque Rivadavia**, Rivadavia 4900, around the *ombú* tree, records, books, magazines, stamps and coins, Sunday 0900-1300, **Plazoleta Primera Junta**, Rivadavia y Centenera, books and magazines, Saturday 1200-2000, Sunday 1000-2000. **Parque Patricios**, Caseros entre Monteagudo y Pepiri, 1000-2000, antiques, books, art and stamps. Saturday market in **Plaza Centenario**, Díaz Vélez y L Marechal, 1000-2100 local crafts, good, cheap hand-made clothes.

Photography

Film developing to international standards. There are many Kodak labs around Talcahuano

Fotospeed, Santa Fe 4838 (20% discount to SAHB owners!) for quality 2-hr service. *Foto Gráfica*, Perón 1253, for black and white developing. *Photo Station*, Díaz Vélez 5504, T49811447, 25% ISIC and GO 25 discount. For developing slides Esmeralda 444, fast service, and *Kinefot*, Talcahuano 244. **Camera repairs** several good shops on Talcahuano 100-400 blocks. Try also *Casa Schwarz*, Perú 989, international brands. *Golden Lab*, Lavalle 630, good prices for film. *Horacio Calvo*, Riobamba 183, all brands and variety of rare accessories. Recommended. Fast service at Tacuarí 75; for Olympus cameras, *Rodolfo Jablanca*, Corrientes 2589. German spoken at *Gerardo Föhse*, Florida 890, fast, friendly. Note that some types of camera batteries are unavailable, includes Panasonic CR-32.

Horseracing... a great evening out

Though the Jockey Club in Buenos Aires was targetted by Peronist revolutionaires as one of the bastions of the elite, horseracing is one of the cheapest forms of entertainment in Buenos Aires. There are three main racecourses (Hipódromos), two in the city itself and one at La Plata. There is always a race taking place at one or other of these continuing with a race every half-hour until 2300.

All racing takes place on the flat with no jumping and the racetracks are typical North American style ovals. Hipódromo Argentino is the smartest, with grass as opposed to a dirt track, and has the best quality racing. All three tracks are, however, comparable with the best European courses, much of the racing being held under excellent floodlighting. The quality of horses and riding is also well up to international standard and the stands are large enough to cope easily with the largest crowds. Entry to the course ranges from US$1 at San Isidro to US$5 at Argentino; for a few dollars more you can enter the best stands. Refreshments are also quite cheap.

There are no on-course bookmakers, betting being by Totalisor only; the large computerised display boards are easy to understand constantly showing the runners and the odds. The crowds are enthusiastic knowing their hosses from the mules. It is a great night out, friendly people and plenty of atmosphere.

Sports

Aerobics try the *Le Parc*, San Martín 645, T43119191, expensive, though has cheaper branch at Rivadavia 4615, monthly membership required *Gimnasio Olímpico Cancillería*, Esmeralda 1042, membership required. **Association and rugby football** are both played to a very high standard. Soccer fans should see Boca Juniors, matches Sun 1500-1800 (depending on time of year), Wed evenings, entry US$10 (La Bonbonera stadium, Brandsen 700, open weekdays for visits; bus 27), or their arch-rivals, River Plate. Soccer season September-May/June, with a break at Christmas. Rugby season April-October/November. **Chess** *Club Argentino de Ajedrez*, Paraguay 1858, open daily, arrive after 2000, special tournament every Sat, 1800, high standards. Repairs for pocket chess computers, T49524913. **Cricket** is played at 4 clubs in Greater Buenos Aires between November and March. **Gambling** weekly lotteries. Football pools, known as *Prode*. *Bingo Lavalle*, Lavalle 842, open to 0300. **Golf** the leading golf clubs are the *Hurlingham*, *Ranelagh*, *Ituzaingó*, *Lomas*, *San Andrés*, *San Isidro*, *Sáenz Peña*, *Olivos*, *Jockey*, *Campos Argentinos* and *Hindú Country Club*. Visitors wishing to play should bring handicap certificate and make telephone booking. Weekend play possible only with a member. Good hotels may be able to make special arrangements. Municipal golf course in Palermo, open to anyone at any time. **Horse racing** at **Hipodromo Argentino** at Palermo and **Hipodoromo San Isidro** in San Isidro. Riding schools at both racecourses. Horseracing is a cheap evening out. **Ice-hockey** is becoming popular. **Motor racing** Formula 1 championship racing has been restored: the Gran Premier de la República Argentina is held at the Oscar Alfredo Gálvez autodrome on the outskirts of the city in Mar/Apr. There are lots of rallies, stock racing and Formula 3 competitions, mostly from Mar to mid-Dec. **Polo**, the high handicap season is October to December, but it is played all year round (low season Apr-June). Argentina has the top polo teams. A visit to the national finals at Palermo in November or December is recommended. **Tennis, squash and paddle tennis** are popular – there are 5 squash clubs. The Argentine Tennis Open is in November, ATP tour. There are many private clubs.

Football in Buenos Aires

Football being the leading sport in Argentina, it is hardly surprising that Buenos Aires has one of the largest numbers of stadia of any city in the world. Although some are old and poorly maintained, those of the bigger clubs, holding 45,000-75,000 spectators, are fine 'theatres' for some of the finest soccer in the world.

Over half the first division clubs are based in Buenos Aires. The rivalry between two, Boca Juniors and River Plate, is particularly fierce. Other big clubs include San Lorenzo, Huracán and Vélez Sarsfield, Independiente and Racing Club.

Tour operators

Tours A good way of seeing Buenos Aires and its surroundings is by 3 hr tour. Longer tours including dinner and a tango show, or a gaucho *fiesta* at a ranch (excellent food and dancing, although the gaucho part can be somewhat showy). Bookable through most travel agents, US$50-65. *BAT, Buenos Aires Tur*, Lavalle 1444, T43712304, almost hourly departures. *Buenos Aires Vision*, Esmeralda 356, T43944682. *Eurotur* (T43126170), in English, or *Autobuses Sudamericanos* (TISA), information and booking office at Bernardo de Irigoyen 1370, piso 1, Offices 25 and 26, T43071956, F3078899. Prices range from US$12 to US$60 (20 night time and *estancia* options), also excursions to Bariloche, Iguazú and Mar del Plata. For reservations in advance for sightseeing tours, with a 20% court esy discount to *South American Handbook* readers, write to Casilla de Correo No 40, Sucursal 1 (B), 1401 Buenos Aires. In USA T (New York) 212-524-0763, First Class Travel Service Ltd. TISA has other branches in Buenos Aires and publishes *Guía Latinoamericana de Omnibus*, organizes Amerbuspass (T43117373 for tickets, or USA 602-795-6556, F7958180) for bus travel throughout Latin America. At same address *Transporte Aereo Costa Atlántica* (TACA), passenger charter services to Pinamar, Villa Gesell, Bariloche, T4267933. Also *Indiana Cars*, T43071956/3005591, for remise, car hire and taxi service with women drivers.

For river tours of Buenos Aires, Charles Cesaire, Dársena Norte, T45534380, Sat, Sun, holidays 1500, 1700, 1900, with bar, US$10. Guided tours of the city by cycle are offered by *Bici-Tour*, T48621327, andresmazzini@hotmail.com 3 hrs, US$20.

Travel agents Among those recommended are *Les Amis*, Santa Fe 810, helpful, efficient. *Exprinter*, Suipacha 1107, T43122519, and San Martín 170, T43313050, Galería Güemes (especially their 5-day, 3-night tour to Iguazú and San Ignacio Miní). *Furlong*, Esmeralda y M T de Alvear, T43183200, T43123043. *ATI*, Esmeralda 561, mainly group travel, very efficient, many branches. *Turismo Feeling*, Alem 762, T43119422, excellent and reliable horseback trips and adventure tourism. *Giorgio*, Florida y Tucumán, T43274200, F3254210. Also at Santa Fe 1653. *Inti Viajes*, Tucumán 836, T/F43228845. Cheap flights, very helpful. *Flyer Viajes y Turismo*, Reconquista 617, piso 8, T43138224, F3121330. Also at Av Fondo de la legua 425, San Isidro, T/F45123101. Specialists on *estancias*, fishing, polo, motorhome rental, English, Dutch, German spoken, repeatedly recommended. *Eves Turismo*, Tucumán 702, T43936151, helpful and efficient, recommended for flights. *City Service*, Florida 890 y Paraguay, piso 4, T43128416/9. *Travel Up*, Maipú 474, piso 4, T43264648. *Proterra Turismo*, Lavalle 750, piso 20 D, T/F43262639. *Folgar*, Esmeralda 961, piso 3 E, T43116937. English is widely spoken.

Transport

Car hire is expensive and has an additional 20% tax. It is difficult to hire cars during holiday periods and best to book from abroad. Use of Avis Car Credit card with central billing in your home country is possible. Driving in Buenos Aires is no problem if you have eyes in the back of your head and nerves of steel. Note that traffic fines are high and police increasingly on the lookout for drivers without the correct papers. **Avis**, Cerrito 1527, T43265542, F3266992. **AL International**, San Luis 3138, T43129475. **Budget**, Santa Fe 869, T43119870, ISIC and GO 25 discount. **Hertz**, Ricardo Rojas 451, T43121317. There are several national rental agencies, eg **AVL**, Alvear 1883, T48054403. **Ricciard Libertador**, Av del Libertador 2337/45, T47998514. **Localiza**, Paraguay 1122, T43143999. **Unidas**, Paraguay 864, T43150777, 20% ISIC and GO 25 discount. **Motoring Associations**: see page 44 for details of service.

Local
For city transport by bus, metro & taxi see page 75

Air Domestic flights operate from Aeroparque (Jorge Newbery Airport). See page 75 for details. *Aerolíneas Argentinas*, *Austral* and *Lapa* offer daily flights to the main cities, for details see text under intended destination, see also page 43 for the Visit Argentina fare. If travelling in the south, book ahead if possible with LADE, whose flights are cheaper than buses in most cases.

Long distance

Road Bus All long-distance buses leave from Retiro terminal at Ramos Mejía y Antártida Argentina (Subte C), for information T3142323. Some bus companies charge extra for luggage (illegally). Fares may vary according to time of year and advance booking is advisable December-March. Some companies may give discounts, such as 20% to YHA or student-card holders and foreign, as well as Argentine teachers and university lecturers. Travellers have reported getting discounts without showing evidence of status, so it's always worth asking. For further details of bus services and fares, look under proposed destinations.

Hitchhiking For Pinamar, Mar del Plata and nearby resorts, take bus for La Plata to Alpargatas *rotonda* roundabout. For points further south, take bus 96 to Route 3 – the Patagonia Rd. Best to hitch from a service station where trucks stop. The police control point at Km 43 (south) is reported to be friendly and will help to find a lift for you. For Mendoza try truck drivers at the wine warehouses near Palermo Subte station (leaving station walk northwest, cross the railway line and turn left into Av Juan B Justo for the warehouses).

Sea The *Buenos Aires Herald* (English-language daily) notes all shipping movements. Flota Fluvial del Estado (Corrientes 489, T43110728) organizes cruises from Buenos Aires, Dársena Sur (dock T43614161/0346) up the Paraná River. South Coast, down to Punta Arenas and intermediate Patagonian ports, served by the Imp & Exp de la Patagonia. Very irregular sailings. For connections with Uruguay, see below.

Train There are 4 main terminals:
  Retiro really 3 separate stations (Belgrano T43115287, Mitre T43126596, San Martín T43118704). Services to **Tucumán** (run by Tucumán provincial government) Mon and Fri, 1600, returning Thu and Sun, 23 hrs, US$50 pullman, US$36 1st class, US$31 tourist); to **Rosario**, 4 a day, US$11 single, US$20 return. Suburban services: to Tigre (US$0.85) via Belgrano, Olivos and San Isidro, every 8 minutes; to Capilla del Señor, US$2.65; to Zárate, US$2.65, every hr and Junin (tickets checked on train and collected at the end of the journey). Information: Trenes de Buenos Aires (TBA), T43174445/4407, office open 0800-1800.
  Constitución T43040024/26, 0900-1800. Frequent services to La Plata, 1 hr, US$1.50. Also services to Ezeiza (US$0.80), Ranelagh (US$0.50) and Quilmes

● ●

☞ *Jorge Newbery*

In the years before 1914, before the advent of cinema and sports stars, Jorge Newbery, the son of an American father and an Argentine mother, was one of the first great popular idols of Buenos Aires.

In 1900, after studying electrical engineering in the United States, Newbery became Director of Lighting for the city. Dashing, handsome and athletic, it was, however, as a sportsman that he was best known, excelling at rowing, boxing, fencing and wrestling. Owner of one of the city's early motor cars, he was a pioneer of motor racing.

His lasting fame, though, was gained as a balloonist and aviator; he was a founding member and the first president of the

Argentine Aero Club. In 1909 his balloon, El Huracán, broke the South American distance record for ballooning; such was the enthusiasm aroused that the name was adopted by a football club founded shortly afterwards. After achieving the South American altitude record for ballooning, he switched to flying the early monoplanes; in 1914 he set a new world altitude record in a monoplane. He was killed shortly afterwards when his plane crashed following take off from Mendoza in an attempt to cross the Andes. His funeral attracted vast crowds and for years afterwards the date of his death, 1 March, drew mourners to his grave in La Chacarita.

● ●

(US$0.90). Daily service to **Rosario**, run by Trenes de Buenos Aires, T43173407/4445. US$11 tourist, US$13 pullman. Services to the following destinations are run by Ferrobaires, an agency of the Buenos Aires provincial government (Reservations T43067919/43040028/43040031): **Mar del Plata**, 8 daily, US$17, 5 hrs; to **Pinamar**, 1 to 3 daily depending on season, US$20; to **Tandil**, one a day, 7 hrs, US$13; to **Bahía Blanca** via General Lamadrid, daily 2130, 12 hrs, Sleeper US$40, Pullman US$25, First US$20, Tourist US$17. Additional service via Azul, Sierra de la Ventana, Mon, Wed, Sat, 2110. The Automóvil Club Argentino provides car transporters for its members.

Once T3312702. Suburban services and services in Buenos Aires province, including trains to Lujan (US$2) and Mercedes (US$3), run by Trenes de Buenos Aires. Also service to **Santa Rosa**, run by Ferrobaires, Mon, Wed, Fri 2000, 11hrs, Pullman U$$21, First US$16, Tourist US$14.

Federico Lacroze This is the Urquiza line station for suburban services to Gral Lemos.T45530044. It is also the head office of *Metrovías* who run the Buenos Aires metro system; metro information available.

International transport

Air **To Brazil** daily services to São Paulo, Rio de Janeiro and other Brazilian cities. **To Chile** foreign and national lines fly daily between Buenos Aires and Santiago, 1½-2hrs. **To Bolivia** services to La Paz and Santa Cruz de la Sierra by *Aerolíneas Argentinas* and *LAB*. **To Paraguay** there are daily air services to Asunción by *Aerolíneas Argentinas* and *Lapsa*. **To Uruguay** to Colonia del Sacramento: from Aeroparque (Jorge Newbery Airport) to Colonia 12 minutes, several airlines, US$30. Buy tickets in advance at weekends when flights are fully booked. Continue by bus to Montevideo. To Montevideo: from Aeroparque, shuttle service known as *Puente Aéreo* run by *Aerolíneas Argentinas* and *Pluna*, daily 0730 and 0910, 40 mins. Book at Aeroparque or T43935122/7730440. To Punta del Este, several flights daily 15 Dec-1 Mar with *Aerolíneas Argentinas, Pluna* and *Lapa* (Thu-Sun), 40 mins, US$90. Out of season, Pluna, Fri only.

Road Four branches of the **Pan-American Highway** run from Buenos Aires to the borders of Chile, Bolivia, Paraguay and Brazil. The roads are paved except when otherwise stated.

To Chile via Villa Mercedes, San Luis, and Mendoza (total: 1,310 km). There are also road connections between Catamarca and Copiapó, Bariloche and Osorno and Puerto Montt, and between Salta and Antofagasta. **Buses** Direct services to Santiago, 23 hrs, US$70-75, eg Ahumada, El Rápido Internacional and others, 1,459 km. US$70-75 to Valparaíso or Viña del Mar, TAC, Fénix Pullman Norte, cheaper to book to Mendoza and then rebook.

To Bolivia via Rosario, Villa María, Córdoba, Santiago del Estero, Tucumán, and Jujuy (total: 1,994 km). The main crossing point is at La Quiaca, but there are also crossings at Aguas Blancas and Pocitos. **Buses** There is no direct bus service from Buenos Aires to La Paz but through connections can be booked. Autobuses Sudamericanos, Bernardo de Irigoyen 1370, piso 1, T43071956 and from Retiro terminal, T43150204, via La Quiaca, US$135, 52 hrs. Atahualpa, T43150601, via La Quiaca, US$95, or Pocitos, US$91, daily, but in all cases a new ticket to La Paz or Santa Cruz must be bought once over the frontier. Cheapest route to Pocitos is by bus to Tucumán, US$40 and then re-book for Pocitos, US$25.

To Paraguay 3 main routes: **1** via Rosario, Santa Fe, Resistencia, Clorinda to Asunción (via toll bridge) (total: 1,370 km). **2** cross the Zárate-Brazo Largo bridges to Route 12, then head west across Entre Ríos to Paraná and take the tunnel to Santa Fe, or head west across Corrientes province to the bridge between Corrientes and Resistencia and then north via Clorinda as above. **3** follow Routes 12 and 14 up the Río Uruguay via Colón and Concordia to Misiones province for Posadas and then take Route 12 to Ciudad del Este via San Ignacio Mini and Puerto Iguazú. **Buses** Take 20-22 hrs, with 11 companies (all close to each other at the Retiro bus terminal). You have choice between executive (luxury service, 15hrs, US$80), *diferencial* (with food, drinks, 18 hrs, US$64) and *común* (without food, but with a/c, toilet, 21 hrs, US$48). Also 5 companies to Ciudad del Este, US$45. Caaguazú goes to Villarrica, and Expreso Río Paraná and La Encarnaceña go to Encarnación, US$46. Tickets can be bought up to 30 days in advance.

To Brazil 3 routes: **1** via Puerto Iguazú (as above under **To Paraguay**). **2** via Paso de los Libres, reached by following the Puerto Iguazú route and crossing the bridge between Paso de los Libres and Uruguaiana. **3** across the Río de la Plata and through Uruguay. This route is a bit cheaper, not as long and offers a variety of transport and journey breaks. **Buses** Direct services to Brazil via Paso de los Libres by Pluma to: São Paulo, 40 hrs, US$145. Rio de Janeiro, 45 hrs, US$163. Porto Alegre, US$71. Curitiba, 38 hrs, US$128. Florianópolis, 32 hrs, US$115. To Rio, changing buses at Posadas and Foz do Iguaçu is almost half price, 50 hrs. Tickets from Buen Viaje, Córdoba 415, 31-2953, or Pluma, Córdoba 461, T43114871 or 3115986.

To Uruguay direct road connections by means of 2 bridges over the Río Uruguay between Puerto Unzué and Fray Bentos and further north between Colón and Paysandú. **Buses** (much slower than the air or sea routes given below). Services to Montevideo, via Zárate-Gualeguaychú-Puerto Unzué-Fray Bentos-Mercedes, Flechabus and Taja, 8½ hrs, US$20.

To Peru via Mendoza, crossing to Chile through the Redentor tunnel and then north through Chile via Coquimbo, Arica, Tacna, Nasca, Ica, Lima. **Buses** Ormeño, T43132259 and El Rápido Internacional, T43935057 have a direct service to Lima, from Retiro bus station, 3½ days, US$160 including all meals, 1 night spent in Coquimbo, Chile (if you need a visa for Chile, get one before travelling).

Buenos Aires and the Río de la Plata

Sea **To Paraguay** occasional river boats to Asunción from May to October, 11 days, bed and private bath, food and nightly entertainment, US$400, reported good. Details from Tamul, Lavalle 388, T43932306/1533.

To Uruguay boats and buses heavily booked December-March, especially at weekends. There are no money changing facilities in Tigre and they are poor elsewhere. Beware of overcharging by taxis from the harbour to the centre of Buenos Aires. **Tax** US$18 port tax is charged on all services to Uruguay; check whether this is included in price quoted. Do not buy Uruguayan bus tickets until you get to Colonia.

Ferry companies *Buquebus*, Córdoba y Madero, T43166500, F43137636, also in Patio Bullrich Shopping Centre, piso 1. Port: Dársena Sur, Ribera Este, T43614161. *Ferrytur*, Maipú 866, T43142051. *Fast Ferry*, Florida 537, Galeria Jardín, piso 1, T43931540, F43009334. Port: Pedro de Mendoza 330, T43620110/7400. *Cacciola* Lavalle y Florida 520,oficina 113, T43936100/43945520. In Tigre: International Terminal, Lavalle 520, T47490329.

To Montevideo (direct) Buquebus daily 0800, 1115, 1600, 1900, 2½ hrs, US$53, vehicles US$93.50-103.50, bus connection to Punta del Este, US$10.

To Colonia del Sacramento Buquebus hydrofoil (*aliscafo*) service 5 times a day, 35mins, US$33, also ferry service, twice a day, 3hrs, US$20. Bus connection to Montevideo US$5 extra. Ferrytur Sea Cat, daily except Fri 0815, 1130, 1915, Fri 0815, 1600, 1900, US$31, 1 hr. Free bus 1 hr before departure from Florida y Córdoba. Connecting bus service from Colonia to Montevideo, US$16, total journey 4 hrs. Fast Ferry, Mon-Thu 0945, 1850, Sat 0800, Sun 0800, 2330, 3 hrs, US$20.

From Tigre to Carmelo boats are operated by Cacciola at 0830 and 1630, 3 hrs, US$13 plus US$8 embarkation tax, to Carmelo. It is advisable to book in advance. Connecting bus from offices to port and from Carmelo to Montevideo.

From Tigre to Nueva Palmira *Delta Argentina* (T47490537, information 47311236) services from Tigre daily 0730, also Sat/Sun US$14, 3 hrs.

Directory

Airline offices Aerolíneas Argentinas, Perú y Rivadavia, T43407800, 0810-22286527, with 4 branches, plus airport offices, reservations T43407777, Mon-Fri 0945-1745; **Austral**, Alem 1134, T43173600. Líneas Aéreas del Estado (LADE), Perú 714, T43617071, erratic schedules, uniformed office. Líneas Aéreas Privadas Argentinas (Lapa), Pellegrini 1075, T41145272 (reservations), or Aeroparque Puente Aéreo section, T47729920, cheapest fares to main tourist centres, good service. **Dinar**, Sáenz Peña 933, T43266374, 7780100. **LAER**, Lavalle 347, piso B, T43115237. **LAB**, Pellegrini141, T43231900, 0800-9093001. **AeroPerú**, Santa Fe 840, T43114115. **Varig**, Carabelas 344, T43299200. **VASP**, Santa Fe 784, T43112699. **Lan Chile**, Paraguay 609 piso 1, T43162200, 3128161 for reconfirmations. **Ecuatoriana**, T43122180. **United**, M T Alvear 590, T43160777. **Lufthansa**, M T Alvear 636, reservations T43190600. **Air France**, Santa Fe 963, T43174700. **British Airways**, Viamonte 590, piso 1, T43206600. **American**, Pueyrredón 1997, T43181111. **KLM**, Reconquista 559, piso 5, T4809473.

Banks Many shops and restaurants accept US dollar bills. Most banks charge very high commission especially on TCs (as much as US$10). Banks open Mon-Fri 1000-1500, be prepared for long delays. US dollar bills are often scanned electronically for forgeries, while TCs are sometimes very difficult to change and you may be asked for proof of purchase. American Express TCs are less of a problem than Thomas Cook. Practices are constantly changing. *Lloyds Bank* (BLSA) Ltd, Reconquista y Mitre, Visa cash advances provided in both US dollars and pesos. It has 10 other branches in the city, and others in Greater Buenos Aires. *Royal Bank of Canada*, Florida y Perón, branch at Callao 291. *Citibank*, B Mitre 502, changes only Citicorps TCs, no commission, also Mastercard; branch at Florida 192. *First National Bank of Boston*, Florida 99. *Bank of America*, JD Perón y San Martín changes Bank of America TCs morning only, US$ at very high commission. *Banco Tornquist*, B Mitre 531, Crédit Lyonnais agents, advance cash on visa card. *Banco Holandés*, Florida 361; *Deutsche Bank*, B Mitre 401 (and other branches), changes Thomas Cook TCs, also Mastercard, both give cash advances.

HSBC, 25 de Mayo 258, changes Thomas Cook TCs without commission. Thomas Cook rep, *Fullers*, Esmeralda 1000 y M T Alvear. *American Express* offices are at Arenales 707 y Maipú, by Plaza San Martín, T43120900, where you can apply for a card, get financial services and change Amex TCs into US$ cash or pesos (1000-1500 only, no commission). *Client Mail* in same building, Mon-Fri 0900-1800, Sat 0900-1300. Mastercard ATMs (look for Link-Mastercard/Cirrus) at several locations, mostly *Banco Nacional del Lavoro* including Florida 40 and Santa Fe y Esmeralda.

There are many *casas de cambio*, some of which deal in TCs. Most are concentrated around San Martín and Corrientes: *Cambio Topaz*, San Martín 13941400, 5% commission. *Casa Piano*, San Martín 345347, changes TCs into pesos or US$ cash for 2-3% commission, *Cambios Trade Travel*, San Martín 967, 3% commission on TCs; *Exprinter*, Suipacha 1107, open from Mon-Fri 1000-1600, Sat closed. *Casa América*, Av de Mayo 959, accepts Thomas Cook TCs. Many *cambios* will exchange US$, TCs for US$ cash at commissions varying from 1.25 to 3%. If all *cambios* closed, try Mercadería de Remate de Aduana, Florida 8, or *Eves*, Tucumán 702, open until 1800. On Sat, Sun and holidays, cash may be exchanged in the *cambio* in some of the large supermarkets (eg Carrefour, Paseo Alcorta Shopping Center, open daily 1000-2200). There is no service charge on notes, only on cheques. Major credit cards usually accepted but check for surcharges. General *Mastercard* office at H Yrigoyen 878, open 0930-1800, T43311022. Another branch at Peru 161 (open 1000-1730). *Visa*, Corrientes 1437, piso 2, T43793300, for stolen cards, helpful. Other South American currencies can only be exchanged in *casas de cambio*.

General Post Office Correo Central – now privatized, Correos Argentinos, Sarmiento y Alem, Mon-Fri, 0800-2000. *Poste Restante* on first floor (US$2.25 per letter), very limited service on Sat (closes 1300). Fax service US$5 per min. Centro Postal Internacional, for all parcels over 1 kg for mailing abroad, at Antártida Argentina, near Retiro station, open 1100 to 1700. Check both Correo Central and Centro Postal Internacional for *poste restante*.

Communications

Internet Prices range from US$2 to US$10 per hr, shop around. Many *locutorios* offer internet access, US$6 per hr. Cybercafes in the centre of Buenos Aires include: *CiberCity*Lavalle 491, T43933360. Mon-Sat 0800-2300, US$3.50 per hr. *Cybercafé*, Maure 1886, Belgrano (bus 29), T47759440, info@cyber.com.ar *Dos H's Bar*, Viamonte 636, T43260878, 0800-2100, closed Sat afternoon, US$3 per hr. *Agua de Fuego*, Rivadavia 1475, T43834930, 0800-2300, US$10 per hr. *Web Café*, alto Palermo Shopping, p3, Santa Fe 3253, T48278000, 1000-2300, US$6 per hr. *www.siemens café*, in Instituto Goethe, Av Corrientes 319, Thur-Tues 1300-1900, T43118964. Many on Florida: *Cyber Express*, No 835. *M@gic-net*, No 578, US$6 per hr. *Net Café*, No 537, p 1, Galería Jardín shop 421, T43938273. Mon-Sat 0800-2100, US$3 per hr. In same Galería, shop 432, *Eagugel*, same hrs, same price, T43220844

Telecommunications The city is split into 2 telephone zones, owned by Telecom and Telefónica Argentina. Local and international calls can be made from *locutorios* which are found throughout the city centre. Local calls can also be made from public telephone boxes, most of which accept *fichas* or *cospeles* (tokens), though some accept coins. *Fichas* cost US$0.50, US$1 for 3, are sold at small tables outside many *locutorios* as well as newspaper stalls, cigarette *kioskos* and Telecom or Telefónica Argentina offices. Many phones now use phone cards costing 5 and 10 pesos: these are inserted into the phone; calls are usually cheaper if made with these cards. The cards are sold with in a protective plastic wrapper and you should not accept unsealed cards. The cards of the 2 companies are interchangeable. International telephone calls from hotels may incur a 40%-50% commission in addition to government tax of about the same amount.

Embassies & consulates
All open Mon-Fri unless stated otherwise

Bolivian Consulate, Belgrano 1670, piso 2, T43810559 Open 0900-1400, visa while you wait, tourist bureau which gives misleading information. **Brazilian Consulate**, Carlos Pellegrini 1363, piso 5, open Mon-Fri, 0930-1400, visa takes 48 hrs, US$24 to US passport holders, T43945255. **Paraguayan Consulate**, Viamonte 1851, 0900-1400, T48120075. **Peruvian Consulate**, San Martín 691, piso 6, T43117582, 0900-1400, visa US$5, takes 1 day. **Uruguayan Consulate**, Las Heras 1907, open 1000-1800, T48073040. Visa takes up to 1 week. **Chilean Consulate**, San Martín 439, piso 9, T43946582. Mon-Thu 0930-1330, 1530-1830, Fri 0915-1430. **Ecuadorean Embassy**, Quintana 585, piso 9 y 19, T48046408. Unless otherwise stated consulates are located in the respective embassy. **United States**, Colombia 4300, T47774533/7007. 0900-1730, visas 0800-1100, calls between 1500 and 1700; **Australia**, Villanueva 1400, T47776580. Mon-Thu

Buenos Aires and the Río de la Plata

English language teaching

If English is your native tongue or you are comfortable using it as a second language, teaching English can be a relatively simple way of making a living in Buenos Aires. You need little start-up capital, demand for teachers always outstrips supply and pay is competitive.

The best place to begin is the Sunday edition of the Herald, where there is usually a good handful of adverts seeking *profesores*. Though a *curriculum vitae is* not necessary, some employers may ask to see an informal summary of your background, even if it is unrelated to English language teaching, and there is always an advert or two which require no teaching background at all. Others may request a CUIT (pronounced "kweet"), a sort of social security number but most employers do not require this and you may be able to pursuade those who do to pay you a slightly lower wage in lieu of it.

Most adverts are placed by *institutos* which run classes on their own premises or send teachers to companies to teach individuals or small groups. Other adverts are placed by *coordinadores who do the* same work but from their homes. Under both systems the teacher receives about 70% of what the companies pay. In time a teacher often makes his/her own contacts through word of mouth and may eventually branch off into private classes. This is more profitable, but it can be risky, since you have no guarantee of a constant supply of students. At holiday-times, when many students leave classes for weeks, only an *instituto* or a *coordinador can fill your* timetable and guarantee you an income. Depending on your persistence and bargaining skills, pay varies from 13 to 20 pesos an hour. Even if you are too shy to bargain you should have no problem finding 15 pesos an hour, while private classes can pay as much as 25 pesos. You are likely to be busiest at the beginning, middle and end of the students' working day, around 0830, 1300 and 1800.

0830-1230, 1330-1730, Fri 0830-1315; **Canada**, Tagle 2828, T48053032. **South Africa**, M T de Alvear 590, piso 7, T43118991/7, Mon-Thu 0900-1300, 1400-1630, Fri 0900-1330. **Israel**, Av de Mayo 701, piso 10, T43421465. **Japan**, Paseo Colón 275, piso 9 y 11, T43432561, 0900-1300, 1430-1800. **Austria**, French 3671, T48022400, 0900-1200. **Belgium**, Defensa 113-8, T43310066/69, 0800-1300. **United Kingdom**, Luis Agote 2412/52 (near corner Pueyrredón y Guido), T48037070, open 0915-1215, 1415-1615. **Denmark**, Alem 1074, piso 9, T43126901/6935, 0900-1200, 1400-1600. **Finland**, Santa Fe 846, piso 5, T43120600/70, Mon-Thu 0830-1700, Fri 0830-1200. **France**, Santa Fe 846, piso 3, T43122409, 0900-1200. **Germany**, Villanueva 1055, Belgrano, T47782500, 0900-1200. **Greece**, Sáenz Peña 547, piso 4, T43424958, 1000-1300. **Ireland**, Suipacha 1380, piso 2, T43258588, 1000-1230. **Italy**, Billinghurst 2577 (consulate M T de Alvear 1149, T48166132, 0900-1300. **Netherlands**, Edificio Buenos Aires, Av de Mayo 701, piso 19, T43343474, 0900-1200, 1300-1530. **Norway**, Esmeralda 909, piso 3 B, T43121904, 0900-1430. **Spain**, Florida 943 (Consulate, Guido 1760), T48110070, 0900-1330, 1500-1730. **Sweden**, Corrientes 330, piso 3, T43113088/9 (Consulate, Tacuarí 147, T43421422), T10001200. **Switzerland**, Santa Fe 846, piso 12, T43116491, open 0900-1200.

Language schools *Instituto de Lengua Española para Extranjeros* (ILEE), Av Callao 339, piso 3 (1022), T/F47827173, www.ilee.com.ar US$19 per hr, groups US$12 per hr. Recommended by individuals and organizations alike, accommodation arranged; *Bromley Institute*, Paraná 641, piso 1 A, T43714113, courses in Spanish, Portuguese, French, English, high standards, well-regarded, recommended. Free Spanish classes at *Escuela Presidente Roca*, Libertad 581, T4352488, Mon-Fri, 1945-2145 (basic level only). Spanish classes also at *Instituto del Sur*, Irigoyen 668, piso 1, T43341487, F43340107, individual lessons, cheap; *Encuentros*, Scalabrini Ortiz 2395 – piso 6 M, T/F8327794; *Estudio Buenos Aires*, San Martín 881, piso 4, T43128936, owner also lets out rooms; *Link Educational Services*, Arenales 2565, piso 5 B, T48253017; *Universidad de Buenos Aires*, 25 de Mayo, offers cheap, coherent courses. CEDIC, Reconquista 719, piso 11 E, T/F43151156, US$16 per hr private tuition, US$11 per hr in groups. Recommended. Graciela Klein T47720918, recommended as private tutor. For other schools teaching Spanish, and for private tutors look in *Buenos Aires Herald* in the classified advertisements. Enquire also at Asatej.

Schools teaching Argentines English *International House*, Pacheco de Melo 2555, British-owned and run; *Berlitz*, Av de Mayo 847; Santiago del Estero 324. *American Teachers*, Viamonte y Florida, T43933331. There are many others. Before being allowed to teach, you must offically have a work permit (difficult to obtain) but schools may offer casual employment without one (particularly to people searching for longer-term employment), if unsure of your papers, ask at Migraciones (address below).

Many dry cleaners and many launderettes, eg Alvear 861, in centre: Junín 15 y Rivadavia, Mon-Sat **Laundry** 0800-2100. Junín 529 y Lavalle; Rivadavia 1340. *Laverap*, Paraguay 888 y Suipacha, Córdoba 466, Local 6, T43125460, US$6.50 per load (10% discount to ISIC and youth card holders, also at Brasil y Bolívar and Rodríguez Peña 100-200), Arenales 894, Solís near Alsina (cheaper). The laundry at Brasil 554 costs US$4 per load, more for valet service. *Marva*, Perón 2000 y Ayacucho. *Lava Ya*, at Libertad 1290 and 832, Paraguay 888, Moreno 417, H Yrigoyen 1294 and Esmeralda 577.

Fundación Banco Patricios, Callao 312, piso 5, Spanish, English, French and some Italian books, **Libraries** Mon-Fri 1000-1900, membership US$15 per month. See also Biblioteca Nacional, page 92.

Innoculations *Centro Médico Rivadavia*, Bustamante 2531 y Las Heras, Mon-Fri, 0730-1900 (bus **Medical services** 38, 59, 60 or 102 from Plaza Constitución), or *Guardia de Sanidad del Puerto*, Mon and Thu, 0800-1200, at Ing Huergo 690, T43341875, free, bus 20 from Retiro, no appointment required (typhus, cholera, Mon-Fri 0800-1200; yellow fever, Tue-Thu 1400-1600, but no hepatitis, take syringe and needle, particularly for insulin and TB). Buy the vaccines in *Laboratorio Biol*, Uriburu 159, or in larger chemists. Many chemists display signs indicating that they administer innoculations. Any hospital with an infectology department will do hepatitis A.

Urgent medical service (day and night) (**Casualty ward** *Sala de guardia*). For free municipal ambulance service to an emergency hospital department, T43424001/4, 107 (SAME). In case of intoxication, T49626666 for information or first aid. Public Hospital: *Hospital Argerich*, Almirante Brown esquina Pi y Margall 750, T49315555. *British Hospital*, Perdriel 74, T4231081, US$14 a visit. Cheap dental treatment at Caseros y Perdriel 76. *German Hospital*, Pueyrredón 1657, between Berutti and Juncal, T48214083. Both maintain first-aid centres (*centros asistenciales*) as do the other main hospitals. *French Hospital*, Rioja 951, T4971031. *Children's Hospital* (Ricardo Gutiérrez), Bustamante 1399, T4865500. *Centro Gallego*, Belgrano 2199, T473061. *Hospital Juan A Fernández*, Cerviño y Bulnes, good medical attention. If affected by pollen, asthma sufferers can receive excellent treatment at the *Hospital de Clínicas José de San Martín*, Córdoba 2351, T48216041, US$6 per treatment. *Dental Hospital*, Pueyrredón 1940, T49415555. *Eye Hospital*, San Juan 2121, T48212721.

Non-Catholic The **Holy Cross**, Estados Unidos 3150, established by the Passionists. **St John's** **Places of** Cathedral (Anglican), 25 de Mayo 282 (services, Sunday 0900 in English, 1030 in Spanish), was **worship** built half at the expense of the British Government and dedicated in 1831. **St Paul's**, **St Peter's**, **St Michael** and **All Angels** and **St Saviour's** are Anglican places of worship in the suburbs. **St Andrew's**, Belgrano 579, is 1 of the 8 Scottish Presbyterian churches. The **American Church**,

Buenos Aires and the Río de la Plata

Corrientes 718, is Methodist, built in 1863, service at 1100. **First Methodist** (American) Church, Santa Fe 839, Acassuso. **Danish Church**, Carlos Calvo 257. **German Evangelical Church**, Esmeralda 162. **Swedish Church**, Azopardo 1422. The **Armenian Cathedral** of St Gregory the Illuminator at the Armenian Centre, and the **Russian Orthodox Cathedral** of The Holy Trinity (Parque Lezama) are interesting. The largest mosque in Latin America was opened in 2000. Part of the **Centro Islámico Rey Fahd**, it is situated at Av Bullrich Y Libertador in Palermo

Synagogue The most important in Buenos Aires are the Congregación Israelita en la República Argentina, Libertad 705 (also has a small museum), and, the oldest, the Templo Israelita at Paso 423 (called the Paso Temple), traditional and conservative. An important orthodox temple is the Comunidad Israelita Ortodoxa, the seat of the rabbis of Argentina, Ecuador 530, T48622701. The Comunidad Betel, Elcano 3424, and the B'nai Tikvah, Vidal 2049, are for reformed worshippers. Congregación Emanu-El (reformed sect), Tronador 1455, take bus 140 from Av Córdoba to Alvarez Thomas block 1600, then turn right into Tronador.

Tourist information On Fri, the youth section of *Clarín* (*Sí*) lists free entertainments. *Página 12* has a youth supplement on Thu called *NO*, the paper lists current events in *Pasen y Vean* section on Fri. Also the weekly, free *Aquí Buenos Aires*, the weekly *La Maga* and Sun tourism section of *La Nación* (very informative). *Where in Buenos Aires*, a tourist guide in English, published monthly, is available free in hotels, travel agencies, tourist kiosks on Florida, and in some news stands. The *Buenos Aires Times* is a bilingual monthly newspaper covering tourist topics, available in some hotels. A good guide to bus and subway routes is *Guía Peuser*. There is 1 for the city and 1 covering Greater Buenos Aires. Similar guides, *Lumi* and *Guía T*, US$5, are available at news stands, US$10. Also handy is Auto Mapa's pocket-size *Plano guía* of the Federal Capital, available at news stands, US$8, or from sales office at Santa Fe 3117. *Auto Mapa* also publishes an increasing number of regional maps, Michelin-style, high quality. Country-wide maps at Instituto Geográfico Militar, Cabildo 301, see page 70.

Tourist offices National office at Santa Fe 883 with maps and literature covering the whole country. Open 0900-1700, Mon-Fri, T43122232, 43125611. There are kiosks at Aeroparque (Aerolíneas Argentinas section), T47739891/05. Mon-Fri, 0830-2000 and Sat 0900-1900, and at Ezeiza Airport, T4800224/0011, Mon-Fri 0830-2200.

Municipal office in the **Municipalidad de Buenos Aires**, Sarmiento 1551, piso 5, T43723612,43747533, www.buenosaires.gov.ar, open Mon-Fri 0930-1730, has an excellent free booklet about the city centre and maps. There are municipally-run tourist kiosks on Florida, junction with Diagonal Roque Sáenz Peña, Mon-Fri 0900-1700 and in the Galerías Pacífico, Florida y Córdoba, piso 1, Mon-Fri 1000-1900, Sat 1100-1900 as well as in the *Café Tortoni*, Av de Mayo 829, Mon-Fri 1400-1600 and Caminito y Lamadrid, in La Boca, Fri/Sat/Sun 1000-1700. Websites www.baxpat.com and www.buenosairesherald.com are good for finding out what's on.

For free tourist information anywhere in the country T0800-5-0016 (0900-2000). Tourist hotline for those overcharged, cheated or suffering from similar minor abuses between 2100 and 0300, T43835331.

Provincial offices There are also *Casas de Turismo* for most provinces. Several are on Av Callao: **Buenos Aires**, No 237, T43717045/7, sub.com@casaprov.gba.gov.ar 1000-1630. Others on Callao are **Córdoba**, No 332, secturcor@arnet.com.ar T43722602, F4762615, 1000-1700. **Chaco**, No 322, T43746531 F43751640, turismo@ecomchaco.com.ar 1000-1630. **La Rioja** No 745, T48151929, 1000-1600. **Mendoza**, No 445, T43717301, F43732580, subturismo@lanet.com.ar 1000-1700. Others: **Río Negro**, Tucumán 1916, T43717078, F43755489, sectur@arnet.com.ar 1000-1600. **Chubut**, Sarmiento 1172, T43828820, chubutur@infovia.com.ar 1030-1700. **Entre Ríos**, Suipacha 844, T/F43289327, 0900-1800. **Formosa**, H Irigoyen 1429, T43812037, F43816290, 0900-1500. **Jujuy**, Santa Fe 967, piso 6, T/F43942295, meconjuj@mail. imagine.com.ar 1000-1700. **Misiones**, Santa Fe 989, T43221907, F43256197, informes@secde turismo.com.ar 0900-1700. **Neuquén**, Perón 687, T/F43266812, casadelneuquen@ciudad.com.ar 0930-1600. **Salta**, Diagonal Sáenz Peña 933, piso 5 A, T43262456, F43260110, infor@turismosalta.com 1000-1730. **Santa Cruz**, 25 de Mayo 277, piso 1, T43433653, F3421667, 1000-1700. **Catamarca**, Córdoba 2080, T/F43746891, casacata@sminter.gov.ar 1000-1700. **Corrientes**, San Martín 333, piso 4, T/F43947432, dgctes@ssdnet.com.ar 1000-1600. **La Pampa**, Suipacha 346, T/F43260511, sindycom@satlink.com.ar 0800-1800. **San Juan**, Sarmiento 1251, T43829241, F43829465, enprotur@ischigualasto.com 0900-1500. **San Luis**, Azcuénaga 1083, T48220426, F48239413,

1000-1730. **Santa Fe**, Montevideo 373, piso 2, T43754570, F43754635, 0930-1530. **Santiago del Estero**, Florida 274, T43269418, F43265915, 0900-1800. **Tucumán**, Suipacha 140, T43220564, 0930-1430. **Tierra del Fuego**, MT de Alvear 790, T43110233, infuebue@satlink.com.ar

Other offices Mar del Plata, Corrientes 1660, oficina 16, T43845613, Mon-Fri 1000-1800, Sat/Sun 1500-2100. **Villa Gesell**, B Mitre 1702, T/F43745098, turismo@gesell.com.ar **Bariloche** hotel, flat and bungalow service in Galería at Florida 520/Lavalle 617, room 116 (cheapest places not listed). **Necochea**, Maipú 633, piso 1, 1200-1900. **Pinamar**, Florida 930, piso 5 B, T43152679, F43152680, 1030-1630. Calafate bookings for *Refugio and Autocamping Lago Viedma*, excursions with Transporte Ruta 3 and lake excursions with Empresa Paraíso de Navegación booked from Turismo Argos, Maipú 812, piso 13 C, T43925460. (For bookings for *Hotel La Loma*, Calafate and further information on the area contact Paula Escabo, Callao 433, piso 8 P, T43719123.) **Estancias Turisticas de Santa Cruz**, Suipacha 1120, T/F43253098/3102, for information and reservations at *estancias* in Santa Cruz. For tourist information on Patagonia and bookings for cheap accommodation and youth hostels, contact Asatej, see below.

Administración de Parques Nacionales Santa Fe 680, opposite Plaza San Martín, T43110303, Mon-Fri 1000-1700, have leaflets on most national parks. Also library (Biblioteca Perito Moreno), open to public Tue-Fri 1000-1700. **Asatej** Argentine Youth and Student Travel Organization, runs a Student Flight Centre, Florida 835, piso 3, oficina 320, T45118700, F43116158, informes@asatej.com.ar Offering booking for flights (student discounts) including 1-way flights at bargains prices, hotels and travel (all payments over US$100 must be in US$ cash). Information for all South America, noticeboard for travellers, the *Sleep Cheap Guide* lists economical accommodation in Argentina, Bolivia, Chile, Brazil, Uruguay and Peru, ISIC cards sold, English and French spoken. Also runs the following: **Red Argentino de Alojamiento Para Jovenes**, same address oficina 319B, T45118712, F43120089, raaj@hostels.org.ar, an Argentine hostal association (affiliated to Hostelling International) which has a network of hostels around the country, International Booking Network for members only, Hostelling International cards sold. *Asatej Travel Store*, oficina 320 and at Santa Fe 2450, piso 3, local 93, selling wide range of travel goods including *South American Handbook* 'at best price'. **Asociación Ornitológica del Plata**, 25 de Mayo 749, T43128958, for information on birdwatching and specialist tours, good library. **Central Police Station** Azopardo 650, T43818041 (emergency, T101 from any phone, free). **Comisión Nacional de Museos y Monumentos y Lugares Históricos**, Av de Mayo 556, professional archaeology institute. **Instituto Antártico Argentino**, Cerrito 1248, Buenos Aires, T48166313/1689, 0900-1500. **Migraciones** (Immigration), Antártida Argentina 1325, T43128661/9, tourist visa extensions 0800-1300. **Municipalidad**, Av de Mayo 525, facing Plaza de Mayo. **Oviajes**, Uruguay 385, piso 8, T43716137, oviajes@redynet.com.ar, also offers travel facilities, ticket sales, information, and issues IYHA, ISIC, ITIC, G025 and FIYTO cards, aimed at students, teachers and independent travellers. **Salvation Army**, Rivadavia 3255. **USIT Tango**, Libertador 2785, Olivos (next to Olivos station), T47948060, turismo@usittango.com.ar, affiliated to USIT World, for cheap fares, travel passes, guided trips and accommodation, also branches at Viamonte 2020, T43724224 and Urguay 969, piso 1, T48167909. **Youth Hostel Association** information for all South America, **Asociación Argentino de Albergues de la Juventud**, Talcahuano 214, piso 3, T43721001 (post code: 1013 Buenos Aires). **NB** A YHA card in Argentina costs US$20, ISIC cards also sold. Secretariat open Mon-Fri 1300-2000. (There are very few hostels near Route 3, the main road south from Buenos Aires.) **YMCA**, (Central), Reconquista 439. YMCA Tucumán 844.

Useful addresses

Buenos Aires and the Río de la Plata

The northern suburbs of Buenos Aires

Northwest of the city along the Plata estuary lie several attractive suburbs, easily reached by train or bus.

Olivos
Population: 160,000

Olivos is the site of the presidential residence is a popular residential district. From the station, walk up Calle Corrientes with its neocolonial architecture and old, shady trees until you reach the river and the Puerto de Olivos, mainly used for construction materials, but there are a marina (private yacht club) and several *parrilladas* that are popular. On Saturday and Sunday a catamaran sails to Tigre taking two hours. The trip is worthwhile. It passes riverside mansions, sailing boats and windsurfers.

Martínez, nearby, is an attractive residential area, with an interesting shopping area. Sailing and windsurfing are well represented and river launches and other craft may be hired.

San Isidro
Population: 80,000

Just beyond Olivos, is one of the most attractive suburbs on the coast and a fashionable nightlife spot, especially along the river bank. There are a number of fine colonial buildings including several *quintas* (country-mansions). One of these, the **Quinta Pueyrredón**, houses the **Museo Pueyrredón**, which contains artefacts from the life of General Juan Martín Pueyrredón. The church, built in 1895, is in French neogothic style. Also French-inspired is the **Villa Ocampo**, built in 1890 and inhabited by the famous writer Victoria Ocampo. San Isidro is a resort for golf, yachting, swimming, and athletics but is most famous for the **Hipodromo San Isidro**, its magnificent turf racecourse.

Tigre
Population: 40,000

On the Río Luján about 29 km northwest, is a popular recreational centre. North of the town is the delta of the Río Paraná, the favourite weekend spot for *porteños* (inhabitants of the city). There are innumerable canals and rivulets, with holiday homes and restaurants on their banks. Regattas are held in November and March. The area is also a profitable fruit growing centre and there is an excellent fruit and handicrafts market at Canal San Fernando on Sunday. The fishing is excellent and the peace is only disturbed by motor-boats at weekends. Regular *lanchas* (launch services) run to all parts of the Delta, including taxi launches – watch prices for these! – from the wharf. Tourist catamarans, run by Interislena (Lavalle 499, T47310261, weekends Lavalle 419, T47310264) leave from next to the Cacciola dock. ■ *Mon-Fri 1330, 1600, 1½ hrs, US$10, different schedule at weekends.* Tren de la Costa (see below) also runs luxury catamaran trips. Longer trips (4½ hours) to the open Río de la Plata estuary are available.

Museums **Museo Naval**, Paseo Victoria 602, T47490608. Covers origins and development of Argentine navy. Worth a visit. ■ *Mon-Thu 0800-1230, Fri 0800-1730, Sat/Sun 1000-1830 US$2, 50 % ISIC discount).* There are also relics of the Falklands/Malvinas War on display outside.

The **Museo de la Reconquista**, Padre Castañeda 470, T45124496. Situated near the location of Liniers' landing in 1806, this celebrates the reconquest of Buenos Aires from the British in 1806-07. ■ *Wed-Fri 1000-1830, free to ISIC card holders.*

Sleeping and eating There are no good hotels in Tigre itself. On the islands of the Delta: **AB** *El Tropezón*, T47281012. With meals, an old inn formerly a haunt of Hemingway, now frequented by affluent *porteños*, highly recommended despite the mosquitoes. **AL** *I'Marangatú*, on Río San Antonio, T47280752. With breakfast, pool, sports facilities. **F** *Canal de San Fernando*, at Río Luján y Abra Vieja, T47280396. Youth hostel, clean, hot showers, table tennis, volleyball, canoes, take all food in advance, there are basic cooking facilities. *Chino*, Cazon 1373, *tenedor libre*, good value. Restaurants on the waterfront in Tigre across the Río Tigre from railway line; cheaper places on Italia and Cazón on the near side.

Transport Bus Take No 60 from Constitución: the 60 'bajo' takes a little longer than the 60 'alto' but is more interesting for sightseeing. Also No 19 or 71 from Once or No 152 from the centre. **Ferries** To Carmelo, Uruguay leave from Cacciola dock (see page 114). Overnight trips to Carmelo (US$72-110 including accommodation) and 3 day trips to Montevideo (US$118 including accommodation) are also available from Cacciola. **Train** By train from Buenos Aires to new Estación Tigre, US$0.65 one way, every 10 mins during peak hrs, otherwise every 15 or 20 mins. Alternatively take train from platform 1 or 2 at Retiro station (FC Mitre) to Bartolomé Mitre and change to the Maipú station (the stations are linked) for the new Tren de la Costa, US$1.50 return, US$2 at weekends, 0700-2300 every 10 mins, 25 mins journey. The terminus, Estación Delta, (T47326000) and several stations (eg San Isidro) on this line have shopping centres (you can get on and off the train as many times as you like on the same ticket).

Situated in the Río de la Plata just off the Uruguayan town of Carmelo and some 45 km north of Buenos Aires, Martín García is now a Provincial Nature Reserve and one of the best excursions from Buenos Aires.

Isla Martín García
Population: 200

The site of Juan Díaz de Solís' landfall in 1516, the strategic position of the island has given it a chequered history. Defended by gun batteries during the War of the Triple Alliance, it became a military base, was used for quarantining immigrants from Europe and served as a prison: four 20th-century Argentine presidents have been detained here including Juan Perón. In 1914 British sailors were interned here, as were survivors from the *Graf Spee* in the Second World War. Evidence of this past can be seen: there are stone-quarries used for building the older churches of Buenos Aires, four gun batteries and a *faro* (lighthouse) dating from 1890. The **Museo Histórico** in the former *pulpería*, houses a display of artefacts, documents and photos.

Wildlife is varied, particularly around the edges of the island and includes laurels, *ceibo* and several species of orchids. Over 200 species of birds visit the island. Take insect repellent.

Sleeping *Hostería Martín García*, owned by Cacciola. For bungalow rental T(0315) 24546. **Camping** *Camping Martín García*, with hostel accommodation.

Isla Martín García

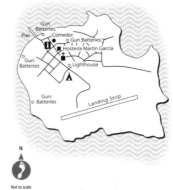

Transport Boat trips daily except Tue and Thu from Tigre at 0800, returning 1700, 3 hrs journey, US$45 including lunch and guide (US$22 transport only), 2-day trip US$120. Reservations can be made through Cacciola, Florida 520, piso 1, Oficina 113, T43945520, who also handle bookings for the inn and restaurant on the island.

Estancias near Buenos Aires

Many *estancias* can be visited relatively easily from Buenos Aires, either to spend a day *(dia de campo)* or longer. The following are arranged in order from north to south, with their distance from the capital. A number of others, especially in San Antonio de Areco, are listed under **The Pampas**. Advanced booking for all *estancias* is recommended, either directly or through a specialist travel agency such as *Turismo Flyer*. All offer horseriding.

Sleeping **LL** *El Metejon*, near Cañuelas, 51 km southwest, T026621728, F013252197. Modern *estancia*, specializing in polo, English spoken, *dia de campo* US$80, also polo classes. **L** *Carmen de Sierra*, near Arrecifes, 185 km northwest, T01-311-0396. A colonial-style *estancia* dating from 1870. No modern comforts (no lights after 2200) but with lots of style and beautiful surroundings. Carriages and fishing. English spoken. *Dia de campo* US$55. **L** *El Cencerro*, T01-743-2319, 3 km from Capilla del Señor, 80 km northwest. Carriages, fishing, walking. *Dia de campo* US$80. **A** *Cabaña los dos Hermanos*, near Zarate, 85 km northwest, T01-765-4320. Not really an *estancia* but has a very good *dia de campo* with swimming, US$50.

From Buenos Aires to La Plata

The 9 de Julio Motorway runs southeast of Buenos Aires, through Avellaneda towards La Plata.

Quilmes Named after the Quilmes Indians who were forcibly moved to this site in 1665 from the famous pre-Inca site in Tucumán Province (see page 254). Now an important industrial town, 27 km south of Buenos Aires, it is the home of one of the world's largest breweries. The **Museo Municipal del Transporte**, Sarmiento 625, houses a collection of carriages and other artefacts from the era of horse-drawn transport. ■ *Mon-Fri 0900-1200, Thu, Sat, Sun 1400-1700.*

Florencio Varela This town, 32 km from the city, is famous as the birthplace of the naturalist and writer W H Hudson. See the box on page 68. The house is now a museum and forms part of the **Parque Ecológico Guillermo E Hudson**, a small nature reserve covering 54 ha, notable mainly as a bird sanctuary (over 100 species visit in Spring). ■ *Wed-Sun 1000-1800. Getting there: Can be reached by train from Constitución station to Florencio Varela and taxi for remaining 7 km.*

Further south the road passes through the **Parque Pereyra Iraola**, 10,000 ha of woodland, a former *estancia* expropriated by the Perón government. The park is in three sectors; the central sector includes the **Estación de Cría de Animales Salvajes**, an animal research centre with exotic species, as well as experimental plant nurseries.

La Plata

Phone code: 022
Colour map 4, grid B6
Population: 545,000
56 km SE of Buenos Aires

The capital of Buenos Aires province is La Plata, situated near the Río de la Plata. A modern city, it was built according to late 19th-century European ideas on urban planning. With its broad avenues, squares and modern public building, it feels quite unlike other major Argentine cities. Though the city has its own port and there is an oil refinery, these are situated some way north of the centre on the Río Santiago. Lovers of the architectural confusion and busy commercial atmosphere of most Argentine cities may, however, find the city rather soulless. Despite this La Plata has one attraction which its rivals lack, the magnificent Museo de Ciencias Naturales.

History

La Plata was founded in 1882 by Dardo Rocha, Governor of Buenos Aires province, as the new provincial capital after the city of Buenos Aires had become federal capital. The site chosen was an estancia; the *Paseo del Bosque* is the site of park of the estancia. Rocha was inspired by the new urban ideas of Parisian architects and the central grid, 5 sq km, was laid down by Pierre Benoit. His design is notable for its wide avenues and total of 23 squares. An international competition was held to design the public buildings: designs were required to consist of two floors and to use only Argentine materials. Most of the winning designs were by Argentines, but the European influence is strong.

Sights

The major public buildings are centred around two streets, Calles 51 and 53, which run northeast from the Plaza Moreno to the Plaza San Martín and from there to the Paseo del Bosque. On the southeast side of **Plaza Moreno** is the magnificent **gothic cathedral**, designed by Benoit, built between 1885 and 1936, and inspired by Cologne and Amiens. The building materials were Argentine but the stained glass windows were made in Germany and France. Its vast interior with its 5 naves holds 12,000 people and covers 7,000 m. ■ *Visits daily 0900-1300, 1500-1800*. Opposite is the **Municipalidad**, in German renaissance style. Two blocks northeast, the **Teatro Argentino** is still under construction after the destruction of the original in a fire in 1977.

La Plata

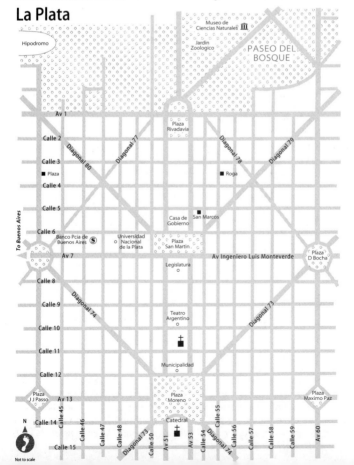

Plaza San Martín is bounded by the **Legislature**, designed by the German architects Heine and Hageman and, opposite, the **Casa de Gobierno** in a mixture French and Flemish renaissance styles. On the northwest side of the plaza is the **Pasaje Dardo Rocha**, designed in Italian renaissance style by the Italian Francisco Pinaroli as the main railway station. It now houses the **Museo Municipal de Bellas Artes** and two theatres. Nearby on Calles 6 and 7 are the imposing **Universidad Nacional** and the **Banco Provincial**.

Among the attractions of the **Paseo del Bosque** are woodlands and an artificial lake as well as the zoological gardens (US$2), astronomical observatory and the Hipodromo, dating from the 1930s and one of the most important racecourses in the country. However, the park is most famous for the **Museo de Ciencias Naturales** (see below).

Museums **Museo de Ciencias Naturals** (also known as Museo La Plata), in the Paseo del Bosque, is one of the most famous museums in Latin America. Founded by Francisco Perito Moreno, it houses an outstanding collection. There are sections on minerology, palaeontology, zoology, anthropology, ethnography, botany and archaeology. The latter includes displays of artefacts from precolumbian peoples throughout the Americas, including a large collection of pre-Inca ceramics from Peru, as well as displays on precolombian civilizations of the northwestern provinces of Argentina. Highly recommended. ■ *Daily, 1000-1900, US$3, closed 1 Jan, 1 May, 25 Dec. Free guided tours, weekdays 1400, 1600, Sat/Sun hrly 1030-1630, in Spanish and in English (phone first, T4257744, F257527) www.unlp.edu.ar/museo/index.html*

Excursions The **República de los Niños**, 8 km west, is an interesting children's village with scaled-down public buildings built under the first Perón administration. ■ *Getting there: Take a green microbus 273 or a red and black 518 to República de los Niños from Plaza San Martín.*

Islas del Río Santiago are northeast of the city. At **Punta Lara**, a holiday resort 12 km northeast, there is a nature reserve protecting the southernmost remaining stretch of riverine forest in South America. In its 31 ha, over 750 plants species, 150 of them medicinal, 270 bird species, 40 species of mammals and 25 species of reptiles have been identified. ■ *Entry is strictly controlled: guided tours on Sun only 1000-1300 and 1400-1800, T021660396 first.*

Parque Costero Sur is a nature reserve 110 km south. Covering 23,500 ha of marshes along 70 km of coastline, it protects a wide range of birds. It includes several *estancias*, including the **Estancia Juan Géronimo**, T/F(01)43270105, which offers accommodation (**L** full board), guided tours, swimming, birdwatching, recommended.

Essentials

Sleeping **L** *Corregidor*, Calle 26 No 1026, T4256800. 4-star, modern, a/c, snack bar, central, expensive. **AB** *San Marcos*, Calle 54 No 523, T42249. Good. **AB** *Acuarius*, Calle 3 No 731, T/F4214229. With breakfast, small beds. **C** *Rex*, Av 44, No 323, T4212703. Modern, a/c. **C** *Roga*, Calle 54 No 334, T4219553, 3 blocks from Paseo del Bosque. **C** *Plaza*, Calle 44 entre Calle 3 y Calle 4, with bath.

Eating *El Fogón*, Av 1 y Calle 49. *Don Quijote*, Plaza Paso. Good value, best in town, can get
Restaurants rarely very crowded. Chinese 'tenedor libre' at *Guinga*, Plaza Paso. *La Linterna*, Calle 60 y Av 1.
open in the evening Upmarket, good value. *El Chaparral*, good *parrillada*, Calle 60 y Calle 117 (Paseo del
before 2100 Bosque). Recommended bar, with steak sandwiches, *El Modelo*, Calle 54 y Calle 5.
Best *empanadas* at *La Madrileña*, a hole-in-the-wall on Calle 60 between Avs 5 and 6.
Best bakery is *El Globo*, Calle 43 y Calle 5.

Tango and tropical music at *El Viejo Almacén*, on Diagonal 74, Calle 2. There are free **Entertainment**
concerts during the summer in the *Teatro Martín Fierro* in the Paseo del Bosque.

Foundation of the City, 19 Nov.   **Festivals**

Turismo San Martín, Calle 51 between Avs 7 and 8, recommended. *ASATEJ*, Av 5 **Tour operators**
No 990, T/F4838673, laplata@asatej.com.ar

Municipal office Calle 47 No 740 between Calle 9 and Diagonal 74, T4258334; Provin- **Tourist offices**
cial office, Torre Municipal, Calles 12 y 53, piso 13, T4295553, F29554, little
information.

Bus To **Buenos Aires**, 1½ hrs, US$3.20, about every 30 mins. From Buenos Aires from **Transport**
Retiro day and night and from Plaza Constitución, daytime. **Train** To/from Buenos
Aires (Constitución) run by TMR, frequent, 1 hr, 10 mins, US$1.50. (At Constitución
ticket office hidden behind shops opposite plat 6).

The Uruguayan Coast

*Along the Uruguayan coast of the Río de la Plata are several attractive little
towns, which are growing in popularity as tourist centres.*

Colonia del Sacramento

A Portuguese colonial gem on the east bank of the Río de la Plata, Colonia del   *Phone code: 0522*
Sacramento is a very popular destination for excursions from Buenos Aires. The   *Colour map 4, grid B6*
modern town, which extends around a bay, is charming and lively; its streets are   *Population: 22,000*
lined with plane trees and the whole town is kept very trim. The small historic sec-
tion is particularly interesting because there is so little colonial architecture in this
part of South America.

There is a pleasant Plaza 25 de Agosto and a grand Intendencia Municipal
(Méndez y Av Gen Flores the main street). The best beach is Playa Ferrando,
2 km to the east (buses from Gen Flores every two hours). There are regular sea
and air connections with Buenos Aires and a free port.

Founded by a Portuguese expedition from Brazil in 1680, Colonia was at the **History**
centre of an intense political and military struggle between Spain and Portugal
for the next 100 years. Its strategic position opposite Buenos Aires challenged
Spanish control of the Río de la Plata and its use as a base for British smugglers
undermined Spanish colonial trading restrictions. Within months of its
founding it was attacked by troops from Buenos Aires and the settlers were
forced to surrender. Refounded in 1683, it was seized by Spain in 1705.
It reverted to Portuguese rule under the Treaty of Utrecht (1713) but was temporarily occupied again by Spanish troops in 1735 and 1762, and destroyed in
1777, after which the Treaty of San Ildefonso between the two countries specified the east bank of the Plata estuary as Spanish. It 1807 it was briefly occupied
by British troops during the attempted seizure of Buenos Aires.

Buenos Aires and the Río de la Plata

The Barrio Histórico

Museums: 1130-1830. Entry by combined ticket bought from Museo Municipal, US$1; not all may be open on the same day

With its narrow streets (see Calle de los Suspiros), colonial buildings and reconstructed city walls, the Barrio Histórico has been declared Patrimonio Cultural de la Humanidad by UNESCO.

The **Plaza Mayor** (Plaza 25 de Mayo) is especially picturesque. At its eastern end is the **Puerta del Campo**, the restored city gate and drawbridge. On the south side is the **Museo Portugués**; see also the narrow **Calle de los Suspiros**, nearby. At the western end of the Plaza are the **Museo Municipal** in the former house of Almirante Brown (with indigenous archaeology, historical items, paleontology, natural history), the **Casa Nacarello** next door, the **Casa del Virrey**, and the ruins of the Convento de San Francisco (1695), to which is attached the **Faro** or lighthouse) built in 1857. ■ *Free – tip or donation appreciated.*

Just north of the Plaza Mayor is the **Archivo Regional**. From here a narrow street, the Calle Misiones de los Tapes, leads east to the river. At its further end is the tiny **Museo del Azulejo** housed in the Casa Portuguesa. Two blocks north of

Colonia del Sacramento

Not to scale

■ **Sleeping**
1 Esperanza
2 Italiano
3 Leoncia
4 Natal John
5 Plaza Mayor

6 Posada del Gobernador
7 Posada del Virrey
8 Posada Los Linajes
9 Posada San Antonio
10 Rincón del Río

11 Royal

● **Eating**
1 El Aljibe
2 El Frijol Mágico

here is the Calle Playa which runs east to the Plaza Manuel Lobo/Plaza de Armas, on the northern side of which is the **Iglesia Matriz**, on Vasconcellos, the oldest church in Uruguay. Though destroyed and rebuilt several times the altar dates from the 16th century. Two blocks north of the church on the northern edge of the old city are the fortifications of the **Bastión del Carmen**; just east of it is the Teatro Bastión del Carmen. One block south of the Bastión, at San José y España, is the **Museo Español**, formerly the house of General Mitre.

Real de San Carlos

Around the bay, 5 km north, is an unusual, once grand but now sad tourist complex. Only the racecourse (Hipódromo) is still operational (US$1 for men, women free) and you can see the horses exercising and swimming in the sea. ■ *Getting there: take blue bus from Flores y Méndez, 30 mins, US$0.40.* The elegant **Plaza de Toros** (bullring) is falling apart. It is closed to visitors but a local guide will take you through a gap in the fence. The casino and its hotel are in decay and, though the huge Frontón court can still be used, the building is rotting. There is also a **Museo Municipal** and by the beach are two restaurants. At Parada 20, about seven stops before Real de San Carlos, is the **Capilla de San Benito**.

To Real de San Carlos

Cnl Arroyo

Alberto Méndez

Av Gen Artigas

Rivera

Dr D Fosalba

Garcia

To Playa Ferrando (2 km)

Budget o   Intendencia o Municipal   ■3

Plaza de Deportes

To Montevideo

Av General Flores

To Real de San Carlos

o Punta Rent a Car

AV F D Roosevelt

18 de Julio

PUERTO

To Buenos Aires

3 El Galeón
4 Español
5 La Torre
6 Mercado del Túnel
7 Yacht Club

Sleeping

Barrio Histórico L-AL *Plaza Mayor*, Del Comercio 111, T/F3193, lovely, English spoken. **L-AL** *Posada del Virrey*, España 217, T/F2223, suites and rooms. **AL** *Posada del Gobernador*, 18 de Julio 205, T3018, with breakfast, charming. Recommended.

Centre A *Beltrán*, Gral Flores 311, T2955, with bath, comfortable. **A** *Esperanza*, Gral Flores 237, T/F2922 (**B** weekdays), charming. **A** *Posada Los Linajes*, Washington Barbot 191, T24181, central, a/c, TV, cafeteria, warmly recommended. **A** *Royal*, General Flores 340, T2169, with breakfast, gloomy, poor restaurant, pool, avoid rooms on street (noisy), noisy a/c. **AB** *Italiano*, Lobo 341, T2103, **B** without bath, good restaurant, hot water but no heating. Recommended. **AB** *Leoncia*, Rivera 214, T2369, F2049, a/c, modern, good. **AB** *Natal John*, Gral Flores 382 on plaza, T2081. **A** *Posada San Antonio*, Ituzaingó 240, T5344, with breakfast, **B** during week. **B** *Hostal de los Poetas*, Mangarelli 675, T/F5457, with bath, quiet, pleasant. Recommended. **B** *Posada de la Ciudadela*, Washington Barbot 164, T2683, pleasant, a/c, simple. **B** *Rincón del Río*, Washington Barbot 258, T3002, shower, with breakfast. **B** *Los Angeles*, Roosevelt 213, T2335, small rooms, no restaurant, English spoken. **C-D** *Hospedaje*

Buenos Aires and the Río de la Plata

Mihanovic's Folly: Real de San Carlos

Real de San Carlos was the brainchild of Nicolás Mihanovic, an immigrant from Dalmatia, who settled in Buenos Aires. Between 1903 and 1912, seeing the potential to attract tourists from Buenos Aires across the Plata estuary to Colonia, Mihanovic built this grand tourist complex, complete with bullring, casino and frontón (court) for Basque pelota. Port facilities were built for Mihanovic's vessels and a railway line transported visitors to the resort.

Mihanovic's entrepreneurial zeal did not take into account the political obstacles. In 1912, 2 years after the bullring was completed, the Uruguayan government outlawed bullfighting. The casino, the nearest to Buenos Aires (where gambling was prohibited) prospered briefly until the Argentine authorities imposed a special tax on Mihanovic's vessels.

Colonial, Flores 436, T2906, recommended but noisy, restaurant below. **D** *Hospedaje Las Tejas* Rosenthal y Fray Bentos, T4096, with breakfast, shower. **D** *Señora Raquel Suárez*, T2916, has spacious rooms to rent, good value. The municipal sports complex has 2 dormitories with 80 beds, which are sometimes available, ask at the tourist office.

Youth hostel *Hotel del Prado*, C Nueva Helvecia, T0554-4169. Open all year, 15 beds, family rooms, no cooking facilities. **Camping** Municipal site at Real de San Carlos, T4444, US$3.50 per person, **C** in mini-cabañas, electric hook-ups, 100 m from beach, hot showers, open all year, safe, excellent. Recommended.

Eating *La Torre*, Av Gral Flores y Santa Rita, in old town, bar and restaurant, loud disco music, but fine panoramic views especially at sunset. *Pulpería Los Faroles*, just off Plaza Mayor, old town. Recommended, friendly. *El Drugstore*, on Plaza Menor, popular. *Yacht Club* (at Puerto de Yates) and *Esperanza* (at hotel) are good. *Mercado del Túnel*, Flores 227, good meat dishes, but encourages eating of fresh vegetables. *El Aljibe*, Flores 248 e Ituzaingó, good fish dishes. *El Asador,* Ituzaingó 168, good *parrillada* and pasta, nice atmosphere, value for money. *El Galeón*, Ituzaingó y 18 de Julio. *Español*, Lobo 377. *Club Colonial*, Gen Flores 382, good value. *El Frijol Mágico*, Galería Americana at Rivadavia y Méndez, good vegetarian food, 1130-1400.

Festivals In the 3rd week of Jan, festivities are held marking the founding of Colonia.

Transport **Air** Flights to Aeroparque, Buenos Aires, most days, generally quicker than hydrofoil.
Book in advance for all sailings & flights in summer, especially at weekends The airport is 17 km out of town along Route 1; for taxi to Colonia, buy ticket in building next to arrivals, US$2. **Road** **Bus** Bus company offices: COT, Flores 432, T3121; Tauril, Flores y Suárez; Tauriño, Flores 436. To **Montevideo**, 2½ hrs, COT and Tauril, ½ hrly service, US$7; to **Carmelo**, 1½ hrs, *Tauriño*), 4 per day (not Sunday), US$2.50 Chadre/Agencia Central. **Car hire** *Budget*, Flores 472; *Punta*, Paseo de la Estación L, on Méndez near Flores; also car hire at airport. Motorcycle and bicycle hire at Flores y Rivera and outside ferry dock, US$5 per hr, US$15 per day, recommended as a good way of seeing the town, traffic is slow. **Sea** Ferries to Buenos Aires are operated by *Buquebus* (T05222975) and *Ferryturismo* (T42919). See under Buenos Aires for details.

Directory **Banks** Banks open in pm only. *Banco Comerical*, on plaza, gives cash against Visa. *Cambio Viaggio*, Flores 350 y Suárez, T2070, Mon-Sat 0900-1200, 1300-1800, Sun 1000-1800 (also outside the ferry dock, with car hire). *Cambio Colonia* and *Banco de la República Oriental del Uruguay* at the ferry port (dollars and South American currencies). **Communications** Post Office: on main plaza. Telephones: *Antel*, Rivadavia 420, open till 2300, does not accept foreign money. **Embassies & consulates** *Argentine Consulate*, Flores 215, T2091, open weekdays 1200-1700. **Tourist**

offices Flores y Rivera, T23700/26140/27000, open Mon-Fri 0800-1830, Sat and Sun 0900-2200, good maps of the Barrio Histórico. Also at passenger terminal at the dock, T4897.

Northeast of Colonia del Sacramento

Route 21 runs northeast through a string of small towns near the Río de la Plata.

Carmelo, on the banks of the Arroyo Las Vacas, is a pleasant town, connected to Tigre by ferry. It has the church, museum and archive of El Carmen on Plaza Artigas. In the Casa de Cultura, 19 de Abril 246, is a tourist office and museum. On the far side of the river from the centre are the Rowing Club, the Reserva de Fauna (with birds and mammals), the casino, the Yacht Club and Playa Seré, Carmelo's beach at the mouth of the river. In summer, several hundred yachts visit Carmelo.

Carmelo
Population 18,000
70 km from Colonia
del Sacramento

Sleeping **AB** *Casino Carmelo*, Rodó s/n, T42314. **B** *Bertoletti*, Uruguay 171, T42030. Modern. **C** *Rambla*, Uruguay y 12 de Febrero, T42390. **D** *Palace*, Sarandí 308, T42622. **D** *San Fernando*, 19 de Abril 161, T42503. Full of character, temperamental showers. Recommended. **D** *Oriental*, 19 de Abril 284. **Camping** At Playa Seré, hot showers.

Transport **Bus** To Montevideo, 1210, 2240, US$8.40, Intertur; to **Fray Bentos** and **Salto**, from main plaza 0710, 1540; to **Colonia**, Tauriño, 4 a day, 1½ hrs, US$2.50. **To Argentina** ferry to Tigre, Cacciola, Constituyente 263, T48062, 3 a day.

Directory Argentina consulate, FD Roosevelt 318, T4266.

Route 21 continues through **Nueva Palmira**, 92 km north, a popular yachting resort with a free zone, **La Agraciada**, some 20 km further north, the historic beach famous for the landing of the 33 patriots on 19 April 1825, which led to Uruguayan independence, **Dolores**, 134 km north, and **Mercedes**, 177 km north, a yachting and fishing centre during the season. Founded in 1788, its charm (it is known as 'the city of flowers') derives from its Spanish-colonial appearance, though it is not as old as the older parts of Colonia.

Route

Buenos Aires and the Río de la Plata

The Pampas

4

The Pampas

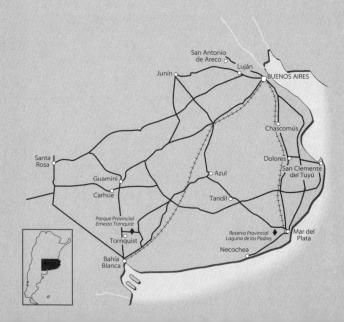

Little visited by most travellers, the pampas is a land of small towns and large estancias, some of which now welcome visitors. Stretching inland from Buenos Aires for hundreds of miles, these broad fertile plains are the economic heart of Argentina producing much of the beef for which the country is famous. Apart from two groups of sierras near Tandil and Bahía Blanca, the surface seems an endless flat monotony. The Sierras de la Ventana are a popular destination for visitors from the capital. To the south and west there is little rainfall and the area becomes known as rise the pampa seca. Here, mobile sand dunes can rise to 30-m high. Where rain falls, filling lakes and lagoons, flamingos, storks, swans and ducks are amongst the prolific birdlife that flock to bathe in those waters.

Along the Atlantic coast, to the south and east of the pampas, are a string of resorts, very popular with Argentines in summer. Mar del Plata, one of the most famous resorts in South America, dates from the late 19th century. It offers a range of attractions including a casino and museums. Inland nearby is Balcarce, which has a museum dedicated to its famous son, the racing driver Juan Manuel Fangio. Apart from Bahía Blanca, one of the largest cities in southern Argentina and an important route centre, the other centres along this coast are almost deserted off season.

Background

Geography

The pampas cover some 40 million ha and extend fanwise from Buenos Aires for a distance of between 550 and 650 km. There are few rivers in this area apart from the Río Salado. Many streams peter out in the desert, often disappearing down a series of fault-lines: around Guaminí these fault-lines have produced a series of lakes. Drinking water is pumped to the surface from a depth of from 30 to 150 m by the windpumps which are such a prominent feature of the landscape.

Climate Over the whole of the pampas the summers are hot, the winters mild, but there is a large climatic difference between various regions, the Atlantic coast being wetter with more moderate temperatures than the interior. South of Buenos Aires around Mar del Plata rain falls all year round and especially in summer. Further south in Bahía Blanca rainfall occurs mainly between October and April. Average daily temperatures along the coast range from 25°C to 14° in Mar del Plata and 30°C to 14°C in Bahía Blanca in summer to 13°C to 5°C in Mar del Plata and 13°C to 3°C in Bahía Blanca in winter. The interior is drier; parts of the western pampas receive as little as 200 mm of rain a year in contrast to over 1,000 mm in Mar del Plata. In Santa Rosa rainfall is heaviest in summer with little in winter. Temperatures in the interior are more variable; summer maxima can reach 40°C and minima can be as low as -8°C.

Wildlife

Chilean flamingos, herons, roseate spoonbills, maguari storks, white- faced Ibis, black-necked swans and coscoroba swans, three species of coots, many species of ducks, the southern screamer and the snail kite inhabit the bodies of water that are found in the pampas and some of the most beautiful birds, such as the many-coloured rush-tyrant and the spectacled tyrant, can be found near aquatic vegetation.

In areas of grassland the greater rhea can still be spotted, though more easy to find are the spotted tinamou, southern lapwing and the guira cuckoo. Birds of prey include the long-winged harrier, the chimango caracara, an opportunistic scavenger and predator. Other species include the burrowing owl, the monk parakeet, which builds huge communal nests, the rufous hornero, which builds an oven nest, the acrobatic fork-tailed flycatcher, the colourful vermilion flycatcher, the aggressive great kiskadee, sandeaters such as the great pampa finch and the grassland yellow finch as well as flocks of cowbirds.

In summer migratory bird species from the northern hemisphere congregate north of Punta Rasa in the lowlands around Bahía Samborombon; these include the red knot, the ruddy turnstone, the white-rumped sandpiper, the hudsonian godwit.

The coypu, a large rodent known locally as the *nutria*, is one of the easiest mammals to find; others include the pampas cavy, the hog-nosed skunk, the white-eared opossum and the grey fox. The pampas deer, an endangered species, is specially proteced in the Reserva Campos del Tuyú.

The Ombu

Native to Argentine Mesopotamia, the Ombu (Phytolacca dioica) was the first tree introduced to the pampas, a status owed to the shade it offered. A vigorous semi-evergreen, it can grow to 20-m high with branches extending over 30 m. Deriving its name from the Guaraní word

for shade, it is also known as the Red Ink plant or Virginian Poke. It has large poplar shaped leaves with racemes of green flowers and dark purple berries. It is a member of the pokeweed family which are all known for the medicinal properties of their leaves, flowers, and bark.

Economy

Agriculture is still central to the economy of the pampas. Buenos Aires province accounts for over half of Argentine cereal production: wheat, maize, sorghum, sunflower seed and soyabeans dominate, though barley for the country's breweries is grown in the Sierra de la Ventana. Over 36% of Argentine livestock are also produced in the province, though there is an important regional division of labour; animals are mainly bred in eastern Buenos Aires and western La Pampa and are fattened in the richer pastures of western Buenos Aires and eastern La Pampa. While the coastal areas, especially around Mar del Plata, rely heavily on tourism, Necochea and Mar del Plata have large fishing fleets; the latter is home to three-quarters of Argentina's trawler fleet and to fish processing industries. Mining is centred in the hills around Olavarria, Azul and Tandil while the petrochemical industry is important to Bahía Blanca, which is an important grain exporting port.

History

When the Spaniards arrived in Argentina the pampas was covered by tall coarse grasses. The cattle and horses they brought with them were soon to roam wild and in time transformed the Indian's way of life. The only part of the pampas occupied by the settlers was the so-called Rim, between the Río Salado, south of the capital, and the Paraná-Plata rivers. Here, on large *estancias*, cattle, horses and mules in great herds roamed the open range. There was a line of forts along the Río Salado: a not very effective protection against marauding Indians. The Spaniards had also brought European grasses with them; these soon supplanted the coarse native grasses, and formed a green carpet which stopped abruptly at the Río Salado.

In the second half of the 19th century the growing urban population of Europe created a demand for cheap food which spurred the occupation and exploitation of the pampas (as well as parts of the United States, Canada and Australia). Agricultural machinery and barbed wire, well-drilling machines and windpumps, roads, railways, and ocean-going steamships, canning and refrigeration all enabled Argentina to become a major exporter of beef, lamb, wheat and wool. By the 1920s the country was the 'breadbasket of the world', with over 23 million ha of land under the plough, 50 million cattle and 30 million sheep.

The transformation of the pampas had important social consequences. Though some politicians argued for colonization schemes which would give immigrants access to smaller landholdings, such schemes were always relegated to poor land, zones near Indian territory or areas some distance from railway lines. From the 1820s onwards governments distributed land, often at very low prices but in such large holdings that only the wealthy could afford to buy. This practice was continued after the 'Conquest of the Wilderness', a war

The Pampas

☞ *Beef, beef and yet more beef*

Though Argentina is famous for beef, cattle were not indigenous to the pampas. After Martín de Garay's expedition brought cattle from Paraguay, the animals roamed wild on the plains, reproducing so quickly that by 1780 their numbers were put at 40 million. By then the pampas Indians were driving herds through the Andean passes to trade with the Mapuche of southern Chile, while gauchos with dogs and boleadoras (lasso with balls) were slaughtering cattle by the thousand for their hides. These were staked out in the sun to dry, while the meat was left to rot.

Such wasteful methods came to an end after 1810 with the opening of saladeros (salting-plants). Hides were exported to Europe as was tallow (animal fat) which was used for candles; the meat was turned into charqui, strips of beef, dried and salted, which were sold to feed the slaves in Brazil and Cuba. Sources of salt were vital to this process and the routes to the salt flats (Salinas Grandes) of southern Buenos Aires province became a key consideration in relations with the Indians.

Although technical developments created the opportunity for Argentina to feed the growing demand for beef in Europe, it was also essential that cattle-farmers improve their herds by introducing new breeds to replace the scrawny pampas cattle and alfalfa was sown as it was better fodder than the native grasses.

The main breeds of cattle which can be seen today were all introduced from Europe. The first Shorthorn bull was imported by the English landowner, John Miller, in 1836. The Hereford, introduced from England in 1862, proved a fine beef

animal, hardy and used to the varied climate of the south: it can be distinguished by its red body and white face and legs. The Aberdeen Angus, also a fine beef animal, was favoured by farmers and railway companies as it has no horns and could be transported by rail more easily. First introduced in 1879, it is very common throughout Buenos Aires province and is distinguished by its black coat. The Holando Argentino, a mixture of breeds from the Netherlands and Switzerland, is the main milk-producer.

Shorthorn

Hereford

Aberdeen Angus

against the Indians in 1878-83 which virtually exterminated them and opened up vast new tracts of the pampas to commercial agriculture. Large *estancias* were often rented out to tenant-farmers who performed the hard work of breaking up the soil by ploughing, destroying pampas grass and replacing it with new strains of grass before their tenancies ended. As a result the pampas did not acquire a population of immigrant smallholders or homesteaders as the United States did.

WH Hudson on the Pampas

Some of the best descriptions of the pampas before their transformation by railways and wire, are to be found in the works of WH Hudson.

"We see all round us a flat land, its horizon a perfect ring of misty blue colour where the crystal-blue dome of the sky rests on the level green world. Green in late autumn, winter and spring, or say from April to November, but not all like a green lawn or field; there were smooth areas where sheep had pastured, but the surface varied greatly and was mostly more or less rough. In places the land as far as one could see was covered with a dense growth of cardoon thistles, or wild artichoke, of a bluish or grey-green colour, while in other places the giant thistle flourished, a plant with big variegated

green and white leaves, and standing when in flower 6 to 10 feet high."

"On all this visible earth there were no fences, and no trees excepting those which had been planted at the old estancia houses, and these being far apart, the groves and plantations looked like small islands of trees, or mounds, blue in the distance, on the great plain or pampa. They were mostly shade trees, the commonest being the Lombardy poplar, which of all trees is the easiest one to grow in that land. And these trees at the estancias or cattle-ranches were, at the time I am writing about, almost invariably aged and in many instances in an advanced state of decay."

WH Hudson, Far Away and Long Ago, Dent, 1985

Since the peak of agricultural exports in the 1920s the economy of the pampas has suffered successive crises, brought on by the Great Depression and changes in the world economy. British entry to the European Union deprived Argentina of what had been her most important market just after an epidemic of foot and mouth disease in Britain, traced to a tin of Argentine corned beef, had led to a ban on beef exports to Britain and a stigma that Argentina still struggles to cast off: only in 1995 was she able to declare herself free of the disease.

Major routes across the Pampas

South to Mar del Plata

Route 2 runs south, past the coastal city of La Plata, through Chascomús and Dolores to Mar del Plata (see page 151), the most famous Argentine seaside resort.

Chascomús lies on a wide plain on the northern shore of Lago Chascomús, one of a group of lakes known as the Lagunas Encadenadas. Around Plaza Independencia are the colonial-style **Municipalidad** and, next door, the **Teatro Nacional Brazzola**. Southeast of the plaza is the **Capilla de los Negros** (1862) which functioned as a religious centre for the local black community ■ *Visits daily 1000-1200, 1700-1900.* West of the plaza is the **Parque Libres del Sud**. In the park is the **Museo Pampeano** which focuses on the Battle of Chascomús and has sections on natural history and early colonization. Beyond the park to the south and east along the shores of the lake runs the pleasant costanera. On the far side of the lake is **La Alameda 1789**, a tourist complex based in a former *estancia* with sports facilities.

Chascomús
Phone code: 02241
Colour map 4, grid B6
Population: 22,200
126 km S of Buenos Aires

Covering 3,000 ha, Lago Chascomús swells greatly in size during the rains. Its slightly brackish water is an important breeding place for *pejerrey* fish, though these have declined due to the introduction of carp. Amateur fishing competitions are held in the winter season. There is a boat club and a regatta

The conquest of the wilderness

Until the 1870s the Indians of the pampas controlled large parts of present-day Argentina, forcing the government in Buenos Aires to defend two frontiers: one in the north which ran west from Santa Fe through Córdoba province and then north towards Santiago del Estero, the other in the south which ran from Azul and Junín west to San Luis and Mendoza. After independence only one campaign was launched against the Indians, in the early 1830s by Rosas in southern Buenos Aires province.

In the 1870s pressure began to grow within the Argentine government for a campaign to defeat the Indians and force their submission to rule from Buenos Aires. However the withdrawal of Argentine troops from the frontier to fight in the War of the Triple Alliance led to a series of increasingly audacious Indian raids. In one of these in 1868, the Indian chief Calfucurá led 2,000 warriors in an attack in Córdoba province which made off with 20,000 head of cattle and 200 prisoners. Altogether this province was attacked nine times in 1868.

With the ending of the War of the Triple Alliance, the Argentine government moved to resist the Indians. Adolfo Alsina, Minister of War, drew up a plan for a chain of forts connected by a moat and ramparts, now known as the Zanja de Alsina. After Alsina's death in 1877, he was replaced by Julio Roca, who had criticized Alsina's plans as too defensive and had called for a war of extermination.

Roca's campaign of 1879 was launched with 8,000 troops in five divisions, one of them led by Roca himself. In a swift offensive five important Indian chiefs were captured along with 1,300 warriors and 2,300 more were killed or wounded. Roca, who expressed the view that "it is a law of nature that the Indian succumb to the impact of civilised man", destroyed villages and forced the inhabitants to choose between exile in Chile or entering reservations. After the campaign the mountain passes to Chile were closed and remaining Indians were forced onto reservations.

Although victory in the "Campaign of the Wilderness" was portrayed as a personal triumph for Roca, it was due more to technological advances. The spread of the telegraph meant that commanders had intelligence reports to offset the Indians' knowledge of the terrain and helped commanders keep in touch with each other. Railways meant that the troops could be supplied quickly. Remington repeating rifles enabled one soldier to take on five Indians and kill them all.

Roca's campaign had important consequences for the whites of Argentina too. Hailed as a hero, Roca was elected President in 1880 and dominated Argentine politics until his death in 1904. More important in the long run was the distribution of conquered land. Roca's campaign had been financed by mortgaging this land in advance: 4,000 bonds were issued, each redeemable by one square league of land but since no one could buy fewer than 4 bonds (costing 4 pesos each) every bond-buyer became potential owner of 25,000 acres at least. Over 20 million hectares of land fell into the hands of about 500 people, many of them friends of Roca.

during Holy Week. Windsurfing is practiced in summer. Further south are two further lakes, La Salada (Km 144) and Lacombe (Km 153), which also offer *pejerrey* fishing, camping and boats for hire.

Sleeping B *Laguna*, Libres del Sur y Maipú, T422808. *Los Vascos*, Av Costanera, T422856. *Nuevo Colón*, Libres del Sur 400, T422567. **C** *El Lago*, Sarmiento y Dolores, T43087. **D** per person *La Toja*, Libres del Sur 102, T422268. **Estancia L** per person *La Mamaia*, 18 km from Chascomús, T/F02241, 424023. Full board, covering 1,000 ha, offering horseriding, swimming pool, cycling and watersports on nearby Lago

Chascomús, *dia de campo* US$60 per person. **Camping** 7 sites, 5 on far side of the lake including *La Alameda*, see above.

Transport Bus To Buenos Aires, US$7, companies: *El Cóndor, El Rápido, Río de la Plata, La Estrella, Antón*. **Train** To **Buenos Aires** (Constitución), 4 daily, US$6 1st class.

Dolores was founded in 1818, destroyed by Indians three years later, and rebuilt. It is a grain and cattle farming centre. Sights include **Museo Libres del Sur**, in the Parque Libres del Sur, which commemorates the revolt of the district against Rosas in the early 19th century. It's interesting and well displayed. ■ *Tue-Sun 100-1700*. Also **Museo de Bellas Artes**, Belgrano 134. ■ *Wed-Sun 1000-1700*.

Dolores
Phone code: 02245
Colour map 4, grid C6
Population: 30,000
204 km S of
Buenos Aires

Sleeping B *Hotel Plaza*, very pleasant. **B-C** *Avenida* Olavarría 362, T47619. 4 blocks from Plaza. Ugly but OK. **Estancias L3** *Haras La Viviana*, 21 km north near Castelli. Full board, watersports, bird-watching, fishing, horseriding. Contact Haras La Viviana, Castelli, Gaspar Campos 671, Vicente López CP138, Prov BsAs, T4541-791-2406. **L3** *Dos Talas*, T443020, F440887. Full board, main house built in 1858, with lovely chapel (copy of Notre Dame de Passy), park designed by Charles Thays, offers horseriding, walking, fishing, cycling, English spoken; dia de campo US$65.

Parrilladas, heladerías & nightlife on Calle Buenos Aires

Transport Bus To Buenos Aires, 3 hrs, Río de la Plata, Buenos Aires 285, Cóndor/La Estrella, Buenos Aires 300 block. **Taxi** Stand at Belgrano y Rico, 1 block from plaza, T43507. **Train** Station 15 mins from centre; to **Buenos Aires**, 4 daily US$8.

Southeast to Bahía Blanca

Route 3 runs southeast via Azul and Tres Arroyos and then east to Bahía Blanca (see page 159).

Azul is an agricultural centre which holds an annual honey festival in June. Around the attractive Plaza San Martín are the French Gothic-style **cathedral** (1906) and the neo-classical French-style **Municipalidad**. Southwest of the centre, along the river are the **Parque Municipal Sarmiento**, with over 200 tree species, and the **Balneario Municipal**. **Museo Etnográfico**, Alvear y San Martín, two blocks northwest of Plaza San Martín, contains a collection of Mapuche silverware and textiles. The tourist office is at Avenida 25 de Mayo 619, T431751.

Azul
Population: 62,000
Phone code: 02281
264 km SW of
Buenos Aires

Azul centre

Sleeping B *Gran Azul*, Colón 626, T422011, excellent cafetéria. **C** *Res Blue*, Mitre 983, T422742, near bus terminal. *Argentino*, Yrigoyen 378, T425953. *Torino*, San Martín 1000, T422749. **Camping** Municipal site, in the Balneario Municipal, hot showers, pleasant, US$2 per person.

The Pampas

The Virgin of Luján

In 1620 a terracotta image of the Virgin was being carried by ox cart from church to church in the area. The cart got stuck and the strenuous efforts of men and oxen to move it all failed. This was taken as a sign that the Virgin willed she should stay there. A chapel was built for the image, and around it grew Luján. The Virgin of Luján, adopted as the virgin of Argentina, Paraguay and Uruguay, has made the city into a major pilgrimage spot. The chapel has long since been superseded by an impressive neo-Gothic basilica.

Southwest to Neuquen

Route 5 runs southwest via Luján, Chivilcoy, Pehuajó and Trenque Lauquen to Santa Rosa de la Pampa.

Luján
Phone code: 02323
Colour map 4, grid B5
Population: 56,500
66 km W of the capital

Behind the cabildo is the river, with restaurants & pleasant river walks & cruises

Museo Histórico Colonial is one of the most interesting museums in the country

Luján is a place of pilgrimage and a very popular spot for weekend trips from Buenos Aires. The **basilica** (1887-1932), rising to 107 m with its twin towers rising to 107 m and stained glass windows, stands on Plaza Belgrano. Its bells were made in Italy from guns used in the First World War. Inside the Virgin stands on the High Altar. Each arch of the church is dedicated to an Argentine province, and the transepts to Uruguay, Paraguay and Ireland. Just off the plaza is the 18th-century Cabildo, the town council building, and next to it, the Casa del Virrey, an 18th-century mansion occupied by the Viceroy escaping the British invasion of 1806. Both buildings are now occupied by museums: **Museo Histórico Colonial** traces the historical and political development of Argentina and includes sections on Argentine presidents, indigenous peoples and gauchos. ■ *Wed-Sat 1200-1730, US$1.* **Museo del Transporte**, containing the best collection of carriages in Argentina as well as *La Porteña*, the first railway engine to operate in the country. ■ *Wed-Sun 1200-1800.* **Salón del Automóvil**, with a large collection of veteran cars in good condition. ■ *Daily 1200-1800, US$2.* **Museo de Bellas Artes**, poor.

Numerous restaurants along the river bank & just off the plaza

Sleeping and eating **B** ***Centro***, Francia 1062, T420667, without breakfast. **B** ***Eros***, San Martín 129, T420797, F21265. Without breakfast, good beds. ***La Paz***, 9 de Julio 1054, T424034. **D** per person ***Carena***, Lavalle 114, T423828. Poor beds, overpriced. Several others around the terminal including **C** ***Venezia***, Alte Brown 100, basic. ***City*** and ***Biarritz***, better. An excellent restaurant is ***L'Eau Vive***, on the road to Buenos Aires at Constitución 2112. It is run by nuns, pleasant surroundings. Another good one is ***La Basílica***, San Martín 101.

Transport **Bus** From **Buenos Aires** (Plaza Once), bus 52, frequent, 2 hrs, US$3.70 or direct service, 1 hr, US$5.50. To **San Antonio de Areco**, 3 a day, US$4, *Empresa Argentina*, 1 hr. **Train** Regular service run by Trenes de Buenos Aires from Once station, Buenos Aires, US$1.50, 2 hrs.

Santa Rosa de Pampa
Phone code: 02954
Colour map 4, grid C2
Population: 70,000
663 km from Buenos Aires

Santa Rosa is the capital of La Pampa province, founded in 1892. The **Teatro Español**, Lagos 44, dates from 1908. Ten blocks west of the Plaza San Martín is Laguna Don Tomás and a park with sports facilities. **Museo de Ciencias Naturales**, Pellegrini 180, displays on archaeology, flora and fauna. ■ *Mon-Fri 0800-1700.* **Museo de Artes**, 9 de Julio 305. ■ *Mon-Fri 0800-1200, Sat 1800-2100.*

The **Parque Luro**, 32 km south of Santa Rosa, covers over 6,500 ha. This provincial park occupies the former estate of Pedro Luro, a local landowner, who

created his own hunting grounds and introduced European species such as the Carpathian red deer and the wild boar. Luro's mansion, a central European style *chateau*, can be visited. Opposite is a *Centro de Interpretación Ecológico*, with displays on the flora and fauna of the Pampas. Nearby is the **Museo de Carruajes**, with a collection of carriages. ■ *Daily 0900-2000. Campsite.*

Sleeping and eating A *Calfucura*, San Martín 695, T423608. 4-star. **C** *Hostería Río Atuel*, Luro 256, opposite terminal, T422597, very good. **D** *San Martín*, Alsina 101, clean, restaurant, parking. **D** *Motel Calden*, Eva Perón y Ferinatti, T424311. Large rooms, good restaurant. **Camping** Municipal site near the Laguna Don Tomás.

Tourist office San Martín y Luro, opposite terminal.

Transport Bus Terminal at San Martín y Luro, 7 blocks east of Plaza San Martín. To Buenos Aires US$25, 8 hrs. To Neuquén, 8 hrs, US$25. **Train** To **Buenos Aires** (Once) Sun, Tue, Thu 1900, 11 hrs, Pullman US$25, First US$20, Tourist US$17.

Route 35 runs south from Santa Rosa to Bahía Blanca, 323 km. At Km 73 Route 152 branches off towards Neuquén. At Km 25 a road leads to **General Acha** after which desert has to be crossed either on Route 20 to Cruz del Desierto and Catriel (no fuel on this stretch), then on to Route 151 to Neuquén, or on Route 152 to Chelforó on Route 22.

South of Santa Rosa de Pampa

Parque Nacional Lihue Calel is situated 240 km southeast of Santa Rosa and 120 km from General Acha and reached by asphalted Route 152. This national park covers 9,901ha of low hills which reach a height of 590 m. Though located in the middle of desert and receiving only 400 mm of rain annually, the park is home to a wide variety of plant species, including a number of unique species of cactus. Wildlife includes pumas, the patagonian hare, vizcachas, guanacos and rheas as well as a wide variety of birds. There are geometric cave paintings of Tehuelche origin over 2,000 years old in the Valle de los Pinturas and the Valle de Namencurá. There are also the ruins of the Estancia Santa María. You are required to keep to the authorized footpaths. **Sleeping** *ACA Hostería* with restaurant, 2 km south of park entrance. **Camping** Site near entrance, good facilities.

The park is best visited in Spring The name derives from the Mapuche for 'place of life'

Santa Rosa

West to San Luis

Route 7 runs west from Buenos Aires via Luján and Junín to San Luis (see page 184).

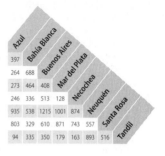

	Azul	Bahía Blanca	Buenos Aires	Mar del Plata	Necochea	Neuquén	Santa Rosa	Tandil
	397							
	264	688						
	273	464	408					
	246	336	513	128				
	935	538	1215	1001	874			
	803	329	610	871	743	557		
	94	335	350	179	163	893	516	

The Pampas: distance chart (km)

Junín
Phone code: 02362
Colour map 4, grid B4
Population: 63,700
256 km W of Buenos Aires

Junín was founded as a fort in 1827. Its main claim to fame is that Eva Perón lived here between the ages of 11 and 15 before moving to Buenos Aires. Near Junín are several lakes including Laguna de Gómez, 12 km west and Laguna el Carpincho, 4 km west, where there is good fishing.

Sleeping and eating A2 *Copahue*, Saavedra 80, T423390, F29041. Faded, ACA discount. *Embajador*, Sáenz Peña y Pellegrini, T421433. Good food is served at *Paraje del Sauce*, Km 258 on Route 7, picturesque but 'don't stop there if you are in a rush' and *El Quincho de Martín*, B de Miguel y Ruta 7.

Transport Train To **Buenos Aires** (Retiro), Fri, Sun 1813, 5 hrs, First US$9, Tourist US$8.

At **Rufino**, 452 km, is the recommended **L** *Hotel Astur*, Córdoba 81, **C** with ACA discount and at **Laboulaye**, 517 km, there are several good and cheap hotels, for example *Victoria*.

Northwest to Cordoba

There are two main routes: Route 9 (713 km) via Rosario (see page 306250) and Villa María (see page 174) and the longer Route 8 (835 km) via San Antonio de Areco, Pergamino, Venado Tuerto, 370 km, and Río Cuarto (see page 175).

San Antonio de Areco
Phone code: 02326
Colour map 4, grid B5
Population: 15,000
113 km NW of Buenos Aires

San Antonio is an attractive town of single-storey buildings, tree-lined streets and a popular costanera. It is a popular centre for visiting *estancias*. Many handicrafts are sold, mainly *gaucho* objects, ceramics, silver, leather, colonial-style furniture.

The **Museo Gauchesco Ricardo Güiraldes**, on Camino Güiraldes y Aureliano, is a modern replica of a typical *estancia* of the late 19th century, containing artefacts associated with gaucho life. ■ *Daily except Tue, 1000-1800*. Güiraldes, a sophisticated member of Parisian literary circles, was an Argentine nationalist who romanticized *gaucho* life. He was born in Paris in 1886 but spent much of his early life on the *Estancia La Porteña*, 8 km from San Antonio. After periods in Paris, where he studied architecture and law, he settled on the estancia. His best-known book, *Don Segundo Sombra* (1926), was set in San Antonio: the *Estancia La Porteña* and sites in the town such as the old bridge and the *Pulpería La Blanqueada* (at the entrance to the museum), became famous through its pages. Güiraldes died in 1927.

Many parrillas on the bank of the Río Areco

Sleeping and eating B *San Carlos*, Zapiola y Zerbione, T453106. Ask in advance for meals. **D** *Res Areco*, Segundo Sombra y Rivadavia, T422166. Good, comfortable, 15% ISIC and GO 25% discounts. *Res El Hornero*, Moreno y San Martín, T42733. **Estancias LL** *La Bamba*, T456293 or Buenos Aires T48069280, www.la-bamba.com Full board. The second oldest *estancia* in Argentina, day visits with *asado* US$70. **LL** *El Ombú*, T492080 or Buenos Aires T48360800, elombu@sinectis.com.ar Full board, beautiful,

The authentic Gaucho town?

Though authentic is an overused word, it best describes San Antonio; a country town set in one of the most fertile areas of the pampas, it has no frills and few hotels; a lick of paint wouldn't go amiss and if you object to flying things or the occasional cockroach in the night, then this isn't for you.

One of the oldest towns in this part of Argentina, San Antonio dates back to the early 17th century and the local school is still run by Irish nuns. In one of the side streets it is still possible to find a pulpería:

in the dark interior, next to the fruit and vegetables, is a small bar around which there are usually a cluster of present day gauchos, wearing the traditional bombachas (baggy trousers) and red neckerchiefs. In the main street there is a silversmith, still making, by hand, the ornamental belt buckles and facones (knives) worn by the gauchos. Nearby are several leather shops and a wonderful old saddlery with the ceilings and walls covered with bridles and boots.

ivy-covered *estancia*. Day visit US$70. **LL** *La Porteña*, T453770, F454157, Buenos Aires T48221325, full board, pool, riding. **L** per person *Los Patricios*, 4 km from town, T/F453823. Caters to groups only. **AB** *La Cinacina*, T452773, aircampo@netline.net.ar Half-board. Mainly caters to day visits which include typical lunch and riding display, recommended. *Don Silvano*, Buenos Aires 47672590, no accommodation, day visit US$20. **Camping** Municipal site at Zapiola y Zerboni, near river. *Club River* on Costanera. *Auto-camping La Porteña*, T43402, 8 km from town on the Güiraldes *estancia*, good access roads.

Festivals *Día de la Tradición*, 10 Nov, is a *gaucho* festival with traditional parades, games, events on horseback, music and dance. There are celebrations throughout the week beforehand (accommodation is hard to find).

Tourist office Arellano 115, T452015, www.arecoturismo.com.ar

Transport Bus From Buenos Aires from Plaza Once, 2 hrs, US$4, every hr; also Chevallier from Retiro bus terminal, US$6, 2 hrs.

The Southern Sierras

Sierra de Tandil

This range of hills runs southeast from near Azul towards the coast near Mar del Plata, a distance of 340 km.

Tandil, situated 350 km south of Buenos Aires and 171 km northwest of Mar del Plata, was founded in 1823 as a fortress. Lying at the heart of the sierras and enjoying a cool, dry climate this city, with its cobbled streets, a relaxed pace and mountain views, is an attractive and convenient base for climbing and exploring the surrounding area. On the south side of the main Plaza Independencia are the neoclassical **Municipalidad** (1923) and **Banco Hipotecario Nacional** (1924) and the **Iglesia del Santisimo Sacramento**, inspired by the Sacre Coeur in Paris. West of the plaza on the outskirts of town is **Cerro Calvario** with the stages of the cross leading to the **Capilla Santa Gemma**, on top. Six blocks south of the plaza, on a hill and offering fine views, is the **Parque Independencia**, with a granite entrance in Moorish style, built by the local Italian community to celebrate the town's centenary. Inside the

Tandil
Phone code: 02293
Colour map 4, grid C5
Population: 125,000

The Pampas

park is a Moorish style castle, built by the Spanish community to mark the same event. South of the park is the **Lago del Fuerte**, where watersports are practised. Another hill **Cerro Centinela**, famous for the giant boulder on top, lies southeast of the Parque Independencia (see box).

Museums Museo Municipal de Bellas Artes, Chacabuco 367, containing works by Argentine artists and a few early 20th-century European works. **Museo Fuerte Independencia**, 4 de Abril 485, displaying a collection of local artefacts including carriages and a reconstruction of a *pulpería*.

Excursions To the **Reserva Natural Sierra del Tigre**, 6 km south, 140 ha, which protects the Cerro Venado, from which there are good views over Tandil. Foxes and guanacos can be seen and there is a small zoo.

Sleeping B *Cabañas Manantial de las Amores*, T45701, F28653, with breakfast, also horseriding, cycle hire, tours. **B** *Libertador*, Mitre 545, T422127, central, good value. **B** *Plaza*, General Pinto 438, T427160. Comfortable and quiet. **C** *Kaiku*, Mitre 902, T423114, basic. **Estancia** *Acelain*, 54 km north of Tandil, Buenos Aires T4322-2784.

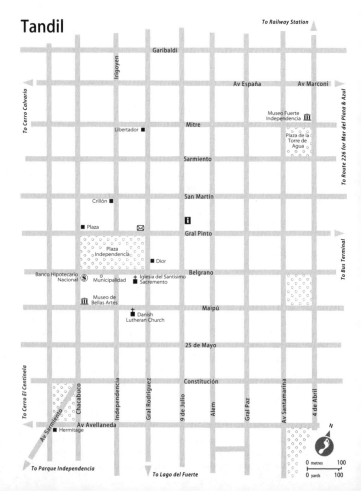

The legend of El Centinela

In the early days of European settlement at Tandil, some soldiers heard the story of a strange and beautiful girl called Amaika who was able to disappear whenever she realized she was being watched. Amaika, who had been brought up by her white father after her Indian mother had died, was regarded as a kind of goddess by the Indians. An Indian boy, the son of a chief, strong and very tall, sat and watched Amaika every day and, as the two fell in love, she began to leave her hiding place more often to sit with him.

Two white soldiers decided to capture the girl. Her frequent appearances to be with the Indian boy gave them the chance to discover her hiding place and seize her. They carried her off to the fort but on arrival she escaped into the night. There was a splash in the deep moat surrounding the fort and Amaika was assumed to have drowned, unable to swim because her arms were tied up.

Though Amaika was never seen again, high up on the hill the Indian boy continued to stand in the vain hope that she might appear. As he waited, standing there in all weathers, he began to look more and more like a rock until one day, miraculously, he was transformed into the enormous rock known as 'El Centinela'.

Andalusian-style mansion dating from 1922, with gardens inspired by the Generalife in Granada and 800 ha of park, offering luxury accommodation, horseriding, polo, watersports. **Camping** *Pinar de la Sierra*, south of the Parque Independencia. *Español*, Rodriguez 543, T425112, US$4 per person. Many others. Restaurants include *El Estribo*, San Martín 759, good atmosphere. Recommended. North of Tandil is *Estancia Acelain*, restaurant and luxury accommodation.

Festivals Holy Week celebrations are outstanding and attract large numbers of visitors: book accommodation in advance.

Transport Air *Lapa* flies 3 times a week to Buenos Aires in summer. **Bus** To Buenos Aires, 6 hrs, US$15. **Train** To Buenos Aires and Bahía Blanca, daily.

Sierra de la Ventana

Situated some 100 km north of Bahía Blanca and running northwest to southeast for some 175 km, this is the highest range of hills in the pampas. It is a popular area for excursions from Bahía Blanca.

Tornquist has an attractive church on the central plaza and an artificial lake. It is a good starting point for excursions into the sierra. Nearby is the Tornquist family mansion, built in a mixture of French styles. Of Swedish origin, Ernesto Tornquist (1842-1908) was the son of a Buenos Aires merchant. Under his leadership the family established the industrial investment bank which still bears his name. Tornquist helped to establish the country's first sugar refinery, meat packing plant and several chemical

Tornquist
Phone code: 0291
Colour map 4, grid C4
Population: 5,672
70 km N of Bahía
Blanca by Route 33

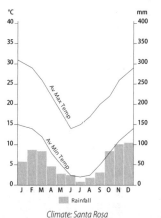

Climate: Santa Rosa

firms. Sleeping at **B** *Gran Central*, 9 de Julio 242, T940035. Seedy but friendly, expensive breakfast. Campsite, US$4 per person. ■ *Getting there: To Buenos Aires and Bahía Blanca daily.*

Parque Provincial Ernesto Tornquist Covering 6,718 ha, 25 km east of Tornquist, this park began with a donation of 3,228 ha by the Tornquist family to the provincial government in 1937. The entrance is marked by the massive ornate iron gates from the Tornquist family home. Nearby is the *Centro de Interpretación Ecológica*, which offers displays, videos and talks. From here it is a three-hour climb to the summit of **Cerro Ventana**, 1,136 m, which offers fantastic views from the 'window' in the summit ridge. Other peaks include Cerro Bahía Blanca, Cerro Chato and Cerro Volante.

Wildlife includes grey foxes, guanacos, pumas and eagles as well as wild horses and red deer. One section of the park is a restricted area in which there are two caves; the **Cueva del Toro** and the **Cueva de las Pinturas Rupestres** which contains petroglyphs. ■ *Excursions are offered from the Centro de Interpretación on Fri and Sun 0900 US$2, 5 hrs.*

Villa Ventana, 10 km east of the Centro de Interpretación on the edge of the park, is a small settlement and the base for climbing **Cerro Tres Picos** (1,239 m), to the south of the park, which is the highest peak in Buenos Aires province. The ruins of the *Hotel Club Casino*, which, when built in 1911 was the most luxurious hotel in Argentina, can be seen; it burned down in 1983. There is an excellent teashop, *Casa de Heidi*, and wholefood is sold at the *Jardín de Aylem*.

Sleeping *El Mirador*, at park entrance, T4941338, 4-star. East of the park on Route 76 are: *La Espadaña*, *Bungalows El Pinar*. **Camping** *Campamento Base*, near entrance, also has dormitory accommodation, T091-940288, hospitable. Municipal site in Villa Ventana, all facilities.

Sierra de la Ventana

● ●

Red flags and white flags

Originally a rural trading post, the pulpería also served as a bar and social club, selling alcoholic drinks, tobacco and hierba maté. A white flag was hung outside to indicate to people at a distance that these were available. A red flag indicated that meat was for sale. The only social institution in many small communities, the pulpería also served as

a bank, the pulpero (or barman) becoming the local money-lender. As the pampas were settled, pulperías were often located near railway stations. The name derives from pulque, the Mapuche word for liquor. Pulperías were frequently violent places: there were always iron bars to protect the pulpero from thieves and discontented customers.

● ●

The town of Sierra de la Ventana, 15 km east of the park at the confluence of the Ríos Sauce Grande, Negro and San Bernardo, is another good centre for exploring the hills. Tres Picos, rising bare and barren from the rich farmlands, is only 6,250 m away. There is a nine-hole golf course, and good trout fishing in the Río Sauce Grande. Excellent tourist information.

Sierra de la Ventana
Colour map 4, grid C4
Population: 900

Sleeping A3 *Provincial*, Drago y Malvinas, T4915025. **D** *La Perlita*, San Martín y Roca, T4915020. **E** per person *Yapay*, Av San Martín near bus terminal, quiet. Recommended. **Youth hostels** *Albergue Sierra de la Ventana* (sleeping bag necessary). **Camping** 3 sites.

Transport Bus To **Buenos Aires**, La Estrella, 1 a day; to **Bahía Blanca**, 2 a day (1 on Sat).

Situated at the northern end of the Sierra, 59 km north of Tornquist, Pigüé is an alternative base for exploring this area with a car. It has a **Museo Regional**, with photographs of the 'Conquest of the Wilderness'. **Sleeping** at *Gran Hotel Pigüé*, España 229, T472460, 3-star and **C** *Central*, San Martín y Belgrano, T473140, friendly.

Pigüé

North of Sierra De La Ventana

Route 33 runs north from Pigüé through a group of lakes known as the **Lagunas del Oeste**, before meeting Route 5, the Buenos Aires-Santa Rosa highway at Trenque Lauquen. The Lagunas del Oeste are popular for fishing: the two main towns for visiting this area are Guaminí and Carhué.

Guaminí is a pleasant summer hill resort on the shore of Laguna del Monte, 202 km north of Bahía Blanca. Sleeping at *Res Turis Guaminí*, San Martín y Alem, T42281 and there is a Municipal campsite at the lakeside.

Guaminí
Population: 3,500

Carhué is a resort situated 38 km west of Guaminí. North of the town is Lago Epecuén, which covers over 10,000 ha and is over 20 times saltier than the sea. It's waters are too salty for fish, and are recommended for the treatment of chronic rheumatism and skin diseases. The ghost town of **Villa Epecuén**, a former health resort 8 km north of Carhué, drowned by the lake in 1985, can be visited (unpaved road). **Museo Regional Adolfo Alsina**, east of the main plaza, behind the town hall, contains artefacts from the wars against the Indians. The tourist office is in the town hall, T42233, F2632.

Carhué
Phone code: 02936
Colour map 4, grid C3
Population: 18,000

Sleeping B *Shalom*, Belgrano 880, T42503, near terminal. 'Eccentric but clean', breakfast extra. *Avenida*, Alsina 1185, T42707. *Termas Carhué*, Dorrego 520,

The Pampas

T/F42887. *Buenos Aires*, Urquiza 313, T42312. *Res Edith*, Mitre 741, T42471. Heating, cafetéria. *Res Isabel García de Sanz*, Dorrego 659, T42438. *Res Maruja*, Alvear 730, T42066. *Res Epecuén*, Martín y Alsina, T42991, restaurant. Restaurant at bus terminal is reasonable. **Camping** Municipal site 9 blocks northwest of main plaza, with *Del Quincho los Almaceneros*, opposite, showers, store. Also at *Balneario La Isla*, on the shores of the lake, full services. *La Chacra*, 5 km east, in 50ha of park, full services.

Transport Bus Terminal one block north of main plaza. To **Buenos Aires**, Empresa Liniers, 9 hrs; to **La Plata**, Empresa Liniers, 10 hrs. To **Mar del Plata**, Pampa, 10 hrs. To **Bahía Blanca**, Ñandú del Sur, 3-4 hrs.

Coastal resorts south of Buenos Aires

Route 36 from Buenos Aires passes La Plata and becomes Route 11 (the *Interbalnearia*) which sweeps around Bahía Samborombón to a string of Atlantic coastal resorts.

San Clemente del Tuyú
Phone code: 02252
Colour map 4, grid C6
Population: 8,000

This is the nearest Atlantic coastal resort to Buenos Aires. It is a family resort with little nightlife and cheaper than the more fashionable resorts further south. To the south of the centre is the **Vivero Cosme Argerich**, a 37 ha park, with woodlands, plant nursery and sports centre. ■ *Daily 1000-1630*. North of the town is **Puerto San Clemente**, a small fishing port with fish restaurants; boats can be hired for fishing trips. North of the port is **Mundo Marino**, the largest oceanarium in South America. Attractions include two orcas, dolphins, elephant seals, sea lions and penguins. ■ *Daily from 1000, closes 1530 May-Sep, 1630 Mar-Apr, Oct-Dec, 1800 Jan-Feb. T421071. Bus 500 from San Clemente.*

Excursions To **Punta Rasa**, 6 km north, where there are an old lighthouse offering superb views over the coast and a nature reserve owned by the Fundación Vida Silvestre, which, in summer, is home to thousands of migratory birds from the northern hemisphere. ■ *US$4.*

The **Reserva Campos del Tuyú** is west of San Clemente, near General Lavalle. Its owned by the Fundación Vida Silvestre, covering 7,500 ha of riverine habitat. Among the wildlife are pampas foxes and the rare pampas deer as well as 150 species of bird including rheas, American swans and flamingoes.

Sleeping and eating The best hotel is *Fontainebleau*, Calle 3, No 2290, 4-star. Several on Av Costanera including *Stella Marina*, T421453. *Costanera*, No 2438, T421110. Several on Calle 1 including **C** *Splendid*, No 2430, T421316 and **B** *Acuario*, San Martín 444, T421357, including breakfast. **C** *Res Bahía*, Calle 4, between Calle 1 and Calle 15, breakfast included, good. Most close out of season. Several campsites. *Restaurante Yo y Vos*, Calle 4 y Calle 17, large and cheap portions, friendly, good.

Tourist offices Calle 2 y 65, T421478.

Transport Bus To **Mar del Plata**, frequent, *Empresa Costamar*, US$11, 5 hrs. To **Buenos Aires**, several companies, US$15-20.

Directory Banks US dollars can be changed at the **Banco de la Provincia de Buenos Aires**, Calle 1 y Calle 4, but TC's are not accepted anywhere in town.

Wild coast

This coast was known by sailors as the costa brava (wild coast); maritime maps advise sailors to keep their distance to avoid the strong tides, sandbanks and the wreckage of over 50 vessels. Some of these wrecks are still visible: the wreck of the Canadian ship Her Royal Highness, sunk in 1883, can be seen at low tide at Las Toninas, as can the remains of the German vessel Margarethe at Mar de Ajó. South of Mar de Ajó, near the Punta Médanos lighthouse, the wreck of the French vessel Karnak, which went down in 1870 can be seen in the dunes.

The Margarethe, wrecked in 1880 when carrying a French theatre company, yielded unusual wreckage. Though crew and passengers were saved, 30 barrels of French wine were lost in the sandbanks. Over 50 years later, when a group of campers drilled a hole for drinking water, their well yielded wine, excellently preserved and extremely drinkable.

South of San Clemente

South of San Clemente is a 65 km stretch of coast lined with resorts and known as the **Atlantida Argentina**, very popular with visitors from Buenos Aires in summer but deserted off seasona and attracting few foreign visitors. The major resorts are **Santa Teresita** (population 9,000; phone code 02246) 17 km south, **Mar del Tuyú** (population 38,000; phone code 02246) 20 km south, **La Lucila del Mar** (phone code 02257) 33 km south, **San Bernardo** (phone code 02257) 35 km south and **Mar de Ajó**, (population 13,000; phone code 02257) 40 km south, which has the largest fishing port on this part of the coast and from where excursions to wrecked vessels are offered.

Sleeping Santa Teresita: best is *Golf Internacional*, Calle 27 y Kennedy, T420469, 4-star. Hotels in centre including *Helénico*, Calle 36 No 238, T420251. *Playa*, Calle 36 No 270, T420579. *Sorrento*, Calle 37 No 35, T420298. Many *hospedajes* including *Alperi*, Calle 2 No 360, T420411. *El Reloj*, Calle 39 No 250, T430536; *Stella Maris*, Calle 39 No 216. **San Bernardo**: best are *Seaboard*, San Bernardo y Chiozza, T461712, 4-star, and *Neptuno Playa*, La Rioja y Hernández, T461789. *Res Ileana*, Chiozza 1621, T460209. Few cheap options. In **Mar de Ajó**: 3-star hotels along Avenida Costanera including *Flamingo*, No 343, T420168. *Mar de Ajó*, No 205, T420023. *Latinoamericano*, No 55, T420254. Cheaper options including *Catalina*, Avenida Costanera 1270, T420249. *Dorin's*, Libertador 166, T420105. *Tupe*, Lebensohn 248, T420189. *Res Asturias*, Montevideo 338. *Saint James*, Montevideo 370. Elsewhere accommodation is more scarce. **Mar del Tuyu**: *Santa Rosa*, Costanera y Calle 68, T420475. *Res Romero*, Calle 58 y 2. **La Lucila del Mar**: *La Maison*, San Juan 5140, T462722. *La Morada del Sol*, San Juan 4878, T462303.

There are lots of hotels in Santa Teresita, San Bernardo & Mar de Ajó

Camping Lots of sites. North of Santa Teresita is *Autocamping El Carmen*, T420220. **Mar del Tuyú** *Camping Mar del Tuyú*, Calle 94 y Calle 13. **San Bernardo** *Weekend*, Gutiérrez y Salta, T460478. In **Mar de Ajó** there is a ACA site next to the plaza and a municipal site 7 blocks south of the plaza.

Pinamar

Pinamar is one of the most attractive resorts with 22 km of beach, a golf course and good water-skiing. Fish, including conger eel (*congrio*) may be bought on the beach from local fishermen. Nearby is the Reserva Dunícola, with sand dunes up to 30-m high. The *estancias* La Victoria and Dos Montes can be visited.

Phone code: 02254
Colour map 4, grid C6
Population: 10,000
89 km S of San Clemente

The Pampas

Excursions   **Ostende**, 6 km south, was founded by Belgian entrepreneurs in 1908 but abandoned when the settlers returned to Belgium on the outbreak of the First World War. The only building surviving from that period is the **Viejo Hotel Ostende**, formerly the Hotel Termas, which was a favourite of Antoine de Saint-Exupéry. Another hotel, **Atlantic City**, unfinished in 1914, now functions as a youth hostel.

General Madariaga is 28 km inland and is where the *Fiesta Nacional del Gaucho* is celebrated on the first weekend in December with processions, singing and dancing. The **Museo del Tuyú**, in the former railway station, has displays of rural artefacts, paintings and local handicrafts. Nearby is the **Estancia Charles Viejo** where a collection of carriages can be seen. From General Madariaga the **Laguna Salada Grande**, the largest lake in the province and be visited; here there is a 40 hectare nature reserve protecting the southernmost examples of the tala.

Sleeping   **AL** *Playas*, Bunge y de la Sirena, T482236, F82226. With breakfast, English spoken. Many, from *Arenas*, Bunge 700, T482444, 4-star, to *Berlín*, Rivadavia 326, T482320. *Sardegna*, Jasón 840, T482760. *Boulogna*, Jasón 523, T482242, all 1-star. All hotels are fully booked throughout Jan-Mar. Houses and apartments can be rented from Dec-Mar: 2-room flats about US$1,000 per month, up to US$5,000 for a mansion. In Mar rates are halved. **Ostende**: best is *Savoia*, Biarritz y Progreso, T486453, 4-star. *Viejo Ostende*, Biarritz y El Cairo, T486081, 3-star. *Rambla*, Biarritz 16, T486028. **Youth hostels** Nuestras Malvinas y Sarmiento, T482908. **Camping** 3 sites all in Ostende (take green *Montemar* bus from terminal): *Saint Tropez*, US$18 per site. *Quintana* and *Nuestras Malvinas*.

Tourist office   Bunge 700.

Transport   **Bus** Terminal 4 blocks north of main plaza. To **Buenos Aires**, Antón, US$20, Río de la Plata US$23, Plusmar *coche cama* US$26. **Train** To **Buenos Aires** (Constitución), US$23 first, US$18 *turista*.

Villa Gesell   Villa Gesell is a modern resort named after the man who planned it in the
Phone code: 02255   1940s, the furniture manufacturer, Carlos Gesell. It is particularly popular
Colour map 4, grid C6   with younger people; it has a chocolate factory, fine beaches, watersports facil-
Population: 16,000   ities and over 100 hotels. In season it is very busy. In January 1994 it attracted
22 km S of Pinamar

Villa Gesell

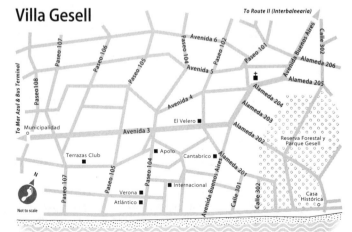

700,000 visitors. Villa Querandi, south, is more simple and peaceful. The **Reserva Forestal y Parque Gesell**, at the northern end of Avenida 3, includes the Casa Histórica, Carlos Gesell's mansion, which functions as a museum. West of the reserve is an open-air amphitheatre where performances are given.

Sleeping *Terrazas Club*, 4-star, suite accommodation, Av 2 entre Calle 104 y 105, T463214. *Colón*, 1-star, Av 4, Calle 104, T462310, restaurant. **A** *Hostería Alpina*, Calle 307 y Alameda 206, T458066, with breakfast, English spoken. **B** *Hostería Gran Chalet*, Paseo 105 No 447 y Av 4-5, T462913, recommended. **C** *Bero*, Av 4 y Calle 141, T466077, opposite bus terminal. **E** per person *Hosp San Hector*, Av 8, No 641, T462052. Many others of all classes. Many apartments for rent (rates as Pinamar). **Youth hostels** *Albergue Camping El Coyote*, Alameda 212 y 306, Barrio Norte, T468448. **Camping** Many sites, including 3 off Av Buenos Aires, north of the centre.

Most hotels are between Avenida 3 & the beach

Sport **Horseriding**: *Tante Puppi*, Blvd y Paseo 102.

Tourist offices In the Municipalidad on Av 3.

Transport **Air** From **Buenos Aires**, *Austral*, US$85, *LAER*, US$60. **Buses** Terminal at Av 3 y Paseo 140, south of town. Direct to Buenos Aires, US$21, *Empresa Antón* and Río de la Plata, book in advance at weekends.

Mar del Plata

The most famous Argentine resort dating from the turn of the century, Mar del Plata is 100 km further south and 400 km from the capital. With its 8 km stretch of beach, it attracts about two million visitors every summer (when the nightlife continues all night). For the rest of the year the town is fairly quiet and good value.

Phone code: 0223
Colour map 4, grid C6
Population: 502,000

The most famous area of the city is around **Playa Bristol** where a broad promenade, the **Rambla**, runs past the fine **casino** (upper floor open to the public) and the **Gran Hotel Provincial**, both of which were designed by Bustillo and date from the late 1930s. Six blocks north along Avenida San Martín is the **Plaza San Martín**, flanked by the attractive cathedral.

Sights

The Rambla runs southeast along Playa Bristol towards Punta Piedras, where, on the headland, stands the **Torreón del Monje**, a Norman style mansion built in 1904. Three blocks inland from Punta Piedras, on top of the hill, are other examples of the *pintoresque* architecture of the early years of this century, among them the Norman style **Villa Ortiz Basualdo** (1909) and the mock Tudor **Villa Blaquier** (1905).

South of Punta Piedras are the rocky promontory of **Cabo Corrientes** and the fashionable **Playa Grande**, with its private clubs and the summer mansions of wealthy *porteños*. Further south is the port, reached by bus, 15 minutes from terminal. There is a large fishing fleet and a huge sealion colony can be seen from the *Escollera Sur* (southern breakwater). Beyond the port are the **Punta Mogotes** lighthouse, built in 1891. ■ *Thu 1330-1700* and the **Bosque Peralta Ramos**, a 400 ha forest of eucalyptus and conifers.

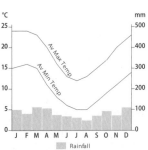

Climate: Mar del Plata

Florentino Ameghino

Born in Luján of Italian parents in 1854, Ameghino started collecting bones and fossils as a boy. Though he lacked any formal scientific training, his reputation spread after he presented his theories to an international congress of archaeologists in Paris in 1878. Before his death in 1911, he published nearly 200 books and articles and became Director of the Museo de Ciencias Naturales in La Plata. He aroused great controversy with his theory that humanity originated and spread from the Argentine pampas.

North of Playa Bristol at **Punta Iglesias** there is a large rock carving of Florentino Ameghino, the palaeontologist. Further north is **Playa La Perla**, with moderately priced hotels. The wooded municipally-owned **Parque Camet**, 8 km north of the centre, has polo grounds and playing fields.

Museums   **Museo de Hombre del Puerto – Cleto Ciocchini**, Padre Dutto 383. Shows the history of the port and its first Sicilian fishermen. ■ *Thu/Fri/Sat 1700-2100, US$2.* **Museo Municipal de Ciencias Naturales**, Libertad 2999, is small but interesting. **Museo Municipal de Arte**, Colón 1189, is housed in the Villa Ortíz Basualdo, which dates from 1909; upper floors of the mansion can be visited, art exhibitions on the ground floor. ■ *Weekdays except Wed 1200-1700, Sat/Sun 1400-1900, US$2, free Tue.* **Centro Cultural Victoria Ocampo**, Matheu 1851, is housed in the Villa Victoria, a beautiful early 20th-century wooden house prefabricated in England, where the famous author spent her summers until her death in 1979; inside are artefacts from her life and temporary exhibition. ■ *Daily 1400-2000, garden opens at 1100, US$2, ISIC cards US$1, free Wed.* **Villa Mitre**, Lamadrid 3870, is in the former mansion of a son of Bartolomé Mitre. Inside are an ecclectic collection of artefacts including photos of the city at different points in its history. **Museo Guillermo Vilas**, Olavarría 2134, is in a beautiful house and concentrate on Vilas' tennis career and the sport in general. ■ *1800-0200, US$5 including video and drink at the bar; also has a high-class restaurant.*

Excursions   **Santa Clara del Mar** is a quiet resort 18 km north, where the **Museo Paleontológico Pachamama**, Niza 1065, can be visited. Beyond, 34 km north, is the **Mar Chiquita**, a lagoon joined to the sea by a narrow channel, offering good beaches, fishing and boating. Also to the Laguna de los Padres and to Balcarce (see below).

Sleeping   There are over 700 hotels and all other categories of accommodation. During summer months it is essential to book in advance. Many hotels open in season only. Out of season, bargain everywhere.

Expensive   AL *Provincial*, Blvd Marítimo 2500, T4916376. Grand hotel overlooking Playa Bristol. **AL** *Argentino*, Belgrano 2225, T432223. Also apartments. Highly recommended. **AL** *Hermitage*, Blvd Maritimo 2657, T4519081, 150 rooms. **AL** *Gran Dora*, Buenos Aires 1841, T4912594. **AL** *Astor*, Entre Ríos 1649, T4921616. Small, no credit cards, 3 mins from beach. **A** *Benedetti*, Colón 2198, T430031/2. Recommended. **A** *Gran Continental*, Córdoba 1929, T48432. **A** *Presidente*, Corrientes 1516, T428819. **AB** *O Sole Mío*, Av Independencia 1277, T426685. Half board, Italian run. Highly recommended.

Midrange B *Cosmos*, Buenos Aires 2481, T4933544, with breakfast. **B** *Boedo*, Almirante Brown 1771, T424695. Hot water, good value, near beaches (open Jan-Feb only). **B** *Canciller*, Gascon 1639, T4512513, with breakfast. **B** *Piemonte*, Buenos Aires 2447, T4954113. With breakfast, good beds. **C** *Monterrey*, Lamadrid 2627, T423266, good. **C** *Niza*, Santiago del Estero 1843, T4951695, (**E** out of season), safe. Recommended. **B** *Alpino*, Balcarce y La Rioja, T4931034. With breakfast, family run, clean, central, open all year. **B** *Europa*, Arenales 2735, T40436. Quiet, hot water. **C** *Hosp Paraná*, Lamadrid 2749, T42825.

Cheaper C *Paley*, Alberti 1752, T4955036. Comfortable, open all year, recommended, good value restaurant. **D** per person *Lima*, Sarmiento 2452, T4518895. Without breakfast, poor beds. **D** per person *Ushuaia*, Gascón 1561, T4510911. With breakfast, pleasant. *La Posada de Güemes*, Flaucho y Güemes, T4514287. **Youth hostels D** per person *Pergamino*, Tucumán 2728, T4957927. Near terminal. Friendly, clean, small IYHA discount. **E** per person *Asociacion Cristina Femenina*, 11 de Septiembre 2700, without bath, kitchen, women only. **Camping** *Pinar de la Serena*, Ruta Provincial 11 y Calle 3. Near Punta Mogotes are *El Griego*, 3 km, T4823471. Also cabins, cycle hire. *El Faro*, 1,500 m, T4660268. Also cabins. Other sites, reasonable prices. Several on the road south.

Area around the bus terminal is full of cheaper places: try especially Alberti, Sarmiento and La Madrid

The Pampas

Mar del Plata centre

N

| 0 metres | 300 |
| 0 yards | 300 |

■ **Sleeping**

1 Astor	3 Dos Reyes	5 Gran Dora	7 Presidente
2 Benedetti	4 Gran Continental	6 Hermitage	8 Provincial

To Centro Cultural Victoria Ocampo & Villa Mitre

Bashful bathing in the 19th century

The fashion for bathing spread from Europe to Argentina in the late 19th century; just as in Europe it raised moral concerns as the Reglamento de Baño (Bathing Regulations) of 1888 *indicated:*

" *Unaccompanied men may not approach bathing women but must maintain a distance of at least 30 metres. Nude bathing is forbidden. The bathing costume* **must** *cover the body from the neck to the knees.*

The use of theatre or opera glasses or similar is forbidden during bathing hours. It is prohibited to use words or actions which are dishonest or contrary to decorum."

Breaches of the regulations could lead to a fine of 2 to 5 pesos or imprisonment for 24-48 hours for a first offence (and 5 to 10 pesos or 48-96 hours imprisonment for a second offence). A third offence could lead to the offender being banned from the beaches for a month.

Apartment rental There are many houses and apartments for rent. Monthly rates for high summer (Jan/Feb) excluding electricity, gas etc: 3 bedroom flats and chalets from US$1,000. The tourist office has a list of companies.

Eating *El Caballito Blanco*, Rivadavia 2534, excellent, German décor. *Gruta de Capri*, Belgrano 2161, not cheap but excellent value. *La Paella*, Entre Ríos 2025, good. Seafood restaurants in the Centro Comercial Puerto including *La Caracola*, good but not cheap. *La Piazetta*, Plaza San Martín, good pasta and salads, vegetarian options. *La Rotisserie*, Av Luro 2696, close to Plaza San martín, small, cosy, good food, service and value. *Teresa*, San Luis 2081, fresh pasta dishes, good value. *Lo de Terri*, Gascón y San Luis, good *parrilla*. *Raviolandia*, Colón y Las Heras, good, cheap, try the seafood with rice. Many *tenedor libre* restaurants of all kinds along San Martín. *Los Inmortales*, Corrientes 1662, good, moderately priced. Good value meals at *La Nueva Glorieta*, Alberti 1821, and *El Nuevo Hispano*, Alberti 1933. **Vegetarian** *El Jardín*, San Martín 2463, *tenedor libre.La Huerta*, Santiago del Estero 1721. *Finca del Sol*, San martín 2459. *Comedor Naturista*, Salta 1571.

There are many seafood restaurants in the modern Centro Comercial Puerto, 3 blocks from the fishing port & cheap restaurants along Rivadavia

Bars *Marienplatz*, Belgrano y Entre Rios, most stylish *confitería* in town, highly recommended but expensive. There are smart bars around Calle Alem that are popular in summer and weekends.

Entertainment **Casino central** Open Dec to end-Apr, 1600-0330; 1600-0400 on Sat. Winter opening, May-Dec, Mon-Fri 1500-0230; weekends 1500-0300. Entrance US$5. Three other casinos operate in summer. **Cinema** *Cine Arte* at Centro Cultural Pueyrredón, 25 de Mayo y La Rioja, every Mon, US$1.50, followed by discussion. On Wed 50% discount at all cinemas. **Disco** Most are on Av Constitución. **Theatre** Reduced price tickets are often available for theatre performances etc from *Cartelera Baires*, Santa Fe 1844, local 33 or from *Galería de los Teatros*, Santa Fe 1751.

Festivals 10 Feb, Foundation of City; 10 Nov, Day of Tradition; 22 Nov, Sta Cecilia.

Sports **Fishing** Good all along the coast and *pejerrey*, *corvina* and *pescadilla* abound; you can charter a private launch for shark fishing.

Transport **Local Car hire** *Primer Mundo*, Jujuy 967, T4739817; *Rent A Car Internacional*, Hotel Dora, Buenos Aires 1841, T4910033; *Weekend*, H Yrigoyen 1967, T4922627; *Dollar*, Córdoba 2270, T4933461; *Avis*, at airport, T4702100; *Budget*, Bolívar 2628, T4956579. Rates for small Fiat including insurance and tax start at US$65 per day. Also **cycle hire**.

Victoria Ocampo

Born into a wealthy Buenos Aires family in 1890, Victoria Ocampo was an essayist and critic who used her wealth to support the arts. In 1931 she launched Sur, a cultural journal and later opened a publishing house of the same name. She argued that the aim of Argentine writing should be to blend and mix the modern literatures from all over the world. Her magazine sought to offer these bridges between cultures through translation (see her own translations of Virginia Woolf, one of her literary models). Ocampo also wrote a highly evocative autobiography and 26 volumes of essays which stressed quotation, translation and interpretation of the universal literary canon in an accessible, almost conversational style. Her work earned her recognition as the first woman to be elected to the Argentine Academy of Literature. Important writers, including Albert Camus, Graham Greene, Aldous Huxley and Rabindranath Tagore, were made welcome at her house and had their works published by her.

An outspoken opponent of both Fascism and Communism, she came into conflict with Juan Domingo and Evita Perón: her imprisonment in 1953 led to a storm of protest abroad. Though she supported women's suffrage and feminism, she was attacked by the left for what they regarded as her elitist views and for her hostility to the Castro regime in Cuba. Argentine nationalists were equally hostile, criticizing her as extrangerizante (a lover of everything foreign).

Long distance Air Camet airport, 10 km north of town. Many flights daily to **Buenos Aires**, *Lapa* (T4922112) and *Aerolíneas Argentinas/Austral* (T4960101). *Southern Winds* to **Córdoba**, **Tucumán** and **Salta**. *Remise* taxi from airport to town, mini bus US$3.50. **Bus** Terminal in former railway station at Alberti y Las Heras, central. To **Buenos Aires**, 6 hrs, US$26, Micromar, Costera Criolla, also has *coche cama*, Empresa Argentina, Chevallier. *El Cóndor* and *Rápido Argentino* to **La Plata**, US$20. To **San Clemente del Tuyú**, *Empresa Costamar*, frequent, US$11, 5 hrs. To **Miramar** hrly, 45 mins, US$4. To **Bahía Blanca**, only *Pampa*, 6 daily, US$25, 5½ hrs. *La Estrella* to **San Martín de los Andes**, US$56. To **Bariloche**, US$60 (none direct, change at Bahía Blanca or Tres Arroyos). For hitchhiking south, take a colectivo to the monument to El Gaucho. **Train** To **Buenos Aires** (Constitución) from Estación Norte, Luro 4599, about 13 blocks from the centre. Buses to/from centre 511, 512, 512B, 541. Services at 0750, 1020, 1715, 1820, Superpullman (sleeper) US$40, Pullman US$25, First US$19, Tourist US$17. Booking offices in bus terminal, Mon-Sat 0800-2000 and at Córdoba y Rivadavia. To Miramar, from Estación Sur, J B Justo y Olazábal, daily except Sun, 0500, 1830, 1½ hrs.

Airline offices *Aerolíneas Argentinas*, Rambla Hotel Provincial, Local 1, T428725. *Austral*, Rambla Hotel Provincial, Local 65, in UK, 54 Conduit St, London, W1R 9FD, T020-7494 1001. **Banks** *Lloyds Bank*, Av Luro 3101. Open 1000-1600, cash advances on Visa. *Casas de Cambio Jonestur*, San Martín 2574, best rates for TCs; *Amex*, Colón 2605, does not cash TCs; *La Moneta*, Rivadavia 2623; *Mar del Plata Cambio*, Buenos Aires 1910; Visa ATM, Santa Fe y Rivadavia. **Cultural centres** La Cultura (formerly Sociedad de Cultura Inglesa): San Luis 2498, friendly, extensive library. **Communications** Post Office: Luro 2460, poste restante, also international parcels office (open till 1200). **Telecommunications** Luro y Santiago del Estero; many *locutorios* around the town. **Laundry** *Laverap*, Buenos Aires 2680, Colón 1716, Entre Ríos y Rivadavia and Moreno y Corrientes. **Tourist offices** Blvd Marítimo 2267, T41325, open 0800-2000 (later in summer), English spoken, good information, including bus routes to all sites of interest; kiosk in Plaza San Martín. **Tours & boat trips** City tours leave from Plaza San Martín and Plaza Colón. Tours also to Miramar and the sierras. Boat trips visiting Isla de los Lobos, Playa Grande, Cabo Corrientes and Playa Bristol leave from the harbour, US$7, 40 mins, summer and weekends in winter. Longer cruises on the *Anamora*, 1130, 1400, 1600, 1800, US$10, T4840103. **Useful addresses** Immigration Office: Chile y Alberti, open mornings.

Directory

The Pampas

Juan Manuel Fangio: gentleman of the track

Considered by many the greatest racing driver of all time, Juan Manuel Fangio was born in Balcarce of Italian immigrants in 1911. His racing debut came in 1936 in a modified taxi but the suspension of the sport in the Second World War interrupted his career and he was aged 37 before he raced in Europe. Despite this he won the world championship in 1951 and dominated the sport until he suddenly retired in 1958, arguing that champions, as well as actors and dictators, should always quit at the top.

Fangio's record is still unrivalled. He won the world championship a record five times, four of them in succession (1954-1957). He won 24 of the 51 Grand Prix races he entered and 102 of the 186 international races he drove in. His greatest triumph came in the German Grand Prix in 1957: after a pit-stop left him nearly a minute behind the leaders, he broke the lap record nine times to win, despite having to wedge himself into the car with his knees after the seat broke. At Monaco in 1950, noticing that the crowd were not watching him as he approached a bend, he braked and was able to avoid a pile up of cars around the corner.

Long before his international triumphs Fangio was a legend in Argentina. In the early 1940s a tango described him as "king of the wheel" though some people later criticized him for cooperating too much with Perón. In 1958 Fidel Castro's guerrillas kidnapped him in Cuba, but he was released two days later and reported that they served his breakfast in bed.

In an epoch when drivers competed for the sake of the sport and gave way to faster rivals with a smile and a wave of the hand, Fangio was renowned for his humility and sense of fairness. A modest family man, he was never accused of driving dangerously. However, foul play can take many forms. Before one important European Grand Prix, Fangio's rivals sent a beauty queen to his room to ensure he would have a short night's sleep. No one knows what ensued, but next day Fangio drove as though he had slept like a log all night, and maybe he really had.

After his retirement from racing, he returned to Balcarce to live in the house where he had been born. He died in 1995.

Inland from Mar del Plata

Route 226 runs northwest to Balcarce and Tandil. The **Reserva Provincial Laguna de los Padres** (entry 19 km from Mar del Plata), contains a reconstruction of the Reducción de Nuestro Señora del Pilar, a Jesuit mission founded in 1746 and abandoned due to Indian attacks in 1751. Nearby in the park is the **Estancia Laguna de los Padres**, which houses the Museo Tradicionalista José Hernández; the writer lived here as a youth and his experiences are said to have inspired Martín Fierro. One section of the park is a natural reserve protecting the *curro*, a rare spikey bush. At Sierra de los Padres, 33 km away, there is a mini-zoo and golf club. The **Laguna Brava**, 38 km away, at the foot of the Balcarce hills, offers *pejerrey* fishing.

Balcarce
Population: 32,000
Altitude: 108 m

Balcarce, 68 km west of Mar del Plata, is a centre for visits to the Cerros Cinco Dedos, five strangely shaped hills. Balcarce is the birthplace of Juan Fangio: just off the Plaza Libertad is the **Museo Juan Manuel Fangio**, which houses all his trophies including a silver cup the same height as Fangio himself. Also on display are many of the racing cars he drove as well as photos and other artefacts associated with the sport. Open daily 1100-1800, US$6. Recommended. Sleeping at **B** *Balcarce*, Calle 17, T422055, good. ■ *Getting there: Frequent buses from Mar del Plata.*

Miramar is known as the 'city of bicycles'. It is cheaper than Mar del Plata and the cliffs backing the beach are higher and the surrounding hills are more picturesque. Founded in 1888, the town was badly damaged by storms in 1911 and 1921. There is a fine golf course at *Hotel Golf Roca* and a casino. Immediately south of the city limits is the **Vivero Dunicola Florentino Ameghino**, a 502 ha forest park on the beach whose vegetation stays green and blooming throughout the year, despite winter night-time temperatures below freezing. Inside the park is the **Museo Municipal**, with displays of animal fossils and of Querandí Indian artefacts.

Miramar
Phone code: 02563
Colour map 4, grid C6
Population: 17,500
53 km SW of Mar del Plata along the coast road

    Mar del Sur, 14 km south, among dunes and black rocks (*Hotel Boulevard Atlántico*) is a peaceful resort with good fishing in a lagoon and bathing on the beach.

Sleeping B *Santa Eulalia I*, Calle 26 No 851, T420808. Friendly but run down. **B** *Villa Cruz*, Calle 19, No 864. Friendly, clean, near the beach. *Gran*, Calle 29, No 586 esquina 12, T420358, 2-star. *Palace*, Calle 23, No 774, T420258, 3-star. **Camping F** per person *El Durazno*, 3 km from town, good facilities, shops, restaurant, take bus 501 marked 'Playas'. Many sites, reasonably priced.

Dozens of hotels & apartments

Tourist office On central plaza, has maps.

Transport Bus To Buenos Aires, Chevallier, Micromar and Costera Criolla, 8 per day, US$31. To Mar del Plata, US$4, *Rápido del Sud*, Pampa. To Necochea, Pampa. **Train** *Ferrobus* daily except Sun to Mar del Plata, 0630, 2000.

Necochea

Necochea is another famous resort, known as the 'Pearl of the South'. Its 24 km long beach is one of the best in the country. There is a large Danish community, Danish club and consulate. It is situated about 110 km further southwest along the coast.

Phone code: 02262
Colour map 4, grid C5
Population: 60,000

The town which lies on the west bank of the Río Quequén, is in two parts, with the centre 2 km inland from the seafront area. On the opposite bank of the river lies **Quequén** (population 14,000), one of the most important grain exporting ports in the country. The two towns are linked by three bridges, one of them a 270 km hanging bridge built in Cherbourg in 1929.

Necochea centre

In the seafront area of Necochea, four blocks southwest of the Plaza San Martín, is the **Parque Miguel Lillo** (named after the Argentine botanist), comprising nearly 600 ha of conifers, nature park, swan lake with paddle boats, an amphitheatre, go-cart track and two museums, the **Museo Histórico Regional** and the **Museo de Ciencias Naturales**. Nearby there is a municipal recreation complex, with a large casino deteriorating in the salt air, various sports facilities, including skating rink, swimming

Sights

The Pampas

The Pampas

pool, bowling, a cinema, discoteque and children's play area. ■ *Open summer daily and winter weekends 2200-0400*. East of Quequén harbour there is a lighthouse built in 1921 (■ *daily 1600-2000*) and fine beaches, particularly the Balneario La Villazón.

Excursions Southeast of Necochea are miles of sand-dunes little visited by tourists. Visits can also be made up the Río Quequén to the **Cascadas de Quequén**, small waterfalls 13 km north. Nearby is the forested Parque Cura-Meucó.

Sleeping

The Hotel Association is at Av 79 y Calle 4. Most close off-season when it is worth bargaining

Seafront area Most hotels are in the seafront area from Calle 2 (parallel with beach) north between Av 71-91. There are at least 100 within 700 m of the beach. Best is *Presidente*, Calle 4 No 4040, T423800, F425974, 4-star. **AB** *Hostería del Bosque*, Calle 89 No 350, T/F420002. 5 blocks from beach, quiet, upper rooms better, nice bar and garden, parking next door. *San Miguel*, Calle 85 No 301, T/F425155, open all year and *San Martín*, Calle 6 No 4198, T/F437000, restaurant, open all year. **AB** *Perugia*, Calle 81, No 288, T422020, a/c, open all year. **B** *Asturias*, San Martín 842, T424524. **B** *Doramar*, Calle 83, No 329, T425815, family run, helpful. **D** *Zure Echea*, Calle 79 No 355, T422167, open all year. **E** *Hosp Bayo*, Calle 87, No 338, T423334. **Centre C** *Hosp Solchaga*, Calle 62, No 2822, T425584, excellent, open all year. **C** *Center*, Calle 59, No 2966, T422013. **D** *Gala*, Calle 57, No 2815, T422447. **Quequén** Hotels include: *Costa Azul*, *Continental*, *Quequén*. The tourist office has a list of companies which rent apartments.

Camping *Río Quequén*, Calle 22 y Ribera Río Quequén, T422145. Sports facilities, bar, cycle hire. *Las Grutas*, Av 2 y Las Grutas. *Puelches*, Calle 111 y Av 32, 500 m from sea, pool. Campsites on beach reported expensive in season. Also in Quequén are: *Doble Jota*, Calle 502 y 529, T426058. *Monte Pasuvio*, Calle 502 s/n, T426064. *El Gringo*, Calle 519 y 520, T425449.

Eating *Centro Basko*, Calle 65, T424939. Typically Basque, good. *Rex*, Calle 62, 'a trip to 1952 Paris', not cheap.

Transport **Air** Airport 12 km northwest of town. To **Buenos Aires**, Aerolineas Argentinas and LAER, US$60-80. **Bus** Terminal at Av 47 y Calle 582, 4 km from the centre; bus 513, 517 from outside the terminal to the beach. Taxi to beach area US$3. To **Buenos Aires**, US$44, La Estrella, Plus-Mar and Costera Criolla; to **Mar del Plata**, Pampa, US$10; to **Bahía Blanca**, Pampa, US$22; to **Tres Arroyos** US$10. **Train** Station in Quequén. To **Buenos Aires** (Constitución) daily, 7 hrs, Pullman US$17, First US$12, Tourist US$10; additional service Mon, Wed, Fri.

Necochea Beach area

Communications Post office in centre, Av 58, No 3086, near beach, Calle 6, No 4099. **Directory**
Telecommunications *Telefónica*, Calle 61, No 2432. **Language schools** *Instituto Argentino de Idiomas*, Galería Monviso, local 8, Calle 62 y 63, recommended. **Sport** Fishing for fishing by boats 3 companies: *La Trucha*, Calle 10 y Calle 59, T428601. *El Gordo*, Calle 10, No 3060, T427812. *El Cornalito*, Calle 59, No 441, T429570. **Horseriding** *Caballo's*, Villa Marítima Zabala y Av 10, T423138. **Tourist offices** On beach front at Av 79 y Av 2, T438333, English spoken. **ACA**, Av 59, No 2073, T422106.

Tres Arroyos lies in an important cattle and wheat growing area. The town was a **Tres Arroyos**
centre of Dutch immigration (Dutch consulate and school). There is also an
important Danish colony, with school, club and consulate. Around the Plaza
San Martín are the **Municipalidad**, in French Bourbon style, and the **Iglesia**
Nuestra Señora de Carmen, which is vaguely French gothic. The **Museo de**
Bellas Artes, a block southwest, contains paintings by Argentine artists.

Phone code: 02983
Colour map 4, grid C5
Population: 44,500
141 km W of Necochea

South of Tres Arroyos are three pleasant resorts. **Claromecó**, reached by a
68 km paved road, is a fishing port with a beautiful beach of dark sand backed
by high dunes. **Orense**, further east, is a centre for watersports, including surfing, wind-surfing and water-skiing. **Reta**, west of Claromecó, is set among
eucalyptus and pine plantations.

Sleeping and eating Tres Arroyos AB *Parque*, Pellegrini 23, T431350, restaurant.
Recommended. **B** *Alfil*, Rivadavia 140, T427002, restaurant, just off Plaza San Martín.
Andrea, Istilart 228, 2 blocks east of Plaza San Martín, T426214, good hotel. *Restaurant*
Di Troppo, Moreno 133, good bites. *Tres Amigos*, Chacabuco 102, popular *parrilla*.
Claromecó Several hotels, restaurants and camping. A good campsite is *Dunamar*,
ACA, US$6 per person, hot showers, fire pits and laundry facilities.

Transport Bus Modern terminal on the outskirts of Tres Arroyos. To Claromecó 2
daily off season, extra buses from mid-Dec in season. To Mar del Plata, Pampa, 4½ hrs.
From Buenos Aires to Claromecó, La Estrella, US$40.

Bahia Blanca

A busy city with an attractive centre based on the Plaza Rivadavia, it is an impor-
tant route centre for heading south or for exploring the Sierra de la Ventana.
Bahía Blanca stands at the head of a large bay at the mouth of the Río Naposta.
The major grain exporting port in the country, the city is also Argentina's most
important petrochemical centre. South of the city are several ports, the most
important of which are Puerto Ingeniero White, which handles oil and chemicals,
and Puerto Galván, which handles grain. Puerto Belgrano, 29 km southeast, is
Argentina's most important naval base.

Phone code: 0291
Colour map 4, grid C4
Population: 260,000

Bahía Blanca was founded in 1828 as a fort, the **Fortaleza Protectora Argen-** **History**
tina, both to control Indian cattle rustling and to protect the coast from Brazil
whose navy had landed in the area in 1827. Though the native population of
the area was defeated in the campaigns of Rosas, the fortress was attacked several times, notably by 3,000 Calfucurá warriors in 1859. An important centre
of European immigration, it became a major port with the building of railways
connecting it with grain-producing areas of the pampas.

The major public buildings date from the early years of this century: around the **Sights**
central **Plaza Rivadavia** are the Municipalidad, the Banco de la Nación and
neo-classical cathedral. Three blocks north is the **Teatro Municipal**. There is a
modest **Jardín Zoológico** in Parque Independencia, Ruta 3 y Av Pringles, on

The Pampas

the outskirts. South of the centre, just over the railway bridge is the **Barrio Inglés** where the foremen and technicians of the port and railway construction teams lived; Brickman Street, just past the railway bridge, is a row of late Victorian semi-detached houses. Managers lived at **Villa Harding Green**, northeast of the centre. There are beaches at Maldonado and Colón, both 3 km south of the city.

Museums **Museo del Puerto**, Torres y Carrega, at Ingeniero White, in former customs building, excellent displays of domestic artefacts from the early 20th century. Serves as a *confitería* on Sun. Highly recommended. ■ *Mon-Fri 0900-1200, Sat/Sun 1530-1930. Bus 500, 504.* **Museo Histórico**, in the Teatro Municipal, Alsina 425, including sections on the pre-conquest period, the conquest and interesting photos of early Bahía Blanca. ■ *Daily 1600-2000.* Outside is a statue of Garibaldi, erected by the Italian community in 1928. **Museo de Bellas Artes**, in basement of Municipalidad, Alsina 65, is small. ■ *Tue-Sat 0930-1300, Thu-Sun 1600-2000, free.* **Museo de Arte Contemporánea**, Sarmiento 450. ■ *Tue-Fri 1000-1300, 1600-2000.*

Excursions **Puerto Belgrano** is Argentina's most important naval base, 29 km southeast, which can be visited daily. **Pehuén-Có** is a quiet resort 84 km southeast is reached by a turning off Route 3. Accommodation is available in the *Hotel Cumelcan* and there are several campsites.

Bahía Blanca centre

To Av de Circunvalación
To Parque Independencia

12 de Octubre
Corrientes
Av Alem
Zeballos
Teatro Municipal & Museo Histórico
Zapiola
Dorrego
10
Alvarado
Lamadrid
Mitre
5
Soler
Zelarrayan
San Martín
Cathedral
Municipalidad & Museo de Bellas Artes
Plaza Rivadavia
Estomba
6
7
Chiclana
Banco de la Nación
9
4
V López
Vieytes
Brown
8
1
Güemes
2
Saavedra
Castelli
Berutti

To Torriquist & the North
11 de Abril
19 de Mayo
Rodriguez
Sarmiento
H Yrigoyen
Alsina
Belgrano
Las Heras
Lavalle
General Paz
Brandsen
Cerri
Israel
Roca
Gorriti
Rondeau
Moreno
Av Colón
O'Higgins
Donado
Fitz Roy
España
Villarino
Undiano
To Bus Terminal

N

0 metres 200
0 yards 200

To Barrio Inglés
To Puerto Ingeniero White

■ **Sleeping**
1 Argos
2 Austral
3 Barne
4 Bayón
5 Belgrano
6 City
7 Chiclana
8 Italia
9 Muñiz
10 Santa Rosa

Monte Hermoso is another fine resort 106 km east. Near Monte Hermoso are **Sauce Grande**, another resort 4 km east along the coast road, and **Laguna Sauce Grande**, a large lake 10 km northeast, where there is *pejerrey* fishing and boats can be hired.

Sleeping in Monte Hermoso Several hotels including *La Goleta*, Costanera y Calle 10, T481142, 3-star. *América*, Valle Encantado 91, T481005. *Santa Isabel*, Bahía Blanca 55, T481030. Hotels open only Jan-Mar. **Camping** Several sites including *El Americano*, good facilities, and *las Dunas*, 30 mins walk west along the beach, US$3 per person, a friendly spot run by an elderly German couple.

The Pampas

AL *Austral*, Colón 159, T4561700, F4553737, haustral@bblanca.com.ar, 4-star, restaurant. **A** *ACA Motel Villa Borden*, Av Sesquicentenario, entre Rutas 3 y 35, T/F4886855, F421098. **A** *Muñiz*, O'Higgins 23, T420021, central, poor breakfast. **B** *Barne*, H Yrigoyen 270, T430864, F550513. With breakfast, helpful, family run. Recommended. **B** *Bayón*, Chiclana 487, T422504, safe. **B** *Belgrano*, Belgrano 44, T/F4564404, hbelgrano@impsat.com.ar, without breakfast, restaurant. **B** *Belgrano*, Belgrano 44, T/F420240/30498, without breakfast, restaurant. **B** *City*, Chiclana 226, T430178, without breakfast, overpriced. **B** *Italia*, Brown 181, T420121, simple, restaurant. **B** *Victoria*, Gral Paz 82, T420522. Basic, quiet. Recommended. **C** *Chiclana*, Chiclana 370, T430436, **D** without bath, basic, poor beds. **C** *Del Sur*, 19 de Mayo 75, T422452, with restaurant, noisy with traffic. **C** *Res Roma*, Cerri 759, T438500, cheaper without bath. **D** *Los Angeles*, Chiclana 367, basic. Other *residenciales* near railway station, eg **D** *Los Vascos*, Cerri 747, T429290.

Sleeping
Most hotels charge extra for parking

Camping *Balneario Maldonado*, 4 km south, T429511, US$5 per tent, US$1 per person, next to petrochemical plant, salt water swimming pool, bus 514 along Av Colón every hr but only when beach is open, ie when sunny and not in evening. *Cala Gogo*, Sarmiento 4000, north of town, US$4.

La Cigala, Cerri 757, very good. *Il Vesuvio*, San Martín 337, good lunch, cheap. *Sergio*, Gorriti 61, good food, large portions, good value. *Café La Bahía*, Chiclana 548, good value. Recommended. A few good fish restaurants at the harbour, eg *Cantina Royal*. Very good seafood and fish at *Ingeniero White*. *Northwestern Café*, Alsina 236, American bar, pizzas, happy hour 1600-1800.

Eating

11 Apr, *Foundation of the City*; 24 Sep, *Our Lady of Mercy*; 10 Nov, *Day of Tradition*.

Local holidays

Municipal market, Donado 151.

Shopping

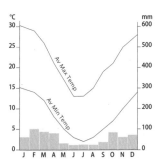
Climate: Bahia Blanca

Local Bus US$0.65, but you need to buy *carnets* (cards) from kiosks for 1, 2 or 4 journeys. **Taxi** *Uni*, T4520000; *San Roque*, T4881524.

Long distance Air Comandante Espora, 11 km northeast of centre. *AR/Austral* (T4552208) and *Lapa* (T4564552) to **Buenos Aires**. *Lapa* to **Comodoro Rivadavia**; *Austral* to **Viedma**; *TAN* (T4552592) to **Neuquén** and **Mar del Plata**. **Trains** Station at Av Gral Cerri 780, T4521571. To Buenos Aires daily 2000, 12½ hrs, sleeper US$30,

Transport

pullman and 1st US$22, tourist US$15, dinner in good restaurant car US$10. **Bus** Terminal in old railway station two and a half km from centre at Estados Unidos y Brown, T4819615. Buses 505, 514, 517 to centre, no hotels nearby. To **Buenos Aires** frequent, several companies, 10 hrs, US$30-34, shop around. To **Mar del Plata**, Río Paraná, US$25, 5½ hrs. To **Córdoba**, US$44, 12 hrs; to **Neuquén**, 6 a day, 8 hrs, US$20. To **Necochea**, Pampa, 5hrs, US$22. To **Zapala**, 3 daily, 11 hrs, US$25, El Valle. To **Río Colorado** US$8, **Viedma**, 3 a day, 4 hrs. To **Trelew**, 3 a week, US$32, 12 hrs. To **Río Gallegos**, Don Otto, US$80. To **Tornquist**, US$4, 0600, 1300, 1720, 1 hr, last return 2020. To **Sierra de la Ventana** (town) 0600, 2040 (not Sat). **Train** Station at Av Gral Cerri 750, T421168. To **Buenos Aires** (Constitución), via Sierra de la Ventana and Azul, 2000 daily, 12 hrs, Sleeper US$39, Pullman US$26, First US$ 20, Tourist US$17. **Hitchhiking** South or west from Bahía Blanca is possible but not too easy. Most southbound traffic takes Route 22 via Río Colorado. North to Buenos Aires on Route 3 is 'virtually impossible'.

Directory **Airline offices** *Aerolineas Argentinas*, San Martín 198, T426934. *LADE*, Darregueira 21, T437697. *TAN*, San Martín 216, Galería Visión 2,000, Local 80, T433610. **Banks** *Lloyds Bank* (BLSA), Chiclana 102; *Citibank*, Colón 58. *Amex*, Fortur, Soler 38, T426209, *poste restante*, English spoken. *Casas de Cambio: Pullman*, San Martín 171, changes US$, TCs to US$ notes, 3% commission on TCs, good rates (closes 1600). *Viajes Bahía Blanca*, Drago 63, good rates. All *casas de cambio* closed at weekends. **Communications** Post office Moreno 34. **Telephones** *Telefónica*, O'Higgins 249. **Consulates** *Chile*, Güemes 102, T4550110, F258803; *Italy*, Colón 446, T4551633; *Spain*, Drago 70, T422549. **Laundry** *Laverap*, Villarrino 87 and at Perú 122. *Daimar*, Mitre 184. **Tour opertators** *ASATEJ*, Zelarrayán 267, T4560666, bblanca@asatej.com.ar **Tourist offices** In town hall on main plaza, Alsina 43, T4564234, F4558803, Mon-Fri 0800-1200. Also in airport in Jan/Feb, helpful.

From Bahia Blanca to Neuquen Route 22 runs direct from Bahía Blanca, cutting across the southern tip of La Pampa to **Río Colorado** (campsite with all facilities), on the river of the same name. Bus to Buenos Aires 0100, 11 hours, US$30. It then runs through northern Río Negro to **Choele Choel** on the Río Negro itself, 308 km from Bahía Blanca. There are large fruit growing areas at Choele Choel and Villa Regina which are irrigated from the Río Negro dam. An unbroken series of groves of tall trees shelter the vineyards and orchards.

Sleeping Choele Choel **B** *ACA Motel* on edge of town, T/F0946-42394, Ruta Nacional 22, Km 1,006. fine modern *Hotel Choele Choel*. Several other hotels. **Camping** Free municipal site beside Río Negro, shady, excellent, no showers. Good restaurant at bus terminal.

The Central Sierras

5

164

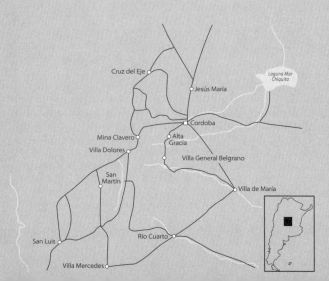

Northwest of Buenos Aires in the provinces of Córdoba and San Luis, the pampas are broken by several ranges of sierras. The Sierra de Córdoba are one of the most popular destinations for Argentine tourists, particularly for walking, hiking and fishing. The Sierra de San Luis are much less visited, though the building of paved roads in recent years is opening this region up to visitors. The scenery is often breathtaking between the Sierras de Córdoba and the Sierra de San Luis; a most spectacular journey is the camino de los Altas Cumbres, which runs west from Córdoba accross the high Pampa de Achala. In the far northwest of the Sierra de San Luis is the Parque Nacional Las Quijadas, an isolated but spectacular national park; its red sandstone cliffs can be seen from miles away.

The other attraction in this region is the city of Córdoba, the second largest in Argentina and the centre of the Argentine motor industry. Though much of Córdoba is modern, it is one of the oldest cities in the country and is an important route centre for visitors to the northwest. At the heart of the city are examples of Spanish colonial architecture, unusual in Argentina. These include several churches and the attractive, arcaded cabildo (town council building) on the main plaza.

Background

Geography

Province population:
Córdoba over 2,700,000;
San Luis under 300,000

While the pampas extend across southern and eastern Córdoba province and the southern part of San Luis provinces, to the north and west five ranges of hills run from north to south. The two provincial capital cities lie on the edge of these hills, Córdoba to the east and San Luis to the west. North of Córdoba and to the east of the sierras is a broad plateau which declines gently from 600 m towards Laguna Mar Chiquita in the northwest of the province.

The sierras are drained by five major rivers flowing east. Though usually known as the Ríos Primero, Segundo, Tercero, Cuarto and Quinto, their prehispanic names are sometimes also used. The two most northerly of these, the Ríos Primero (or Suquía) and Segundo (or Xanaes) flow northeast and empty into Laguna Mar Chiquita, a large inland sea. Further south the Ríos Tercero and Cuarto flow into the Río Saladillo, which as the Río Carcarañá empties into the Paraná. The Río Quinto, the main river draining the Sierras de San Luis, flows southeast and disappears into the pampas. Two other rivers in San Luis are worth noting, the Río Conlara, which flows north before drying up, and the Río Salado which drains the west of the province and forms the boundary with the province of Mendoza. The main rivers have been dammed forming a number of artificial lakes, which provide irrigation, hydro-electric power and watersports facilities. These are particularly important in Córdoba: the province has 15 dams, nine of which generate electricity.

Climate This area enjoys a dry continental climate. Average daily temperature in the two provincial capitals range from 4°C to 18°C in winter and from 17°C to 30°C in summer, but temperatures are lower in the sierras and higher in the plains to the south and east. Rainfall occurs mainly in summer, being higher in the sierras and lower in the plains where it drops to 200 mm a year. Some areas in the sierras, notably Merlo, enjoy special microclimates. The city of San Luis is noted for a strong southerly wind, the *Viento Chorrillero*, which blows almost daily.

Economy

The city of Córdoba is one of the most important industrial centres in the country, the home of Argentina's car and aviation industries: there are Renault, Iveco and Fiat car plants, as well as a Lockheed aircraft maintenance centre. While the south and east of Córdoba province and the south of San Luis province are areas of cereal production and cattle ranching, agriculture in the sierras is more varied with olives, vines, cotton and honey being produced. The sierras are also of growing importance for mining, marble being extensively mined in Córdoba, tungsten, quartz, feldspar, mica, graphite, onyx and gold in San Luis.

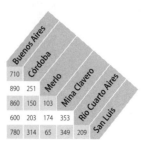

	Buenos Aires	Córdoba	Merlo	Mina Clavero	Río Cuarto Aires	San Luis
	710					
	890	251				
	860	150	103			
	600	203	174	353		
	780	314	65	349	209	

The Central Sierras: distance chart (km)

The Jesuits in Córdoba

Though less well known than the missions of Paraguay and the Argentine province of Misiones, Córdoba was one of the most important Jesuit centres in Latin America. The first Jesuits arrived in the city in 1587 and, shortly afterwards Córdoba became the headquarters of the Order's activities in South America. The need to train priests led to the foundation of a Jesuit College in the city, which in 1621 became the University of San Carlos, one of the first universities in the continent. Novices studied Latin,

theology and the arts; tuition was free. The university became the focus of local cultural life and by the 18th century Córdoba Docta (learned Córdoba) was recognized as the cultural capital of the Viceregency of La Plata.

The cost of maintaining the university with its 40 Jesuit teaching staff was met from the produce of nearby farms and estancias which were bequeathed to the University. Several of these can still be seen today: at Alta Gracia, Jesús María, Santa Catalina and La Candelaria.

Córdoba

The Central Sierras

Situated on the Río Primero Córdoba is capital of Córdoba province. Despite its age and significance in the colonial period, it is a busy modern industrial city, home of two universities and one of the best shopping centres in the country. At the heart of the city, around the relatively peaceful Plaza San Martín, are several colonial buildings, particularly significant because of the lack of colonial architecture in Argentina. Most accommodation is a few blocks southeast of Plaza San Martín in the streets near the bus terminal. The city is a convenient centre for day-trips into the Sierras de Córdoba.

*Phone code: 0351
Colour map 4, grid A2
Population: 1,200,000
713 km NW of
Buenos Aires*

Founded in 1573 by an expedition from Santiago del Estero led by Jerónimo Luis de Cabrera, Córdoba was an important city in colonial times, situated at the junction of the routes from Chile and Alto Peru to Buenos Aires. In 1810 when Buenos Aires backed independence, the leading figures of Córdoba voted to remain loyal to Spain. After independence the city was a stronghold of opposition to Buenos Aires. Since the 1940s Córdoba has grown from a cultural, administrative and communications centre into a large industrial city.

History

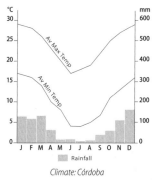

Climate: Córdoba

Most of the older buildings lie within a few blocks of the **Plaza San Martín**, which dates from 1577. In the centre is a fine statue of the Liberator. On the west side is the former **Cabildo**, dating from 1610 and built around two interior patios. It has served as a prison, courthouse, local legislature and police headquarters. Part is now occupied by tourist offices and part by the **Museo de la Ciudad**. Next to it stands the **cathedral**, the oldest in Argentina (the present building dates from 1697-1782), with a neo-baroque interior, attractive stained-glass windows and a richly-decorated ceiling: see the remarkable cupola. In the vault of the central nave you can see the works of the Codoban painter Emilio Caraffa. Just south of the cathedral at Independencia

**The Old City:
A walking tour**
A good way of viewing the city is on the City Tour operated by the municipality, leaving from the cathedral corner of Plaza San Martín at 1100 & 1730, US$6, T4469796

The Central Sierras

122 is the 17th-century **Carmelite convent** and chapel of **Santa Teresa**. The convent, dating from 1628, has a fine portal built in 1770.

From Plaza San Martín walk west one block to the pleasant **Plaza del Fundador**, where there is a statue to the city founder Jerónimo Luís de Cabrera. On the west side of the Plaza is the convent and church of **Santa Catalina de Siena**, founded in 1613 but rebuilt in the late 19th century. The convent contains a rich collection of paintings from colonial Peru as well as colonial Spanish tapestries and carpets. From here walk two blocks south along Obispo Trejo to the former Jesuit church of **La Compañía**. Though its façade was rebuilt in the 20th century, the church dates from about 1650: the barrel vaulted ceiling and cupola of its Capilla Doméstica, built entirely of Paraguayan cedar, are unique. The main altar was the work of local Indians. Next to La Compañía are two other former Jesuit institutions, the main building of the **Universidad Nacional de Córdoba** and the **Colegio Nacional de Montserrat**. One block west of the latter at Vélez Sarsfield 351 is the neo-classical **Teatro Libertador General San Martín** (1891), the oldest existing theatre in the country. From the Colegio Nacional walk two blocks east to Calle Buenos Aires; the convent and church of **San Francisco** at Entre Ríos y Buenos Aires, dating from the late 18th century, contains fine examples of Indian woodcarving. From here walk two blocks north across Plaza San Martín to Rosario de Santa Fe and one block east to reach the **Casa del Virrey Marqués de Sobramonte**, the sole remaining colonial house in the city which houses the Museo Histórico Provincial. Continue one block north along Ituzaingó and then one block west along 9 de Julio to reach the basilica of **La Merced** at 25 de Mayo 83; built in the early 19th century, it has a fine gilt wooden pulpit dating from the colonial period. On its exterior, overlooking Rivadavia, are fine ceramic murals depicting scenes from the history of Córdoba by the local artist Armando Sica.

Córdoba centre

■ **Sleeping**
1 Argentino	4 Ducal	7 Mediterráneo	10 Windsor
2 Cristal	5 Felipe II	8 Panorama	
3 Dorá	6 Garden	9 Sussex	

Not to scale

Other sights

The church of **San Roque**, Obispo Salguero y San Jerónimo, is notable for its Indian-carved pulpit. The neo-gothic church of the **Sagrado Corazón**, built in 1933, at Buenos Aires y Yrigoyen, is also worth a visit.

The magnificent **Mitre railway station**, near the bus terminal, is now almost closed though its beautiful tiled *confitería* is still in use. South of the centre in the large **Parque Sarmiento** is a good **zoo**, with animals in clean spacious environments, US$3. On the western outskirts of the city alongside the river is the **Parque del Oeste**, with sporting facilities, and the **Parque General San Martín**.

Córdoba

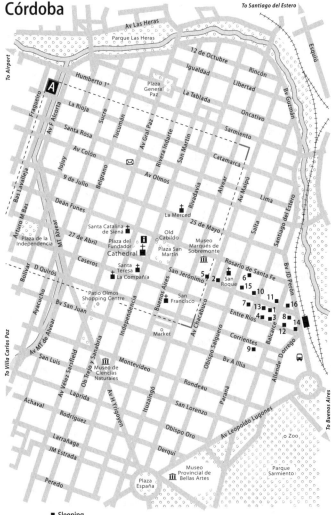

N

Not to scale

■ **Sleeping**			
1 Corona	5 Felipe II	9 Mi Valle	13 Rosa Mística
2 Dallas	6 Florida	10 Ritz	14 Royal
3 Del Sol	7 Harbor	11 Riviera	15 Thanoa
4 Entre Ríos	8 La María	12 Roma Termini	16 Viña del Italia

Related map
A *Córdoba centre*, see
page opposite

• •

 Radical Córdoba

Always at odds with Buenos Aires, Córdoba has acquired a reputation for opposition to the central government and support for the Radical party. Its most famous hour came in 1969 when disturbances in the city ignited opposition to military rule throughout the country. The Cordobazo of May 1969 *began with student protests in support of their fellows in Corrientes, but gained support among the car workers who took over the city and were only defeated by the use of the army. More recently, Córdoba was the stronghold of Radical party opposition to the Peronist government of Carlos Menem.*

• •

Museums **Museo Marqes de Sobremonte**, in the 18th-century Casa del Virrey Marqués de Sobremonte, Rosario de Santa Fe 218. Local history museum with displays on the 18th and 19th century. ■ *Tue-Fri 0900-1300, 1500-1900, Sat 0900-1300, Sun 1000-1300, US$1.* **Museo de la Ciudad**, in the Cabildo Histórico, Plaza San Martín. Includes photographs of Córdoba. ■ *Tue-Sun 0900-1300, also daily 1600-2100.* **Museo de Ciencias Naturales**, Yrigoyen 115. ■ *Mon-Fri 0830-1230, 1430-1800, US$1.* Good guided tours (in Spanish), 'interesting skeletons of prehistoric glyptodonts'). **Museo de Zoología**, Velez Sarsfield 299, piso 2, many birds but poorly displayed with no labels. ■ *Mon-Fri 0900-1200, Wed-Fri 1600-1800.* **Museo Provincial de Bellas Artes**, Plaza España, in a French-style mansion dating from the early 20th century. Permanent collection on the development of Córdoban painting to the present day. ■ *Daily 0900-2100.* **Museo Municipal de Bellas Artes**, Gral Paz 33. Paintings and sculptures from the 19th century to the present. ■ *Tue-Fri 0930-1330, 1630-2100, Sat/Sun 1000-2000.* **Centro de Arte Contemporáneo**, in the Chateau Carreras, a late 19th-century mansion in the Parque San Martín. ■ *Tue-Sun 1600-2000, US$2.* **Museo de Meteorología Nacional**, Laprida 808. ■ *Mon-Fri 0830-1330*; nearby is Argentina's main observatory, ■ *Wed 2000-2200.* **Museo de Arte Religioso**, in the convent of Santa Teresa, Independencia 122. ■ *Wed-Sat 0930-1230.*

Essentials

Sleeping **Expensive** **Centre** **L** *Córdoba Plaza International*, San Jerónimo 137, T4268900.
Blvd Perón is often referred to as Blvd Reconquista Large comfortable rooms, parking. **L** *Córdoba Park*, San Juan 165, T4207000. Modern. **L** *Panorama*, Alvear 251, T4204000. Good, pool, central, new. **AB** *Cañada*, Alvear 580, T4214649. Good, including conference facilities with full technical back-up, a/c, restaurant, laundry. **AB** *Windsor*, Buenos Aires 214, T4224012. Comfortable, very good.

On San Jerónimo A *Felipe II*, No 279, T4255500. Bar, good. **AB** *Ritz*, No 495, T4215031. With breakfast, 'clean but dilapidated'. **AB** *Sussex*, No 125, T4229071. Comfortable, roomy, discounts for ACA members. **AB** *Dallas*, No 339, T/F4216091. With breakfast, parking, a/c. Recommended. **AB** *Viña de Italia*, No 611, T/F4226589. With breakfast, parking, restaurant, good value. **AB** *Del Sol*, Balcarce 144, T4242969, F433961. Fan, a/c extra. Recommended. **A** *ACA Hotel Dr Cesar C Carman*, Av Sabattini 459, T4583825, **AL** for non-members, very good.

Cheaper **On Corrientes C** *Bristol* Pasaje Oliver (just off Corrientes) No 64, T4239950. A/c. **C** *Res Mi Valle*, No 586. Fan, small, family-run, poor beds.

On San Jerónimo B *Felipe II*, No 279, T444752. Adequate. **B** *Corona*, No 571, T4228789. Without breakfast. **D** *La María*, No 628. Parking, good value. **D** per person *Rosa Mistica*, No 532. Also monthly rates. **D** *Res Thanoa*, No 479, T4222807. With bath, cheaper without, old fashioned, good value.

On Balcarce B *Mallorca*, No 73, T4239234. Quite clean and near bus terminal, noisy. **B** *Riviera*, No 74, T4223969. With breakfast, parking. **D** *El Progreso*, No 140, basic.

On Entre Ríos B *Regins*, No 629, T4232825. Without breakfast. **B/C** *Roma Termini*, No 687, T4218721. Without breakfast, welcoming. Recommended. **B/C** *Entre Ríos*, No 567, T4230311. With breakfast, parking, family run, good value.

Elsewhere C *Nuevo Florida*, Rosario de Santa Fe 459, T426373. Recommended, some rooms with a/c. **B** *Royal*, Bv Perón 180, T4227155, F4553492. With breakfast and parking. **B** *Garden*, 25 de Mayo 35, T4214729. Central, secure. Highly recommended. **C** *Harbor*, Paraná 126, T/F4217300. Without breakfast, good value. **C** *Quetzal*, San Jerónimo 579. With breakfast, parking, clean, quiet. **D** *Wonder*, San Jerónimo 519, T4229321. With bath, parking, friendly, good value. **E** per person *Gral Paz*, 25 de Mayo 240, T4210198. With bath, run down, clean.

The following offer 10% discount to ISIC card holders: *del Sol*, Balcarce 144 (see above) and on Arturo Illia, *del Boulevard*, No 182, T4243718, *Heidy*, No 619, T4218906.

Camping Municipal site, Gral San Martín, at the back of the Complejo Ferial (bus 31).

When the weather is good in the Cerro de las Rosas district, on the northern outskirts, there are plenty of places to dine al fresco. Many cheap restaurants along San Jerónimo including *San Carlos*, No 431. Good food and service. *Casino Español*, Rivadavia 63, good. *La Mamma*, Santa Rosa y Figueroa Alcorta. Excellent Italian, pricey. *Il Gatto*, Gral Paz 120. Great pasta and pizzas, reasonably priced. *Romagnolo*, Perón y San Jerónimo, opposite the Mitre railway station, recommended. *Betos*, San Juan 494. Best *lomitos* in town, *parrilla*, recommended, pricey. *Minoliti*, Entre Ríos 358, excellent homemade pastas, inexpensive, limited menu. Highly recommended. *Firenze*, 25 de Mayo 220. Busy, pleasant, traditional café. *Meeting*, 27 de Abril 248, good café. *Sorocabana*, San Jerónimo 98, 24-hr café. Excellent fruit juices (*licuados*) at *Kiosco Americano*, Tucumán 185 and at Gral Paz 242. Good *empanadas* at *La Vieja Esquina*, Belgrano y Caseros. *Mandarina*, Obispo Trejo 171, salads, Chinese, reasonably priced, good food. *Empanadería La Alameda*, Obispo Trejo 170, reasonable food, good student atmosphere, best 2200-2400. Ice-cream at branches of *Dolce Neve* throughout town. *Soppelsa's* ice cream is also highly recommended, with several outlets.

Eating

Asociación Argentina de Cultura Británica, Yrigoyen 496, good library with books, magazines, newspapers, English teaching materials, videos and a small reading room, open Mon-Fri 0900-2000. **Goethe Institut**, Illia 356, T4224358. Open Tue-Fri 1700-2045, Fri 0930-1230.

Cultural centres

Cinema Modern multi-screen ones in new shopping centres, US$7. *Cine Teatro Córdoba*, 27 de Abril 275, foreign language films, slightly cheaper, nice atmosphere. *General Paz*, Rivadavia 50. *Gran Rex*, Gral Paz 174, 4 screens. Another at Colón 345. Programmes in local newspaper, *La Voz del Interior*.

Entertainment

Bars *Noé*, Independencia 345, billiards, young clientele, crowded. *Rock & Feller's*, Yrigoyen 320, very popular and fashionable, restaurant and bar, nice atmosphere, reasonable prices. *Picadilly Pub*, Yrigoyen 464, British-style pub/restaurant, owner

The Central Sierras

speaks English, busy at lunchtime. *La Fenice*, Buenos Aires y Yrigoyen, popular late night bar at weekends. *La Luna*, Independencia y Yrigoyen, crowded bar. Av Yrigoyen between Ituzaingo and the Patio Olmos shopping centre is a very popular restaurant, disco and bar area on Fri and Sat eveings.

Nightclubs Several on Av H Yrigoyen, expensive and in Cerro de las Rosas including *Estación Victorino*, Nuñez y Victorino Rodriguez, fashionable. **Folk music** *Pulpería El Viejo Rincón*, Dumesnil y Mendoza. Excellent music till 0500. **Tango** *Confitería Mitre*, Mitre railway station, Sun 2130.

Local holidays 6 Jul, *Foundation of the City*; 30 Sep, *St Jerome*, 7-10 Oct.

Shopping In the centre the main shopping area, with lots of *galerías*, is off Plaza San Martín.
On Sat shops (apart There are 3 **modern malls** (open 1000-2200): *Patio Olmos*, Vélez Sarsfield y San Juan,
from those in shopping varied shops, smart; *Córdoba Shopping Centre*, Goyechea 2851, Barrio Villa Cabrera,
centres) close at 1330 in with good views of the city, 12-screen cinema; *Nuevo Centro Shopping*, 4-screen cin-
summer, 1830 in winter ema, Av Duarte Quirós, Barrio Santa Ana (has a 24 hr supermarket).The following **supermarkets** open on Sun: *Spar*, in the bus terminal; *Americanos*, Corrientes 161, also at Entre Ríos y Chacabuco and Obispo Trejo y Ituzaingo; *Disco*, Velez Sarsfield 138. **Handicraft market** in Rodríguez y Canada, Sat/Sun 1600-2300, over 200 artisans dis-playing ceramics, leather, woodcrafts and metalware. **Bookshops** *Librería Blackpool*, Dean Funes 395, for imported English books. **Health foods** Health food shops in *galería* on 27 de Abril opposite Plaza Fundador.

Tour operators *ASATEJ*, Caseros y Belgrano, T4265225, F4247503, cordoba@asatej.com.ar Youth travel specialists; *Argentina Turística*, Vélez Sarsfield 30, T4243236. Recommended. *Alexandria*, Belgrano 194, planta alta, T4237421, for budget travel.

Transport **Local Bus** municipal buses and electric buses (trolleys) do not accept cash; you have to buy tokens (*cospeles*) or cards from kiosks, normal US$0.80, *diferencial* US$1.30. **Car hire** *Avis*, Corrientes 452, T4227384, F4222483 and airport, T4816473. *A1*, Entre Ríos 70, T4224867. *Budget*, Figeroa Alcorta 50, T4244822. *Dollar*, Chacabuco 185, T4210426. *Localiza*, Castro Barros 1155, T4747747. At the airport are *Avis*, *A1*, *Hertz*, *Localiza* and *American Remis*.

Long distance Air Pajas Blancas airport, 13 km north of city, has shops, post office, a good restaurant and a *casa de cambio* (open Mon-Fri 1000-1500). A taxi to the airport costs US$9. Bus service, known as Travellers' Airport Service (TAS), between airport and hotels, US$3.50, run by *Ecuador* (24 hr reservations T0800-5550224), punctual, good service. Local bus services (cheaper but less convenient): *Ciudad de Córdoba* bus from the terminal (ticket office 34) US$1, 40 mins; Bus No 55 from Chacabuco between Rosa de Santa Fe y San Jerónimo, US$0.80, 40 mins. There are several flights to **Buenos Aires** daily, about 1 hr, *Aerolíneas Argentinas*, *Lapa*, *Southern Winds*. *Andesmar* fly to **Tucumán**, **La Rioja**, **Salta**. To **Puerto Iguazú**, *Southern Winds*, US$147. *Southern Winds* also fly to **Mendoza, Tucumán, Salta, Neuquén, Bariloche, Mar del Plata** and **Rosario**. *AR*, *TAN* and *Kaiken* fly to most major Argentine cities. International flights with *TransBrasil* and *Varig* to Brazil, with *Americana* to Peru, and to Uruguay direct, others via Buenos Aires.

Bus Large terminal conveniently situated at Blvd Perón 300. In the basement are a bank with ATM (does not change TC's) and left luggage offices, US$1 per bag per day; the ground floor has booking offices and a very helpful tourist information office; there are shops and cafés on the first floor and a restaurant, supermarket, pharmacy, *locutorio*, and showers on the top floor. Very busy at peak travel periods. Remises can be hired at the southern entrance.

To **Buenos Aires**, *Ablo*, *Costera Criolla*, *Chevallier* or *Cacorba*, 10 hrs, US$30 *común*, US$50 *diferencial*: to **Salta** (US$30) and **Jujuy** (US$35), *Panamericano*, 4 daily, *La Veloz del Norte*, twice, about 12 and 15 hrs. To **Mendoza**, 10 hrs, 6 a day with *TAC*, slow, 1 daily with *Uspallata* US$40, avoid La Cumbre. To **Tucumán**, US$24, 8 hrs, about 8 a day, *Panamericano* has more than other companies. To **Posadas**, *Expreso Singer*, *Crucero del Norte* (very good buses), *Encon*, US$34, 18 hrs. To **Santa Fe**, frequent, 5½ hrs, US$22. To **Rosario**, *Ablo*, frequent, US$22. To **Trelew** US$69, 17 hrs. To **Comodoro Rivadavia**, US$88, 24 hrs, *TUS*. To **Río Gallegos** US$95, 36 hrs, *El Pingüino*. To **Mar del Plata** US$45-55. To **La Rioja**, 4 a day, 6½ hrs, US$20. Some go on to Catamarca, US$16. To La Rioja-Aimogasta-**Tinogasta**-**Fiambalá**, *El Cóndor*, daily 1500, 2320 (*Fiambalá* Mon, Thu only). To **La Rioja**, *Chevallier*, 6½ hrs, US$20, also *coche cama*. To **Catamarca**, *Chevallier*, 4 a day, US$20, 6 hrs. To **Belén** (Catamarca), *La Calera*, Mon, Wed, Fri, 2100, US$28.

In general, it is best to travel from Córdoba if you are going north, as it may be hard to get a seat if boarding en route

To the Sierras de Córdoba To **Alta Gracia**, 1 hr, every 15 mins from the *Plataforma Auxiliar*, US$2, by ticket on bus. To **Villa Carlos Paz**, US$2, *SATAG*, fast, efficient,1 hr, every 15 mins, continues to **Cosquín**, US$3.50, and **La Falda**, US$5, *SATAG*. To **Villa Carlos Paz**, also *Car-Cor* minibus service, from town centre (Humberto 1° 57) every 40 mins, US$3.

International services To **Asunción** (Paraguay) direct, US$57, 16-18 hrs, *Brújula*, Sat 1400, *Cacorba*, Wed/Sun 1400. To **Montevideo** (Uruguay), US$57, 16 hrs, *Encon*, Tue, Fri, Sun, 1700, *EGA*, Mon, Wed, Sat 1745. To **Santiago** (Chile), US$40, 16 hrs, *Tas-Choapa*, Wed, Fri, Sun 2100, *El Rapido*, daily 2130. To **Lima** (Peru), 65 hrs, US$110, via Chile, *Tas-Choapa*, Wed/Sun, *El Rapido*, Tue, Fri, Sun. To **Pocitos** (Bolivian border), US$50, *CMP Express*, *Panamericano*, *Atahualpa* and *Andesmar*, daily 18 hrs.

Train One daily service only from the Mitre station (opposite bus terminal) to **Villa María**, 1830, 2½ hrs, US$6, T4282114. The *Tren de las Sierras*, a tourist train to Capilla del Monte, runs on Sat/Sun only, from Rodríguez del Busto station (15 km out of town), which is reached by buses 51, 53, 54 and 56. Departs 0900, returns 1530, US$20 return, T4822252.

Airline offices *Aerolíneas Argentinas/Austral*, Colón 520, T4267601/2, open 0900-1730. *Lapa*, Figueroa Alcorta 181, T4258000. *LAB*, Colón 119, piso 3, T4216458, open 0900-1300. *Southern Winds*, Colón 540, T4266626. *Dinar*, Colón 533, T4331700. **Banks** *Lloyds Bank*, *Banco de Galicia*, *Boston Bank* and *Banco de la Nacion*, all on Plaza San Martín, all have ATMs. Many *casas de cambio* on Rivadavia just off Plaza San Martín as well as ATMs. ATMs also at branches of *Banco de Córdoba* at Rosario de Santa Fe y Ituzaingo, San Jerónimo 258 and Gral Paz 44. Amex agents: *Simonelli Viajes*, Alcorta 50, T426186. **Communications** Post office Colón 201, parcel service on the ground floor beside the customs office. **Telecommunications** Many *locutorios*. **Internet** Many places including: *Internet Workstation*, Independencia 362, T4262841, private booths and high quality printers; *Cyber Cabildo*, in the Cabildo (entrance on Dean Funes) US$1.50 per hr, open 0900-1800. Others at Obispo Trejo 167, open Sun nights. 27 de Abril 223. Yrigoyen y San Luis. Indarte 73, cheap US$3 per hr. Rosario de Santa Fe 225. San Jerónimo 167. Chacabuco 674. Ayacucho y Dean Funes. Buenos Aires 32. Perón y Entre Ríos, US44 per hr. **Consulates** *Bolivia*, San Juan 639, piso 3, T4231672. *Chile*, Crisol 280, T4692010. *Denmark*, Nuñez del Prado 2484, T4810171. *Finland*, Chacabuco 716, T4208200. *France*, Ayacucho 46, T4221129. *Germany*, Eliseo Canton 1870, T4890826 (Honorary Consul: Carlos Dechsle). *Israel*, Velez Sarsfield 84, piso 2. *Italy*, Ayacucho 131, T4221020. *Peru*, Belgrano 313, T4210266. *Spain*, Chacabuco 875, T4697490. *Sweden*, Alvear 10, T4240111. *Switzerland*, Colón 184, piso 1, T4232170. **Language schools** Usual rates of pay for teaching English in private language schools US$7-10. *Casa de Lenguas*, General Bustos 401, T4226260, F4299402, cordoba@casadelenguas.com, small Spanish language classes, activities. *Comisión de Intercambio Educativo*, San José de Calasanz 151, T4243606, offers classes mainly pre-arranged in Germany. (Contact Kommission für Bildungsaustausch, Wrangelstr 122, DW-2000 Hamburg 20.) *Interswop*, Sucre 2828, Alta Cordoba, T4710081, F4220655, organizes stays abroad

Directory

The Central Sierras

and language classes (about US$180 per week, 25 hrs of classes) and accommodation at about US$10 per day, also exchange programmes for any nationality. Applications and details: Interswop, Bornstrasse 16, 20146 Hamburg, Germany, T/F40-410-8029. **Laundry** *Laverap*, Chacabuco 313, also at Rivera Indarte 289, and Paraná y Rondeau. *La Lavandería*, Av 182, local 4. *Lavadero Bahía*, San Jerónimo 478, open late Sunday night. others at Rosario de Santa Fe 338 and San Juan between Velez Sarsfield and Alvear. Most charge US$5 per load. **Medical services** *Hospital Clínicas*, public hospital, T4337051. *Hospital de Urgencias*, T4215001. English-speaking doctor, *Ernesto J MacLoughlin*, Centro Asistencial Privado de Enfermedades Renales, 9 de Julio 714, home Pérez del Viso 4316, T4814745. Dentist, *Dra Olga Olmedo de Herrera*, Fco J Muñiz 274, T4804378, daughter speaks English. **Tourist offices** *Dirección Provincial de Turismo*, Tucumán 25. Provincial tourist office, T4331980/2 and municipal tourist office, T4337542, both in the old *Cabildo*, on Plaza San Martín, open Mon-Sat 0930-1200, 1630-1900. The municipal office offers free maps, detailing self-guided walking tours in Spanish and English and extensive information on accommodation, helpful as well as a tour guide service to major sites, US$2, munturis@cordoba.gov.ar Provincial office Mon-Fri 0800-2000, Sat/Sun 0900-1300, 1400-2000. There are also information offices in the bus terminal, T4331980 and at the airport. For free tourist information (in Spanish) on the province T0800-4-0107. A useful information booklet is the free monthly, *Plataforma 40*, published by Nueva Estación Terminal de Omnibus de Córdoba (Netoc). *Club Andino* Deán Funes 2100, open Wed after 2100, closed Jan.

The Sierras de Córdoba

Three ranges of undulating hills rise from the pampas, their lower slopes often wooded, particularly in the south. The central range, Sierra Grande, is the longest and highest, extending for some 600 km and including the peaks of Champaquí (2,790 m), Los Gigantes (2,370 m), La Bolsa (2,260 m) and Las Ovejas (2,206 m). To the east is the Sierra Chica with its highest peak, Uritorco (1,949 m) and to the west is the Sierra de Guasapampa and its continuation, the Sierra de Pocho. In some places the peaks are separated by high plains, known as *pampas*. West of Córdoba the three ranges are 150 km wide.

At the foot of the Sierra Chica the rivers have been dammed to form large lakes: Lago San Roque on the Río Primero, the Embalse Los Molinos on the Río Segundo, and a sequence of four lakes on the Río Tercero. There are two other large dams in the hills, at Cruz del Eje and La Viña. They provide power and irrigation, and the lakes themselves are attractive. Sailing and fishing are popular.

A network of good roads gives pleasant contrasts of scenery. The climate is dry, sunny and exhilarating, especially in winter. There are innumerable good hotels and *pensiones*; names are therefore not always given. Many services are closed out of season.

Southeast of Córdoba

Routes From Córdoba two routes run southeast across the Pampas towards Buenos Aires. Route 9 (713 km) passes through **Villa María**, Km 130, a prosperous agricultural town and important route centre at the junction of Route 9 with the highway linking central Chile with Paraguay, Uruguay and Brazil. **Sleeping** at **B** *City*, Buenos Aires 1184, T420948, and **C** *Alcázar*, Alvear y Ocampo, T425948, near bus station, good value.

The other route, Route 38 runs across flatlands and rolling hills to Río Cuarto, where it joins Route 8. About half-way the road runs across the retaining wall of the great Río Tercero dam. The town of **Río Tercero** (*population* 42,657; several hotels) is a modern industrial centre with an armaments factory and petrochemical works.

Río Cuarto, 203 km south of Córdoba, is situated on the river of the same name. Founded in 1786, it has a fine Municipalidad (1932) and cathedral (1890). The **Museo Histórico Regional**, Fotheringham 178, contains displays on early white settlement and the wars against the Indians. In April to May one of the country's biggest motor races is held here.

Río Cuarto
Colour map 4, grid B2
Population: 138,000
Altitude: 439 m

Sleeping AB *Opera*, 25 de Mayo 55, T4634390, 4-star, a/c, parking; **B** *Gran*, Sobremonte 725, T433401, 3-star; **C** *Alihué*, Sarsfield 58, good value, very friendly, big rooms. Near bus terminal on Sobremonte 100-200 block are 3 cheap *Residenciales*, *El Ciervo*, *Hosp El Bambi*, *Res Monge*, all **C. Camping** Municipal site, *El Verano*.

Transport Bus To Buenos Aires, US$34, frequent service; to **Mendoza**, US$24; to Córdoba, US$10; to **Santiago, Chile**, frequent.

Directory Banks Lucero Viajes, Constitución 564, T433656, only place changing TCs, 3% commission.

North and east of Cordoba

Provincial route 57 runs north from Córdoba through pleasant little townships such as Villa Allende, Río Ceballos, Salsipuedes and La Granja. At El Manzano, Km 44, an unpaved road branches west to La Cumbre. At **Candonga** (altitude 1,000 m), 15 km along this road, there is a chapel built in 1730 as an oratory of the Jesuit Estancia of Santa Gertrudis. ■ *Tue-Sun 0900-1300, 1500-1800.*

Route

Ascochinga is an unremarkable village but 14 km further north is **Santa Catalina**, which was the most important Jesuit *estancia* in the Sierras de Córdoba. Founded in 1622, the site includes the church with its twin towers and elegant façade, the cemetery with a baroque gateway and the residence. Only the church can be visited: the key is kept at the house to its right. ■ *Getting there: Buses from Jesús Maria, twice a day.*

Ascochinga
Colour map 4, grid A2
61 km N of Córdoba; 20 km W of Jesús María

Sleeping and eating Río Ceballos D *La Gloria*, Av San Martín 5495. Affiliated to IYHA, warmly recommended. 3 campsites. Several campsites also at **Salsipuedes**. **Candonga** *Hostería Candonga*, good meals. **Ascochinga B** *Hostería El Cortijo*, full board only, good value, small swimming pool and river outside, horses for rent, US$1 per hr. Campsite at Tres Cascadas falls, 5 km west, open all year.

North along Route 9

Route 9 is the main road north to Santiago del Estero.

This is the site of another former Jesuit *estancia*: though dating from the 16th century, most of the buildings are 18th century. Apart from the fine church and the former residence, there is, in the cloisters, an excellent **Museo Jesuítico**, one of the best on the continent; it also has an important archaeological collection. ■ *Mon-Fri 0800-1200 & 1400-1900, Sat & Sun 1600-2000.* The remains of the famous winery can also be visited: wine from Jesús María was reputed to have been the first American wine served to the Spanish royal family. South of the town centre is the **Casa de Caroya**, another former Jesuit property now housing the excellent **Museo de Immigración**, which focuses on the settlement of the large Italian community in **Colonia Caroya**, 3 km south Jesús María. At **Sinsacate**, 4 km north of Jesús María, is a fine colonial posting inn, with long, deep verandah and chapel attached, which is now occupied by the **Museo Rural**

Jesús María
Phone code: 03525
Colour map 4, grid A3
Population: 21,000
Altitude: 533 m
51 km N of Córdoba

The Central Sierras

de la Posta. ■ *Summer Tue-Sun 1500-1900; winter Tue-Sun 1400-1800.* Each January Jesús María celebrates a popular gaucho and folklore festival, lasting 10 nights from second week. Good fishing in winter.

Sleeping *Rizzi*, Tucumán 664, T420323, 2-star. *Napoleón I*, España 675, T421273. *Hosp Del Plata*, Tucumán y Colón. **Camping** *Los Nogales*, on western outskirts near river.

Transport Bus Direct to Córdoba, US$2, 1½ hrs; to Buenos Aires, *TAC*, US$30.

Parque Arqueológico y Natural Cerro Colorado

This provincial park covering 3,000 ha with eagles, white woodpeckers and foxes, containing about 30,000 rock paintings scattered among some 200 sites, some of them underground. Painted by the Comechingones Indians between the 10th century and the arrival of the Spanish, the paintings, in red, black and white, portray animals, hunting scenes and battles against the Spanish. There is also a small archaeological museum. ■ *US$1, includes guide.*

In the centre of the park there is a village: among the houses is the former home of the Argentine folklore singer and composer Atahualpa Yupanqui, now a museum, which can be visited, US$2, ask in the village for the curator.

The park can only be visited with a guide: guides available from the administration building, the tour lasts one to 1½ hours. There is a hostería and campsite. ■ *Getting there: By an unpaved road, 12 km, which branches off Route 9 at Rayo Cortado, 104 km north of Jesús María. Daily bus from Jesús María at 1610.*

Villa de María
Population: 2,400

This is the birthplace of Leopoldo Lugones, a poet of country life. His house is a museum. It lies 136 km north of Jesús María.

Laguna Mar Chiquita
At times the water is so salty you can float in it

This large salt-lake is fed by three rivers: from the north by the Río Dulce which flows through a large area of marshland known as the **Bañados del Río Dulce** and from the south by the Ríos Primero and Segundo from the Sierras de Córdoba. As the lake is shallow (maximum depth 12 m) and has no outlet, its size varies – 65 to 80 km by 30 to 40 km – according to rainfall patterns. The lake and its coastline form the **Reserva Natural Bañados del Río Dulce y Laguna Mar Chiquita**, an important nature reserve providing a feeding area in summer for migratory birds from the northern hemisphere. The vegetation is similar to the wetlands of the Chaco. There is fishing for *pejerrey* all year round and during the summer it is very popular with visitors; its salt waters are used in the treatment of rheumatic ailments and skin diseases. Park administration is situated in **Miramar** on the southern shore. This Mar Chiquita and Miramar should not be confused with the other Mar Chiquita and Miramar on the Atlantic coast. It is situated on the southern margin of the Chaco, 211 km northeast of Córdoba and about 320 km southeast of Santiago del Estero.

Sleeping *Savoy*, San Martín y Sarmiento, cheap, very friendly. **Camping** *Autocamping Lilly*, Bahía de los Sanavirones.

The Punilla Valley

Situated between the Sierra Chica to the east and the Sierra Grande to the west, the Punilla valley is the most popular tourist area of the Sierras de Córdoba. Its rivers are drained by two reservoirs, Lago San Roque, 27 km west of Córdoba, in the south, and Embalse Cruz del Eje, in the north. From Villa Carlos Paz Route 38 runs north along the valley through a string of resorts where there are many hotels and campsites. The northern resorts are quieter and more interesting than the southernmost ones, particulary in Argentina holiday periods.

Villa Carlos Paz, situated on Lago San Roque 35 km west of Córdoba, is a large and rather uninteresting resort with many hotels and often crowded. Tours available on catamarans to the two dams on the lake (daily 1500, US$10, 1½ hours); launch trips also available. A chair-lift runs (0900-1900) to the summit of the Cerro de la Cruz, which offers splendid views. There is also a museum of meteorites, entry US$2.

Villa Carlos Paz
Phone code: 03541
Colour map 4, grid A2
Population: 46,000

Excursions Cerro Los Gigantes, (2,374 m), west of Villa Carlos Paz, is a paradise for climbers. It is reached by an unpaved road which runs through **Tanti** (15 kilometres west; population 3,200; altitude 900 m; accommodation) over the Pampa de San Luis to Salsacate. At Km 30 a road branches west to Los Gigantes, the base for climbing the granite massif. Tanti can be reached by local bus for Villa Carlos Paz and local buses connect Tanti with Los Gigantes. Club Andino has a *refugio*; details in Villa Carlos Paz. Further west at Km 65 a road branches off to **La Candelaria**, 25 km north, where there is a former Jesuit *estancia* and a church dating from 1693. From here a road runs west to La Higuera. The **Observatorio Bosque Alegre**, 31 km south, can also be visited, see page 183.

Sleeping C *El Monte*, Caseros 45, T422001, F422993. Very good. Recommended. **C** *Mar del Plata*, Esquiú 47, T422068. Recommended. **C** *Villa Carlos Paz Parque*, Santa Fe 50, T425128. Full board available, recommended. **D/E** per person, *Acapulco Hostel*, La Paz 75, T421929, F431030, acapulco@hostels.org.ar Hostelling International, breakfast extra, kitchen and laundry facilities, pool. **D** *Wanda*, Alvear 479, T/F421760, nice garden. **Camping** ACA site, San Martín y Nahuel Huapi, T422132. *Club de Pesca*, España y Av Atlántica, and *Los Pinos*, Curros Enríque y Lincoln, open all year. Many others.

Plenty of hotels in all price categories

Shopping Best buys leather mats, bags, pottery.

Tour operator *Recep Tur Carlos Paz*, in bus terminal, T421725, offer tours to Capilla del Monte US$13, to La Cumbrecita US$24.

Transport Bus Terminal at San Martín y Belgrano, near centre. To Córdoba every 15 mins in summer, US$2; taxi to/from Córdoba airport, US$10.50. To/from **Buenos Aires**, *Ablo*, US$26; also *Cacorba*, *Chevallier*, *General Urquiza*.

Directory Banks *Banco de Córdoba*, San Martín, accepts US$ cash only. **Communications** Post office and telephone San Martín 190. **Laundry** San Martín y Libertad. **Tourist offices** San Martín 400, near terminal, T421624.

On the banks of the Río Cosquín, Cosquín is known as the National Folklore Capital. It is the site of Argentina's most important folklore festival, beginning in the last week in January. There is also a national *artesanía* festival in the same month. There are good views over the Punilla valley from Cerro Pan de Azúcar (1,260 m), situated 7 km east of town in the Sierra Chica. Chairlift to top (all year round). **Museo Camin Cosquín** on Route 38, 3 km north of centre, minerals and archaeology. Recommended.

Cosquín
Colour map 4, grid A2
Population: 16,400
26 km N of Villa Carlos Paz,
63 km from Córdoba

Sleeping Several places near the bus terminal including: **C** *La Serrana*, P Ortiz 740, T451306, good. **C** *Italia*, Ternengo y Vértiz, T452255. Recommended. **D** *Ideal*. Several campsites.

Tourist office Plaza Próspero Molino; 0700-2100 daily in high season, 0800-2000 daily off season.

The Central Sierras

Transport Bus To **Córdoba**, US$3.60, 1½ hrs, *Empresa La Calera* via the San Roque dam or Satag via Carlos Paz.

La Falda
Phone code: 03548
Colour map 4, grid A2
Population: 14,000
82 km N of Córdoba

La Falda is a good centre for walks in the surrounding hills. The **Hotel Edén**, built 1897 as a grand hotel, visited by illustrious figures early this century, but closed since the 1960s, can be visited. ■ *Guided tours only; daily 0930-1200, 1600-1900 in season, 1000-1200, 1500-1800 off season, US$3.* There is also a **Model Railway Museum** at **Las Murallas Zoo**. ■ *Daily 0930-2000 in season, Sat/Sun only 1000-1200, 1500-1900 off season. Las Murallas 200* and **Museo Arqueológico Ambato** that is privately run, well displayed. ■ *Thu-Sun and public holidays 0900-2000, US$0.50. Cuesta del Lago 1467.*

Excursions Valle Hermoso is 5 km south. Here is the old restored chapel of San Antonio which is a gem and well worth a visit. There is a small museum; displays include palaeontology and archaeology. Horseriding is available. **Huerta Grande** (971 m), 3½ km north, is a bathing resort with good fishing and medicinal waters. The *Estancia El Silencio*, 11 km east, T424809, offers trekking and horseriding.

Walk A good circular route is to the **Cascadas de Olaén** via a road west from La Falda. At Km 16 turn left and follow for 2 km to the crossing marked 'Cascadas de Olaén', from where it is 4½ km further to the falls via the Capilla Santa Bárbara, a Jesuit chapel dating from 1747. Return to the crossing and turn right; follow dirt road for about 12½ km until you reach Route 38 from where it is a further 12 km north to La Falda.

Sleeping About 80 hotels in all categories, all full in Dec-Feb holiday season; La Falda is visited mostly by the elderly, many hotels belong to pension funds. **AL** *Nor Tomarza*, Edén 1603, T422004 and **AL** *Tomaso di Savoia*, Edén 732, T423013. **AB** *La Scala*, La Plata 59, with breakfast, pool. **D** *Hostería Los Abrojos*, Goya s/n, Valle Hermoso, T/F470430. Hot water, also full board, sports, excursions. **E** per person *Malvinas*, 2 blocks from terminal, meals available. Houses for rent 1 Mar to 30 Nov on a monthly basis. **Camping** *Balneario 7 Cascadas*, T423869, west of centre, hot water, cafétéria.

Eating *El Cristal*, San Lorenzo 39, where the locals eat. *La Parrilla de Raúl*, Buenos aires 111, *tenedor libre.*

Tour operators *Aventura Club*, 9 de Julio 541, T/F423809. Trekking, jeep tours, camping, birdwatching etc. *Wella Viajes*, Av Edén 412, loc 12, T0548-21380. Offers 15% discount to ISIC and youth card holders for trekking, climbing, etc to Cerro Champaquí.

Transport Bus To **Córdoba**, US$4, 2 hrs; to **Buenos Aires**, Cacorba, Cita, US$40.

Directory Banks *Banco de la Nación* and *Banco de Suquía* for exchange. **Communications** Post office Av Argentina y 9 de Julio. **Telecommunications** Telecom, San Martín 6. **Tourist offices** Av España y de la Torre.

La Cumbre offers fine views from the statue of Christ the Redeemer on the hill. Trout streams with good fishing from November to April. Swimming, golf, tennis; hang gliding and parapenting nearby at Cuchi Corral. The **Estancia El Rosario**, 6 km southeast of La Cumbre, offers horseriding, parapenting, excursions and sports, daily 0830-1830. **Cruz Chica**, 2 km north of La Cumbre (altitude, 1,067 m), is a wealthy residential area with English-style houses and gardens in pine woods. The **Museo Manuel Mujica Laínez**, occupies the former house of the Argentine writer, US$3, in season daily, off season at weekends only 1400-1800. **Los Cocos**, 8 km north of La Cumbre, is a popular mountain resort with good hotels and many holiday houses.

La Cumbre
Colour map 4, grid A2
Population: 6,500
Altitude: 1,141 m
12 km N of La Falda

Climb up El Mastil &
beyond for the views
& birds

Sleeping and eating **La Cumbre AL** *Lima*, Moreno y Dean Funes, T451727. With breakfast, excellent facilities, pool, quiet. **C** per person *Victoria*, Posadas s/n, T451412. Charming, small. *Res San Antonio*, Caraffa 449, T451338. **C** *Res Peti*, Paz y Rivadavia, good. *Pizza Luis*, Rivadavia 267. Recommended. **Cruz Chica** *Reydon*, T/F451056, reydon@coopvg.agora.com.ar, beautiful setting, English spoken. **Los Cocos** *Blair House*, Grierson, T492147. English-style. Recommended. *Host Walcheren*, T/F492049. *Host del Mediterraneo*, Los Tulipanes s/n, T492023. *Los Pinos*, Grierson s/n, T492002, F492188. *Los Molles*, Grierson s/n. T492001. **Camping** *El Cristo*, Cabrera s/n, T451839.

Tourist office Caraffa 300, T451154 near bus terminal.

Transport **Bus** To **Córdoba**, US$4.50.

Capilla del Monte is the best centre for exploring this part of the Sierras. The location of many sightings of unidentified flying objects, the area is popular for 'mystical tourism' and there are tours to meditation and 'energy' centres. There are good opportunities for walking, windsurfing on the El Cajón reservoir, parapenting from Cerro Las Gemelas and rock-climbing. Horse riding costs US$20 per half day.

Capilla del Monte
Phone code: 03548
Colour map 4, grid A2
Population: 7,620
Altitude: 979 m
109 km N of Córdoba

Excursions **Cerro Uritorco**, with an altitude of 1,979 m, 6 km northeast, is a four-hour climb, via La Toma, 4 km, where there are medicinal waters and from here there are further walking opportunities. A trip to **Los Alazanes** dam *(altitude 1,400 m)*, 10 km southeast, can be reached via La Toma. **San Marcos Sierra** *(altitude 680 m)*, 22 km west, is known as *capital de la miel* for the quality of its honey. There is an 18th-century church, several hotels and campsite. From here it is another 12 km northwest to the Cruz del Eje dam; there are parakeets and small farmhouses and good views along the way. The **Quebrada de la Luna**, 14 km north, is the highest point in the Sierra Chica.

Sleeping **AB** *Cerro Uritorco*, Alem 671, T482069. Pool, trekking, horseriding and camping. **B** *Hosp Italia*, Rivadavia 54. Clean, showers, opposite bus terminal. **D** per person *la Loma*, Frías 123, T481138, pool. *Roma*, Corrientes 387, T481083. Pool, a/c. **D** per person *Las Gemelas*, Alem 967, T481186, F481239, 7 blocks from centre, half board. **C/D** *Hosp Centro*, Irigoyen y Funes, T482116. Many others in all categories. **Camping** Municipal site *Calabalumba*, 600 m north of the centre, **E** per tent, hot water, recommended, also *cabañas*. *Witcoin* on road to La Toma, T481801. *Cabañas La Toma*, US$10 per tent.

Tourist office In old railway station, T481341, open daily 0830-2030, some English spoken.

The Central Sierras

Transport Bus To **Córdoba**, 3 hrs, US$10; to **Buenos Aires**, many companies, US$38.

Cruz del Eje
Phone code: 03549
Colour map 4, grid A2
Population: 25,500

Cruz del Eje, 39 km further northwest near the dam, is an uninteresting town famous for its olives. Boats for hire on the reservoir where there is good fishing. **Sleeping** at **AB** *Posta de las Carretas*, Ruta 38 y Rua Moyano, T42517. Good, service station and restaurants. **C** *España*, Caseros y Alsina, T42702, friendly, family-run. **Camping** is possible at foot of dam.

The Traslasierra Valley

Its name, meaning 'Across the Sierra', implies an isolation from Córdoba on the far side of the Sierra Grande

Situated west of the Sierra Grande and east of the Sierra de Guasapampa, this valley is much less developed than the Punilla Valley and offers better opportunities for the independent traveller. Sandy soils limit agriculture in the valley but potatoes, olives and grapes are grown. Three rivers, the Ríos Los Sauces, Mina Clavero and Panaholma, provide irrigation. From Cruz del Eje a road runs south through the valley to Villa Dolores and into San Luis province.

Camino de las Altas Cumbres

The main road to the valley from Córdoba is the most spectacular route in the Sierras. The road, running southwest from Villa Carlos Paz passes **Ycho Cruz**, by the Río San Antonio (**D** *Hostería Avenida*, with bath; several campsites) before climbing into the Sierra Grande and crossing the Pampa de Achala, a huge desert plateau of grey granite and descending into the Traslasierra valley near Mina Clavero.

The **Parque Nacional Quebrada de los Condoritos**, covering 40,000 ha of the Pampa de Achala and the surrounding slopes was created in 1995 to protect the spectacular Quebrada de Los Condoritos, an 800 m deep gorge. It is reached by a 7 km track. This is the easternmost habitat of the condor which nests in the walls of the gorge: they are best seen from a rocky outcrop known as *El Balcón*. Information from *guardaparques* or from Club Andino in Córdoba.

Sleeping B per person *La Posta*, Km 101, T/F03544-70887, with breakfast. **AL** per person full pension, beautifully situated, great views, also has an *Albergue*, **C** per person, with breakfast, without bath, reservations advisable.

Transport Bus From **Córdoba** to Ycho Cruz, US$2, *Cotap*; to El Cóndor US$5.

South of Cruz Del Eje

The road from Cruz del Eje passes through several uninteresting towns and across the flat Pampa de Pocho before reaching Mina Clavero (Km 139). South of Salsacate a road branches off east across the Sierra Grande to Villa Carlos Paz via Los Gigantes (see above) and another branches west towards Chepes via the **Quebrada de la Mermela**, Km 87, a gorge which is entered by passing through five tunnels. Beyond the gorge, at Km 107 a turning leads off to the **Parque Natural Chancani**, 4,920 ha, which protects one of the last remnants of *Chaqueño* forests in this area.

Mina Clavero
Phone code: 03544
Colour map 4, grid A2
Population: 5,100
140 km W of Córdoba

Mina Clavero lies at the confluence of the Ríos Panaholma and Mina Clavero and at the foot of the **Camino de Las Altas Cumbres**; it is a good centre for exploring the high *sierra*. Black ceramics are a traditional product of this area. There is a fascinating museum, **Museo Rocsen**, 13 km south and about 5 km from the village of Nono. ■ *Daily 0900 till sunset, US$3, taxi from Mina Clavero US$5.* The road south of Nono, near the Embalse La Viña, a reservoir surrounded by forests, is lined with hotels and campsites.

The Museo Rocsen

The Museo Rocsen is perhaps one of the most unusual museums in Argentina. The life's work of Juan Santiago Bouchon, a native of Brittany, France, it contains over 12,000 items arranged under 56 themes. Though there are sections on archaeology, geology, anthropology and oceanography, it also contains European furniture, musical instruments, vehicles, machinery and much more.

At the age of 8 Bouchon discovered a clay figure of a Roman soldier 2,000 years old while digging in a Roman amphitheatre: the discovery changed his life. After studying anthropology and fine arts and teaching himself natural sciences, he moved to Argentina in 1950 with 8,000 kilograms of luggage.

Working for the French tourist office in Buenos Aires, he travelled the country, before settling in Nono in 1959. The first museum building, covering 100 square-metres, was opened in 1969; it now occupies 1,325 sq-m. The great façade of the building is marked by 49 human statues, designed by Sr Bouchon to trace human history; not one is of a military figure; the last is of Martin Luther King. The museum is staffed by members of Sr Bouchon's family.

Though his museum may appear to be a collection of everything and anything, Sr Bouchon is clear about his aim, believing that single-theme museums bore most visitors, and he plans to extend the museum by a further 2,700 sq-m.

The Central Sierras

Sleeping and eating B *La Posada*, Sarmiento 1394, T470179. With breakfast. C *Ferrari*, Oviedo 1334, T470172. With breakfast. C *Marengo*, San Martín 518, T470224. With breakfast. D per person *La Morenita*, Urquiza 1142, T470347. With breakfast, parking. D per person *Las Leñas*, Muiño 1208, T470714. E per person *El Parral*, Vila 1430, T470005. E per person *Res Jonathan II*, Mitre 1208, opposite terminal, with breakfast. **Camping** Several sites including *La Siesta*, at north end of town and 3 sites west of centre. **On the road south of Nono** C *Las Mil y Una*, Km 13, T498167, excellent, restaurant, helpful. D per person *Castillo Villa La Fontana*, Km 20, between Los Hornillos and Los Rabanes, E per person without bath, in beautiful 1920s Italianate palace, attractive gardens, English spoken, cooking and laundry facilities, highly recommended. *Rincón Suizo*, Champaquí 1200, serves good pastries.

There are over 70 hotels, though many close off season

Sport Climbing *Traslasierra Turismo*, Mitre y Merlo, T/F470929, organize day trips to Champaquí, minimum 4 persons, US$40 per person including equipment. **Horseriding** *Mis Montañas*, at Los Hornillos, Km 22 south, T0544-49015, F0544-94435, German and English spoken.

Transport Bus Terminal in centre at Av Mitre 1191. To **Córdoba**, US$10, 6 a day, 3 hrs; to **Buenos Aires**, *TAC*, US$40, 12 hrs; to **Mendoza**, 8½ hrs, US$26.

An uninteresting town Villa Dolores lies 45 km south of Mina Clavero and 187 km southeast of Córdoba. However, as an administrative centre and market town, it is the most important centre in the valley. The **Museo de la Ciudad**, Sarmiento y San Martín, contains displays on natural history and archaeology and a model of the Sierras de Córdoba. ■ *Mon-Fri 0800-1200, 1500-1900*. South of here the road continues to Merlo and Villa Mercedes.

Villa Dolores
Colour map 4, grid A2
Population: 21,000

Sleeping B *Sierras Grandes*, San Martín 9, T/F420088. Without breakfast, gloomy, overpriced. D per person *Vila Plaza*, on Plaza, T421691. Without breakfast, parking, poor beds. D *Hosp Cáceres*, Brizuela 390. D *Res Champaquí*, Germán 166, T422358. D per person *Hosp Sonia*, Brizuela 415, T422938, opposite terminal, without breakfast. At Las Tapias, 10 km east is B per person *La Posta de Mistal*, T420893. Half board, pool, tennis, restaurant. **Camping** Nearest site at Piedra Pintada, 6 km northeast, pleasant village well situated for walks into mountains.

Tourist office 25 de Mayo 1, Monday-Friday 0800-1400.

Transport Bus Terminal at Brizuela y Tomás Edison. To **Buenos Aires**, *Chevallier cama*, US$40, 12 hrs; to **San Luis** 5¼ hrs. To **Córdoba**, several companies, US$8-10, 5 hrs. To **Mendoza**, *TAC*, US$26, 8 hrs; to **Mina Clavero**, frequent, US$3, 1½ hrs.

Champaqui   The highest peak in the Sierras (2,884 m), Champaqui is topped by a bronze bust of San Martín. It can be climbed from Las Rosas, 15 km east of Villa Dolores, or from San Javier, 12 km southeast. The route from San Javier goes by La Constancia, a ruined *estancia* set in a river valley with pine and nut trees. To the summit takes eight to 10 hours, the descent to La Constancia four hours. Neither route should be attempted in misty weather. The easiest way to climb Champaquí is from Villa General Belgrano in the Calamuchita valley, see page 183. Some 2 km south of San Javier, at the foot of Champaquí, in a region of woods and waterfalls is **Yacanto**, which has curative waters.

Sleeping Available in both San Javier and Las Rosas. A good base is *Vai Kunta* (Postal address 5885 Las Rosas), 2-hr walk from Los Molles, run by Rolf Graf (Swiss), good food, guides. Taxis to Los Molles from *pizzería* near bus station in Las Rosas.

The Calamuchita Valley

Situated south of Córdoba, west of the Sierra Chica and east of the Sierra Grande, this valley is a prosperous agricultural zone, producing cereals, alfalfa and fruit. It provides fine walking opportunities in wooded countryside. Route 5 runs from Córdoba south past Alta Gracia before climbing through the hills around the Embalse Los Molinos and continuing to the artificial lakes of the Río Tercero, 117 km south of Córdoba.

Alta Gracia   Alta Gracia occupies the site of a 17th-century Jesuit *estancia*. With the arrival
Phone code: 03547   of the railway and the building of the Hotel Sierras (1908), the town became a
Colour map 4, grid A2   popular resort for sufferers from respiratory diseases, among them the young
Population: 39,000   Che Guevara. Che grew up here after his parents left his birthplace of Rosario
39 km SW of Córdoba   to live in the more refreshing environment in the foothills of the Andes. He had
started to suffer from asthma which would plague him for the rest of his life.

The major buildings of the *estancia* are situated around the plaza. The church, completed in 1762, with a baroque façade but no tower, is open for services only. ■ *Summer Mon-Sat 2000, Sun 1000 & 1800; winter Mon-Sat 1800, Sun 1000 & 1800.* To the north of the church is the former Residence, built round a cloister and housing the **Museo del Virrey Liniers**. ■ *Tue-Fri 0900-1300, 1500-1830, Sat, Sun 0930-1230, 1530-1830, US$1 (all day in summer).* To the south of the church are the former workshops, now occupied by a school. North of the residence is the **Tajamar**, an artificial lake built by the Jesuits. The clock tower, on its corner, dates from 1938: its figures include those of a gaucho, an Indian, a Jesuit and a conquistador.

Northwest of the centre in parkland is the abandoned Sierras Hotel, and, beyond it, the **Museo Manuel de Falla**, the house where the Spanish composer spent his final years. ■ *Closed Monday, entry US$0.30. Pellegrini.* There are beautiful views from the Gruta de la Virgen de Lourdes, 3 km west of town.

The Graf Spee

The Graf Spee, a German 'pocket' battleship launched in 1934, was small enough to avoid the restrictions put on the German navy in 1919 but was more heavily gunned than any cruiser afloat and faster than any vessel which could outgun her. In 1939, the Graf Spee sank nine merchant ships in the Atlantic before being cornered on 13 December by three British cruisers. After a 14 hour battle in which one British ship was badly damaged, the Graf Spee's commander, Captain Hans Langsdorff, retreated into the neutral port of Montevideo, where the 36 German crewmen killed were buried. Langsdorff asked to stay in Montevideo for 2 weeks to repair his ship; the Uruguayan government, under British pressure, gave him 2 days. On 17 December the Graf Spee sailed out to sea. Crowds, lining the shore in fading light to watch the expected battle, saw the vessel sink within minutes. All the remaining crew and 50 captured British seamen on board were rescued. Hitler had given the order to scuttle the vessel rather than allow it to be captured. Two days later, in Buenos Aires, Langsdorff wrapped himself in the flag of the Imperial German Navy and committed suicide.

Most of the crew were interned in Argentina where they were warmly welcomed by the German community of Buenos Aires. British pressure forced the Argentine government to disperse them: groups were sent to Mendoza, Córdoba, San Juan, Santa Fe and Rosario and over 200 were kept on Isla Martín García. Their reception in the towns of the interior varied: in Córdoba they were welcomed by the governor, while in Mendoza they were stoned by locals and beaten up by the police. Many of the officers escaped and returned to serve with the German navy, much to the annoyance of the British who suspected Argentine government connivance. The German embassy, meanwhile, tried to enforce military discipline and to prevent the men from getting friendly with local women.

In 1945 the US and British governments demanded the repatriation of all the men to Germany. Nearly 200 sought to avoid this by marrying Argentine women and a further 75 escaped, but in 1946 the British navy deported over 800 men to Germany. Many, after 6 years in Argentina, had no wish to return to a country shattered by defeat and within 2 years all those who wished to return to Argentina were allowed to do so.

Excursions To the **Observatorio Bosque Alegre**, 17 km northwest, which at the time of construction contained the largest telescope in South America. ■ *Thu 1600-1800, Sun 1000-1200 & 1600-1800.* The surrounding area affords good views over Córdoba, Alta Gracia and the Sierra Grande.

Sleeping *Covadonga*, Quintana 265, T421456. *Hostería Reina*, Urquiza 229, T421724, good. **Camping** *Los Sauces* in the Parque Federico Garcia Lorca.

Tourist office Tourist office inside clock tower by Lago Tajamar.

Transport Bus To **Córdoba**, US$2, every 15 mins, 1 hr.

A pleasant and popular resort in attractive countryside, it is a good centre for excursions in the surrounding mountains. The town is very German looking. Founded in the 1930s, its German character was boosted by the arrival of interned seamen from the *Graf Spee*, some of whom later settled here. There is a monument to the crew in the Plazoleta Graf Spee. Genuine German smoked sausages and cakes are sold. The *Confitería Chocolate*, San Martín 8, owner, Héctor F de la Fuente, sells such delights. He is also very informative on local hikes and activities.

Villa General Belgrano
Phone code: 03546

Population: 4,500
85 km S of Córdoba

Museums The **Museo Arqueológico Ambrosetti**, collection of artefacts from the Comechingon Indians, the original inhabitants of the valley. The **Museo del Carruaje**, old carriages and cars. The **Museo Ovni**, on southern outskirts, dedicated to unidentified flying objects, but with archaeological exhibits and a good library, US$3.

Excursions **La Cumbrecita**, with an altitude of 1,450 m, is a charming German village 40 km west, where there is good walking and riding. At Km 6 there is an 18th-century chapel, the oldest in the valley. South of La Cumbrecita is **Villa Alpina**, a small resort 55 km west along a poor gravel road and the base for climbing Champaqui.

Sleeping **AB** *Bremen*, Route 5 y Cerro Negro, T461133. Restaurant, sports facilities. **A** *Edelweiss*, Ojo de Agua 295, T461317, F461387. Pool, excellent food. *Berna*, V Sársfield 86, T/F461097. **B** *Hostería Alfred*, Uruguay y Roca, T461119. With breakfast, very good, French spoken, horseriding. **C** *Res Alpino*, Roca y 25 de Mayo, T461355, F462177. Without breakfast, kitchen facilities. **Villa Berna**, 25 km west: *Cougar Hill*, T0546-87018, English, French, German spoken, very helpful. **La Cumbrecita** **AB** *Cascadas*, T481015, with pool, tennis etc. **AB** *Panorama*, higher up hill (T498406). *La Cumbrecita*, T498405, F481052. *Las Verbenas*, T481008. Also *Las Verbenas*,T481008, *Kuhstall* and *Casa Rosita* (**C**, cheapest). Restaurants *Tirol* and *Raices*, both good. **Villa Alpina** chalets; youth hostel, T0571-21947. **Youth hostels** **C/D** per person *El Rincón*, in beautiful surroundings 600 m from terminal, cooking and laundry facilities, highly recommended (reservations: Patricia Mampsey, Casilla 64, T461323, cordoba@hostels.org.ar). *Estancia Alta Vista*, T462238. 14 km from town on route to La Cumbrecita, both offer discounts to ISIC and YHA card holders (20% and 25% respectively). **Camping** *San José*, 2 km north of town, T462496. *Camping Arroyo* and municipal site, both near Arroyo El Sauce.

Festivals *Oktoberfest* beer festival in Oct; *Fiesta de la Masa Vienesa*, Easter week; *Festival del Chocolate Alpino* in Jul.

Transport **Bus** To/from **Córdoba**, 2 hrs, US$6, hrly (sit on the left). To **Mendoza**, US$28. To **Buenos Aires**, *San Juan Mar del Plata*, daily 2000, 11 hrs, US$48, several other companies. To **La Cumbrecita** by taxi (US$33, 1-1½ hrs) or by 7 *Lagos* bus, 4 a day, US$8.

San Luis Province

South of the city of San Luis is flat and of little interest but in the northern part of the province three ranges of hills run from north to south: the Sierra de las Quijadas in the west, the Sierra de San Luis in the Centre and the Sierra de Comechingones to the east. In the first of these is the spectacular Parque Nacional Sierra de las Quijadas.

San Luis

Phone code: 03652
Colour map 4, grid B2
Population: 110,000

San Luis is the provincial capital. Founded by Martín de Loyola, the governor of Chile, in 1596, it is a modern city and good centre for exploring the Sierra de San Luis. It lies 770 km west of the capital.

Sights On the south side of Plaza Independencia is the **Convento de Santo Domingo**, the oldest building in the city, dating from the 18th century; the adjacent church is modern. Visit the **Centro Artesanal San Martín de Porras**, next to the monastery, where rugs are woven. ■ *Mon-Fri 0700-1300*.

Just outside the city are two artificial lakes, Embalse Potrero de los Funes, 15 km northeast, surrounded by woods and picnic areas, and Embalse Cruz de Piedra, 10 km east, which offers good fishing. Just north of the latter is El Volcán, a *balneario* with camping and picnic.

Excursions

Pres Illia A *Quintana*, No 546, T/F438400. Best, without breakfast, large rooms, restaurant. **AB** *Aiello*, No 431, T425609, F425694. With breakfast, a/c, spacious, garage. Rrecommended. **AB** *Gran San Luis*, No 470, T425049, F430148. With breakfast, restaurant, pool. **AB** *Gran Hotel España*, No 300, T437700, F437707, also cheaper rooms **B**, gloomy but clean.

Sleeping

Elsewhere AB *Grand Palace*, Rivadavia 657, T422059. With breakfast, parking, central, spacious, good lunches. *Intihuasi*, La Pampa 815 (behind Casa de Cultura). Spotless, TV, lounge. Highly recommended. **C** *Iguazu*, Ejercito de los Andes 1582, T422129, basic. **C** *Rivadavia*, Rivadavia 1470, T422437. Without breakfast, good beds, gloomy, opposite bus terminal. Next door is **D** *17 de Octubre*, which should be avoided, gloomy, basic, run down. **D** *San Antonio*, Ejército de los Andes 1602, T422717. Without breakfast, restaurant. *Res Buenos Aires*, Buenos Aires 834, T424062. *Res Los Andes*, Ejercito de los Andes 1180, T422033.

Outside the city L *Hotel Potrero de los Funes*, T430125/20889, F423898 (Buenos Aires, 25 de Mayo 516, 11th floor, T4313-4886, F4312-3876). Luxury resort and casino on lake of the same name, sports and watersports, lovely views. *Villa Andrea*, at El Volcán, F494009. Pool, restaurant. Several hotels along Route 20 to El Volcán.

Camping 3 sites in El Volcán: *El Volcán*, T427447, F421337. *El Rincón*, and *Salto Colorado*.

Most close at weekends; hotel restaurants are closed Sunday, *San Luis'* closes Sat too. *El Cantón de Neuchatel*, San Martín 745. Opposite Cathedral on main plaza, is open Sun, modest. *Michel*, Lafinur 1361, good food and service. *Campo La Sierra*, 18 km west on Route 20. Swiss run, also offers horseriding and trekking.

Eating

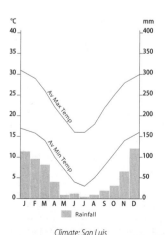

Climate: San Luis

Bus terminal at Vía España between San Martín y Rivadavia. To **Buenos Aires**, US$33-45. To **Santiago** (Chile), 9-10 hrs, *Turbus* US$30, *Tas Choapa* US$25. To **Mendoza**, US$16, 3 hrs. To **Córdoba**, US$20, 7½ hrs.

Transport

Banks Very difficult to change TC's, try **Banco de Galicia**, Rivadavia y Belgrano, 1.5% commission. **Tourist office** Junín y San Martín, excellent. Subsecretaría de Turismo, 9 de Julio 934, T433853, www.sanluis.gov.ar

Directory

The most direct route to Córdoba, is by Route 146 which runs north from San Luis to the west of the Sierras de Córdoba through San Francisco del Monte de Oro, Luján and Villa

Routes

Dolores. An alternative is Route 20 which runs east through La Toma to meet Route 148 (see above) which follows north to Villa Dolores along the western edge of the Sierras. Route 7 leads across the pampas to Buenos Aires via Villa Mercedes, 99 km southeast.

Parque Nacional Sierra De Las Quijadas
97 km NW of San Luis Excursions can be organized from San Luis

Situated in the northwestern corner of the province, the park covers 150,000 ha including the **Potrero de Aguada**, a huge natural amphitheatre of nearly 4,000 ha surrounded by steep red sandstone walls, eroded into strange shapes. Archaeological remains include evidence of dinosaurs and pterosaurs. The vegetation is largely scrub though species such as the *quebracho*. Wildlife includes guanaco, collared peccaries, cougars, tortoises, crowned eagles and peregrine falcons and condors. It is worth a visit but there are no facilities and no wardens: take everything with you including water. ■ *Getting there: By an unpaved road which turns off from Route 147 (San Luis to San Juan) at Hualtarán.*

San Luis centre

The Sierra de San Luis

Situated northeast of the city of San Luis, this range of hills is little known to travellers but is becoming more accessible with the building of paved roads. The sierra is a centre for mining green onyx.

San Luis to Carolina

The western edge of the sierras, around Carolina, can be visited by taking Route 9 north from San Luis.

El Trapiche
Km 42

An attractive village set on the Río Trapiche in wooded hills; there are summer homes, hotels and picnic sites. **Sleeping** at **A** *Hostería Los Sauces*, T493027, *El Parque*, T493058 and *Hostal Los Pinos*, T493009. **Camping** at the municipal site, south near the Embalse La Florida. *Schmidt* is further north by the river. Nearby is the La Florida reservoir which offers good fishing. ■ *Getting there: Bus from San Luis, US$4 return.*

Carolina
Km 84

Carolina is a former gold-mining town at the foot of Tomolasta (2,018 m) which offers great views. It is accessible by four-wheel drive vehicles. Though the goldmine is closed, it can be visited. A statue of a gold miner overlooks the main plaza. Gruta de Intihuasi, 21 km southeast, is a cave formed by a natural arch. The paved road ends at Carolina: an unpaved track leads north over the Cuesta Larga to San Francisco del Monte de Oro, from where it is possible to follow Route 146 to Villa Dolores. **Sleeping** at *Hostería Las Verbenas*, T424425.

San Luis to San Martín

The central part of the sierras is best reached by Route 20 to La Toma, from where a paved road runs north to San Martín.

La Toma is the cheapest place to buy green onyx. From here you can make an excursion to Cerros Rosario, interesting hills and rock scenery, 10 km northwest. **Sleeping C** *Italia*, Belgrano 644, T421295, hot showers.

La Toma
84 km E of San Luís

Known as **San Martín**, this is a good centre for exploring the rolling hills of the northern sierra. The Dique La Huerta, 7 km west, offers good fishing for *pejerrey*. From San Martín an unpaved road runs north to reach Route 146. **Sleeping** at **E** per person, *Hostería Eva Perón*, with bath and breakfast, meals served, good value, recommended. ■ *Getting there: Buses from San Luis 1 daily; from Villa Mercedes 2 a day in summer*.

Libertador General San Martín
75 km N of La Toma

Eastern San Luis

Founded in 1856 as a fortress, Villa Mercedes is an important route centre with little of interest. The old municipal market (Chacabuco y Mitre) is now an arts and community centre.

Villa Mercedes
Population: 77,000
Phone code: 03657

Sleeping and eating ACA hotel **B** *San Martín*, Lavalle 435, T422358. Restaurant, parking. **C** *Libertador*, near bus terminal, with bath, without breakfast. Some cheaper places on Mitre.

Transport Air Airport at Villa Reynolds, southeast. **Bus** Terminal on Plaza San Martín opposite Municipalidad. To Buenos Aires US$28. To **Villa Dolores** 1 hr.

Lying east of the Sierra de San Luis and west of the Sierra de Comechingones, this broad valley runs into the Traslasierra Valley to the north. From Villa Mercedes Route 148 runs north through **San José del Morro**, Km 49, where there is an 18th-century chapel. Nearby is the Sierra del Morro, the remnants of a collapsed giant volcano; inside its crater are small volcanic cones (there is a model in the Museo de Ciencias in Buenos Aires). Lots of rose-quartz can be found here. From here Route 148 follows the Río Conlara north towards Villa Dolores (see page 181). More scenic is Provincial Route 1 which runs parallel to the east along the base of the Sierra de Comechingones through a string of pretty villages like Villa Larca, Cortaderas, Carpintería and Merlo.

The Conlara Valley

Situated almost at the San Luis-Córdoba border, some 150 km north of Villa Mercedes, Merlo is a small town on the steep western slopes of the Sierra de Comechingones. A popular holiday centre, Merlo claims a special microclimate: its altitude makes it cooler than the pampas and it is sheltered from the humidity of the damp easterly winds. Locals claim that it also benefits from specially high levels of ionization, atmospheric ozone and nitric oxide, which are purported to be beneficial for the nervous system. These high concentrations are explained by the presence of uranium in the local rocks. The area is being promoted for its rich wildlife, particularly birds. On the plaza is the church dating from 1720, though the town itself was only founded in 1797. There are many good walks especially in the Sierra (for example the climb to Cerro Linderos Alto via the hill with a cross; the Circuito de Damiana Vega, three to four hours) and excursions to *balnearios*, waterfalls and other attractions. Some 8 km north of Merlo is **Piedra Blanca**, a small settlement in attractive surroundings. Nearby is a giant *algarrobo* tree, known as the *agarrobo abuelo*.

Merlo
Phone code: 03656
Colour map 4, grid A2
Population: 6,000
Altitude: 895 m

The Central Sierras

Sleeping and eating Most in Merlo are along Av del Sol. **A** *Rincón del Este*, T475306. 5 km from centre, recommended. **AB** *Altos del Rincón*, De los Cesares 2977, T476333. Small but pleasant rooms. **AL** *Parque*, Av del Sol 821, T475110. With breakfast, tennis, golf, pool. At Villa Elena, 26 km south, is **B** per person *Posada del Sol*, T420017, half-pension, pool, tennis, restaurant, English spoken.

Tour operators Mountain biking, trekking, horse riding and fishing are all available. *Valle del Sol*, T476109, offer tours to the Sierra de las Quijadas US$45 per person, minimum 6 persons. For tours to the Sierra del Morro contact Carlos Lasalle, Hostería Naschel, T491277. **Tourist office** Mercau 605, T476078.

Transport Bus Terminal 3 blocks from the plaza. Frequent services to **San Luis**. To **Buenos Aires**, *TAC*, *Sierras Cordobesas* and *Chevallier*, US$35, 12 hrs. To **Córdoba**, *TAC*, 7 hrs.

The West

6

The West

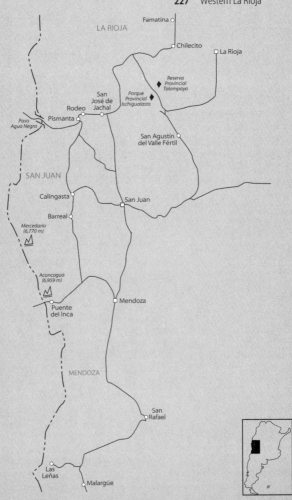

The Provinces of Mendoza, San Juan and La Rioja stretch east from the Pampas to the heights of the Andes and the Chilean frontier. Mendoza is the most dynamic city in this region; lying on the main Andean crossing to Chile, it is at the heart of the main fruit-growing and wine making area in Argentina. Winter sports and climbing are popular in the mountains to the west of the city; the most popular climb is Aconcagua, the highest peak in the world outside Asia. The route to Chile, through the Cristo Redentor tunnel is spectacular, though less so than the descent on the Chilean side of the frontier; highlights on the Argentine side include the Puente del Inca, a natural stone bridge regarded as one of the natural wonders of South America. Further afield from the city of Mendoza are other attractions. In the far south of Mendoza province there are two centres for adventure sports, at Valle Grande, in the steep sided Cañon de Atuel, and at Malargüe; nearby is the international ski resort of Las Leñas.

San Juan and La Rioja, both north of Mendoza, are less popular with travellers than Mendoza but both offer diverse and spectacular landscapes, especially at the Ischigualasto and Talampaya parks which lie on the border between these provinces.

The West

Background

Geography

Provincial populations:
Mendoza 1,412,481;
San Juan 528,715;
La Rioja 220,729.
Population capitals:
Greater Mendoza
773,559; Greater San
Juan 353,456;
La Rioja 110,494

The western parts of these three provinces are dominated by the two ranges of the Andes. The *Cordillera Principal* or western range and the *Cordillera Frontal* or eastern range. Between them are high upland valleys. The western range, which is the highest and forms the frontier with Chile, declines in altitude south of Mendoza. The mountain passes are over 3,000 m in Mendoza but over 4,000 m further north. Highest peaks are Aconcagua (6,959 m), Tupungato (6,800 m), Ramada (6,410 m), de la Pollera (6,235 m), del Plomo (6,120 m), San Juan (6,111 m), Marmolejo (6,070 m), San José (6,099 m) and Juncal (6,060 m) in northern Mendoza, Mercedario (6,770 m) in southern San Juan and Pissis (6,882 m), Bonete (6,759 m), Veladero (6,436 m), Reclus (6,335 m), Olivares (6,220 m), El Toro (6,160 m), Los Gemelos (6,130 m), De Las Tórtolas (6,105 m), Famatina (6,097 m) and Calinga (6,028 m) in La Rioja.

East of the Andes lie discontinuous ranges of mountains, rising as high as 4,000 m and known as *precordillera*: between these and the Andes, running north-south, are high valleys such as Uspallata, Uco, Calingasta, Iglesia and Vinchina. The eastern half of these provinces is arid steppe, part of a great geological depression into which flow the major rivers. Two of these, the Ríos Mendoza and San Juan, flow into the Lagunas de Guanacache (also known as Huanacacha), a great expanse of marshland on the provincial borders of San Juan, Mendoza and San Luis, which is the source of the Río Desaguadero and thence into the Río Salado. The latter, which also receives the waters of the Ríos Atuel and Diamante from southern Mendoza, dries up before reaching the coast.

Climate Annual temperature ranges vary according to altitude. In the high Andes winter temperatures can drop to -30°C though even in winter daytime temperatures can rise rapidly. On the plains maximum summer temperatures range from 36°C to 43°C in La Rioja: winters in the plains are cool, but rarely below -3°C. The high valleys west of the *cordillera frontal* often enjoy the most

West Andean peaks

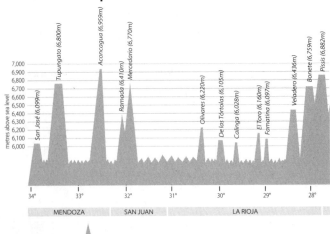

pleasant climate with winter minima of -14°C in July and summer maxima of around 30°C in February.

Sheltered from the Pacific Ocean by the Andes, these three provinces generally receive little rain. Rainfall is lowest in La Rioja, especially in the eastern steppe and highest in southern Mendoza. Although snow falls in the mountains of Mendoza in winter, snow is less common in San Juan or La Rioja. Rainfall is concentrated in the summer months and often falls as heavy storms.

Wildife

Among birds are the lesser rhea and the elegant crested-tinamou, species in which males incubate the eggs of different females. Birds of prey and scavengers include the andean condor, the turkey-vulture and the caracara. Amongst other birds are the burrowing parrot, the spot-winged falconet, the crested-gallito, the white-throated cacholote, the austral negrito, the black-crowned monjita and the white-banded mockingbird.

Mammals are mainly nocturnal. There are different species of armadillo, ranging from the small endangered pichiciego to the common wailing pichi. Among rodents are the plains vizcacha, the mara, the cavy and the tucotuco. There are also grey foxes and hog-nosed skunks. Reptiles include several species of lizards, the arboreal boa and land turtles. The wild boar, introduced first into Parque Luro in La Pampa, from Europe, is now found in large areas of the west.

Economy

In this area of slight rainfall, little can be grown except under irrigation. In Mendoza only 4% of the 15 mn ha of land are cultivated, most of it in the two important oases formed by the Ríos Mendoza and Tunuyán in the north and around the Ríos Diamante and Atuel, 160 km to the south around San Rafael. Wine dominates the provincial economy: of the cultivated area 40% is given over to vines, 25% is under alfalfa grown for cattle, and the rest is devoted to olive groves, fruit trees and vegetables. Petroleum is produced in the south of the province, and there are important uranium deposits. The main manufacturing industries are petrochemicals, chemicals and machinery.

San Juan and La Rioja are less fortunate. San Juan relies heavily on agriculture and is Argentina's second largest wine producer; La Rioja is more varied: agriculture is important, but there is also considerable mining activity for gold, silver, copper, lead, zinc and other minerals and industry includes food processing, textiles, chemicals and electronics.

The West

Mendoza

Buenos Aires	Chilecito	Las Rioja	Las Cuevas	Mendoza	San Juan	San Rafael	Ischigualasto
1230							
1175	194						
1236	864	776					
1030	668	612	196				
1150	503	447	364	165			
990	895	870	423	227	392		
1258	226	202	469	273	108	500	

The West: distance chart (km)

Situated at the foot of the Andes and surrounded by the broad plain of the Río Mendoza, the city lies at the centre of the largest conurbation in western Argentina: nearby are the towns of Las Heras, Guaymallén, Godoy Cruz, Luján del Cuyo and Maipú. Irrigation and intensive cultivation has made this the heartland of Argentine wine cultivation. The city is also an important route centre, particularly for travellers

Phone code: 0261
Colour map 3, grid A2
Population: 121,000
1,060 km from Buenos Aires

●●

The Zonda

Though the zonda, a warm, dry, westerly wind, can occur throughout western Argentina and at any time of year, it most commonly affects Mendoza and San Juan between August and October. Beginning over the Pacific as a wet wind, the zonda deposits its humidity on the Chilean side of the Andes; as it drops on the eastern side of the cordillera, its temperature increases 1°C for every 100 m. By the time it reaches the plains it is very dry and very warm, in winter causing an unseasonal

increase in temperatures and provoking snowfalls in the mountains. Though it blows away the dust in the atmosphere, allowing you to see clearly over long distances, Argentines often stress its negative effects: apart from the physical damage to houses and crops, it is said to cause headaches and sickness. The Pirelli guide to Argentina warns that it provokes "emotional instability, an increase in delinquency and even alterations in sexual behaviour!"

●●

to Chile via the Redentor tunnel, as well as a convenient base for climbing expeditions to Aconcagua. Lively and dynamic, Mendoza is more prosperous and stylish than most other Argentine provincial centres especially around Avenida San Martín, the broad main street, and the nearby Paseo Sarmiento. Away from the centre and in the streets of the surrounding towns, however, there is much less bustle and life is much more leisurely.

History Founded from Chile in 1561, the city was named after García Hurtado de Mendoza, then governor of Chile. In the colonial period it was of little significance, being governed from Chile and having little contact with modern-day Argentina. The city was completely destroyed on Easter Saturday 1861 by an earthquake which killed some 4,000 of its 12,000 inhabitants. After 1861 a new centre was planned, several blocks to the west; this modern city with its broad avenues and attractive plazas was planted with trees watered by a network of irrigation channels 500 km long.

Sights The centre of the city is the **Plaza Independencia**, a large square in the middle of which are the Museo de Arte Moderno and a theatre. On the western side and dating from the 1920s is the *Plaza Hotel*, which has accommodated Argentine presidents including Juan Perón and Evita, on their visits to the city. Though run down it is worth a visit. Next door is the Teatro Independencia which can also be visited. Off the corners of Plaza Independencia are four smaller squares: of these the most attractive is the **Plaza España**, pleasantly tiled and with a mural displaying historical episodes and scenes from *Don Quijote* and *Martín Fierro*.

East of Plaza Independencia and linked to it by pedestrianized Paseo Sarmiento is **Avenida San Martín**, the city's main boulevard and a popular meeting place. Most of the city's public buildings lie five blocks south of Plaza Independencia in the *Barrio Cívico*. The original city centre, destroyed in 1861, now known as the **Area Fundacional**, is about 10 blocks north of the centre: here there are a

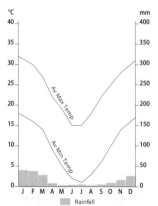

Climate: Mendoza

Mendoza and San Juan

"To be between San Juan and Mendoza" is an Argentine expression for alcoholic excess. Yet of the two provinces, it is Mendoza which dominates wine production. In an average year 71% of all Argentine wine is made within its boundaries (23% comes from San Juan) and almost all the leading wineries are based in Mendoza. Lying at about the same southern latitude as the northern latitudes of France, Italy and California, the province is favoured by its temperate climate, clearly defined seasons and lack of extremes of temperature.

The 130,000 ha of vineyards in the province are located in two main regions: in the north centred around the provincial capital and in the south around San Rafael. A third area, semi-separated from Mendoza, can be found tucked at the foot of the Andes, due west of the capital

around the small town of Tupungato.

While a few vineyards are found below 500 m, the best, in the departments of Maipú and Lujan del Cuyo, are situated at between 700 m and 1,000 m. Tupungato vineyards are at 900 m to 1,300 m. The local soils are sandy and/or calcareous, often with pebbles and limestone, and occasionally clay. The vineyards, in common with all Argentine vineyards except for a few exceptions in Salta, are planted on flat, slightly sloping land, so as to allow for efficient irrigation.

Grape picking is still almost entirely by hand, mechanical harvesting being rare. The season starts in the second half of February and ends in the first 10 days of April, though the dates vary slightly from area to area. As a result Argentine wines are ready about 6 months before European wines in any given year.

museum and the ruins of the Jesuit church of **San Francisco**. The best shopping centre is **Avenida Las Heras**, where there are good souvenir, leather and handicraft shops. At **Plaza Pellegrini**, Avenida Alem y Avenida San Juan, an attractive little square, wedding photos are taken on Friday and Saturday nights.

Ten blocks west of Plaza Independencia are the wrought iron entrance gates to the great **Parque San Martín**, covering some 420 ha and containing over 50,000 trees of 750 species, as well as watercourses, a 1 km-long artificial lake, where regattas are held, a sports stadium, an amphitheatre and the **Jardín Zoológico**, daily 0900-1730, US$3, and **Eureka**, an 'interactive science park' dealing with 'the universe, man, environment, communication and energy'. ■ *Summer: Wed/Fri/Sun 0930-1230, 1630-2130. Rest of year Tue-Fri 0930-1730, Sat/Sun 1030-1830.* There are views of the Andes (when the amount of floating dust will allow) rising in a blue-black perpendicular wall, topped off in winter with dazzling snow, into a china-blue sky. On a hill above the park is the **Cerro de la Gloria**, crowned by the **monument to San Martín**: a great rectangular stone block with bas-reliefs depicting various episodes in the equipping of the Army of the Andes and the actual crossing. In front of the block, San Martín bestrides his charger. ■ *Getting there: To reach the park entrance take*

Gran Mendoza

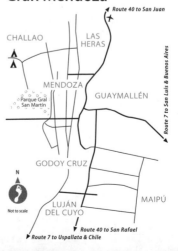

bus 110 (Zoo) from Sarmiento west of Plaza Independencia or the trolley from Sarmiento y 9 de Julio. An hourly bus ('Oro Negro') runs to the top of the Cerro de la Gloria from the east end of the park, on Avenida Libertad – it's a long walk (45 mins).

Tours
Official tours of the city are generally poor value

A large sign in Plaza Independencia shows a walking tour which takes about two hours. The municipal tourist office runs a bus service (*Bus Turístico*) around the city, with commentary by the driver every two hours from 1000 to 1800 daily from Garibaldi y San Martín, US$10, children under 12 US$5. There are 14 stops (clearly marked) and the bus waits for 15 minutes at Cerro de la Gloria: tourists can leave or join the bus at any point; tickets are valid for 24 hours. Map of route available from municipal tourist office.

Museums

Museo del Area Fundacional, Alberdi y Videla Castillo. Includes ruins of the *cabildo* of 1749 and many archaeological artefacts from the area including the mummified body of a child found on Aconcagua. The best organized museum in Mendoza. Recommended. ■ *Reached by Bus T or 110. Tue-Sat 0830-1500, Sun 1500-2100, US$1.* **Museo Histó- rico San Martín**, Avenida San Martín 1843. Housed in San Martín's former residence, this contains arms and other artefacts from San Martín's campaigns and from later wars including the Falklands/Malvinas War, 1982. Poorly organized. ■ *Mon-Fri 0930-1200, US$1.*

The West

Mendoza centre

N

0 metres 200
0 yards 200

■ **Sleeping**

1 27 de Agosto	5 Balcarce	9 Escorial	13 Necochea
2 Aconcagua	6 Cervantes	10 Galicia	14 Nutibara
3 Argentino	7 City	11 Huentala	15 Pacífico
4 Balbi	8 Crillón	12 Imperial	16 Palace

Museo Municipal de Arte Moderno, underground (*subsuelo*) in Plaza Independencia, very small unless there is a special exhibition. ■ *Mon-Sat 0900-1300, 17002100, Sun 1700-2100, US$1.50.* **Acuario Municipal**, underground at Buenos Aires e Ituzaingó, although the aquarium is small its worth a visit. ■ *US$0.50, daily 0900-1230, 1500- 2030.* **Museo Provincial de Bellas Artes** in the Casa de Fader, Carril San Martín 3671, Mayor Drumond, T4960224, on the road south to Luján de Cuyo. Excellent dedicated of works by Argentine artists, with sculpture in gardens. ■ *Tue-Fri 0830-1330, 1500-1930, Sat/Sun 1430-1930. US$41.50. Reached by bus 200, 40 mins.* For the **Museo Nacional del Vino**, see below.

Wine cellars
Prices at the bodegas have roughly a 00% mark-up from supermarket prices

Many tourist agencies include the *bodegas* in their half-day or day-long tours (US$10-13) but these visits are too short, with too few guides and little tasting – only of the cheaper wines, usually in plastic cups. Many *bodegas* welcome visitors and visiting times are available from the tourist office. Most are situated outside the city, the closest being **Bodegas Escorihuela**, Belgrano 1188, Godoy Cruz, T4242744, which also has a restaurant run by Francis Mallman. ■ *Tours Mon-Fri 0930, 1030, 1130, 1230, 1430, 1530. Easily reached by Bus T from 9 de Julio or bus 170 (subnumber 174).*

There are several *bodegas* in **Maipú**, 15 km southeast of Mendoza. Here you should see the lovely plaza and eat at the *Club Social* which offers good simple food. **La Colina de Oro**, Ozamis 1040, T4972592 has a short tour, good tasting. ■ *Getting there: bus 150 (subnumber 151) marked 'Maipú' every hr, 0900-1230, 1500-1800 from terminal, US$1.* Nearby is the **Museo Nacional del Vino**, in the Casa de Giol, Ozamis 914, T4975004. Others include: **López**, Ozamis 375, T4972406, also reached by bus 150 (subnumber 151); **'La Rural'** (**Bodega Rutini**), Montecaseros s/n, Coquimbito, T4973590, a small traditional bodega, is worth visiting. ■ *Bus 170 (subnumber 173) from La Rioja y Garibaldi, US$1.60. Tours Mon-Sat 1000-1630, Sun 1000-1200.* Also has museum. In **Guaymallén**, east of Mendoza, is **Santa Ana**, Roca y Urquiza, T4211000. ■ *Visits 0930, 1045, 1200, 1200, 1545, 1700; take the bus turístico (see above) or bus 20 (subnumber B-25) from P. Mendocinas at Plaza Independencia.*

South of the city, **Luján del Cujo: Pequeña Bodega**, Ugarte 978, La Puntilla, T4392094, is a small *bodega* with a museum. A visit is recommended. ■ *0900-1300, 1600-2000. Take bus 10 (Ugarte) from 25 de Mayo.* **Norton,** at Perdriel, Km 23.5, Ruta Provincial 15, T4880480. ■ *Tours at 0900, 1000, 1100, 1200, 1400, 1500,*

To Area Fundacional

Córdoba
San Luis ■9
Entre Rios
Acuario Municipal
■15
Rioja
Plaza Sarmiento
Av San Juan
Buenos Aires
Salta
Moreno
Av Gobernador Videla
Ituzaingó
Monte Caseros
Lavalle
Catamarca
GUAYMALLEN
Saavedra
Garibaldi
Plaza Brown
■11
■10
Av Alem
20
V López
Palacios
Don Bosco
Don Bosco
Pardo
Av Zapata
P de La Rita
Rondeau
Salta
25 de Mayo
Florida
Rep de Siria
Tte 1° Ibáñez
N Laprida
A Calle
Grl Flores
To San Luis & Buenos Aires
Av General José de San Martín
Av San Juan
Morón
Rioja
J V González
J G Godoy
Pedro Venegas

To Chile
To San Rafael

The West

La Colina de Oro

The Giol bodega, La Colina de Oro occupies a special place in the development of the Mendoza wine industry. Once the largest bodega in the world, it was named after the birthplace of Bautista Gargantini, who, with Juan Giol, founded Bodegas Giol in 1896. Oak casks for storage were imported from France, one of which, with a capacity of 75,000 litres was the largest in the world. Selling its wines under the labels La Colina and El Toro, the company expanded rapidly: at its height it employed over 800 workers, 400 of them making barrels, 180 as carters and 220 in the bodega itself. Some 1,200 mules were used for transport and the first aerial vinoducto (wine aqueduct) in the world, 3 km long, was built between the winemaking plant and one of its bodegas. Juan Giol eventually sold out to the Banco Español and in 1954 the company was taken over by the state. It was split up and privatized in 1988; the bodega is now owned by a cooperative of local vinegrowers.

1600, 1700. Bus 380 from the terminal. Further south is **Chandon**, one of the newer *bodegas*, Ruta Provincial 15, Km 29, T4980830. ■ *Tours Mon-Fri 0930, 1100, 1230, 1400, 1530, Sat (in summer only) 0930, 1100, 1230. Bus Mitre (no 380) from the terminal (platform 53 0r 54, 0745, 0800, 0840, 0930, 1030), 1 hr, US$1.60.* The **Orfila** bodega in San Martín, T02623-420637, 40 km east, located in the house of San Martín, also has a wine museum.

Excursions Trips can be made to the thermal springs at **Cacheuta**, 29 km west, and at **Villavicencio**, 47 km north, see page 204. **Embalse El Carrizal**, an artificial lake 60 km south, has yachting and fishing, campsites and picnic areas. As for climbing Aconcagua, see page 207.

Essentials

Sleeping **L** *Aconcagua*, San Lorenzo 545, T4204499, F4202083. Good service, good but expensive restaurant, pool, tourist advice and bookings available. **L** *Cervantes*, Amigorena 65, T/F4201782. Central, modern. **L** *Huentala*, Primitivo de la Reta 1007, T4200766, good. **L** *Park Hyatt*, Chile 1124 on main plaza, due to open 2001.

A *Crillón*, Perú 1065, T4238963, F4239658. Small, clean but overpriced. **A** *Nutibara*, Mitre 867, T4296628, F4296761. Central, a/c, parking, with breakfast, pool. Recommended. **AB** *Palace*, Las Heras 70, T/F4234200. A/c, with breakfast, good beds, central. **B** *San Martín*, Espejo 435, T4380677. Recommended. **A** *Vecchia Roma*, España 1615, T4232529. Next door to restaurant of same name, comfortable, safe. **A** *Balbi*, Las Heras 340, T4233500, F4380626. Pool, a/c, nice rooms, helpful. **AB** *Argentino*, Espejo 455, Plaza Independencia, T/F4254000. With breakfast, garage. **AB** *del Sol*, Garibaldi 82, T4204296, F4204820. With breakfast, good beds. Recommended. **AB** *Gran Ritz*, Peru 1008, T4235115. With breakfast. **AB** *Vendimia*, Godoy Cruz 101, T4250675, F4233099. Good.

B *Milena*, Babilonia 17 (off San Juan), T4202490. With breakfast, small rooms, quiet, fan, cozy. **B** *Acapulco*, Patricias Mendocinas 1785, T4230454, F4320124. **B** *Imperial*, Las Heras 88, T4234671. Old fashioned, central, with breakfast. **B** *City*, General Paz 95, T4251343. Including breakfast, helpful. **B** *27 de Agosto*, Amigorena 36, T4200035, F4200023. With breakfast. **B** *Petit*, Perú 1459, T4232099, without breakfast. Recommended. **B** *RJ*, Las Heras 212, T/F4380202. With breakfast, comfortable, helpful, English spoken. Recommended. **B** *Pacífico*, San Juan 1407, T/F4235444. Modern, comfortable, good value. **B** *Balcarce*, San Martín 1446, T4252579. Old fashioned, with

San Martín the Liberator

Among the independence heroes of Spanish America José Francisco de San Martín stands equal to Simon Bolívar. Like Belgrano, he advocated a monarchy rather than a republic and like Bolívar he hoped to unite Spanish America after independence. Though he failed to achieve either aim, his military genius played a major role in securing independence. This genius lay mainly in his grasp of detail and his organizational ability even when leading troops scattered by large distances and mountainous terrain. His epic crossing of the Andes in 1817 was a turning point in the Wars of Independence; the campaigns which followed in Chile and Peru ended Spanish rule in South America.

Born in Yapeyú, Corrientes in 1778 and educated in Spain, San Martín served in the Spanish army in North Africa, Spain and France, gaining his first combat experience at the age of 15. In 1811 he resigned from the army and sailed for London where he made contact with Francisco de Miranda and other supporters of South American independence. Arriving in Buenos Aires the following year, he was appointed to train a new cavalry regiment. In December 1813 he replaced Belgrano as commander of the northern armies. Arguing against the view that the way to defeat the Spanish stronghold of Peru was by an offensive through Alto Peru (Bolivia), San Martín resigned in 1814. His request to be appointed governor of Cuyo province, based on Mendoza, was granted and he spent the next 2 years preparing to carry out his plan for the capture of Peru by means of a giant flanking movement through Chile and then up the coast to Lima.

The nucleus of his Army of the Andes was drawn from regular troops sent by Buenos Aires. Financed by reorganizing the taxation system of Cuyo, the army was armed by setting up arms factories around Mendoza. San Martín personally reconnoitred the mountain passes to plan the crossing to Chile. Realizing the importance of deception, he called a meeting of Pehuenche Indian chiefs in September 1816 and asked permission to cross their territory to invade Chile via the passes south of Mendoza; as expected spies carried this news across the Andes, leaving San Martín free to use a more northerly route. Though the main force crossed by the Los Patos and Uspallata passes, smaller columns crossed further north and south. Setting out on 18-19 January 1817, 3,778 men with equipment, support services and 10,791 horses and mules crossed the Andes in 21 days, arriving on time at their intended destinations. Within days the army defeated the Spanish at Chacabuco and entered Santiago in triumph, but conclusive victory was delayed until the Battle of the Maipú (5 April 1818). With Chilean independence secure, San Martín led his forces by sea to Peru in 1820. Avoiding battle against the larger Spanish forces, he negotiated a truce and encouraged enemy desertions. Finally entering Lima in triumph, in July 1821, he assumed political and military command of the new republic of Peru.

San Martín's three meetings with Simon Bolívar in Guayaquil, Ecuador, in July 1822 are one of the most famous, and mysterious, episodes of his career. Afterwards San Martín returned to Lima, resigned his post and returned to his small farm in Mendoza. In 1824 he left for Europe, settling first in Brussels and later in Grand Bourg, France. He died in Boulogne-sur-Mer in 1850. In 1880 his remains were returned to Buenos Aires and placed in the Cathedral. Symbolizing to many Argentines the virtues of sacrifice, bravery and lack of personal gain, he is remembered by countless statues in squares across the country and by street names in even the smallest towns.

The West

breakfast. **B** *Andino*, Patricias Mendocinas 1532, T4202609, F4290059. With breakfast, parking, comedor. **B** *Royal*, 9 de Julio 1550, T4380522. Breakfast included, a/c. **B** *Sol Inn*, Lateral Norte de Av Acceso Este 400 block, Guaymallén. Near bus terminal, with bath, parking, English spoken. **B** *Las Viñas*, Martinez de Rosas 1668, T4232501.

C *Mallorca*, Roca 719, T4233079. Very clean, simple, English spoken, helpful. **C** *Castillo*, Gutierrez 572, T4231766. Clean, quiet, good value. **C** *San Remo*, Godoy Cruz 477, T4234068. With breakfast, quiet, small rooms, rooftop terrace, secure parking. Highly recommended. **C** *El Piño Azul* apartments, San Martín 2848, T4304240. **C** *Center*, Alem 547, T/F4237234. With breakfast, parking, family run, good value. **C** *Mayo*, 25 de Mayo 1265, T4254424. With breakfast, good value. Recommended. **C** *Zamora*, Perú 1156, T4257537. Reasonable. **C** *Necochea*, Necochea 541, T4253501. Pleasant, cheerful, English spoken. **C** *Escorial*, San Luis 263, T4254777. Recommended. **C** *Viena*, Las Heras 240, T420046, with breakfast. **On Juan B Justo: C** *Ideal*, No 270, T4256842, transport to bus terminal. **C** *Embajador*, No 365, T4259259. a/c, good value. **C** *Margal*, No 75, T4252013. Central, safe, good, with fan.

D *Galicia*, San Juan 881, near Alem, T4202619. Gloomy, kitchen facilities, a/c. **D** *Res Tayna*, Gral Paz 469, T4251546. With bath, **E** without, quiet. **D** *Aladym*, Patricias Mendocinas 876, with bath, central, quiet. **E** per person *Res Savigliano*, Palacios 944, T4237746, savigliano@hotmail.com Near bus terminal, with bath and breakfast, kitchen facilities, rooftop terrace, internet access. 'best hostel in South America'. Highly recommended. **E** per person *Hosp Eben-Ezer*, Alberdi 580, T4312635. Quiet, German spoken. **E** *Veris Tempus*, Tirasso 2170, T4263300. Dormitories, often has school groups, take bus 26B, 'Paraguayo', 20 mins, ask driver. **E** per person *Campo Base*, Mitre 946, T4290707, info@campo-base.com.ar Hostelling International discounts, dormitories, cooking and laundry facilities, internet access, cycle rental, very helpful, information on climbing and permits for Aconcagua. Highly recommended. **E** per person *Hostel Internacional Mendoza*, España 343, T4240018, www.hostel mendoza.net Central, dormitories, Hostelling International discounts, also rooms with bath, kitchen and laudry facilities, climbing wall, internet access, book exchange. **E** *Balear*, Mitre 998, Guaymallen (reached by bus 20), T453516. With bath, clean, excellent value.

Camping In Parque General San Martín, T/F4296656. 2 cheaper sites at El Challao, 6 km west of the city centre, reached by *colectivo* No 110 leaving every hr: *Camping Suizo*, Av Champagnat, 6 miles from city, T4411406, US$10 per site, modern with pool, barbecues, hot showers, friendly, recommended. Bus 110 (El Challao) from Calle Rioja. At Guaymallén, 9 km east: *Saucelandia*, Tirasso s/n, T4511409. Take insect repellent.

Eating *La Marchigiani*, Patricias Mendocinas 1550, good varied menu, expensive *Trevi*, Las Heras 70, good food and service. Recommended. *Posta Las Marías*, San Martín 914, English spoken, speciality is roast kid, pricey but good. *Sarmiento*, Av Sarmiento 658 (*parrilla*), good. *Parrillada Arturito*, Chile 1515, good steak, good value, popular with locals. *Montecatini*, Gral Paz 370, wide variety, good food, good value. Recommended. *Mesón Español*, Montevideo 244, good food and atmosphere, pricey, Charlie the blind pianist plays requests. *Centro Catalá*, San Juan 1436, good fixed menu. Recommended. *La Margarita*, Colón 248, pizzas, sanwiches, large patio, pleasant. *La Vuelta*, San Lorenzo 65, *parrilla libre* US$5, also pastas, sandwiches, chivito. Recommended. *Club Alemán*, Necochea 2261, Godoy Cruz. Recommended. Ice cream at *Soppelsa*, Las Heras y España and at Paseo Sarmiento 55. Recommended. *Sr Cheff*, De la Reta 1075, *parrillada*, fish, pastas, *tenedor libre*. *Il Tucco*, Emilio Civit 556, also in centre at Paseo Sarmiento 68, excellent Italian restaurants, reasonable prices. *Boccaduro*, Mitre 1976, *parrilla*, good. Good value, and big 'super pancho' sandwiches in many places, including *Pizzería Sebastián*, Alem 431. *Pizzería Mi Querencia*, Las Heras 523,

The Fiesta de Vendimia

This grand street festival, held at the beginning of March to celebrate the start of the wine harvest, is perhaps the highlight of the year in Mendoza. Its climax is a great procession through the city and along Avenida San Martín; the great array of floats celebrates aspects of the city's culture and promotes local produce. On the Saturday there is a great

outdoor extravaganza in the Parque San Martín, where a crowd of 40,000 including the Argentine President are treated to 2½ hour show which culminates in the crowning of the festival queen and a fantastic laser and firework performance. Tickets are in such demand that the event is repeated the following day.

good pasta dishes and atmosphere. *Aranjuez*, Lavalle y San Martín, nice café, good meeting place. *Mankie Snack Bar*, Las Heras y Mitre, excellent breakfasts; several good snack bars (known as *carrito* bars): *Tío Paco*, Salta y Alem; *Torombola*, San Juan 1348; *Don Claudio*, Benegas 744. *El Gran Lomo*, Rivadavia 56, Zapata 334, Belgrano 886, recommended. There are several cheap eating places near the terminal along Alem opposite the hospital. Note that toasted sandwiches (elsewhere called *tostado*) are known as *Carlitos*. **Vegetarian** *El Retaño*, Garibaldi 93, no indoor tables, cheap.

Casino 25 de Mayo 1123, daily 2100-0300. **Cinema** *Cine de Arte Eisenchlas*, known as the *microcine*, 9 de Julio 500, Thu-Sun 2200. *Cine de la Universidad del Cuyo*, Lavalle 77. Also cinemas in the Mendoza Plaza Shopping and Palmares shopping malls. **Nightclubs** *Saudades*, San Martín 213; *Treinta y Pico*, La Rioja 1339, also at 25 de Mayo 3118, discos for the over 30s. *Fechurías*, La Rioja 1523, also for the over 30s. **Nightlife** *Soul Café*, San Juan 456, T4320828, popular for jazz, lambada, blues, also theatre performances. Recommended. *Blues Bar*, Aristides Villanueva 687, very popular, reservations for eating T4290240. Several other pleasant bars along same street.

Entertainment
The most popular discos are S of the city in Chacras de Coria. Quieter bars & restaurants along Colón

18 Jan, *Crossing of the Andes*; 25 Jul, *Santiago Apóstol*; 8 Sep, *Virgin of Carmen de Cuyo*. Hotels fill up fast at the beginning of March for the *Fiesta de la Vendimia* (wine vintage festival). Prices rise at this time, and in Jul (the ski season) and Sep (the spring festival).

Local holidays

Shopping centres *Centro Comercial Plaza Mendoza*, known as *Mendoza Plaza Shopping*, about 5 km east T4490100, F4490290. Has supermarkets, shops, fast food and cinemas; take bus T or 100. *Palmares*, 7 km south, includes supermarket, shops, cinema, good restaurants; take bus T on 9 de Julio. **Camping equipment** *Casa Orviz*, Juan B Justo 532-5.500, T/F 261-4251282, www.orviz.com Sales and rental, transport, guides, information. **Handicrafts** *Mercado Artesanal*, San Martín 1133, for traditional leather, baskets, weaving. Leather goods are good and cheap, try *Alain de France*, Belgrano 20, T4285065. *El Turista*, Las Heras 351, has most of the traditional local souvenirs. **Books** *Centro Internacional del Libro*, Lavalle 14, small selection of classics and paperbacks in English located behind the counter. English language magazines and *Buenos Aires Herald* usually available from kiosks on San Martín.

Shopping
Most shops close between about 1300 & 1600

Ballooning Known as *globonautica*, this is increasingly popular, T 4217993 for information. **Gym** *Stadium*, San Juan y Buenos Aires, piso 1. Also a municipal gym at Paso de los Andes, T4200463. *Marina Natación*, indoor swimming pool, San Lorenzo 765, T4236065; municipal pool at Montecaseros y Sobremonte, T4200463. **Mountain climbing** Information from tourist office. *Club Andinista*, F L Beltrán 357, Gillén, T4319870. There is a 3-day (Thu-Sat) climbing and trekking expedition via Godoy Cruz and Cacheuta to Cerro Penitentes (4,351 m), sleeping in mountain refuge, food included. See also page 207. **River rafting** Popular; US$20-30 for 1 hr, including

Sports
The best skiing in the province is at Las Leñas, south of San Rafael (see page 210)

The West

equipment. **Skiing** Ski resorts near Mendoza are: Los Penitentes, 165 km west and Vallecito, 79 km west, both on the route to Chile (see below) and Manantiales, 63 km west of Tunuyán (south of Mendoza). Equipment hire *Piré*, Las Heras 615, T4257699 and other agencies.

Tour operators *Cuyo Travel*, Paseo Sarmiento 133, Local 14. 10% discount for ISIC and youth card
Lots, especially on holders for trekking and climbing on Aconcagua. *Turismo Sepeán*, De la Reta 1008,
Paseo Sarmiento T4204162. Friendly and helpful, have branch in Santiago (Chile). *Road Runner*, in bus teminal, trekking, horseriding, rafting. *Viajes Mendoza*, Paseo Sarmiento 129, T4380480. Trips to *El Cristo Redentor*. *ASATEJ*, San Martín 1360, T/F4290029, mendoza@asatej.com.ar *Huentata*, Las Heras 695, T4257444. *Aymara Turismo*, 9 de Julio 1023, T4205304, aymara@satlink.com For adventure tourism and climbing Aconcagua. Many agencies, including those in the terminal, run tours in high summer to the *Cristo Redentor* statue via Puente del Inca, US$28, 12 hrs, only 15 mins at statue. Other local tours offered include Mendoza city tour, US$20. Wine tour US$13; Puente del Inca, US$28. Agencies also offer longer excursions including to the Valle de la Luna, US$80, 22 hrs and to San Luis province, US$39, 15 hrs.

Transport **Local Bus** All city buses have 2 numbers: one is large and ends in zero (eg 140); below it is a smaller number (eg 141, 142, 143, etc), which is the one to look for. Local directions will usually give both numbers, eg 140, sub-número 145. The bus fare is US$0.55 per journey; tickets for 2, 4, 10 and 25 journeys can be bought at kiosks, some shops, at the terminal or at Mendobus ticket offices (there is one at Patricios Mendocinas y España on Plaza Independencia). On entering bus punch your ticket into the machine. Alternatively you can buy a single ticket (for US$0.70) on the bus. **Car hire** *Herbst*, in *Hotelera del Sol*, Garibaldi 82, T4289403, reliable vehicles from US$70 per day including mileage and insurance. Recommended. *Avis*, De la Reta 914, T4296403. *Dollar*, De la Reta 936, T4299939. *Localiza*, Mitre 1356, T (cellular) 155139000. *Aires*, San Juan 1012, T4202666. *Thrifty*, Coón 241, T4235640. **Cycles** *El Túnel*, at exit from bus terminal, buys and sells cycles, also repairs, friendly. **Cycle hire** *Piré*, Las Heras 615, T4257699, US$8 per day. Also at *Campo Base* (details under **Sleeping**). **Motorcycle repairs** César Armitrano, Rubén Zarate 138, 1600-2100. Highly recommended for assistance or a chat; he will let you work in his workshop.

Long distance Air El Plumerillo airport, 8 km north of centre, T4480017/4480944, has *casa de cambio,* a few shops, restaurant and *locutorio* but no left luggage. Plastic wrapping of luggage by *Secure Bag*, US$6. Car hire at *Avis*, *Localiza* and *Herts*. Reached from the centre by bus No 60 (subnumber 63) from Alem y Salta, every hr at 35 mins past the hr, 40 mins journey; make sure there is an 'Aeropuerto' sign on the driver's window. Taxi to/from centre US$8; to/from terminal US$10. Private cars which stay more than 15 mins are charged US$2. To **Buenos Aires**: 1 hr 50 mins, *Aerolíneas/Austral*, *Lapa*, *TAN* and *Dinar*. To **Santiago** (Chile) *Lan Chile*, daily. To **Córdoba**, *Aerolíneas Express*, *Southern Winds*. *TAN* to **Neuquén**. *TAPSA* to **Neuquen**, **Comodoro Rivadavia**, **Río Gallegos** and **Ushuaia**. *Southern Winds* to **Córdoba**, **Tucumán** and **Salta**. In the bus terminal airline information can be obtained from the *TAC* office.

Bus Terminal on east side of Av Videla, 15 mins walk from centre, T4310543, with shops, cheap restaurant, children's play room, post office, left luggage lockers, tourist information and supermarket (open Mon-Sat 0800-2130, Sun 0900-1330, 1700-2130).

Provincial services To **San Rafael**, many daily, *Empresa Uspallata, TAC, Andesmar, El Rapido*, 3½ hrs, US$10. To **Malargüe**, *Empresa Uspallata*, *TAC*, 5½ hrs, US$19, also *combi* service, *Transportes Viento Sur*, 2 a day, 4 hrs, US$20. To **Potrerillos**, *Empresa*

Uspallata, TAC, 5 a day, 1 hr, US$3. To **Uspallata**, *Empresa Uspallata* 5 a day, 2 hrs, US$8. To **Puente del Inca**, *Uspallata*, 2 a day (luggage limit 15 kgs).

Further afield To **Buenos Aires**, 15 hrs, 2nd class US$30-40, 1st class, US$55, companies include *Chevallier, TAC, Jocoli, El Rápido, Expreso Uspallata, La Estrella*, very few *coche-cama* services (*TAC* 1800, *Sendas* 1800). To **Bariloche**, *Andesmar* daily, US$70, 22 hrs, book well ahead (alternative is *TAC* to Neuquén and change). To **Córdoba**, *TAC*, frequent, several other companies including San Juan Mar del Plata, 9 hrs, US$35, *coche-cama* services operated by *TAC* and *San Juan Mar del Plata*. To **San Luis**, *TAC* frequent, several other companies including *Jocoli*, US$14, 3 hrs. To **San Juan**, *TAC*, frequent, *San Juan Mar del Plata*, *Andesmar* and several other companies, US$11, 2 hrs. To **Tucumán**, US$29, *Andesmar, Autotransportes Mendoza, TAC* and other companies (TAC *coche-cama*), all via **San Juan**, **La Rioja** (US$25, 10 hrs) and **Catamarca** (12 hrs, US$25). To **Salta**, *Andesmar, America* and other companies (via San Juan, La Rioja and Catamarca), 20 hrs, US$52. To **Mar del Plata**, *TAC* daily, 8 hrs. To **Neuquén**, *Andesmar* 3 daily, *Alto Valle coche-cama* service, 12 hrs. To **San Martín de los Andes**, *TAC*, daily with change at Neuquén, 20 hrs. To **Comodoro Rivadavia**, *Andesmar* 2 a day, *TAC* 1 a day, US$100, 32 hrs. To **Río Gallegos**, *Andesmar* and *TAC* daily 1900. To **Santa Fe**, *TAC*, Villa María, 13 hrs. To **Rosario**, US$30, 12 hrs. No services to **Puerto Iguazú**, travel via Corrientes, to **Corrientes**, TAC direct, daily, also La Estrella, with change in Tucumán, 24 hrs.

International services To **Santiago**, Chile US$20, 7-8 hrs depending on border crossing, *TAC* and *El Rápido*, 5 daily, *Tur Bus, CATA* and *Chile Bus*, 2 daily, also *Ahumada coche-cama* service, *Chile Bus*. Highly recommended; some adverse reports on *El Rápido*. Passport required when booking, tourist cards given on bus. Children under 8 pay 60% of adult fare, but no seat. Book at least 1 day ahead, shop around. The journey over the Andes is spectacular (see page 204 for a description). If you want to return, buy an undated return ticket Santiago-Mendoza; it is cheaper. There are also minibus services, US$30, 5½-6 hrs, run by Chiar, 4 a day, and Nevada, 2 a day. These run only if they have a minimum of 10 passengers. When booking, ensure that they will pick you up and drop you at your hotel; have this written on your receipt; if not you will be dropped at the bus terminal. Taxi to Santiago costs about US$90 for 4-5 people. To **Viña del Mar**, 7 hrs, US$20-25, *Tur Bus* 2 daily, *Tas-Choapa* 3 daily, *TAC, CATA* and *El Rápido* daily; to **La Serena**, 12-14 hrs, US$45, *El Rápido, CATA, Corvalle*. To **Lima**, 56 hrs, *El Rápido*, US$140, Mon, Wed, Sat 0830, *Ormeño*, US$120, Wed, Thu, Sun 0700. To **Montevideo**, 10 hrs, US$66, *El Rápido*, Tue 2000, also *EGA*, Sun 1600.

Hitchhiking Between Mendoza and Buenos Aires is quite easy. If hitching to San Juan, take bus No 6 to the airport which is near Route 40. Hitching from Mendoza to Los Andes (Chile) is easy; go to the service station in Godoy Cruz suburb (bus No 6), from where all trucks to Chile, Peru and elsewhere leave.

Airline offices *Aerolíneas Argentinas/Austral*, Paseo Sarmiento 82, T4204143. *Andesmar*, **Directory**
Espejo 189, T/F4380654 and bus terminal. *Lapa*, Rivadavia y España, T4231000, airport 4487961. *Southern Winds*, Catamarca 63, T4291413. *Ecuatoriana/VASP/TAN*, España 1008, T4340240. *Dinar*, Paseo Sarmiento 119, T/F4205138. *Lan Chile*, Rivadavia 135, T4257900. *Iberia*, Rivadavia 180, T4296248. *Varig/Pluma*, Rivadavia 209, T4293706.

Banks *Lloyds Bank* (BLSA), Gutiérrez 60. *Banco de Crédito Argentino*, España 1168. *Citibank*, San Martín 1099, gives US$ cash for TCs. *HSBC*, Espejo y 9 de Julio, low commission and good rates on TCs. Many ATMs around San Martín. Many *casas de cambio* along San Martín, including *Exprinter*, No 1198, 1.5% commission on TCs. *Santiago*, No 1199. Recommended. *Maguitur*, No 1203, 1.5% commission on TCs. *Casas de cambio* open till 2000 Mon-Fri, and some open Sat morning.

The West

Communications Post office San Martín y Colón, T4290848, Mon-Fri 0800-2000, Sat 0900-1300. *Poste restante* located in the 'sector de abonados', US$1.50, letters held for 2 months. **United Parcel Service**, 9 de Julio 803, T4237861. **Telephone** *Telefónica de Argentina*, Chile 1584. There are many *locutorios* around the centre. **Internet** *Internet Web House*, Rivadavia 56, open Sun evening. Also at *locutorios* at: Espejo 599 (open Sun). Sarmiento 202 (open daily until midnight), Zapata 191 (English spoken), Catamarca 148, Catamarca 16, San Martin 940, Garibaldi 90 and 9 de Julio 1106.

Consulates *Bolivia*, Garibaldi 380, T4292458. *Chile*, Emilio Civit 599, T4254344. *Belgium*, Cuadros 156, Godoy Cruz, T4396338. *Spain*, Agustín Alvarez 455, T4253947. *Italy*, Necochea 712, T4231640. *France*, Houssay 790, T4298339. *Germany*, Montevideo 127, 1st floor D6, T4296539. *Finland*, Boulogne Sur Mer 889, piso 6, T4340777. *Israel*, Lamadrid 838, T4282140. **Cultural centres** *Alianza Francesa*, Chile 1754. *Instituto Dante Alighieri* (Italy), Espejo 638. *Instituto Cultural Argentino-Norteamericano*, Chile 985. *Instituto Cuyano de Cultura Hispánica* (Spain), Villanueva 389. *Goethe Institut*, Morón 265, Mon-Fri, 0800-1200, 1600-2230, German newspapers, Spanish classes, very good.

Language schools *Sra Inés Perea de Bujaldon*, Rioja 620, T4290429, teaches Spanish to German speakers. Recommended.

Laundry *Lavemas*, Garibaldi 142, US$5 per load, full service. *Lava Ya*, San Martín 559; *Lavandería Necochea*, Necochea 733. *La Lavandería*, San Lorenzo 338.

Medical services Central hospital near bus terminal at Alem y Salta, T4248600. **Lagomaggiore**, public general hospital (with good reputation) at Boulogne Sur Mer 2500, T4299364. **Hosptal Materno y Infantil Humberto Notti**, bandera de los Andes 2600, T4450045. Medical emergencies T4280000. **Late night pharmacies** *Del Aguila*, San Martín y Buenos Aires, T4233391; *Del Puente*, Las Heras 201, T4259209, both open 0800-2400. There is a private gynaecological clinic at Gral Paz 445, T4233560, Mon-Fri 0830-1200, 1530-2000, Sat 0830-1200, helpful and relatively inexpensive.

Tourist offices Provincial office, San Martín 1143, T4202800. Municipal offices at Paseo Sarmiento/Garibaldi y San Martín, T4201333, central, very helpful, open 0900-2100, and at Las Heras 670, T4296298. Also at bus terminal (opposite Plat 30), T431300 and airport, T4306484, helpful (frequently closed). They have a list of reasonable private lodgings and a hotel booking service (**B** range and upwards), and other literature including lists of *bodegas* and an excellent free town and province map.

Useful addresses *ACA*, Gob Videla y Reconquista, T4313510. *Migraciones*, San Martín 1859, T4380569. *Travelling Student*, San Martín 1366, local 16, T4290029/30.

From Mendoza to Chile

This route, Route 7, via the Redentor tunnel, is the most important border crossing between Argentina and Chile, giving access to the Chilean capital, Santiago, and the surrounding district. It is an area of great beauty. From Mendoza the road rises steadily on the Argentine side; climbing the steep sided valley of the Río Mendoza. Beyond Uspallata the valley broadens before narrowing again and climbing steeply to reach Puente del Inca. There are fine views of the Tupungato volcano in the distance and of Aconcagua which dominates the crossing. The most spectacular section of the crossing is, however, on the Chilean side where the road descends via a series of steep hairpin bends towards the Chilean town of Los Andes; on a clear day there are superb views over the Chilean countryside.

This route is sometimes blocked by snow in winter (June-October): if travelling by car in these months enquire about road conditions from ACA in Mendoza. Officially, driving without snow chains and a shovel is prohibited between Uspallata and the border. ACA and Chilean Automobile Club sell, but do not rent, chains, but ask at YPF station in Uspallata about chain rental.

If driving in mountains remember to advance the spark by adjusting the distributor, or weaken the mixture in the carburettor, to avoid the car seizing up in the rarified air. Document work for leaving Argentina can be carried out in advance at *Migraciones* in Mendoza or in Uspallata or at the frontier.

There are two alternatives of Route 7 from Mendoza as far as Uspallata; the southern route following the Río Mendoza via Cacheuta, is much easier than the northern one which runs through Villavicencio. Look out for detours between Santiago and Uspallata caused by the construction of a dam between Cacheuta and Uspallata.

Villavicencio is noted for its hot springs and pleasant walks nearby. The town attracts many tourists. The *Gran Hotel* is under restoration but the park can be visited. Beyond Villavicencio the road is unpaved over the spectacular **Cruz del Paramillo**. At an altitude of 3,050 m it offers fine views of Aconcagua, Tupungato and Mercedario and round the *Caracoles de Villavicencio*, 365 bends which give the route its name, *La Ruta del Año* (Route of the Year). ■ *Getting there: There are no bus services but Viajes Mendoza (see page 202, tour operators) use this route for excursions to the mirador, Wed, Sat, Sun, 0930, US$17.*

Villavicencio
Altitude 1,700 m
Km 47

Along the southern route to Uspallata, 42 km west of Mendoza, Cacheuta has thermal springs. Entry costs of US$8. There are indoor thermal baths for a variety of ailments but they are for residents only.

Cacheuta
Altitude: 1,245 m

Sleeping L *Hotel Termas*, T4316085, full board. *Hostería Mis Montañas*, 400 m west. **Camping** 2 sites *Camping Termas de Cacheuta*, T4259000. *Camping Don Elias*, 4 km west.

Transport From Mendoza take bus 40 to Luján and change.

This is a charming resort situated at the foot of the Cordón del Plata mountains which is excellent for birdwatching in the summer. A 21 km road turns off here to the south and runs to the ski resort of **Vallecito** (season July-September) which has a ski-lodge, four *refugios*, ski school, restaurant. In summer you can hike to Vallecito from Potrerillos taking two days. On the first you see desert scenery, blooming cactus flowers, birds and an occasional goat or cow and on the second you walk surrounded by peaks, a steep but not difficult climb to the San Antonio refuge, usually open with beds and meals. **Sleeping** at **AL** *Gran Hotel*, T0624-82010 (or via *Hotel Plaza*, Mendoza) with meals. **Camping** at an ACA campsite. *Restaurant Armando* is recommended.

Potrerillos
Altitude: 1,354 m
Km 58

This is the only settlement of any size between Mendoza and the Chilean frontier. A former silver and zinc mining town, it lies in the valley of the Río Uspallata. A road follows the valley north to Barreal (108 km) and Calingasta (see page 216), unpaved for its first part and tricky when the snow melts and floods it in summer. North of the town are Las Bóvedas, several metal foundries built of *adobe* and an Inca *tambería*. There is a small, interesting museum.

Uspallata
Colour map 3, grid A2
Population: 3,000
Altitude: 1,751 m
Km 100

Sleeping A *Valle Andino*, Ruta 7, T0624-20033. Good rooms and restaurant, heating, pool, including breakfast, ACA discount. **AB** *Uspallata*, T420003. Nice location, but run down, good service. **C** *Hostería Los Cóndores*, T420002, good restaurant. *Donde Pato*, Ruta 7, good food and service. **Camping** Municipal site, US$3 per tent, hot water.

Transport Bus From Mendoza, 0700, 1000, US$10.

West of The road crosses a vast, open, undulating plain, wild and bare. On all sides
Uspallata stand the grey, gaunt mountains. On the far side of this plain the valley narrows
till Río Blanco is reached, the road climbs steeply and the mountain torrents
rush and froth into the river. The majestic cone of **Tupungato**, one of the
giants of the Andes, rising to 6,800 m, can be seen by looking left up the
Tupungato valley about 2 km after Punta de Vacas. **Walking tours** in the
Tupungato area can be arranged by Quinche Romulo, Alte Brown, Tupungato
(a town 73 km southwest of Mendoza), T0622-88029.

Los Penitentes A small ski resort named after the majestic mass of pinnacled rocks. From their
Altitude: 2,580 m base (easily reached with a guide from Puente del Inca – see below), the higher
Km 165 rocks look like a church and the smaller, sharper rocks below give the impression of a number of cowled monks climbing upwards. Skiing is good with only
a few people on slopes. There are 28 pistes with a total length of 24 km and eight
lifts. ■ *May-Sep. Daily ski hire US$35, lift pass US$30.*

Sleeping AB-B *Ayelén*, T4259990, comfortable. **C** *La Taberna del Gringo*, Km 151,
Villa Los Penitentes. Recommended. *Hostería Penitentes*, and others. **B** *Cruz de Caña*
ski club, 1 km west, only open in season, with comfortable dormitories, including
meals, and a good restaurant. The owner organizes trekking expeditions to Plaza de
Mulas on Aconcagua; US$50 a day full board during expedition, and US$20 per mule.

Puente del Inca Puente del Inca is a sports resort set among mountains of great grandeur. The
Colour map 3, grid B1 natural bridge after which the resort is named is one of the wonders of South
Population: 100 America. It crosses the Río Mendoza at a height of 19 m, has a span of 21 m,
Altitude: 2,718 m and is 27 m wide, and seems to have been formed by sulphur-bearing hot
Km 172 springs. Watch your footing on the steps as they are extremely slippery. There
Puente del Inca is are hot thermal baths just under the bridge that are very dilapidated but a new
the best point for bath has been built between the bridge and the small church which is good for a
horseriding excursions soak and the scenery is magnificent. West of the village (you can walk along the
into the higher old railway), to the right, there is a fine view of Aconcagua sharply silhouetted
Andean valleys against the sky. Los Horcones, the Argentine customs post, is 1 km west. To
visit the Laguna Horcones in the Parque Provincial Aconcagua see below.

Sleeping AB-B *Hostería Puente del Inca*, T4380480. Less off-season, very pleasant
atmosphere, friendly service, good food, more expensive if booked in Mendoza. **E** *La
Vieja Estación*, per person, old railway station, T4321485. Dormitory, kitchen facilities,
meals served. If both places are full, ask at the army office (big building north side of
the road, 400 m from the *Hostería* towards Chile), they have beds for US$10.
E *Parador del Inca*, per person, with breakfast, dormitories, sleeping bag essential,
cheap meals. **Camping** *Los Puquios*, 1 km east; also possible next to the church, if
your equipment can withstand the winds. Better site near Laguna de los Horcones in
the Parque Provincial Aconcagua.

Transport Bus *Expreso Uspallata* from Mendoza, US$10, 5 hrs, 0700 and 1000,
returning from Puente del Inca 1130 and 1615; local buses also go on from Puente del
Inca to Las Cuevas, *Expreso Uspallata*, US$12 return (**NB** Take passport). Most buses
from Mendoza to Santiago de Chile refuse to drop passengers here but *El Rápido* will
do so if you book in advance. To continue to Santiago take *Tur Bus* service, 1000, 1400,
US$16 but make sure you ask for an international ticket.

The West

The mountain gets its name from the Quechua for 'stone sentry'. Five great glaciers hang from its slopes. While its north face is relatively easy to climb (the list of successful ascents includes two Italians on bicycles in 1987 and four blind climbers in 1994) the south face is almost impossible. The north face was first climbed by Zurbriggen of the Fitzgerald Expedition in 1897. In 1985, a complete Inca mummy was discovered at 5,300 m. Best time for climbing is from end-December to February.

Aconcagua
The highest peak in the world outside Asia Altitude: 6,959 m

The **Parque Provincial Aconcagua**, 75,000 ha, includes 30 other peaks over 4,000 m, nine of them over 5,000 m. Entry is via the Valle de los Horcones, 2 km west of Puente del Inca; here is a Ranger station, excellent views of Aconcagua, especially in the morning; free camping, open climbing season only. From here the route leads past the **Laguna de los Horcones** with reflections of Aconcagua in its green waters. At **Confluencia** (3,200 m), three hours further walking, there is a campsite (recommended if pacing yourself). Confluencia is the meeting point of two valleys: Horcones Superior and Horcones Inferior, which lead to the **Plaza de Mulas** and **Plaza de Francia** base camps respectively. There is no drinking-water after Confluencia: take your own.

At Plaza de Mulas (4,370 m), 38 km from Puente del Inca, there is a rescue patrol. The area is crowded in summer. Plaza de Francia (4,200 m), 25 km from Puente del Inca, is less crowded.

Here is the highest hotel in the world

Permits A permit is required for trekking or climbing between November 15 and March 15. This must be obtained in advance from Dirección de Recursos Naturales Renovables, Parque Gral San Martín, Mendoza, T4252090, open Monday-Friday 0800-1900 high season, 0800-1200, 1600-2000 low season, Saturday/Sunday (all year) 0800-1200 (the office is 50 m from the main gate). Seven-day trekking January US$40, December/February US$30, rest of year US$10. For climbing a 20-day permit is required (foreigners: January US$120, December/February US$80, rest of year US$30, Argentines half-price).

Access Allow at least one week for acclimatization at lower altitudes before attempting the summit. There are two access routes: Río Horcones and Río Vacas, which lead to the two main base camps, Plaza de Mulas and Plaza Argentina respectively. Río Horcones starts a few kilometres from Puente del Inca, at the Horcones ranger station. About 80% of climbers use this route. From here you can go to Plaza de Mulas (4,370 m) for the North Face, or Plaza Francia (4,200 m) for the South Face. The intermediate camp for either is Confluencia (3,300 m), four hours from Horcones. Río Vacas is the access for those wishing to climb the Polish Glacier. The Plaza Argentina base camp is three hours from Horcones and the intermediate camps are Pampa de Leñas and Casa de Piedra. From Puente del Inca mules are available (list at the Dirección de Recursos Naturales Renovables, about US$250 for 60 kg of gear one way; arrange return before setting out for a reduced two-way price. At Plaza de Mulas is the highest hotel in the world (see below) and a accident prevention and medical assistance service (climbing season only); crowded in summer. The same service is offered at Plaza Argentina in high season only. Climbers are advised to make use of this service to check for early symptoms of mountain sickness and oedema.

Equipment Take a tent able to withstand 100 miles per hour winds, and clothing and sleeping gear for temperatures below -40°C. Equipment hire at hotel.

The West

Sleeping *Hotel Plaza de Mulas*, the highest hotel in the world, **L** per person full-board, **B** per person without meals, good food, information, medical treatment, recommended, also camping area, open high season only.

Climbing information Trekking and climbing programmes can be booked through agencies in Mendoza and Buenos Aires (eg *Proterra Turismo*, Lavalle 750, p 20 D, T/F4326-2639). Prices from US$990 to US$1,890 for 10 days. Treks and climbs are also organized by: Sr Fernando Grajales, the famous climber who lives in Penitentes in summer but can be contacted via his family at Moreno 898, Mendoza, T493830, grajales@satlink.com or via Eduardo Ibarra, manager of the *Hotel Plaza de Mulas;* Roger Cangiani at *Campo Base* in Mendoza. Highly recommended. *José Orviz*, Juan B Justo 536, Mendoza, T/F4251281, for hire of mules, transportation and equipment. Also recommended in Mendoza are Rudy Parra, *Aconcagua Trek*, T4317003, aconcagua@rudyparra.com; *Daniel Alessio Expediciones*, T4962201, aconcagua@ alessio.com.ar. See also tour operators, page 202. Further information from **Dirección de Recursos Naturales Renovables**.

Las Cuevas
Altitude: 3,112 m
Km 188

A collection of eight buildings, Las Cuevas is advertised as a skiing resort (though there is no ski-lift as yet). Beyond, the road goes through the 3.2 km Cristo Redentor Tunnel to Chile (open 24 hours, US$2 for cars and buses; cyclists are not allowed to ride through, ask the officials to help you get a lift). Before the opening of the tunnel the route led over La Cumbre pass and the statue of **El Cristo Redentor** (Christ the Redeemer) at 4,200 m, erected jointly by Chile and Argentina in 1904 to celebrate the British arbitration in 1902 of boundary disputes between the two countries. The bronze statue, 8-m high and weighing six tons, is completely dwarfed by the bare mountainous landscape. Though the pass is now closed, the statue may be visited by taking the old road, though this is closed in winter. To walk from Las Cuevas, allow four and a half hours up, two hours down: you should be in good condition and the weather should be fine. Agencies in Mendoza also offer 12-hour excursions in summer (see page 202).

Sleeping and eating A *Hostal Internacional Aconcagua Las Cuevas*, no phone, book in advance through *Campo Base* in Mendoza. Food supplies from *Hostería Las Cuevas* (no accommodation).

Frontier with Chile

The Chilean border is beyond Las Cuevas, but all Argentine entry and exit formalities are dealt with at Punta de Vacas, 30 km east of Las Cuevas. Argentine customs are near Los Horcones, 2 km west of Puente del Inca. At Chilean customs there is a thorough search of vehicles entering Chile for fruit, vegetables and dairy products. If crossing by private vehicle car drivers can undertake all formalities in advance at Uspallata while refuelling. Members of ACA need only the *Libreta de Pasos por Aduana*, otherwise you need the *Documento de Exportación* to enter Chile. See page 204 for details of the Chilean consulate. No visas into Chile are available at the border. Tourist cards are given out on international buses. It is possible to hitchhike, or possibly bargain with bus drivers for a seat, from Punta de Vacas to Santiago, but if you are dropped at the entrance to the tunnel in winter, one cannot walk through. Travellers report that customs officers may help by asking motorists to take hitchhikers through to Chile.

Southern Mendoza

The main settlements in southern Mendoza lie in the oases of the valleys of the Ríos Atuel and Diamante where irrigation has made large-scale fruit growing possible. West of the main city of San Rafael lie the ski resort of Las Leñas and the small town of Malargüe.

The second city in the province and a service centre for this agricultural area, San Rafael lies north of the Río Diamante, 273 km southwest of San Luis, 242 km south of Mendoza. The **Parque Mariano Moreno**, 2 km south of the centre on Isla del Río Diamante (reached by Iselin bus along Av JA Balloffet) includes botanical gardens, a zoo and the **Museo Municipal de Historia Natural**, with displays on anthropology, archaeology, and palaeontology. ■ *Tue-Sun 0800-1200, 1500-1900, free.* Visits can be made to two wine *bodegas*. **Bianchi** at Montecaseros y Civit is recommended, and **Suter** on Route 143 west of the centre.

San Rafael
Phone code: 02627
Colour map 3, grid B2
Population: 95,000
Altitude: 688 m

Excursions Southwest is the **Cañon de Atuel**, a spectacular gorge with polychrome rocks. In the space of some 50 km the Río Atuel drops some 500 m, cutting through the rocks of the Bloque de San Rafael. Most of the gorge lies between two lakes 46 km apart, Valle Grande (508 ha) and El Nihuil (9,600 ha) formed by damming the river to generate electricity. A *ripio* road runs through the gorge offering fantastic and changing views. Around Valle Grande there is plenty of accommodation and campsites, river rafting and horse riding. ■ *Getting there: From San Rafael 3 buses a day go to the Valle Grande at the near end of the gorge, 35 km, US$3 but there is no public transport through the gorge to the El Nihuel dam. Travel agencies in Mendoza run all-day excursions to the canyon, but these involve long hours of travel.*

A centre for adventure tourism, rafting, horseriding & fishing

Sleeping *España*, San Martín 292, T424055. **C** *Kalton*, Yrigoyen 120, T430047. Excellent, safe, good value. **D** per person *Hosp Rex*, Yrigoyen 56, T422177, with breakfast. **D** per person *Hosp Jardin*, Yrigoyen 283, T434621, with breakfast. *Hosp Cerro Nevado*, Yrigoyen 376, T428209. **Youth hostel E** per person *Puesta del Sol*, Deán Funes 998, 3 km, T434881, puestaso@hostels.org.ar. **E** per person *Albergue Municipal*, El Pino s/n, with breakfast. **Camping** two sites (one of them ACA) at Isla Río Diamante, 2 km southeast. Several campsites near the Valle Grande dam.

Sport *Complejo Turistico Portal del Atuel* at Valle Grande, T/F423583, offers varied activities including rafting, trekking, canoeing.

Tour operators Many including *Ever Green*, San Martín 265, T421950. *Rumbo*, Coronel Day 45, T424871.

Tourist offices At Yrigoyen y Balloffet, very helpful, T424217. Ask for Aldo or Hector Seguín at España 437 for trekking and climbing information. **ACA**, Yrigoyen y 9 de Julio.

Transport Bus Buses to **Mendoza**, frequent, US$9; to **Neuquén**, US$20.

A paved road leads from San Rafael west across the plain of the Río Atuel, passing saltflats and marshland. **El Sosneado**, Km 138, set on the Río Atuel near oilwells, is the only settlement along this road. A *ripio* side road leads off and follows the valley of the Río Atuel northwest to Laguna El Sosneado, 42 km, the Termas el Sosneado, 55 km (the *Hotel Termas El Sosneado* is in ruins) and the Overo volcano (4,619 m). **Sleeping** at **D** per person *Hosteria El Sosneado*, T0627-71971, with breakfast, good beds.

From San Rafael to Las Leñas

Some 28 km southwest of El Sosneado and 166 km southwest of San Rafael, a *ripio* road follows the Río Salado west into the Andes. It passes **Los Molles**, Km 30, where there are thermal springs and accommodation. Opposite Los Molles a *ripio* road leads to the *refugio* of the Club Andino Pehuenche and on 8 km to the **Laguna de la Niña Encantada**, a beautiful little lake and shrine to the Virgin. At Km 37 are the **Pozo de las Animas**, two natural pits, both filled

The West

Alive!

Some 8 km from the Hotel Termas El Sosneado a plaque marks the site of the crash of an Uruguayan airforce plane in October 1972. The plane, a Fairchild F-27 en route from Montevideo to Santiago, carried 45 passengers and crew, including the members of a rugby team. The pilot, co-pilot and several passengers died on impact. Despite the efforts of the Chilean and Argentine airforces, the wreckage was not found. Two of the survivors crossed the mountains to Chile and finally brought help to the remaining 14 survivors who had spent 70 days on the Las Lágrimas glacier. The incident inspired the best-selling book 'Alive' by Piers Paul Read and the films 'Survive' (1976) and 'Alive' (1992).

with water (the larger is 80 m deep); when the wind blows across the holes, a ghostly wail results, hence the name (Well of the Spirits).

Las Leñas
Colour map 3, grid B1
Altitude: 2,250 m

Internationally renowned Las Leñas, 49 km off the San Rafael-Malargüe road, is the most expensive ski resort in Argentina (season July-October). Set in the middle of five snow-capped peaks, it has 41 pistes with a total length of 65 km and 11 ski-lifts. Ski passes in high season are US$40 per day, US$30 per half-day and ski hire is US$20 daily. Beyond Las Leñas the road continues into **Valle Hermoso**, a beautiful valley accessible December-March only.

Budget travellers should consider staying in Malargüe

Sleeping Las Leñas: **L+** *Piscis*, 5-star. *Aries*, *Escorpio*, *Acuario* and *Geminis*, T for all 471100. There are cheaper apart-hotels and dormy houses, US$1,200 per week for 5 people. For cheaper accommodation you have to stay in **Los Molles** where there are: **AB** per person *Hostería Lahuen-co*, T/F02627-427171. Full pension, run down, old fashioned. **AB** *Hotel Hualum*, same phone.

Transport Bus From **San Rafael**, daily 1000, US$5; from **Buenos Aires**, 15 hrs, in skiing season only.

Malargüe
Phone code: 02627
Colour map 3, grid B2
Population: 15,000
Altitude: 1,426 m
96 km SW of San Rafael

Malargüe sees itself, somewhat grandly, as the national centre for adventure tourism. It is an excellent alternative base for skiing at Las Leñas. The small **Museo Regional**, on the northern outskirts, includes displays on archaeology, minerology and local history. Nearby is a restored mill, used until cereal-growing was devastated by the eruption of the volcano Descabezado in 1932.

Excursions The **Fortín Malal Hue**, ruins of a fort dating from 1847, 12 km south. **Caverna de las Brujas** are privately owned caves, 70 km southwest (last 7 km *ripio*, difficult in wet weather), which take two to three hours to visit. Your own vehicle plus a guide is essential. Available for hire in Malargüe, US$20. **Laguna Llancanelo**, 37 km southeast, is one of the main Argentine nesting areas of the Chilean flamingo. The lake is best visited in spring when the birds arrive. Details from the tourist office. Fishing licences from the Dirección de los Bosques, next to the tourist office.

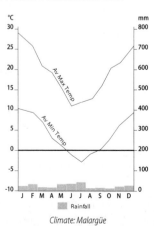

Climate: Malargüe

Sleeping **AB** *El Cisne*, Villegas 278, T471350, good value. Recommended. **AB** *Bambi*, San Martín 410, T/F471237, with breakfast, overpriced. **AB** *Río Grande*, Route 40 north, T471589, with breakfast, pleasant. **AB** *Reyen*, San Martín 938, T/F471429, with breakfast. **B** *Hotel del Turismo*, San Martín 224, T/F471042. With breakfast, heating, good restaurant, comfortable. Recommended. **B** *Portal del Valle*, Route 40 north, T471294, F471811. Sauna, pool, restaurant, also suites. **B** *Llancanelo*, T470689, with breakfast. **B** *Rioma*, Inalicán 68, T471065, with breakfast, heating. **C** *Valle Hermoso*, Torres 151, T471360, F470470. Several others. **Camping** *Polideportivo Marlargüe*, T/F471060; *La Costa*, Route 40 south, Km 7.

High season (Jan/Feb & Jul/Aug) prices given: off-season prices much lower

Sports **Caving** *Epecuén*, Fortín Malargüe y Meneses, T471747. **Climbing** *Kieniv Aventuras*, Pueblas 157, T471297. **Cycling** *Ciclotours*, Pueblas 908, T470336. **Horseriding** *Pincheira Aventuras*, Ortega 423, T471823. *Yaima*, Ortega 1043, T471202.

Tour operators *AGAPE Mendoza*, Asociación Grupo Antropo Paleonto Espeleológico, contact Dora de and Héctor Rofsgaard, Beltrán 414, T471536. *Expresos Payún*, Av Roca 430, T471426. *Karen Travel*, San Martín 1056, T470342, horseriding, trekking, rafting, excursions. *Turimalal*, San Martín 193, T/F470812, offer rock climbing, US$10 per person per half day, horseriding, cycle hire, skiing and fishing equipment hire; *Extremis*, San Martín 550 and several other shops on same street also rent out skiing and fishing equipment.

Malargüe

Tourist office Route 40 on the northern outskirts, T471659.

Transport Air Airport on southern edge of town, T471265. There are flights from Buenos Aires in the skiing season. **Bus** *TAC* and *Expreso Uspallata* from Mendoza. Also minibus service, *Transportes Viento Sur*, 4 hrs, US$20.

South of Malargüe

Route 40 continues to Chos Malal (see page 365), 294 km (road *ripio* from Km 114). At Km 72 a dirt road turns off to the petrified forests of **Llano Blanco**.

Frontier with Chile

Paso Pehuenche (2,553 m) is reached by a *ripio* road which branches off Route 40, 66 km south of Malargüe. On the Chilean side the road continues down the valley of the Río Maule to Talca. The border is open from December to March 0800-2100 and April to November 0800-1900.

The West

San Juan Province

The province of San Juan extends from the provincial capital, which lies in the broad valley of the Río San Juan, north and west to the Chilean frontier. The San Juan valley is the second most important wine producing area in the country; beyond it to the west the foothills of the Andes rise in ranges separated by valleys which are sparsely populated. Further north and west still are several Andean peaks, including Mercedario, and the crossing to Chile at Paso Agua Negra. Northeast of the San Juan valley, on the provincial border with La Rioja, are two parks, famous for their fantastic desert landforms.

San Juan

Phone code: 0264
Colour map 3, grid A2
Population: 122,000
Altitude: 650 m
168 km N of Mendoza

San Juan, home to over 90% of the population of the province, is the provincial capital in the valley of the Río San Juan. A modern city, rebuilt after the 1944 earthquake, its streets are lined with trees and there is a modern cathedral on the plaza.

History San Juan was founded 1562 by Don Juan Jufré de Loaysa y Montese and moved to its present site in 1593 to avoid the flooding of the Río San Juan. An earthquake which struck San Juan on 15 January 1944 was the most powerful in Argentine history, measuring 7.8° on the Richter Scale. Over 10,000 people were killed and the aftershocks continued for months afterwards. At a fund-raising event at Luna Park in Buenos Aires for the victims of the tragedy, Juan Perón met Eva Duarte, the radio actress who became his second wife.

Sights One of the country's largest wine producers, *Bodegas Bragagnolo*, on the out-
The main street, skirts of town at Route 40 y Avenida Benavídez, Chimbas, can be visited.
Av San Martín, is often ■ *Bus 20 from terminal; guided tours daily 0830-1330, 1530-1930, not Sunday.*
called Libertador **Museo Casa Natal de Sarmiento**, Sarmiento 21 Sur. The birthplace of Domingo Sarmiento, see box. ■ *Daily 0830-1330, also 1500-2000 Tue-Fri and Sun. US$1, free on Sun.* **Museo de Ciencias Naturales**, Predio Ferial, España y Maipú, includes fossils from Ischigualasto Provincial Park (see below). ■ *Mon-Sat, 0800-1300. US$0.50.* **Museo Histórico Celda de San Martín**, Laprida 97 Oeste, including the restored cloisters and two cells of the Convent of Santo Domingo, destroyed in 1944. San Martín slept in one of these cells on his way to lead the crossing of the Andes. ■ *Mon-Sat 0900-1400. US$1.*

Excursions The **Parque Sarmiento**, 10 km northwest on the banks of the Río San Juan, includes a small zoo. The **Embalse de Ullum**, 7 km further, offers rowing, sailing and fishing. The Club Bahía de las Tablas, about 2 km after crossing the dam, has a club-house, restaurant, pool, showers, US$10. **Parque de Zonda**, 17 km west, includes the Quebrada de Zonda, a 4 km long gorge and the **Museo Geografico Municipal Albert Einstein**, situated in a tunnel under the hill. ■ *Tue-Sun*

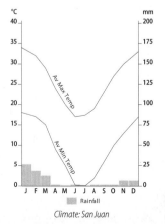

Climate: San Juan

Sarmiento

Born, the son of a soldier, in 1811, San Juan's most famous son Domingo Faustino Sarmiento was the colossus of Argentine public life in the 19th century. In a career which extended over some 60 years as writer, educator, journalist, historian, linguist, diplomat and politician, he consistently advocated education as the solution to Argentina's problems. While still a teenager he taught in local schools, but was forced to flee to Chile in 1829 after fighting in the defeated Unitarist forces against the Federalists. An early advocate of women's education, he founded a girls' secondary school in San Juan after his return to the city in 1836. He also started a newspaper, `El Zonda', in which he put forward his ideas on education and agriculture. In 1840, as a result of his opposition to Rosas, he was again forced into exile in Chile, where he was on friendly terms with prominent politicians and writers. Head of a teacher training college and tirelessly promoting his educational theories, he was an important influence on the development of the Chilean educational system.

Sarmiento's fame as a writer is based primarily on his work, Facundo: Civilisation and Barbarism, published in 1845. Focussing on the career of Juan Facundo Quiroga, the Federalist caudillo (military leader) of La Rioja, the book was a passionate attack on Rosas. Expressing the views of a sector of the Argentine elite which opposed Rosas attempts to close the country to outside influences, Sarmiento presented the struggle in terms of a war between civilization and barbarism. The latter was equated with the backward interior, provincial caudillos, the gaucho as an inferior social type and introverted nationalism. Civilization could be found in adopting European patterns in the political, cultural and social spheres. Argentina had to open up its trade to the rest of the world, attract European immigrants and acquire values of sociability and respectability that would lead the country out of fragmentation caused by excessive individualism.

Rosas replied by trying to have Sarmiento extradited, but the Chilean government sent him to study educational methods in Europe and the United States. Though he participated in the overthrow of Rosas, he soon fell out with his successor, Urquiza. In 1855 he became head of education for Buenos Aires province, though his support for universal public education with an emphasis on science and gymnastics for both boys and girls met with fierce opposition. After serving as Senator for San Juan he was sent as a diplomat to Peru and the United States.

As President of Argentina, 1868-1874, he encouraged European immigration, greater trade, improvements in public health and the building of schools, public libraries, roads and railways. His presidency was, however, not without its ironies: despite his lifelong hostility to caudillos, he exhibited many of the characteristics of the personalist leader; though a native of the frontier province of San Juan, he strengthened the power of the Federal Government, crushing provincial opponents; an advocate of the rule of law, he ruled by decree when he deemed the law inadequate.

Between leaving office and his death in 1888 he worked tirelessly in a succession of government posts and still found time to found a newspaper and an educational journal. His complete writings filled 53 volumes. Somewhere he found time to marry, leave his wife for another woman and father a son who was killed fighting against Paraguay in the War of the Triple Alliance.

The West

16000-2000. The **Museo Arqueológico** of the University of San Juan at La Laja, 26 km north, contains an outstanding collection of prehispanic indigenous artefacts including several well-preserved mummies. Inexpensive thermal baths nearby. ■ *Daily 0930-1700, US$2. Getting there: Bus No 20 from San Juan, 2 daily but you need to take the first (at 0830) to give time to return.*

Vallecito, 64 km east, is the site of a famous shrine to the **Difunta Correa**, an unofficial saint whose infant (according to legend) survived at her breast even after the mother's death from thirst in the desert. Some 700,000 pilgrims visit the shrine every year, up to 100,000 of them in Holy Week, some crawling 100 m on their knees. See the remarkable collection of personal items left in tribute, including number plates from all over the world and even one policeman's detective school diploma! For information, consult Fundación Vallecito at Caucete. Accommodation includes *Res Difunta Correa*.

Sleeping   **AL** *Alkázar*, Laprida 82 Este, T4214965, F214977. Including breakfast, garage, good. **A** *Nogaró*, de la Roza 132 Este, T4227501/5. Pool, a/c, central, TV, parking (ACA and US AAA discounts). **AB** *Capayan*, Mitre 31 Este, T4214222. With breakfast, very good. **AB** *Central*, Mitre 131 Este, T4223174. Quiet, good beds, welcoming owner. **AB** *Embajador*, Rawson 25 Sur, T4225520. Large rooms, pleasant, café, good value. Several residenciales (**B**) along Av España, blocks 100-600 Sur. **AB** *Jardín Petit*, 25 de Mayo 345 Este (ACA discount with cash), T4211825. Hot water, pricey, parking next door. **AB** *Bristol*, Entre Rios 368 Sur, T4222629. A/c, hot water. **B** *Plaza*, Sarmiento 344 Sur, T4225179. **B** *Selby*, Rioja 185 Sur, T4224777. A/c, parking, quiet, central. **B/C** *Breschia*, España 336 Sur, T4225708. With fan, quiet. **D** *Res 12 de Diciembre*, (no sign) Sarmiento 272 Norte. Fan, clean, family run, also monthly. **C/D** *Hispano Argentino*, Estados Unidos 381 Sur, T4210818. Just outside bus terminal, with bath, also **E** without bath, with breakfast, fan, snack bar. **D** *Roy*, Entre Ríos 180 Sur, T4224391. Reasonable, clean, ask for room away from the street. **D** *Santa Fe*, Santa Fe 35 Oeste. Clean. **D** *Capri*, Acha 633 Sur. Clean. **D** *9 de Julio* (no sign), 9 de Julio 147 Oeste, also **E** without bath, cheap, quiet.

Camping   campsite in the Parque Sarmiento; also *Camping Municipal Rivadavia*, in the Parque Zonda, free, no facilities. Take insect repellent.

Eating   *Club Sirio Libanés 'El Palito'*, Entre Rios 33 Sur. Pleasant decor, good food. *El Castillo de Oro*, de la Roza 199 Oeste. Central, reasonable, large *parrillada* at the back. *Fono Bar*, Sarmiento Sur y Mitre Oeste, 24 hr snack bar and *locutorio*. *Las Leñas*, San Martín 1670 Oeste, *parrilla*, pricey. Recommended. Eat under thatched roof (*quincho*). *Listo el Pollo*, San Martín y Santiago del Estero, very good. Many *pizzerías*, *confiterías*, and sidewalk cafés. *Marilyn Bar*, San Martín y Mendoza, late night drinks. *Parrilla Bigotes*, Las Heras 647 Sur, inexpensive 'all you can eat' meat, chicken, salads. *Soychú*, de la Roza 223 Oeste. Excellent vegetarian food. *Wiesbaden*, Circunvalación y San Martín. German-style, pleasant setting.

Entertainment   **Cinema** On Plaza at Mitre 41 Este, 2 screens.

Shopping   *Mercado Artesanal* at Av España y San Luis, worth a visit. Apart from its wines, San Juan is well known for its fine bedspreads, blankets, saddlebags and other items made from sheep, llama and guanaco wool from Calingasta. Other items include leather, wooden plates and mortars from Pampa del ChaNar and sheepskin from Niquivil.

Tour operators   *San Juan Viajes y Turismo*, General Acha 17 Norte, T4220864. Tours to Ischigualasto subject to demand, US$50 per person plus US$3 national park entry fee. *Fascinatur*, San Martín 1085 Oeste, T/F4343014. Guide: Rafael Joliat. Recommended for 4WD treks to remote areas, also horseback and mountain bike excursions, English, French, German spoken. Guide: Raul Horacio Despous, Mendoza 4619 Sur, T4242688, cellular 156606960. Tours to Parque Provincial Ischigualasto and other parts of the province by car or minibus. Highly recommended.

Local Bicycle repairs *Petit Bicicletería*, San Martín y La Rioja, helpful. **Car hire Transport** **Parque Automotor**, España y San Martín, T4226018. Cash discount on request. **Localiza**, España 274 (Sur), T4229243.

Long distance Air Chacritas Airport, 11 km southeast. Bus 19 or 22 (Triunfo) to/from centre, 4 a day, 30 mins, US$1. *Remis* from city, prices vary, shop around. To **Buenos Aires** *Aerolíneas Argentinas/Austral, Lapa*, several daily, US$91. *Aerolíneas Argentinas* also to San Luis, US$39. **Bus** Terminal at Estados Unidos y Santa Fe, 9 blocks east of centre, T4221604. Bus 33 and 35 for city centre. To **La Rioja**, *Socasa, Andesmar, Autotransportes Mendoza, El Rapido*, 6 hrs, US$18, also *coche cama* service. To **Catamarca**, *Andesmar, TAC, El Rapido, La Estrella*, 8 hrs, US$29. To **Córdoba**, direct, *Socasa, 20 de Junio, San Juan Mar del Plata, semi-cama*, US$22, *coche-cama*, US$27. Also services via Mendoza. To **Tucumán**, *Andesmar, TAC, El Rapido, La Estrella*, socasa, US$35. To **Buenos Aires**, San Juan Mar del Plata, *TAC, La Estrella, semi-cama* US$45, *coche-cama* US$55. To **San Agustín**, *Vallecito*, 3 a day, 4 hrs, US$14. To **Mendoza**, several companies, every hr, US$11, 2 hrs. To **San Luis**, frequent, US$15, 4 hrs. Also services to provincial tourist destinations including **San Agustín del Valle Fertil** (for Parque Provincial Ischigualasto), *Vallecito*, 0700, 1900, 4 hrs, US$23. **To Chile**: To **Santiago** direct services, 8½ hrs, US$20, Covalle, Mon, Wed, Fri 2200, TAS-Choapa, Wed, Sun 1000. The alternative is *TAC* via Mendoza, 0600, 0830, 1930 with onward connection to Santiago. **Hitchhiking** To **La Rioja**, take route 141 to Chepes (ACA *Hostería*), then north to Patquía; more traffic on provincial Route 29, a well paved, but less interesting road than that via San Agustín or Jachal (see below).

San Juan centre

Sleeping
1 Alkázar
2 Bristol

3 Jardín Petit
4 Nogaró
5 Plaza

● **Eating**
1 Sirio Libanés
2 Soychú

Directory **Airline offices** *Aerolíneas Argentinas/Austral*, San Martin y Sarmiento, T08008886527, airport 4250487. *Lapa*, De la roza 176 Este. *Southern Winds*, De la Roza 278 Este, T4200010. *TAN*, De la Roza 278 Este, T4200010. **Banks** Banks open 0700-1200. Banelco ATMs at *Boston Bank*, Laprida Oeste y Mendoza Sur, *Banco Río*, Mendoza 170 Sur, *Banco Francés*, Rivadavia 64 Este, *Bansud*, Rivadavia 70 Este, *HSBC*, De La Roza 145 Este. Link ATM at *Banco de San Juan*, Mendoza Norte y San Martín Este. *Casas de cambio: Cambio Santiago*, Gral Acha 52 Sur. *Banco de San Juan*, De la Roza 85 Oeste. *Banco Transandino*, Gral Acha 41 Sur. **Communications** Post Office De la Roza 259 Este. **Internet** *Cyber Café*, Rivadavia 12 Este, T4201397/9, *Interredes*, Laprida 362 Este, T4275790, *IAC*, Acha 142 Norte, T4277104. Also Rivadavida y Acha (on plaza) (open Sun), Acha 282 (on plaza), Mendoza 379 Sur (open Sun), Mendoza 139 Sur (open Sun), San Martín 49 Oeste. **Cultural centres** Centro Cultural San Juan Gral Paz 737 Este, concerts and other events. **Alianza Francesa**, Mitre 202 Oeste, library open to public, pleasant reading room, Mon/Wed 0900-1300, 1800-2100. **Laundry** *Marva*, San Luis y Rioja. *Laverap*, Rivadavia 493 Oeste. *Fast*, 9 de Julio y Sarmiento. **Medical services** Gral Paz y Estados Unidos, T4222272. Medical emergencies at *ECI*, Mendoza 474 Sur, T4226088/4221919. There is a 24 hr pharmacy at Gral Paz Oeste y Mendoza Sur. **Tourist offices** Sarmiento Sur 24 y San Martín, T4222431/4210004, F4225778, helpful, good brochures, Mon-Fri 0730-2030, Sat/Sun 0900-2000; also at bus terminal. Large-scale provincial maps available at bookshops. *ACA*, 9 de Julio y Rawson, T4223781, useful information on routes, helpful.

The Calingasta Valley

100 km W of San Juan

Separated from the city by the Sierra del Tontal, this valley is drained by the Río de los Patos and the Río Castaño Viejo, which join to form the Río San Juan. Inhabited since at least 10,000 BC, the valley formed part of the route of the Camino del Inca, which ran south to the Uspallata Valley and north to the Iglesia Valley. In the 19th century mining was important and abandoned mine workings can still be seen. From the 1930s it became the centre of the Argentine cider industry, before losing out to the Río Negro valley in the 1970s.

Route The valley is reached from San Juan by the scenic Provincial Route 12 though this has been disrupted by work on two dams and is only open after 2000 and Sunday (one-way system as above). Alternative, unpaved roads are in use, north via El Puntudo (Rutas 436/412), south via Los Berros but neither are very good. Cyclists in this area should note that there is very little shade on any of these roads, water is in short supply (fill up at every opportunity) and the police should be consulted before cycling from Calingasta to San Juan. Provincial Route 412 runs along the valley, linking it to Uspallata in the south and Iglesia in the north. About half way between Calingasta and Barreal, this passes, to the east, the Cerros Pintados, a range of red, white and grey stratified hills.

Calingasta Calingasta lies at the confluence of the Ríos de los Patos and Calingasta, 135 km west of San Juan. Set in attractive surroundings, it produces cider and holds an annual cider festival in April. Nearby are sulphate and aluminium mines. The Jesuit chapel of Nuestra Señora del Carmen dates from 1739.

Population: 2,000
Altitude: 1,430 m

Sleeping **B** *Calingasta*, T422014. Remodelled, pool, full board available. **C** *La Capilla*, T421033. Including breakfast, basic but very clean, family run, the family also sells the TAC bus tickets, and has the only public telephone in the village. **Camping** Municipal site. Take insect repellent.

North of Calingasta Route 412, unpaved from Calingasta, climbs the valley of the Río Castaño Viejo. At **Villa Nueva**, 33 km north, the **De Cordelier** cider plant can be visited. Here the road forks: Route 412 continues north to Iglesia and Las Flores, a route described as scenic but lonely, while the other fork continues up the valley to disused gold mines at Mina Castaño Viejo.

Barreal lies 40 km south of Calingasta, 108 km north of Uspallata. From here excursions can be made east into the Sierra de Tontal, rising to 4,000 m with views over San Juan, Mercedario and Aconcagua, and south following the valley of the Río de los Patos to Las Hornillas (54 km) where there is fishing and a *refugio* and then runs west towards the Chilean frontier and Mercedario (see below).

Barreal
Phone code:02648
Colour map 3, grid A2
Population: 1,800
Altitude: 1,650 m

Sleeping AB *Barreal*, San Martín s/n, T41000. Reservations through *Nogaró* in San Juan, T4227501. Poor restaurant, pool, riding. *Cabañas Alamos-Cordilleranos*, T41025/41139, on plaza next to *Supermercadito El Angel*. *Cabañas Doña Pipa*, Mariano Moreno s/n, T41004. Sleep 5, with bath, kitchen, sitting room, comfortable. **E** *Hotel Jorge*, clean, very simple. *Posada San Eduardo*, San Martín y Los Enamorados, T41046. Colonial-style and patio with old trees, small, most rooms with bath, pleasant and relaxing. Accommodation with Sr Patricio Sosa or Sr Cortez. **Camping** Municipal site, also *cabañas*, T San Juan 223745.

Eating *Isidoro*, Roca s/n, owned by local baker and sandyacht champion, reasonable, good set meals; food also available at *Mama Rosa*.

Tour operators For rafting trips contact Sr Eduardo Conterno. Sr Ramón Luis Ossa, physical education teacher at the high school, runs mule treks into the Andes, crossing the foothills in summer, from 10-21 days between Nov and Apr; contact via *Cabañas Doña Pipa*, address above.

Transport Bus From San Juan daily, *El Triunfo*, 0700, plus Mon, Wed, Fri, Sun at 2030 (return Mon, Wed, Fri, Sun 1330, 1600, Tue, Thu 1400, Sat 1600), 5 hrs, US$11. *Remise* service San Juan-Calingasta-Barreal, US$17 per person, T San Juan 262121 daytime or 252370 1900-2300; in Barreal, Sr Pachá, *Restaurante Isidoro*; also Silvio, T San Juan 252370, Barreal 41257, US$14. Recommended. *Omnibus Vitar* from Mendoza (Las Heras 494, T4232876) Thu and Sat via Uspallata, continuing to Tamberías and Calingasta (return Fri and Sun); fare Barreal-Calingasta US$7.

Covering 76,000 ha of the eastern slopes of the Sierra de Tontal and rising to over 4,000 m, this reserve includes two observatories. To the west there are fine views of Mercedario and other peaks in the *cordillera*. The environment is semi-arid; fauna includes guanacos, red and grey foxes, and peregrine falcons. ■ *Observatories: visits daily 1000-1100, 1600-1800, US$3; no public transport; tours can be arranged from San Juan, Avenida España 1512 Sur, T4213653, or at Hotel Barreal. Getting there: Unpaved road (17 km) which turns off the Route 412, 22 km south of Barreal. Ranger post at entrance; no facilities, take all supplies.*

Reserva Natural El Leoncito

Known in Chile as **El Ligua** and rising to 6,770 m , Mercedario lies southwest of Calingasta. It was first climbed in 1934 by a Polish expedition which went on to climb the nearby peaks of Pico Polaco (6,050 m), La Mesa (6,200 m), Alma Negra (6,120 m) and Ramada (6,410 m).

To climb Mercedario, from Barreal go to Casas Amarillas on the Río Blanco, about 100 km on a gravel road. It may be possible to hire a Unimog 4x4 from the Gendarmería Nacional. Guides (*baqueanos*) may also be hired who can provide mules if necessary. The best time is mid-December to end-February. The types of terrain encountered are gravel, snow and rock. There is no rescue service.

Mercedario
No authorization is required, but it is advisable to inform the Gendarmería Nacional at Barreal

Information From Club Andino Mercedario in San Juan, which meets at the Circulo Aleman, Urquiza, between Laprida and Rivadavia, T4220756; alternatively contact the Club President, Guillermo Raimie, T4201092 or Vice-President Faustino Varas, T4236448. **NB** It is illegal to cross the frontier to/from Chile in this region.

The West

The Río Jachal Valley

The valley of the Río Jachal is an oasis some 180 km north of San Juan. Flowing south from the mountains of La Rioja through the valley of Iglesia, the Jachal flows east through a narrow gorge (the Quebrada del Jachal) before continuing southeast into the Río Bermejo. The river has been dammed to create an artificial lake, the Embalse Cuesta del Viento, covering 3,000 ha. The main town is San José de Jachal, east of the gorge.

Route From San Juan the Jachal valley is reached by Route 40, the principal tourist route on the East Andean slope. At Talacasto, Km 55, Route 436 branches northwest towards Iglesia (Km 166), Las Flores (Km 180) and the Chilean border at Paso Agua Negra (see below).

San José de Jachal
Colour map 3, grid A2
Population: 15,000
Altitude: 1,157 m

An oasis town 157 km north of San Juan by Route 40, San José de Jachal is a wine and olive-growing centre with many adobe buildings. From here, the undulating Route 40, paved but for the first 25 km to the La Rioja border runs north to Villa Unión (see below), crossing dozens of dry watercourses; it is unpaved north of the La Rioja border.

Sleeping and eating C *Plaza*, San Juan 545, T420256. *San Martín*, Juan de Echegaray 387, T420431. **Camping** *El Chato Flores*, restaurant, good; . also behind ACA station at northeast edge of town. another site 3 km west.

Transport Bus *Expreso Argentino* bus from San Juan at 0730 arrives at 0940.

Rodeo
Colour map 3, grid A2
Population: 1,600
Altitude: 1,900 m

Rodeo lies 42 km west of San José along a scenic road which runs through several tunnels as it passes through the Quebrada de Jachal. There are good facilities for fishing and watersports. Ing Meglioli raises guanaco and vicuña, and sells local produce and crafts. From here a *ripio* road runs north along the Jachal valley to **Angualasto**, Km 20, where the **Museo Arqueológico Luis Benedetti**, contains a 400-year-old mummy.

Reserva de la Biosfera San Guillermo
Best visited between Oct & Apr. Inaccessible when the Río Blanco is high

Situated north of Angualasto, this park protects 860,000 ha of the upper valley of the Río Blanco, rising from 3,300 m to peaks of over 5,000 m. Vegetation is sparse, consisting mainly of steppe grasses and cacti, but the park is home to over 5,000 vicuña as well as vizcachas, guanacos, pumas, grey foxes, white eagles, falcons and condors. The park is also the site of important archaeological remains. Several burial sites of prehispanic peoples have been found.
■ *Getting there: Reached from Angualasto. Register with the police in Angualasto and report to the rangers in the park. Guides are available in Angualasto and Las Flores.*

Pismanta
Altitude: 1,724 m

Pismanta is an oasis town with thermal springs 22 km southwest of Rodeo and 182 km north of San Juan. There is a Jesuit chapel, dating from 1640, 3 km away. Nearby are other thermal springs, Termas Rosales and Termas Centenario, but these have few facilities.

Sleeping B *Termas de Pismanta*, T4227501. With breakfast, rooms for 120 guests, thermal baths between 38°C and 44°C, a large swimming pool, medical attention, bowling, bingo occasionally, covered parking, good value. Reservations in Buenos Aires (Maipú 331) and San Juan (San Martín y Sarmiento). **E** *La Olla*, family run, clean, restaurant.

Transport **Bus** From San Juan, *TAC*, 2 daily, *Empresa Iglesia* 4 weekly; also from Mendoza.

Paso Agua Negra is 100 km west of Pismanta, the first 60 km is poor asphalt, the last 35 km *ripio*. The crossing is spectacular, particularly the views of fields of *penitentes* (ice needles) about 5 km east of the pass. This route is only open January to early April; in winter it is closed by snow, in summer it may be closed by rain. On the Chilean side the road continues to Vicuña, 172 km west, and La Serena, 238 km west. First fuel is at Rivadavia, 154 km west.

Frontier with Chile
Altitude: 4,600 m

Immigration and customs Argentine immigration and customs at Las Flores is open 24 hrs for entry, 0800-1700 only for departures. Police checkpoint 40 km west of Las Flores. Chilean immigration and customs are at Las Juntas, 84 km west of Paso Agua Negra, open 0800-1700; US$2 per vehicle 1700-2200.

Sleeping First accommodation in Chile at Huanta (Guanta on some maps), 126 km west, **G**, clean, basic, ask for Guillermo Aliaga. No food between the frontier and Huanta.

Transport No public transport on this route. Check road conditions with ACA in Las Flores.

North and east of San Juan

The West

Two of the most popular attractions in this region are the Parque Provincial Ischigualasto and the Parque Nacional Talampaya, situated near each other on the San Juan/La Rioja provincial border (Ischigualasto is in San Juan; Talampaya in La Rioja). From San Juan these are reached by taking Route 20 east through Caucete and joining Route 141, via Difunta Correa to Marayes, then turning north onto Route 510 (paved but poor in parts) for 135 km.

San Agustín is a textile-weaving town, 102 km north of Marayes along Route 510, which has become a base for visiting the parks. There is fishing in the nearby Embalse San Agustín. Tourist information on the plaza. Local weavers sell ponchos and blankets.

San Agustín del Valle Fértil
Phone code: 0246
Population: 3,000

Sleeping **AB** *Hostería Valle Fértil*, Rivadavia s/n, T420015/7. Breakfast extra, excellent views over Dique San Agustín. **AB** *Cabañas Villa del Lago*, fully equipped. *Res Andacollo*. **E** per person *Hosp Los Olivos*, Santa Fe y Tucumán, T420115, with bath, fan, spacious, restaurant, excellent value. **D** *Hosp Romero*, T420342. **E** per person *Hosp Santa Fe*, T420357, with bath, welcoming. Recommended. private houses also provide lodging. **E** per person *Hosp Ischigualasto*, Mitre y Aberstain, T420146, with bath, clean, fan. **Camping** Municipal site next to the Embalse. Supermarket, Rivadavia y Sarmiento.

During Holy Week all accommodation is fully booked

Transport **Bus** To San Juan, US$9, Vallecito, 2 daily, 4 hrs, 23 hrs. To **Chilecito**, Vallecito daily, 4½ hrs; from **La Rioja**, Mon-Fri 1215, US$10, 4 hrs.

Popularly known as the **Valle de la Luna** (Valley of the Moon), this park covers 62,000 ha of spectacular desert landforms, the site of important archaeological discoveries. Named after a Huarpe Indian chief, the site occupies a large basin, formerly filled by a lake, lying, at an average altitude of 1,200 m, between the red Cerros Los Colorados to the east and the green, black and grey rocks of Los Rastros to the west. Many of the rocks have bizarre shapes and are named accordingly: 'The Submarine', 'The Kiosk', 'The mushroom.' Fossils from all the

Parque Provincial Ischigualasto
Colour map 3, grid A2

Talampaya

There are 600-year-old petroglyphs with pictures depicting animals. The whole area is said to have been covered with water long ago; now there are two visible strata, the tarjado and the talampaya. After that

one enters a canyon with 'balconies', sheer overhanging walls. Coming out of the canyon there are rocks shaped like a cathedral, a bird, a castle, a chessboard, a monk, and three kings on a camel.

geological periods of the last 250 million years old have been found; among these have been fossils of the oldest dinosaurs known, including *Eoraptor*, 225 million years old and discovered in 1993. Vegetation is scrub and bushes; fauna include guanacos, vizcachas, patagonian hares, red foxes, pumas and rheas.

All private vehicles must be accompanied by rangers whose knowledge and interest vary greatly, no fee but tip appreciated. The circular route, 2½ hrs on unpaved roads covers only a small part of the park, though it covers most of the interesting sites. The route takes you to *Gusanos* (Worms), *La Cancha de Bochas* (the Bowling Green), *El Submarino* (the Submarine) and *El Hongo* (the Mushroom).

■ *Getting there: Entrance at Cerro El Morado, 1,800 m, reached by a side road 17 km long, turning off Route 510 at a police checkpoint near Los Baldecitos, 56 km north of San Agustín del Valle Fértil. Entry US$5.*

Transport Local bus from San Juan Mon and Fri to police checkpoint and on Sat afternoon, if demand is sufficient.

Tours Run by agencies from San Juan, US$55, 14 hrs, with breakfast in San Agustin and lunch which are not included in the price; from San Agustín US$18 for a guide (ask at tourist office). Taxi from San Juan US$55, more out of season.

Parque Nacional Talampaya

Extending over 215,000 ha at an altitude of 1,200 m, Talampaya occupies a basin between the Cerros Los Colorados to the west and the Sierras de Sañogasta to the east. Though the park's fossils have been less significant to scientists than those of Ischigualasto, the rock formations are just as interesting and in some places petroglyphs can be seen. The most popular part is the gorge of the Río Talampaya, the walls of which rise to 143 m. At one point the gorge narrows to 80 m wide where there is a 'botanical garden'. Vegetation and fauna are similar to Ischigualasto. ■ *Getting there: Access is by a paved side road, 12 km long, which turns off Provincial Route 26, at Km 144, 61 km north of the police checkpoint at Los Baldecitos and 55 km south of Villa Unión. Entry US$3. 0800-1630, entrance US$3. Best time to visit in the morning, avoiding strong winds in the afternoon.*

Sleeping *Refugio* near the entrance, sleeping bag essential. Free campsite next to park administration. In Pagancillo, a village 28 km north on Route 26, accommodation can be arranged by Sr Páez, Park Director (eg with **D** per person *Familia Flores*, including breakfast and dinner).

Transport Chilecito-San Juan buses pass Talampaya. Patquía-Villa Unión buses pass through Pagancillo. Tours through the gorge of the Río Talampaya in 4WD vehicles are operated by park rangers, 5 tours of different lengths offered, prices per truck, US$30-110, not including entrance. Tours arranged through Dirección Provincial de Turismo in La Rioja, through the tourist office in Chilecito or Sr Páez, Park Director, in Pagancillo.

La Rioja Province

The eastern part of the province consists of a plain which stretches south and east to the Sierras de Córdoba. Extending over some four million hectares, and including large areas of saltflats, this area is sometimes known as the Llanos de los Caudillos. Water is sparse and vegetation is scrub and poor grassland, used for cattle ranching. To the west several ranges of mountains run north-south, extending to the Andes in the far west. Between these ranges lie two valleys, the Valley of Famatina and the Valley of Vinchina. Communications between these valleys are difficult. About 50% of the population live in the capital.

La Rioja

La Rioja, the provincial capital, is situated on the edge of the plains at the foot of the Sierra de Velasco. Founded in 1592, it is known as 'City of the Orange Trees', but there are also many specimens of the contorted, thorn-studded palo borracho tree. Despite a major earthquake in 1894, some colonial buildings survive. It is a quiet provincial city which can easily be explored on foot.

Phone code: 02822
Colour map 1, grid C2
Population: 106,000
Altitude: 498 m

Sights The city centre is on Plaza 25 de Mayo. Here are the early 20th-century cathedral and the neo-colonial Casa de Gobierno. The **Convent of San Francisco**, one block northwest at 25 de Mayo y Bazán y Bustos, contains the Niño Alcalde, a remarkable image of the infant Jesus as well as the cell (*celda*) in which San Francisco Solano lived and the orange tree, now dead, which he planted in 1592. To visit the tree when the church is closed, ring the bell at 25 de Mayo 218 next door. The **Convent of Santo Domingo**, Luna y Lamadrid, is the oldest surviving temple in Argentina, dating from 1623. The **Casa González**, at Rivadavia 950, is a brick 'folly' in the form of a castle. On the outskirts of the city, 3 km west, is the **Parque Yacampis**, with a swimming pool and zoo.

Museums **Museo Folklórico**, Pelagio Luna 811, includes displays on mythology, handicrafts and cooking. ■ *Tue-Fri, 0800-1200, 1600-2000, Sat/Sun, 0900-1200, US$1.50.* **Museo Arqueológico Inca Huasi**, Alberdi 650, owned by the Franciscan Order, contains a huge collection of fine Indian ceramics and other artefacts. ■ *Tue-Fri, 0900-1200, US$1.* **Museo del Traje**, Rivadavia 537, is a costume museum which includes 19th-century clothing and advertisements. ■ *Mon-Sat 0800-1200.* **Museo Histórico de la Provincia**, Dávila 87, has a varied collection which includes furniture and weapons. ■ *Tue-Sat 0800-1200.* **Museo Municipal de Bellas Artes**, Pelagio Luna y Calchaquí, houses works by local, national, and foreign artists. ■ *Tue-Sat 0700-1300.*

Excursions The most popular excursions are to Los Padercitas and the Embalse Los Sauces, situated to the west of the city (see page 223).

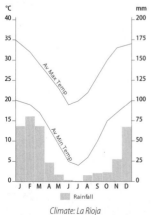

Climate: La Rioja

The West

Sleeping

Avoid arriving on Sat night as most things are shut on Sun

Accommodation, especially in the cheap range, can be difficult to find

Turismo Internacional, San Nicolas de Bari y 9 de Julio (Plaza 25 de Mayo). 5 star, under construction. **L** *Plaza*, Mitre y 9 de Julio (Plaza 25 de Mayo), T425215, F422127. With breakfast, pool, bar, parking. Recommended but street noisy. **L** *King's*, Quiroga 1070, T422122. With buffet breakfast, a/c, pool, confitería. **AB** *Libertador*, Buenos Aires 253, T427794, F427474. With breakfast, a/c, parking, good value. **AB** *Embajador*, San Martín 250, T/F438580. Breakfast extra, a/c, good beds, bar, parking. **A** *Turismo*, Perón y Quiroga, T422005. With breakfast, a/c, confitería, parking. **AB** *Prisma*, Buenos Aires 104, T421567. Apartments with kitchen, a/c, parking. **B** *Imperial*, Moreno 345, T422478, helpful. **B** *Res Petit*, Lagos 427, basic, hospitable. **B** *Talampaya*, Perón 951, T424010. With breakfast, a/c, confitería. **C** *Savoy*, Roque A Luna 14, T426894. Excellent value, hot shower. **C** *Res Florida*, 8 de Diciembre 524, basic, poor beds. Tourist office keeps a list of private lodgings, such as Sra Vera, Dávila 343. **Camping** ACA site in the Parque Yacampis; at Balneario Los Sauces, 15 km west.

Eating

Very few places open on Sun

Alike, Sarsfield y Catamarca, Chinese, *tenedor libre* US$8. *Club Atlético Riojano*, Santa Fe 536, eat in gymnasium, no atmosphere but cheap, open Sun. *Comedor Sociedad Española*, 9 de Julio 233, excellent pastas. *Il Gatto*, Plaza 25 de Mayo, good pastas and salads. *La Pomme*, Rivadavia y San Martín, open-air terrace, popular meeting place. *La Vieja Casona*, Rivadavia 449, pricey but good, open Sun. *Taberna Don Carlos*, Rivadavia 459, good fish and service. **Cafés**: *Café Corredor*, San Martín y Pelagio Luna,

La Rioja centre

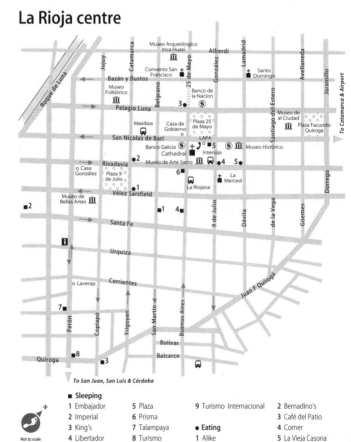

- ■ **Sleeping**
- 1 Embajador
- 2 Imperial
- 3 King's
- 4 Libertador
- 5 Plaza
- 6 Prisma
- 7 Talampaya
- 8 Turismo
- 9 Turismo Internacional
- ● **Eating**
- 1 Alike
- 2 Bernadíno's
- 3 Café del Patio
- 4 Corner
- 5 La Vieja Casona

Not to scale

good, cheap. *Corner*, Riviadavia y 9 de Julio. *Bernadino's*, Rivadavia y Irigoyen. *Café del Patio*, Pelagio Luna y 25 de Mayo, open air.

Yafar Turismo, Lamadrid 170, tour to Ischigualasto and Talampaya parks. To visit the **Tour operators** parks by private car with guide costs US$190 for up to 5 people, plus park entry fees. *Tierra Riojana*, Plaza 25 de Mayo, next to cinema, T420222.

Long distance Air To/from **Buenos Aires**, *Aerolíneas Argentinas* (T427257) and **Transport** *Lapa* (T435197). *Lapa* also to **Catamarca**, *Aerolíneas Argentinas* to **Tucumán**, *Andesmar* to **Córdoba** and **Mendoza**. **Bus** Terminal 7 blocks south of the Cathedral at Artigas y España. To **Buenos Aires**, *General Urquiza*, US$47, combine with Ablo, via Córdoba. To **Córdoba**, *Chevallier*, 6½ hrs, US$15, also *coche cama*. To **Mendoza** (US$25) and **San Juan** (US$19), *La Estrella*, *Libertador* and *Andesmar*, 8 hrs. To **Tinogasta**, 0620, 2200, daily, US$11. To **Tucumán** (US$15), with Sol y Valle and La Estrella. To **Salta**, Andesmar, 10 hrs, US$33. To **Chilecito**, *combis* (minibuses), US$8, 2 hrs, several companies including *La Riojana*, Buenos Aires 132, T435279; *Maxibus*, San Nicolas de Bari 743, T423134; *Interioja*, Rivadavia y González, T421577.

Banks US$ cash changed at *Banco de Galicia*, Plaza 25 de Mayo (no commission on Visa cash **Directory** advance), and *Banco de Crédito*, San Nicolás 476. TCs difficult to change – try *Banco de la Provincia*, Bazán y Bustos, commission 8%. **Communications** Post office Perón 258. **Telecommunications** Perón 764. **Internet** *Telecom*, San Nicolas de Bari 540 (Plaza 25 de Mayo). **Laundry** *Laverap*, Perón 944. **Tourist office** Perón y Urquiza, T/F428839.

Northeastern La Rioja

Two roads head north from La Rioja. Route 38 runs northeast to Catamarca at Km 33 and then Provincial Route 9 (later 10) branches off north for **Villa Mazán**, Km 99. Some 7 km north of Villa Mazán is **Termas Santa Teresita**. Here there is **AB** *Hostería Termas Santa Teresita*, T420445 which has open air thermal pool, thermal baths in all rooms, good set menu, breakfast included. Highly recommended. The other road, Route 1 to Aimogasta, is more interesting, passing through Villa Sanagasta, Aminga and Anillaco.

This is the site of the remains of the 16th-century adobe building where San **Las Padercitas** Francisco converted the Indians of the Yacampis valley. The ruins are pro- *Km 8* tected by a stone temple. Beyond is the **Quebrada de los Sauces**, the gorge of the Río Los Sauces, and an artificial lake, Km 15, with swimming and fishing. The **Cerro de la Cruz** (1,680 m), Km 27, is a centre for hang-gliding, where condors and falcons may be sighted.

Villa Sanagasta is attractively set among orchards. There is a chapel dating **Villa Sanagasta** from 1801. From here the road climbs steeply over the Cuesta de Huaco (1,800 *Population: 1,600* m) and runs north; at Km 83 a turning (2 km) leads to **Chuquis**, where there *Altitude: 1,000 m* is a small museum. *Km 32*

Aminga is a small village with several wine *bodegas*. The vines are grown between **Aminga** rows of orange and walnut trees. The **De La Fuente** *bodega* may be visited. *Population: 600*
Altitude: 1,360 m
Km 88

Anillaco, 3 km off the road at Km 93, is the hometown of former-President **Anillaco** Carlos Menem. This small town, with two fine hotels is becoming a tourist *Population: 900* attraction: it styles itself *Capital de la Fe* on account of its proximity to the *Señor* *Altitude: 1,300 m* *de la Peña* (Our Lord of the Rock), a giant boulder 25 km west said to resemble

Carlos Saul Menem

At the beginning of this century there was only a crystalline brook at Anillaco (Ilaco or yaco is Quechua for water and ani is Quechua for shade). Shortly afterwards a Syrian immigrant family called Menehem settled here and started a vineyard. The fine grapes, pressed at their own bodega, produced a tasty white wine.

The eldest son, Carlos (who altered his surname to Menem) became active in the Partido Justicialista (Peronist party), being elected to the La Rioja parliament in 1955 and rising to become provincial governor by 1973. Imprisoned for five years by the military government which seized power in 1976, he was re-elected governor on the return to civilian rule in 1983.

Menem was victorious over Antonio Cafiero for the Peronist presidential nomination in 1989 which came as a surprise to many observers. La Rioja is one of the smallest provinces and Menem had a reputation as a playboy with an appetite for publicity stunts such as appearing in the national football team in a friendly match. As President (1989-1999) he sprang further surprises. While the media, especially abroad, continued to focus on his lifestyle and marital difficulties (he was once famously locked out of the presidential palace by his then-wife) and the alleged corruption associated with his family and former business associates, his government was credited with stabilising the currency, eliminating inflation, reducing taxes and

privatising many industries, in the process reversing many of the policies associated with his party's founder, Juan Perón. In 1993 he pursuaded the opposition Radicals to support reforms to the constitution which enabled him to stand for another term in office. Despite a campaign to alter the constitution again to enable him to be the Peronist candidate in 1999, he was forced to step down. The Peronists, badly divided, lost the ensuing presidential election to the Radical, De La Rua. Menem's supporters marked the inauguration of De La Rua in December 1999 by launching his candidacy for the 2003 presidency.

The rise of its most famous son has brought fame and prosperity to Anillaco. When Menem first became Governor of La Rioja he pursuaded the Argentine Automobile Club to build a handsome hostería in his hometown. Once Menem became President the town became a kind of unofficial second capital of Argentina, where the president held cabinet meetings and press conferences. Planning for his retirement, Menem built himself a spacious private residence and a mountain retreat nearby. A further building project, the construction of an airstrip for medium sized commercial jets a few kilometres from town fuelled criticism and the kind of allegations of misuse of public funds which were a hallmark of Menem's decade in the presidential palace.

the figure of Christ; it is a site of Holy Week pilgrimages. **Sleeping** at *ACA Hostería* with a restaurant and *Hostería Los Amigos*. **Camping** at a municipal site, US$2 per person.

Aimogasta
Population: 7,700
Altitude: 830 m
Phone code: 02827
Km 117 at the junctions of Routes 1, 9 & 60

Aimogasta is the largest town in this part of the province. Known as the 'National olive capital', it holds the National Olive Festival on May 24. Nearby at Arauco there is an olive tree dating from the 16th century, which has the distinction of having escaped the royal decree of 1770 to cut down all the olive trees in the Spanish colonies. **Sleeping** at *Hostería Brigite* on the plaza and *Hostería Arauco*, T420206. **Camping** at *Los Nacimientos*.

The Famatina Valley

This valley lies between two ranges of hills. To the east the Sierra de Velasco, rising to 4,257 m, separates it from La Rioja and to the west is the Sierra de Famatina. From La Rioja the valley is reached via Patquía, 69 km south of the capital, but a new road is being built to link the valley directly with the provincial capital. Once an important mining area, the valley is famous for its tasty wines, olives and walnuts.

The second town in the province, Chilecito lies on the Río Famatina in an area of vineyards and olive groves. Founded in 1715, its name derives from the influx of Chilean miners in the 18th and 19th centuries. There are good views of the Sierra de Famatina, especially from the top of El Portezuelo, an easy climb from the end of Calle El Maestro. It is also a base for climbing Cerro Negro Overo (6,097 m) in the Famatina massif. On the southern outskirts of town you can see the first station of the cable car system to the La Mejicana mine; the first station has a small historical museum. At Los Sarmientos, 2 km north of town, is a chapel, dating from 1764, with a fine wooden door, the work of Indian craftsmen.

Museo de Ciencias Naturales Samay Huasi, 2 km southeast of town, in the house of Joaquín V González, founder of La Plata University. ■ *Mon-Fri 0800-1300, 1330-1930, Sat/Sun 0800-1200, 1400-1830.* There are pleasant gardens and good views of Chilecito and the Sierra de Famatina.

Chilecito
Phone code: 02825
Colour map 1, grid C2
Population: 20,000
Altitude: 1,074 m

Sleeping **AB** *Chilecito*, Gordillo y Ocampo, T422201, **B** for ACA members, without breakfast, a/c, in lovely gardens, confitería, good value. **B** *Riviera*, Castro Barros 133, T423382. Without breakfast, lounge with photos and articles on Carlos Gardel. Recommended. **D** *Res Americano*, Libertad 68, T422804. Per person, without breakfast, fan, good beds, clean. **AB** *Belsavac*, 9 de Julio y Dávila (Plaza Sarmiento), T422977. With breakfast, a/c. **C** *Wamatinag*, Galeria Victoria (Plaza Sarmiento), T423419. Without breakfast, run down, overpriced. **C** *Hermosina*, Castro Barros 182. With

The tourist office has a list of families offering accommodation, but not for singles

Chilecito centre

To Route 40 to Famatina

San Nicolás · San Francisco · J Hernández · San Román · Av Pelagio B Luna · 19 de Febrero · D de Castro y Bazán · Gobernador Gordillo

o El Portezuelo

San Vicente · Ocampo

Juan XXII

Gobernador Moita

🏛 Museo Samay Huasi

La Plata

4

Banco de la Nación Argentina

Joaquin V González

Cordoba · Uruguay · Gordillo · Ocampo

5

2

La Rioja · El Maestro

1 Yotamar · **3** o La Rioja

8

B Mitre · 25 de Mayo

o Interioja

7 **2**

1

6

Castro Barros

Dávila

3

4

H Yrigoyen · Famatina · Maxibus

San Martín · Libertad · Martínez · 9 de Julio

Independencia

To Museo Cable Carril

N
Not to scale

■ **Sleeping**		● **Eating**	
1 Belsavac	4 Hosp Josesito	7 Riviera	1 Capri	4 Creisy
2 Chilecito	5 Mary Pérez	8 Wamatinag	2 Chaplin	5 El Quincho
3 Hermosina	6 Res Americano		3 Chloé	

La Mejicana

The La Mejicana cable car gives some idea of Chilecito's importance as a mining centre in the early 20th century. Built in 1903-5, it linked the La Mejicana mine in the Sierra de Famatina with the foundry at Santa Florentina and the railhead in Chilecito, and replaced mules as the only means of supplying the mine and transporting the ore. Built by the Bleichert company of Leipzig, Germany, it was, at the time, the longest cable railway in the world, 34.6 km long and climbing from 1,075 m in Chilecito to 4,063 m at the mine. There were 262 towers, 9 stations, a tunnel 160 m long and a viaduct; the 2 ends were linked by

one of the first telephone systems in the country. 450 wagons, each with a capacity of 250 kg, carried the gold, silver and copper ore from the 40 mine workings, at a speed of 8 kmph, powered by a steam engine fed by quebracho wood brought from Santiago del Estero.

After the mine closed in 1926, some regular maintenance was carried out by railway company until 1974. In 1990 the municipal government began restoration work: tourist services are operated on special occasions between Chilecito and the Santa Florentina foundry on a branch line 6 km away.

breakfast, clean. **D** *Mary Pérez*, Dávila 280, T423156. Per person, with bath and breakfast, with fan, patio, very comfortable. Recommended. **E** *Hosp Josesito*, La Plata y 19 de Febrero, T424329, opposite bus terminal. Per person, with bath, without breakfast, basic, clean. **Camping** At Santa Florentina, 6 km northwest of Chilecito and Las Talas, 2 km beyond.

Eating *El Gallo*, Perón e Illia, excellent. On Plaza Sarmiento: *Chaplin*, parrillada. *Capri*, light meals and drinks. *Chloé*, restaurant/bar. *Creisy*, bar. *El Quincho*, restaurant. *Ferrito*, Pelagio Luna 661, very good.

Tour operators For tours in the Reserva Natural Laguna Brava (see below) contact Jorge Humberto Llanos, T422171, or Adolfo and Daniel at *Laguna Brava ETV*, T422348, F423330. For treks, and trips to see gold washers at Famatina or to Talampaya, ask for Carlos de Caro, or enquire at tourist office, at bus terminal, T424978, F424888.

Transport Air J Facundo Quiroga airport at Anguinán, 7 km south. *Líneas Aéreas Riojanas* to **La Rioja**, 20 mins. **Bus** To **Buenos Aires** via Córdoba, *Urquiza* and *ABLO*, daily, US$66. To **San Juan**, *Vallecito*, daily, US$22. To **Mendoza**, *Vallecito*, daily US$26. To **Tinogasta** (Catamarca), Mon-Fri, direct at 0700 via Route 11. To **La Rioja**, *combi* service run by *Interioja*, Plaza Sarmiento, T425949. *La Riojana*, El Maestro 61, T424710, *Yotamar*, kiosk in Plaza Sarmiento. *Maxibus*, 25 de Mayo 112, T423134. To **Villa Unión** daily, *Cotil*. To **Catamarca** and **Córdoba** via *La Rioja* only.

North of Chilecito Route 40 continues north from Chilecito. **Famatina** (*Population* 2,000; *Altitude* 1,470 m), Km 31, is a sleepy hamlet amid nut plantations with a *hostería* and restaurants. From here Provincial Route 11 (*ripio*) goes north to Tinogasta, while Route 40 heads north to **San Blas** (*Population* 2,800; *Altitude* 1,050 m), which has a church dating from 1734. 12 km further north Route 40 meets Route 60, the Aimogasta-Tinogasta road.

Western La Rioja

The westernmost inhabited valley in La Rioja is that of the Río Vinchina, which flows along the west side of the Sierra de Famatina. The valley is reached from the provincial capital via Patquía and Route 150, then north along Route 26 via the Parque Nacional Talampaya, or from Chilecito by Route 40, which branches off, at Nonogasta, 16 km south and runs westwards through the Cuesta de Miranda, one of the most spectacular routes in the province. Winding its way between the Sierra de Famatina to the north and the Sierra de Sañogasta to the south, it rises to 2,010 m and drops again, passing through 320 bends in its 11,500 m.

Some 92 km west of Nonogasta, Villa Unión is the largest settlement in the valley and is a base for visits to the Parque Nacional Talampaya, 67 km south. **Sleeping** at *Dayton* on the main street and **E** *Hosp Paola* on the main street opposite the police station, basic. Next door is **E** *Hosp Changuito* wth a restaurant.

Villa Unión
Population: 3,500
Altitude: 1,240 m

Provincial Route 26, unpaved, runs along the Río Vinchina valley. From **Vinchina**, where there are several basic *hospedajes* and fuel, Km 73, it passes through the Quebrada de la Troya before reaching **Jagüe** at Km 117.

North of Villa Union

This park covers some 405,000 ha of mountain-valleys, rising from 3,800 m to 4,360 m. Laguna Brava, a salt lake, 4,271 m, 16 km long, 3 km wide, lies further northwest beyond the Portezuelo del Peñón. There superb views over the lake, with some of the mightiest volcanoes on earth in the background. From the left these are the perfect cone Veladero (6,436 mm), Reclus (6,335 m), Los Gemelos (6,130 m), Pissis (6,882 m) the highest volcano in the world, though inactive, and Bonete (6,759 m) which is visible from Villa Unión and Talampaya. The park is home to flamingoes and over 3,000 vicuñas. The building of a new international road to Chile, planned to run through the park, along the north side of Laguna Brava and through the Paso de Pircas Negras (4,195 m), will make this area much more easily accessible. ■ *Getting there: From Jagüe, 4WD essential. Entry US$10. For tours in this area see opposite page.*

Reserva Natural Laguna Brava
Colour map 1, grid C1

The West

The Northwest

7

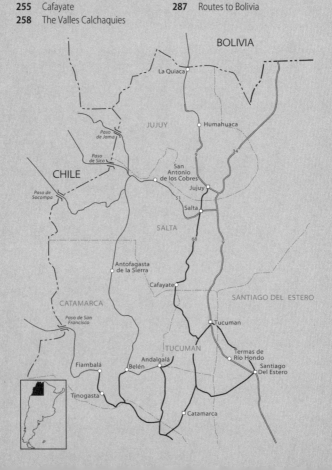

The Northwestern provinces of Catamarca, Santago del Estero, Tucumán, Salta and Jujuy provide some of the biggest contrasts in Argentina. The west of the region, Catamarca, Salta and Jujuy, offers Andean landscapes. Catamarca is little visited by travellers, Salta, however, is one of the great tourist centres of Argentina and a base for exploring the beautiful mountain valleys further west. It is also the starting point for the famous 'Tren a las Nubes' (train to the clouds). Jujuy, north of Salta, offers its own attractions, the most popular of which is the Quebrada de Humahuaca, a wonderful long gorge with strata of rock of contrasting colours. At higher altitudes in Salta and Jujuy there is a bleak landscape reminiscent of parts of Bolivia: saltflats, flamingoes and mining towns populated by indigenous peoples. By contrast, eastern Jujuy and Salta, on the steep eastern edges of the Andes, includes Argentina's three cloudforest parks.

Southeast of Salta is Tucumán, the smallest province in Argentina, much of which is subtropical lowlands, the home of the Argentine sugar industry. Santiago del Estero, further southeast still is mainly covered by the arid Chaco desert. One of the few areas of Argentina with an indigenous population, this is also a region of major prehispanic ruins. The most important of these are at Tafí del Valle, Quilmes and Santa Rosa de Tastil.

The Northwest

Background

Geography

In the northwest the crest of the Andes rises to include some of the highest peaks in the Americas. East of the Andes lies the *puna*, a windswept, stony and treeless plain, geologically a remnant of the Brazilian massif of hard ancient crystalline rocks. Parts of the *puna* are not drained by rivers: rainfall and snowfall collects in lakes and forms large areas of saltflats. Rivers flow east from the *puna* through steeply cut valleys or *quebradas*, which are particularly important as routes to the *puna*. East of the *puna* and running north-northeast to south-southwest are several ranges of hills. Between these ranges are lowlands known as the *valles*. The easternmost ranges fall steeply towards the plains of the Chaco which occupy the southeasternmost parts of this region.

Though many rivers and streams flow east from the *puna*, they feed into three main rivers: the Bermejo, the Juramento and the Dulce. The Bermejo is easily the largest, flowing south from Bolivia and receiving the waters of the Río San Francisco, which flows north from Salta, and of the smaller rivers which flow east in Jujuy. The Dulce flows south into Laguna Mar Chiquita in Córdoba province while the Juramento feeds into the Río Salado and is part of Argentina's longest river system, the Paraná.

The highest peaks in this region are: Ojos del Salado (6,864 m), Tres Cruces (6,749 m), Walther Penk (6,683 m), Incahuasi (6,638 m), Nacimientos (6,493 m), El Muerto (6,488 m), Pico Ata (6,445), El Cóndor (6,373 m), De Los Patos (6,239 m) and San Francisco (6,016 m) in Catamarca; Llullaillaco (6,739), Antofalla (6,440 m), Cachi (6,380 m), Socompa (6,031 m) and Quewar (6,102 m) in Salta and Chañi (5,896 m) in Jujuy.

Climate There are distinct climatic zones. In the *puna* wide variations in daytime temperatures occur: from 35°C to -2°C in summer; from 15°C to -26°C in winter. Though snow falls on the mountains above 5,500 m, rainfall is low, in some area below 50 mm a year. In the valleys temperatures are less extreme; rainfall

Northwest Andean peaks

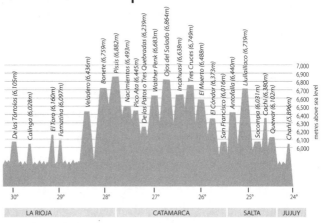

Volcano   Mountain

Teeming with wildlife

The puna is home to a variety of birdlife including the lesser rhea, a non-flier which compensates by running fast, the andean lapwing, the puna plover, the mountain caracara and the andean condor. The lakes of the puna attract different species according to the season and are outstanding for bird-watchers. There are huge flocks of flamingoes (three species of which the Chilean is the most common), andean geese, puna ibis, andean gulls and various species of coots and ducks including the puna teal and the crested duck.

Camelids are the most impressive mammals, with herds of wild vicuña and guanaco as well as the domesticated llama. Rodents include the chinchilla.

In the valleys of the prepuna you can see andean woodpeckers, grey-hooded parakeets, giant hummingbirds, ghiguano thrushes and seedeaters such as the green yellow-finch, the black-hooded sierra-finch and the black siskin. Lesser rheas, andean geese, guanacos and vicuñas can be seen in winter.

is heavier in the eastern valleys. The eastern hills experience a very different climate, with heavy rainfall, up to 2,000 mm a year, carried by easterly winds from the Atlantic. Temperatures in the east rise rapidly with declining altitude. Rainfall throughout the northwest occurs mainly in summer, when many roads become impassable.

Economy

The economy of the northwest is as varied as its landscapes. Tucumán and eastern Jujuy are the centres of Argentine sugar production, while tobacco is also an important crop. Cafayate is renowned for its wines and the valleys of western Catamarca also produce grapes and other fruit. Industry tends to be limited to food-processing but minerals are important in some parts of the northwest, particularly in Jujuy. Antimony and tin are mined in Rinconada, while Sierra del Aguilar and Nevado del Chañi have the richest deposits of lead, zinc, silver and iron in Argentina and iron ore from the Zapala mine is processed at Palpalá. Oil is extracted from around Libertador General San Martín in eastern Salta. Tourism is also important for the local economy, especially in Salta which has become one of the major tourist centres in Argentina.

History

The northwest was one of the most important areas of prehispanic settlement as the extensive archaeological sites of Quilmes, Tafi del Valle and Santa Rosa de Tastil indicate. This was also one of the first areas of Spanish settlement. The first Spanish expedition, led by Diego de Almagro from Cuzco (Peru), entered Argentina in 1536. A little later a better and lower route was discovered through the Quebrada de Humahuaca. Along this new route the Spanish founded a group of towns: Santiago del Estero, Tucumán, Salta, and Jujuy. Throughout the colonial period these were the centres of white settlement. Attempts to subdue the Amerindian population of the valleys included the imposition of *encomiendas*, the establishment of Jesuit and Franciscan missions and military conquest, but resistence was fierce, especially in the Calchaquí and Humahuaca valleys.

Trade followed the pattern of Spanish advance into the northwest: just as the area had been settled from the north, colonial trade was oriented towards Potosi and other mining areas. Trade was largely in mules and other goods

The Northwest

Colonial churches of Salta and Jujuy

Some of the most attractive colonial churches in Argentina are to be found in the provinces of Salta and Jujuy. Despite the ravages of time, natural disasters, war and restoration work, many retain their charm, especially away from the two provincial capitals.

The main influence on church architecture in this region was the city of Sucre (today in Bolivia), which was capital of the audiencia of Chuquisaca and seat of an archbishop. The architecture of Sucre, in its turn, was influenced particularly by the medieval churches of Seville. The basic structure, with adobe

walls and wooden-framed roof, had a single nave with side-chapels, sacristy and a single tower. In the valleys, where the population was entirely Amerindian, an atrium or covered area outside was added in front of the church: this was used for teaching the unconverted and often became the social centre of the village.

Away from the cities, the easiest churches to visit are those in the Valles Calchaquíes and the Quebrada de Humahuaca. Among the less accessible are some of the most outstanding, notably Casabindo and Yavi in northern Jujuy.

were carried by mules. The larger cities of the northwest grew in importance as they served this route. Mules were bred mainly in the plains between Rosario, Santa Fe, and Córdoba, and driven to Salta for the great fair in February and March. In 1679 Crown officials estimated that 40,000 cattle and 20,000 mules were passing through Salta each year on their way north. Tucumán was strategically important: the routes of the Ríos Salado and Dulce forced mule traffic to pass through it on the way to Salta. Jujuy was intended to protect the trade route from attacks by the Humahuaca and Calchaquí indians.

Although the economy of the cities continued to rely on the trading route to Bolivia, by the 18th century the Spanish had developed cattle ranching, tobacco, wheat, oranges and rice in the valleys. The break up of the Spanish Empire and the loss of trade links with Bolivia and Peru hit the area badly. Jujuy was invaded 11 times by royalist forces and was badly devastated during the wars of independence. The whole area suffered from the political instability which followed.

Catamarca Province

Catamarca can be divided into three areas, the eastern sierras, the Alta Cordillera or High Andes, and the puna. There are three main valleys: the Valle de Catamarca, the most populated part of the province, situated between the Sierra de Ancasti and the Sierra de Ambato; the Campo de Belén, a wide basin west of the Sierra de Ambato and south of the Sierra de Belén; and the valley of the Río Abaucán between the Sierra de Fiambalá and the Sierra de Narváez. West of the Sierra de Fiambalá is another valley, the Valle de Chaschuil, almost uninhabited, west of which tower the High Andes. North of Belén, the northern part of the province is puna, a high rolling, largely barren plain. The province is scattered with thermal springs. Cattle, fruit, grapes and cotton are the main agricultural products, but it is also renowned for hand-woven ponchos and fruit preserves. There are traces of Amerindian civilizations, including extensive agricultural terraces (now mostly abandoned), throughout the province.

Catamarca

The provincial capital, known officially as San Fernando del Valle de Catamarca, Catamarca was founded in 1683 and lies on the Río del Valle. Though it is a pleasant city, it is one of the less visited provincial capitals in Argentina. Several of the public buildings date from the late 19th century and were designed by the Italian architect Luigi Caravati.

Phone code: 03833
Colour map1, grid C3
Population: 111,000
153 km NE of La Rioja &
240 km S of Tucumán

Sights

The centre of the city lies around the attractive Plaza 25 de Mayo, which has an equestrian statue of San Martín. On the western side of the plaza are the rose coloured **cathedral** (1878) and the white **Casa de Gobierno** (1891), both designed by Caravati. The cathedral interior is richly decorated; frescoes on the ceiling depict scenes from the life of Christ. Four blocks east of the plaza is the **Seminario Conciliar**, also by Caravati, which has a double bell-tower and an Italianate façade,but it is closed to the public. One block north of the plaza is the **Convento de San Francisco** with a church dating from 1891. Fine views over the city can be had from the **Paseo General Navarro**, five blocks west of the plaza, a small park, rather run down but with a variety of attractive tree species.

Museums

Museo Arqueológico, Sarmiento 450. An important collection of pre-Hispanic artefacts including stone and ceramic pipes used for smoking drugs on ceremonial occasions. ■ *Mon-Fri 0730-1230, 1430-2030, Sat/Sun 0830-1230, 1530-1830.* **Museo Folklórico**, underground (*subsuelo*), Paseo Gral Navarro. Displays of traditional handicrafts as well as weaving looms and musical instruments. ■ *Mon-Sat 0800-1230, 1500-2000, Sun 0900-1230.* **Museo Histórico Provincial**, Chacabuco 425, T437562. Includes furniture and portraits as well as a 1886 plan of the city. ■ *Mon-Fri 0800-1200, 1500-1900, Sat 1500-1900.* **Museo Antropológico,** Belgrano 300. Includes pieces from the Aguada culture. ■ *Mon-Fri 0800-1300, 1500-2100.* **Museo de la Ciudad**, Rivadavia 1050, in the former mansion of Caravatti. Dsiplays on the history of the city and local customs. ■ *Mon-Fri 0900-1230, 1630-2000, Sat 0900-1300.*

Excursions

At **Capillas del Valle**, there are churches in the Valle de Catamarca, just north of the city. The first of these, at **San Isidro**, 5 km east, was designed by Caravati. At **Villa Dolores**, 1 km further north, there is a church built in colonial style in 1847, **San Antonio**. It dates from 1802 but was remodelled in 1830 and 1845. Nearby is a **zoo** with guanacos, vicuñas, alpacas and llamas in a park. **San José**, 4 km further north, is another colonial church dating from 1780 while **La Señora del Rosario**, 2 km east, a simple white building dating from 1715, is the oldest of all the churches in the area. Three kilometres further north is **Los Milagros** (1793) which has a 19th-century tower. **Dique Las Pirquitas** is a lake in the same valley, 25 km north of Catamarca, where there is good fishing and watersports as well as trekking and mountain-biking. ■ *Getting there: Bus No 1A from bus terminal, every 30 mins,*

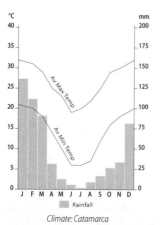

°C / mm
40 / 200
35 / 175
30 / 150
25 / 125
20 / 100
15 / 75
10 / 50
5 / 25
0 / 0
J F M A M J J A S O N D

Av Max Temp
Av Min Temp

▨ Rainfall

Climate: Catamarca

The Northwest

stops at Hostería de Turismo (with restaurant) at Villa Pirquitas, from where it is about 45 mins walk to the lake.

For fine panoramic views over the Valle de Catamarca head for the **Cuesta del Portezuelo**, a hill 20 km northeast on the road to Lavalle and Santiago del Estero. At the village of Portezuelo, Km 18, there is a police checkpoint before the Cuesta which is 20 km long and which rises through 13 hairpin bends to 1,680 m. From the top the road continues via El Alto (altitude 950 m; hosteria), near which is the Dique Ipizca (good *pejerrey* fishing) to Lavalle. For transport along this route see transport, page 238.

Sleeping **L** *Casino Catamarca*, Pasaje César Carmen, T/F430891, hcasino@infovia.com Pool, restaurant and full facilities. **AL** *Ancasti*, Sarmiento 520, T430617, F435952. Central, restaurant, also apartments. **A** *Arenales*, Sarmiento 542, T431329. **A** *Leo III*, Sarmiento 727, T431090. Rooms and suites, restaurant. **AB** *Pucará*, Caseros 501, T 430688. Good value. **AB** *Grand*, Camilo Melet 41, opposite Paseo General Navarro, T436715. **AB** *Inti Huasi*, República 297, T435705. A/c, snack bar, parking. **B** *Colonial*, República 802, T423502. Recommended, welcoming, good value. **AB/B** *Suma Huasi*, Sarmiento 547, T435699, F432595. Breakfast, a/c, parking, good beds, gloomy, restaurant *Las Tinajas*. **C** *Residencial Delgado*, San Martín 788, T426109. Bath, basic. Several *residenciales* near bus terminal including **C** *Res Ambato*, Güemes 841, T422242, with bath. **C** *Res Tucumán*, Tucumán 1040, T422209. With bath, modern. **C** *Res Avenida*, Güemes 754, T422139. With and without bath. **C** *Res Yunka Sumu*, Vicario Segura 1255, T 423034. With and without bath. **D** *Hosp Menem*, Güemes 797, T424755. Opposite terminal. Discounts to ACA members at *Ancasti, Inti Huasi*, and *Suma Huasi*. Provincial tourist office has a list of families who rent rooms.

Catamarca centre

■ Sleeping			● Eating
1 Ancasti	6 Hosp Menem	11 Res Avenida	1 Augustus
2 Arenales	7 Inti Huasi	12 Res Delgado	2 La Criolla
3 Casino Colonial	8 Leo III	13 Res Tucumán	3 Montecarlo
4 Colonial	9 Pukará	14 Res Xunka Sumu	4 Richmond Bar
5 Grand	10 Res Ambato	15 Sumay Huasi	5 Sociedad Española

Festivals of the Northwest

Though Argentina is an ultramodern country in some respects, it still preserves ancestral customs dating back to before the Spanish conquest. Such indigenous customs survive in the interior of the country, especially in the Northwest. The most colourful of the region's local festivals are summarized below:

Date	Event	Place(s)
20 December-6 January	Virgin of Belín	Belín (Catamarca)
1-15 January	Pre-Carnival festivities	Humahuaca (Jujuy)
15-31 January	January festival	Tilcara (Jujuy)
2 February	Virgen of Candelaria	Humahuaca
6 February	Pachamama (Mother Earth)	Purmamarca (Jujuy); Amaichá del Valle (Tucumán)
Feb/March (variable)	Carnival	Humahuaca
19 March	San José (patron saint of workers)	San Jos, and Cachi (Salta)
March/April (variable)	Holy Week	Throughout the Northwest
March/April (in Holy Week)	Festival of Yavi	Yavi (Jujuy)
March/April (in Holy Week)	Procession accompanying Virgin of Punta Corral	From Punta Corral to Tumbaya (Jujuy)
March/April (in Holy Week)	Pilgrimage to El Señor de la Peña	Aimogasta (La Rioja)
4 May	Santa Cruz	Uquía (Jujuy)
24 June	San Juan, Rinconada, Conchinoca, Santa Catalina	San Juan Bautista (John the Baptist)
24/25 July	Santiago Apóstol (St James)	Humahuaca
26 July	Santa Ana	Tilcara (Jujuy)
15 August	Toreo de la Vincha (only bullfight in Argentina)	Casabindo (Jujuy)
30 August	Santa Rosa de Lima (Patron-saint of America)	Purmamarca (Jujuy)
15 September	Our Lord and the Virgen of the Miracle	City of Salta
First Sunday in October	Adoration of the Cachis	Iruya (Salta)
Third Sunday in October	Fiesta de las Ollas (pots)	La Quiaca (Jujuy)
1, 2 November	All Souls Day; Day of the Dead	Towns in the Quebrada de Humahuaca (Jujuy)
8 December	Virgen del Valle (Virgen of the Valley)	City of Catamraca
December-January	Adoration of the Child Jesus (nativity plays)	Many places in the Northwest.

Eating

Many cheap restaurants near bus terminal & around the Plaza 25 de Agosto

Sociedad Española, Virgen del Valle 725. *Las Tinajas*, Sarmiento 533. Excellent, pricey, live music. Warmly recommended. Several restaurants around Plaza 25 de Mayo including *La Criolla*, República 546, *parrillada*, and *Montecarlo*, República 520, *trattoria*. Two interesting bars are *Richmond Bar*,Plaza 25 de Mayo, superb decor dating from 1920s with period furniture, and *Augustus*,República 488, *confitería* in an elegant setting. There are several bars and cafés along Rivadavia including *Marco Polo Bar*, No 916, drinks, snacks.

Festivals

Pilgrimages to the church of the Virgen del Valle. Jul, regional handicrafts are sold at *Festival del Poncho*, a *feria* with 4 nights of music, mostly folklore of the northwest.

Shopping

Catamarca specialities from *Cuesta del Portezuelo*, Sarmiento 571 and 588. *Mercado Artesanal*, Virgen del Valle 945, T 437598. Wide range of handicrafts.Supermarkets *Lozano*, Plaza 25 de Agosto. *Sin Nombre* and *Tia*, both on Rivadavia 900 block. Camping and fishing equipment from *El Ferretero* in bus terminal.

Transport

Local The major sights and services in the city can be visited on foot.

Air Aeropuerto Felipe Varela, 20 km south, T430080. *Aerolíneas Argentinas*, *Southern Winds* and *Lapa* to Buenos Aires and La Rioja.

Bus Modern terminal with shops, cafeteria, ATM and telephone office 5 blocks southeast of plaza at Güemes y Tucumán. Taxi to/from Plaza 25 de Mayo US$1. To **Tucumán**, *Transportes Mendoza*, *El Rapido*, *Sierras de Córdoba*, 4 hrs, US10. To **Buenos Aires**, several companies daily, 15 hrs, US$50, *cama* US$55. To **Córdoba**, *Chevalier*, 3 daily, 5½ hrs, US$20. Also *Robledo*, *Sierras de Córdoba*. To **Santiago del Estero**, 1630, US$12. To **Mendoza**, several companies, daily. To **Santiago de Chile** via Mendoza, US$45, 18 hrs, daily. To **La Rioja**, several companies, US$8, 2 hrs. To **Belén** via Aimogasta and Londres, *Rubimar* and *Cacorba*, 5 hrs, US13. To **Andalgala**, *Cacorba* 2 a day, *Lazo* 4 a day, *Gutierrez* 3 a day, 4½ hrs, US$13.

To Santiago del Estero province No service over the Cuesta del Portezuelo to Lavalle but *Empresa 25 de Agosto* service to Frías, further south, uses this route, departing 1330 daily, returning 0300. From Frías buses run to Lavalle and on to Santiago del Estero. Minibuses to the Portezuelo are run by *Anquinilabus*, T421058. To Frías via Totoral, Mon-Fri, Sadji,0300. To Lavalle via Totoral, same No 18, leaves Tue, Thu, and Sun 1100, 4 hrs.

Tour operators

Yokavil, Rivadavia 916, Local 14, T430066, offers excursions to Cuesta de El Portezuelo, US$15, 4 hrs.

Directory

Airline offices *Aerolíneas Argentinas*, Sarmiento 589, T424460 *Lapa*, Sarmiento 506, F434450. *Southern Winds*, Prado 357, T431006. **Banks** *Banco de Catamarca*, Plaza 25 de Mayo, changes US$ cash but not TCs, ATM, Visa, Mastercard. *Banco de Galicia* Rivadavia 554, changes TCs, high commission, ATM. **Communications** Post office San Martín 753, slow, open 0800-1300, 1600-2000. **Telephone** Several *locutorios* including *Rivadavia* 758, open 0700-2400, daily. **Internet** *CEDECC*, Esquiu 414.*Telecom*, Sarmiento 741.*Telefónica*, Rivadavia 650. **Laundry** *Laverap*,Mota Botello 339. *Lave Centro*, Salta 648, Mon-Sat 0800-2200, US$7 per load, wash and dry. **Tourist offices** Sarmiento 535, T437595, has information on route to Chile via Paso de San Francisco. Provincial tourist office, Roca y Virgen del Valle, T/F437594, Mon-Fri 0700-1300, 1400-2000. Also office in airport. In small towns in the province, go to the municipalidad for information and maps.

From Catamarca to Chile

Route 60 (later Route 45) runs northwest along the provincial border with La Rioja passing through Aimogasta (see page 224) before following the Río Colorado to Tinogasta. Beyond Tinogasta Route 60 continues north along the Río Abaucan and east of the high Sierra de Fiambalá as far as Fiambalá. From here the road runs west along the Río Guanchín and then, 50 kilometres west of Fiambalá through the narrow gorge of the Río Chasquil before climbing north along the Valle de Chasquil; to the west there are fine views of Cerro de la Coipa (5,150 metres) and Cerro Agua Caliente (5,517). In the dry upper reaches of the valley the main vegetation is the cactus. At the northern end of the valley is the Cordillera de San Buenaventura and here Route 60 turns west before climbing to the Chilean frontier at Paso San Francisco, 203 km northwest of Fiambalá. This road, ripio from the beginning of the Valle de Chasquil to the frontier, has been described as 'quite some washboard' but it does not require a four-wheel drive vehicle.

A former-copper mining town in the broad valley of the Río Abaucán, it is an oasis of vineyards, olive groves, and poplars. This was an important area of pre-hispanic settlement and there are two small archaeological museums. The **Museo Arqueológico Municipal**, in the Casa de la Cultura, Constitución 430, displays objects from the fortress of Batungasta. ■ *Mon-Fri 0700-1300, 1400-2000.* The **Museo Doctor Alanis**, Copiapó y Tucumán. ■ *Mon-Fri 0700-2000.* Excursions may be made to the **Termas de Aguadita**, 15 km west along a dirt road which turns off Route 60, 10 km north of Tinogasta. Further north along this road, at km 24 an unpaved road leads off ½ km to the Diaguita Indian archaeological site of **Batungasta**, from where it is possible to walk west through an impressive red sandstone gorge. ■ *Getting there: Both Termas de Aquadirta and Batungasta can be reached by taking the Tinogasta-Fiambalá bus.*

Tinogasta

Phone code: 03837
Colour map 1, grid C2
Population: 9,000
Altitude: 1,203 m
277 km W of Catamarca

Sleeping and eating **B** *Provincial de Turismo*, Moreno y 25 de Mayo, T423911. Clean but run down, restaurant. **C** *Hostería Novel*, Córdoba 200, T442009. Near airport, friendly. **C** *Familiar*, Perón 231, T420028. With fan. **C** *Res Le Miraje*, Moreno 748, T420323. With fan. **D** *Res Don Alberto*, A del Pino 425, T420323. **Camping** At Balneario Municipal. Restaurants *Persegani*, Tristán Villafañe 373, and *Rancho Huairapuca*, on Moreno.

Tour operators *Varela Viajes*, Copiapó 156, T/F420428 for 4WD excursions to the Alta Cordillera; Omar Monuey, La Espiga de Oro, 25 de Mayo 436 for expeditions and horse riding.

Transport **Bus** To **Tucumán**, Empresa Gutiérrez, Tue, Fri, Sun 1700, Mon, Tue, Fri, Sun 0615, Fri 0845, US$22. Return Tue, Fri, Sun. To **Catamarca** 1700 and 0030 daily. To **La Rioja** and **Córdoba** 0930, El Cóndor, US$11. Services twice a week to **Chubut**, **Comodoro Rivadavia**, and **Caleta Olivia**, with Empresa Ortiz, reflect that this is the source region for labour in the Patagonian oilfields.

In the Abaucán valley in an area of vineyards, Fiambalá is the last town before the frontier. It was founded in 1702 near the site of a mission. The church of San Pedro on the outskirts 2 km south dates from 1702. Near the plaza in the Centro Cultural is the **Museo del Hombre** which includes two Indian mummies found recently in the Alta Cordillera. ■ *Tue-Sun 0900-1300, 1600-1900.* There are thermal springs nearby, the **Termas de Fiambalá**, 14 km east, temperatures from 30°C to 54°C. They can be visited by taxi (make sure taxi fare includes wait and return), and the **Termas de Saujil**, 15 km north.

Fiambalá

Population: 1,800
Colour map 1, grid B2
Altitude: 1,550 m
49 km further N

The Northwest

Sleeping C *Hostería Municipal*, Almagro s/n. Good value, restaurant, bar. *Complejo Termal Municipal*, at the Termas de Fiambalá, T 496016, cabañas **E** per person, bungalows **D** per person. **Camping** At the Termas de Fiambalá.

Tour operators For excursions into the Alta Cordillera on foot or in 4WD contact Jonson and Ruth Reynoso, T0766-90271, F0837-96154 (check state of vehicles). 4WD vehicles may be hired in Fiambalá: ask at the Intendencia.

Transport Bus *Empresa Gutiérrez* daily at 1345 to Catamarca via Tinogasta (1500) and Cerro Negro junction (1610). Connect with *Coop Catamarca* bus to Belén (from Catamarca), about 2 hrs by bad road. Also 0530 departure from Fiambalá.

Climbing in the Alta Cordillera Fiambalá and Tinogasta are the starting points for expeditions to several inactive volcanic peaks along this part of the frontier near the San Francisco pass. These include **Pissis** (6,882 m), the second highest mountain in South America, first climbed in 1937. You have to register at the police station outside Fiambalá, take passport. Other climbing possibilities include Bonete (6,759 m) Walther Penck (6,658 m), El Fraile (6,062 m), Incahuasi (6,638 m), Nacimientos (6,493 m), Tres Cruces (6,749 m), El Muerto (6,488 m) and San Francisco (6,016 m). Ojos del Salado (6,864 m) is best attacked from the Chilean side. The most favourable periods for climbing are short: November-December and March-April. In winter temperatures in this area can drop to to -35°C. For transport and guides see under Tinogasta.

Frontier with Chile Fiambalá is the starting-point for the crossing to Chile via the **Paso de San Francisco** (4,726 m), 203 km northwest. This road is officially open all year but liable to be closed by snow between June and October. Take enough fuel for at least 400 km as there are no service stations from Fiambalá to just before Copiapó. Argentine immigration and customs is at La Gruta, 21 km east of the pass. On the Chilean side roads run to El Salvador and Copiapó. Chilean customs are near the Salar de Maricunga, 100 km west of the pass.

Catamarca to Antofagasta De La Sierra

Two roads, Route 46 to Andalagá and Route 40 to Belén and Antofagasta de la Sierra, run north to give access to the valleys of western Catamarca. Route 46 (paved) branches off Route 60 at El Empalme and runs northwards between the Sierra de Ambato to the east and the saltflats of the Salar de Pipanaco to the east.

Andalgalá
Phone code: 03835
Colour map 1, grid B2
Population: 7,800
Altitude: 962 m

Renowned for its strong alcoholic drinks

The main town along this road, Andalgalá lies 134 km north of El Empalme, in an area of olives, walnut trees and fruit growing. Originally a fortress, the town is situated at the foot of Mount Candado (5,450 m) in a zone rich in archeological remains. The **Museo Arqueológico Provincial**, Libertad 50 in the Centro Civico, contains artefacts from the Belén culture. ■ *Mon-Fri 0800-1300, 1700-2100, Sat 0900-1300*. The **Mayorazgo de Huasán**, 3 km south, is a colonial mansion which can be visited (T422493 to arrange). At Minas Capillitas, 66 km north of the town, rhodochrosite, Argentina's unofficial national stone is quarried which can be bought at shops around the plaza.

Sleeping B *Aquasol*, Carranza s/n, T422615. Breakfast, pool. C *Hotel de Turismo*, Sarmiento 444, T422210. Restaurant, pool, sports facilities. D *Res Galileo*, Nuñez del Prado 757, T422247, bar. D *Res Alex*, Barcena Oeste s/n, T 1-5697112. Breakfast, laundry facilities. D *Res Andalgalá*, Belgrano 26, T422351. Without bath. D *Res Don Carlos*,

Belgrano 46, T422024. Breakfast, a/c. **Estancia** *Condado de Huasan*. Apartments, tours and horseriding. **Camping** *Autocamping La Aguada*. Pool, US$5 per tent.

Transport 3 bus lines to Catamarca.

Founded in 1681 at the entrance to the gorge of the Río Belén, the town lies north at the northern edge of a wide basin, the Campo de Belén and is noted for its olives, walnuts and peppers. This region is also famous for its weavings, ponchos, saddlebags and rugs. There are good views from the new statue of the Virgin of Belén, 450 m above the town, at the summit of the path beginning at Calle General Roca. The **Museo Condor Huasi**, Lavalle 393, contains one of the largest collection of Diaguita artefacts in the country. ■ *Mon-Fri 0800-1200, 1700-2000, Sat 1700-2000*. Belén lies 85 km west of Andalgalá along Route 46 at the junction with Route 40 which runs north from Route 60 at Cerro Negro, 79 km west of El Empalme. North of Belén there are thermal springs at La Ciénaga, 22 km along Route 40.

Belén
Phone code: 03835
Colour map 1, grid B2
Population: 8,800
Altitude: 1,240 m

Belén is known as national capital of the poncho

Sleeping and eating B *Samay*, Urquiza 349, T461320. Recommended. C *Internacional*, Calchaqui 213, T 1-5697071, pool. D *Turismo*, Belgrano y Cubas, T461501, good. Recommended. D *Doña Pilar*, Lavalle 459, T461235. Both with and without bath. **Epp** *Albergue Belén*, Arquez y Esquiú, T461539. **Epp** *Albergue Municipal*, Calchaqui s/n. T/F461878. **Camping** At Balneario Municipal. Good breakfast at bus terminal. *Restaurant Dalesio*, near YPF gas station, excellent and cheap. *El Amigazo*, behind church, good.

Transport Bus To **Catamarca** via Andalgalá; *Coop Catamarca* via Saujil, Poman, Chumbicha, Tue, Thu 1000, Fri, Sun 1300, 8 hrs. To **Santa María** Tue 1330, Fri and Sun 2020. Return Tue and Thu 0930, Sun 1945. To **Salta** via Hualfín, Santa María, Cafayate Thu 0600. To San Antonio de los Cobres via Villavil, Tue, Thu, Sun 0800 (returns from Villavil at 1830). Sit on right-hand side for best views of impressive canyon and Río Bolsón reservoir.

Festivals *Fiesta de Nuestra Señora de Belén*, 20 Dec-6 Jan; *Festival Nacional del Poncho*, Jul/Aug.

Londres was founded in 1558 and is the second-oldest town in Argentina though its site was moved several times. It was named in honour of the marriage of Mary Tudor and Philip II: the municipalidad displays a glass coat-of-arms of the city of London and a copy of the marriage proposal. There are poorly reconstructed ruins of a prehispanic settlement at Shinkal, 4 km northwest. ■ *Mon-Fri 0730-1330, 1700-1900*. There are no hotels but several *hospedajes* and a campsite on the route to Shinkal. Snacks from the shops around the plaza.

Londres
Population: 1,850
Altitude: 1,300 m
15 km S of Belén on Route 40

There are two routes north to Salta. The most direct is via Route 40 which runs northeast another 176 km, largely unpaved, to Santa María at Tucumán provincial border (see page 253), and on to Cafayate (page 255) and Salta.
    The alternative is via Route 43, which branches west off Route 40 at a point 52 km north of Belén and runs across the high *puna* to Antofagasta de la Sierra and San Antonio de los Cobres (see page 277). This route is almost impassable for passenger cars after heavy rains. The stretch just after the junction with Route 40 is very difficult with 37 km of fords. At Km 87 is Cerro Compo (3,125 m), from which the descent is magnificent; at Km 99 the road turns right to Laguna Blanca, where there is a museum and a small vicuña farm (don't go

North of Belén

straight at the junction). There are thermal springs along this road at **Hualfín**, 10 km north of the junction, and at **Villavil**, 13 km further north, that are open from January to April. There is a *hostería* here (**D**). For transport, see page 241.

This route requires enough fuel for 600 km at high altitudes on unmaintained roads. Fuel consumption of carburettor engines at these altitudes is almost double that in the lowlands. Fill up at Hualfín and San Antonio de los Cobres.

Antofagasta de la Sierra
Colour map 1, grid B2
Population: 900
Altitude: 3,365 m

The main township in sparsely populated northwest Catamarca, Antofagasta de la Sierra, is situated on the Río Punilla, 260 km north of Belén and 557 km northwest of the provincial capital. It is surrounded by lunar landscapes and volcanoes. To the west are the salt flats of the Salar de Antofalla. There are many peaks over 5,000 m, including Cerro Galán (5,912 m) a volcano with a giant caldera 40 km x 25 km. Deposits of marble, onyx, sulphur, mica, salts, borates, and gold can be found in the area. Wildlife includes vicuña, guanaco, vizcacha, flamingos, foxes and ostriches. In the Centro Cultural there is a small archeological museum. No petrol station, but fuel obtainable from *intendencia*. North of Antofagasta the road continues via the Salar de Hombre Muerto to San Antonio de los Cobres.

Sleeping and eating **D** *Albergue Municipal*, T471001, without bath, hot water. **E** per person *Pensión Darío*, blue door just off main square. **E** per person *Res Florida*, Catamarca 6. Several others. *Almacén Rodríguez*, Belgrano y Catamarca, serves meals, including breakfast.

Transport **Bus** From Belén Tue, Thu, Sun 0800, or hire a pickup or hitch.

Santiago del Estero

Phone code: 0385
Colour map 1, grid B3
Population: 201,000

Situated on the Río Dulce on the western edge of the Chaco, Santiago del Estero lies 435 km north of Córdoba. On the opposite bank of the river is the town of La Banda. Capital of its namesake province, it is a commercial centre for the Chaco.

History
Founded in 1553 by Francisco de Aguirre, Santiago was at one time an important city, the base for expeditions to found six other cities in the northwest. In 1570 it became a bishopric and in 1577 was made capital of the Spanish province of Tucumán. Sited near large Indian communities it was a centre of Jesuit missionary activity. Though Santiago proudly sees itself as the oldest city in Argentina, virtually none of this past has survived.

Sights
On the **Plaza Libertad** stand the **Municipalidad** and, next to it, the **Jefatura de Policia**, built in 1868 in the style of a colonial cabildo. On the west side is the **cathedral**, the fifth on the site, dating from 1877. The fine modern **Casa de Gobierno** is on Plaza San Martín, four blocks northwest. Two blocks southeast of the plaza, at Urquiza y 25 de Mayo, is the **Convento de Santo Domingo**, containing one of two copies of the 'Turin Shroud', given by Philip II to his 'beloved colonies of America'. ■ *Daily 0800-1200, 1700-2000*. On Plaza Lugones, three blocks east of Plaza Libertad, is the church of **San Francisco** (1895), at the back of which is the cell of San Francisco Solano, which forms part of a museum. East of the centre on the banks of the Río Dulce, is the pleasant **Parque Francisco de Aguirre**.

The Northwest

Museo de Ciencias Naturales y Antropología, Avellaneda 353. This contains an important collection of pre-Hispanic artefacts from the Chaco. There are displays on cave paintings, funerary customs, ceramics and musical instruments. The basis of the museum was a collection of over 90,000 pieces which were the lifework of Emilio and Duncan Wagner, the sons of a French diplomat. Born in Scotland and educated in Switzerland, the brothers arrived in the city in 1885 and dedicated themselves to collecting artefacts from pre-conquest Indian civilizations in the Chaco. ■ *Mon-Fri, 0800-1300, 1500-2000, Sat/Sun 0930-1200, free.* **Museo Histórico Provincial**, Urquiza 354. Located in a 200-year old mansion, this contains a wide variety of 18th- and 19th-century artefacts from wealthy local families. ■ *Mon-Fri, 0700-1300, 1400-1900, Sat/Sun 0930-1200.* **Museo Andrés Chazarreta**, Mitre 127. Located in the musician's former house, this displays artefacts from his life including a range of musical instruments. ■ *Mon-Fri 1600-2000.* **Museo de Arte Sacro**, Avellaneda 716. This includes the cell of San Francisco Solano, patron saint of Tucumán, who stayed in Santiago in 1593. ■ *Mon-Fri 0830-1200, 1730-2000, Sat 0830-1200.*

Museums

AB *Gran*, Avellaneda e Independencia, T4224563. *Libertador*, Catamarca 47, T4218730. **AB** *Rodas*, Gallo 432, T4218804. Safe. **C** *Res Emausi*, Av Moreno 600 block. Good value. *Santa Rita*, Santa Fe 273. Near bus terminal, basic. **Camping** *Las Casuarinas*, Parque Aguirre, T4211390. Insect repellent essential.

Sleeping

Restaurant Sociedad Española, Independencia 236. Popular, good value. *Centro de Viajes*, Buenos Aires 37. Good value lunches. *Mía Mamma*, 24 de Septiembre 16, on Plaza. Good restaurant/salad bar, pricey.

Eating

Carnival when virtually everything throwable gets thrown by everyone at everyone else.

Festivals

The Northwest

Santiago del Estero centre

The Northwest

Andres Chazarreta

Celebrated as the man who put Argentine folk music and dance "on the map", Andres Chazarreta was born in Santiago del Estero in 1876. From early childhood he learned to play the guitar and other instruments by ear. His first formal musical studies, at the age of 26, oriented him towards European opera and the light classics, then all the rage in Argentina which looked to France and Italy for musical inspiration.

In 1905, however, Chazarreta became fascinated by gaucho literature. Inspired by José Hernández's epic poem "Martín Fierro" and the novels of Eduardo Gutierrez which were adapted for the stage and performed by travelling groups of players, Chazarreta began arranging and performing

traditional folk tunes, beginning with the celebrated Zamba de Vargas. In 1911 in Santiago del Estero he produced a stage performance of traditional music and dance by a group of rural artists. Despite predictions of disaster, the show was a great success, but Chazarreta and his troupe of musicians and dancers had to wait another decade until they achieved their ultimate goal, a similar triumph in Buenos Aires.

In 1941 Chazarreta founded the Academy of Native Dance in Buenos Aires and by the time of his death he had made over 250 records. His versions of traditional songs and dances, mainly based on Santiago, continue to dominate Argentine folk music to this day.

Transport **Air** Mal Paso airport on northwestern outskirts. *Austral* to Buenos Aires and Jujuy. **Bus** Terminal at Gallo 480, 4 blocks from centre. To **Buenos Aires**, several daily, 12 hrs, US$37, *Cacorba, La Unión* and *Atahualpa*. To **Resistencia**, 3 a day, *El Rayo*, via Quimili and Roque Sáenz Peña, 8 hrs, US$25. To **Córdoba**, 12 a day, 7 hrs, US$16. To **Tucumán** via Río Hondo US$8; 4 a day to **Salta**, US$23, *Panamericano*, 5½ hrs, and to **Jujuy**, 7 hrs.

Directory **Airline offices** *Aerolíneas Argentinas*, Buenos Aires 60, T4224088; *Austral*, Libertad 766, T4214612. **Banks** *Banco Francés*, 9 de Julio y 24 de Septiembre; *Noroeste Cambio*, 24 de Septiembre 220, good rates. *Amex*, El Quijote Paladea Turismo, Independencia 342, T4213207. **Tourist offices** On Plaza Libertad, T4214243.

Termas de Río Hondo
Phone code: 03858
Colour map 1, grid B3
Population: 25,000
Altitude: 265 m
65 km N of Santiago del Estero

On the Río Dulce, this is the most popular spa town in Argentina. The thermal waters, over 30°C are recommended for blood pressure and rheumatism and good to drink. There are two pools: La Olla near the river and the Pileta Municipal in the Parque Güemes, both southeast of the centre. The huge Río Hondo dam, 4 km west on the Río Dulce, forms a lake of 33,000 ha, used for sailing and fishing. **Museo Municipal de Bellas Artes**, Belgrano between San Lorenzo and Sarmiento in the Centro Cultural, contains works mainly by local artists. ■ *Mon-Fri 0900-1300, 1600-1900, Sat 0900-1300.*

Sleeping There are over 170 hotels, but at national holiday periods, and especially in Aug, accommodation is hard to find, so book well in advance. *Grand Hotel Río Hondo*, Yrigoyen 552, T421195.

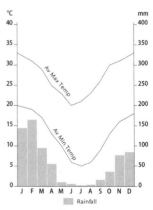

Climate: Santiago del Estero

Los Pinos, Maipú 201, T421043. Pleasant. **B** *Ambassador*, Libertad 184, T421196. *Aranjuez*, Alberdi 280, T421108. **Camping**   2 sites, both on Yrigoyen y Ruta 9: *Del Río*, US$5 rent a tent, US$4 own tent, very well run. *La Olla*, opposite. Also ACA site 4 km from town. *El Mirador*, Ruta 9 y Urquiza.

Tourist office Caseros 132, T421721.

Transport Bus   Terminal Las Heras y España, north of centre near Route 9. To **Santiago del Estero**, 1 hr, US$2 and to **Tucumán**, 2 hrs, US$4; several to **Buenos Aires** US$38.

Tucumán

The city of Tucumán (full name San Miguel de Tucumán) lies 159 km northwest of Santiago del Estero on a broad plain on the west bank of the Río Sali: to the west towers the Sierra de Aconquija. Capital of the smallest province in Argentina, it is the largest and most important city in the north. Dynamic and bustling, Tucumán is often very hot and sticky in summer. Away from the Plaza Independencia a jumble of contrasting building styles make it one of the least visually appealing cities in the Northwest. The city does, however, have its own charm; in summer the climate and the local sugar economy give it something of the feel of the Caribbean. The Parque Nueve de Julio, east of the centre, is one of the finest urban parks in Argentina.

Phone code: 0381
Colour map 1, grid B3
Population: 400,000

Founded in 1565 and transferred to its present site in 1685, Tucumán became an important centre for mule trains on the routes from Bolivia to Buenos Aires and Mendoza. With a colonial economy based on sugar, citrus fruit and tobacco, it developed a landed aristocracy distinct from those of Buenos Aires and Córdoba. The city was the site of an important battle during the Wars of Independence: Belgrano's victory here in 1812 over a royalist army ended the Spanish threat to restore colonial rule over the River Plate area. However, Tucumán is more famous for the meeting of the leaders of the anti-Spanish resistance. The Congress of Tucumán, which met from 1816 to 1820, was attended by 29 representatives from 14 provinces, including three which are now part of Bolivia. Although unable to agree on a constitution, its famous independence declaration on 9 July 1816 was an important statement of the aims of the leaders of the movement against Spanish rule. In the 19th century the province received relatively few immigrants, retaining its colonial flavour and traditional social structure into the 20th century when it began to industrialize with the growth of sugarmills, chemical plants, distilleries and textile mills.

History

The administrative centre of the city lies around the main **Plaza Independencia**. The oldest building here is the neoclassical **cathedral** (1852) with its distinctive cupola. Inside, near the baptismal font, is an old rustic cross used when founding the city. On the west side is the ornate **Casa de Gobierno** (1910) where there is a small museum (see below): next to it is the church of **San Francisco** (1891), with a picturesque façade and tiled cupola.
   South of the plaza, on Calle Congreso, is the **Casa Histórica**: only the original room where the Declaration of Independence was drafted remains, the rest being a modern reconstruction housing a museum (see below). There is a *son et lumière* programme in the garden. ■ *Nightly not Tue except in July at 2030. Adults US$2, children US$1, tickets from tourist office on Plaza Independencia, no seats.*

Sights
Fine views over the city may be obtained from Cerro Jabriel, reached by bus 118

The Northwest

Several of the former mansions of wealthy families are now occupied by museums, including the **Casa Padilla**, Plaza Independencia, and the **Casa Sortheix**, San Lorenzo y Lillo.

The **Parque Nueve de Julio**, east of the centre, was the work of Charles Thays who the Parque Tres de Febrero in Buenos Aires. Extending over 400 ha, it was the property of Bishop Colombres who played an important role in the development of the local sugar industry: his house is a museum (see below). The park contains a wide range of sub-tropical trees as well as a lake and sports facilities.

Museums **Casa de la Independencia Nacional** in the Casa Histórica (see above), Congreso 151. Displays include silverwork and furniture. The hall where independence was signed is lined with the portraits of the representatives. ■ *Wed-Mon 0900-1300,1530-1930, US$1*. **Museo de la Industria Azucarera**, in Bishop Colombres's house in the Parque 9 de Julio. Outside is his first mill which crushed the sugar between wooden beams and an 1883 French steam mill. Inside there is a display on sugar-making, but there are few explanations. ■ *Mon-Fri 0700-1300, 1400-1900, Sat/Sun 0700-1900, US$2*. **Museo de Ciencias Naturales**, 25 de Mayo 265 in University building. A fine collection which includes funerary urns and other artefacts from the pre-Hispanic cultures of the Calchaquí valleys. ■ *Mon-Fri, 0800-1330*. **Museo Folklórico Provincial**, 24 de Septiembre 565. Collections of silverwork from Peru, woollen goods and musical instruments. ■ *Mon-Fri 0900-1200, 1500-2000, Sat 0930-1230, 1530-2030. Free*. **Museo Iramaín**, Entre Rios 27. Memorial to the sculptor Juan Carlos Iramain. ■ *Mon-Fri 1100-2000*. **Museo de Bellas Artes**, 9 de Julio 44. Works by Tucumán artists. ■ *Tue-Fri, 0900-1230, 1700-2030, Sat/Sun 1700-2030*.

Excursions **Alpa-Puyo** is a private park in Tafi Viejo, 14 km north. It can be reached by white minibuses from Calle Santiago. The **El Cadillal** dam, in the gorge of the Río Sali, 26 km north, supplies electricity and water for the city and permanent irrigation for 80,000 ha. There are places to eat, a good ACA campsite, sailing and good swimming, and a small archaeological museum at the dam. ■ *Getting there: Sierras y Lagos, every 1½ hrs approximately, US$1.50, 45 mins, last buses back 1715 and 1945)*.

Simoca, 45 km south on Route 157, is known as the *capital del sulky* because of the widespread use of sulkies (carriages). It has a Saturday morning handicrafts and produce market. ■ *Getting there: Posta bus, several 1½ hrs, US$2.50; essential to get there early*.

The **Reserva Biológica San Javier**, (14,172ha) at **Horco Molle**, 14 km west on the edge of the Sierras de Aconquija, contains a wide range of subtropical plants. ■ *Getting there: Take Bus No 100 ('Reserva') and ask driver to let you off at gates*.

During the sugar cane harvest (*zafra*) some *ingenios* (mills) offer tours (ask tourist office for details). The easiest to visit is **Ingenio Concepción**, on the outskirts of Tucumán, which has guided tours (in Spanish). ■ *Mon-Sat, 0930 and 1030, no booking required. Getting there: Take Aconquija bus for Santo Cristo US$1, 15 mins*.

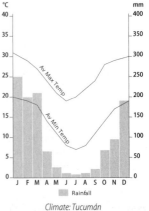

Climate: Tucumán

Essentials

L *Grand de Tucumán*, Los Proceres 380, opposite Parque 9 de Julio, T4502250. Rooms
with even numbers quieter, outstanding food and service, pool (open to
non-residents), tennis courts, disco. **L** *Metropol*, 24 de Septiembre 524, T4311180,
F4310379, metropol@amet.com.ar With buffet breakfast, Swiss restaurant, pool, parking, large rooms, central. **A** *Carlos V*, 25 de Mayo 330, T/F4311666. Central, good service,
a/c, bar, restaurant. Recommended. **AL** *Del Sol*, Laprida 35, T4311755, F4311755,
hotel_delsol@arnet.com.ar Central, pool. **AB** *ACA Motel Tucumán*, Siria 2080,
T4276037. **A** *Premier*, Alvarez 510, T/F4310381, info@redcarlosv.com With breakfast,
restaurant, parking, a/c, good. **AL** *República* , Rivadavia 71, T4310481. With breakfast,
parking. **AB** *Colonial*, San Martín 35, T4311523. Modern, fan, good breakfast, parking.
Recommended. **A** *Mediterraneo*, 24 de Septiembre 364, T4310025, F4310080. 20% discount to *South American Handbook* readers. **B** *Astoria*, Congreso 88, T/F4213101. With
breakfast, bar/restaurant, good beds. **B** *Francia*, Alvarez 467, T/F4310781. With breakfast, bar, good beds, good value. **B** *Versailles*, Alvarez 481, T4229760, F4229763. With
breakfast, 18th-century French style, restaurant, good beds. **B/C** *Viena*, Santiago del
Estero 1050, T4310313. **C** *La Vasca*, Mendoza 281, T4211288. Safe. Recommended.
C *Casa de Huéspedes María Ruiz*, Rondeau 1824. Safe. Recommended. **C** *Florida*, 24 de
Septiembre 610, T4226674. Without breakfast, a/c, helpful. **C** *Independencia*, Balcarce,
entre San Martín y 24 de Septiembre. With fan, quiet, poor water supply on 1st floor.
C/D *Palace*, 24 de Septiembre 233, without breakfast, central, run down. **C** *Petit*,
Alvarez 765, T4214902. Spacious, old fashioned, pleasant patio.

Near train station AB *Dallas*, Corrientes 985, T4218500. With breakfast. **B** *Miami*,
Junín 580, T4310265. With breakfast, parking, discounts for *Hostelling International*
members. **C/D** *Nuevo Tucumán*, Catamarca 573, T/F4221809. With bath, also **D** without bath, fan, confiteria, good value.

Near terminal D *Alcázar*, Saenz Peña 33, not very clean, friendly, noisy. **E** *Estrella*,
Araoz 38, T4229880, without bath, very hospitable.

Outside the city At San Javier **AB** *Hostería San Javier* T4929004, F229241. Beautiful
location, clean, pool, restaurants. At Villa Nougués **AB** *Hostería Villa Nougués*,
T4310048. Small, excellent, great views.

Camping   Avoid the sites in the Parque 9 de Julio. 2 roadside campsites 3 km east
and northeast of city centre.

There are several popular restaurants and cafés in Parque 9 de Julio and on Plaza
Independencia. *El Fondo*, San Martín 848, T4222161, good service, 'best steakhouse
ever'. Arab restaurants include *Ali Baba*, Junín 380, intimate, inexpensive. Recommended, closed lunchtime. *El Emir*, Catamarca 605. *Sociedad Sirio-Libanesa*, Maipú
575. *El Fogón*, Marcos Paz 630, good, show. *El Alto de la Lechuza*, 24 de Septiembre y
Avellaneda. *La Leñita*, 25 de Mayo 377, expensive, smart, good meat. *La Parrilla de La
Plaza*, San Martín 391, excellent, reasonable prices. *Las Brasas*, Maipú 740, good but
not cheap. *Cipriani*, San Juan y Junín, pizzas. *Il Postino*, 25 de Mayo y Córdoba, pizza
bar, popular. *Augustus*, 24 Septiembre y Buenos Aires, good café. *El Griego*, Muñecos
y Córdoba, café/bookshop.*Sir Harris*, Laprida y Mendoza, bistro. *Pastísima Rotisería*,
Mendoza y Laprida and at San Martín 964, good cheap snacks, take out service.
Panadería Villecco, Corrientes 751, good bread, also 'integral'. In this part of Argentina 'black beer' (eg Salta Negra) is available.

Casino Sarmiento y Maipú, open Fri, Sat, Sun, 2100-0230.

Local holidays 24 Sep, *Battle of Tucumán*; 29 Sep, *San Miguel*; 10 Nov, *Día de la Tradición*.

Shopping *Artesanía El Cardón*, Alvarez 427, excellent handicrafts. *Mercado Artesanal*, at the
All shops close tourist office in Plaza Independencia, small, but nice selection of lace and leather
1200-1630 work. *Regionales del Jardín* , Congreso 18, good selection of local jams, *alfajores* etc.
Other shops selling local produce nearby. *Lozano* supermarket, San Martín just east of
Plaza Independencia. Market *Mercado del Norte*, on block bounded by Córdoba,
Mendoza, Junín and Maipú.

Transport **Local Bus** Operate on *cospeles*, US$0.60, which you buy in advance in kiosks. **Car
hire** *Avis*, Congreso 76, T4875674, F431184 and airport. *Liprandi*, 24 de Septiembre
524, T4311210. *Movil Renta*, San Lorenzo 370, T4310550, F08007773682 (toll free),
rentacar@movilrenta.com, and at airport. *Localiza*, San Juan 959, T4311352. **Car**

Tucumán centre

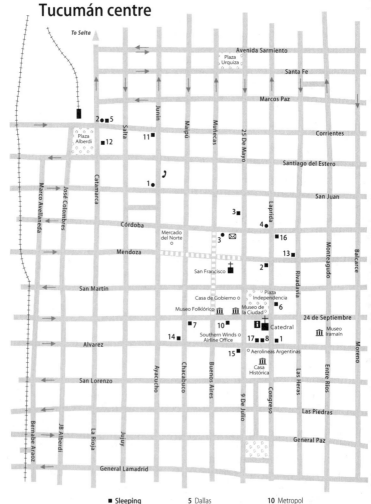

N
Not to scale

■ **Sleeping**	5 Dallas	10 Metropol
1 Astoria	6 Del Sol	11 Miami
2 Bristol	7 Florida	12 Nuevo Tucumán.
3 Carlos V	8 Francia	13 Palace
4 Colonial	9 Gran	14 Petit

Situated 160 km north of Rosario de la Frontera and 196 km east of Salta, this park covers 44,162ha of the eastern foothills of the Andes rising to 1,600 m. The park is bounded by two ranges of hills: the Cresta del Gallo to the northwest and the Serrania del Piquete to the southeast: between these ranges clear streams with fishing feed the Río Popayán. There are several small lakes.

Parque Nacional El Rey
Best time to visit: May-Oct

Vegetation varies with altitude, humidity and rainfall. The lower parts of the park are covered with Chaco-type scrub, including algarrobos and talas; higher up is cloudforest. Wildlife includes the red-legged seriema, the chaco chachalca, the coati as well as foxes, tapirs, brockets and peccaries. The rivers are inhabited by river-otters and *mayuato* (crab-eating racoons) and there are 152 species of birds. Mosquitoes, ticks and chiggers thrive; take lotion. Horse-riding is available.

Climate Mean temperatures range from 12°C in winter to 27°C in summer. Mean annual rainfall is 600-700 mm in the valleys, but up to 1,800 mm in the upper areas of the park. Most rainfall is in summer, when the park can be inaccessible.

Access Via a poor road which branches off Route 5, 44 km east of Lumbreras and runs north 46 km, fording the river 9 times; passable for ordinary cars except in the wet season.

Sleeping None while *Hostería El Rey*, 12 km north of the entrance, is closed (it is due to be transferred to private hands). Camping is free, there are several sites, but few facilities.

Information Park office, España 366, 3rd floor, Salta (helpful). There are *guardaparques* at the park entrance.

Transport No public transport; ask the park office in Salta about alternatives, or take a tour from an agency, US$50 per person for at least 6.

Parque Nacional El Rey

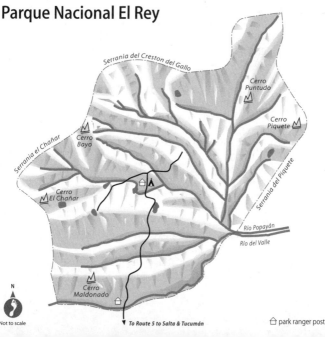

Serrania del Creston del Gallo

Cerro Puntudo

Cerro Piquete

Serrania el Chañar

Cerro Bayo

Cerro El Chañar

Serrania del Piquete

Río Popayán

Río del Valle

N

Cerro Maldonado

Not to scale

To Route 5 to Salta & Tucumán

⌂ park ranger post

The Northwest

The route via Cafayate

Route 38 runs southwest from Tucumán towards Catamarca; at Km 42 Route 307 branches off northwest towards Cafayate, climbing through sugar and citrus fruit plantations before passing through the Quebrada del Río los Sosa. At Km 69 there is a statue to El Indio, with picnic area.

Tafi del Valle
Phone code: 03867
Colour map 1, grid B3
Population: 2,600
Altitude: 2,100 m

Tafi del Valle (Km 107) lies in the valley of the Río Tafí, a sacred valley of the precolumbian Indian peoples. The southern part of the valley is filled by an artificial lake, Embalse La Angostura. The valley has its own microclimate, much cooler in the lowlands in summer: often, with the cloud formed by warm air moving up from the lowlands hanging low and wisps of white cloud rising like smoke over the lake, you can appreciate the sacred importance of the valley. There is a local cheese festival in February. Most services are along Avenida Perón, the main street.

South of the lake is **El Mollar**. Nearby is the **Parque de los Menhires**, a park with 129 granite standing stones marked with engraved designs of unknown significance. Originally found in different locations in the valley, they were moved to their present site in 1977.

Capilla Jesuíta y Museo La Banda, in the 16th-century chapel of San Lorenzo, contains archaeological pieces from pre-Hispanic Tafi cultures as well as European furniture and other items. ■ *Mon-Sat 1000-1600, Sun 0900-1200.*

Sleeping **AL** *Lunahuana*, Gobernador Critto 540, T/F421330. Half pension, expensive restaurant, apartments, gymnasium, solarium. **A** *Mirador del Tafí*, 2 km outside town, T/F421219. With breakfast, good beds, spacious, heating, restaurant, excellent views. **B** *Hostería Tafi del Valle*, T421027, ACA, San Martín y Campero, opposite terminal. With breakfast, in attractive grounds with fine views. **AB** *Hotel Tafí*, Belgrano s/n, T421007, F421452, hoteltafi@impsat1.com.ar With breakfast, bar, heating. **AB** *La Rosada*, Belgrano 322, T421323. Good beds, lovely building, cycle hire, trekking expeditions. **AB** *Huayra Puca*, Los Menhires 71, T421111, huayrapuca@infovia.com.ar With breakfast, **B** off-season, large rooms, good beds. **AB** *Sumaj*, T0381-155958705, with breakfast. **C** per person *Hostería Los Cuartos*, T/F421444, with breakfast, **B** per person half-pension, restaurant, heating, good views, good beds. **C** *Colonial*, T421067. Closed out of season, no singles. **D** per person *Hostal ATEP*, Los Menhires y Campero, near terminal. Run down, also half board. **D** per person *Hospedaje El Valle*, Perón 56, T421641. With bath, **E** per person without bath, without breakfast, clean, good beds, good value. **E** per person *Hosp Celia* Belgrano, T421170. Near church (ask for Profesora Celia), dormitory accommodation. Recommended. Cheaper accommodation can also be found along Miguel Critto.

Outside town There are bungalows (**B**) at El Pinar del Ciervo, 5 km north on Route 307. At La Banda, 1 km southwest is **AL** *La Hacienda Le Pepe*, with breakfast, English and French spoken, horses for rent. *Hostería Castillo de Piedra*, T421199. There is plenty of accommodation in El Mollar, including *Cabañas El Mollar*, T/F4303086. Sleep 4 to 7, fully-equipped, also offer horseriding, excursions. **Camping** *Autocamping Los Sauzales*, T421084, US$4, run down. Also several sites in El Mollar.

Estancia *Estancia Los Cuartos*, T03867-421127 or Tucumán (0381)-4226793, mercedes_chenaut@hotmail.com. Offers lunches (US$35), teas and activities including horseriding.

The Sacred Valley

As in other parts of the ancient world, the dependence of the early inhabitants on crops and wildlife and the ever-present risk of drought, floods or some other type of natural disaster meant that appeasing the gods assumed great importance. They built sacred sites and erected statues as images of the gods.

Situated in a hollow covering 100 sq km at an altitude of 2,000 m and surrounded by hills, Tafí del Valle was densely populated: the sides of the valley were covered in agricultural terraces and traces of the large numbers of underground dwellings can still be seen. Curiously they have a floral pattern, each of the circular rooms leading off a circular central patio. The many ritual circles can be identified by the circles of stones with a larger rock in the centre. What stands out above all are the menhires. These were gods which protected the fields and the dwellings. Due to the number of these Tafí is thought to have been the most sacred place of the indigenous population of northwestern Argentina.

A complete circuit of the valley can be made by road, a distance of 38 km, beginning in Tafí and passing through La Banda, San Isidro, El Rincón, El Mollar and La Angostura. At the last of these, on a hill, there are 129 menhires, brought together from all over the valley in the early years of this century. Smooth, hand-worked or sculptured, each dolmen is a small work of art, each worthy of being studied in the context of the large population that which once lived in Tafí.

Eating Most places are along Av Perón including, *El Rancho de Félix*. Recommended. *Parador Tafinista*, *parillada*. *El Buon Mangiare*, pastas. *El Portal de Tafí*, good, has video room (movies in summer only).

Shopping For local cheeses try the shops runs by *Estancia Las Carreras* and *Estancia Los Cuarton*, both on Miguel Critto.

Tour operators Tours to El Mollar and Tafí are available from travel agencies in Tucumán, US$15 each for 4 people minimum. Daniel Carrazano, T421241 offers guided tours, horseriding and fishing. Off season contact the tourist office to arrange excursions by taxi, US$15 per person. **Tourist office** *Casa del Turista*, in centre, poor.

Transport Bus To **Tucumán**, Aconquija, sit on right side, 9 a day in summer, fewer off season, 3½ hrs, US$9. To **Cafayate** 4 a day, 4 hrs, US$10. To **El Mollar** several daily, US$1. Buses to Tucumán stop at El Mollar on request.

Directory Banks *Banco de Tucumán*, Miguel Critto 311, ATM, Visa, Mastercard. *Banco Popular*, ATM.

Northwest of Tafi del Valle

From Tafí Route 307 continues northwest, climbing out of the valley and offering very fine views. At Km 130 it crosses the Abra del Infiernillo (3,042 m) and then drops through the attractive arid and rocky landscape of the valley of the Río del Amaichá to join Route 40 which follows the Río Santa María north to Cafayate.

Amaicha del Valle

Phone code: 03892
Population: 400
Altitude: 1,997 m
163 km NW of Tafi

Amaicha del Valle claims to have 300 sunny days a year. It has an important Pachamama festival at end of Carnival. Just outside the town there is a small museum with displays on local geology and anthropology. ■ *Daily 0900-1800.* The road forks at Amaichá: Route 357 continues north through a rocky landscape covered with scrub for 14 km to the junction with Route 40 while Route 337 branches off south to join Route 40 at Santa María.

The Northwest

The fall and rise of Quilmes

Of all the indigenous peoples of northwestern Argentina, perhaps the most tragic fate was that which awaited the inhabitants of Quilmes. At the heart of the resistance to Spanish rule, in the 17th century Quilmes had a population of some 3,000, though it is estimated that 7,000 people in the surrounding area were also under its rule. Defeated by being cut off from water and food supplies, the 270 surviving families were marched out of the

northwest and were settled in a reservation 27 km south of Buenos Aires. Forced to work in a quarry, most lost their lives in a smallpox epidemic in 1718. By 1730 only 141 remained and when the reservation was closed in 1812 there were no survivors.

Today the Quilmes are chiefly remembered by the name of the largest brewery in Argentina, which gets its name from the town built on the site of the reservation.

Sleeping *Hostal Colonial*, T421046. *Casa del Piedra*, new, semi-luxurious. **Camping** *La Coplerita*, with hot water.

Transport Bus To Tucumán, US$7, sit on the right.

Santa María
Colour map 1, grid B2
Population: 7,500
Altitude: 1,800 m
22 km S of Amaicha

Santa María lies on the Río Santa Maria on the site of a Franciscan mission. The **Museo Arqueológico Eric Boman**, on the plaza contains an important collection of pre-Hispanic artefacts. ■ *Mon-Sat 0830-1300, 1700-2100*. From Santa María Route 40 leads north along the valley to Cafayate (55 km) and south to Belén (176 km, see page 241). Along this road are several archaeological sites which can be visited including Ampajango, 27 km south, Fuerte Quemado 15 km north and Quilmes (see below).

Sleeping AB *Plaza*, San Martín 285, T420309. On plaza, small rooms. **B** *Provincial de Turismo*, San Martín 450, T420240. Recommended, restaurant, heating, pool. **B** *Amancay*, Belgrano 471, T421013. Heating. **B** *Caasama*, 9 de Julio s/n, T421627, bar, pool, tennis court. **C** *Res Inti-Huaico*, Belgrano 146, T432047. With bath, clean, friendly, lovely gardens. Recommended. **C** *Res San Silvestre*, Mitre 592, T421544. Both with and without bath. **D** *Res Reinoso*, 1 de Mayo 649, T420306. Without bath. **F** per person. *Albergue Municipal*, Sarmiento s/n, T421083. Without sleeping bag, **G** per person with own sleeping bag. **Campsite** Municipal campsite at end of Sarmiento.

Transport Bus To Tucumán, Aconquija, 4 hrs, Mon-Sat 5 a day, Sun 4 a day, US$8.50. To **Cafayate**, 1 hr, *El Indio* daily 0700, 1615, US$10. *Empresa Bosio* to **Catamarca**, Sat. Via Tucumán Sun 1230, 9 hrs. *Cayetano* to **Belén** 4 hrs, Mon, Wed, Fri 0500.

Directory Tourist office in the municipalidad, T 421083, F420898.

Quilmes
Colour map 1, grid B2
32 km N of Santa María,
5 km along a dirt road
off Route 40

Quilmes is one of the most important archaeological sites in Argentina. Situated on the slopes of the Sierra de Quilmes at an altitude of 1,850 m, were a central fortification flanked to north and south by two other fortresses which controlled the valley. Its strategic situation and the width of its walls, up to 3 m, made it impregnable. Southeast of the main ruins are others which stretch as far as a dam several kilometres distant. There are splendid views and interesting cacti. ■ *Guide 0700-1730, entry US$2. Best seen 1600-1700*. Near the entrance there is an archaeological museum. ■ *Daily 0800-1800*.

Sleeping and eating A *Parador Ruinas de Quilmes*, T0892-21075, at the site, comfortable, underfloor heating in winter, a/c in summer, owners are tapestry and ceramics experts; shop selling good indigenous crafts, particularly textiles; good restaurant, bar and camping facilities.

Transport For a day's visit take 0630 Aconquija bus from Cafayate to Santa María, alight at site, or take 0700 bus from Santa María; in each case take 1100 bus back to Cafayate. Taxi from Cafayate US$60 return.

Cafayate

Cafayate, 231 km northwest of Tucumán, lies 78 km down the valley from Santa María. Founded in 1863 on the site of Jesuit and Franciscan missions, it is a popular summer holiday centre for Argentines. Surrounded by vineyards, it is an important centre of wine production and home of several renowned bodegas: the white wines are reputed to be the best in Argentina. North of the town is Ceramica Cristófani, where you can watch the whole process of making pots.

Phone code: 03868
Colour map 1, grid B2
Population: 8,432
Altitude; 1,660 m

There are 5 *bodegas*, all of which can be visited. In town are **Nanni**, on Chavarría 1 block east of the plaza, and **Domingo Hermanos**, 3 blocks south of the plaza on 25 de Mayo. North of town are **Vasija Secreta**, (on outskirts, next to ACA *hostería*), T421503, perhaps the most interesting because it is the oldest in the valley, English spoken, and **La Rosa**, reached by turning right 500 m past the ACA *hostería*. ■ *Visits Mon-Fri, 0800-1230, 1500-1830, weekend mornings only, no need to book, 30 min tours and tasting*. Nearby is an old water mill which is still in use. **Etchart**, 2 km south on Route 40, T421310 F421529. ■ *Offers tours Mon-Sat 0900-1700, Sun 1000-1300*.

Bodegas

Museo de la Vid y El Vino on Güemes Sur, two blocks south of the plaza, in an old *bodega*. Includes a collection of old wine-making equipment and a display on the history of wine. Recommended. ■ *Mon-Fri 1000-1300, 1700-2000*. **Museo Arqueológico Rodolfo I Bravo**, Calchaquí y Colón. The life work of the late Sr Bravo, a collection of pre-Inca funerary and religious artefacts, some dating back to the 4th century, as well as Inca ceramics, all excavated withing 30 km of Calafate. ■ *Open on request (T421054), US$1*.

Museums

Cerro San Isidro, 5 km west, has cave paintings and fine views across the Aconquija chain in the south and Nevado de Cachi in the north.

Excursions

Accommodation in single rooms, may be hard to find in holiday periods (Jan, Easter and late-Jul). Prices are much lower off season. **AB** *Asturias*, Güemes Sur 158, T421328, asturias@infonoa.com.ar Best in town, with breakfast, pool. Recommended. **B** *Briones*, Toscano 80, main plaza, T421270. With breakfast, German, English, French spoken, elegant colonial style, open high season only. **AB** *Hostería Cafayate* (ACA), T421296. With breakfast, confitería, colonial-style patio with gardens, poor beds, run down. **B** *ASEMBAL*, Güemes Norte y Almagro, T421065. Nice rooms, good restaurant. **AB** *Gran Real*, Güemes Sur 128, T421016. With breakfast, pool, good beds, also apartments. **B** *Tinkunaku*, Diego de Almagro 12, 1 block from plaza, T421148. Recommended. **D** per person *Hostería Docente*, Güemes Norte 160, T421810. Dormitories, with bath, without breakfast, kitchen facilities, clean. **E** per person *El Cardón*, Almagro 134, T421233. Poor beds, charming patio, pool. **E** per person *Hostal del Valle*, San Martín 243, T421039. Breakfast extra, nice patio, kitchen facilities. **D** per person *El Hospedaje*, de Niño y Salta, T421416. Without bath or breakfast. **C** *Confort*, Güemes Norte 232, T421091. Breakfast extra, fan, good value, very helpful, also has *cabañas* **AB**, sleep 6, with kitchen, pool, heating. **C** *La Posta del Rey*, Güemes Sur 415, T421120. **C** *Pensión Arroyo* (no sign), Niño 160. Recommended. **D** *Familia Herrero*, Vicario

Sleeping

Toscano 237, T421269. **E** per person *Hostal Kutiy-Ashpa*, Córdoba 135 T421566, pabloyfer@connmed.com.ar Dormitories, with kitchen. **E** per person *Albergue Juvenil*, Güemes Norte 441, T421440. Small, hot water, stores luggage, tours arranged, English and Italian spoken. **E** per person *Mirta Alcira Daurich*, Rosario 153, T421098. Dormitory style, basic, kitchen. Accommodation in private houses is available.

Campsite Municipal site on southern outskirts, T421051, hot water, pool, well maintained, bungalows for rent, **D** for 4 people. *Camping Luz y Fuerza*, also on southern outskirts, quiet, better value (US$2 per person). *El Divisadero*, 6 km north.

Estancia AB *Finca La Indústria*, T421480. Accommodation, meals, horseriding, adventure tourism.

Eating *Cafayate Confitería La Barra. El Gordo. La Carreta de Don Olegario*, Güemes Norte y Quintana. Recommended. *El Criollo*, Güemes Norte 254. Recommended. *El Quincho de Cabra*, Mitre 151, cane roof, informal, good value. *Cafetería Santa Barbara*, Güemes Norte 151, billiards, ice-cream. *Helados Miranda*, Güemes Norte 170, wine-flavoured ice-cream. *El Rincón del Amigo*, San Martín 23. *La López Pereyra*, Güemes 375, good food, friendly. Several *comedores* along Güemes Norte 200 block.

Festivals *Serenata Cafayateña*, just after Carnival, the most important music festival in the area.

Shopping Handicrafts are made in the town: tapestries are interesting but very expensive, visit the Calchaquí tapestry exhibition of Miguel Nanni on the main plaza. For silver work try Jorge Barraco, Colón 157, T421244. Oil paintings, woodcarving, metalwork and ceramics by Calixto Mamani can be seen in his gallery, Rivadavia 452, or contact him at home (Rivadavia 254). Ceramics are also made by Manuel Cruz, Güemes Sur 288 (the building itself is worth seeing). Handicrafts in wood and silver by Oscar Hipaucha near the Bodega Encantada.

The Northwest

Cafayate

To Bodegavajilla Secreto
Ceramica Cristófani

Río Chuschas

Buenos Aires · Bartolomé Mitre · Avenida Güemes Norte · Salta

Lamadrid · Sevilla
La Banda · Brachieri
Alvarado · Córdoba
Lavandería Arco Iris · Banco de la Nación Argentina
Rivadavia · Aconquija Bus Terminal
Banco de Jujuy
Market
San Martín · Q de Niño
Municipalidad
Mercado o Artesanal
El Indio Bus Terminal
Toscano · Belgrano
Nuestra Señora del Rosario
Museo Arqueológico · Bodega o Nanni
Colón · Hurtado
Calchaquí
Museo de la Vid y el Vino
Chacabuco · Peñalva
25 de Mayo
Bodega Domingo Hermanos
Av Güemes Norte
Municipal Campsite
Río Loro Huasi

To Bodega Etchart

N
Not to scale

■ **Sleeping**
1 Asembal
2 Asturias
3 Brionés
4 Colonial
5 Confort
6 El Hospedaje
7 Gran Real
8 Hostal del Valle
9 Hosteria Cafayate
10 Hostería Docente
11 Tinkunaku

● **Eating**
1 El Quincho de Cabra
2 El Rincón del Amigo
3 La Carreta de Don Olegario

Pachamama

Pachamama, the goddess of mother earth, is a deity venerated for the fertility of the earth, animals and crops. Pachamama is important throughout the Andes, but there are great regional variations in beliefs and practices. While the term Pachamama is Quechua, it is widely used by Spanish speakers. Ironically Quechua speakers in rural Bolivia refer to her by the Spanish term Virgen. Although after the conquest llamas replaced humans as sacrificial victims, today Pachamama usually has to make do with offerings of cigarettes, alcohol and coca leaves. As she is also the deity of travellers, it is particularly important to make offerings to her before setting out on a journey. It is also customary, on reaching a mountain pass, to add a rock to the

apacheta (pile of stones) built up over the centuries.

Of the few surviving pachamama festivals in the northwestern Argentina that in Amaichá is reckoned to be the most important. Celebrated over several days, the final day is particularly colourful. A woman chosen from the most elderly of the village takes on the role of Pachamama: dressed up, she is mounted on a horse or on a cart drawn by oxen. She is accompanied by other deities, El Yastay, the god of animals and hunting, La Nusta, a young maiden celebrating fertility, and El Pujillay, the fawn-like spirit of carnival. At the height of the festivities Pachamama offers everyone wine from the new harvest and is in turn toasted by the people.

Pancho Silva has a workshop on 25 de Mayo selling and their own and locals' handicrafts. Local pottery is sold in the *Mercado Municipal de Artesanía* on the plaza. Souvenir prices are generally high.

Local Bicycle Cycle hire is very popular. One hire place on the plaza, another just off the plaza on Güemes Norte, US$2 per hr, US$15 per day. **Horse** Can be hired from La Florida, Bodega Etchart Privado, 2 km south of Cafayate, or from Tito Stinga (ask around). **Transport**

Long distance Bus To **Tucumán**, Aconquija, Mon-Sat 0215, 0600, plus 1800 in high season, Sun 0600, 1800, 5 hrs, US$20, alternatively take *El Indio* service to Santa María and change. To **Salta** via the Quebrada de Cafayate, *El Indio*, 4 a day Mon-Fri, 3 daily Sat/Sun, US$12 (worth travelling in daylight). To **Angastaco**, *El Indio*, 1100 Mon-Sat. 1515 Sun, US$4, 2½ hrs, sit on the right, leaves Angastaco for the return journey at 0630 Mon-Sat, 10.30 Sun. To **Santa María**, (for Quilmes) *El Indio*, daily 1100, 2230, 1 hr.

Cafayate can also be visited by organized excursion from Salta, US$40, including lunch & visit to a bodega

Banks *Banco de la Nación*, Alvarado y Córdoba, ATM. TC's and credit cards not accepted. *Banco de Jujuy*, Rivadavia y Mitre. **Laundry** *Lavandería Arco Iris*, Mitre y Córdoba, open all year, good service. **Tourist office** Kiosk on the main plaza, high season daily 0900-2100, off season Mon-Fri 0900-2100, Sat/Sun 1000-1300, 1800-2100 Sat/Sun. **Directory**

North of Cafayate the Río Santa María joins the Río Calchaquí to form the Río de las Conchas which flows north into the Embalse Cabra Corral. Route 40 climbs the Calchaquí valley northwest from Cafayate to San Antonio de los Cobres. For a description of this route see page 258, Valles Calchaquies. Route 68 branches off north of Cafayate and follows the Río de las Cochas northeast to Salta, passing through the spectacular Quebrada de Cafayate. **North of Cafayate**

The gorge of the Río de las Conchas, known as the Quebrada de Cafayate, starts about 20 km north of Cafayate and extends for about 65 km. For most of its length it is a desert landscape, with rocks of contrasting colours. The **Quebrada de Cafayate**

The sun is very hot, take lots of water

The Northwest

●●●

☞ *The Calchaquí Wars*

The Calchaquí valleys were the scene of the strongest resistance to Spanish rule in the Argentine northwest. In 1630, following the failure of Jesuit missionaries to christianize the local indigenous peoples, the Spanish Governor of Tucumán tried to bring them under control of Spanish landowners. The uprising which ensued quickly spread beyond the valley and was only ended with the arrival of reinforcements from Chile. Chamelin, the Indian leader of the uprising, was hanged and quartered, his head being exhibited in La Rioja and his right arm in Londres.

A second uprising in 1657 was sparked by the arrival of a Spanish adventurer, Pedro de Bohórquez, who claimed to be a descendent of the last Inca. The response of the Governor of Tucumán was to clear the valleys of their inhabitants: 5,000 people were taken prisoner and 11,000 more were dispersed throughout the northwest as gifts to Spanish settlers.

●●●

winding road offers constantly changing views and many wild birds, including *ñandúes* (rheas) can be seen. The gorge is particularly famous for the unusual rock formations found in the southern section, all signposted. These include *Los Castillos* (The Castles) Km 20, *El Obelisco* (The Obelisk), Km 23, *El Fraile* (The Friar) Km 29, *El Sapo* (The Toad) Km 35, *El Anfiteatro* (The Amphitheatre) Km 48, and *La Garganta del Diablo* (The Devil's Throat) Km 49.

One way of seeing the Quebrada is by taking the El Indio bus towards Salta and then walk back (catching a returning bus from Salta) from Los Loros, Km 32, or the Garganta del Diablo; alternatively hire a bike in Cafayate and take it on the 0545 El Indio bus and then cycle back.

Embalse Cabra Corral North of the Quebrada the road runs along the west side of the Embalse Cabra Corral through Col Moldes and El Carril to Salta. Cabra Corral, 81 km south of Salta, is one of the largest artificial lakes in Argentina; water skiing, fishing, camping site, restaurant and sailing club; the **B** *Hostería Cabra Corral*, T/F4905022, is 4 km from the lake, half board, swimming pool, 'delightful'. Recommended.

The Valles Calchaquies

The Río Calchaquí rises at above 5,000 metres on the slopes of the Nevado de Acay and flows south between the Sierra de Pastos Grandes to the west and Cumbres del Obsipo to the east. In its 210 kilometres course before its confluence with the Río Santa María just north of Cafayate, the river drops some 3,400 metres and gathers the waters of 34 streams and rivers. Originally it continued south along the Río Santa María and into the Quebrada de Belén.

The lower part of the main valley, that of the Río Calchaquí itself, is dotted with small settlements linked by Route 40 which follows the course of the river. Attractions of this section include the Quebrada de las Flechas, a gorge now bypassed by the road, and the village of Cachi, the most popular place in the valley for an overnight stop. Vegetation varies with altitude but the area around these villages are cultivated with orchards and vines. Away to the west the lower ranges of the Andes can be viewed. The upper valley, north of Cachi, is more sparsely populated and the only real centre is the village of La Poma.

History The valleys of the Río Calchaquí and its tributaries were densely populated in prehispanic times. After the defeat of the indigenous population in the Calchaquí Wars, the Spanish established missions and *haciendas* in the valley. Some of these *haciendas* surivived until the 20th century, before being seized by the Perón government in the 1940s. During the colonial period the valley prospered, providing pasturage for mules-trains and herds of cattle *en route* over the mountain passes into Chile and Alto Perú (Bolivia). After independence lower parts of the valley became the chief wheat growing and wine producing area for the provincial capital but the local economy declined in the late 19th century when the building of railway lines linking Salta with the south brought cheap wheat from the pampas and when local wines were hit by the expansion of wine production in Mendoza.

From Cafayate Route 40 climbs up the valley to the Abra del Acay and then continues to San Antonio de los Cobres. The road is mainly gravel and can be very difficult after rain, but the views of the Andean-foothills with their strange rock formations & unexpected colours, are fascinating. Most of the villages along the road grew up around colonial *haciendas*. Fuel is available in Cachi, Molinos and Angastaco.

Route 40

San Carlos was the most important village in the valley until the growth of Cafayate. The first settlement on the site in 1551 was destroyed by Indians and three further attempts met a similar fate. The main buildings are on the plaza, including the church, the largest in the valley, which was built between 1801 and 1860. Its zinc roof replaced the original made of cactus which was destroyed by an earthquake in 1930. Nearby there is a small archaeological museum which includes a mummified infant. ■ *Daily 1000-1400*. Also on the plaza are artisans' shops and workshops and a craft market; the crafts are cheaper than in Cafayate, but the range is limited.

San Carlos
Colour map 1, grid B2
Population: 1,500
Altitude: 1,710 m
Km 24

Sleeping **C** *Hostería de San Carlos*, on plaza, T4218937, with bath, without breakfast. **E** per person *El Bagualero*. *Hospedaje* on the plaza, another nearby. Municipal campsite.

Transport **Bus** 5 services a day to **Cafayate**, *El Indio*, 30 mins, US$1.

This gorge, just south of Angastaco, is bypassed by a new section of Route 40. Formed by the Río Calchaquí and remarkable for its formations and colours, the quebrada is named after the arrow-shaped rocks found particularly about 10 km south of Angastaco.

Quebrada de las Flechas

Angastaco is a modern village, with a small archaeological museum in the civic building. The church is modern but a much older one, the **Iglesia del Carmen de Angastaco** (1800) lies about 8 km further north on the Finca El Carmen. There is a small archaeological museum in the Centro Civico which contains artefacts from an Indian cemetary 3 km away. This area is famous for *vino patero*, a sweet wine, red or white, which is supposed to be made by treading the grapes in the traditional manner: sample it in a house close to the bridge in Angastaco. The Fiesta Patronal Virgen del Valle is held on the second weekend of December, with processions, folk music, dancing, many gauchos and rodeos.

Angastago
Colour map 1, grid B2
Population: 600
Altitude: 1,900 m
2 km off Route 40
at Km 77

Sleeping **B** *Hostería de Angastaco*, T15639016, with breakfast, negotiable in low season, meals on request, pool, knowledgeable. Highly recommended. **E** per person *Hostería El Cardón*, with bath, also rooms without bath, breakfast extra, good, clean, comfortable.

Transport **Bus** To Cachi and Salta (US$5.50), Fri, 1100 only. To **Cafayate** via San Carlos, *El Indio*, 0630 Mon-Sat, Sun 1030). Taxi to Molinos US$40, ask at police station for address of Orlando López; no transport for hitching.

The Northwest

Molinos
Colour map 1, grid B2
Population: 500
Altitude: 2,000 m
2 km off Route 40
at Km 118

Molinos was founded in 1659. The church, with its fine twin-domed bell-towers, built about 1720, contains the mummified body of the last Royalist governor of Salta, Don Nicolás Isasmendi Echalar (to protect it from visitors plucking its hair, this relic can no longer be viewed by the public). The priest is very knowledgeable about local history. A pleasant walk is down from the church, crossing a creek and then climbing a gentle hill, from which there are good views of Molinos and surrounding country. Fiesta del Poncho in February.

Sleeping A *Hostal de Molinos*, T494002/4. With breakfast, good meals. In 18th-century Casa de Isasmendi, which also contains a small archaeological museum. Also offers horseriding. *Sra de Guaymas* (known as 'Sra Silvia') runs a restaurant and rents rooms, **E**, basic, clean. There are other rooms to rent around the main plaza.

Transport Bus To Salta via Cachi, Thu, Fri, Sat, Mon at 0645, also Mon, Thu, Sat at 1315, Marcos Rueda; 2 hrs to Cachi, US$4.50, 7 hrs to Salta. To Angastaco, Thu morning.

Seclantás
Population: 183
Altitude: 2,200 m
Km 135

Seclantás is a small village with a church dating from 1835. Many of the houses are in colonial style with verandas in front. Eight kilometres south along the old road are a disused mill and the archaeological site of Churcal. **Sleeping** at *El Reposo del Guerrero*.

Cachi
Phone code: 03868
Colour map 1, grid B2
Population: 1,400
Altitude: 2,280 m
Km 180

Cachi is a beautiful town at the foot of the Nevado del Cachi (6,380 m). Founded in 1694, it is renowned for its weaving, other crafts and invigorating climate. The roof of the 18th-century church is made from the wood of the *cardón* cactus. The **Museo Arqueológico** presents a small but interesting survey of pre-colonial Calchaquí culture. ■ *Mon-Fri 0800-1900, Sat 1000-1400, Sun 1000-1300 US$1.* There are fine views from the cemetery, 10 mins walk from the village.

Excursions Cachi Adentro, 6 km west, has more fine views. Horses can be hired, US$5 per hr and fishing is also possible. ■ *Getting there: 3 buses a day from Cachi.* The Indian ruins at **Las Pailas**, 18 km northwest, are not in themselves especially impressive but the view is breathtaking, with huge cacti set against snow-topped Andean peaks. ■ *Getting there: By foot (4 hrs one way), or by bus from Cachi. Ask for directions or a guide in Las Pailas village.*

Sleeping AB *ACA Hostería Cachi*, T491105, with breakfast, on hill above the town, good, pleasant, ACA reductions. **B** *El Cortijo*, T491034, clean, friendly, good breakfast. **E** per person *Res Pajarito*, with bath, basic. **E** *Albergue Municipal*, also has good municipal campsite with swimming pool and barbecue pits, on hill at south end of town. **At Cachi Adentro B** *Hostal Samay Huasi*, T421631, a restored *hacienda*, pleasant and helpful owners, heating and hot water at all times. **AL** *El Molino de Cachi Adentro*, T491094 (Salta 4219368, Buenos Aires 48039399), a restored working mill, beautiful views, horse riding. Recommended, minimum stay 3 days, book in advance, Buenos Aires T48039339, F44762065.

Transport Bus To Salta, 1530 daily except Wednesday, also at 0900 Thu, Fri, Sat, Mon, 5 hrs, US$14. **To Molinos** 1200 daily; *El Indio* from Cafayate Thu morning only, returning Thu afternoon.

La Poma
Population: 300
Altitude: 3,015 m
5 km off Route 40
at Km 234

La Poma is the last village in the valley. It is situated near two extinguished volcanoes and has views over the Nevado de Palermo (6,172 m). It was destroyed by an earthquake in 1930: the ruins lie 2 km north of the modern village. **Sleeping** at **B** *Hosteria La Poma*, T491003, with breakfast. Recommended.

North of La Poma Route 40 continues over the Paso Abra del Acay (4,900 m), **La Poma to San**
Km 282, the highest pass in South America negotiable by car. Road conditions **Antonio de los**
vary depending on the weather and whether the bulldozer has passed recently. **Cobres**
A high clearance four wheel drive vehicle is advisable. The critical part is south
of the pass at Mal Paso, Km 257, where summer rains can wash the road away.
There are no buses on this road. North of the pass the road runs across the
puna to San Antonio de los Cobres (see below), Km 324.

At Payogasta (new *Hostería*), 11 km north of Cachi, Route 33 (mainly paved) **Cachi**
turns off Route 40 and runs east along a dead-straight stretch of 10 km known **to Salta**
as **La Recta del Tin-Tin** and over the Piedra del Molino pass (3,347 m), Km
43, before dropping through the Cuesta del Obispo. This part of the road runs
through the **Parque Nacional Los Cardones**, a new national park covering
70,620 ha at altitudes between 2,700 and 5,000 m and intended to protect the
huge candelabra cacti. If you want to spend some time in the park, take the
0700 Marcos Rueda bus from Salta towards Cachi, get off at La Recta del
Tin-Tin and catch returning bus around 1600.

From the end of the Cuesta del Obispo the road runs through the **Quebrada
de Escoipe**, a narrow gorge 34 km long, which can be flooded in wet weather.
The road is paved from Chicoana, Km 115, 5 km east of the gorge (*hostería*). It
joins Route 68 at El Carril, 119 km from Cachi and 37 km south of Salta.

Salta

Situated on the Río Arias in the wide Lerma valley, Salta lies in a mountainous   *Phone code: 0387*
and strikingly beautiful district. Founded in 1582 the city still possesses a number   *Colour map 1, grid B3*
of fine colonial buildings. Capital of its province, it is a great handicraft centre   *Population: 375,000*
and the major starting place for tours of the northwest.   *Altitude: 1,280 m*
  1,600 km N of
  Buenos Aires

An interesting pedestrian tour of the centre is marked by ceramic pavement   **Sights**
plaques. The central **Plaza 9 de Julio** is one of the most outstanding squares in
the country and the only one with verandas all round. The **cathedral**, open
mornings and evenings, on the north side was built 1858-1878. It contains the
images of the Cristo del Milagro and of the Virgin Mary and has a rich interior
mainly in red and gold, as well as a huge late baroque altar. Opposite the cathedral is the **Cabildo**, built in 1783 (the upper floor was added in 1807; the arches
are slightly out of line).

One block west of the Cabildo are three colonial mansions: the **Casa
Leguizamón**, Caseros y Florida, the **Casa Arias Rengel**, next door (now
housing the Museo de Bellas Artes)
and the **Casa Hernández**, Florida y
Alvarado. A fourth, the **Casa
Uriburu** (see below) lies one block
east of the Plaza at Caseros 421. Just
beyond is the **San Francisco** church,
at Caseros y Córdoba (1796), one of
the city's landmarks with its magnificent façade and red, yellow and grey
coloured tower (1882) rising above
the city centre skyline. ■ *Getting
there: 0700-1200, 1730-2100, in theory.* Two blocks further east is the

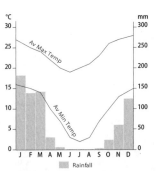

Climate: Salta

The Northwest

Convent of **San Bernardo**, Caseros y Santa Fe, built in colonial style in 1846; it has a famous wooden portal of 1762. Nuns still live here so the inside of the convent is not open to visitors.

East of the city centre is the **Cerro San Bernardo** (1,458 m), at the foot of which is an impressive statue by Víctor Cariño, 1931, to General Güemes, whose *gaucho* troops repelled seven powerful Spanish invasions from Bolivia between 1814 and 1821. The top of the hill can be climbed by a steep path (1,136 steps) with Stations of the Cross from behind the nearby Museo Antropológico or by cable car (*teleférico*). ■ *Daily except Thu, 1400-2000, US$6 return, children US$3, from Parque San Martín.* At the top there is an old wooden cross, together with restaurant and artificial waterfalls. At the bottom near the *teleférico* station is a lake where rowing boats can be hired. ■ *US$3 for 20 mins.*

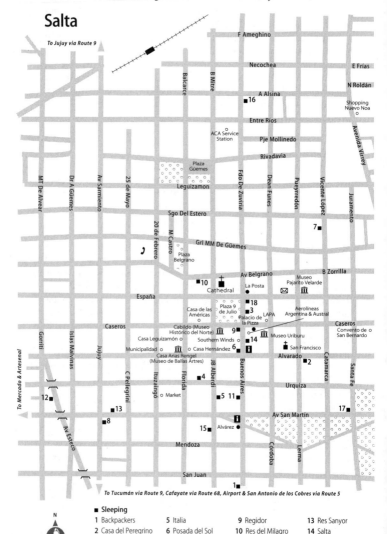

Salta

Sleeping

1 Backpackers	5 Italia	9 Regidor	13 Res Sanyor
2 Casa del Peregrino	6 Posada del Sol	10 Res del Milagro	14 Salta
3 Colonial	7 Posada Samir	11 Res Elena	15 Sol de la Vina
4 Crystal	8 Premier	12 Res San Jorge	16 Tampu Huasi

Not to scale

Museo Histórico del Norte, in the Cabildo Histórico, Caseros 549. Colonial and 19th-century artefacts including a fine 18th-century pulpit. Guided tour in Spanish. Recommended. ■ *Tue-Sun 0930-1330, Tue-Fri 1530-2030, Sat/Sun 1700-1930, US$1.* **Museo Antropológico**, Paseo Güemes, behind the statue. This contains a large and important collection of ehnographic material from the northwest, and includes many objects from Tastil (see page 271). The recently-opened Sala de Alta Montaña includes a mummy discovered high up in the Andes. ■ *Mon-Fri 0800-1800, Sat/Sun 0900-1300, US$1.* **Museo de Bellas Artes**, Florida 20. Located in a fine 18th-century mansion with 2-m thick walls, this includes displays on colonial, 19th-century and 20th-century art. ■ *Mon-Fri 0900-1300, 1600-2030, Sat 1000-1300, US$1 (closed Jan).* **Museo Histórico Uriburu**, Caseros 421. Situated in the former mansion of the Uriburu family, the most distinguished of *salteño* families, this contains artefacts from the lives of the two former presidents. ■ *Tue-Sat, 0930-1330, 1500-2000, US$1.* **Museo Pajarito Velarde**, Pueyrredón y España, has paintings, furniture and artefacts from the life of Pajarito Velarde, a famous patron of the bohemian artists of the city. ■ *Mon-Fri 1700-2000, Sat 1000-1200.* **Museo de Ciencias Naturales**, in Parque San Martín, displays over 20,000 specimins including more than 150 regional stuffed birds and an interesting collection of armadillos. Recommended. ■ *Tue-Sun 1400-1800, US$0.50.* **Museo de la Ciudad 'Casa de Hernández'**, Florida 91, is located in a 19th-century mansion. This contains a collection of 18th- and 19th-century furniture as well as plans and photographs which trace the development of the city. ■ *Mon-Fri 0900-1300, 1600-2030, Sat 1000-1300.*

Museums
In summer check opening times at tourist office as many close

Salta is the starting point for several popular longer excursions, including **Cafayate** and the **Valles Calchaquies** (see page 258), allow two to three days by car; **Parque Nacional El Rey** (see page 251) and **San Antonio de los Cobres** (see page 271). Agencies also offer tours to the **Quebrada de Humahuaca** (see page 278) but these are not recommended: it is much better to visit the quebrada from Jujuy.

Excursions

The Northwest

AF Cornejo
A Figueroa
Dr Linares
M Sola
J Uriburu
Rep De Israel
Paseo Güemes
Dr G Pulo
San Lorenzo
A Saravia
Dr I Gómez
Klein
Abrahán Cornejo

Av Uruguay
Del Milagro
Toledo
Lavalle
Las Heras
Avenida Yrigoyen
J Tobias
Dr Mariano Boedo

Cerro 20 de Febrero
ⅲ Museo Antropológico
Monument to General Güemes
Av Ejército del Norte
Fco De Gurruchaga
To Cerro San Bernardo
To Ruta 34, Gral Güemes
Talavera

Parque San Martín
ⅲ Museo de Ciencias Naturales

17 Travellers
18 Victoria Plaza

The miracle of Salta

According to legend the famous images of Christ and the Virgin Mary in Salta Cathedral were found in a box floating in the sea off Callao, Peru, in June 1592 and later given to the city. Their fame comes from their intervention during a series of terrifying earthquakes which hit the city in September 1692. In a dream José Carrión, a priest, received the revelation that only when the images were paraded through the streets would the earthquakes cease. The apparent success of this strategy is celebrated every year between 6 and 14 September, culminating on 15 September when the images repeat their historic journey through the city.

Sleeping Salta is a favourite convention town. Some hotels close for a vacation during the Christmas season until Jan 10, so check. Accommodation is scarce in the last 2 weeks in Jul because of holidays and around 10-16 Sep because of the celebrations of Cristo del Milagro.

AL *Portezuelo*, Del Turista 1, T4310133, F4310133, hprtzelo@salnet.com.ar Breakfast extra, some rooms a/c, also apartments, English, German, French, Italian spoken, pool, helpful, good restaurant. Recommended. **L** *Salta*, Buenos Aires 1, in main plaza, T4310740, hotel@salnet.acom.ar 1st class, pool, good restaurant. **A** *Provincial*, Caseros 786, T/F4322000, www.hotelprovincial.com.ar, central, helpful, good restaurant. Recommended. **A** *Posada del Sol*, Alvarado 646, T4317290, hpdelsol@salnet.com.ar Near main plaza, also suites. **AB** *Victoria Plaza*, Zuviría 16, T4310634. With buffet breakfast, expensive but good restaurant, the foyer overlooking the plaza is one of the centres of *salteño* life. **AB** *Colonial*, Zuviría 6, T4310805, F4314249. With breakfast, a/c. Recommended, but 1st floor rooms good, 2nd floor rooms cheaper but poor. **AB** *Crystal*, Urquiza 616, T4310738, F4222059. Without breakfast, helpful. **B** *Las Lajitas*, Pasaje Calixto Guana 336, T4233796. With breakfast, modern, good value, ACA reduction. Recommended. **AB** *Petit*, H Yrigoyen 225, T4213012. Pleasant, small, with breakfast, rooms around patio with small swimming pool, a/c extra, French spoken. **AB** *Regidor*, Buenos Aires 10, T4311305. With breakfast, a/c, English-speaking owner, good value lunch, comfortable. **AB** *Cristian*, Islas Malvinas 160, T4319600. With breakfast, parking, clean, English spoken. Highly recommended. **AB** *El Portal de Salta*, Alvarado 341, T4313674, F4321125, porsalta@satlink.com, small pool, modern. **AB** *Premier*, San Martín y Jujuy, T4310815, breakfast extra.

B *General Güemes*, España 446, T4314800, F4311050, with breakfast. **C** *Astur*, Rivadavia 752, T4212107. Recommended. **B/C** *España*, España 319, T4320898. Central but quiet, simple. Recommended. **B/C** *Res del Milagro*, Belgrano 657, T4218819, resmilagro@starmedia.com With bath, also **C** without bath, with breakfast, fan, very central. Also has **E** per person *La Casona del Milagro*, Paraguay 2800, T4271251. Large dormitories, pool, horseriding, sports facilities. **B/C** *Florida*, Florida y Urquiza 718, T4212133. Stores luggage. Recommended. **C** *Italia*, Alberdi 231, T4214050, breakfast extra, next to jazz club/casino. Recommended. **C** *Res Elena*, Buenos Aires 256, T4211529. Without breakfast, quiet, 'charming' with attractive patios, safe. **C** *Res Balcarce*, Balcarce 460, T4318135. Friendly, clean. **C** *Res Provincial*, Santiago del Estero 555, T4319344, with bath.

C *Res Crisol*, Ituzaingó 166, T4214462, good meeting place. **D** per person *Sanyor* San Martín 994, T4214440. Laundry facilities. **C** *Res San Jorge*, Esteco 244 y Ruiz de los Llanos 1164 (no sign), T/F4210443, hotelsanjorge@arnet.com.ar With bath, **E** per person without. Parking, safe deposit, laundry and limited kitchen facilities, heating, parking, homely, horse-trekking advice by proprietor, also organizes local excursions by car, good value, highly recommended (take buses 3 and 10 from bus terminal to San Martín y Malvinas). **D** *Casa de familia de María del Toffoli*, Mendoza 915 (about 10 blocks from bus station), T4320813. Nice atmosphere, comfortable, roof terrace, cooking facilities, also rooms at Nos 917 and 919, **D-C**, belonging to Sra Toffoli's sisters (reservations at No 917), all highly recommended. *Sra Dora de Batista*, Mendoza 947, T4310570. Recommended, laundry facilities.

E per person *María Galleguillos*, Mendoza 509, T4318985. With breakfast. Recommended. *Mercedes Anchezar*, 20 de Febrero 197, 5th floor, T4320701, F313595. Without breakfast. **E** *Hosp Doll*, Pasaje Ruiz de los Llanos 1360 (7 blocks from centre), with bath, safe. Recommended. **E** per person *Casa del Peregrino*, Alvarado 351, T4320423. Dormitories, breakfast extra, clean, modern. **E** per person *Travellers*, San Martín 104, T4214772, travellersalta@hotmail.com Dormitories, kitchen and laundry facitilies. **D** *Sol de la Viña*, Alberdi 374, T4219137, hostalsoldelvinia@infovia.com.ar Central, with bath, with breakfast. Other cheap hotels near railway station including **D** *Tampu Huasi*, Zuviria 832, T4212164, tampuhuasi@arnet.com.ar Cooking facilties. **E** *Internacional*, Ameghino 651. Hot water, basic, with good cheap restaurant), but few near bus terminal. **E** per person *Backpackers*, Buenos Aires 930, T/F4235910, hostelsalta@impsat1. com.ar Bus 12 from bus terminal or 30 mins walk. Affiliated to *Hostelling International*. Small dormitories, laundry and kitchen facilities, stores luggage, internet access, budget travel information, bar,English, Greek and Hebrew spoken, frequently recommended, noisy, crowded and popular. **E** per person *No Me Olvides*, Av de los Pioneros, Km 0.800. Shared rooms, cooking facilities. Recommended. **E** per person *Posada Samiri*, Vicente López 3534, T4314579, samirisalta@ hotmail.com Kitchen facilities.

Do not be tempted by touts at the bus terminal offering convenient accommodation

Outside Salta AB *Hostería Punta Callejas*, Campo Quijano, 30 km west at the entrance to the Quebrada del Toro, T4904086. With breakfast, very clean and comfortable, a/c, pool, tennis, horseriding, excursions, meals. **B** *Hostería de Chicoana*, in Chicoana, 47 km south, T/F4907009, martinpek@impsat1.com.ar Pool, gardens, English and German spoken, horses for hire. Recommended.

Estancias AB per person *Finca San Antonio*, El Carril, T/F4908034, rcornejo@salnet.com.ar Accommodation, pool, horseriding, other activities. **B** per person *Eaton Place*, at San Lorenzo, 12 km from Salta, T4921347. Meals, horseriding, country activities. **B** *Finca Los Lapachos*, at Perico, north of Salta on Route 66, a sugar estate, comfortable. **L** per person *Finca El Bordo de las Lanzas*, at El Bordo, 45 km east of Salta, 12 km from General Güemes, T4310525, bordlanz@cpsarg.com Full board, excursions. Recommended. **AB** per person *Finca Arnaga*, T4921478, F921513. Cycling, walking, French and English spoken. Recommended. **AB** per person *Finca Los-Los*, 4 km from Chicoana, 47 km south, T4317258, F4215500. Full board, horseriding, trout fishing. **AB** per person *Finca El Manantial*, 25 km from Salta, T/F4395506, elmanantial@arnet.com.ar Beautiful views, swimming, sports. Recommended. *Finca Santa Anita*, at Coronel Moldes 60 km from Salta, T/F4313858, elewis@salnet.com.ar Accommodation, horseriding, activities. *Hostal de Castellanos*, 15 km from Salta, T4921816. Accommodation, meals, walking, horseriding. **B** per person *Casa de Campo Arnaga*, in San Lorenzo, 15 km from Salta, T4921478, tbuena@impsat1.com.ar With breakfast, also horseriding, cycle-hire, activities. **L** per person *Finca Puerta del Cielo*, near Encon, 35 km from Salta, T156830747, F4317291. Full board accommodation, excursions, horeriding.

In Salta estancias are known as fincas

Camping *Camping Carlos Xamena*, by river, 300 m artificial lake (popular Dec-Feb). Bus 13 to grounds. There is no signposting: leave the city heading south on Calle Jujuy, after 3 km you will see the Coca Cola plant on your left; turn left before the plant and then take the 1st road right. Charges US$3 per tent plus US$2 per person. Free hot showers available if there is gas (not often), safe, bathrooms run-down, disappointing. At ACA's *Motel Huaico*, Bolivia y P Costas, T4310571. *Municipal Campsite* at Campo Quijano, 30 km west of Salta, at the entrance to Quebrada del Toro gorge, hot showers, bungalows, plenty of room for pitching tents. Recommended, bus from Salta bus terminal.

Eating

Cheapest food is from the numerous superpanchito stalls

Cheap restaurants near the bus terminal, which is also the cheapest places for breakfast. Many restaurants are lunch only, especially on San Martín near the Municipal Market. *El Monumento*, Gurruchaga 20 (opposite Güemes monument). Good food, slow service, good atmosphere, reasonably priced. *La Posta*, España 476, food and atmosphere both excellent, reasonable prices. Highly recommended. *El Viejo Jack*, Virrey Toledo 145. Good meat dishes, huge portions. *Palacio de la Pizza*, Caseros 459. Wide range, popular. *Cantina*, Caseros y 20 de Febrero. Pizzas, steaks. *9 de Julio*, Urquiza 1020. Excellent lunch. *El Mesón de Pepe*, Rivadavia 774. Fish specialities, good but pricey. Several good places on Plaza 9 de Julio, including *Confitería Monaco*, *Café Van Gogh*, good breakfasts, *Confitería Regidor* and *Café Venus*. Pleasant outdoor restaurants in Parque San Martín, at foot of Cerro San Bernardo. *Sociedad Española*, Balcarce 653. Excellent cuisine. *de Pablo*, Mitre 399. Excellent set lunch. *JT*, San Martín y Yrigoyen. Good food. *Santana*, Mendoza y Catamarca. Good. *Alvarez*, Buenos Aires y San Martín. Cafetéria style, cheap and good. *La Casona del Molino*, Caseros 2500. Colonial house, good food and drink, good value, entertainment provided by guests. *Pub Yo Juan*, Balcarce 481. Popular, live music at weekends. *Cafemania*, Caseros 860. Good breakfasts. *Café del Paseo* at *Hotel Colonial*, Zuviría 6. Open 24 hrs, superb breakfast, good value (ask for Té Paseo). *Cafe Río*, Mitre 40. Good breakfasts.

Entertainment

Some bars charge around US$7 per person for music, but don't display charges

Music *Peña* (folk music show) and evening meal at *Boliche Balderrama*, San Martín 1126, 2200-0200, US$20. *Gauchos de Güemes*, Uruguay 750, 2130-0200, US$20. *Casa Güemes*, España 730. For something less touristy try *Manolo*, San Martín 1296 or *La Casona del Molino*, Luis Burela y Caseros, T4316079, folk music and *empanadas*, after 2300.

Festivals

15 Sep, Cristo del Milagro (see above); 24 Sep, Battles of Tucumán and Salta. 16-17 Jun, Commemoration of the death of Martín Güemes, with folk music in afternoon and *gaucho* parade in mornings around his statue. Salta celebrates Carnival with processions on the four weekends before Ash Wednesday at 2200 in Av Belgrano (seats optional at US$2-4); also Mardi Gras (Shrove Tuesday) with a procession of decorated floats and dancers with intricate masks of feathers and mirrors. It is the custom to squirt water at passers-by and *bombas de agua* (small balloons to be filled with water) are on sale for dropping from balconies.

Shopping

Mercado Municipal, San Martín y Florida, for meat, fish, vegetables, *empanadas*, *humitas* and other produce and handicrafts, closed 1200-1700 and Sun. Good supermarket, *Disco*, Alberdi y Leguizamon. **Shopping Nuevo Noa**, Virrey Toledo y Cornejo, modern shopping centre. **Mercado Artesanal** on the western outskirts of the city in the Casa El Alto Molino, a late 18th-century mansion. San Martín 2555, T4219195, Mon-Fri 0800-2000, Sat 0900-2000 (sometimes closes in summer) take bus 2, 3, or 7 from Av San Martín in centre and get off as bus crosses the railway line. Excellent range of goods but expensive. Woodcarvings of birds etc from *Tres Cerritos*, Santiago del Estero 202. For objets d'art and costume jewellery made of onyx, visit *Onix Salta*, Chile 1663. *Feria del Libro*, Buenos Aires 83; *Librería Rayuela*, Buenos Aires 96, foreign-language books and magazines; *Plural Libros*, Buenos Aires 220, helpful. Arts and handicrafts are often cheaper in surrounding villages. Camping shops: *HR Maluf*, San Martín y Buenos Aires, and 1 at La Rioja 995. Cheap **hairdressing** by students at the *Academía de Peluquería Miguel Angel*, Alvarado 911.

All agencies charge similar prices for tours (though some charge extra for credit card **Tour operators**
payments). Salta city US$15. Quebrada del Toro US$18. Cachi US$45. Humahuaca US$50
(too long in the bus: go from Jujuy). San Antonio de las Cobres US$75. Cafayate (1 day)
US$40. 2-day tour to Cafayate, Angastaco, Molinos, Cachi, US$80. Out of season, tours
often run only if there is sufficient demand; check carefully that tour will run on the day
you want. *Movitren*, Caseros 447, T4314984, F411264. For Tren a las Nubes and full
programme of tours. *Saltur*, Caseros 485, T4212012, F4321111, saltursalta@arnet .com.ar
Very efficient and recommended for local tours (no English-speaking guides). *Norte
Trekking*, T/F4396957, fede@nortetrekking.com Tours over the Paso de Jama to San
Pedro de Atacama (Chile) and Salar de Uyuni (Bolivia) *Puna Expediciones*, Braquiquitos
399, T4341875, punaexp@ciudad.com.ar (well qualified and experienced guide Luis H
Aguilar can also be contacted through the *Res San Jorge*), organizes treks in remote areas,
US$25 a day including transport to trekking region, food, porters. Highly recommended.
Ricardo Clark Expeditions, Caseros 121, T4215390, specialist tours for bird watchers, Eng-
lish spoken, books on flora and fauna in several languages sold. Highly recommended.
Norte Trekking, Los Juncos 173, T4396957. 4WD vehicle, hiking, horseriding, all with expe-
rienced guide Federico Norte. Recommended. *Hernán Uriburu*, organizes trekking and
horseriding expeditions, Rivadavia 409, T4310605, expensive but highly professional.
Juan Kühl, Córdoba 202, T4216525, F311772, tours by light aeroplane, horseback, cara-
van, boat, German and English spoken, highly recommended, also runs photographic
company. *Martin Oliver*, T4321013, F91052, adventure tourism guide. *Movitrack*, Buenos
Aires 68, T4316749, F4315301, www.movitrack.com.ar Offer range of safaris in 4WD truck,
to San Antonio de los Cobres, Humahuaca, Cafayate and Iruya, one or two days. Also special charter to Chile via the Paso de Sico, 5 days, and rafting on the Río Juramento, US$30
plus US$20 for transport. German, English spoken, book in advance direct from company
or via Kraft Travel Service, Lamarca 343, 1640 Martínez, Buenos Aires, T/F47934062. *Turismo San Lorenzo*, Dávalos 960, T/F4921757, tsan_lorenzo @impsat1.com.ar, for rafting,
horseriding and adventure tourism. *Sucamalú*, Buenos Aires 186, T/F4219015,
info@sucamalu.com German and French spoken.

Local Car hire *Avis*, Alvarado 537, T4317575, F311184, US$100 per day. Recom- **Transport**
mended. *Rent A Car*, Caseros 489 and 221. Local companies reported to be cheaper: *Care hire is very*
ALE, Caseros 753, T4223469. *López Fleming*, Buenos Aires 33, T4211381, new cars, *expensive. It may be*
cheapest, friendly. *Ruiz Moreno*, Caseros 225, in *Hotel Salta*, good cars, helpful. *Renta* *cheaper & more*
Autos, Caseros 400, also good. *Jet*, Alvarado 537, T4317575. *MPC*, Buenos Aires 8, *convenient to hire a*
T4317270, F4313402. *Integral*, Buenos Aires 88, T4155844478. **Bicycle** *Pogoni*, *taxi for a fixed fee*
España 676, helpful. *Parra*, Caseros 2154, T4225326, helpful. *Manresa*, Pellegrini 824,
imported equipment. Helpful mechanic, *S Fernández*, Urquiza 1051.

Long distance Air Airport 12 km south, reached by airport bus run by *Empresa San
Cayetano*, T4236629, US$3. Taxi from airport to bus terminal US$9. *LAB* to **Santa Cruz**
(Bolivia) twice a week, once via Tarija, continuing to Cochabamba. *Austral*, *Dinar* and
Lapa fly to **Buenos Aires**, 2 hrs, minimum. *Dinar*, *Lapa*, *Andesmar* to **Tucumán**.
Andesmar also to **Córdoba** and **Mendoza**. *Southern Winds* to **Córdoba**, **Tucumán**,
Rosario, **Mendoza**, **Neuquén**, **Bariloche** and **Mar del Plata**.

Bus Terminal is 8 blocks east of the main plaza (T4214716 for information). The terminal is being rebuilt during 2000/2001 which may result in disruption. Behind terminal is a 24 Shell station serving cheap snacks. To **Buenos Aires**, several daily, US$80,
19 hrs (*Atahualpa*, *La Estrella*, including snacks, dinner and breakfast in restaurant,
comfortable. Recommended, 4 daily) US$86 with *La Veloz del Norte* (20% ISIC dis-
count). To **Córdoba**, 4 a day, 12 hrs, US$41, *Expreso Panamericano* (T4212460), twice
daily, *Veloz del Norte*. To **Santiago del Estero**, 6 hrs, US$23. To **Tucumán**, 4 hrs, several
firms (*La Veloz del Norte* recommended, *La Estrella*), US$18. To **Puerto Iguazú**, via

The railway line to the clouds

The line from Salta to the Chilean frontier at Socompa, a distance of 570 km, is one of the great feats of South American railway construction. Work began in 1921 on the basis of French plans drawn up in 1911, it was the most outstanding achievement of Richard Maury, an engineer from Pennsylvania who arrived in Argentina in 1906 and who is commemorated by the station at Km 66 which bears his name. Though in 1922 President Yrigoyen ordered its completion within 500 days, it would be 1948 before this occurred, by which time developments in road and air transport had reduced its importance. Delays were not only the result of construction difficulties: on several occasions work was halted through lack of funding.

Some idea of the problems faced by Maury can be gained from the statistics. The line includes 21 tunnels, with a total length of 3.2 km; 19 of them are on the 178 km stretch between Campo Quijano and the La Polvorilla viaduct; there are also 31 bridges, 13 viaducts and 1,279 bends.

From the station in Salta (1,487 m) the line runs to Campo Quijano (Km 40, 1,520 m) and then climbs steeply up the

Quebrada del Toro. At El Alisal (km 50) and Chorrillos (km 66) there are switchbacks as the line climbs the side of the gorge. At Km 122 and Km 129 the line goes into 360°C loops before reaching Diego de Almagro (3,304 m). At Abra Munaño (3,952 m) the road to San Antonio can be seen below to the left, zig-zagging its way up the Quebrada del Toro. From here the line drops slightly on its way across the puna to San Antonio, Km 196.

The viaduct at La Polvorilla, 22 km further west, is one of the most spectacular engineering feats on the line: 224 m-long, 63 m-high and curved, it weighs 1,724 tons and is held up by 6 towers. Built in Italy, it was erected in 1929-1930. The highest point on the line, Abra Chorrillos (4,475 m), is reached 13 km further west, from where the line runs across the puna, 3,500-4,000 m above sea level, for another 335 km before reaching Socompa (3,865 m). On the Chilean side the line continues to Calama and Antofagasta, 901 km west of Salta. For further details of the building of this line see Federico Kirbus's book: El Fascinante Tren A Las Nubes (Ateneo, 1996).

Tren a las Nubes

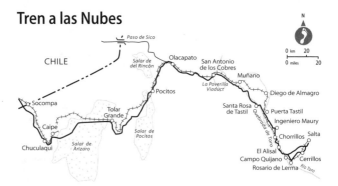

Tucumán or Corrientes, US$70. To **Mendoza** via Tucumán, several companies, daily, US$52, 20 hrs. To **Embarcación** daily with *Atahualpa* at 0700, US$14.50. To **Tartagal**, *Veloz del Norte, Atahualpa* (poor buses), US$22. To **Jujuy**, many companies including *Balut, La Veloz del Norte* and *Atahualpa* frequent between 0700 and 2300, 'directo', US$7, 2 hrs. To **La Rioja**, US$33. To **Belén**, Wed, US$26. To **Cafayate**, US$11, 4 hrs, *El Indio*, 4 a day. To **Santa María**, *El Indio*, 6½ hrs, 0700. To **Cachi**, 5 hrs, US$14, **Angastaco** (depart Thu 1300) and **Molinos** (7 hrs) *Marcos Rueda* daily (except Tue,

Thu) at 1300, unreliable on Sun (sit on left). To **Rosario de la Frontera**, US$5, 2½ hrs. To **San Antonio de Los Cobres**, 5½ hrs, *El Quebradeño*, Mon-Sat 1600, Sun 1930, US$14. Extra service on Thu 1030 continues to the Tincalayu mining camp (arrives 2140), returning to Salta on Fri 1200, passing San Antonio at 1800. This bus is the only public transport going further into the *puna* than San Antonio.

To Paraguay Salta provides the most reliable cheap land connection between Bolivia and Paraguay. Direct service to Asunción, *Empresa Sol*, US$42, overnight, 14 hrs. Alternatively travel to **Resistencia**, buses daily 1700, US$40 with *La Veloz del Norte* (20% reduction for students), *Sáenz Peña* or *Panamericano*, 12 hrs, then change. For description of road, see page 327. Salta-**Formosa** with Atahualpa, which provides the quickest route to Asunción (change at Orán), operates only twice weekly because of the state of the road – Wed and Sun at 0630, 12 hrs, US$40.

To Chile Services to Calama, San Pedro de Atacama, Antofagasta, Iquique and Arica were operated by *Tramaca* once or twice a week 12 hrs, via Jujuy and the Paso de Jama. Book well in advance, may be difficult to get a reservation, so try just before departure for a cancellation. Be prepared for delays at the frontier and take warm clothes (at night ice sometimes forms on the insides of bus windows), plenty of water, food, a sheet to protect luggage against dust. This route is usually closed for at least part of the winter and is liable to closure at other periods of the year. At the time of going to press the future of this service was not clear after *Tramaca* went bankrupt.

Chilean customs will not allow fruit in

To Bolivia To **La Quiaca**, on Bolivian frontier, about 10 buses daily, *Atahualpa*, US$27, 11 hrs (via Jujuy, prolonged stop), can be very cold, dusty, not recommended, best change to *Panamericano* in Jujuy. Also *Balut*, 3 a day, US$23, 7 hrs. To **Orán** (see page 267), 6 hrs, and *Aguas Blancas* for Bermejo, Bolivia; thence road connection to Tarija. To Yacuiba, via **Pocitos** (Bolivian frontier, see page 142), for Santa Cruz, US$17 with *Atahualpa* to Pocitos, 7-10 hrs, very full, road paved.

Train Station at 20 de Febrero y Ameghino, 9 blocks north of Plaza de Armas, taxi US$2. Trains only on the line to Socompa on the Chilean frontier (see below for a description of the line). On all journeys on this line beware of *soroche* (altitude sickness): do not eat or drink to excess.

Tren a las Nubes (Train to the Clouds) between Salta and La Polvorilla viaduct operates most Sat throughout the year, weather permitting, and on additional days in the high season (Jul/Aug), depart 0700, return to Salta 2215, US$95, without meals, credit cards not accepted, US$250 from Buenos Aires. The train is well-equipped with oxygen facilities and medical staff, restaurant car and snack bar. Explanations are available in English, Spanish, French and Italian. Book in advance (especially in high season) through **Movitren**, address above, **Trenes y Turismo**, Caseros 431, T4314984, trenes&turismo@salnet.com.ar *La Veloz del Norte*, Esmeralda 320, 4th floor, T4326-9623, Buenos Aires, or through any good travel agency (seats are limited and booking in Salta can be difficult as the train is often booked up from Buenos Aires). There is also a new service to the Quebrada del Inca, with folklore show, on Wednesdays, shorter and cheaper than the Tren a las Nubes, details and booking through Movitren.

Regular services Freight trains run between Campo Quijano and the borax mine at the Salar de Pocitos, but they are not supposed to carry passengers. There is also a weekly freight train with 1 or 2 passenger carriages which leaves Salta Fridays about 0900 for San Antonio, 12 hrs, and Socompa, 26 hrs, returns Sun: tickets from office to right of station entrance from 0800 on day of departure or in advance from yellow building to left of entrance. Officially this train is restricted to locals only; if refused passage in Salta boarding is usually possible in Campo Quijano and Rosario de Lerma

Cardoons

Cardoons *(Trychocereus pasacana)*, a slow-growing cactus, is found only at altitudes between 2,000 and 3,500 m and is very susceptible to changes in climate. Full grown cardoons reach a height of 6 m and are thought to be 100-200 years old. Its wood, which is marked by long thin holes, is so hard that it has been used for centuries for making furniture and building houses: many older churches in the Andes have ceilings of cardoon. Overexploitation of such a slow growing plant has led to restrictions on its use.

There are many stories about the cardoon: according to one from the War of Independence, General Belgrano's troops

used to clothe cardoons in ponchos and hats to hide their numerical inferiority from the opposing Spanish armies.

(reached by bus from Salta 1800): ask in the brake van and offer the guard yerba mate, sugar and cigarettes. Restaurant car, no heating, extremely cold; long delays are common and you may do much of the journey in the dark. Take food, water, sleeping bag and warm clothing. Fare US$30. From Socompa irregular freight trains run to Augusta Victoria, Baquedano or Antofagasta in Chile: officially the Chilean railway authorities do not permit passengers to travel on this line. Options are to return to Salta or wait, perhaps for several days, for a lift by train or truck. There is no food or accommodation in Socompa; if stuck try the Chilean customs building.

Directory **Airline offices** *Austral*, Caseros 475, T4310258. *Lapa*, Caseros 492, T4317080. *Dinar*, Buenos Aires 46, T/F4310606. *Lloyd Aéreo Boliviano*, Buenos Aires 120, T4217753 (will hold luggage and schedule a *colectivo* taxi). **Banks** Open 0730-1300, do not advance cash against credit cards as all have ATMs. *Banco de la Nación*, Mitre y Belgrano. *Banco Salta*, España 526 on main plaza, low commission on TC's. *Banco de Credito Argentino*, Alvarado 777, for Mastercard and Visa. *Banco Nacional del Lavoro*, Florida y Urquiza, cash on Mastercard. *Banco de Galicia*, Balcarce y Belgrano. *Banco HSBC*, Mitre 143, good rates, 1% commission on Amex TC's for US$ cash, changes Thomas Cook TC's (go to *Comercio Exterior* desk). *Dinar*, Mitre 101. *Chicoana Turismo*, Belgrano y Zuviria 255, Amex agent, does not cash TC's. Many *cambios* on España including *Maguitur*, No 666, only cash. *Golden Life*, Mitre 95 (Plaza 9 de Julio), local 1, 1st floor, best rates for cash. Difficult to buy US$ on cards or TC's. **Communications** Internet *Chat Café*, Vicente López 117. **Post office** Deán Funes 160, between España and Belgrano *poste restante* charges US$1.15 per letter. **Telephone** *Telecom*, Alvarado 595. Many *locutorios* including *Telecentro Zuviria*, on Plaza 9 de Jul. **Consulates** *Bolivia*, Mariano Boedo 32, T4211040, open Mon-Fri, 0900-1400 (unhelpful, better to go to Jujuy). *Chile*, Santíago del Estero, T4215757. *Paraquay*, Mariano Boedo 38, T/F4321401, friendly. *Peru*, 25 de Mayo 407, T4310201. *Spain*, República de Israel 137, T4312296, F4310206. *Italy*, Alvarado 1632, T4314455. *France*, Santa Fe 156, T4314726. *Germany*, Córdoba 202, T4216525, F4311772, consul Juan C Kühl, who also runs travel agency (see below), helpful. *Belgium*, Pellegrini 835, T4234252. **Cultural centres** *Alliance Française*, Santa Fe 20, T4210827. **Laundry** *Sol de Mayo*, 25 de Mayo 755, service wash. *Laverap*, Santiago del Estero 363, (open Sun morning) good, fast service, US$6 for 1 load. *Marva*, Juramento 315. *La Baseta*, Alvarado 1170. *Alvarado*, Alvarado 183, Mon-Sat 0800-1300, 1600-2000. **Tourist offices** *Provincial Tourist Office (Emsatur)*, Buenos Aires 93 (1 block from main plaza), T4310640. Open Mon-Fri 0800-2100, Sat/Sun 0900-2000. Municipal Tourist Office, San Martín y Buenos Aires, T4310641. Open Mon-Fri 0800-2200, Sat/Sun 0900-2000. Both offices arrange accommodation in private houses in high season (Jul) and can arrange horse-riding, US$50 full day, US$30 half-day including guide and meals. Recommended. Offices also at bus terminal and at the *teleférico* station in the Parque San Martín. **Useful addresses** Immigration office Maipú 35, 0730-1230.

From Salta to San Antonio De Los Cobres and Chile

San Antonio and the Chilean frontier can be reached by road and by rail **Route** (though see above for problems of rail travel). All roads are *ripio* apart from Route 51 between Salta and San Antonio, which is being paved. Route 51, runs west from Salta. From **Campo Quijano**, Km 30, it climbs along the floor of the Quebrada del Toro, fording the river repeatedly before reaching **Ingeniero Maury** at altitude of 2,350 m, Km 65, where there is a police control point. From Km 96, now paved, the road climbs the Quebrada de Tastil, leaving the railway which continues through the Quebrada del Toro.

Santa Rosa de Tastil at an altitude of 3,200 m, Km 103, is the site of an impor- **Santa Rosa** tant pre-hispanic settlement of over 400 houses and over 2,000 people. There **de Tastil** is a small museum. ■ *Daily 1000-1800, US$0.50. Recommended.*

Sleeping and eating In Santa Rosa Basic accommodation next door to the museum, no electricity or heating, take food, water and candles. Try the *quesillo de cabra* (goat's cheese) from Estancia Las Cuevas. **At El Alfarcito**, 5 km south of Santa Rosa, there is a good restaurant with 1 double room.

Transport *El Quebradeño* bus (see below). Alternatively take a tour from Salta, or share a taxi.

Beyond Tastil the road mainly paved climbs over the Abra Blanca pass **Route** (4,050 m), though the old route, over the Abra Muñano in a long series of steep zig-zags, is still passable. At the top of the pass, the road drops and runs across the *puna*, offering views of Chañi (5,896 m) to the left, Acay (5,716 m) to the right, and Quewar (6,102 m) in the far distance. At Km 123 Route 51 meets Route 40, the road from La Poma over the Abra del Acay.

San Antonio de los Cobres, 136 km northwest of Salta, is a squat, ugly mining **San Antonio** town situated in a hollow in the *puna* surrounded by hills. Beware of soroche: *Altitude: 3,750 m* avoid eating heavily or drinking alcohol until acclimatized.

Sleeping AB *Hostería de las Nubes*, on the eastern outskirts, T4909058, F490959. Modern, including breakfast, restaurant, comfortablle. Recommended. **E** per person *Hostería Inti Huasi*, opposite Aduana, T4909041. With breakfast, restaurant, clean. *Hosp El Palenque*, Belgrano s/n, T4909019. Also café, family run. **D** *Hosp Belgrano*, T4909025. Very friendly, evening meals.

The road to the Chilean frontier crossings at Paso de Sico at Paso de Socompa **From San** runs through very beautiful scenery, crossing saltflats with flamingos and **Antonio to Chile** impressive desert. Obtain sufficient drinking water before setting out from San *Hitchhiking along* Antonio. Most traffic uses the Paso de Sico crossing: there is virtually no traffic *these roads is not* on the other road. A third crossing, via the Paso de Huaytiquina, shown on *recommended* many maps, is closed. Because of snowfalls, these routes may be closed two or three times a year, for two or three days each time. Immigration and customs officials in San Antonio may be able to advise about road conditions but truck drivers using it are more reliable.

Route 51 continues across the *puna*; at Km 149 there is a turning which runs below the La Polvorilla railway viaduct. At Km 163 the highest point on the road, the Abra de Chorrillos (4,650 m) is reached. At Cauchari (3,993 m), Km 204 on the southern edge of the Salar de Cauchari, the road forks. One branch, Route 27 follows the railway line south and west across the giant Salar de

The Northwest

Arizaro to the Chilean frontier at Paso de Socompa. At Pocitos, 40 km south of Cauchari, Route 17 branches off Route 27 and runs south to Antofagasta de la Sierra. Route 51 continues west from Cauchari before forking again at Km 210, where Route 70 leads off north towards the Chilean frontier crossing at Paso de Jama while Route 51 runs to the frontier at Paso de Sico (4, 079 m).

Frontier
with Chile
The Argentine immigration offices are in San Antonio de los Cobres at the other end of town from aduana. There is a police checkpoint at Catúa, 26 km east of Paso de Sico. There is a police checkpoint in Toconao but customs and immigration for Chile is in San Pedro de Atacama. Note that fruit, vegetables and dairy products may not be taken into Chile (search 20 km west of Paso de Sico). From Paso de Sico the road continues on the Chilean side via Mina Laco and Socaire to Toconao (the road is very bad between these two points), San Pedro de Atacama and Calama. From Paso de Socompa a poor road runs to Pan de Azúcar from where there are roads west to the Pan American Highway south of Antofagasta and north via the Salar de Atacama to San Pedro de Atacama. No fuel is available until San Pedro or Calama.

Jujuy Province

From Salta
to Jujuy
There are two routes: the direct road, Route 9 (92 km) via La Caldera and El Carmen, is more interesting. North of La Caldera it winds through the Sierra de Chañi, passing through areas of cloudforest before reaching the Abra de Santa Laura (1,600 m) and dropping to El Carmen. The other route via Güemes is better for hitchhiking.

Jujuy

Phone code: 03882
Colour map 1, grid A3
Population: 182,000
Altitude: 1,260 m

The city of Jujuy lies on the edge of a broad valley at the southern end of the Quebrada de Humahuaca. Though the original city was sited between two rivers, the Ríos Grande and Xibi Xibi (or Chico), it has sprawled south beyond the latter. Capital of one of the smallest, and poorest, provinces in the country, Jujuy is a pleasant stop en route to or from Bolivia and a convenient stepping off point for excursions into the puna and to the national parks further northeast. Wars and earthquakes have ensured that the city has few colonial remains. Many of the streets are lined with bitter orange trees.

History
Founded first in 1561 and then in 1575, when it was destroyed by the Indians, the city was finally established in 1593. The province of Jujuy bore the brunt of fighting during the Wars of Independence: between 1810 and 1822 the Spanish launched 11 invasions down the Quebrada de Humahuaca from Bolivia. In August 1812 General Belgrano, commanding the republican troops, ordered the city to be evacuated and destroyed before the advancing Spanish army. This event is marked on 23-24 August by festivities known as *El Exodo Jujeño* with gaucho processions and military parades. As a tribute to the city for obeying his orders, Belgrano donated a flag which is displayed in the Casa de Gobierno: a painting of this ceremony can be seen inside the Cathedral.

Sights
In the eastern part of the city is the **Plaza Belgrano**, a fine square also lined with orange trees; in the centre is an equestrian statue of Belgrano. On the south side of the plaza stands the **Casa de Gobierno**, an elaborate 18th-century French-style palace, built in 1920. Inside, in the Salón de la Bandera, is the flag donated to the city by Belgrano. ■ *Mon-Fri, 0800-1200,*

What's your name again?

The city's formal title is San Salvador de Jujuy and it is usually referred to by locals as San Salvador. Jujuy is said to be corruption of Xibi Xibi, one of the rivers on which the city is sited. The two previous cities founded by the Spanish on this site

went by the names of La Ciudad de Nieva (after the then-Viceroy of Peru), 1561, and San Francisco de la Nueva Provincia de Alava, 1575. Travellers usually refer to the city as Jujuy (pronounced 'Hoo-Hooey').

1600-2000. Around the building are four statues representing Justice, Liberty, Peace and Progress by the Argentine sculptor, Lola Mora. On the west side is the **cathedral**, built in the late 19th century to replace the original which was built between 1598 and 1653 but which was destroyed by an earthquake in 1843. Inside are several fine 18th-century paintings as well as a superb gold plated wooden pulpit, carved by Indians in the Jesuit missions, a colonial treasure without equal in Argentina. Nearby, on the north side of the plaza, is the **Cabildo**, built in 1867 and now occupied by the police.

The church of **San Francisco**, Belgrano y Lavalle, two blocks east of the plaza, is modern but contains another fine colonial pulpit. The church of **San Bárbara**, San Martín y Lamadrid (1777) is similar in style to the colonial churches in the Quebrada de Humahuaca. The **Teatro Mitre** (1901) is two blocks further north at Alvear y Lamadrid.

Museo Histórico Provincial includes displays of colonial and 19th-century artefacts as well as a section on General Juan Lavalle, an opponent of Rosas, who was killed here in 1841. According to the story, he was hit by a bullet which passed through the door as he approached it from the other side. The door in the museum is a copy; the original is in the Museo de Historia Nacional in Buenos Aires. ■ *Mon-Fri 0800-1300, 1600-2000, Sat/Sun 0900-1200, Lavalle 250. US$1.* **Museo Municipal de Bellas Artes**, San Martín 230. Includes 20 works by the 'child painters of Chucalezna', a village north of Humahuaca. ■ *Mon-Fri, 0900-1230, 1700-1900, Sat/Sun 0900-1300, 1600-2100.* **Museo Histórico Franciscano**, in the Iglesia San Francisco at Belgrano y Lavalle. Includes 17th-century paintings and other artefacts from Cuzco. ■ *Daily 0900-1300, 1600-2100.* **Museo Arquológico Provincial**, Lavalle 434. Includes two mumified adults as well as ceramics from the Yavi and Humahuaca cultures. ■ *Daily 0900-1200, 1500-2000.* **Museo Histórico en Maquetas y Miniaturas**, Gordaliza 1511. Models and miniatures illustrating key events in Argentina and world history. ■ *Mon-Fri 0800-1230, 1600-2200, Sat/Sun 0900-1200, 1500-2000.*

Museums

Climate: Jujuy

Termas de Reyes, at an altitude of 1,800 m, 19 km northwest, is a thermal resort with the *Hotel Termas de Reyes*, a grand neo-classical hotel set among magnificent mountains. **AB** with breakfast or half-board, **A** full board, run down, restaurant. Camping US$5 per person with use of thermal pool, take insect repellent. Non-residents can use the hotel's thermal pool for US$3 (weekends

Excursions

The Northwest

US$5), and there are also municipal baths. ■ *Daily 0800-1200 and 1400-1700 (Thu 1400-1700 only), US$1.* ■ *Getting there: 6 buses a day from Jujuy bus terminal between 0630 and 1945, returning 0700-2040, US$1 1 hr.*

Sleeping **L** *Panorama*, Belgrano 1295, T4234089. Highly-regarded. **L** *Jujuy Palace*, Belgrano 1060, T/F4230433, jupalace@imagine.com.ar With buffet breakfast. **A** *Augustus*, Belgrano 715, T4230203. VIP section very good, standard section overpriced, modern, comfortable but noisy. **A** *Internacional*, Belgrano 501 (Plaza Belgrano), T4231599. With breakfast. **AB** *Fenicia*, 19 de Abril 427, T/F4231800. Tower block on riverside, good views from upper floors. **B** *Avenida*, 19 de Abril 469, T4236136. On riverside, with good restaurant (**C** off season, cafétéria only). **AB/B** *Sumay*, Otero 232, T4235065. Central, friendly. Recommended. **AL** *Altos De La Viña*, Route 56, Km 5, on northeastern outskirts, T4261666, lavina@mail.imagine.com.ar Attractive, swimming pool. **C** *Huaico*, Av Bolivia 3901, T4235186, F4228353. Breakfast extra, *confiteria*, solarium, pool. **C** *Res Los Andes*, República de Siria 456, T424315. Hot water, a bit prison-like. Opposite is **C** *Res San Carlos*, República de Siria 459, T4222286. Modern, some rooms a/c, parking. **C** *Paso de Jama*, Ramirez de Velazco 561, T4236118. With bath, without breakfast, modern. On Alvear: **C** *Chung King*, No 627, T4228142. Dark,

Jujuy centre

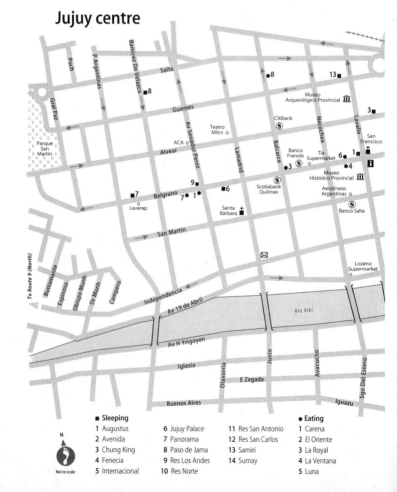

■ **Sleeping**
1 Augustus
2 Avenida
3 Chung King
4 Fenicia
5 Internacional
6 Jujuy Palace
7 Panorama
8 Paso de Jama
9 Res Los Andes
10 Res Norte
11 Res San Antonio
12 Res San Carlos
13 Samiri
14 Sumay

● **Eating**
1 Carena
2 El Oriente
3 La Royal
4 La Ventana
5 Luna

Not to scale

very noisy, also **D** without bath, good restaurant. **D** *Res Norte*, No 444, T4222721, restaurant, basic. **D** *El Aguila*, Alvear 400, restaurant, basic. Near the bus terminal only **C** *San Antonio*, Lisandro de la Torre (opposite), modern. Recommended. **D** *Res Río de Janeiro*, Av José de la Iglesia 1536, very basic, run down. **E** per person *Samiri*, Balcarce 569, T4238425, youth hostel, kitchen, central.

Outside the city **AB** *Hostería Posta de Lozano*, Route 9, Km 18 north, T4980050, F4980028, posta@imagine.com.ar Good restaurant, pools with fresh mountain water, covered parking **E** per person *El Refugio*, in Yala, Route 9, 14 km north T/F4909344, elrefugio@arnet.com.ar, youth hostel, restaurant, trekking and horseriding excursions.

Camping *Camping Municipal*, Av República de Bolivia west of town near the Río Grande. US$4 per tent, ask for a cheaper rate for 1 person. *Autocamping*, 3 km north outside city at Huaico Chico. Buses 4 or 9 frequent, hot showers (if you remind the staff), laundry facilities, very friendly.

Former Railway Station

Sarmiento

Gorriti

5●
10■

Cabildo

5■

2● Cathedral
LAPA
Plaza Gen Belgrano

Otero

Paseo de las Artesanías

Casa de Gobierno

Arganaras

14■

■2   4■

Av H Yrigoyen

Dorrego

J Newberry

M Gorriti

Campero

R De Siria

R Del Líbano

9■ ■12

Municipal o Market

Urdininea

Leandro N Alem

■11

L De La Torre

6 Madre Tierra
7 Montecarlo
8 Savoy
9 Sociedad Espánola

El Cortijo, Lavalle y San Martín. Interesting salads, good vegetarian food, reasonably priced. *Sociedad Española*, Belgrano y Pérez, elegant setting, good set price meals. *Confitería La Royal*, Belgrano 770. Good but expensive. *La Victoria*, Av El Exodo 642, away from centre, good. *Confitería Carena*, Belgrano 899. Good for breakfast. *El Oriente*, Güemes 723, Arab specialities. *Montecarlo*, Belgrano y Pérez. Attractive café. *Luna*, Belgrano 134, Chinese *tenedor libre*. *La Vanguardia*, San Martín y Ramirez de Velasco. Pizza. *La Ventana*, Belgrano 751. Good cheap menu, good service, à-la-carte menu expensive. *La Rueda*, Lavalle 320. Good food and service, very popular, expensive. *Madre Tierra*, Belgrano y Otero. Vegetarian, fixed price lunch. Highly recommended. *Krysys*, Balcarce 272, excellent atmosphere, good food, pricey. *Ruta 9*, Lavalle 287. Good local food, Bolivian owners. Cheaper places on Santiago del Estero and Alem behind bus terminal. Very good ice cream at *Helados Xanthi*, Belgrano 515, made by Greek owner. *Opus-Café*, Belgrano 856. Good coffee, music and atmosphere. Good bread and cake shop at Belgrano 619. Good sandwiches at *Rada Tilly*, 2 locations on Belgrano.

Eating

The Northwest

Chung King, Alvear 627. Live music and dancing at weekends. *Savoy*, Alvear y Urquiza, live music.

Entertainment

Belgrano

Though among Argentine independence heroes, General Manuel Belgrano stands second only to San Martín, his plans to establish a constitutional monarchy after independence were a failure and his military career was marked more by defeat than victory. He is, however, honoured as the creator of the Argentine flag although when he first unfurled the now familiar blue and white banner on the banks of the Río Paraná in 1812, he was reprimanded by senior officers who opposed what they saw as a declaration of independence from Spain.

Born into a wealthy merchant family in Buenos Aires in 1770, Belgrano was educated in Spain, returning to become a leading figure in a circle of intellectuals influenced by the European enlightenment. As secretary of the Buenos Aires merchant guild, he promoted ideas of free trade through his writings. He was therefore an enthusiastic supporter of moves to break away from Spanish colonial rule with its trading restrictions. In 1811 he commanded a military expedition to Paraguay; convinced that the Paraguayans would support his cause, his force of 700 men was overwhelmed by 5,000 Paraguayans and defeated. Placed in command of the northern armies, he defeated royalist forces at Tucumán (September 1812) and Salta (February 1813). His attempt to end Spanish control over Upper Peru (Bolivia) by siezing Potosi failed: defeated, he was forced back to Tucumán, where he was replaced by San Martín.

In 1815 Belgrano was sent to Europe to pursuade Spain to accept Argentine independence under a king from the Spanish royal family. After the failure of this mission he participated in the Congress of Tucumán; though he successfully argued for a declaration of independence, his schemes for a monarchy under a descendent of the Incas were again rejected. After a further period with the northern army he died in Buenos Aires in 1820.

Festivals Festival on 6 Nov. *El Exodo Jujeño*, 23/24 Aug (hotels fully booked).

Shopping Handicrafts are available at reasonable prices from vendors on Plaza Belgrano near the cathedral and from the *Paseo de las Artesanías* on the west side of the plaza. *Regionales Lavalle*, Lavalle 268. *Centro de Arte y Artesanías*, Balcarce 427. *Librería Rayuela*, Belgrano 636, good maps and travel guides. *Librería Belgrano*, Belgrano 602, English magazines and some books. *Farmacia Avenida*, Lavalle y 19 de Abril, 0800-2400. *Tierrita*, Necochea 508, fishing and camping equipment. Municipal market at Dorrego y Alem, near bus terminal. Supermarkets: *Tia*, Belgrano 825 and *Lozano*, 19 de Abril y Necochea.

Tour operators Many along Belgrano *Alicia Viajes*, No 592, T422541. *Giménez*, No 775, T42924. *Turismo Lavalle*, No 340. *Pasajes Turismo* No 722. *Grafitti*, No 731. *Be Dor Turismo*, No 860 local 8, 10% for ISIC and youth card holders on local excursions. All offer tours along the Quebrada de Humahuaca, 10 hrs, US$35. For information on bird watching, contact Mario Daniel Cheronaza, Peatonal 38, No 848-830, Viviendas 'El Arenal', Jujuy.

Transport **Local Car hire** *Avis*, Hotel Jujuy Palace, T4911501, F311184 and airport.

Long distance Air Aeropuerto El Cadillal, 32 km southeast, T491505. *Tea Turismo* vans leave *Hotel Avenida* to meet arrivals, 1 hr, US$4.50. *Austral* flies to **Buenos Aires**, 1 a day direct, **Salta** and **Santiago del Estero**. *LAB* to Tarija twice a week. *Austral* offers bus connection with its Buenos Aires flight to Tartagal (in the northeast of the province) via San Pedro and Embarcación.

Bus Terminal at Iguazú y Dorrego, 6 blocks south of centre. To **Buenos Aires**, US$89, several daily with *Balut, La Estrella, La Internacional*. To **Córdoba**, *Panamericano* and *La Veloz del Norte*, daily. To **Tucumán** 5 hrs, US$25, and **Córdoba**, 14 hrs US$45, *Ledesma*. To **Puerto Iguazú**, 2 a week, US$80, 30 hrs. To **Salta** hrly from 0700, 2¾ hrs, US$6. To **La Quiaca**, 6½ hrs, several companies, US$16, reasonably comfortable, but very cold at night, best is *Veloz del Norte*, fastest is *El Quiaqueño*. To **Humahuaca**, US$7, 3 hrs, sit on left side. To **Tilcara** 1½ hrs, US$5. To **Orán** daily at 1700. To **Embarcación**, US$7 Balut, via San Pedro. To **Purmamarca** (1 hr) and **Susques**, 3½ hrs, *El Quiaqueño*, Fri and Sun. **To Chile** To **Antofagasta** via the Paso de Jama, San Pedro de Atacama and **Calama** (15 hrs), *Tramaca*, Tue and Fri, US$50 including cold meal, breakfast. To **Iquique**, Wed and Sat, *Panamericano*, US$50. Check weather conditions in advance.

Airline offices *Aerolíneas Argentinas*, San Martín 745. *LAPA*, Belgrano 616. **Banks** At banks **Directory**
Banco Jujuy, Lamadrid, ATM, changes US$ cash only. *Scotiabank Quilmes*, Belgrano y Balcarce, ATM, Amex TCs changed at 1% commission while *Banco de Galicia*,Alvear, charges US$10 commission. Visa and Mastercard ATMs at *Citibank*, Güemes y Balcarce. *Banco Francés*, Belgrano 872. *Banco Salta*, San Martín 785. nowhere to change Thomas Cook TCs; *Horus*, Belgrano 722, good rates for cash; *Dinar*, Belgrano 731. Travel agencies on Belgrano also change cash. If desperate, ask the dueña of the *confitería* at bus station, rates not too unreasonable. **Communications** Post office at Independencia y Lamadrid, in Galería Impulso, Belgrano 775. **Telecoms** Plenty. Senador Pérez 141, open 0700-0100 and at Alvear 870, Belgrano 730. **Internet** *Cybercafé*, Belgrano y Balcarce. **Consulates** *Bolivia*, Belgrano 250, open 0900-1300. *Spain*, Ramirez de Velasco 362, T428193. *Italy*, Av Fascio 660, T423199. *Paraguay*, Tacuarí 430, T428178. **Laundry** *Laverap*, Belgrano y Ramirez de Velasco. **Tourist offices** Belgrano 690, T4221326, F4221325, setjujuy@imagine. com.ar 28153, very helpful, open till 2000. **ACA**, Pérex y Alvear. **Useful addresses** Migración Antardida 1365.

From Jujuy to Chile

This route via the Paso de Jama, an alternative to the route via the Paso de Sico *No fuel is available*
(see above), is now the road most used by traffic, including trucks, crossing to *between Jujuy & San*
northern Chile. *Pedro de Atacama*
except at Susques
 Near Purmamarca (see below), 61 km north of Jujuy on Route 9, Route 52 *& then only if they*
(*ripio*) leads west through the quebrada de Purmamarca and over the Abra *have electricity*
Potrerillos (4,170 m) to reach the *puna*. From here the road runs northwest, crossing, at Km 127, Route 40, which runs between San Antonio de los Cobres and Abra Pampa. From the crossing to Susques the road is paved. At Km 131-136 the road crosses Salinas Grandes (3,500 m), one of the largest areas of saltflats in the country where there are amazing views especially at sunset. In the winter months, on both sides of the road, three different ancient types of salt mining by hand can be seen. At Km 180-200 the road winds through the Quebrada de Mal Paso crossing the Tropic of Capricorn several times.

The only settlement between Purmamarca and the frontier, Susques lies in a **Susques**
hollow at the confluence of the Ríos Susques and Pastos Chicos. The church, *Phone code: 03882*
dating from 1598, is one of the outstanding examples of colonial architecture *Colour map 1, grid A2*
in the region, with a roof of cactus-wood and thatch. Inside is an old *Population: 700*
Altitude: 3,700 m
bellow-organ. *Km 213*

Sleeping **E** per person *Res La Vicuñita*, San Martín 121, T4790207, F490229. Opposite church, without bath, hot water, breakfast.

Transport **Bus** To **Jujuy**, El Quiaqueño, Mon, Fri 3½ hrs.

The Northwest

Route West of Susques Route 16 (*ripio*) continues through the Quebrada de Taire to meet Route 70 (Km 261), which runs south along the west side of the Salar de Cauchari to meet Route 51, the San Antonio de los Cobres-Paso de Sico road.

Frontier **Paso de Jama**, (4,750 m) 360 km west of Jujuy, is reached by a 60 km road **with Chile** which branches off Route 70. Argentine customs and immigration are at Susques. On the Chilean side the road continues (unpaved) to San Pedro de Atacama (Km 514), where fuel and accommodation are available, and Calama. Chilean customs and immigration are at San Pedro de Atacama.

North from Jujuy

Route 9 runs north from Jujuy, through the **Quebrada de Humahuaca** and then across the *puna* to the Bolivian frontier at **La Quiaca**. Drivers heading off main roads in this area should note that service stations are far apart: there are ACA stations at Jujuy, Humahuaca and La Quiaca and YPF stations at Tilcara and Abra Pampa. Spare fuel and water must be carried. In the rainy season (January-March) ask the highway police about flooding on the roads. There are frequent **bus** services along the Quebrada which stop at the main towns; most services from Jujuy to Humahuaca, fewer north of Humahuaca. Companies: Panamericano, Veloz del Norte, Cotta Norte, Balut, Atahualpa.

Quebrada de Humahuaca

The road through this gorge offers some of the most attractive landscapes in the northwest. The rock strata are a spectacular variety of contrasting colours and giant cacti grow in the higher, drier parts. Although the most famous views of the rock strata are from Purmamarca, there are outstanding views also from Route 9, particularly around Maimará and, further north, around Tilcara. The main centres for visiting the Quebada are Tilcara and Humahuaca.

The Quebrada de Humahuaca has some of the most interesting **festivals** in the region. The pre-Lent carnival celebrations are picturesque and colourful. At Easter in Tilcara and Humahuaca pictures of the Passion are made of flowers, leaves, grasses and seeds and a traditional procession on Holy Thursday at night is joined by thousands, especially in Yavi.

Purmamarca Purmamarca lies on Route 52 to Paso de Jama (see above). Overlooking the *Colour map 1, grid A3* village to the west is *la colina de las siete colores*, a hill in seven contrasting *Population: 200* colours can be distinguished in the rock strata. There are good views from the *Altitude: 2,100 m* road entering the village that are best seen in the early morning or at least *3 km W of Route 9* before noon. On the plaza is the church of Santa Rosa (1648, rebuilt 1778) with *at Km 61* adobe walls and a cactus roof. Next to the church is an *algrarrobo* tree thought to be 500-years old.

Sleeping **B** *La Posta*, T/F490804029. With bathbreakfast, triple rooms only, good restaurant. **B** *Zulma*, T4908023, with bath. **C** *Aramayo*, T4908028, without bath. **D** *Hostal Bebo Vilte*, T/F4908038, without bath, camping space. **E** per person *Ranchito del Rincón*, Sarmiento, new, owners Yolanda and Zulma are helpful. Highly recommended. **E** per person *El Poro*, T4908003, accommodation and camping. The *comedor* on main square has good, cheap, local food and helps find accommodation.

Transport **Bus** to Jujuy US$4, 1 hr.

Maimará lies at the foot of the *Paleta del Pintor*, sloping rock strata in contrasting colours. Just off the road, 3 km south, is **La Posta de Hornillos**, one of the chain of colonial posting house which used to extend from Buenos Aires to Lima. Restored, the building now houses a historical museum with a collection of 18th- and 19th-century funtiture as well as weapons and historical documents. ■ *Wed-Mon 0900-1800, free.* **Sleeping** at **C** *Pensión La Posta*, the owners' son is a tourist guide and has helpful information, 5 km from Maimará and **camping** at *Centro Turístico*, T156822067.

Maimará
Population: 1,600
Altitude: 2,150 m
Km 75

Situated near the confluence of the Ríos Grande and Huasamayo, Tilcara is a green oasis surrounded by steep mountains with attractively coloured rock strata. The village is centred around a pleasant tree-lined plaza. South of the village, some 2 km, overlooking the Río Grande is a *pucará*, or Indian fortress, uncovered in 1903 and reconstructed in the 1950s. At the entrance there are botanical gardens containing a variety of cacti and other high altitude plants. From the pucara there are fine views along the quebrada. ■ *Daily 0800-1230, 1400-1830.*

Tilcara
Phone code: 0388
Colour map 1, grid A3
Population: 2,900
Altitude: 2,460 m
Km 84

Fiestas on weekends in Jan

Museums **Museo Arqueológico**, Belgrano 445 on the plaza, attached to the University of Buenos Aires. Contains a fine collection of precolumbian ceramics from the Andean regions of present day Argentina, Bolivia and Peru. ■ *0900-1300, 1400-1830, highly recommended, US$2, free entry Tue. Admission includes entry to the pucará and vice-versa.* **Museo Regional de Pintura**, Rivadavia 459. Paintings by José Antonio Terry and other artists on the customs and traditions of Tilcara. ■ *Tue-Sat/Sun 0900-1900, Sun 0930-1200, 1500-1800.*

Sleeping **L** *Casa de los Alamos*, T4955172, juylosalamos@arnet.com.ar With breakfast, meals served. **A** *Casa de La Nona*, Belgrano 553, T/F4955068, ccaliari@imagine.com.ar With breakfast, also **L** half-pension. **L** *Villar del Ala*, Padilla 100, T/F4955100. Half-pension, English spoken. **B** *Turismo*, Belgrano 590, T/F4955002, tilcahot@imagine.com.ar Municipally run, restaurant, pool (usually dry), gym, also dormitory accommodation **E** per person. **B** *Malka*, San Martín s/n, 5 blocks from plaza, T4955197. Bungalows with kitchen and laundry facilities, also **E** per person dormitory accommodation, kitchen facilities, Hostelling International affiliated, horse and bike rental, meals provided. **C** *El Antigal*, Rivadavia s/n, T4955020, good restaurant, colonial style, stores luggage. Recommended. **C/D** *Hostería La Esperanza*, Belgrano 335, T4955106, without bath, spacious rooms, arranges walking tours. **C** *Res Frami*, Lavalle y Bolívar, T4955045, with bath, **D** without. **C** *Hosp Pucará*, Padilla s/n. 3 blocks from plaza, T4955050, with bath, **D** without, cosy, friendly. Recommended, also camping. **E** *Edén*. **Camping** Municipal campsite, dirty. *Camping El Jardín*, T4955128, US$5, clean, hot showers. *El Enano*, T 4955242.

Eating *Pucará*, good value. *Café del Museo*, good coffee.*El Cafecito*, on plaza, home made cakes and bread.

Shopping There are excellent craft stalls and shops around the main plaza, selling ponchos, sweaters and wooden items.

Transport **Bus** *El Vallarta* local serices to **Maimara** and **Humahuaca**, cheaper, poor buses, regular service . **Cycle hire** *Bicicletería Tilcara*, US$2 per hr, US$5 per half-day.

The Northwest

Huacalera Huacalera lies 2 km north of the Tropic of Capricorn; a sundial 20 m west of
Population: 100 the road marks the exact location. The church, several times restored, has a
Altitude: 2,700 cactus-wood roof and a small museum. **Sleeping** at **B** *Hostal La Granja*,
Km 90 T0388-4561766, restaurant, solarium, very good.

Uquía Situated near striking red mountains, Uquía has one of the oldest churches is
Phone code 03887 the region. Built in 1691, the 1-m thick walls of the naves are hung with
Altitude 2,818 m 17th-century paintings of winged angels in military dress: the so-called *ángeles*
Km 105 *arcabuceros*. Note also the baroque altarpiece. **Sleeping** at **AB** *Hostal de*
Uquía, T/F490508, elportillo@cootepal.com.ar With breakfast, clean, English
spoken and **B/C** *El Molino*, T490515.

Humahuaca

Phone code: 03887 *Humahuaca is the largest and most important town between Jujuy and the Boliv-*
Colour map 1, grid A3 *ian frontier. Founded in 1591 on the site of a prehispanic settlement, it has the air*
Population: 6,000 *of the archetypal Andean colonial town with narrow streets and one-storey adobe*
Altitude: 2,940 m *buildings: in fact it was mostly rebuilt in the late-19th century. Coach trips from*
126 km N of Jujuy *Salta and Jujuy congregate here at midday but few tourists stay for more than a*
couple of hours. It is an attractive and peaceful centre from which to explore the
Quebrada de Humahuaca.

Sights The church, **La Candelaria**, completely rebuilt in 1873-80, has a bell from 1641.
Carnival celebration The modern **Cabildo**, in Californian neo-colonial style is incongruous: from it a
is 1 of the most mechanical figure of San Francisco Solano blesses the town at 1200. Overlooking
outstanding in the NW the town is the massive **Monumento a la Independencia Argentina**, made of
& 2 Feb, bronze and weighing 60 tons, built in 1936-50 and sited here because the valley
La Candelaria was the scene of the heaviest fighting during the Wars of Independence. There is
a good **Feria Artesanal** on Avenida San Martín (on the far side of the railway
line), but avoid the middle of the day when the coach parties arrive.

Museums **Museo Folklórico Regional**, Buenos Aires 435, run by Sixto Vásquez Zuleta.
Traditional native customs, free entry, guided tour (recommended) US$5.
■ *0800-2000*. Inside the museum is *La Chicera*, a restaurant serving
pre-Hispanic, colonial and present-day indigenous food. **Museo Ramoneda**,
Salta y Santa Fe, private collection of contemporary art in 19th-century mansion. ■ *Daily 1030-1300, 1330-1900*.

Excursions **Coctaca**, 10 km northeast, has an impressive and extensive (40 ha) series of
pre-colonial agricultural terraces, the largest archaeological site in Jujuy which
is puzzling. The terrain is not very hilly.

Sleeping **AB/B** *Turismo*, Buenos Aires 650, T421154, F421067. With breakfast, large rooms with
balcony overlooking mountains, restaurant, cafeteria, heating run down, poor service,
modern building sadly out of keeping with surroundings. *Hostería Camino del Inca*,
Ejercito del Norte s/n, T421007. **C** *Res Humahuaca*, Córdoba y Corrientes, 1 block
north of bus terminal, T421141, **D** without bath, some a/c, poor breakfast extra.
B/C *Res Colonial*, Entre Ríos 110, near bus terminal, T421007, some windowless
rooms. **D** without bath, laundry facilities. **E** per person *Albergue Humahuaca*, Buenos
Aires 447, T421064. Dormitories and family rooms, clean, laundry and limited cooking
facilities, cafetéria, cold, Hostelling International affiliated, special price discounts for
ISIC and youthcard holders, German spoken. Offers tours, all with accredited local
guides to popular and lesser-known sites, horse riding, trekking, local festivals, also to
the Pacific via Lagunas Colorada and Verde (Bolivia) and the Ruta de Che Guevara

(Bolivia). **E** per person *Youth Hostel Posada El Portillo*, Tucumán 69, T421288, elportillo@cootepal.com.ar Dormitories, without bath, restaurant, kitchen facilities. **D** *El Cardón*, cabaña with kitchen.

Camping Across bridge by railway station, small charge including use of facilities. *Bella Vista*

Many restaurants open only during the day, difficult to find breakfast. Beware of **Eating** *soroche*: eat light meals and avoid alcohol until acclimatized. *La Cacharpaya*, Jujuy 295. Excellent, pricey, Andean music. *Humahuaca Colonial*, Tucumán 22. Good regional cooking, good value, but invaded by coach parties at midday. *El Rancho*, (no sign) Belgrano 346, just around the corner from market, good value, where the locals eat.

Bus To **Jujuy**, US$8. To **La Quiaca**, US12.   **Transport**

Banks *Banco de Jujuy* on plaza, ATM. Credit cards are not accepted anywhere. **Laundry** in the   **Directory** *Albergue Humahuaca*, US$4 per load. **Tourist offices** Kiosk in main plaza in high season.

North of Humahuaca

North of Humahuaca Route 9 rises steadily as far as Tres Cruces offering more views of colourful rock strata as it climbs out of the Quebrada. From Tres Cruces it continues across the bleak and barren puna to La Quiaca on the Bolivian border. At Km 146 a road turns off northeast to Iturbe and then over the 4,000 m Abra del Cóndor before dropping steeply into the Quebrada de Iruya to Iruya.

Humahuaca centre

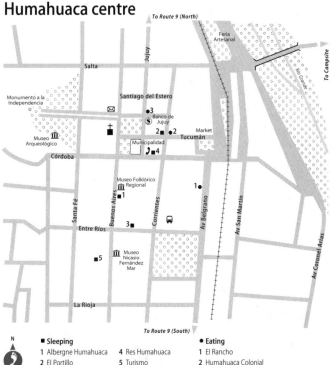

Sleeping		Eating
1 Albergne Humahuaca	4 Res Humahuaca	1 El Rancho
2 El Portillo	5 Turismo	2 Humahuaca Colonial
3 Res Colonia		3 La Cacharpaya

Not to scale

Iruya
Colour map 1, grid A3
Population: 300
Altitude: 2,713 m
77 km from
Humahuaca

Iruya is a beautiful walled village wedged on a hillside. Probably founded in 1741, it was a colonial stopover point for mule trains to Bolivia. It is a pleasant and friendly centre for horseback or walking trips in the area (take sleeping bag). At Titiconte 7 km away, there are unrestored pre-Inca ruins (take guide). There is a colourful Rosario festival on the first Sunday in October.

Sleeping and eating AB *Hostería de Iruya*, T482001, with breakfast. **F** per person *Albergue Belén*, very basic. **F** per person *Hosp Tacacho*, clean, friendly, *comedor*, on the plaza. Food at *Comedor Iruya*.

Tour operators *Puna Expediciones* (see page 267) runs a 7-day trek, Salta-Iruya-Nazareno-La Quiaca, walking between Iruya and Nazareno along remote paths, sleeping in local schoolhouses; rest of route is by truck.

Transport Bus Daily bus service from Jujuy and Humahuaca to Iturbe by *Panamericano*, 1400 and 1900, 45 mins. In Iturbe you may be able to get a seat on a truck. *Empresa Mendoza* bus from Humahuaca, 1015, Mon, Wed, Fri, Sat and Sun, 3½ hrs, US$7 1 way, waits 2-3 hrs in Iruya before returning. Service varies according to time of year and may be suspended in rainy season (esp Feb and Mar) details from *La Cacharpaya* restaurant in Humahuaca, T421016.

Tres Cruces
Altitude: 3,693 m

A village of one storey adobe buildings, Tres Cruces (Km 190) is where customs searches are made on vehicles from Bolivia. From here a private paved road runs south to the Mina Aguilar where lead zinc and silver are mined. **Sleeping** at **E** per person *El Aguilar* (no sign) without bath, clean, basic.

Abra Pampa
Population: 4,000
Altitude: 3,484 m

Originally known as Siberia Argentina, Abra Pampa (Km 217) is an important mining centre. Route 9 continues north from here to La Quiaca and three roads branch off: southwest to Casabindo, west to Cochinaca and northwest to the Laguna de los Pozuelos and Rinconada. There is a small archaeological museum, ■ *Mon-Sat 0900-1200, 1600-1800*. At **Miraflores**, 15 km south west of Abra Pampa on the Casabindo road, is a vicuña farm, the largest in Argentina. ■ *Getting there: Buses Mon-Sat mornings from Abra Pampa. Information offered, photography permitted.*

Sleeping *Res La Coyita*, Gobern- ador Fascio 123, T/F491052, with bath, heating. **F** per person *Res El Norte*, Sarmiento 530, shared room, clean, hot water, good food. *Res Cesarito*, clean, restaurant.

Laguna de los Pozuelos

Route 7 to La Quiaca

Yoscaba

Pasajes

Sierra de Rinconada

Río Chico

Rodeo

Lagunillas

Laguna de los Pozuelos

To Rinconada

Río Cincel

Sierra de Cochinaca

Ranger Post

N

Not to scale

steppe covered by bushes
grassland
unpaved roads

The Northwest

El Toreo de la Vincha

Each year on 15 August Casabindo celebrates the Assumption of the Virgin by holding El Toreo de la Vincha, the only corrida de toros (bullfight) held in Argentina. Bullfighting was outlawed in Argentina shortly after independence, but this is no ordinary bullfight. To start with, the bull is not killed; instead, in front of the church, he challenges onlookers to take a ribbon and silvercoins which he

carries on his horns. The coins are offered to the Virgin. The event is said to symbolize the struggle between the Virgin (whose defenders are the men) and the Devil (the bull). There is, however, another aspect to the celebrations: just before the toreo, in another part of the village, coca leaves and alcohol are buried as a tribute to Pachamama.

Casabindo was founded in 1602. Its magnificent church with twin towers dates from 1772 and is called 'the cathedral of the Puna': (Federico Kirbus). Inside are frescos of archangels in military uniforms (*angeles arcabuceros*). **Sleeping** at **E** per person *Albergue*, T03887-491129. ■ *Getting there: La Quiaqueña bus daily on Route 40 from Jujuy to La Quiaca passes through Casabindo.*

Casabindo
Altitude: 3,500 m
62 km SW of
Abra Pampa

Laguna de los Pozuelos is a flamingo reserve extending over 16,245 ha. Some 36 bird species have been identified but in recent years lack of water has led to the departure of many flamingos. Temperatures can drop to -25°C in winter; if camping warm clothing, drinking water and food are essential. There is a ranger station at the southern end of the Laguna with a campsite nearby. At Lagunillas, further west, there is smaller lagoon, which also has flamingos. ■ *Getting there: Mon-Fri 0930, 2 hrs, US$3. Southern entrance is from the Abra Pampa-Casabindo rd. There is also an entrance north of Guayatayoc, northwest of the Laguna and 5 km east of Route 7.*

Laguna de los Pozuelos
Altitude 3,650 m
50 km NW of from
Abra Pampa

La Quiaca lies on the Río La Quiaca, which is usually dry, marks the frontier with Bolivia. It is linked with Villazón on the Bolivian side by a bridge. A modern town, it dates from the opening of the railway line in 1907. There are very few shops as most commercial activity has moved to Villazón where everything is cheaper.

La Quiaca
Population: 11,500
Altitude: 3,442 m
Phone code: 03885
292 km N of Jujuy

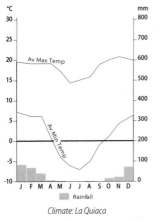

Climate: La Quiaca

Excursions Yavi, with a population of 300 and at an altitude of 3,300 m, is 16 km east along a good paved road. Founded in 1667, this provided the crossing point to Bolivia until rail and road connections were built through La Quiaca. The church of **San Francisco** (1690) is a colonial gem though the roof has been replaced. It has magnificent gold decoration and windows of onyx. Find the caretaker at her house and she will show you round the church. ■ *Tue-Sun 0900-1200 and Tue-Fri 1500-1800.* Opposite is the **Casa del Marqués Campero y Tojo**, the austere former mansion of the family who were granted large parts of the *puna* by Philip V of Spain. It

The Northwest

contains a historical museum of family artefacts including two early editions of *Don Quijote*. ■ *Mon-Sat 0900-1200, 1400-1800*. There is a colourful evening procession in Holy Week. East of here a precarious road for trucks and pick-ups only leads over the Abra de Lizoite (4,500 m) to Santa Victoria, Km 116. **Sleeping** at *Hostal de Yavi*, T03887-421288, elportillo@cootepal.com.ar Bath, heating, restaurant. Accomodation is also available in private houses and there is a municipal campsite. ■ *Getting there: Taxi remise from La Quiaca, US$12 return, including 1 hr wait.*

The Mancafiesta (festival of the pots): the Third Sunday in Oct

Santa Catalina, with a population of 200 and at an altitude of 3,900 m, is 67 km west along a poor road. There is a 19th-century church and a small museum of artefacts from local history housed in the oldest building in the village. **Sleeping** at **G** per person Albergue Santa Catalina. ■ *Getting there: From Jujuy to Santa Catalina via La Quiaca, 19 hrs, Mon and Fri.*

La Quiaca & Villazón

Sleeping and eating AB *Turismo*, Siria y San Martín, T/F422243. With bath. Recommended, modern, comfortable, restaurant. **B/C** *Crystal*, Sarmiento 543, T422255. **E** per person without bath, clean, run down, hospitable. **C** *Victoria*, good hot showers. *Alojamiento Pequeño*, Bolívar 236, cheap, basic. **D** *Hotel Frontera*, Belgrano y Siria, without bath or breakfast, also restaurant with good value menu. *Sirio-Libanesa*, near *Hotel Frontera*, good restaurant, cheap set meal. **Camping** *Camping Municipal*. Camping is also possible near the control post on the outskirts of town and; also at the ACA service station about 300 m from near the frontier.

Transport Bus Terminal at España y Belgrano, luggage storage. Taxi to frontier US$1.50. To **Salta**, 6-8 a day, 10 hrs, US$27. Cheapest company *Balut*, US$23 via Humahuaca, 3 hrs, US$12 and Jujuy with change in Jujuy. To **Jujuy**, US$21.50, 5 hrs, *Panamericano*, 5 a day, *Balut* 4 a day. To **Jujuy** via Route 40, *NorBus* and *El Quiaqueño* daily, US$15. To **Buenos Aires**, via Jujuy, US$89 including meals, 28 hrs.

Directory Banks Lots of *casas de cambio* in Villazón (Bolivia), none in La Quiaca. **Medical services** There is a good hospital south of the centre. *Farmacia Nueva*, half a block from church, has remedies for *soroche* (mountain sickness).

■ **Sleeping**
1 Cristal
2 La Frontera
3 Residencial Bolivia
4 Turismo
5 Victoria

N

Not to scale

The frontier bridge is 10 blocks from La Quiaca bus terminal, 15 mins walk. **Frontier** This crossing is the scene of a lot of illegal (but tolerated) smuggling: searches **with Bolivia** of locals are thorough. Contrary to popular belief, there is no fee to cross the border either way, and any attempts to levy a surcharge or tax are illegal. You should be on your guard at all times at this border crossing; stories of illegal practices are rife.

Immigration and customs Argentine immigration and customs offices open 0700-2000; buses arriving outside these hrs have to wait, so check before travelling. Formalities for those entering Argentina are usually very brief but thorough customs searches are made just south of La Quiaca and at Tres Cruces, 102 km south, where documents are also checked. Avoid carrying items such as packets of coca leaves or similar derivatives of the plant. The Bolivian immigration office is in Villazón on Av República de Argentina immediately after the frontier bridge open 0700-1900, Mon-Sat. Bolivia is 1 hr behind Argentina from Oct-Apr. From May-Sep Argentina loses an hr and keeps Bolivian time. The Argentine consulate in Villazón is 3 blocks south of the main plaza at the intersection of Av República de Argentina and Calle Río open weekdays 1000-1200 and 1400-1700, closed weekends and holidays. The Bolivian consulate in La Quiaca is on República Arabe Siria y San Juan open from 0830-1100 and 1400-1700 weekdays, Sat 0900-1200 (in theory). Travellers who need a visa to enter Bolivia are advised to get it before arriving in La Quiaca.

An uninspiring town, Villazón lies on the north bank of the river 898 km south **Villazón** of La Paz, the Bolivian capital. Avenida República de Argentina, the road from *Colour map 1, grid A2* the frontier bridge is lined with shops. *Population: 13,000* *Altitude: 3,443 m*

Sleeping Villazón has a surprising number of lodgings, all very cheap and offering little beyond the basic amenities. Dollars, bolivianos and Argentine pesos are accepted, but not credit cards. **D** *Residencial El Cortijo*, 20 de Mayo 338, T4696209. The best of the lot, intermittent hot water, restaurant. **F** per person *Grand Palace*, behind bus terminal, safe. **F** *Res Martínez*, opposite *Grand Palace*, T4696562. Hot water. Recommended. Next door is **F** *Res 10 de Febrero*, very basic. **F** *Res Panamericano*, Av República de Argentina, laundry facilities. Recommended. **F** *Res Bolivia*, 1 block from border, small rooms, run down, good value breakfast, hot showers extra.

Eating The town's culinary offerings are limited. The only bona fide restaurant is *Charke Kan*, next door to the *Hotel Grand Palace*. Off the plaza is *Snack El Pechegón*. There are also a handful of dubious-looking food stalls near the bus terminal, all of which are equally unappetizing. Most travellers suggest crossing the border to eat in La Quiaca.

Transport Bus Terminal is near the plaza, 5 blocks north of the border. To **Potosí**, several between 0830 and 1830, 10-15 hrs, US$7-8 (up to 24 hrs in wet weather). To **Tupiza**, 0700 and 1500, US$2.50. To **Tarija**, a beautiful journey but most buses go overnight only, daily at 1900/2000, US$6.50, 6 hrs. To **La Paz**, several companies, 25 hrs, US$17.25, even though the buses are called 'direct', you may have to change in Potosí, perhaps to another company. Argentine bus companies have offices opposite the terminal but buses leave from La Quiaca. Taxi to the frontier bridge US$0.50. **Train** Station about 1 km north of the frontier on the main road; taxi US$2.50. To **Oruro** (very dusty and cold), via Tupiza, Atocha and Uyuni, Mon and Thu at 1630, US$5.60; Tue and Fri at 1600, US$7.50. Latest reports suggest that trains go no further than Uyuni. The ticket office opens at 0800; expect long queues.

The Northwest

Directory Banks There is no bank in town but there are several *casas de cambio* on Av República de Argentina approaching the border: **Cambio Porvenir** is rumoured to be the best, but rates vary. Hotels and shops probably change small amounts only. Difficult to change TC's and terrible rates offered. Credit cards are not accepted anywhere. Communications **Post office** and **Entel** are in the same building, on Av República de Argentina opposite bus terminal. Both are open weekdays 0700-1800 (Entel sometimes until 2100) and Sat 0800-1200.

Northeast from Jujuy

Route 34 follows the valley of the Río San Francisco which flows along the base of the eastern foothills and into the Río Bermejo. The road provides alternative routes to Bolivia and access to two of Argentina's three cloudforest parks.

San Pedro de Jujuy
Phone code: 03844
Population: 50,000
Altitude: 578 m

A sugar town San Pedro de Jujuy lies 63 km east of Jujuy. The Ingenio La Esperanza, 4 km east, is a sugar-mill with hospital, housing and a recreation centre, formerly owned by the English Leach brothers. There is a small historical museum in the Centro Cultural, with displays on local archaeology and folklore. ■ *Mon-Fri 0900-1300, 1600-2000.*

Sleeping and eating C/D *Alex II*, Leach 467, T420526, fan. C*Alex I*, Tello 436, T420299, also **D** without bath. **C** *Vélez Sarsfield*, V Sarsfield 154, T422310, also **D** without bath. **C/D** *Nasa*, Alsina 54, T422577, with breakfast. An excellent restaurant is at *Sociedad Sirio-Libanesa* on the plaza.

Transport Bus To Jujuy, US$2.50, 1½ hrs. To **Embarcación**, Atahualpa, US$6.50, 2½ hrs.

Libertador General San Martín
Phone code 03866
Km 113

Commonly known as Libertador, this is another sugar town with a big sugar mill, the Ingenio Ledesma, on the southern outskirts. Of little interest, it is the stepping off point for the Parque Nacional Calilegua. Sleeping and eating at **AB** *Posada del Sol*, Ceibo s/n, T424900, with breakfast, pool, **E** *Res Gloria*, Urquiza 270, hot water and *Sociedad Boliviana*, Victoria 711, which is where the locals eat.

Parque Nacional Calilegua
125 km NE of Jujuy

Vegetation varies dramatically according to altitude

This park, covering 76,360 ha, protects an area of peaks, sub-tropical valleys and cloudforest on the eastern slopes of the Serranía de Calilegua. The highest peaks are Cerro Amarillo (3,720 m) and Cerro Hermoso (3,200 m). Several rivers flow southeast across the park into the Río Ledesma. There are over 300 species of bird including the red-faced guan and the condor. Among the 60 species of mammal are tapirs, pumas, otters and *taruca* (Andean deer).

Route 83 unpaved climbs northwest across the park, providing access to the southeast sections and splendid views. The best trek is to the summit of Cerro Amarillo, three days round trip from the entrance. At Alto Calilegua near the base of Cerro Amarillo, there is an interesting shepherds' settlement. It is possible to walk west from the park to Humahuaca and Tilcara (allow at least four days).

Climate Subtropical with a dry season. Mean temperatures range from 17°C in winter to 28°C in summer. Mean annual rainfall is 2,000 mm, falling mainly in summer.

Access Park entrance is at Aguas Negras, 12 km northwest of Libertador General San Martín, reached by Route 83 which runs off Route 34 just north of town. Hitching possible. Best time for visiting is outside the rainy season (November-March).

Park services   Park headquarters are on San Lorenzo s/n, in Calilegua, 4 km north-east of Libertador, T(0886) 22046. There are 2 ranger stations, at Aguas Negras and at Mesada de las Colmenas, 13 km further northwest along Route 83.

Camping   site at Aguas Negras (drinking water from river nearby, and some cook-ing facilities and tables). To camp at Mesada de las Colmenas ask permission at Aguas Blancas.

Transport   Trucks run by *Empresa Valle Grande*, Libertad 780, leave Libertador, Tue and Sat, 0730, 6 hrs if road conditions are good, very crowded, returning Sun and Thu 1000. Check with Sr Arcona (the driver, everyone knows him) in Libertador whether the truck is going. Weather unpredictable. Or contact Gustavo Lozano at Los Claveles 358, Barrio Jardín, T421647, who will contact Angel Caradonna to pick you up.

Routes to Bolivia

There are two routes into Bolivia from this area, one via Pocitos and the other via Aguas Blancas. The route via Aguas Blancas is the shorter of the two and provides the opportunity to visit the spectacular cloudforests of the Parque Nacional Baritú, one of the most inaccessible national parks in Argentina. The route via Pocitos is longer (though this may shorten your journey in Bolivia) and recom-mended in wet weather when roads into Bolivia from Aguas Blancas are difficult.

From Libertador General San Martín, Route 34 runs northeast 244 km, to the Bolivian frontier at **Pocitos**.

Via Pocitos

Parque Nacional Calilegua

N

Not to scale

Route 83 to Valle Grande ►

Cerro Amarillo

Serranía de Socabón

Cerro Hermoso

Mesada de las Colmenas

Route 34 to Tartagal ►

Aguas Blancas

Calilegua

Río San Lorenzo

Libertador General San Martín

Río Ledesma

▼ Route 34 to Güemes & Jujuy

park ranger post
— unpaved road

The Northwest

Embarcación
Phone code: 03878
Population: 13,000
217 km NE of Jujuy

Embarcación was built as the western terminus of the Trans-Chaco railway line to Formosa which no longer operates. Two km out of town is the Loma Protestant mission for Matuco and Toba Indians, who sell unpainted pottery.

Sleeping and eating B *Punta Norte*, España 434, T471035, clean, a/c, friendly. **D** *Centro*, Yrigoyen y 9 de Julio, T471073, a/c. *Del Pilar*, España 117, T471195, breakfast extra, a/c. Restaurant of *Sociedad Sirio-Libanesa*, H Yrigoyen and 9 de Julio, cheap and good.

Transport Bus To **Orán**, 1 hr, US$1.70. To **Pocitos** change at Tartagal, making sure your ticket is stamped with the next bus time or you won't be allowed on it. To **Buenos Aires** US$91. To **Salta** US$14.50, 3 a day. To **Formosa** daily at 1300, 17 hrs, US$40, Atahualpa, but frequently cancelled; alternative is to take bus to Pichanal, US$1.25, several companies, change for J V Gonzales, US$10, 1600, and change again for Resistencia, 2215, then take a bus to Formosa.

Tartagal
Population: 35,000
Altitude: 350 m
Phone code: 03875
Km 306

An agricultural centre with a small museum featuring displays on animals of the Chaco and regional folk art. ■ *Mon-Fri 0700-1300, 1500-2100.* The director, Ramón Ramos, is very informative about the region. Animal masks and pottery are made by Indians at Campo Durán, 32 km north.

Sleeping B *Tropico*, Rivadavia 571, T421341. A/c, expensive but clean. **AB** *Argentino*, San Martín 617, T421117. With breakfast, also suites. **B** *Espinillo*, San Martín 122, T421007, a/c, without breakfast. **B** *Res City*, Alberdi 79, T421558. Without breakfast, a/c. **C** *America*, 20 de Febrero 525, T421404. Without breakfast. **Camping** At the Complejo Deportivo, southeast of centre.

Frontier
with Bolivia

Pocitos lies on the frontier 56 km north of Tartagal and 362 km northeast of Jujuy. Crossing can take time here, depending on the availability of officials. Argentine customs and immigration at the frontier. Beware that theft at customs has been reported. **Sleeping** at **E** *Hotel Buen Gusto*, just tolerable.

Transport Bus Daily service to **Buenos Aires**, via Salta, La Internacional; frequent services to **Tartagal** and **Embarcación**.

Into Bolivia The road continues via Yacuiba, 4 km north of the frontier, to Tarija, 280 km north. From Yacuiba there are regular bus services to Tarija and Santa Cruz de la Sierra, departing mainly 1700-1900.

Via Aguas
Blancas

At Pichanal, 88 km northeast of Flamingos, 16 km before Embarcación, Route 50 crosses Route 34 and runs along the valley of the Río Bermejo to the Bolivian frontier at Aguas Blancas 69 km north.

Orán
Population: 35,000
Altitude: 350 m
Phone code: 03878
Km 20

Formally San Ramón de la Nueva, Orán is the only town along this road but it is one of little interest. There is a small museum in the Centro Cultural at San Martín y López y Planes which includes displays on the local sugar industry and on local indigenous cultures.

Sleeping AB *Alto Verde*, Pellegrini 671, T421214. Parking, pool, a/c. **C** *Crillón*, 25 de Mayo 225, T421101. Breakfast extra. **B** *Argentino*, Bolivia 65, T421910. Without breakfast. **C** *Colonial*, Pizarro y Colón, T421103. With breakfast, parking, a/c. **E** per person *Centro*, Pellegrini 332, T421615. **C** *Res Crisol*, López y Planes, hot water, friendly. Recommended.

Transport **Bus** To **Aguas Blancas** every 45 mins, US$2. To **Güemes**, 8 a day, US$10. To **Salta**, *Veloz del Norte* and *Atahualpa*, 3 daily each, US$17.50. To **Tucumán**, direct, at 2130, connecting for *Mendoza* bus which leaves at 1300. To **Jujuy** at 1200 daily. To **Formosa** (connection for Paraguay), US$28, 14 hrs, leaving Tue, Thu, Sat at 0930. To **Embarcación**, US$3. To **Tartagal** daily at 0630 and 1800.

Buses are subject to searches for drugs & contraband: long delays are possible

Aguas Blancas lies 49 km north of Orán on the west bank of the Río Bermejo, opposite the Bolivian town of Bermejo to which it is linked by a bridge. There is no accommodation, nowhere to change money and Bolivianos are not accepted in Argentina south of here. There are shops and several restaurants including *El Rinconcito de los Amigos*. The Argentine customs and immigration is open from 0700 to 1200 and 1500 to 1900; insist on getting an exit stamp. There is no exit tax.

Frontier with Bolivia

Transport **Bus** To **Orán** every 45 mins, US$2, luggage checks on bus.

Into Bolivia Bermejo has a population of 13,000 and is at am altitude 415 m. There are several hotels and 2 *casas de cambio*, both on the main street. From Bermejo the road continues (unpaved except for 50 km) following the east bank of the Río Bermejo towards Tarija, 210 km north. The views are spectacular (sit on the left). This route is not recommended during or just after the rainy season. There are buses to Tarija, twice daily, 5 hrs.

Situated northwest of Aguas Blancas on the west bank of the Río Bermejo, this is one of the most inaccessible parks in the country. Covering 72,439 ha of the

Parque Nacional Barítú

Parque Nacional Barítú

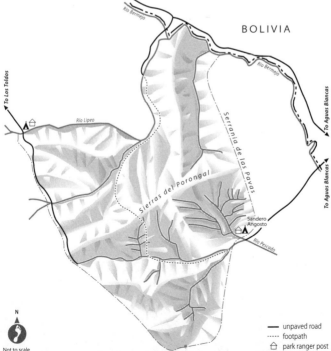

Not to scale

— unpaved road
···· footpath
⌂ park ranger post

eastern slopes of the Andean foothills and rising to around 2,000 m, the park is crossed by several streams which feed north into the Río Lipeo (and thence into the Bermejo) and south into the Río Pescado. Most of the park is covered by cloudforest, vegetation varying with increasing altitude. Fauna is also abundant and varied. There are no facilities apart from ranger posts and campsites at the entrances.

Climate Mean temperatures vary from 21°C in winter to 30°C in summer. Mean annual rainfall is 2,000 mm, with the heaviest rainfall in summer.

Difficult during & immediately after wet weather

Access There are 3 entrances, all of them difficult to reach: at Sendero Angosto, reached by a dirt road which runs west, 30 km, from near the customs post in Aguas Blancas; at Los Pozos, north of the park, which can be reached by crossing into Bolivia from Aguas Blancas, following the road north along the Río Bermejo and then recrossing the frontier at La Mamora; from Los Toldos to the west of the park, reached by following the same route through Bolivia and recrossing the river further north.

The Northeast

8

The Northeast

The great attraction of this region is, without question, Iguazú Falls. Situated on a tributary of the Alto Paraná on the frontier with Brazil, these are the most magnificent waterfalls in South America and one of the most popular destinations for visitors to Argentina.

However the region has other gems. South of Iguazú lie the provinces of Misiones, Corrientes and Entre Ríos, each of which is markedly distinct. Misiones has a hilly landscape and red soil, much of it covered with forests of pine and cedar and broad-leaved trees, reminiscent of parts of Brazil. Corrientes is marshy and deeply-wooded, with low grass-covered hills rising from the marshes. Entre Ríos is covered by plains of rich pasture land. West of the Río Paraná lie the provinces of Santa Fe, Chaco and Formosa All three are covered by flat plains, the latter two by the Argentine Chaco, much of which is arid desert.

The Río Uruguay, little visited by non-Argentine travellers, includes several popular Argentine weekend resorts among them Guayeguaychú and Colón. Along the Río Paraná are the important cities of Rosario, Santa Fe, Paraná, Corrientes and Resistencia; while none of these could be considered a major tourist destination, they all offer distinct perspectives on Argentine life. Rosario is one of the most vibrant centres of popular culture, home to some of Argentina's best rock musicians and artists.

The centre of the most famous complex of Jesuit missions can be seen at Misiones; the best can be seen at San Ignacio Mini. Nature lovers, particularly bird-watchers, will want to visit the marshes of Iberá and parts of the Chaco.

Background

Geography

The northeast is dominated by the river systems of the Paraná/Paraguay and the Uruguay. Between the rivers, a distance which varies from about 210 km near Santa Fe to 390 km in northern Corrientes, lies Argentine Mesopotamia: the provinces of Entre Ríos, Corrientes, and Misiones. The normal rainfall is about 2,000 mm, but the rains are not spread uniformly and drain off quickly through the sandy soil. On the west bank of the Paraná the pampas extend north across most of Santa Fe province, the soil becoming gradually poorer further north. North of Santa Fe is the Argentine Chaco, a great plain which stretches west from the Paraná to the foothills of the Andes.

Climate   Winters are mild; summers are hot with rain falling in short, sharp storms. Both Entre Ríos and Corrientes often suffer from summer drought. In Misiones the rainfall is heavy: twice as heavy as in Entre Ríos. The days are hot, and the nights cool.

Economy

Santa Fe is an important agricultural province, producing some 35% of the country's wheat and over 50% of its sunflower seeds; other crops include flax, lentils, soya and potatoes. Much of Entre Ríos and Corrientes is still pastoral, a land of large *estancias* raising cattle and sheep. Maize is largely grown in southern Entre Ríos, which is also the most important producer of linseed and poultry in Argentina. The northeastern part of the province, around Concordia, is the main citrus fruit area in the country; rice is also grown in this area and commercial forestry is important. In Corrientes, along the banks of the Paraná between the cities of Corrientes and Posadas, rice and oranges are grown. Misiones is the largest producer of *yerba mate*: 180,000 ha are dedicated to its cultivation. Citrus, tobacco, timber and tung oil are also produced. The Chaco is mainly devoted to cattle ranching, though tannin and cotton are also cultivated.

Communications   Communications in the area are by road and by the Ríos Uruguay and Paraná, neither of which is very good for navigation. Bridges connect Fray Bentos (Uruguay) and Puerto Unzué, near Gualeguaychú, and Paysandú (Uruguay) and Colón, and there is a road link over the Salto Grande dam from Concordia to Salto (Uruguay).

History

Mesopotamia was first colonized by Spaniards pushing south from Asunción to reoccupy Buenos Aires; Santa Fe was founded in 1573, Corrientes in 1588. From about 1880 there were Jewish agricultural settlements in Entre Ríos, promoted by Baron Hirsch for victims of pogroms in the Czarist Empire (see 'Los gauchos judíos' by Alberto Gerchunoff). Vestiges of these settlements remain at Domínguez (museum) and Basavilbaso, and across the river in Moisesville (Santa Fe).

Misiones Province was first occupied by the Jesuit Fathers fleeing from the Brazilian Alto-Paraná region with their devoted Indian followers. During this century Misiones has attracted large scale immigration from Eastern Europe, from Paraguay and from the rest of Mesopotamia.

On a mission

Between 1609, when they built their first reducción or mission in the region of Guaíra in present day Brazil, and 1767, when they were expelled from Spanish America, the Jesuits founded about 50 missions around the upper reaches of the Ríos Paraná, Paraguay and Uruguay. In 1627 the northern missions around Guaíra were attacked by the slave-hunting Bandeirantes from São Paulo, forcing them to flee southwards. Some 10,000 converts, led by the priests, floated on 700 rafts down the Río Parapanema into the Paraná, only to find their route blocked by the Guaíra Falls. Pushing on for 8 days through dense virgin forest on both sides of the river, they built new boats below the falls and continued their journey. Some 725 km from their old homes, they re-established their missions and trained militias which protected them from further attacks.

Copying the layout of Franciscan missions, the Jesuits built their reducciones around a central square, with the church in the middle of one side: alongside the church were the cloisters, workshops, priests' quarters and the cemetery. The living quarters of the Guraraní occupied the remaining three sides. Each mission was run by two priests, other Europeans being strictly excluded. Often occupying rich lands and efficiently organized, the missions prospered: the Guaraní grew traditional crops such as manioc, sweet potatoes and maize, plants imported from Europe like wheat and oranges as well as looking after herds of cattle, horses and sheep. The missions became major producers of yerba maté, favoured by the Jesuits as an alternative to alcohol. Apart from the common lands, used for crops and animals, the Guaraní farmed individual plots.

The decision by Carlos III to expel the Jesuits from South America in 1767 was made under conditions of the highest secrecy: sealed orders were sent to the colonies with strict instructions that they should not be opened in advance. On the appointed date over 2,000 members of the order were put on ships for Italy after which Jesuit property was auctioned. The Jesuit schools and colleges were taken over by the Franciscans and Dominicans; the missions fell into disuse and many were destroyed in 1817 on the orders of the Paraguayan dictator Rodríguez de Francia.

Controversial since the founding of their first missions, the Jesuits had attracted many enemies. The wealth and economic power of the missions angered landowners and traders, their control over Guaraní annoyed landowners short of labour and rumours circulated that the missions contained mines and hoards of precious metals. Also in 1750 a treaty between Spain and Portugal settling their border disputes in the area placed seven missions under Portuguese control. The Jesuits resisted with arms, justifying Spanish and Portugese suspicion of the power of the order.

Disagreement over the role of the Order has continued to the present day: some, such as R B Cunninghame Graham, saw them as a 'vanished arcadia' and a kind of primitive socialism; others have accused the Jesuits of enslaving the Guaraní and forcing them to adopt Christianity. The Order's supporters stress its role in defending the Guaraní from enslavement and exploitation by the Spanish and Portugese and refer to missions as 'lost cities'.

Only four of the missions show signs of their former splendor: San Ignacio Mini in Argentina, Jesús and Trinidad in Paraguay and São Miguel in Brazil. The first three can be visited with ease from Posadas or Encarnación, as can several others, including Santa Ana, Loreto and San Cosmé y Damián, all of which are described in the book.

The Río Uruguay

The Río Uruguay is formed by the waters of two rivers, the Pelotas and the Canoas, which rise in the Serra do Mar in southern Brazil. It is over 1,600 km long and its widest, on the bend between Puerto Unzué and Fray Bentos, it is 25 km across. The river is Argentina's eastern boundary with Uruguay and Brazil.

There are no regular passenger shipping services. From Buenos Aires Route 9 runs northwest to Zárate, where the Paraná de las Palmas and Paraná Guazú rivers, and the Isla Talavera which lies between, are crossed by the beautiful Zárate and Brazo Largo suspension bridges (toll US$6). From here Route 14 continues north along the west bank of the Río Uruguay. At Ceibas, 76 km from Zárate, Route 12 branches northwest to Gualeguay.

Gualeguay
Phone code: 03444
Colour map 2, grid C1
Population: 30,000
134 km from Zárate

Gualeguay lies on the west bank of the Río Gualeguay and is situated in the centre of one of the richest cattle and sheep ranching regions in Entre Ríos. Inside the **Iglesia San Antonio**, on the central Plaza Constitución, there are frescos which include reproductions of works by Rafael, Rembrandt and Rubens. The tourist office is on eastern outskirts of town, eight blocks east of centre.

Sleeping and eating **AB** *Gran Gualeguay*, Monte Caseros 217, T423085. Poor value. **E** *Italia*, Palacios 1, T424575, with bath, friendly. There is a municipal **campsite**. In the centre there are practically no restaurants, but the *Jockey Club* and the *Club Social*, both on the main square close to the *Gran Hotel Gualeguay*, cater also for non-members. The *Club Social* has a very nice atmosphere, good food, and you might be invited to see films on certain nights.

Sport There is good fishing at the confluence of the Ríos Gualeguay and Pavón, 43 km south. Excursions are offered in launches, minimum 2 days, details from tourist office.

Gualeguaychú
Phone code: 03446
Colour map 2, grid C1
Population: 64,500
220 km N of Buenos Aires
13 km E of Route 14

There is a lively pre-Lenten Carnival

A pleasant town, with an attractive costanera, Gualeguaychú has become a popular weekend resort for *porteños* since the opening of the Zárate-Brazo Largo Bridges. On the opposite bank of the river is the Parque Unzué, 110 ha, with sports facilities and sailing clubs. There is a large German immigrant population. There are some interesting museums. **Museo de la Ciudad**, San Luis y Jujuy, in a former mansion built in 1835, US$1. **Museo Arqueológico**, in the Casa de la Cultura, 25 de Mayo 734, with artefacts from indigenous cultures of the Uruguay basin. **Solar de los Haedo**, San José y Rivadavia (on Plaza), in the oldest house in the city, which served as Garibaldi's headquarters when he sacked the city in 1845. Filled with artefacts of the Haedo family. ■ *Guided tour (Spanish) US$1, Wed-Sat 0900-1145, Fri/Sat also at 1600-1945.*

Scarce at weekends (few single rooms to be found) & during Carnival. The tourist office has a list of family accommodation

Sleeping **AB** *Embajador*, San Martín y 3 de Febrero, T424414. Casino. **AB** *Alemán*, Bolívar 535, T426153. German-spoken, without breakfast. Recommended. **AB** *París*, Bolívar y Pellegrini, T423850, F26260. With breakfast, fan, restaurant, comfortable. **A** *Berlin*, Bolívar 733, T/F425111. German spoken, with breakfast, comfortable. **AB** *Viedma*, Bolívar 530, T424262, garage extra. **B** *Victoria*, Bolívar 565, T426469. Opposite terminal, small rooms, modern, with breakfast. **C** *Brutti*, Bolívar 591, T426048. Shabby, good value, without breakfast, fan. **C** *Amalfi*, 25 de Mayo 571, T425677. With breakfast, good beds. **D** *Mayo*, 3 de Febrero y Bolívar, T427661. Uncomfortable beds, with bath.

Camping *La Delfina* in the Parque Unzué, T422293. *Costa Azul*, T423984. *Puerta del Sol*, T423700, and *Playa Chica*, T425709, all near river. *Ñandubaysal*, 15 km east, T426009, best.

£4000 worth of holiday vouchers to be won!

... that can be claimed against any exodus, **Peregrine or Gecko's holiday, a choice of around 570 holidays that set industry standards for responsible tourism in 90 countries across seven continents.**

exodus

The UK's leading adventurous travel company, with over 25 years' experience in running the most exciting holidays in 80 different countries. We have an unrivalled choice of trips, from a week exploring the hidden corners of Tuscany to a high altitude trek to Everest Base Camp or 3 months travelling across South America. If you want to do something a little different, chances are you'll find it in one of our brochures.

Peregrine

Australia's leading quality adventure travel company, Peregrine aims to explore some of the world's most interesting and inaccessible places. Providing exciting and enjoyable holidays that focus in some depth on the lifestyle, culture, history, wildlife, wilderness and landscapes of areas that are usually quite different to our own. There is an emphasis on the outdoors, using a variety of transport and staying in a range of accommodation, from comfortable hotels to tribal huts.

Gecko's

Gecko's holidays will get you to the best places with the minimum of hassle. They are designed for younger people who like independent travel but don't have the time to organise everything themselves. Be prepared to take the rough with the smooth, these holidays are for active people with a flexible approach to travel.

To enter the competition, simply tear out the postcard and return it to Exodus Travels, 9 Weir Road, London SW12 0LT. Or go to the competition page on www.exodus.co.uk and register online. Two draws will be made, Easter 2001 and Easter 2002, and the winner of each draw will receive £2000 in travel vouchers. The closing date for entry will be 1st March 2002. If you do not wish to receive further information about these holidays, please tick here. ☐ No purchase necessary. Plain paper entries should be sent to the above address. The prize value is non-transferable and there is no cash alternative. Winners must be over 18 years of age and must sign and adhere to operators' standard booking conditions. A list of prizewinners will be available for a period of one month from the draw by writing to the above address. For a full list of terms and conditions please write to the above address or visit our website.

To receive a brochure, please tick the relevant boxes below (maximum number of brochures 2) or telephone (44) 20 8772 3822.

exodus	Peregrine	Gecko's
☐ Walking & Trekking	☐ Himalaya	☐ Egypt, Jordan & Israel
☐ Discovery & Adventure	☐ China	☐ South America
☐ European Destinations	☐ South East Asia	☐ Africa
☐ Overland Journeys	☐ Antarctica	☐ South East Asia
☐ Biking Adventures	☐ Africa	☐ India
☐ Multi Activity	☐ Arctic	

Please give us your details:

Name: --

Address: --

Postcode: --

e-mail: --

Which footprint guide did you take this from?

----

getaway tonight on **www.exodus.co.uk**

exodus
The Different Holiday

getaway tonight on

www.exodus.co.uk

exodus
The Different Holiday

---

exodus
9 Weir Road
LONDON
SW12 0BR

BUSINESS REPLY SERVICE
Licence No SW4909

Transport Air Airport west of town. **Bus** Terminal in centre of town at Bolívar y Chile. To **Fray Bentos**, 1 hr, US$3, 2 a day, *ETA*. To **Mercedes**, 1½ hrs, US$4, 2 a day, *ETA*. To **Concepción del Uruguay**, **Colón** and **Concordia**. To **Buenos Aires** US$15, 4 hrs, *Flechabus* and *El Rápido*, 6 a day each.

Directory Banks *Banco Internacional Cooperativa*, 25 de Mayo y Perón, changes cash; *Casa de Cambio: Daniel*, 3 de Febrero 128. **Tourist offices** Costanera y 25 de Mayo, open 0800-2000.

Situated 33 km south of Gualeguaychú, the **Libertador General San Martin Bridge** (5.4 km long) provides the most southerly route across the Río Uruguay, to Fray Bentos. Vehicle toll US$4; pedestrians and cyclists can only cross on motor vehicles, though officials may arrange lifts.

Frontier with Uruguay

Customs and immigration At opposite ends of the bridge. This is a very uncomplicated crossing, formalities taking about 10 mins. The Argentine consulate is at Sarandí 3195, Fray Bentos. Passport details are noted when booking bus tickets and passed to officials at border. Passports are inspected on the bus.

Fray Bentos is the southernmost port on the east bank of Río Uruguay. A friendly little town with an attractive *costanera*, Fray Bentos is famous for its none other that its meat-packing factory (*frigorífico*) known as **El Anglo**, which has been restored as the **Museo de La Revolución Industrial**. ■ *Daily except Mon, entry by guided tour only, US$1.50, 1000, 1430 (1000, 1130 and 1700 in summer), tour 1½ hrs in Spanish, may provide leaflet in English.*

There are beaches to the northeast and southwest and also at Las Cañas, 8 km south (where there is a tourist complex including motels, T2597, **C**, campsite, sports facilities and services).

Into Uruguay: Fray Bentos
*Population: 22,000
44 km SE of
Gualeguaychú;
7 km W of the
international bridge*

Gualeguaychú

■ Sleeping
1 Alemán   4 Brutti   7 Victoria
2 Amalfi   5 Embajador   8 Viedma
3 Berlin   6 París

The Northeast

Corned beef and oxo

To generations of British people brought up in the early and mid-20th century, Fray Bentos means corned beef: the name was the most famous trademark of what for many was a staple part of the diet. Dating from 1859 and situated on the edge of one of the best natural harbours on the Río Uruguay, the frigorífico (meat-packing plant) became the first factory in Uruguay to produce a meat extract by a method invented by the German chemist Julius Leibig. This extract was sold in Britain under the name Oxo. Operating with British capital the Leibig Extract of Meat Company expanded the frigorífico until by the 1930s it was employing some 5,000 workers of the town's population of 12,000. By then 2,500 cattle were being killed by every 8 hr shift of 200 workers and over 6,000 tons of meat were being processed daily and loaded straight onto vessels in the plant's own port. Peak production periods were during the two World Wars as the frigoríficos tried to meet the demand for corned beef and other products to feed the British and allied armed forces. Nothing was wasted: animal remains were turned into fertilizers and it was said that the only part of an animal not used was the 'moo'.

The frigorífico was sold off to the Uruguayan government in 1961, though the Fray Bentos name had long been turned into a trade mark for products which had no connection with the town. The factory was closed, at very short notice, in 1980. Ten years later work began to turn it into a museum and business park.

There were many other frigoríficos in this part of South America, some of which, now modernised, still operate. What makes Fray Bentos unusual, if not unique, is the preservation of buildings and machinery from its heyday. Covering some 55 ha, the buildings include the offices, beautifully restored and lacking only personnel. Much of the machinery, though old, is still in working order. Outside, in the Barrio El Anglo, the workers' and managers' housing can be seen. Among the 30 enterprises to move into the business park have been a restaurant, 'Wolves', and a discotheque called 'Fuel Oil'.

Sleeping **A** *Gran Hotel Fray Bentos*, Paraguay y Zorilla, T2358, overlooking river, casino. **B** *Plaza*, 18 de Julio y 25, T2363. Comfortable. **D** *Colonial*, 25 de Mayo 3293, T2260. Attractive old building with patio. **E** per person *25 de Mayo*, 25 de Mayo y Lavalleja, T2586, basic. **Camping** At the *Club Remeros*, near the river and at Colegio Laureles, 1 km from centre, T2236.

Eating *Olla*, 18 de Julio near Plaza Constitución, seafood and pasta, good value. Several other cafés and pizzerias on 18 de Julio near Plaza Constitución.

Transport Terminal at 18 de Julio y Blanes, buses call here, but do not alight as buses also call at company offices around Plaza Constitución. To **Montevideo**, *CUT*, 4½ hrs, 6 a day, US$11.75, also Chadre, US$12.50. To **Buenos Aires**, *bus de la carrera*, 3½ hrs, US$18. To **Gualeguaychú**, 1 hr, US$3, 2 a day.

Directory Banks Cambio Fagalde, Plaza Constitución, open Mon-Fri 0800-1900, Sat 0800-1230. **Tourist offices** In Museo Solari, Plaza Constitución, T2233, very friendly.

Concepción del Uruguay

Phone code: 03442
Colour map 2, grid C1
Population: 65,500
74 km N of
Gualeguaychú

Situated opposite several islands on the Río Uruguay, Concepción del Uruguay is a major port and service centre for a prosperous agricultural region. Founded in 1783, it was capital of Entre Ríos province between 1813-21 and 1860-1883.

The old town is centred on **Plaza Ramírez**; on its west side is the Italian neo-classical-style **Basílica de la Concepción Inmaculada**, which contains the remains of General Urquiza. Next to it is the **Colegio Superior del Uruguay**, considered the first secular school in the country, though sadly its 19th-century buildings were largely replaced in 1935. **Banco Pelay**, 5 km northeast, is a 3 km stretch of beach, considered the longest riverine beach in South America. **Museo Casa del Delio Panizza**, Galarza y Supremo Entrerriano, is in a mansion dating from 1793 and contains 19th-century furnishings and artefacts. The tourist office is on 9 de Julio 844, T425820.

Sights

Palacio San José, 35 km west of the town, is the former mansion of General Urquiza. Now a museum with artefacts from Urquiza's life and a collection of period furniture, the palace stands in a beautiful park with an artificial lake. ■ *Mon-Fri 0900-1300, 1400-1800, Sat/Sun 0900-1245, 1400-1745, US$1.50, written explanations in Spanish, French and English. Highly recommended. Getting there: Reached by Itape buses to 3 km from the Palacio, US$3, 45 mins.*

Excursions

L per person *Estancia San Pedro*, outside Concepción, T427459. Owned by descendents of Urquiza, old rooms full of antiques, very good. **B** *Res Fiuri*, Sarmiento 779, T427016, attractive. **B** *Carlos I*, Eva Perón 117, T426776. **C** *Gran*, Eva Perón 114, T422851. **C** *Virrey*, González 2075, T425017, F25007. **C** *Ramírez*, Martínez 50, T425106. Above bus terminal. **E** *Hosp Los Tres Nenes*, Galarza 1233, near terminal, good. **Camping** *Banco Pelay*, 5 km northeast, T424003. *El Canguro*, opposite terminal, good food, reasonably priced. *Rocamora*, Rocamora y Millán. Bus terminal bar for *tenedor libre* meals.

Sleeping & eating

Fiesta Nacional de la Playa, second half of Jan, with water and beach sports; Carnival.

Festivals

Bus Terminal at Rocamora y Los Constituyentes, 11 blocks west of Plaza Ramírez (bus 1 to centre or remise, US$1). To **Buenos Aires**, frequent, 4½ hrs, US$15. To **Paraná**, 5 hrs. To **Colón** 45 mins. To **Paysandú** (Uruguay) 1 hr, US$4.

Transport

Colón was founded in 1863 as a port for the Swiss colony of San José, 10 km north. The river is more picturesque here with an attractive *costanera*, 7 km of sandy beaches, and cliffs visible from a considerable distance. Nearby is a bridge linking Colón with Paysandú, Uruguay. The town is known for *artesanía* shops along 12 de Abril, and there is a large handicrafts fair at Carnival time. Just outside the town is the Complejo Termal Colón, with open-air thermal pools, US$2. The tourist office is on Avenida Costanera y Gouchón.

Colón

Phone code: 03447
Colour map 2, grid C1
Population: 15,000
45 km N of Concepción del Uruguay

Sleeping **L** *Quirinale*, Quirós s/n, T421978. Casino. **AB** *Plaza*, 12 de Abril y Belgrano, T421043. With breakfast, a/c, modern. **AB** *Holimasú*, Belgrano 28, T421305, F21303. With breakfast. **B** *Palmar*, Ferrari 285, T421952, good. **B** *Vieja Calera*, Bolívar 344, T421139. With breakfast, a/c. **C** *Ver-Wei*, 25 de Mayo 10, T421972. Without breakfast, new ownership. **Families** rent rooms – the Boujon family, Maipú 430, **C**, good breakfast and other meals extra. Recommended. **Apartments** for rent from Sr Ramón Gallo, Paysandú, T472-3280, with kitchen, bathroom, hot showers, close to bus terminal. **Camping** 2 sites on river bank: *Camping Municipal Norte*, T421484, excellent facilities, cheapest. *Piedras Coloradas*, T421451/423548. Recommended.

Eating *Comedor El Rayo*, Paysandú 372. *Pizzería Luisa*, San Martín 346. *La Rueda*, San Martín y 3 de Febrero. *Marito*, Gral Urquiza y Andrade. *El Viejo Almacén*, Urquiza y Paso, good fish.

Urquiza

The most important figure in the history of Entre Ríos, Justo José de Urquiza, is a contradictory figure. While his fame rests on his role in the overthrow of the dictator Rosas, Urquiza was a provincial caudillo leader whose decision to resist Rosas was based more on political calculation and personal interest than on principle. An autocrat who, after the defeat of Rosas was known in Buenos Aires as 'the other Rosas', Urquiza was a lifelong advocate of educational improvement and in later life an enthusiastic promoter of railway- building.

Born in 1801, Urquiza's early life was perhaps typical of the landowner of the period: mixing business with provincial politics and playing a leading role in the warfare between provincial caudillos of the 1830s and 1840s, he became provincial governor in 1841. Business interests as well as political rivalry brought him into conflict with Rosas: though the biggest landowner in the province and owner of meat-salting plants, his landholdings were of little value as long as Rosas blockaded the Río Paraná to enforce the dominance of Buenos Aires.

After his victory over Rosas at Caseros (1852), Urquiza led his troops into Buenos Aires where they massacred Rosas's supporters. Named director of the Argentine Confederation, he later became its first president. Following the defeat of the Confederation armies by Buenos Aires in 1861, he retired to the Palacio San José, where he dedicated himself to his business and philanthropic interests. By 1869 his personal fortune was said to include 600,000 cattle, 500,000 sheep, 20,000 horses and nearly a million hectares of land. Like so many caudillos he met a violent death, assassinated in 1870 in his own house by agents paid by his former ally, López Jordán, the caudillo of Santa Fe.

Transport Bus Terminal at Paysandú y Sourigues. To **Buenos Aires**, 4 a day, US$18, 5 hrs. To **Concepción del Uruguay**, Copay and Paccot, 4 a day, 2 on Sun, US$2. To **Concordia**, US$6 (2½ hrs) and **Paraná** daily. To **Córdoba** 4 a week. To **Paysandú, Uruguay**, US$3, 45 mins.

Frontier with Uruguay Seven kilometres south of Colón, the General Jose Artigas Bridge gives access to the Uruguayan city of Paysandú. Toll US$4.

Customs and immigration Argentine and Uruguayan formalities are both dealt with at Argentine end of the bridge. Easy crossing.

Into Uruguay: Paysandú
Population: 100,000
Phone code: 03722

Situated on the eastern bank of the Río Uruguay, 6 km from the international bridge, Paysandú is the second largest city in Uruguay. There are several fine late 19th- and early 20th-century buildings. Note particularly the **Teatro Florencio Sánchez** (1876), the **Jefatura de** Policia and the **Basílica de Nuestra Señora del Rosario** dating from 1860. Also worth a look is the **Monumento a la Perpetuidad**, the old cemetery. Museums include the **Museo de la Tradición**, north of town at the Balneario Municipal, which is worth a visit. ■ *Tue-Fri 1230-1700, Sat 0900-1200, Sun 1330-1700, reached by bus to Zona Industrial, gaucho articles*; and the **Museo Salesiano**, Florida 1278, attached to cathedral, interesting. ■ *Mon-Fri 0830-1130.*

Tourist offices Plaza de la Constitución, 18 de Julio 1226. Open Mon-Fri 0800-1900, Sat-Sun 0800-1800. For full details of accommodation and other services see the *South American Handbook*.

Yatay Palm

This tall and graceful palm (Syagrus yatay) is now mainly confined to the El Palmar National Park to which it gave its name. This palm was once found across the entire Pampas region, but particularly close to the Rio Uruguay and its tributaries. The introduction of widespread cattle ranching was to prove devastating: the young seedlings were just as tasty as the grass and now only full grown 150-200 year old palms are to be found except in protected areas where seedlings and young specimens of less than 30 years old may be found. The palms grow in groves or palmares and the trunks may reach 12 m in height with the fronds or leaves some 2 m in length.

On west bank of the Rio Uruguay, the park occupies a former *estancia* and covers 8,500 ha of gently undulating grassland and mature palm forest, which includes Yatay palms up to 12 m-high, some of which are hundreds of years old. Along the Río Uruguay and the streams (*arroyos*) which flow into it, there are gallery forests of subtropical trees and shrubs. There are also Indian tombs; on the edge of the Río Uruguay there are beaches and the remains of an 18th-century quarry and port. Fauna includes capybaras, foxes, otters and vizcachas as well as rheas, monk parakeets and several species of woodpecker.

The administration centre is in the east of the park, near the Río Uruguay. Nearby there are camping facilities (US$6 per person, electricity, hot water) with restaurant opposite, and a small shop. There is a small hotel 8 km north of the park. ■ *Getting there: Buses from Colón, 40 mins, US$2.50, will drop you at the entrance and it is easy to hitch the last 6 km to the park administration. Entry US$5.*

Parque Nacional El Palmar
51 km N of Colón and 53 km S of Concordia
Best to stay overnight: wildlife is more easily seen early morning or at sunset. Very popular at weekends in summer

Concordia

Situated a little downriver from the city of Salto, Uruguay, Concordia is an important service centre for the local agricultural economy. At Salto Grande, 18 km north, there is a large Argentine-Uruguayan hydro-electric dam, which

Phone code: 0345
Colour map 2, grid C1
Population: 93,800
104 km N of Colón

The Northeast

Parque Nacional El Palmar

creates an artificial lake, 80,000 ha, with excellent fishing. The dam provides a crossing to Salto. Above Salto Grande the river is generally known as the Alto Uruguay. Founded in 1832, Concordia soon became the most prosperous Argentine city on the Río Uruguay.

Sights The city centre lies about 1 km inland from the port, around the **Plaza 25 de Mayo**; on the southwestern side of the plaza is the cathedral (1899). Around the plaza are some fine buildings, notably the French style. Seven blocks further northwest, just off the Plaza Urquiza, is the **Palacio Arruabarreba**, a family mansion built in French style in 1919; it houses the **Museo Regional**, which has local and natural history collections. ■ *0800-2100 daily, entry free.* Some 5 km northeast is **Parque Rivadavia**, 70 ha of gentle hills and woodlands, in the centre of which are the ruins of the **Palacio San Carlos**. In 1888, two years after his arrival in Concordia, the Conde Eduardo de Machy, son of a French banker, bought the lands of the Parque Rivadavia from the descendents of the Urquiza family. After ordering the building of a mansion, he set up factories producing jams and ice, bringing in the best machinery from Europe and employing over 700 building workers. Three years later, in 1891, the Count left for Europe, never to return. The factories and the *palacio* were sold several times, before being burned down in 1938. The park offers good views of the river and there is also a motor-racing track. ■ *Getting there: Take bus No 2, one block from Plaza 25 de Mayo, to corner of Av Justo and Av Salto Uruguay, from where entrance is 1 block north.*

Sleeping **AL** *Salto Grande*, Urquiza 581, T/F4210034. With breakfast, comfortable. **A** *Palmar*, Urquiza 521, T4216050, F215020. Bright, comfortable, also **B** in older part, with breakfast. **A** *Federico 1°*, 1° de Mayo 248, T4213323. With fan. **A** *Centro*, La Rioja y Buenos Aires, T4217776, F217746. A/c, comfortable, *comedor*. **B** *Embajador*, San Lorenzo 75, T4213018. Near bus terminal, neat. **C** *Argentino*, Pellegrini 560, T4215767. With bath, old fashioned, nice patio. **C** *Central*, 1° de Mayo 148, T4212842. Reasonable, but shared bathrooms not too clean. **C** *Colonial*, *Pellegrini 443*, T4221448. Without breakfast, fan, pleasant. **C** *Concordia*, La Rioja 518, T4216869. With fan, good. **E** per person *Aatrac*, Quitana 131, T4210708. **D** *Colón*, Pellegrini 611, T4215510. Fan, attractive but run down, poor beds. **Camping** *La Posada de Suárez – Club Viajantes* on Av Costanera south of Parque Mitre. Warmly recommended, with good *parrillada* alongside, but beware of the cats. Also site in Parque Rivadavia. North of the city near Salto Grande are: *La Tortuga Alegre*, Km 11, T4211340. With restaurant, store. *Las Palmeras*, Km 18, T4218359. *Punta Viracho*, Km 18.

Eating *La Estancia*, Plaza 25 de Mayo, good value. *Comedor Las Dos Naciones*, Plaza

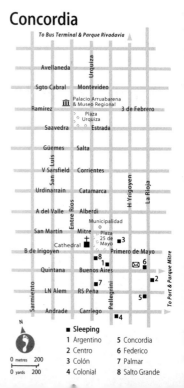

Concordia

To Bus Terminal & Parque Rivadavia

Avellaneda

Urquiza

Sgto Cabral — Montevideo

Palacio Arruabarena & Museo Regional

Ramírez

3 de Febrero

Plaza Urquiza

Saavedra — Estrada

Güemes — Salta

San Luis

V Sarsfield — Corrientes

Urdinarrain — Catamarca

H Yrigoyen

La Rioja

A del Valle — Alberdi

Entre Ríos

Municipalidad

San Martín — Mitre

Plaza 25 de Mayo ■3

Cathedral ■

B de Irigoyen — Primero de Mayo

■8 ⊠6

■1

Sarmiento

Quintana — Buenos Aires

■2

■7

LN Alem — RS Peña

Pellegrini

5■

Andrade — Carriego

■4

To Port & Parque Mitre

N

0 metres 200
0 yards 200

■ **Sleeping**
1 Argentino   5 Concordia
2 Centro   6 Federico
3 Colón   7 Palmar
4 Colonial   8 Salto Grande

25 de Mayo y Av 1° de Mayo, good, moderate prices, large portions. *Mafalda*, corner of Plaza Urquiza and Entre Ríos, very good home made ice cream and cakes.

Fiesta Nacional de la Pesca de la Boga, a fishing festival, third week in Jan. *Fiesta* **Festivals**
Nacional de Citricultura (citrus fruit festival), Dec, includes crowning of the national citrus fruit queen.

Local The city centre can be negotiated on foot. To get to and from the bus terminal **Transport**
take No 2 bus. From the bus terminal to the port take No 4 bus marked 'Puerto'.

Long distance Air *Líneas Aéreas Entre Ríos* (LAER) flies from Aeroparque, Buenos
Aires to Paraná and Concordia with low fares; enquire at Puente Aéreo desk at
Aeroparque. **Bus** Terminal at Justo y Yrigoyen, 13 blocks north west of Plaza 25 de
Mayo. To **Buenos Aires**, 6 daily, US$17, 6½ hrs. To **Córdoba**, US$25, Expreso Singer, at
2200 and 0300, 9 hrs. To **Paraná** 5 a day, to **Posadas** at 1800 and 2300, Expreso Singer
(8½ hrs, US$32), to **Iguazú** at 1810, 13½ hrs US$32, to **Corrientes** US$11. To **La Paz**
(Entre Ríos) – see page 315, 1100, US$10.50, 8 hrs. To **Paso de los Libres** direct, El
Recreo 1500 Mon, Sat and several at 0300, US$11, 3½ hrs. **Sea** To **Uruguay** ferry pas-
senger service to Salto operated jointly by Sancristobal and Río Lago, US$3-4, 5 depar-
tures Mon-Fri, 4 departures Sat, 2 departures (0800 1800) Sun, 20 mins, tickets
obtainable at a small kiosk, which shuts 15 mins before departure, outside building
marked 'Resguardo'.

Banks *Banco Río de la Plata*, on plaza, no commission on Visa advances; *Casa Julio*, 1 de Mayo, **Directory**
half a block from plaza; *Casa Chaca*, on plaza; *Tourfé* on Mitre. **Communications** Post office
La Rioja y Buenos Aires. **Telephone** San Luis 700 block, open 24 hrs. **Internet** Dampermic,
Sarmiento 55, US$8 per hr. **Tourist offices** Plaza 25 de Mayo, open 0700-2400 daily.

The most northerly of the three main crossings between Argentina and Uruguay **Into Uruguay:**
is via the Salto Grande dam. This is an uncomplicated crossing; all formalities are **Salto**
dealt with on the Argentine side. Salto is situated on the east bank of the Río *Population: 80,000*
Uruguay and is a centre for cultivating and processing citrus fruit. Shrove *13 km S of Salto Grande;*
Tuesday is celebrated with a colourful carnival. **Museo de Bellas Artes**, is in *39 km from Concordia*
the French style mansion of a rich *estanciero* and is well worth a visit. ■ *1400,*
Uruguay 1067. Near Salto are three sets of hot springs. **Fuente Salto**, 6 km
north; **Termas del Daymán**, 10 km south; and **Termas del Arapey**, 96 km
northeast. Both Daymán and Arapey have hotels. For full details see the
South American Handbook.

Transport Bicycles Cycles are not allowed to cross the international bridge but officials will help cyclists find a lift. **Bus** *Flecha Bus* and *Chadre* 2 a day each, US$3, pass-
ports checked on bus.

North of Concordia

Route 14 continues north, inland from the giant Salto Grande lake, and then runs
northwest following the west bank of the Río Alto Uruguay. Above Monte Caseros
and Bella Unión, the river forms the boundary between Argentina and Brazil.

A small port near the confluence of Ríos Quarem and Alto Uruguay. On the **Monte Caseros**
opposite bank of the Alto Uruguay is the Uruguayan town of Bella Unión, on the *Population: 19,600*
Brazilian border. Regular ferry lauches cross to Bella Unión. **Sleeping** at *240 km N of Concordia*
Paterlini, Colón y Salta, T4219, *Conte*, Salta 463, and *Cortez*, 2 de Febrero 1663.

The Northeast

Into Uruguay: Situated just south of the frontier between Uruguay and Brazil, Bella Unión lies
Bella Unión 144 km north of Salto. The Brazilian frontier is crossed by the Barra del
Population: 12,000 Cuaraim bridge.

Sleeping 3 hotels and a campsite in the Parque Fructuoso Rivera (T0642-2261), insect repellent needed.

Transport Bus to **Salto**, US$6, 2 hrs. To **Montevideo**, US$26.15, El Norteño, Chadre. Buses to Barra del Cuareim (the 'town') leave every 30 mins, US$0.60, from Plaza 25 de Agosto.

Directory Consulate Brazil, Lirio Moraes 62, T454.

Paso de los Paso de los Libres lies opposite the larger Brazilian town of Uruguaiana: a
Libres bridge joins the two. Paso de los Libres was founded in 1843 by General
Population: 34,000 Madariaga; it was here that he crossed the river from Brazil with his 100 men and
96 km N of Monte annexed Corrientes province for Argentina. Carnival is a colourful affair.
Caseros

Sleeping A *Alejandro I*, Coronel López 502, T424100. Pool, cable TV, best.**C** *Uruguay*, Uruguay 1252, T425672. Not clean but friendly, good *comedor*. Opposite is **C** *26 de Febrero*. **C** *Las Vegas*, Sarmiento 554, T423490, modern. Near terminal are **C** *Capri*, T424126. With bath, and several others. **Camping** *Camping Municipal*, near the international bridge in a park with views over the river and Uruguaiana; also nearby at Laguna Mansa.

Transport Bus Terminal 1 km south of town centre, on road to the frontier. To **Buenos Aires**, US$25. To Corrientes US$10.

Directory Tourist offices Near Argentine customs office at end of the bridge.

Frontier The international bridge, 1,500-m long, lies 2 km south of the centre of Paso de
with Brazil los Libres.

Customs and immigration Argentine and Brazilian formalities are carried out at opposite ends of the bridge. Exchange and information are available in the same building as Brazilian immigration (exchange rates are better in Uruguaiana than at the border).

Transport Minibuses run between Paso de los Libres and the bridge, US$0.60. Buses run between the town centres and bus terminals, every 30 mins, but do not wait at immigration posts and bus tickets are not transferable. No bus service on Sun – taxi charges US$20.

Into Brazil Just over the international bridge on the east bank of the Río Uruguay,
Population: 117,460 **Uruguaiana** is an agro-industrial city serving western Río Grande do Sul.

Sleeping AL *Hotel Glória*, Rua Domingos de Almeida 1951, T412-4422. Good. **D** *Palace*, Praça Rio Branco, without breakfast. *Fares Turis Hotel*, Pres Vargas 2939, T/F412-3358, may let you leave your bags while you look around town. **D** *Barcelona*, next to terminal, good.

Transport Bus To **Uruguay**, Planalto buses run from Uruguaiana via Barra do Quaraí/Bella Unión (US$4.50) to Salto and Paysandú.

The site of a Jesuit mission (1626) little of which remains, Yapeyú is famous as the birthplace of the liberator, José de San Martín. Part of the house where he was born is preserved as a museum. There is also an interesting Jesuit Museum. **Sleeping** at **B** *San Martín*, next to the municipalidad, T493120. There is camping by the river and **B** *Bungalows*, near river, *cabañas*, good. The Carillo family on the main plaza rent rooms, **E**, good.

Yapeyú
Population: 1,200
58 km NW of Paso de los Libres

Buenos Aires to Paraguay: The Ríos Paraná

The Río Paraná is formed by the rivers Paranahyba and Grande which rise in Brazil. From their confluence the Paraná flows 2,570 km before entering the Río de la Plata: its total length is 3,470 km and it drains an area of 1,510,000 sq km. Its major tributary, the Río Paraguay, which flows south from central Brazil across the Pantanal, drains an area of 1,095,000 sq km. Slow-moving due to its low gradient, the river is braided south for the 440 km south from Diamante to the outskirts of Buenos Aires. The only long-distance passenger services up the Río Paraná from Buenos Aires are to Asunción, Paraguay.

Buenos Aires to Rosario

Route 9 heads north west out of the capital and runs north west along the west bank of the Paraná to Rosario.

Situated off Route 9 at Km 68, this reserve covers 2,600 ha on the banks of the Río Paraná. Vegetation varies from medium-sized trees such as willows, *ceibos* and alders to areas of tall grasses. Parts of the reserve are regularly flooded; here there are rushes, tussock grass and white grass. Fauna include the thick-tailed opossum, the capybara and the marsh-deer. Over 240 species of birds have been identified, including two banded warblers, rufous-capped antshrikes, rushbirds, rush-tyrants, coots, ducks and swans. A trail leads from the Administration Centre to an observation sight which offers extensive views over the floodplains.

Reserva Natural Otamendi
Colour map 4, grid B5

The Northeast

Lying 90 km northeast of Buenos Aires on the west bank of the Río Paraguay, Zárate is an industrial centre with large *frigoríficos* and paper works. Route 14 branches off here and runs north across the Zarate and Brazo Largo bridges.

Zárate
Phone code: 0328
Population: 77,000

Sleeping and eating **B** *San Martín*, Ameghino 773, T422713. **Camping** Several sites over the Zarate bridge on Isla Talavera including *Camping Club La Isla*. *Restaurant La Posta de Correa*, cheap, good service. Along the waterfront are many *parrillas* and restaurants.

Transport **Bus** From **Buenos Aires** (Plaza Once) US$3, every 30 mins.

Some 50 km further north west on the edge of the Laguna San Pedro, this is the most attractive town on this part of the Río Paraná. The town is centred on Plaza Constitución, in the centre of which is the **Iglesia de Nuestra Señora del Socorro** (1872). On the corner of the plaza, in the Municipalidad, is the **Museo Histórico Regional**. **Sleeping** at *Turismo*, Blvd Paraná 450, T425459, *Obligado*, Mitre 425, T424225 and there are many camping sites along the edge of the laguna.

San Pedro
Population: 35,500

Rosario

Phone code 0341
Colour map 4, grid A5
Population: 1,000,000
320 km N of
Buenos Aires

Rarely visited by travellers, Rosario has a lively cultural scene and is the home of many popular rock musicians and modern artists and so the nightlife is good, as are the theatres. The third largest city in Argentina it is also one of the most important industrial and export centres in the country. It has a racecourse, two boat clubs and a golf club.

Route There are two routes from Buenos Aires. The best is by Route 8 (marked Córdoba) to Pergamino, and then, following signs, by Route 188, and then 178 to Rosario. This is better than lorry-packed Route 9.

History Unlike most Spanish American cities Rosario was never officially founded.

Che Guevara was born here is 1928

Though a fort was established in 1689 by Luis Romero de Pineda, it remained little more than a port for the export of mules and tobacco throughout the 18th century. The opening of a railway line connecting the port with Córdoba in 1870 and the growth of shipping along the Paraná led to its sudden growth in the late 19th century: its port became a major exporter of grain and beef, while new industries were established, including metal-working, breweries, grain mills, textiles, leather industries and chemical works. By the 1920s it was being compared with Chicago as a major grain-exporting centre with a large immigrant population from Italy.

Sights The old city centres on the Plaza 25 de Mayo. Around it are the **cathedral**, in somewhat eclectic style and containing the Virgen of Rosario, and the **Palacio Municipal**. One block east is the **Monumento de la Bandera**, an imposing and austere memorial built between 1930 and 1955 on the site in which General Belgrano who raised the Argentine flag for the first time. The tower, 75 m high, reached by lift (US$0.50), offers the best available views over the city, the river and its islands. Below is the Sala de las Banderas, containing the flags of all the American states (except Canada).

See the Paseo del Siglo at night. It is a very popular spot especially at weekends

The demolition of the old railway and warehouse facilities along the river has opened up this area. South of the Monumento de La Bandera is is the **Parque Urquiza**, with sports facilities. Further north, at the foot of the monument, is the **Parque de la Bandera**, beyond which is the **Parque de España**, a modern development which incorporates the old railway arches as an exhibition centre (Tue-Sun 1500-2000, US$1) and offers fine views over the Río Paraná. Further north is the bar *Aux de Magaux*, a good spot for resting and watching passing boats. Beyond, another park is under construction.

Boulevard Oroño runs southwest to the **Parque Independencia**, 126 ha, with lakes and monumental gardens and several museums (see below).

Museums **Museo de Bellas Artes J B Castagnino**, Pellegrini 2202, just outside the Parque Indepdencia. Houses a large collection of European paintings, particularly French impressionist, Italian barroque and Flemish works as well as individual works by El Greco and Goya and one of best collections of Argentine

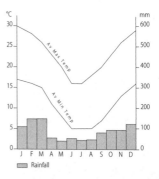

Climate: Rosario

The golden age of Rosario

At the height of its prosperity (1880-1950), Rosario became a city noted for its French and Italian-inspired architecture. Sadly, serious damage was done in the 1970s as some of the finest buildings were demolished and replaced by ugly 10 and 12 storey tower blocks, destroying the harmony and uniformity of the streets and replacing it with a untidy and irregular appearance.

Interesting examples of its former glory do remain however. Some of the mansions of the rich can be seen along Boulevard Oroño, one of the finest avenues in the city. The stretch of Calle Córdoba which runs from Boulevard Oroño to Avenida San Martín has been titled the Paseo del Siglo; plaques (in Spanish) identify some of the most important surviving buildings. The Victoria shopping mall, Córdoba y San Martín, and the Falabella store, Córdoba y Sarmiento, which occupies the former La Favorita building, once the great department store of Rosario, are particularly impressive. Further west, at Córdoba y Corrientes, is the Bolsa de Comercio (stock exchange); opposite is La Fénix, the former mansion of one of the cities grain exporting barons.

paintings. ■ *Tue-Sat 1200-2000, Sun 1000-2000*. **Centro Cultural Bernardino Rivadavia**, San Martín 1080, 0800-2000 daily, free, contemporary art, also cinema, theatre. **Museo de Arte Decorativo Firma y Odilio Estévez**, Santa Fe 748, former private collection including 16th-century Flemish tapestries, silverware from 18th-century Potosi and pre-Columbian ceramics from Peru as well as a replica of Titian's famous portrait of Philip II. Few explantions, all in Spanish. ■ *Thu-Sun 1500-2000*.

Balneario La Florida, about 8 km north, is a beach where you are able to swim. There are also several islands, with woods and beaches nearby in Río Paraná. Launches run regularly every 15 minutes in summer and less frequently off season, summer US$2 return winter US$1 return. The islands can also be visited at weekends on board the *Ciudad de Rosario,* which leaves the Estación Fluvial near the Monumento de la Bandera, Sat/Sun 1400, 1630, also Sun 1000.

Excursions

On the opposite bank of the Río Paraná is the **Estancia La Margarita**, near Victoria, T0436-22159, F0435-21623. **L** per person with homemade food, horseriding, fishing, watersports, beautiful surroundings. Recommended.

San Lorenzo is 28 km north and the site of one of the largest chemical works in Argentina. In the centre near the river is the restored former Franciscan monastery of **San Carlos de Borromeo**. Nearby is the **Campo de la Gloria**, site of the battle of San Lorenzo (3 February 1813), at which, Spanish troops disembarking from their boats, were attacked and routed by San Martín's forces, who had been concealed behind the monastery. The monastery, built in 1780 and used as a hospital during the battle, is now a museum. Visitors can see the room used by San Martín as well as a pine tree grown from a cutting of the tree under which the Liberator rested after the battle. The chapel contains paintings and sulptures from the 17th and 18th centuries.

AL *La Paz*, Barón de Mauá 36, T4210905. Quiet. Recommended. **AL** *Presidente*, Corrientes 919, T4242854. Good. **AL** *Plaza*, Barón de Mauá 26, T47097. **A** *Europeo*, San Luís 1364, T4240382. With breakfast, modern. **AB** *Benidorm*, San Juan 1049, T4219368. With breakfast, central, overpriced. **B** *Rosario*, Corrientes 900, T4242170. With breakfast, parking, large rooms, good beds. **B** *Savoy*, San Lorenzo 1022 near San Martín, T4480071. Built 1900 and retaining original bathrooms, with breakfast, **D**

Sleeping
Camping at Balneario La Florida, 8 km N

The Northeast

without bath, large rooms, cheap restaurant, good value. **C** *Río*, Rivadavia 2665, T4396421. Pleasant. **C** *Normandie*, Mitre 1030, T4212694, helpful, central. **D** per person *Bahía*, Maipú 1262, T4217271. Without breakfast, poor beds.

Around terminal on Av Santa Fe **B** *Micro*. No 3650, T4397192. Uninspiring. **B** *América*, No 3746, T4386584. Without breakfast, best value on this street. **B** *Casas*, No 3600, T4304717. Without breakfast, a/c, pleasant. Recommended. **B** *Confort*, No 3500, T4380486. Poor beds. **B** *Embajador*, No 3554, T4384188. With breakfast, a/c extra, good. **B** *Nahuel*, No 3518, T/F4397292. With breakfast, gloomy, modern. **B** *Le Nid*, Iriondo 660, T4388762. Without breakfast, a/c, modern, pleasant. Recommended.

Eating Excellent quality and value meals at the supermarket at Tucumán y Corrientes. Along the river are good cheap restaurants and fishing club barbecues, good atmosphere. Several parrillas and ice-cream parlours along Pellegrini. *Don Rodrigo*, Sante Fe 968, and *Fénix*, Santa Fe next to Citibank, are both very good. *La China*, Santa Fe 1882, US$5 *tenedor libre*. *Gaucho*, Roca 725, churrasquería. *Capote*, Corrientes y Urquiza. *La Máquina*, Urquiza y Entre Ríos, bar with some food, popular with young people and artists. *Mamacita*, 9 de Julio 2246, Mexican. *Vegetariano*, Mitre 710. *Casa Uruguaya*, Alvear 1125 (T469320), away from centre, good. *Marialronn*, Santa Fe y Pres Roca, recommended for dancing.

Entertainment **Bars** *Café de la Opera*, Mendoza y Laprida, next to *Teatro El Círculo*, cabaret, live music, highly recommended, friendly; *La Puerta*, Entre Ríos 639, *La Nuestra*, San Luis y Rosas; *Berlín*, Pasaje Zabala (Sarmiento 300); *Pasaporte*, Maipú 509, very good. Several good bars along the *Paseo del Siglo* (Córdoba 1600 to 1800) and nearby including *Miscelánea*, Roca 755; *Play Off*, Santa Fe y Roca, as well as on Tucumán 800 to 1,000 blocks in the El Bajo district. **Nightclubs** *L'Infierno*, Córdoba 2300; *María*, Santa Fe y Roca.

Rosario

Not to scale

A revolutionary life

One of the most enduring images of youthful revolutionary zeal is that of Che Guevara staring proud, implacable and defiant under that trademark black beret. It is an image that has graced many student walls. Rosario is strangely coy about its links with Guevara perhaps because his parents soon moved with their asthmatic child to the healthier climate of the Sierras de Córdoba. The future revolutionary was born here in 1928 in a house at Entre Ríos y Urquiza into a middle class family.

Che's eyes were soon opened to the plight of South America's poor during a journey around the continent on a beat-up old motorcycle and rather than pursue a career in medicine which he had studied prior to his journey he would dedicate the rest of this life to the fight for 'liberation of the American continent'.

In 1956 he met Fidel Castro in Mexico and together they planned to create the ideal socialist model in Cuba as well as establish links with other, sympathetic nations. But his overriding ambition had always been to spread the revolutionary word and take the armed struggle to other parts. Bolivia seemed the obvious choice for Fidel and Che to begin their mission to 'liberate South America', especially as it bordered Argentina. It had always been

Che's dream to create a socialist state in this home country but conditions were not right and would have to be prepared from neighbouring Bolivia. He spent a little time in La Paz and them travelled to a guerrilla base at Nanchuazú. However the constant movements of the group aroused the suspicion of neighbours (who had little sympathy for the movement, the government having successfully played on their patriotism of this 'foreign invasion') and the army were alerted. They fled and spent several months wandering the steep valleys of eastern Bolivia. In August 1967 they were ambushed by Bolivian troops. Che was executed and buried in an unmarked grave. In 1997 his body was exhumed and returned to Cuba .

Local holidays *Fiesta de las Colectividades*, first 2 weeks of Nov, with music, dance and food in front of the Monumento de la Bandera. In the second week of Sep the Sociedad Rural hosts a large fair.

Shopping Main shopping street is the pedestrianized Av Córdoba. There is a handicrafts fair in front of the tourist office, Sat and Sun from 1500. **Bookshop**: *Stratford*, Mitre 726, for imported English books.

Transport **Air** **Fisherton airport**, 8 km west of centre. Minibus operated by *Transportes Ayolas*, Dean Funes 1525, T4839863, connects with flights, US$4, to and from hotels and *AR* office. Taxi or *remise* US$10. Several flights daily to **Buenos Aires** with *Aerolíneas Argentinas / Austral* and *Southern Winds*; *Andesmar* to **Córdoba** and **Mendoza**. *Southern Winds* to **Córdoba**, **Tucumán**, **Salta**, **Neuquén**, **Bariloche** and **Mar del Plata**. Also *Pluna* to **Montevideo**, *Varig* to **São Paulo**, **Belo Horizonte**, **Curitiba**, **Porto Alegre** and **Florianópolis**.

Bus Terminal at Santa Fe y Caferatta, about 25 blocks west of the *Monumento de la Bandera*. Bus to centre 115, 119, US$0.50, taxi US$4. Terminal has post office, shops

☞ *Canallas and leprosos*

Rosario is the home of two of Argentina's oldest and most famous football clubs: Rosario Central and Newell's Old Boys. Central, founded in 1889 by workers on the Central Argentine Railway, draw their support mainly from the north of the city. Newells, who were founded by ex-pupils of the Anglo-Argentine school led by the Englishman Isaac Newell, are supported mainly by the southern part of the city.

Rivalry between the two clubs is understandably intense and, if partly based on social class, is heavily influenced by tradition. At their peak Central won the championship four times, once fewer than Newell's. On Sundays the city divides in more ways than one: fans of Central head north to Lisandro de la Torre to watch their team, while Newell's fans go to their stadium in the Parque Independencia. They are easily distinguishable: Central wear blue and white, while Newell's wear red and black. Travellers should perhaps exercise care in using the nicknames commonly used: Central are known as the canallas (politely translated as 'rabble') while Newell's are less than affectionately known as leprosos or lepers.

and restaurants. To **Buenos Aires**, Chevallier hrly, US$20-22, 3-4 hrs, also Ablo, General Urquiza, La Unión. To **Córdoba**, 6½ hrs, US$18, several companies. To **Santa Fe**, US$10. To **Mendoza**, US$30, 10 hrs. To **Mar del Plata**, TIRSA, US$47, 12 hrs. To **Bariloche**, TIRSA, US$97, 24 hrs. To **Puerto Iguazú**, US$50.

Sea Ferries to Victoria, on the east bank of the Río Paraná, which has a municipal campsite.

Train The Buenos Aires-Tucumán service stops in Rosario. To Tucuman, US$15, 13 hrs, Mon and Fri.

Directory **Airline offices** *Aerolíneas Argentinas*, Santa Fe 1410. **Banks** *Lloyds Bank* (BLSA), La Rioja 1205; **Citibank**, Santa Fe 1101; *First National Bank of Boston*, Córdoba y Mitre. Open 1000-1600. Most banks charge 2% commission on cheques and cash. *Amex*, Grupo 3 de Turismo, Córdoba 1147, T4244415. *Casas de Cambio: Transatlántica*, Córdoba 992; *Exprinter*, Córdoba 960; **Carey**, Corrientes 802; *Carbatur*, Corrientes 840. **Communications** Post OfficeCórdoba y Buenos Aires. **Telecommunications**San Luis, between San Martín and Maipú. **Laundry** Santa Fe 1578. **Tourist offices** *ETUR*, Belgrano y Buenos Aires, T4802230/1, 0800-2000 daily, helpful, maps, English spoken. **Useful addresses** *Scrivanti*, Corrientes 653, 6th floor, T4253738, for budget travel information.

Santa Fe

Population: 350,000
Colour map 4, grid A5
Phone code: 0342
165 km N of Rosario

Santa Fe lies near the confluence of the Ríos Santa Fe and Salado in a low-lying area with lagoons and islands just west of the Río Paraná. It is connected with the smaller city of Paraná, on the east bank of the river, by road bridges and a tunnel. Santa Fe is capital of its province and the centre of a very fertile region.

History Founded by settlers from Asunción in 1573 and transferred to its present site in 1660, it was, in the colonial period, one of the main centres of Jesuit and Franciscan influence in the country and an important port on the voyage between Buenos Aires and Asunción. After independence it suffered badly from the struggles between provincial *caudillos*.

Sights The southern part of the city, around the **Plaza 25 de Mayo** is the historic centre. On the plaza itself is the **cathedral**, dating from 1751 but remodelled in 1834, with its twin towers capped by blue cupolas. On the east side is **Iglesia de**

Santa Fe: cradle of the constitution

Santa Fe calls itself the "Cradle of the Constitution" and the "city of conventions". It was here that the constitution of 1853 was drafted; though replaced by Perón in 1949, and abused,

suspended and broken at will by military governments, it is still in force. Conventions to consider reforms to the constitution have also met in the city, in 1860, 1866, 1957 and 1994.

Nuestra Señora de los Milagros, dating from 1694, richly decorated with an ornate dome. Next door is the **Colegio de la Inmaculada Concepción**, established by the Jesuits. On the northern side is the majestic **Casa de Gobierno**, built in 1908 in French-style on the site of the historic Cabildo in which the 1853 constitution was drafted.

One block south of the plaza is the **Iglesia y Convento de San Francisco** built in 1680. The church has walls nearly 2-m thick and fine wooden ceilings, built from timber floated down the river from Paraguay, carved by indigeneous craftsmen and fitted without the use of nails. Inside are the remains of Estanislao López (see below). The pulpit and altar are 17th-century baroque. A block west of the Plaza at 3 de Febrero y 9 de Julio is the **Iglesia de Nuestra Señora del Rosario**, part of the 19th-**Convento de Santo Domingo**, which has a fine patio and museum; north of the centre at Javier de la Rosa 623, is the modern neo-gothic style **Iglesia de Nuestra Señora de Guadalupe**, with attractive stained glass windows. ■ *Daily 0730-2000, bus 4 from the centre, 20 mins.*

Museo Histórico Provincial, 3 de Febrero y San Martín, in a building dating from 1680 (one of the oldest surviving civil buildings in the country), includes pieces from the former Jesuit mission of San Javier, as well as artefacts associated with the dictator Rosas and with Urquiza, who overthrew him. There are portraits of both men and of Estanislao López, Rosas's ally who ruled Santa Fe. ■ *Tue-Fri 0830-1230, 1430-1900, Sat/Sun 1500-1800*. **Museo Etnográfico y Colonial**, 3 de Febrero y 25 de Mayo, includes large collection of artefacts from Santa Fe La Vieja (the original site of the city) and items from indigenous cultures in the Santa Fe area. ■ *Mon-Fri 0900-1200, 1530-1900, Sat 1530-1830, Sun 1000-1200, 1530-1830*. **Museo de Bellas Artes**, General López, Tue-Sun 1730-2030, exhibitions of local artists' work.

Museums

AL *Conquistador*, 25 de Mayo 2676, T/F4551195. Sauna, pool, gym. **A** *Río Grande*, San Gerónimo 2586, T4551025. Modern. Recommended. **A** *Corrientes*, Corrientes 2520, T4592126. With breakfast, garage, restaurant, comfortable. **A** *Hostal de Santa Fe de la Vera Cruz*, San Martín 2954, T4551740. Best, genial, well-kept and run. **AB** *Castellar*, 25 de Mayo y Falucho, T4520141. A/c, parking. **AB** *Hernandarias*, Rivadavia 2680, T4529752. Fan, gloomy. **AB** *Suipacha*, Suipacha 2375, T4521135. Safe, a/c, garage, pleasant. Recommended. **B** *Niza*, Rivadavia 2755, T4522047. Very nice, without breakfast, a/c. **B** *Emperatriz*, Irigoyen Freyre 2440, T4530061. Pleasant, good value.

Sleeping

Near the terminal AB *Bertaina*, H Yrigoyen 2255, T/F4553068. Parking, a/c, good beds, well maintained. **AB** *Zavaleta*, H Yrigoyen 2349, T/F4551840. Cafetéria, with breakfast. **B** *Colón*, San Luis 2862, T4545167. **D** without bath, pleasant, large rooms. **B-C** *Royal*, Irigoyen Freyre 2256, T4527359. OK, fan, gloomy. **C** *Apolo*, Belgrano 2821, T4527984. Old fashioned, gloomy, poor beds, basic. **B** *Brigadier*, San Luis 3148, T4537387. 2 blocks from bus station. Good, a/c, some English spoken, parking. **B-C** *Carlitos*, Irigoyen Freyre 2336, T4531541. **C** *Humberto*, Crespo 2222, T4550409. Without breakfast, poor beds, basic.

Santa Fe

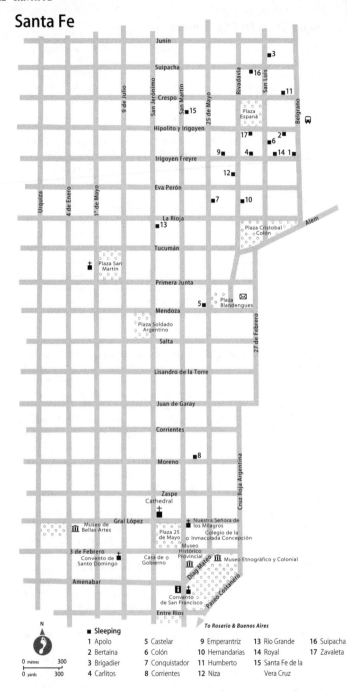

Camping Several sites on the lakes and rivers outside town including: *Náutico Sur*, on the Río Santa Fe. *Luz y Fuerza*, 7 km north near Laguna Guadalupe. *Cámara del Hogar*, 4 km east on Route 168. *Túnel Subfluvial*, 300 m before the Hernandarias tunnel to Paraná, 17 km east.

El Quincho de Chiquito, Obispo Príncipe y Almirante Brown, excellent and good value, classic fish restaurant, huge helpings. Excellent grills including *surubí* (local fish) at *Gran Parrillada Rivadavia*, Rivadavia 3299. *Surubí* also at *España*, San Martín 2644. *Baviera San Martín*, San Martín 2941, good salads. *Café de la Paix*, San Martín y Santiago del Estero.

Eating Many good ones, offering excellent meals with good wine

30 Sep, *San Jerónimo*; 15 Nov, *Foundation of City*.

Local holidays

Swimming on river at Guadalupe beach; local bus.

Sports

Air Airport at Sauce Viejo, 17 km south. Daily flights to and from Buenos Aires, Aerolíneas Argentinas, (T4599461), Southern Winds and LAER; LAER also to Paraná. **Bus** Terminal near the centre at Belgrano 2910. To **Córdoba**, US$18, 5 hrs. To **Buenos Aires**,many companies, US$19-28. To **Paraná**, Etacer and Fluviales del Litoral, frequent US$2, 1 hr. To **Rosario** very frequent, 2½ hrs by *autopista*, US$10. To **Mendoza** daily. To **Posadas**, 12 hrs, US$30, several companies. To **Santiago del Estero/Tucumán** (2010). To **Concordia** 4½ hrs, US$16.50. To **Asunción** (Paraguay), daily overnight, La Internacional US$31, común, US$57 diferencial.

Transport

Banks Lloyds Bank (BLSA), 25 de Mayo 2501, open 0715-1315. **Citibank**, San Martín 2609. Amex representative, **Vacaciones Felices**, San Martín 2347. **Casas de Cambio** Camsa, 25 de Mayo 2466 Carbatur, San Martín 2520 Tourfé, San Martín 2901,Sat 0830-1230, changes TCs. **Laundry** *Servi Rap*, Rivadavia 2834 (open Sat 0800-1300), *Laverap*, San Martín 1687. **Tourist office** San Martín 2836 and at the bus terminal: maps, friendly.

Directory

The cities are 27 km apart and separated by several islands, linked by bridges and the Hernandarias tunnel which is almost 3 km long. From Santa Fe the route runs northeast crossing Laguna Guadeloupe onto Isla Crucesitas and then across the Río Colastine (Km 9) onto Isla Santa Candida. The tunnel is at Km 19, toll US$2 per car. Trucks with dangerous loads cross the river by a launch which also carries pedestrians and operates Monday-Sat, 0600-2100, 20-mins journey, frequency depending on demand from trucks.

Santa Fe to Paraná

Paraná

Capital of Entre Ríos province, Paraná is situated on the east bank of the Río Paraná. The centre is situated on a hill offering fine views over the river and beyond to Santa Fe.Although the area was populated long before, the city was founded in 1730 by settlers from Santa Fe. From 1853 to 1862 the city was capital of the Argentine Confederation.

Phone code: 0343 Colour map 4, grid A5 Population: 210,000 495 km N of Buenos Aires

Though nothing remains from the colonial period, there are many fine 19th- and 20th-century public buildings. In the centre is the **Plaza Primero de Mayo**, where there are fountains and a statue of San Martín. On the east side is the **Cathedral**, notable for its fine stained glass windows, its portico and its interior. Just around the corner from the cathedral is the **Colegio del Huerto**, seat of the Senate of the Argentine Confederation between 1853 and 1861. Also on the plaza are the **Municipalidad** (1890) and the **Club Social** (1906), for years the elite social centre of the city. Several blocks north of the plaza are the **Teatro 3**

Sights

de Febrero (1908), the **Casa de Gobierno** (1900), on the Plaza Carbo, which has a grand façade and the **Iglesia San Miguel** (1895) on Plaza Alvear.

The city's glory is **Parque Urquiza**, northwest of the centre. Extending over 44 ha and planted with lapachos, palos borrachos and pines, it has an enormous statue to General Urquiza, and a bas-relief showing the battle of Caseros, at which he finally defeated Rosas; also an open-air theatre. There are pleasant walks along the river bank and around the fishing port of **Puerto Sánchez**.

Museums **Museo de Bellas Artes**, Buenos Aires 355. **Museo Histórico**, Buenos Aires y Laprida, including a fine collection of silverware. ■ *Tue-Fri 0700-1300, 1500-2000, Sat 0900-1200, 1600-1900 (winter), 1700-2000 (summer), Sun 0900-1200.*

Excursions **Parque Nacional Diamante**, 44 km south, covers 2,458 ha of marshland and riverine forest. It is 6 km south of the town of Diamante. This new park is a good spot for birdwatching: over 140 species have been indentified. Before visiting you must contact the *guardaparque* at H Yrigoyen 396, Diamante.

Sleeping There is a shortage of hotel space, especially at peak periods (Semana Santa and Jul), when the tourist office arranges accommodation with families. There is a greater selection of hotels – at lower prices – in Santa Fe. **AL** *Mayorazgo*, Etchevehere y Córdoba, on Costanera Alta, T4230333. 5-star, with fine view of park and river, has

Paraná

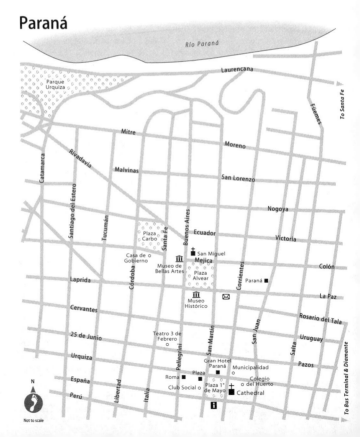

casino and swimming pool. **A** *Paraná*, 9 de Julio 60, T4231700. With breakfast, pleasant. **A** *Gran Hotel Paraná*, Urquiza 976, T4223900. **B** *Super Luxe*, Villaguay 162, T4232835. **C** *Bristol*, Alsina 221, T4313961. Close to the bus terminal, basic. **C** *Plaza*, San Martín 915, T4210720. **C** *Roma*, Urquiza 1069, with bath, basic, central.

Camping *Balneario Thompson*, just west of the tunnel. *Balneario Los Arenales*, east of the tunnel.

Air General Urquiza airport, 12 km south east of town. **Bus** New terminal 1 km southeast of centre on Av Ramírez. East across Entre Ríos to **Concordia** on Río Uruguay, 5 a day, 5 hrs. To **Buenos Aires**, US$22. **Transport**

Laundry *Laverap*, Belgrano 650 and San Juan 273. **Tourist offices** 25 de Mayo 44. **Directory**

North of Santa Fe and Paraná

Two roads lead north, one on either side of the Río Paraná. East of the river Route 12 runs from Paraná to Corrientes passing through small towns such as La Paz and Goya while Route 11 runs to the west of the river through Reconquista to Resistencia.

La Paz, 173 km north of Paraná, is a small port in an area popular for fishing. It has a regional museum, riverside park and golf club. **Sleeping** at *Milton*, Italia 1029, T422232. 2-star, *Res Plaza*, San Martín 862, T421208 and others. **Camping** at *El Eucaliptal*, information from España 1157, T421496, F21918. Also cabins, sleep 4-6. **La Paz**
Phone code: 03437
Colour map 4, grid A5
Population: 16,700

Situated at the centre of an important tobacco growing region, Goya is the second town of the province of Corrientes. The town lies on the Riacho Goya, a tributary of the Paraná and is centred around the **Plaza Mitre**; on the northwest corner is the fine cathedral (1861-1892), designed by the italian Francisco Pinaroli. One block north of the plaza is the **Museo Juan Esteban Martínez**, housed in a fine 19th-century mansion. West of Goya, 14 km inland from the western bank of the Río Paraná is **Reconquista** (*population* 52,000), a town situated on the site of a former Jesuit mission. The town is centred on the Plaza 25 de Mayo; on the east side is the neo-romantic cathedral (1942); on the north side is the **Casa Roselli** (1880), the oldest building in town. A vehicle ferry across the Río Paraná connects Puerto Reconquista (14 km south) with Goya. **Goya & Reconquista**
Phone code: 03777
Colour map 1, grid C6
Population: Goya, 56,700; Reconquista, 52,000 Km 374

Sleeping Goya *Cervantes*, Gómez 723, T/F422864. 3-star. *Turismo*, Mitre 860, T/F422926. 3-star. *Colón*, Colón 1077, T422682. 1-star. Several others. **Camping** Many sites including *Club Social y Deportivo*, on road to port, T422735.

Mercedes is a good base for visiting the **Esteros del Iberá**. About 27 km south of Mercedes are the strange Ita Pucú rock formations, remnants of a mountain massif long disappeared. **Sleeping** at *Turismo*, Caaguazú y Sarmiento, T4317 and *Plaza*, San Martín 699, the cheapest. **Mercedes**
Population: 20,750
Phone code: 03777
140 km E of Goya

This reserve protects nearly 800,000 ha of marshland known as the **Esteros del Iberá**. Similar to the Pantanal in Brazil, the Esteros are the old course of the Río Paraná. From their outlet into the Río Corrientes, which flows south west into the Río Paraná, the marshes extend some 250 km northeast to Ituzaingó on the Alto Paraná and are some 150 km wide at their greatest extent. Though the waters are under 5 m deep, there are several deep lagoons along the **Reserva Provincial del Ibera**

The Northeast

☞ Camilla

Though no traces remain of the house in which they lived, Goya provided refuge in 1848 for two famous fugitives, whose story formed the basis of the film Camilla by Maria Luisa Bemberg. Camilla O'Gorman, the daughter of one of the most aristocratic families in Buenos Aires, eloped with a priest. Escaping the moral disapproval of Buenos Aires, they lived here incognito for several months, but were recognized, arrested and shot on the orders of Rosas. Many people who disapproved of their morals were shocked by Rosas's brutality and their fate contributed to the overthrow of the dictator.

southeastern edge. Wildlife are very similar to the Wet Chaco (see below): species include the endangered *aguará-guazú* (maned wolf), the marsh deer and the broad snouted caiman as well as capybaras, brocket deer, curiyús (yellow ananconda) and tegú lizards. About 300 species of bird have been identified, among them the jabirú (or Juan Grande) stork – the largest stork in the western hemispere, southern screamers and several species of ducks.

Esteros del Iberá

Access is 2 km from **Colonia Carlos Pellegrini**, 110 km northeast by dirt road from Mercedes. Here there is a visitors centre, camping and shop. The tap water here is not drinkable, but bottled water can be bought.

Sleeping AL per person *Posada de la Laguna*, T/F0376929827, iberalaguna@starmedia.com, Elsa Güiraldes, full pension, English spoken, tours arranged. *Ñande-Reta Inn*, T011354773-20155, www.tierrabuena.com.ar/tb.php3/niandereta, full board, also riding, boat trips, trekking, English spoken. Also rooms in the house of Pera Roque, **E** per person, basic. **Estancias** for *estancias* on the northern edge of Iberá see under Ituzaingó.

Tours can be arranged through agencies in Mercedes and Corrientes: in Corrientes try Marcus Moncada, of *Turismo Aventura 4WD*, Junín 1062, Loc 4. Workers at the visitors centre take boat trips in small punts, US$10 per hr, a recommended way of discovering the wildlife quietly.

Transport Bus Daily bus and minibus from Mercedes.

Parque Nacional Mburucuya Situated north of the Esteros del Iberá and and south east of the city of Corrientes, this park covers 15,060

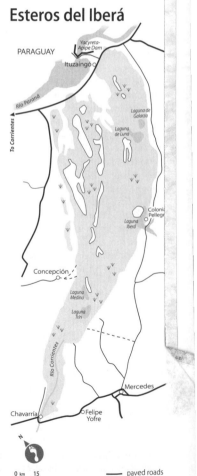

PARAGUAY

Yacyreta-Apipe Dam

Ituzaingó

Río Paraná

To Corrientes

Laguna de Galarza

Laguna de Luna

Colonia Pellegr

Laguna Iberá

Concepción

Laguna Medina

Laguna Trin

Río Corrientes

Mercedes

Chavarría   Felipe Yofre

N

0 km   15
0 miles   15

—— paved roads
—— unpaved roads

The Northeast

Mburucuyá

Almost unpronounceable in Spanish or English, Mburucuyá is the Guaraní name for the passion flower (Passiflora caerula), found in hot climates across the world. Its Spanish name pasionaria was given by missionaries who saw similarities with the Passion of Christ: its three stigmas representing the three nails, the five anthers the five wounds, the corona the crown of thorns, the ten tepals the faithful apostles (no Judas or Peter), and the lobed leaves and tendrils by which it climbs the hands and scourges of the persecutors.

Well adapted to its environment, it secretes a sweet substance which attracts ants, which defend the plant from caterpillars and insects. It flowers over a long period during the summer and its orange/red berries are poisonous.

ha, stretching north from the marshlands of the Río Santa Lucía, which forms its southern limit. Formerly two *estancias*, the park includes varying natural environments, ranging from Wet Chaco to *Espinal* types. Flora includes yatay and caranday palms and quebrachos as well as areas of savanna. Wildlife includes the rare *aguará guazu* (maned wolf), monkeys, mountain foxes and about 300 bird species. No infrastructure.

Access By Provincial Route 86, 12 km east of the town of Mburucuyá, 107 km northwest of Bella Vista. The *guardaparque* lives in Mburucuyá.

Corrientes

Capital of Corrientes province, the city is mainly a service centre for its agricultural hinterland which produces beef, cotton, tobacco, rice and yerba maté. Although Corrientes is less important than Resistencia as a route centre and more expensive than the latter, it is a pleasant place for a stopover. The city centre, with its peaceful traditional streets and squares, is well preserved; its costanera is one of the most attractive in the country. The national capital of Carnival, the city is also famous as the location of Graham Greene's novel 'The Honorary Consul'. The river can make the air heavy, moist and oppressive, but in winter the climate is pleasant.

Phone code: 03783
Colour map 1, grid B6
Population: 268,000
586 km N of Paraná
25 km W of Resistencia
by the General
Belgrano bridge

Founded on a relatively high promontory in 1588 by an expedition from Asunción, Corrientes became important as a port on the route between Buenos Aires and Asunción. Several Franciscan missions were built nearby to settle the Indians. **History**

The main **Plaza 25 de Mayo**, one block inland from the costanera, is one of the best preserved in Argentina. On the north side is the **Jefatura de Policia**, built in 19th-century French style. On the east side are the Italianate **Casa de Gobierno** (1881-6) and the **Ministerio de Gobierno** (1882). On the south side is the church of **La Merced**, while the **Casa Lagraña**, built in 1860 for the governor, lies one block south. Two blocks east at Quintanta y Mendoza is the **Convento de San Francisco**, rebuilt in 1861 on the site of the original which dated from 1608. The **Cathedral**, built in 1874 is on Plaza Cabral where there is a statue to the sergeant who saved San Martín's life at the battle of San Lorenzo. **Sights**

The Northeast

The church of **La Cruz de los Milagros** (1897) houses *La Madera*, a miraculous cross placed there by the founder of the city, Alonzo de Vera – Indians who tried to burn it were killed by lightning from a cloudless sky.

Calle Junín is pedestrianized, with restaurants and shops, crowded at night. The attractive Avenida Costanera, lined with *lapachos* and *palos borrachos*, leads along the Río Paraná to **Parque Mitre**, from where there are good views of sunsets over the river. Up river from the bridge to Resistencia, is a **zoo** with animals of the region.

Museums **Museo Histórico Regional**, 9 de Julio 1044. ■ *Tue-Fri 0800-1200, 1600-1800, Sat 0900-1200, US$1*. **Museo de Bellas Artes**, San Juan 643. ■ *Tue-Fri, 0800-1200, 1600-2100, Sat, Sun, 0900-1200, 1800-2000*. **Museo de Ciencias Naturales**, San Martín 850. ■ *Daily except Tue, 0800-1200, 1600-2000*. **Museo de Artesanía**, Buenos Aires y Quintana. ■ *Mon-Fri, 0730-1200, 1500-2000, Sat 0900-1200, 1600-1900*.

Excursions
There are several interesting towns northeast along Route 12

Santa Ana de los Guacarás, Km 17, is the site of a 17th-century Fransiscan mission. The chapel, restored in 1889, dates from 1771. The old railway station has been preserved as a museum to the Ferrocarril Provincial El Económico, a narrow-gauge railway line which operated from 1890 to 1960. **Paso de la Patria**, Km 38, lies on the Alto Paraná opposite its confluence with the Río Paraguay. A paradise for *dorado* fishing, it is very popular during the *Fiesta del Pesca Dorada* in August. **Sleeping AB** *Hostería Don Julián*, T494021, full board. Lots more including cabins. **Itatí** at Km 73, is a tiny port on the Alto Paraná and the site of a festival (June 16) which celebrates the crowning of the

Corrientes centre

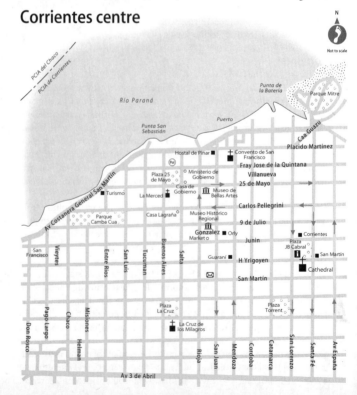

Graham Greene in Corrientes

Corrientes is the setting of one of Greene's most famous novels, The Honorary Consul (1973), the story of the kidnapping of the British Honorary Consul by opponents of the Paraguayan dictator, General Stroessner (never named in the novel). In his memoirs, Ways of Escape (1980), Greene explains how he first visited Corrientes in 1966 en route to Asunción to research his novel Travels With My Aunt; the boat stopped for half an hour:

"A few lights along the quay, a solitary sentinel outside a warehouse, a small public garden with something resembling a classical temple and the slow tide of the great river". (Ways of Escape, Penguin 1981.)

Five years later returning for a two week stay Greene found the inspiration for

The Honorary Consul from a newspaper story. The Paraguayan consul in a town near Corrientes was kidnapped by mistake for the Paraguayan Ambassador; General Stroessner, on a fishing holiday in Argentina, refused to respond. However, although several characters in the novel were also based on people Greene met, there are few descriptions of the city:

"The city was beginning to wake up for the evening hours after the long siesta of the afternoon. A chain of cars drove by along the riverside. The white naked statue in the belvedere shone under the lamplight, and the Coca Cola sign glowed in scarlet letters like the shrine of a saint. Through the darkness the ferry boat was screaming a warning to the Chaco shore". (The Honorary Consul, Penguin 1974).

Virgin of Itatí. According to one version of the story, the Virgin appeared before local Indians who were attacking the settlers in Itatí and persuaded them to cease fighting. The Basilica, built in 1942, has a dome 83-m high, 26-m diameter and it seats 9,000 people. **Sleeping** *Antártida*, 25 de Mayo s/n, T493060. *El Promesero*, 25 de Mayo s/n, T493129. *El Colonial*, Desiderio Sosa 672, T493050. **Camping** at 2 sites.

A *Gran Hotel Guaraní*, Mendoza 970, T423663, F24620. With breakfast, very good, a/c, restaurant. **AB** *Corrientes*, Junín 1549, T465019, F65025. With breakfast, a/c, parking, good value for Corrientes, good restaurant. **AB** *Turismo*, Entre Ríos 650, T/F433173. One block from river, breakfast, restaurant, pool, laundry service, parking. A *Hostal de Pinar*, Martínez y Italia, T469060. Modern, with breakfast, parking, sauna. **AB** *Orly*, San Juan 867, T427248. With breakfast, a/c, parking. **AB** *San Martín*, Santa Fe 955, T465004, F32326. With breakfast, good beds, restaurant, parking. In the centre **C** *Robert*, La Rioja 437. Basic, clean, without bath. Several near the terminal including **C** *Caribe*, Av Maipú Km 3, T469045. Cheaper accommodation is scarce.

Sleeping
More expensive than Resistencia

Camping Near bus terminal is *Camping-club Teléfono*, Av Maipú, hot showers or bath, friendly. 4 sites along Route 12 heading east.

El Nuevo Balcón, Pellegrini 962, good food, clean, reasonable prices. *Las Brasas*, Av Costanera y San Martín (near beach). Many others, and various *pizzerías*. Several tea rooms on San Juan, and on Junín. Try *chipas* (maize delicacies).

Eating

Nightclubs *Metal*, Junín y Buenos Aires; *Savage*, Junín y San Lorenzo.

Entertainment

Carnival is very colourful.

Festivals

Local Car hire *Avis* at *Gran Hotel Guaraní* and airport; only credit cards accepted from foreigners. **Long distance Air** Camba Punta Airport, 10 km east of city reached by Route 12. Bus No 8 from Av Costanera y La Rioja. *Austral* (T427442) and

Transport

The Northeast

Lapa (T431625) to Buenos Aires and Formosa. **Bus** To **Resistencia** US$1.30, Cota, every 15 mins, 40 mins journey, labelled 'Chaco', leaving from Av Costanera y La Rioja. Terminal 5 km south of centre, bus No 6 or 11 from Av Costanera y La Rioja, US$0.50. To **Posadas** US$18, 5½ hrs, road paved. To **Buenos Aires**, US$30, but there are more services from Resistencia to Buenos Aires, Rosario and Santa Fe. To **Paso de los Libres**, 5 hrs, US$10. To **Concordia** US$11, Empresa Gualeguaychú, 2 a day. To **Asunción** (Paraguay) US$18.

Directory **Banks** *Banco de la Provincia*, 9 de Julio y San Juan, cash advance on Mastercard; *Banco de Iberá* for cash advance on Visa and Mastercard; *Scotiabankquilmes*, San Juan 740, changes TC's. *Casa de Cambio El Dorado*, 9 de Julio 1343, accept Amex TC's, 5% commission.**Communications** **Post office** San Juan y San Martín. **Telecommunications** Pellegrini y Mendoza. **Internet** *Cybermate*, Jujuy 1087, open 24 hrs. **Tour operators** *Turismo Aventura 4WD*, Galería Paseo del Sul, Junín 1062, T427698, F33269. *Quo Vadis*, Carlos Pellegrini 1140, T423096 Amex representative. **Tourist offices** Plaza Cabral.

Resistencia

Phone code: 03722
Colour map 1, grid B6
Population: 228,000

The hot and energetic capital of the Province of Chaco, Resistencia, is the commercial centre for the Chaco region with the port of Barranqueras, just south on the Río Paraná. It is also an important route centre for travellers between Asunción, Salta and Iguazu. A city of little architectural interest, it is known as the 'city of the statues', there being many of these in the streets.

History   Founded in 1750 near the site of a Jesuit mission, Resistencia was abandoned after the expulsion of the Jesuits and refounded by immigrants from Fruili, Italy, in 1878.

Sights   The **Fogón de los Arrieros**, Brown 350, entre López y French, is a famous club, very interesting. ■ *Open to non-members Mon-Sat, 0800-1200, Tue, Wed, Thu only, 2130-0100, US$2, highly recommended*. **Museo Histórico Regional**, Donovan 425. ■ *Mon-Fri, 0800-1200, 1600-1800*, in the Escuela Normal Sarmiento, traces the development of the city. **Museo de Bellas Artes**, Mitre 150, collection of 19th- and 20th-century local works. ■ *Tue-Sat, 0730-1200, 1500-1900*. **Museo Del Hombre Chaqueño**, Illia 655, sections on indigenous peoples, European immigration and the fauna of the Chaco. **Museo Policial**, Roca 233. Sections on marijuana and other drugs (closed May 2000). ■ *Mon-Fri 0800-1200, 1800-2000, Sat 0800-1200*

Excursions   The **Parque Nacional Chaco**, see page 328. The **Reserva Natural Colonia Benitez**, 13 km north, protects 10 ha of wet Chaco marshlands with savanna and Caranday palms. The **Isla del Cerrito**, an island 63 km northeast of Corrientes at the confluence of the Ríos Paraná and Paraguay, forms a provincial nature reserve of 12,000 ha, covered mainly with grassland and palm trees. At the eastern end of the island, on the Río Paraná, is Cerrito, a tourist complex with white sand beaches, accommodation and

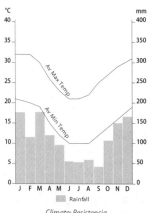

Climate: Resistencia

restaurants, which is very busy during the *Fiesta de la Pesca Dorada* in Paso de la Patria. ■ *Getting there: Follow Route 16 east and turn north just before the bridge to Corrientes: from here a road, the last 20 km of which are dirt, leads to a bridge, from where it is 17 km further to Cerrito. A ferry service connects Cerrito with Paso de la Patria. There are occasional buses from the city. Hitching difficult.*

AB *Colón*, Sta María de Oro 143, T422862. Old fashioned, comfortable. **Sleeping**
AB *Covadonga*, Güemes 182, T44444, F43444. Small rooms, a/c, *Tabaré* snack bar.
B *Hotel AMCSAPCH* (known as Esmirna), H Yrigoyen 83 on corner of Plaza, T422898. Owned by local police, with bath, good value, a/c. **C** *Alfil*, Santa Maria de Oro 495, T420882. A/c extra, English spoken. **C** *Celta*, Alberdi 210, T422986. With bath, basic. **C** *Res San José*, Rawson 304, basic. **C** *Res Alberdi*, Alberdi 317, **E** without bath, basic but clean, restaurant. Recommended. **D** *Aragón*, Santiago del Estero 154.

Camping 2 sites north of town: *Parque Dos de Febrero*, Av Avalos, very pretty, near artificial lake, US$5 per tent. *Parque Avalos*, free.

Restaurant Sociedad Italiana, Yrigoyen 204, excellent cuisine, smart, pricey. *Charly*, **Eating** Güemes 213, snacks, good breakfast, good value.

Regionales Pompeya, Güemes 154, sells local handicrafts and has an Indian handi- **Shopping** craft display. Excellent leather goods at *Chac*, Güemes 160.

Resistencia centre

To Museo de Ciencias Naturales

Corrientes — Don Bosco
Liniers — R de Escalada de San Martín — Pueyrredón — Mitre — Av Sarmiento — Güemes
Santa Fé — Brown
Covadonga — Fogón de los Arrieros
Museo de Bellas Artes 🏛 — Amscapch (Esmirna) ✉
MT de Alvear — H Yrigoyen
Plaza 25 de Mayo
Av 25 de Mayo — Av 9 de Julio
Cathedral ✝ — ℹ
JA Roca — Juan B Bustos
🏛 Museo Policial
■ Colón
Juan Domingo Peron — Presidente Illia
Celta ■
Salta — Donovan — Necochea — General Vedia — Santa Maria de Oro — Av Alberdi — Rawson — General Obligado — JM Paz — R Sáenz Peña
Santiago del Estero — F Ameghino
🏛 Museo Histórico Regional
Plaza 9 de Julio
■ Alfil
Av Moreno — Av Rodríguez Pena
N
0 metres 100
0 yards 100
To Bus Terminal
To Museo del Hombre Chaqueño

The Fogón de los Arrieros

Unique in Argentina and with few parallels in South America, the Fogón de los Arrieros was founded in the late 1930s by a group of friends led by the poet and sculptor Juan de Dios Mena. The club building, with bar, library and workshop, is decorated with local art and 'objets'. A meeting-place for artists and other local characters, it welcomes visits from travellers.

The Fogón was also the inspiration for the city's statues and murals. In 1961,

deciding to create an 'open air art gallery', the club began to promote the placing of statues and sculptures in the streets and plazas: there are now nearly 200, including 26 in Avenida Sarmiento alone, some by local artists, some by outsiders. This, along with the murals in the city's public buildings, can be seen as an expression of the club's view that art is an important part of the development of the city and of the Chaco.

Transport **Local Car hire** *Avis*, French 701 and at airport. *Localiza*, Roca 460, T439255. **Long distance Air** Airport 8 km west of town (no bus). *Austral* (T445550) and *Lapa* (T430201) to/from Buenos Aires; *Aerolíneas Argentinas/Austral* to Formosa; *Lapa* to **Posadas**. *Southern Winds* (T443300) to **Córdoba**, Mendoza, Rosario, Slata and Tucumán. **Bus** Modern terminal on south outskirts (bus 3 or 8 to centre, 20 mins, US$0.70; remise US$4). To **Corrientes** over the Río Paraná bridge, every 15 mins from Av Alberdi near Plaza 25 de Mayo, 40 mins, US$1.30. To **Buenos Aires** 14 hrs, US$35 several companies, most services overnight. To **Santa Fe**, 8 hrs, US$26. To **Córdoba**, 12 hrs, US$43. To **Formosa** 2½ hrs, US$10. To **Iguazú** US$34. To **Posadas**, 5½ hrs, US$18. To **Tucumán** *El Rayo*, 1930 and 2200, 12 hrs, US$21. Buses to Tucumán and Santiago del Estero from Resistencia, or Corrientes, travel at night to avoid the heat; even on a/c buses the dust manages to get in and cover everything. To **Salta** (for connections to Bolivia), *Veloz del Norte*, *Burbuja* and *Central Sáenz Peña*, daily 1830 and 1900, 15 hrs, US$40. To **Bolivian border at Aguas Blancas/Bermejo**, take bus for Salta, change at Güemes, for direct connection to Orán. To **Clorinda** and Paraguayan border US$17, 5 hrs. To **Asunción** daily, via Formosa, *La Internacional*, 6½ hrs, US$21. **To Paraguay** To **Clorinda** and border US$17, 4 hrs. To **Asunción** daily, via Formosa, *La Internacional*, 6 hrs, US$21. **To Bolivia** To frontier at Aguas Blancas/Bermejo, take bus for Salta, change at Güemes, for direct connection to Orán (*Atahualpa* buses every 2 hrs approximately), from where it is 45 mins to border.

Directory **Banks** *Banco del Chaco*, Plaza 25 de Mayo, cash only. *Banco de Crédito*, Justo 200 block, cash advance on Mastercard. *Banco de Iberá* changes TCs (3% commission). *Banco Corrientes*, Alberdi 300 block, cash on Visa card. *Cambio El Dorado*, 9 de Julio 201, changes TCs at reasonable rate. **Communications** Post office Plaza 25 de Mayo, Mon-Sat, 0700-1200, 1500-2000. Telecommunications Justo y Paz. **Laundry** *Tokio*, Güemes y Brown. **Tour operators** *Puerto Aventura*, Saavedra 557, T/F432932, very helpful. **Tourist offices** Santa Fe 178, T/F423547.

North of Resistencia

Route 11 runs north to Formosa and the Paraguayan frontier near Clorinda. Crossing low lying pastures with streams and Caranday palms, this route offers views of the diverse birdlife of the Wet Chaco and is beautiful in the evening.

Formosa
Phone code: 03717
Colour map 2, grid A1
Population: 155,000
240 km N of Corrientes

Formosa is the capital of Formosa Province and the only Argentine port of any note on the Río Paraguay. Boats cross the river to **Alberdi**, a Paraguayan duty-free spot, which can be visited only if you have a multiple entry visa. **Museo Histórico Regional**, 25 de Mayo y Belgrano, has a large collection of artefacts with no particular logic. ■ *Mon-Fri 0730-1200, 1500-1930, entry free.*

Sleeping A *Turismo*, San Martín 759, T426004. Best, parking, a/c. **AL** *Colón*, Belgrano 1068, T426547. Noisy, a/c, colour TV, spacious, **B** without a/c, good, with breakfast. **B** *San Martín*, 25 de Mayo 380, T426769. A/c, with breakfast, run down. **B** *Plaza*, Uriburu 920, T426767. 2-star. **C** *Rivas*, Belgrano 1395, T420499. **E** without bath, cold water, basic, run down. **C** *Colonial*, San Martín 879, T426345. Basic, a/c, parking. **C** *Casa de Familia*, Belgrano 1056, good. Opposite bus terminal is **D** *Hosp El Extranjero*, Gutnisky 2660, T428676. Modern, a/c, with bath, also short stay.

Camping *Club Caza y Pesca* southwest of town, on the Río Paraguay southwest of town. To the south of Formosa, reached by Route 11: *Camping Banco Provincial*, Km 4, good facilities including pool, tennis courts, T429877, US$10 per person. *Las Arianas*, 10 km south (turn off Route 11 at El Pucu, Km 6), T427640.

Eating *Ser San*, 25 de Mayo y Moreno, good. *Pizzería Italia*, 25 de Mayo y Rivadavia. Also on 25 de Mayo: *El Tono María*, No 55, good Italian food, nice atmosphere, expensive. *Parrillada La Cascada*, No 335.

Formosa

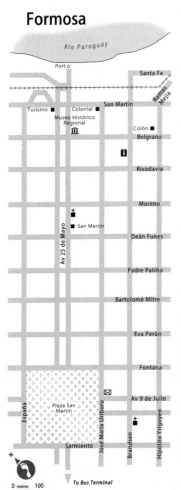

Tour operators *Turismo de Castro*, Brandzen 75, T434777; *Turinfort*, Moreno 58, T427011.

Transport Local Bus 4 or 11 from the terminal to and from the centre. The centre can be traversed on foot. **Long distance Air** El Pucu Airport, 7 km north; *Aerolíneas Argentinas/Austral* and *Lapa* (T435979) to Buenos Aires. **Bus** Modern bus terminal on western outskirts (bus 4 or 11 to/from centre). To **Asunción**, 0400, 0800 and 1730, 3 hrs, US$10.50; easier to go to Clorinda on the border (US$6.50) and then take a bus to Asunción. To **Resistencia**, 6 a day, US$10. To **Buenos Aires** US$41, La Internacional. Bus services to **Embarcación** are frequently cancelled (scheduled daily 1200. Do not rely on this as a route to Bolivia, better to go from Resistencia to Salta and then north). **Train** There are no longer passenger services on the line across the Chaco to Embarcación.

Directory Banks Close at noon and there are no *casas de cambio*; buy pesos in Asunción or Clorinda. **Tourist offices** Brandzen 117, T426502, also at bus terminal very helpful.

Clorinda

Phone code: 03718
Population: 40,000

Clorinda lies on the Río Pilcomayo, 13 km upstream from its confluence with the Río Paraná. It has a banana festival in early October. It is 118 km north of Formosa.

The Northeast

Sleeping **B** *Embajador*, San Martín 166, T421148. **C** *Helen*, San Martín 320, T421118. **C** *Res 9 de Julio*, San Martín y Roque Sáenz Peña, T421221. With a/c. *Res San Martín*, 12 de Octubre 1150, T421211 **Camping** at *YPF* station south of town on road to frontier.

Transport Bus From Argentine end of Puente Loyola: to **Formosa**, 10 a day; **Resistencia**, US$14, 4 a day, and **Santa Fe/Rosario/Buenos Aires** 3 daily.

Parque Nacional Río Pilcomayo
65 km NW of Clorinda

This park covers 48,000ha of Wet Chaco environment on the western bank of the Río Pilcomayo. The western part, near the entrance, is mainly marshland; further east is savanna studded with groves of trees including quebrachos, caranday palms and palos borachos. Along the Río Pilcomayo are areas of riverine forest. Among the protected species are aguará-guazú, giant anteaters and tapirs. Caimans, tagú lizards, black howler monkeys, rheas and a variety of birds can also be seen. You need at least a day to visit the western parts of the park and must be accompanied by *guardaparques*. Vehicles should have four-wheel drive. ■ *Getting there: Buses run to Laguna Blanca, 4 km from the park entrance; 3 km further is the guardaparque office, near which camping is permitted.*

Frontier with Paraguay

There are two routes into Paraguay. The easiest crossing is by road via the Puente Loyola, 3 km north of **Clorinda**. From Puerto Falcón, at the Paraguayan end of the bridge, the road runs 20 km east and crosses the Río Paraguay to reach Asunción.

Asunción

■ **Sleeping**
1 Ambassador *A1*
2 Cecilia *B6*
3 Chaco *B4*
4 Continental *B2*
5 Embajador *B2*
6 Española *C4*
7 Excelsior *D3*
8 Gran Armele *B1*
9 Gran Renacimiento *B3*
10 Guaraní *C3*
11 Ñandutí *B2*

Immigration Formalities for entering Argentina are dealt with at the Argentine end, those for leaving Argentina at the Paraguayan end. Easy crossing, open 24 hrs.

Transport Bus Local services to Asunción, *Empresa Falcón* US$1, every hr, last bus to the centre of Asunción 1830.

The other route is by ferry from Puerto Pilcomayo, close to Clorinda (bus US$0.40) there is is a vehicle ferry service to Itá Enramada (Paraguay), US$0.65, 20 minutes journey every 30 minutes. Then take bus 9 to Asunción.

Immigration Argentine immigration at Puerto Pilcomayo, closed at weekends for tourists. Paraguayan immigration at Itá Enramada.

Asunción

The capital and largest city in Paraguay, Asunción sprawls south and east of its original site on the shore of a bay on the eastern bank of the Río Paraguay. Most of the public buildings are near the river; most can be seen by following El Paraguayo Independiente southeast from the Aduana (Customs House).

Phone code: 021
Population: over
1,200,000

The **Palacio de Gobierno**, built 1860-1892 in the style of Versailles. ■ *Open Sun*. In **Plaza Independencia** or **Constitución** stands the **Congreso Nacional** (debates can be attended during the session from April to December, on Thursday and sometimes Friday). On the northwest side of the Plaza is the **Antiguo Colegio Militar**, built in 1588 as a Jesuit College and now housing the Casa de la Cultura and the military history museum (see below). On the southeast side of the Plaza is the **cathedral**. Two blocks southwest, along Calle Chile, is **Plaza de los Héroes**, with the **Pantéon Nacional de los Héroes** based on Les Invalides in Paris, begun during the War of the Triple Alliance and finished in 1937. Near the **Plaza Uruguaya** is the railway station, built 1856, and a steam engine, the *Sapucai*, dating from 1861. The **Cementerio Recoleta**, the national cemetery resembling a miniature city with tombs in various architectural styles, is on Avenida Mariscal López, 3 km southeast of the centre.

Sights

The best of several parks is **Parque Carlos Antonio López**, set high to the west along Colón and, if you can find a gap in the trees, with a grand view. The **Jardín Botánico** covering 250 ha is 6 km east, on Avenida Artigas y Primer Presidente. The gardens lie along the Río Paraguay and

To Parque Caballero, Jardín Botánico, Puerto Falcón, Argentina & Chaco

To Airport & Luque

Museo Dr Andrés Barbero

Av España

Río Monday

Bogado (Rutas 1 & 2)

San Roque

Eligio Ayala

Mcal Estigarribia

25 de Mayo

Cerro Corá

Plaza Uruguaya

To Av Mcal López, Airport & Luque

Av Estados Unidos

Paraguari

Antequera

Tacuary

5

6

To Itá Enramada

12 Orly *D3*
13 Paraná *B4*
14 Plaza *B5*
15 Presidente *C3*
16 Sabe Center *B4*
17 Zaphir *B1*

contain only trees (no labels, but nice and shady), an 18-hole golf course, and a little zoo, which has inspired some unfavourable comments and protests. ■ *Getting there: Bus Nos 2, 6, 23, and 40, US$0.15, about 35 mins from Luis A Herrera, or Nos 24, 35 or 44B from Oliva or Cerro Corá. Entrance fee US$0.50.* In the gardens are the former residences of two Presidents: that of Carlos Antonio López, a one-storey typical Paraguayan country house with verandahs, which now houses a **Museo de Historia Natural** and a library, and that of Francisco Solano López, a two-storey European-inspired mansion which is now the **Museo Indigenista.** ■ *Both museums open Mon-Sat 0730-1130, 1300-1730, Sun 0900-1300, both free, neither is in good condition.* The beautiful church of **Santísima Trinidad** (on Santísimo Sacramento, parallel to Avenida Artigas), dating from 1854 with frescoes on the inside walls, is well worth a visit. It is a 10-minute walk from the zoo entrance. The **Maca Indian reservation** is north of the gardens. The Indians, who live in very poor conditions, expect you to photograph them (US$0.25). ■ *Getting there: Bus 42 or 44, entrance US$0.15, guide US$0.80.*

Museums **Museo Nacional de Bellas Artes,** Iturbe y Mariscal Estigarribia, a good collection of Spanish paintings including works by Tintoretto and Murrillo; also an interesting selection of 20th-century Paraguayan art. ■ *Tue-Fri, 0700-1900, Sat-Sun 0800-1200.* In the **Casa de la Independencia** (14 de Mayo y Presidente Franco) is an interesting historical collection. ■ *Tue-Fri 0700-1200 and 1430-1830, Sat and Sun 0800-1200, entry free.* **Museo Histórico Militar** in the Antiguo Colegio Militar, on Plaza de la Independencia. Containing collections focussing on the War of the Triple Alliance and the Chaco War. ■ *Mon-Fri 0730-1200, 1330-1800, Sat-Sun 0800-1200.* **Museo Dr Andrés Barbero,** España y Mompox. With a good collection of tools and weapons, et cetera, of the various Guaraní cultures. Recommended. ■ *Mon-Fri 0700-1100, and Mon, Wed, Fri 1500-1700, anthropological, free.* **Centro de Artes Visuales,** at Isla de Francia, access via Avenida Gral Genes, bus 30 or 44A from the centre. ■ *Daily, except Sun and holidays, 1600-2030*; contains **Museo Paraguayo de Arte Contemporáneo,** with some striking murals, **Museo de Arte Indígeno** and **Museo de Barro,** containing ceramics. Highly recommended.

Tourist offices *Dirección General de Turismo,* Palma esquina Alberdi, open Mon-Fri 0800-2000, T441530, F491230. Free map, information on all parts of Paraguay, but you may need to be persistent. Another map is sold in bookshops.

Directory **Immigration** O'Leary 625, 8th floor. Ministerio de Relaciones Exteriores, O'Leary y Presidente Franco. For full details including accommodation, restaurants, embassies, travel agents and excursions see the *South American Handbook.*

The Argentine Chaco

The Chaco is mostly cattle country, a vast low-lying plain some 900 km across and covering about half of Paraguay, areas of Bolivia and Brazil and parts of northern Argentina. Though this sprawling alluvial lowland rises gradually from east to west, its rise is so gentle (200 m in 900 km) that the rivers which cross it are slow and meander.

Little visited by travellers, its wildlife makes it a worthwhile destination for nature lovers. Though poor roads and lack of public transport make much of the Chaco inaccessible, there are several parks: two are described below while a third,

The Quebracho

Though large areas of quebracho forest have been destroyed, the tree continues to symbolize the Chaco. There are in fact two species of quebracho: white (Aspidosperma quebracho blanco) and red (Schinopsis Balansae). White quebracho is found throughout northern Argentina. Growing as high as 23 m, it has a grey trunk up to 1 m in diameter and pointed leaves. The Indians used its bark for medicinal purposes. The red quebracho, found only in the Chaco, has very hard wood and is the purest known source of tannin (up to 30%) which is of great value for curing leather.

the Parque Nacional Pilcomayo, near Clorinda, is described above. There are two distinct zones: the Wet Chaco along the Ríos Paraná and Paraguay and the Dry Chaco further west. The Wet Chaco is covered mainly by marshlands with savanna and groves of Caranday palms. Further west, as rainfall diminishes, scrubland of algarrobo, white quebracho, palo borracho and various types of cacti are found.

The Chaco is one of the main centres of indigenous population in Argentina: it is home to two of the largest minorities, the Tobas and the Wichi or Mataco as well as the less numerous Mocovi.

Climate Rain falls mostly in summer; in the east annual rainfall is about 1,200 mm, dropping to 400-700 mm in the centre. Higher rainfall (1,700 mm a year) occurs in the far west near the Andean foothills, but most is lost through evaporation. South America's highest temperatures, exceeding 45°C, have been recorded here, but winters are mild, with an occasional touch of frost in the south.

Economy The Chaco has large *estancias* and low stocking rates: some estimate that the minimum size for an *estancia* to return a profit is 7,500 ha. Tannin and cotton are the traditional industries, although acreage planted to sunflowers has increased dramatically, along with maize and sorghum. Tannin is struggling against competition from synthetic tannin and the huge mimosa plantations in South Africa. The more accessible eastern forests have nearly disappeared; deforestation of all species is proceeding rapidly in the north and west of the province, which produces charcoal for a military steel foundry in Jujuy. Small roadside factories also produce custom furniture.

Cities in the Chaco The most important cities are on the edge of the Chaco: Resistencia and Formosa are on the west bank of the Ríos Paraná and Paraguay (see page 320 and 322, respectively). For Santiago del Estero, on the western edge of the Chaco, see the North West section. The other towns are located along the two main routes which cross the Chaco, Route 16 and Route 81. Most roads in the Chaco are poor.

Route 16

Running northwest from Resistencia through Roque Sáenz Peña to Salta province where it connects with Route 9 (the main northern highway) at a point north of Metán, this is the best route between Paraguay and Northwest Argentina. It is mostly paved, several tolls.

The Northeast

Wildlife of the Wet Chaco and Iberá marshlands

The open landscapes of the Wet Chaco and the Iberá marshlands offer incredible opportunities for observing wildlife. Reptiles include the yellow anaconda, black caiman and broad-snouted caiman, the tegu lizard and the water turtle. The colorful bird life is outstanding: among species which may be seen are the white-necked herons, black-headed parakeets, and turquoise parrots, scarlet-headed blackbirds, yellow-winged blackbirds and screaming cowbirds. Species of duck include the muscovy and tree-ducks. Amongst the birds of prey are the black-collared hawk and the savannah hawk.

The Chaco and Iberá are also probably the best environments in Argentina for viewing land mammals. Worth watching out for are the capybara (the largest rodent in the world), the black howler monkey and the crab-eating fox. There are also armadillos and two species of brockets. Peccaries, tapirs and collared anteaters are more difficult to find. Endangered species are the long-legged maned wolf, the giant anteater and the marsh deer, which is restricted mainly to the marshlands of Iberá.

Most of these mammals can also be found further west in the Dry Chaco, though here you may also find the peccari quimilero as well as endangered species such as the giant armadillo and jaguar. The Dry Chaco is also home to reptiles such as the red ground lizard and the arboreal boa.

Capybaras

Maned Wolf

Parque Nacional Chaco
115 km W of Resistencia
Best visited in autumn & spring

The park extends over 15,000 ha and protects one of the last remaining untouched areas the Wet Chaco. Along the banks of the Río Negro, which crosses the park, are areas of riverine forest. There are 10 km of tracks, which lead through different types of environment including lagunas and streams, savanna with Caranday palm groves and forests of quebracho and palo borracho. It is a good place to see the region's abundant birdlife. The *guardaparques* offer a one to two hour walk, explaining the region's plants and animals. Recommended. "The mosquitos are more voracious than we've ever encountered in Asia or South America, but the birds were good".

Access The park is reached by Provincial Route 9, which branches off Route 16, 56 km west of Resistencia. Route 9 is paved for 15 km, but the remaining 23 km to the park entrance are unpaved and difficult in wet weather. Entry US$5.

Sleeping Camping facilities, good, free, cold showers, but the nearest supplies are in Capitán Solari, 6 km from the park entrance.

Transport Bus From Resistencia 4 daily, 2½ hrs, US$6, as far as Capitán Solari from where local transport is available, ask around.

Penetrating the inpenetrable

El Impenetrable is the name sometimes given to a large northwestern expanse of the Argentine Chaco. Covering some 4 million hectares and largely uninhabited, it has resisted attempts at settlement and commercial exploitation during the past century.

In the years before the First World War two railway lines were begun across the Chaco, from Barrancas to Métan, and from Formosa to Embarcación. These were intended to open the Chaco up for settlement and for transporting the products of the region out to the ports of the Río Paraná. Towns were built along these lines and the new settlers, attracted by the rise in world cotton prices during the First World War, turned the area into a major producer of cotton. In the 1950s

competition from natural fibres, soil exhaustion and changes of government policies led to a collapse in cotton production and the abandonment of towns and villages.

The railways struggled on, though lack of investment, declining revenues and competition from road transport, made their timetables ever more fictional. By the early 1990s the trip from Formosa to Embarcación, 20 hours in a cochemotor with wooden seats and no refreshments, was decidedly for the adventurous, though those who made it reported that the birdlife was wonderful. The 1994 decision of the Argentine government to transfer responsibility for passenger rail services to the provinces dealt the final blow to passenger trains on these two lines.

Roque Sáenz Peña is the most important centre on Route 16. Since the early 1980s it has acquired the status of a spa town: its thermal waters, 35-42°C are 30% more salty than the sea and are claimed to be the best in the country. Founded in 1912, the city attracted large number of immigrants from Central Europe during the 1920s. Its principal attraction is the **Parque Zoológico**, 3 km south of the centre and covering 28 ha, one of the best in the country, containing a wide variety of animals native to the Chaco, as well as a botanical reserve of local species. The **Museo Histórico de la Ciudad**, San Martín y Sarmiento, displays on the founding and early growth of the city. ■ *Tue-Fri 0730-2000, Sat/Sun 1430-2100*. The **Casa de la Cultura**, Calles 12 y 9, has exhibitions of indigenous handicrafts, archaeology, anthropology.

Presidencia Roque Sáenz Peña
Phone code: 03714
Population: 65,000
160 km NW of Resistencia

Excursions Quitilipi, 23 km east along Route 16, where there is a Toba community and a free municipal campsite. At **Castelli**, 114 km north, there is a large Toba Indian community and an *artesanía* shop. ■ *Getting there: Buses Central Sáenz Peña services at 1100, 1530 and 2000*.

Sleeping A *Gualok*, San Martín 1198, T420521. Including use of thermal baths (also available to non-residents for a small charge), run down, parking. **AB** *Augustus*, Belgrano 483, T422809, a/c. **B** *Orel*, San Martín 130, T420101. *Res Asturias*, Belgrano 402, T420210, fair. *Res Sáenz Peña*, Sub Palmira 464, T420320, near bus station, cheap. **E** *Hotel Guc*, basic. **Camping** *El Descanso*, municipal site, 1 km east of centre.

Entertainment Thermal baths Brown 541, with sauna, massage and other services.

Transport Bus To **Buenos Aires**, daily 2000, US$40 (from Buenos Aires also daily 2000), *La Estrella* and *La Internacional* alternate days. To **Santiago del Estero** and **Tucumán**, *Empresa El Rayo* daily. To **Resistencia** (connection for Salta 1700 daily), 2 hrs, US$4.

The Northeast

Northwest
of Roque
Sáenz Peña

At **Avia Terai**, 31 km northwest, the road forks. Provincial Route 94 goes southwest to General Pinedo, then continues paved as National Route 89 to Quimilí and Santiago del Estero. Along this road, near Gancedo, 141 km south of Avia Terai on the border of Chaco and Santiago del Estero provinces is the **Campo del Cielo**, a meteorite impact field about 15 km by 4 km where about 5,000 years ago a planetoid broke before landing into 30 main pieces. Some of the meteorites are on display in Buenos Aires (the Rivadavia Museum and the Planetarium), but the largest, 'El Chaco' (33.4 tonnes), is on display at the Campo. ■ *Getting there: A 15 km dirt road south from Gancedo.*

From Avia Terai, Route 16, runs straight northwest through **Pampa del Infierno**, Km 232, to the Santiago del Estero border. In Santiago province the road is good as far as Los Tigres, Km 387, then less good to the Salta border. From this border to **Macapillo**, Km 539, it is straight and well-paved. From Macapillo the road runs north following the Río Juramento to **Joaquín V González**, Km 575, around which it is appalling and difficult after rain. From here it continues through Ceibalito and El Tunal to meet Route 9 just north of Metán. At Km 585 and Km 593, roads run north to connect with provincial Route 5 (passing Parque Nacional El Rey, see page 251) and Route 9 at Lumbreras. The Joaquin V González stretch can be avoided by a dust-road which branches off just past Macapillo and runs to El Tunal, via Corral Quemado.

Essentials   There are service stations at Roque Sáenz Peña, Pampa del Infierno (ACA *Hostería*), Pampa de los Guanacos (good hot, clean and free showers at the YPF station, and good value set dinner at the *comedor* next door), **Taco Pozo** (basic *Hospedaje* half a block from ACA station), **El Quebrachal** (gaucho festival in late Nov) and J V González (last fuel before Güemes *en route* to Salta). Fuel cannot be pumped during the frequent power cuts.

Route 81

Running northwest across the Chaco from Formosa to Embarcación, this is the other route across the Chaco. It is paved as far as Las Lomitas, Km 299, from where it is dirt and often in very poor condition, especially after rain.

Reserva
Nacional
Formosa
210 km NW of Las
Lomitas; 500 km NW of
Formosa
Best time to visit:
spring & autumn

This park stretches between the Río Teuquito to the north and the Río Bermejo to the south. Covering 10,000 ha and located at the heart of the Dry Chaco, the park covers 10,000 ha of woodlands broken by the floodplains of the Río Teuquito. The park is one of the few habitats in Argentina of the endangered *tatú carreta* (priodontes maximus), the largest surviving species of armadillo. Other wildlife includes carayá monkeys, mountain foxes, pumas, peccaries and a wide variety of bird species.

Access   Park entrance is reached by Provincial Route 39 which runs 62 km south from Ingeniero Juárez, situated 459 km northwest of Formosa. 4WD vehicle advisable. No accommodation, take supplies from Ingeniero Juárez.

Along the Alto Paraná

The Alto Paraná is difficult to navigate, being shallow in parts, braided in others, its various channels embracing mid-stream islands. Much rice is grown on its banks. Yerba mate, tea and tobacco are grown in the area around Posadas.

Ituzaingó lies on the northern edge of the Esteros del Iberá. There are good views of the birdlife of Iberá from the road. It is a modern town serving the nearby Yacyretá-Apipé hydroelectric project, which can be visited: free buses run to Centro de Relaciones Públicas, where a video is shown and other information given.

Ituzaingó
Population: 10,000
Colour map 2, grid B2
227 km E of Corrientes

Sleeping Several hotels including **AB** *Ituzaingó*, Entre Rios y Iberá, T420601. **E** *Hosp Dos Hermanos*, Pellegrini y Posadas, clean, friendly. **Estancias** *San Gará*, Route 12, Km 1237, about 15 km west, full board **A** per person, or in dormitory with hammock-style accommodation, **C** per person, including pool and all excursions into the Iberá marshes, by boat, jeep or on horseback a lovely place with extraordinary hospitality. Recommended. Book in advance: T0786-20550, in Posadas 0752-27217, in Buenos Aires, 01-811-1132, F476-2648 (office at Av Alvear 1668, piso 5); ask for owner Sr Pablo Prats. Take any bus between Posadas and Ituzaingó and walk 1,500 m from turning to the *estancia*; **A** per person *San Juan Poriahú*, on the northern edge of the Iberá marshes, near Loreto, 83 km southwest of Posadas, 16,500 ha, devoted to cattle ranching and cereals. Open March-November to groups of 4-12. Transport from Corrientes US$45. T/F Buenos Aires 4791-9511, from US$75 per person per day, advance booking essential.

Posadas

The main Argentine port on the south bank of the Alto Paraná, Posadas is 320 km east of Corrientes. Founded in 1879, the city flourished as a river port and is now capital of Misiones.

Phone code: 03752
Colour map 2, grid B2
Population: 211,000

The centre of the city is the Plaza 9 de Julio on which stand the **cathedral** and the **Gobernación**, in French neogotic style. There are fine views over the river from the **Parque Río del Paraguay**, 11 blocks north, where there is also a good **Mercado Artesanal.** ■ *Mon-Fri, 0800-1200.* **Museo del Hombre**, General Paz 1865, houses archaeological pieces from the areas to be flooded by the Yacyretá hydroelectric project and a section on the Jesuit missionary era. ■ *Mon-Fri, 0700-1300, 1400-1900.* A good way of seeing the city is to take the No 7 bus ('Circunvalación') from Calle Junín. On the opposite bank of the river lies the Paraguayan town of Encarnación, which can be reached by the San Roque bridge.

Sights

The Northeast

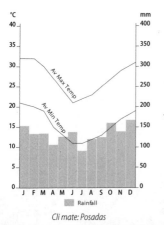

Cli mate: Posadas

San Miguel Apóstoles, 65 km south, is a prosperous town founded by Ukrainian and Polish immigrants, where a maté festival is held in November. **Sleeping** at **D** *Hotel Misiones.* **Estancia Santa Inés**, 20 km south (Route 105), T0752-36194, F0752-39998, 2,000ha, grows much *yerba maté.* Activities include walking, horseriding and, between February and October, helping in *maté* cultivation. **AB** full board; half-day activities US$20, taxi from Posadas, US$15.

Excursions

All streets have been given numbers instead of names: the central plaza is bounded by Calles 36, 38, 39 and 41;

Essentials

Uruguay, for instance is now Calle 54. Also, the bus terminal which used to be at Uruguay/54 y Mitre has now been coverted into the *Paseo Cultural La Terminal* and a new terminal built on the outskirts.

Sleeping
Cheaper accommodation is available in Embarcación

Best is **A** *Libertador*, San Lorenzo 2208, T437601, F39448. With breakfast, also cheaper rooms for travellers. **A** *Continental*, Bolívar 314, T438966, F35302. Comfortable but noisy, restaurant, parking, breakfast. **A** *Posadas*, Bolívar 1949, T40888, F30294. Garage, a/c, TV, comfortable, good service, snack bar, laundry, highly recommended. **B** *Turismo*, Bolívar 171, T437401. Modern, a/c. **B** *City*, Colón 280, T433901. A/c, central, good value, good restaurant. **B** *Res Marlis*, Corrientes 234, T425764, German spoken, highly recommended. **B** *Le Petit*, Santiago del Estero 1630, T436031, parking. Recommended. **Near bus terminal** is **B** *Carioca*, Mitre 2437, T424113, next to expreso Singer. **B** *Colonial*, Barrufaldi 2419, T436149. **B** *Horianski*, Líbano 2655, T422675. Garage, fan, poor value. **C** *Res Misiones*, Azara 382, basic, helpful. **C** *Gran Hotel Misiones*, Libano y Barrufaldi, T422777. Run down, with breakfast. **B** *Res Marlis*, Corrientes 234, T425764. German spoken, highly recommended. **B** *Le Petit*, Santiago del Estero 1630, T436031, parking. **C** *Res Andresito*, Salta 1743, T423850, youth hostel style, noisy. **D** *Res Nagel*, Calle 58 No 2146 (formerly Pedro Méndez 211), 2 blocks from *Paseo Cultural La Terminal*, small rooms, shared shower, no hot water, shady patio, no breakfast. **E** per person *Pension Andresito Guacubari*, Salta 1743, T423850.

Camping Municipal site, Av Gendarmeria Nacional, on the river, off Route 12, electric showers, dirty, shop, reached by buses 4 or 21 from centre;.

Eating *El Tropezón*, San Martín 185, good, inexpensive. *El Encuentro*, San Martín 361, good value. *La Ventana*, Bolívar 1725, excellent. *Sociedad Española*, La Rioja 1848, good food, popular lunches. *El Estribo*, Tucumán y Ayacucho, good cooking in attractive atmosphere. Recommended. *La Querencia*, Bolívar 322, on Plaza 9 de Julio, good

Posadas

Not to scale

value. Recommended. *Pizzería Los Pinos*, Sarmiento y Rivadavia, excellent and cheap. *Pizzería La Grata Alegría*, Bolívar y Junín, good. *Sukimo*, Azara near San Martín, good for breakfast. The restaurant at San Martín 1788 serves excellent meals, good value. Several cheap places on Mitre near the *Paseo Cultural La Terminal*, near the market and on the road to the port.

Discos *Los Años 60*, San Lorenzo y Entre Ríos. *Power*, Bolívar between 3 de Febrero y 25 de Mayo. Another at San Martín y Jujuy, open 0100-0500 Thu-Sun. **Entertainment**

Air General San Martín Airport, 12 km west, reached by Bus No 8 or 28 from near bus terminal (ask at kiosk opposite terminal) in 20 mins, US$0.45, taxi US$13. To **Buenos Aires**, Lapa and Austral, both once a week via Corrientes; Lapa also to **Iguazú**, Austral to **Formosa**. **Transport**

Bus New terminal about 3 km out of the city on the road to Corrientes. To **Buenos Aires**, 15 hrs, shop around off season for best deal. Singer and Tigre each have several buses a day. *Común* US$47.50, *diferencial* US$58, *ejecutivo* (with hot meal) US$70; some go via Resistencia, some via Concordia. From the Argentine side of the international bridge bus tickets to Buenos Aires are sold which includes taxi to bus terminal and breakfast. Frequent services to San Ignacio Miní, 1 hr, US$3.50, and Puerto Iguazú, *servicio común* US$16, 7 hrs, *expreso*, US$23, 5 hrs. To **Corrientes** US$18. To **Formosa**, US$8. To **Córdoba** with *Singer* and *Litoral* on alternate days at 1200, 15 hrs, US$34. To **Tucumán**, *La Estrella*, daily 1315, 17 hrs, US$55. To **Salta**, *La Nueva Estrella* daily at 1315, arrives 0700 next day, US$62, change bus in Resistencia, book in advance, T455455. to **Resistencia**, 6-7 hrs, US$18. To **Concordia**, Singer, US$32, 2100 daily, 10 hrs. To **Concepción del Uruguay**, Singer, US$29, 11 hrs.

International For buses to *Encarnación* see below under Frontier Crossing. To **Asunción**, Singer, daily 1400, 7 hrs, and Empresa Godoy, US$14. To **Montevideo**, a roundabout journey because the main Asunción-Montevideo route passes through Corrientes; alternative is Singer to the junction for Colón, at Villa San José (ACA hostel, C), local bus to Colón, bus over the bridge to Paysandú, then on to Montevideo. To Brazil via Uruguaiana, Singer, US$10-14, 6 hrs, 3 daily to **Paso de los Libres**, then cross the international bridge. Singer to **Porto Alegre**, via Oberá, Panambí, Santo Angelo and Carazinho, Tue, Thu, Sun at 1400, arriving 0345 next day.

Airline offices *Lapa*, Junín 2054, T40300; *Austral*, Ayacucho 264, T432889. **Banks** *Banco de Iberá*, Bolívar 1821 (main plaza), changes Amex TCs (4-5% commission). *Banco de La Nación*, Bolívar 1799, opens 0700-1215. *Banco Francés*, San Martín y San Lorenzo, Visa cash advance (morning only). *Banco Nacional del Lavoro*, Plaza 9 de Julio, ATM accepts Mastercard and Visa. *Cambio Mazza*, Bolívar 1932 and Buenos Aires 1442, open Sat 0800-1200, TCs accepted. Amex agent, *Express Travel*, Félix de Azara 2097, T4237687 Street money changers on southwest corner of Plaza 9 de Julio. If stuck when banks and *cambios* are closed, cross the river to Encarnación and use the street changers. **Communications** Post Office Bolívar y Ayacucho. **Consulates** *Brazil*, Mitre 631, T424830, 0800-1200, visas issued free, photo required, 90 days given. *Paraguay*, San Lorenzo 179. **Laundry** *Lavemaster*, Santiago del Estero y San Lorenzo, efficient. **Tour operators** *Viajes Turismo*, Colón 1901, ask for Kenneth Nairn, speaks English, most helpful, good tours to Iguazú and local sights. **Tourist offices** Colón 1985 y La Rioja, T424360, helpful, maps and brochures in English of Posadas, Formosa and Iguazú Falls. Municipal kiosk on Plaza 9 de Julio, open 0800-1200, 1400-2000 daily. Hotel listings for Misiones province. **Directory**

The **Puente San Roque** is the only route between the two cities: the ferry service across the river is for locals only (no immigration facilities). Pedestrians and cyclists are not allowed to cross the bridge; cyclists must ask officials for assistance. Pesos are accepted in Encarnación, so there is no need to change **Frontier with Paraguay**

The Northeast

them back into dollars. Paraguay is one hr behind Argentina, except during Paraguayan summer time.

Immigration and customs Formalities are conducted at respective ends of the bridge. Argentine side has different offices for locals and foreigners; Paraguay has one for both. Delays are common entering Argentina.

Transport Buses leave from opposite terminal every 15 mins, *servicio común* US$1.50, *servicio diferencial* (faster service at frontier) US$3. Buses do not wait for formalities. Alight, keep your ticket and luggage, and catch a later bus. Taxi US$5.

Encarnación (Paraguay)

Phone code 071
Population: 60,000

Founded in 1614, Encarnación is the third largest city in Paraguay. It exports the products of a rich agricultural area: timber, soya, maté, tobacco, cotton, and hides. The old centre is due to be drowned when the Yacyretá-Apipé dam is finally completed: though badly neglected, it forms the main commercial area, selling a wide range of cheap goods to visitors from Argentina and Brazil. A modern, but less interesting, centre has been built on higher ground. Tourist goods, electrical equipment and accommodation are much cheaper than in Posadas.

Excursions
There are several Jesuit missions nearby worth visiting

Trinidad, 28 km east, was founded in 1706 and designed by the architect Juan Bautista Prímoli; it is now a UNESCO World Cultural Heritage site. The Jesuit church, once completely ruined, has been partially restored. Also partially rebuilt is the bell-tower which is near the original church (excellent views from the top). You can also see another church, a college, workshops and the Indians' living quarters. ■ *US$1.* **Jesús**, 10 km northwest of Trinidad, is a much later Jesuit construction, dating from 1763-1767. The massive construction programme included a church, sacristy, *residencia* and a baptistry, on one side of which is a square tower. ■ *Closed 1130-1330, US$1.* **San Cosmé y Damián**, about 90 km west of Encarnación, was also unfinished in 1767 when the Jesuits were expelled from South America. A huge completion project has recently been carried out following the original plans.

Sleeping
For full details of services see the South American Handbook

AL *Novohotel Encarnación*, first class, on outskirts Route 1, Km 2, T4131. Comfortable, very well run, highly recommended. **A** *Cristal*, Estigarribia 1157, T2371. Restaurant. **B** *Paraná*, Estigarribia 1414, T4440. Good breakfast, helpful. Recommended. **C** *Acuario*, Mallorquín 1550, T2676. With breakfast, central, pleasant, parking. **C** *Viera*, 25 de Mayo 413, T2038. With breakfast and a/c, **D** with fan. **D** *Central*, Mcal López 542, T3454. With breakfast, nice patio, German spoken. **D** *Germano*, Cabañas y C A López, opposite bus terminal, T3346, **E** without bath, German and Japanese spoken, small, very accommodating. Highly recommended. **D** *Itapúa*, C A López y Cabanas, T/F5045. Opposite bus station, dark rooms, modern. **D** *Hotel Liz*, Av Independencia 1746, T2609. Comfortable, restaurant, parking. Recommended. **D** *Viena*, PJ Caballero 568, T3486. Beside Antelco, with breakfast, German-run, good food, garage. **E** *La Rueda*, C A López y Memmel near bus station, a bit run down but OK.

Directory Tourist offices Wiessen 345, 3 blocks from bus terminal, helpful, open 0800-1200; street map of city.

San Ignacio Mini

San Ignacio Mini is a small town which is the site of the most impressive remains of a Jesuit mission in the Misiones region, 63 km east of Posadas. The site is maintained by UNESCO as a national monument. The town is also a good base for visiting other Jesuit ruins nearby and for walking.

Phone code: 03752
Colour map 2, grid B2
Population: 4,300 m

History

San Ignacio Mini ('small' in comparison with San Ignacio Guazu – 'large' – on the Paraguayan side of the Río Paraná) was founded on its present site in 1696. At the height of its prosperity in 1731, the mission housed 4,356 people but after the expulsion of the Jesuits in 1767 its decline was rapid. By 1784 there were only 176 Guaraní and by 1810 none remained. In 1817, by order of the Paraguayan dictator, Rodriguez de Francia, San Ignacio was set on fire. The ruins, like those of nearby Santa Ana and Loreto, were lost in the jungle until discovered again in 1897. In 1943 control over the site was handed to an agency of the Argentine government. Some of the craft work produced at San Ignacio can be seen in two museums in Buenos Aires: the Museo colonial Isaac Fernández Blanco and the municipal Museo de Arte Colonial.

San Ignacio Mini

NB This includes buildings no longer standing

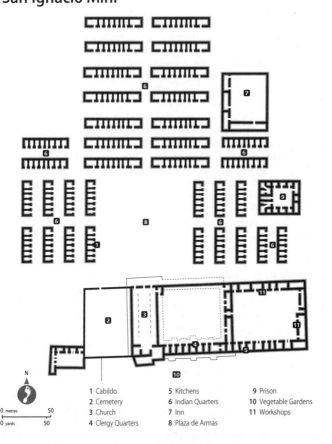

The Northeast

1 Cabildo	5 Kitchens	9 Prison
2 Cemetery	6 Indian Quarters	10 Vegetable Gardens
3 Church	7 Inn	11 Workshops
4 Clergy Quarters	8 Plaza de Armas	

0 metres 50
0 yards 50

The ruins

*Son et-lumière show,
2000 (not Mon or Tue),
weekends only out of
season, cancelled in wet
weather, Spanish only,
tickets from museum*

Like other Jesuit missions San Ignacio Mini was constucted around a central plaza: to the north, east and west were about 30 parallel one-storey buildings, each with a wide veranda in front and each divided into 10 small, one-room dwellings. The roofs have gone, but the massive metre-thick walls are still standing except where they have been torn down by the *ibapoi* trees. The public buildings, some still 10 m high, are on the south side of the plaza: in the centre are the ruins of the church, 71 m x 28 m, finished about 1724. To the right is the cemetery, to the left the cloisters, the priests' quarters and the workshops. The masonry, a red sandstone, was held together by a sandy mud. There is much bas-relief sculpture, mostly of floral designs.

The **Centro de Interpretación Jesuítico-Guaraní**, generally known as the 'Museo Vivo', 200 m inside the entrance to the ruins, is an exhibition which includes representations of the lives of the Guaraní before the arrival of the Spanish, the work of the Jesuits and the consequences of their expulsion, as well as a fine model of the mission in its heyday; well laid out. There is also a small **Museo Provincial**, which contains a collection of artefacts from Jesuit reducciones. ■ *0700-1900 daily.*

■ *0700-1900, entry US$2.50, US$10 with guide, tip appreciated if the guards look after your luggage). Allow about 1½ hrs for a leisurely visit. Go early to avoid crowds. There are heavy rains in Feb. Mosquitoes can be a problem.*

Excursions

The ruins of the mission of **Loreto** are reached by a 3 km dirt road (signposted) which turns off the main road 6 km west of San Ignacio. Moved to its present site in 1686, it was the site of the first printing press in the area. Little remains of this once large establishment other than a few walls, though excavations are in progress. Note the number of old trees with stones encased between their buttresses and main trunk. **Sleeping** at *Colonial*, at entrance, secluded, recently opened.

The **Santa Ana** are the ruins of another Jesuit mission, 16 km west. Moved to its present site in 1660, Santa Ana was the site of the Jesuit iron foundry. Much less well preserved than San Ignacio, the ruins are 1½ km along a path from the main road (signposted). ■ *US$1.*

The **Casa de Horacio Quiroga** is the former house of an Argentine writer born in Uruguay, situated 2 km southwest of town in beautiful gardens. Recommended. ■ *US$2.* From here the path leads to Puerto Nuevo on the Río Paraná, from where, during summer, boats cross to Paraguay.

*From here there are
panoramic views over
the Río Paraná*

The **Parque Provincial Tetú-Cuare**, 11 km south, is a 75 ha reserve which includes the Peñon Tetú-Cuare, a 150-m high hill also known as the Peñon Reina Victoria because of its supposed resemblance to the facial profile of the British queen. From here the path continues 1 km to a riverside picnic spot.

Sleeping

B *Hostería San Ignacio*, T470064. With breakfast, nice rooms, pleasant grounds. **C** *San Ignacio*, San Martín 823, T470047. Good, *cabañas*. **C** *Hosp El Descanso*, Pellegrini 270, T470207. Modern, quiet, owner speaks German, poor breakfast but otherwise recommended, excellent camping. **D** per person *El Sol*, Chatsa 73, with breakfast, nice garden. **E** *Hosp Italia*, San Martín 1291, artists' house, dormitory style, laundry facilities. Recommended. **E** per person *Hosp Alemán Los Salpeterer*, Sarmiento y Centenario, 100 m from bus terminal, without bath, kitchen, nice garden, run down but pleasant, 'pool'. Recommended,

Camping At Hosp Alemán Los Salpeterer and house opposte. 2 pleasant sites by small lake about 5 km south of San Ignacio, on Route 12, cold showers only.

Eating *Restaurant Don Valentín*, good and cheap lunches. There are 2 *comedores* near the entrance to the ruins: *El Coco*, large choice, good food; *Santa Clara*, cheap, tasty, simple.

Tours and excursions on foot, on horseback and by canoe are offered by Dante and **Tour operators**
Eva Perroue, details from tourist information. Also Jorge and Diana, in house opposite
Hosp Alemán Los Salpeterer, offer horses, canoeing, tours.

Bus Though some buses leave from the terminal at Sarmiento y Quiroga, many **Transport**
through services stop only at the entrance to San Ignacio. Buses to/from **Posadas**
every 30 mins-1 hr, US$3.50, last return bus at 2100. To **Puerto Iguazú**, US$14.
To **Buenos Aires**, US$35 including meals, 24 hrs, 1800, 1900.

San Ignacio to Puerto Iguazú

From San Ignacio Route 12 continues northeast, running parallel to Río Alto Paraná,
towards Puerto Iguazú. With its bright red soil and lush vegetation, this is an attrac-
tive route which provides a good view of the local economy: plantations of yerba maté,
manioc and citrus fruits can be seen as well as timber yards, manioc mills and yerba
maté factories. The road passes through several small modern towns including Jardín
America, Puerto Rico, Eldorado and Wanda.

Eldorado is a prosperous small town surrounded by flourishing *mate*, tung, **Eldorado**
citrus, eucalyptus and tobacco plantations. The ACA office is very helpful and *Phone code: 03751*
has a large illuminated map of Eldorado and its surroundings. For information *Colour map 2, grid A3*
on the **Misiones Rainforest Reserve**, contact Daphne Colcombet, *Population: 38,000*
T0751-21351. *Km 123*

Sleeping and eating AB *Hostería ACA*, T421370. Pool, good facilities. **B** *Alfa*,
Córdoba y Rioja, T421097. **C** *Atlántida*, San Martín 3087, T421441. A/c, pool, parking,
good restaurants. Recommended. **C** *Esmeralda*, San Martín, Km 8, basic. **C** *Ilex*, San
Martín, Km 9, safe. *Gran Riojano*, San Martín 314, T422217. 5 mins walk from main
road crossing, with restaurant. **Camping** Municipal site in Parque Schweim, San
Martín, Km 1, T42154. Free, good. **Estancia AL** per person *Las Mercedes*, 7 km from
town, T431511, F31448. 620 ha of *maté* and pine plantations, plus cattle, offers
birdwatching, horseriding, swimming pool, fishing, canoeing, English, German, Russian spoken. Recommended.

Wanda is famous as the site of two open-cast amethyst and quartz mines which **Wanda**
sell gems. There are free guided tours to one of them, Tierra Colorada, daily. *Population: 7,500*
Sleeping at **C** per person *Hotel Las Brisas*, at Puerto Esperanza, Swiss owned, *Km 165*
English and German spoken, discount for Swiss nationals. ■ *Getting there:*
Buses between Posadas and Puerto Iguazú stop near the mines and the hotel.

The interior of Misiones

An alternative route through Misiones is along Provincial Route 14 which runs
from San José, 42 km south of Posadas, northeast through the heart of Misiones to
Bernardo de Yrigoyen, on the Brazilian frontier. Along this route several roads
connect with Route 12.

At **Leandro N Alem**, 52 km east of San José, Provincial Route 4 runs south to **Route**
San Javier, 43 km south on the Río Uruguay, in an area famous for sugar cultivation and fishing. **Cerro Monje**, a hill 6 km north, is the site of a chapel which
attracts pilgrims in Holy Week. There is a Museo Histórico and just west of
town are the ruins of the Jesuit mission of San Francisco Javier. Some 26 km
west along Provincial Route 2 (unpaved) are the ruins of another Jesuit Mission, **Santa María La Mayor**. **Sleeping** at *ACA Hotel*, Plaza del Cerrito.

The Northeast

Transport Frequent ferry service across the river to Porto Xavier in Brazil from the port, 4 km from town. Buses to Posadas.

Oberá

Phone code: 03755
Colour map 2, grid B3
Population: 42,000
79 km NE of San José;
95 km from Posadas

Oberá is located in an area of tea and *yerba-maté* plantations. The factories for drying the leaves can be visited. One of the biggest centres of 20th-century European immigration in the province, it is the second largest town in Misiones. Its immigrant origins can be seen in its different churches. East of the centre is the **Parque de Naciones**, with houses to commemorate the 17 nationalities who settled here. Nearby, at Haiti y Diaz de Solís, is the **Criadero de Pájaros Wendlinger**, housing a collection of local birds. There are waterfalls, Salto Berrondo, set in a park 6 km west on Route 103. In the first week of October there is a *Fiesta Nacional del Inmigrantes*.

There are two museums: the **Museo de Ciencias Naturales**; Gobernador Barreyra y José Ingenieros. ■ *Tue-Fri 0600-1200, 1600-1800, Sat 0600-1200.* And the **Museo Municipal**, in the Municipalidad, Gobernador Barreyra y José Ingenieros, with displays on the foundation of the town. ■ *Mon-Fri 0600-1200, 1700-2000.*

Sleeping *Premier*, 9 de Julio 1164, T421214. 3-star. *Cuatro Pinos*, Sarmiento 853, T421306. Good value. **C** *Real*, opposite bus terminal, T422761. Basic, hot showers. *Res Anahi*, Santiago del Estero 36, T421127. Many others. Cheap accommodation at Centro Deportivo. **Camping** *Santa Rita*, Route 14 m 3 km from town. *Salto Berrondo*, at the falls, swimming pool.

Eating *Enqüete* restaurant, Cabeza de Vaca 340, good. Excellent *empanadas* at *Bar Terminal* next to bus terminal.

Tourist office Plazoleta Güemes, Libertad 90, open 0700-1900, Sat 0700-1300, very helpful, lots of maps.

Transport Bus To **Posadas**, 2 hrs, US$5.50, Singer; once a day to/from **Puerto Iguazú**, 5 hrs.

From Oberá to
Bernardo De
Yrigoyen

Route 14 continues northeast from Oberá passing through a string of small towns including **Aristobolo del Valle**, Km 135, and **Dos de Mayo** (**C** *Hotel Alex*, clean), Km 159.

Paraíso, Km 243, Provincial Route 21 (a dirt track) runs south 82 km to the Río Uruguay and the **Saltos del Moconá**; an alternative route is via El Soberbio, reached by paved Provincial Route 212 which turns off Route 14 at San Vicente (Km 178), but whichever route you take if you want to see the falls you will get wet: at least to your knees in the dry season while in wet weather it is impossible. The area has been declared a provincial park and there is fine fishing but no infrastructure.

Beyond Paraíso Route 14 continues to **San Pedro**, Km 255, 9 km north of which Route 20 (paved) runs north and joins up with Route 17 which runs west through lovely vegetation to Eldorado; Route 14 becomes a dirt track leading through **Tobuna**, where there are the Alegría falls to Bernardo de Yrigoyen.

Sleeping Near the Saltos del Moconá **AB** *Posada La Bonita*, T03755-680380. Cabañas with bath and breakfast, also fishing, trekking, riding, canoeing. At **San Pedro C** *American Hotel*, Güemes 670, T43364. Meals served. At **Palmera Boca**, 3 km from San Pedro **C** *Posada Itaroga*, T0751-70165. A family farm with log houses beside a lake, swimming and rowing boats, includes breakfast, cooking facilities, peaceful, relaxed and friendly, recommended, also camping.

Birds and the beasts

Although birds and mammals are not easily seen by visitors, the wildlife of subtropical rainforests is the most diverse in Argentina. Some 500 species of birds have been identified in the forests of Misiones. Among mammals are the tapir, the largest mammal in South America, as well as brockets, peccaries, brown capuchin monkeys, crab-eating racoons and several species of cats, including the puma, the ocelot, the margay and the yaguarundi. Most species of bats, rodents and opossums can be found: the easiest to spot are the coatí, the grey squirrel and the paca. Among endangered species are the jaguar (the largest cat in the Americas), the giant otter, the bush-dog, the giant anteater, the

harpy eagle (the most powerful eagle in the world), the brazilian merganser (a duck with a serrated bill) and the broad-snouted caiman (now recovering from near extinction).

Coati

Situated on the Brazilian frontier, Bernardo de Yrigoyen lies in the highest part of the hills of Misones. From here the direct (dirt) road north to Puerto Iguazú, 142 km, crosses the National Park of Iguazú, via the quiet attractive villages of Andrecito, Cabuneí and San Antonio, offering fine views of rainforest. The **Reserva Natural San Antonio**, 600 ha of forest on the banks of the Río San Antonio, protects one of the few remaining areas of Paraná pine, which only 40 years ago covered large areas of the province.

Bernardo de Yrigoyen
Phone code: 03741
Colour map 2, grid A3
Population: 3,700
Altitude: 805 m

Sleeping Bernardo de Yrigoyen C *ACA Motel*, Ruta Nacional 14, Km 1435, T0751-92026. Clean, friendly. *Yrigoyen*, Libertad s/n. **Andrecito: C** *Res Los Robles*, clean, quiet.

Transport Bus There are services to B Yrigoyen from Eldorado and Oberá; local buses also run in dry weather from Yrigoyen to Puerto Iguazú through the national park.

Iguazú Falls

The Iguazú Falls are the most overwhelming and spectacular waterfalls in South America and are justifiably one of the most popular attractions in Argentina. Situated on the Río Iguazú (in Guaraní guazú is big and I is for water), the river receives the waters of about 30 rivers before reaching the falls. There are rapids for 3½ km above the falls which are a 60 m high precipice, over which the water plunges in 275 falls over a frontage of 2.7 km at an average rate of 1,750 cubic metres a second. They are 20 m higher than Niagara and about half as wide again causing them to be described as making Niagara look like a mere dripping tap. They are immense. The most spectacular part is the Garganta del Diablo, visited from the Argentine side. Above the impact of the water upon basalt rock hovers a perpetual 30 m high cloud of mist in which the sun creates blazing rainbows. Viewed from below, the tumbling water in its setting of begonias, orchids, fern and palms with toucans, flocks of parrots and cacique birds, swifts dodging in and out of the very falls, and myriad butterflies (at least 500 different species), is majestically beautiful, especially outside the cool season (when the water is much diminished, as are the birds and insects).

The Northeast

History The first European visitor to the falls was the Spaniard Alvar Núñez Cabeza de Vaca in 1541, on his search for a connection between the Brazilian coast and the Río de la Plata: he named them the Saltos de Santa María. Though the falls were well known to the Jesuit missionaries, they were forgotten, except by local inhabitants, until the area was explored by a Brazilian expedition sent out by the Paraguayan president, Solano López in 1863. In the 20th century, the falls have become recognized globally as a major attraction; this did not, however, impress Malcolm Slesser in the 1960s: "Except for a night on the tiles in Rio de janeiro, Brazil's greatest tourist attraction is the Iguaçu falls. This huge cataract eclipses Niagara. These falls are a splendid frolic of 300 falls, 270 feet high, almost three miles wide, filling the place with spray. Here is a large government hotel, luxurious with absolutely nothing to do except eat, drink and lounge – and look at the falls. We did not go, on the principle that a waterfall was a waterfall" (*Brazil: Land Without Limit*, George Allen and Unwin, London, 1969, pages 151-2). Do not follow his example!

How to visit
Sunset from the Brazilian side is a worthwhile experience

Bridges connect the Argentine town of Puerto Iguazú with the Brazilian city of Foz do Iguaçu and that city in turn with the Paraguayan city of Ciudad del Este. Both Argentine and Brazilian sides of the falls are described below: this is followed by descriptions of Puerto Iguazú, Foz do Iguaçu and Ciudad del Este. Most of the falls lie in Argentina; Argentines say "Argentina puts on the show and Brazil charges for the view". In both parks the subtropical rainforest benefits from the added humidity in the proximity of the falls, creating an environment rich in vegetation and fauna.

Around the Iguazú Falls

N
Not to scale

The Brazilian park offers a superb panoramic view of the whole falls and is best visited in the morning when the light is better for photography. The Argentine park (which requires a day to explore properly) offers closer views of the individual falls and is much more interesting from the point of view of seeing the forest with its wildlife and butterflies, though to appreciate these properly you need to go early and get well away from the visitors areas. Both parks can, if necessary, be visited in a day, starting at about 0700, but the brisk pace needed for a rapid tour is exhausting for the non-athletic in the heat.

Busiest times are holiday periods and on Sundays when helicopter tours over the falls from the Brazilian side are particularly popular (and noisy). Both parks have visitors centres, though the information provided by the Argentine Centre is far superior to that in the Brazilian Centre. Despite the massive popularity of the falls, the remaining parts of the parks are surprisingly little visited.

There are many advantages in staying in Foz and commuting to the Argentine side, better and cheaper hotels and restaurants, for example. Whichever side you decide to stay on, most establishments will accept Brazilian *reais*, Argentine pesos or dollars. Cross border transport usually accepts Paraguayan *guaraníes* as well.

Between October and February (daylight saving dates change each year) Argentina is one hour behind Brazil and, from December to February, one hour behind Paraguay.

Parque Nacional Iguazú (Argentina)

Created in 1934, the park extends over an area of 67,620 ha, most of which is covered by sub-tropical rainforest. It is crossed by Route 101, a dirt road which runs southeast to Bernardo de Yrigoyen on the Brazilian frontier. Buses operate along this route in dry weather, offering a view of the park.

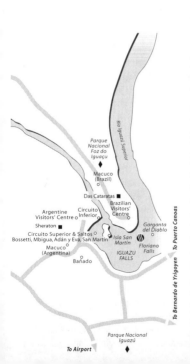

Very little of the wildlife in the park can be seen around the falls: even on the nature trails described below you need to go in the early morning. Jaguars, tapirs, brown capuchin monkeys, collared anteaters and coatimundi live alongside over 400 species of birds, amoung the most commonly visible are the black-crowned night heron, the black vulture, the plumed kite, the white-eyed parakeet, the blue-winged parrolet, the red-rumped cacique which builds hanging nests on pindo palms, and fruiteaters like the magpie tanager and the colourful purple-troated euphonia. Over 100 species of butterflies have been identified, among them the colourful shiny blue *morpho*, the poisonous red **Wildlife**

The Northeast

and black *heliconius* and species of Papilionidae and Pieridae.

The falls

The catwalks & platform get very crowded in mid-morning after tour buses arrive

From the visitor centre two sets of catwalks (the *Circuito Inferior*) lead down to the lower falls but the catwalks to the **Garganta del Diablo** (Devil's Throat) were damaged by floods, most recently in 1986. Instead boats (US$4) link Puerto Canoas with the remains of the catwalks which lead to a viewing platform above the Garganta, particularly recommended

Toco Toucan

in the evening when the light is best and the swifts are returning to roost on the cliffs, some behind the water. Puerto Canoas can be reached by bus – see below – or by car, parking US$1). The catwalk network is being rebuilt. Work is also in progress on a monorail from the Visitors' Centre to Puerto Canoas.

Below the falls a free ferry leaving regularly subject to demand, connects the Circuito Inferior with **Isla San Martín**. A path on the island leads to the top of the hill, where there are trails to some of the less visited falls and rocky pools (take bathing gear in summer to cool off).

Other attractions

There are two nature trails near the falls: the **Sendero Macuco** 4 km, starting from near the visitor centre and leading to a natural pool (El Pozón) fed by a waterfall and good for swimming; the **Sendero Yacaratia**, leading from near the start of the Macuco trail to Puerto Macuco (this has been criticized as not being a 'serious' nature trail).

Activities

A number of activities are offered, both from the visitor centre and through agencies in Puerto Iguazú. These include: *Aventura Náutica*, a journey by launch along the lower Río Iguazú, US$15 per person; *Safari Náutico*, a 4 km journey by boat along the Río Iguazú above the falls, US$15 per person; *La Gran Aventura*, a boat trip down the lower Río Iguazu to Puerto Macuco, followed by a trip back in four wheel drive vehicle along the Yacaratiá Trail, US$33 per person; *Full Day*, which includes the *safari náutico*, *aventura náutica*, US$30 per person (5 hrs), or US$45 with *gran aventura* (7 hrs), lunch extra (November 1999 prices from *Iguazú Jungle Explorer* at the *Hotel Sheraton Iguazú*, T421600, F420311; also have an office in the bus terminal, local 3, T422722).

There are also night-time walking tours between the *Hotel Sheraton* and the falls when the moon is full; on clear nights the moon casts a blue halo over the falls. Mountain bikes and boats can also be hired, US$3 an hr. For serious birdwatching and nature walks with an English speaking guide contact Daniel Samay (*Explorador* agency) or Miguel Castelino, Apartado Postal 22, Puerto Iguazú (3370), Misiones, T420157, FocusTours@aol.com, highly recommended. A useful guidebook is *Iguazú, The Laws of the Jungle* (in Spanish, *Iguazú, las leyes de la selva*) by Santiago G de la Vega, Silvestre Ediciones (1999).

Park information

The park is open 0800-1900 every day. Entry US$5, payable in pesos or dollars only (guests at *Hotel Sheraton* should pay and get tickets stamped at the hotel to avoid paying again). The visitor centre includes a museum of local wildlife and an auditorium for periodic slide shows (on request, minimum 8 people), no commentary, only music; it also sells a good guide book on Argentine birds. Food and drinks are available in the park but are expensive so it is best to take your own. There is a Telecom kiosk at the bus stop. There is *Camping Puerto Canoas*, 600 m from Puerto Canoas, tables, but no other facilities, nearest drinking water at park entrance. In the rainy season, when water levels are high, waterproof coats or swimming costumes are advisable for some of the lower catwalks and for boat trips. Cameras should be carried in a plastic bag. Wear shoes with good soles, as the rocks can be very slippery in places.

Transportes El Práctico buses run every hour from Puerto Iguazú bus terminal, stopping at the national park entrance for the purchase of entry tickets and continuing to Puerto Canoas. Fares US$4 return to visitor centre, a further US$0.50 to Puerto Canoas, payable in pesos, dollars, guaraníes or reais. First bus 0740, last 1940, last return 2000, journey time 30 mins. These buses are sometimes erratic, especially when it is wet, even though the times are clearly indicated. There are fixed rates for taxis, US$15 one way, up to 5 people. A tour from the bus terminal, taking in both sides of the Falls, costs US$40. Hitchhiking to the Falls is difficult, but you can hitch up to the Posadas intersection at Km 11, then it is only a 7 km walk. For transport between the Argentine and Brazilian sides see under Foz and Puerto Iguazú, below. Motorists can park overnight in the National Park, free. **Transport**

Parque Nacional Foz do Iguaçu (Brazil)

The Brazilian National Park was founded in 1939 and the area was designated a World Heritage Site by UNESCO in 1986. The park covers 170,086 ha, extending along the north bank of the Rio Iguaçu, then sweeping northwards to Santa Tereza do Oeste on the BR-277.

Most frequently encountered are little and red brocket deer, South American coati, white-eared opossum, and a sub-species of the brown capuchin monkey. Much harder to see are the jaguar, ocelot, jaguarundi, puma, margay, white-lipped peccary, bush dog and southern river otter. The endangered tegu lizard is common. Over 100 species of butterflies have been identified, among them the electric blue *Morpho*, the poisonous red and black *heliconius*. The bird life is especially rewarding for the birdwatcher. Five members of the toucan family can be seen: toco and red-breasted toucans, chestnut-eared araçari, saffron and spot-billed toucanets. Bird and mammal information supplied by Douglas Trent, *Focus Tours*. **Wildlife**

From opposite the *Hotel das Cataratas* a 1½ km paved walk runs part of the way down the cliff near the rim of the falls, giving a stupendous view of the whole Argentine side of the falls. It ends up almost under the powerful Floriano Falls: from here an elevator carries visitors to the top of the Floriano Falls (from 0800; US$0.50) and to a path leading to Porto Canoa (if there is a queue it is easy and quick to walk up). A catwalk at the foot of the Floriano Falls gives a good view of the Garganta do Diabo. There are toilets and a lanchonete/restaurant on the path down and more toilets at the top of the elevator. **The falls**

The **Macuco Safari Tour**, US$30 (Amex accepted), leaves from near the falls, with trailers taking the visitors down the trail. The guides speak Portuguese, English and Spanish and it is highly recommended (take insect repellent). *Macuco Safari de Barco*, Caixa Postal 509, 85851-001, Foz do Iguaçu, Paraná, T0XX45-5744464. Expeditions can also be organized, by prior arrangement, for photographers, botanists and others, and boat hire can be arranged for up to 80 people, by the hr, or by the day. **Helicopter tours** over the falls leave from *Hotel das Cataratas*, US$60 per person, 10 minutes. Apart from disturbing visitors, the helicopters are also reported to present a threat to some bird species which are laying thinner-shelled eggs: the altitude has been increased, making the flight **Tours**

The Northeast

The Macuco safari

After about 20 minutes ride on the trailer you get off and begin hiking your way down the side of the Iguaçu gorge to the Macuco Falls which cascade into a deep dark plunge pool. Steps cut into the rock allow you to descend to the foot of the falls but beware: they are slippery and steep. Good walking shoes are a must. The tour is taken at a relaxed pace so there is no pressure to rush back up those steps. After the falls you descend to the banks of the river, where you take to the water in inflatable rafts capable of carrying 20 people. The ride is bumpy, but make sure you look up at the steep sides of the gorge. As the boat comes up to the edge of the falls there is a deafening roar from above as the boat begins to turn and the spay is so powerful you have to shut your eyes. You will get very wet. Plastic raincoats are sold at the launch site and plastic bags are provided for cameras if you ask. The view of the falls is unbeatable. Once back on dry land you are whisked up to the top of the canyon by jeep to rejoin the trailer to the entrance. From here a free shuttle bus transfers you through the park to the top of the falls.

less attractive. Many **hotels** organize tours to the falls: these have been recommended in preference to taxi rides. If visiting the Brazilian side from Puerto Iguazú by bus, ask the driver to let you off shortly after the border at the roundabout for the road to the falls (BR-469), where you can get another bus.

Park information Park entry is US$3 (6 reais, payable only in Brazilian currency), payable at the entrance. There is a Banco do Brasil *câmbio* at the entrance (0800-1900). If possible, visit on a weekday when the walks are less crowded. The Brazilian side of the falls is closed on Monday until 1300 for maintenance. Non-residents can eat at the *Hotel das Cataratas*, midday and evening buffets.

Transport Buses leave Foz do Iguaçu, from the *Terminal Urbana* on Av Juscelino Kubitschek, opposite the Infantry Barracks. The green Transbalan service (marked `Cataratas') goes to the falls every hr, 0715-1800, past the airport and *Hotel das Cataratas*, 40 mins US$0.80 one way, payable in *reais* only (the driver waits at the Park entrance while passengers purchase entry tickets, which are checked by a park guard on the bus); the *Parque Nacional* bus runs every 22 mins, US$0.40, to the park entrance only (from where you will need to take a `Cataratas' bus the rest of the way which works out more expensive). Both buses can also be picked up at any of the stops on Av Juscelino Kubitschek. Return buses 0800-1900. Taxi US$4, plus US$5.50 per hr for waiting.

Puerto Iguazú

Population: 19,000
Altitude: 210 m
Phone code: 03757

Puerto Iguazú stands high above the river, 18 km northwest of the falls, on the Argentine side near the confluence of the Ríos Iguazú and Alto Paraná. A modern town which serves mainly as a centre for visitors to the falls, its prosperity has varied in relation to the difference in prices between Argentina and Brazil.

Sights
Puerto Iguazú is an easy town to walk around; less frenetic than Foz

The port lies to the north of the town centre at the foot of a hill. From the port you can follow the Río Iguazú downstream towards Hito Argentino, a *mirador* with views over the point where the Ríos Iguazú and Alto Paraná meet and over neighbouring Brazil and Paraguay. There are souvenir shops, toilets and *La Barranca* pub here; bus US$0.50.

La Aripuca is a large wooden structure housing a centre for the appreciation of the native species and their environment. Turn of Ruta 12 just after *Hotel Cataratas*; T423488, English and German spoken. At **Güira Oga** (Casa

The Northeast

de los Pájaros) birds that have been injured are cured and reintroduced to the wild. There is also a trail in the forest and a breeding centre for endangered species. Turn off Ruta 12 at *Hotel Orquídeas Palace*; cellular T15670684.

Museo Mbororé, San Martín 231, Mon-Sat 1700-2100, US$1, exhibition on Guaraní culture, also sells Guaraní made handicrafts, cheaper than shops. **Museo Imágenes de la Selva**, Calle Los Cedros y Guatambú, one block west of Av Victoria Aguirre, displays the sculptures in wood of Rodolfo Allou, mostly from materials found in the forest. He was related to Jules Verne. ■ *US$2, 0800-1200, 1500-1800.*

Crowded during summer (Jan-Feb), Easter and Jul holiday periods. Accommodation is expensive but there is plenty of choice; outside the high season be prepared to shop around and to bargain.

Sleeping

LL-L *Sheraton Internacional Iguazú Resort*, T421600, F491800, www.sheraton.com, pool, casino, good restaurants, business facilities, overlooking the falls, being completely remodelled, rooms with garden views cost less, excellent, check-out can take ages. *Cataratas*, Route 12, Km 4, T421100, F421090, www.fnn.net/hoteis/cataratas-ar, pool, gymnasium. **L** *Esturión*, Av Tres Fronteras 650, T420020. Last hotel before *Hito Argentino*, clean, comfortable, swimming pool, good restaurant. **A** *Orquídeas Palace*, Ruta 12, Km 5, T420472. Very comfortable, English, German spoken, pool. **A** *Saint George*, Córdoba 148, T420633, F420651, www.hotelsaintgeorge.com With breakfast, comfortable, pool and garden, good, expensive restaurant, close to bus station. Highly recommended.

B *Alexander*, Córdoba 685, opposite bus station, T420249, T420566. With breakfast, a/c, pool. Recommended. **B** *Hostería Casa Blanca*, Guaraní 121, 2 blocks from bus station, T421320. **C** in low season, with breakfast, fan, large rooms with phone. Recommended. **B-C** *Hostería Los Helechos*, Amarante 76, off Córdoba, behind *Saint George*, T/F420338. With breakfast, cheaper rooms have no TV, owner speaks German, pleasant, a/c or fan, pool. **B** *El Libertador*, Bompland 110, T/F420984. Modern, central, helpful, large bedrooms and public rooms, rooms at back have balconies overlooking garden and swimming pool. **B** *Residencial Lilian*, Beltrán 183, T420968. Two blocks from bus terminal, with breakfast, a/c, cheaper with fan, TV, helpful, safe. Recommended. **C** *King*, Aguirre 915, T420360. Pool, hot showers, good value. **C** *Residencial Paquita*, Córdoba 158, opposite terminal, T420434. Some rooms with terrace, a/c extra, nice setting. Recommended. **C** *Residencial Ríoselva*, San Lorenzo 140, at end of street, T421555. Laundry facilities, large garden, pool, communal barbecue. Highly recommended. **C** *Residencial San Fernando*, Córdoba y Guaraní, near terminal, T421429. With bath and breakfast, popular. **C** *Tierra Colorada*, Córdoba y El Urú 28, T420649, F420572. Fan or a/c, cheaper without breakfast, pool, trips arranged. Very good. **E** per person *Bompland*, Av Bompland 33, T420965. **D** with a/c, with bath, barbecue, central.

E per person *Residencias Gastón*, Félix de Azara 590, T423184. With bath, breakfast, a/c, youth hostel style, by river. **F** per person *Noelia*, Fray Luis Beltrán 119,

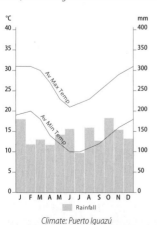

Climate: Puerto Iguazú

Rainfall

°C 40 35 30 25 20 15 10 5 0

Av Max Temp
Av Min Temp

mm 400 350 300 250 200 150 100 50 0

J F M A M J J A S O N D

The Northeast

T420729. Not far from bus terminal, good value, with bath. **Youth hostel D** per person *Hospedaje Uno*, Beltrán 116, T420529. With bath and breakfast, **E** in dormitory accommodation, friendly, clean, recommended, tour to Itaipú, Foz de Iguaçu and Brazilian side of the falls. **E** per person *La Cabaña*, Tres Fronteras 434, T420564, F420393, iguazu@hostels.org.ar The tourist office has a list of family accommodation (**E** per person), though it may be reluctant to find private accommodation unless the hotels are full. **Camping** For the site in the national park see above. Municipal site, Corrientes y Entre Ríos. Reported as `grim'. *Camping El Pindo*, Av Aguirre, Km 3 at the southern edge of town, US$1.50 per person, plus charge for tent and for use of pool, friendly, but very run down. There are also facilities at *Camping El Yaguarete*, Route 12, Km 5, T420168. Opposite is *El Viejo Americano*, which also has camping. Pool open to non-guests, US$2.50. In pleasant, wooded gardens, but no food; US$3 per person, US$3 per car, US$3 per tent.

Eating *La Rueda*, Córdoba 28. Good food at reasonable prices. *El Charro*, Córdoba 106. Good food, *pizzería* and *parrilla*, popular with locals, no credit cards. *El Criollito*, Tres Fronteras 62. Recommended. *Jardín de Iguazú*, Córdoba y Misiones, at bus terminal. Good. *Fechoría*, Ingeniero Eppens 294. Good *empanadas*. On Aguirre, next to *Turismo Dick* is a group of restaurants: *Pizzería y Restuarante Imperial*, Fast Food (tenedor libre, ie fixed price), *Blanco Paraíso parrillada*. *Panificadora Real*, Córdoba y Guaraní. Good bread, open Sun evening; another branch at Victoria y Brasil in the centre.

Tour operators *Turismo Dick*, Aguirre 226, T420778, turismodick@interiguazu.com.ar, open Mon-Sat 0830-1300, 1630-2000. *Turismo Caracol*, Aguirre 563, T420064. All-day tour of both sides of falls, including good meal in Brazil, but mainly for `non-English speaking clients with an interest in shopping'. *Turismo Cuenca del Plata*, Amarante 76, T421330, F421458, cuencadelplata@fnn.net 10% discount to ISIC and youth card holders on local excursions. *IGRTur*, Terminal de Omnibus, local 5, T/F422983, all tours sold, mountain bike hire US$3/hr, 2-hr circuit in forest on quadbikes US$30, information on hostels and other accommodation. *Aguas Grandes*, Mariano Moreno 58, T421140, F423096,

Puerto Iguazú

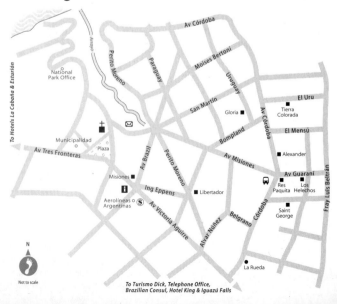

www.aguasgrandes.com.ar tours to both sides of the falls and further afield: Saltos de Moconá, 5,000 m wide (overnight US$190 all included); Puerto Península, using old logging trails, rope ladders in trees and abseiling down (US$40 per person); Sendero de los Saltos, giant ferns, abseiling down waterfalls, swimming; Raices Guaraníes to an indigenous community (US$25 per person); bilingual and local guides, flexible. *Cabalgatas por la Selva*, Ruta 12, just after the Rotonda for the road to the international bridge, cellular T15542180. For horse riding. *Exploradaor Expediciones*, Perito Moreno 217, 1 B, T/F421632 and in *Hotel Sheraton*. Trips in the forest leaving from the Visitors' Centre 1030 and 1500, photographic safaris. Recommended taxi-guide, Juan Villalba, T420973 (radiotaxi 044). Good value, speaks basic English. Agencies arrange day tours to the Brazilian side (lunch in Foz), Itaipú and Ciudad del Este (US$25) though more time is spent shopping than at the Falls, and to a gem mine at Wanda, the Jesuit ruins at San Ignacio Miní and a local zoo (10 hrs driving time, US$30, not including entry fees, may be cheaper for more than 2 in a taxi or hired car).

Local Car hire *Avis* at airport. *Localiza*, at airport and Aguirre 279, T0800-9992999. Cars may be taken to the Brazilian side for an extra US$5. **Taxi**, T420973, fares: to airport US$15, to Argentine falls US$15, to Brazilian falls US$20, to centre of Foz US$15, to Ciudad del Este US$20, to Itaipu US$30 return, to Wanda gem mines with wait US$35.

Transport

Long distance Air Airport is south of Puerto Iguazú near the falls. *Expreso del Valle* buses (T420348) between airport and bus terminal connect with plane arrivals and departures, US$3. Check times at *Aerolíneas Argentinas* office. Taxis charge US$10 to *Hotel Sheraton*, at least US$18 to Puerto Iguazú, US$14 to Foz do Iguaçu and US$25 to the Brazilian airport. *Aerolíneas Argentinas* and *Lapa* fly direct to Buenos Aires, 2 hrs, flights are very crowded.

For the best view on landing, sit on the right side of the aircraft

Bus The terminal, at Av Córdoba y Av Misiones, has a phone office, a Municipalidad office, various tour company desks (see below) and bus offices. To **Buenos Aires**, 21 hrs, *Expreso Singer, Tigre Iguazú, Crucero del Norte, ViaBariloche*, daily, US$33-40 *semi cama*, US$50 *cama* (some offer student discounts). It is cheaper to take a local bus to Posadas and then rebook. To **Posadas**, stopping at San Ignacio Miní, frequent, 5 hrs, US$19, *expreso*, 7 hrs, US$16 *servicio común*. To **San Ignacio** Miní, US$16 *servicio común. Agencia de Pasajes Noelia*, local 3, T422722, can book tickets beyond Posadas for other destinations in Argentina, ISIC discounts available.

Airline offices *Aerolíneas Argentinas*, Brasil y Aguirre, T420194; *Lapa*, Perito Moreno casi Bompland, T420390. **Banks** Several *cambios* on Aguirre near the outskirts of town towards the Falls. *Turismo Dick* (address below), changes TCs at high commission (up to 10%). Rates vary so shop around. Alternatively pay in US$. Nowhere to get cash on Visa. **Communications** *Telecentro*, Victoria Aguirre y Horacio Quiroga, T420177, phone, fax, post office and Banelco ATM. **Embassies and consulates** *Brazilian*, Av Guaraní 70, T/F420131. **Tourist information** Aguirre 396, T420800. Mon-Fri 0800-1300, 1400-2000, Sat-Sun 0800-1200, 1630-2000.

Directory

This crossing via the Puente Tancredo Neves is straightforward. If crossing on a day visit no immigration formalities are required. Argentine immigration is at the Brazilian end of the bridge. If entering Argentina buses stop at immigration. The Brazilian consulate is in Puerto Iguazú, Guaraní y Esquiu, 0800-1200.

Frontier with Brazil

Transport Buses leave Puerto Iguazú terminal for Foz do Iguaçu every 20 mins, US$2 but do not wait at the frontier so if you need exit and entry stamps keep your ticket and catch the next bus (bus companies do not recognize each other's tickets). Taxis: between the border and Puerto Iguazú US$15; between the border and *Hotel Internacional Iguazú* US$35.

Frontier with Paraguay The ferry service from the port in Puerto Iguazú to Tres Fronteras is for locals only (no immigration facilities). Crossing to Paraguay is via Puente Tancredo Neves to Brazil and then via the Puente de la Amistad to Ciudad del Este. Brazilian entry and exit stamps are not required unless you are stopping in Brazil. There is a US$3 tax to enter Paraguay. The Paraguayan Consulate is at Bompland 355.

Transport Direct buses (non-stop in Brazil), leave Puerto Iguazú terminal every 30 mins, US$2, 45 mins, liable to delays especially in crossing the bridge to Ciudad del Este. Taxi from Puerto Iguazú to Ciudad del Este, US$70 one way.

Foz do Iguaçu (Brazil)

Phone code: 045
Population: 232,000

A rapidly developing and improving town, Foz lies 28 km from the falls, with a wide range of accommodation and good communications by air and road with the main cities of southern Brazil and Asunción in Paraguay.

There are **artificial beaches** on Lake Itaipu (see below for the Itaipu dam itself). The closest to Foz de Iguaçu are at Bairro de Três Lagoas, at Km 723 on BR-277, and in the municipality of Santa Terezinha do Itaipu, 34 km from Foz. The relaxing leisure parks have grassed areas with kiosks, barbecue sites and offer fishing as well as bathing, US$2.50. It is also possible to take boat trips on the lake. The **Parque das Aves** bird park, entrance US$8, at Rodovia das Cataratas Km 18, just before the falls, has received frequent good reports. It contains Brazilian and foreign birds in huge aviaries through which you can walk, with the birds flying and hopping around you. There is also a butterfly house. For a guided tour T45231007. The parque is within walking distance of the *Hotel San Martin*; the *Paudimar* youth hostel (see below) offers a discount for its guests.

Sleeping
A wide selection;
many offer excursions
to the falls

If you know which hotel you wish to stay in touts may say it no longer exists, or quote room rates below what is actually charged. In high season (eg Christmas-New Year), you will not find a room under US$15 but in low season there are many good deals.

In Foz do Iguaçu **L** *Internacional*, Almte Barroso 2006, T45214100, F5745201. Very well-appointed and decorated, good. **A** *Lanville Palace*, Jorge Schimmelpfeng 827, T/F5231511. Restaurant, bar, pool. **A** *Rafain Centro*, Mcal Deodoro 984, T/F5231213. Good restaurant, pool. **A** *Recanto Park*, Costa e Silva 3500, T/F5223000. Comfortable accommodation with restaurant, coffee shop, pool, sauna. **A** *Suiça*, Felipe Wandscheer 3580, T45253232, F5253044. Swiss manager, helpful, pool. **A** *Bogari*, Brasil 106, T45232243, F5722123, bogari@fnn.net Excellent restaurant, swimming pool, a/c, safe. **B** *Foz do Iguaçu*, Brasil 97, T45234455, F5741775, hotelfoz@purenet.com.br Good, expensive laundry, luggage store. **B** *Foz Presidente*, Xavier da Silva 1000, T/F5724450. Restaurant, pool, with breakfast, convenient for buses. Recommended. **B** *Foz Presidente II*, Mcal Floriano Peixoto 1851, T45232318. Smaller but a little more expensive, also with pool, bar and restaurant.

C *Dany*, Brasil 509, T/F5231530, danyhotel@danyhotel.com.br Comfortable, a/c, TV, good buffet breakfast. **C** *Luz*, Costa e Silva Km 5, near Rodoviária, T45223535, F5222474. Recommended. **C** *San Remo*, Kubitschek e Xavier da Silva 563, T45722956. A/c, Good breakfast. Recommended. **D** *Minas*, Rebouças 809, T45745208. Basic, hot water, safe, no breakfast. **D** *German Pension*, Rebouças 1091, T45745603. Recommended. **D** *Maria Schneider* , Jorge Schimmelpfeng 483, T45742305. German spoken. **D** *Ortega*, Brasil 1140, T45231288. Good breakfast. **D** *Pousada Evelina Navarrete*, Irlan Kalichewski 171, Vila Yolanda, T/F5743817. Lots of tourist information, English, French, Italian, Polish and Spanish spoken, helpful, lots of information, good breakfast and location, near Chemin Supermarket, near Av Cataratas on the way to the Falls, warmly recommended. **D** *Pousada da Laura*, Naipi 671, T/F5723374. Good breakfast, hot water, bathroom, central, friendly, secure, kitchen, laundry facilities, good place to meet other travellers, Spanish, English, Italian and French spoken, excellent. **D** *Tarobá*, Tarobá 1048, T45743670/3890. Helpful, a/c, clean, small pool, good breakfast. Recommended. **E** *Athenas*, Almte Barroso 2215 e Rebouças, T45742563. Good value, special rates for backpackers, some rooms with shared bath, fan, breakfast extra. **E** *Trento*, Rebouças 829, T45745111. A/c, with bath, without breakfast, noisy, but recommended. **E** *Pousada Verde Vale*, Rebouças 335, T45742925. Cramped, cheap, very basic, open high season only.

Youth hostel There are two branches of the *Paudimar* youth hostel, both **F** per person (in high season IYHA members only): *Paudimar Campestre*, Av das Cataratas Km 12.5, Remanso Grande, near airport, T/F5722430, paudimarcampestre@ paudimar.com.br From airport or town take Parque Nacional bus (0530-0100)and get out at Remanso Grande bus stop, by *Hotel San Juan*, then take the free shuttle bus (0700-1900) to the hostel, or 1.2 km walk from main road. IYHA, camping as well, pool, soccer pitch, quiet, kitchen and communal meals, breakfast. Very friendly and highly

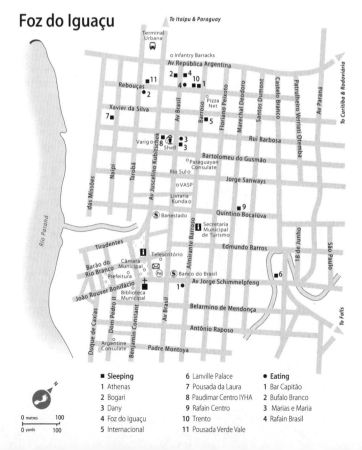

Foz do Iguaçu

■ Sleeping	6 Lanville Palace	● Eating
1 Athenas	7 Pousada da Laura	1 Bar Capitão
2 Bogari	8 Paudimar Centro IYHA	2 Bufalo Branco
3 Dany	9 Rafain Centro	3 Marias e Maria
4 Foz do Iguaçu	10 Trento	4 Rafain Brasil
5 Internacional	11 Pousada Verde Vale	

recommended. For assistance, ask for Gladis. *Paudimar Centro*, Rui Barbosa 634, T/F5745503, paudimarcentro@paudimar.com.br Safe, laundry, kitchen, TV, central, convenient for buses to falls, also very friendly. Recommended. For assistance, ask for Lourdes. English, Spanish and Portuguese spoken. Hostel will pay half taxi fare from rodoviária or airport if staying more than two days. Both hostels have telephone, fax and internet for use of guests. You can stay at one hostel and use the facilities of the other. Tours run to either side of the falls. *Paudimar* desk at rodoviária. **Camping** Pretty cold and humid in winter. *Camping Pousada Internacional*, Manêncio Martins, 600 m from turnoff. For vehicles and tents. *Camping Clube do Brasil*, by the National Park entrance 17 km from Foz, T45238599, US$10 per person (half with International Camping Card), pool, clean. Park vehicle or put tent away from trees in winter in case of heavy rain storms, no restaurants, food there is not very good, closes at 2300. Camping is not permitted by the *Hotel das Cataratas* and Falls. Sleeping in your car inside the park is also prohibited.

Outside Foz do Iguaçu L-AL *Hotel das Cataratas*, directly overlooking the falls, 28 km from Foz, T45217000, F5741688. 40% discount for holders of the *Brazil Air* Pass. Generally recommended but caters for lots of groups, attractive colonial-style building with pleasant gardens (where a lot of wildlife can be seen at night and early morning) and pool. Receipt of email for guests only. Check the exchange rate if paying in dollars. Non-residents can eat here, midday and evening buffets (mixed reports); also *à-la-carte* dishes and dinner with show. On the road to the Falls (Rodovia das Cataratas) are **L** *Bourbon*, Km 2.5, T45231313, F5741110. Top quality, excellent buffet dinner, open to non-residents (US$12). **L** *San Martin*, Km 17, T45232323, F5743207, www.fnn.net/hoteis/sanmartin/new 4-star, a/c, TV, pool, sports, nightclub, several eating options, luxury, comfortable (any problems ask for Miguel Allou). Recommended. **AL** *Carimã*, Km 10, T45231818, F5743531. 4-star, pool, restaurant, bars. Very good value. Recommended. **A** *Colonial*, Km 16, T45231777, F5258585. 1 km from the airport, pool, fine location, price includes breakfast and mediocre dinner, no English, credit cards accepted, packages including transport and tours can be booked with a good discount at hotel booking office at the airport. **A** *Panorama*, Km 12, T45231200, F5231456. Good value, pool.

Eating
Many stay open till midnight & accept a variety of currencies

Bufalo Branco, Rebouças 530. All you can eat churrasco for US$15, good salad bar. *Cabeça de Boi*, Brasil 1325. Live music, buffet. Churrasco but coffee and pastries also. *Rafain*, das Cataratas, Km 6.5, with Paraguayan harp trio, good *alcatra* (meat), excellent buffet, US$25 for all you can eat. *Rafain Brasil*, Brasil 157, a collection of food stalls for different tastes and budgets, with live music and dancing 2000 to 0200, bingo, lively. Recommended. *Scala*, Santos Dumont e Xavier da Silva. Good atmosphere and value. *Sorvete Italia*, Kubitschek 553. Very good ice cream. *Tropicana*, Juscelino Kubitschek 228. All-you-can-eat pizza or *churrascaria* with salad bar, good value. *Vira Lata*, Juscelino Kubitschek e Jorge Sanways. Good value. *Zaragoza*, Quintino Bocaiúva 882, T45743084. Spanish. *Marias e Maria*, Brasil 50. Good *confeitaria*.

Bars & nightclubs
Oba! Oba!, das Cataratas 3700, T45742255/5724217 (Antigo Castelinho). Live samba show Mon-Sat 2315-0015, very popular, US$9 for show and one drink. *Churrascaria Rafain Cataratas*, das Cataratas Km 6.5. With floor show and food, see above. *Capitão Bar*, Schimmelpfeng 288 y Almte Barroso, T45721512, popular nightspot for drinks, open from 1730.

Entertainment Cinema On Barão do Rio Branco beside the former *Hotel Salvatti*.

Sports Fishing For *dourado* and *surubi* fishing contact Simon Williams at Cataratas late Club, Gen Meira, Km 5, T45232073.

Kunda Livraria Universitária, Almte Barroso 1473, T45234606. Guides and maps of **Shopping** the area, books on the local wildlife, novels etc in several languages including French and English.

Beware of overcharging for tours by touts at the bus terminal. There are many travel **Tour operators** agents on Av Brasil. *Caribe Tur* at the international airport and *Hotel das Cataratas*, T45231230, runs tours from the airport to the Argentine side and *Hotel das Cataratas*. Recommended guides, *Wilson Engel*, T45741367, friendly, flexible. *Ruth Campo Silva*, STTC Turismo, Hotel Bourbon, Rodovia das Cataratas, T45743849, F5743557 (American Express); *Chiderly Batismo Pequeno*, Almte Barroso 505, Foz, T45743367.

Local Car hire *Localiza* at airport, T45234800, Juscelino Kubitschek 2878, **Transport** T45221608, and Rodovia das Cataratas Km 2.5, *Hotel Bourbon*, T45231632.

Long distance **Air** Iguaçu international airport, 18 km south of town near the Falls. In Arrivals is *Banco do Brasil* and *Caribe Tours e Câmbio*, car rental offices, tourist office (see below) and an official taxi stand, US$10 to town centre (US$11 from town to airport). Transbalan (Parque Nacional) town bus for US$0.50, first at 0530, does not permit large amounts of luggage but backpacks OK. Many hotels run minibus services for a small charge. Daily flights to Rio de Janeiro, São Paulo, Curitiba and other Brazilian cities. **Bus** For transport to the falls see above under Parque Nacional Foz do Iguaçu. Long distance terminal (*Rodoviária*), Av. Costa e Silva, 4 km from centre on road to Curitiba; bus to centre, any bus that says `Rodoviária', US$0.65. Book departures as soon as possible. As well as the tourist office (see below), there is a Cetreme desk for tourists who have lost their documents, Guarda Municipal (police) and luggage store. **To Curitiba**, *Pluma, Sulamericana*, 9-11 hrs, paved road, US$15. **To Guaíra** via Cascavel only, 5 hrs, US$10. **To Florianópolis**, *Catarinense* and *Reunidas*, US$22, 16 hrs; *Reunidas* **to Porto Alegre**, US$30. **To São Paulo**, 16 hrs, *Pluma* US$30, *executivo* 6 a day, plus one *leito*. **To Rio** 22 hrs, several daily, US$38. **To Asunción**, *Pluma*, *RYSA* (direct at 1430), US$11.

Airline offices *Rio Sul*, J Sanways 779; *TAM*, T45238588 (offers free transport to Ciudad del Este for **Directory** its flights, all cross-border documentation dealt with); *Transbrasil*, Brasil 1225, T45743836; *Varig*, Kubitschek 463, T45232111; *Vasp*, Brasil 845, T45232221. **Banks** It is difficult to exchange on Sun but quite possible in Paraguay where US dollars can be obtained on credit cards. There are plenty of banks and travel agents on Av Brasil. *Banco do Brasil*, Brasil 1377. High commission for TCs. *Bradesco*, Brasil 1202. Cash advance on Visa. *Banespa*, Barroso e Schimmelpfeng, good rates for Visa, quick service. *Banestado*, Kubitschek e Bocaiúva, has *câmbio*. *Banco 24 Horas* at Oklahoma petrol station. *Itaú* ATM at airport. **Communications** **Post office** Praça Getúlio Vargas 72. **Telecommunications** Phone calls from *Telescritório*, Rio Branco 606, T45232167, also fax, email (US$2.50 per hr), telescritorio@foznet.com.br, open Mon-Fri 0730-2230, Sat-Sun 0800-2200. Phone calls also from *Telepar* on Edmundo de Barros. **Internet** *Cafe PizzaNet*, Rebouças 950, T/F5232122, www.foznet.com.br 0900-2300, US$4 per hr; also phone and fax. See also *Telescritório* above. **Electric current** 110 volts AC. **Embassies and consulates** *Argentine*, Travessa Eduardo Bianchi 26, T45742969. Open Mon-Fri 1000-1430. *French*, Federico Engels 48, Villa Yolanda. *Paraguayan*, Bartolomeu de Gusmão 480, T45232898. **Medical services** There is a free 24-hr clinic on Av Paraná, opposite Lions Club. Few buses: take taxi or walk (about 25 mins). **Security** Av Kubitschek and the streets south of it, towards the river, have a reputation as being unsafe at night as a favela is nearby. Take care if walking after dark. Taxis are only good value for short distances when you are carrying all your luggage. **Tourist information** 24-hr kiosk on Rio Branco, by Praça Getúlio Vargas. *Secretaria Municipal de Turismo*, Almte Barroso 1300, T45230222, T/F5742196. There is a 24-hr tourist help line number, T0800-451516. Very helpful. Kiosk on Av Brasil, by Ponte de Amizade (helpful), books hotels. Airport tourist information is also good, open for all arriving flights, gives map and bus information. Helpful office, free map, at the rodoviária, English spoken. A newspaper, *Triplice Fronteira*, carries street plans and other tourist information.

The Northeast

Frontier with Paraguay The Ponte de Amizade/Puente de Amistad (Friendship Bridge) over the Río Paraná, 12 km north of Foz, leads straight into the heart of Ciudad del Este. Crossing is very informal but keep an eye on your luggage and make sure that you get necessary stamps – so great is the volume of traffic that it can be difficult to stop, especially with the traffic police moving you on. It is particularly busy on Wed and Sat, with long queues of vehicles. Pedestrians from Brazil cross on the north side of the bridge allowing easier passage on the other side for those returning with bulky packages.

Immigration Paraguayan and Brazilian immigration formalities are dealt with at opposite ends of the bridge. There is a US$3 tourist charge to enter Paraguay. Remember to adjust your watch to local time.

Transport Buses (marked Cidade-Ponte) leave from the Terminal Urbana, Av Juscelino Kubitschek, for the Ponte de Amizade (Friendship Bridge), US$0.60. **Crossing by private vehicle**: if only intending to visit the national parks, this presents no problems.

Into Paraguay: Ciudad del Este
Population: 83,000

Founded as Ciudad Presidente Stroessner in 1957, the city grew rapidly during the construction of the Itaipú hydroelectric project. Described as the biggest shopping centre in Latin America, it attracts Brazilian and Argentine visitors in search of bargain prices for electrical goods, watches, perfumes et cetera. Dirty, noisy, unfriendly and brashly commercial, it is worth a visit just for the people-watching, but you should be careful with valuables and take particular care after dark. Accommodation is expensive. (For full details of services see the South American Handbook).

Excursions may be made to the Paraguayan side of the **Itaipú** hydroelectric project (see above under Foz do Iguaçu). ■ *Getting there: Buses run from Rodríguez y García, outside the terminal to the visitor centre, open Mon-Sat 0730-1200, 1330-1700, Sun and holidays closed. Free conducted tours of the project include a film show (versions in several languages – ask) 45 mins before bus tours which start at 0830, 0930, 1030, 1400, 1500, 1600, check times in advance. Take passport.* Some 10 km south of Ciudad del Este are the **Cascada del Monday** (Monday Falls), where the Río Monday drops into the Paraná gorge. Worthwhile. There is good fishing below the falls. ■ *Return fare by taxi US$20.*

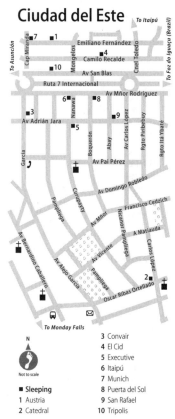

Ciudad del Este

N

Not to scale

■ **Sleeping**
1 Austria
2 Catedral
3 Convair
4 El Cid
5 Executive
6 Itaipú
7 Munich
8 Puerta del Sol
9 San Rafael
10 Tripolis

The Lake District

9

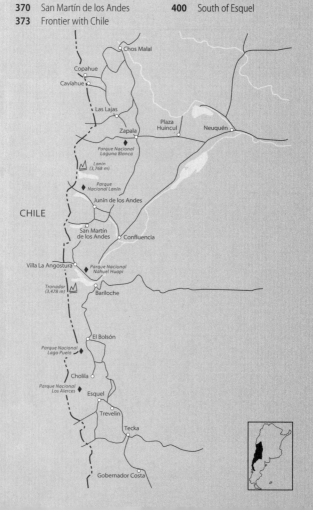

Stretching along the western side of the Andes in the province of Neuquén and in western parts of Río Negro and Chubut are a string of glacial lakes. The western ends of these cut deeply into the mountains, their water lapping the forested skirts of some of the most spectacular snow-capped peaks in the world; their eastern ends are contained by the frontal moraines deposited by the ancient glaciers which gouged out these huge lakes. The water is a deep blue, sometimes lashed into white froth by high winds. Four national parks have been created to protect this environment.

The most important centre is the city of Bariloche, the base for exploring the Parque Nacional Nahuel Huapi, one of the largest and most spectacular national parks in Argentina and a popular destination for lovers of climbing, winter sports, walking and fishing. Bariloche is also the departure point for one of the most beautiful and famous crossings into Chile, the route by boat across Lago Todos Los Santos. Further north is the Parque Nacional Lanín, less popular with travellers, but no less attractive; the main centres for visiting this park are San Martin de los Andes and Junin de los Andes. South of Bariloche lie two more parks: Lago Puelo, reached from the small town of El Bolson, and Los Alerces, reached from Esquel. The latter town is also famous as the southern terminus of La Trochita, the little railway made famous by Paul Therroux as 'the Old Patagonian Express'. Further north, Neuquén has become famous for the discovery of the largest fossils of carnivorous dinosaurs found on Earth.

Southern beech forests

Although the southern beech forests extend across a wide range of latitudes, wildlife found there varies little. Bird species found in the forests include the fantastically named chilean flicker, the magellanic woodpecker, the green-backed firecrown (the only hummingbird found at these latitudes) and the rufous-tailed plantcutter. More typical of the Valdivian forest are the chucao tapaculo and the huet-huet. Lakes and rivers are inhabited by species of grebes and ducks including the lake duck and the torrent duck. Near open areas the black-faced Ibis, fire-eyed Diucon and the austral blackbird may be seen.

Mammals are harder to find. Native species include the red fox and the Patagonian hog-nosed skunk as well as several endangered species: the pudú (the smallest deer in the world), the huillín (a species of river otter) and the huemul or Andean deer.

Among species introduced are the red deer (most common in Neuquén) and Canadian Beavers, European rabbits and muskrats, all of which have flourished in Tierra del Fuego. Salmon and trout have been introduced to most of the rivers and lakes in the Lake District, Patagonia and Tierra del Fuego, mainly for sport.

Background

Eastern areas of Neuquén are covered by the foothills of the Andes, rising steadily westwards. The Andes themselves are much lower than further north: most peaks range from 2,000 m to 2,500 m, though three volcanoes tower above this, Tromen (3,978 m) Lanín (3,768 m) and Copahue (2,953 m), as well as two other peaks, Domuyo (4,709 m) and Tronador (3,478 m).

A few rivers, notably the Ríos Hua Hum, Puelo and Futaleufú which between them drain most of Chubut, flow west into the Pacific Ocean via Chile. Most of the lakes (except Lago Lácar) drain into the Atlantic via the Río Negro. This river, the most important in Argentina apart from those which form the Río de la Plata flows into the ocean 637 km further west. The northern lakes, including Lagos Aluminé, Ñorquinco, Quillén and Tromen, flow into the Río Aluminé, which flows south, west of the Sierra de Catan Lil. Most of the southern lakes drain via Lago Nahuel Huapi into the Río Limay which forms an impressive gorge as it flows north to meet the Río Neuquén. Huge reservoirs have been built to harness the waters of the major rivers and produce electricity which is distributed throughout the country: the artificial lakes include Cerros Colorados on the Río Neuquén, Ezequiel Ramos Mexía, Piedra del Aguila and Alicurá on the Río Limay, and Amutui Quimei, south of Esquel.

A series of national parks has been created to protect the environment of the largest lakes: the most important of these are Lanín, Nahuel Huapi and Los Alerces: the main centres for exploring these are, respectively, San Martín de los Andes, Bariloche and Esquel.

Climate Annual rainfall varies in relation to the proximity of the Andes, from 200-400 mm in Eastern Neuquén to over 3,000 mm in some of the westernmost forest areas. Outside these westernmost areas rainfall mainly occurs between May and August. Summer temperatures range between 31°C and 13°C in Neuquén and between 21°C and 6°C in Esquel. Winter temperatures vary between 13°C and 0°C in Neuquén and between 6°C and -3°C in Esquel.

Off season, mid-Aug to mid-Nov, excursions, boat trips, etc, run on a limited schedule, if at all. Public transport is also limited

The Monkey Puzzle Tree

The Pehuen (Araucaria araucana) is perhaps better known as the monkey puzzle tree; other names include the Chilean pine, umbrella tree or parasol tree. Very slow growing, it can grow to 40-m high. Some are believed to be 300 years old. Though its natural habitat is on both sides of the Andes between 37 and 39 south, it is much more widespread in Chile than Argentina and

is the Chilean national tree. A true conifer, its a descendent of the petrified pines found in the Bosques Petrificados. Its cones and its sharp leathery leaves were eaten by the Mapuche for centuries. Some isolated trees are still seen as sacred by the Mapuche who leave offerings to the tree's spirit. The characteristic cones can weigh up to 1 kg so take care sitting underneath!

Neuquén Province

Bounded to the west by the Andes, the north by the Río Colorado and the south by the Río Limay, the province of Neuquén is the main gateway to the Lake District from Buenos Aires. It is reached by Route 22 which runs west from Bahía Blanca, crossing the Río Colorado at the town of Río Colorado and the Río Negro at Choele Choel. This route passes through the valley of the Río Negro which is particularly beautiful in April to May when the leaves of the poplars turn yellow. Most buses from Buenos Aires do not follow this route; instead they follow Route 20 across the province of La Pampa, a monotonous almost straight line 200 km across the desert, and then take Route 151 to Neuquén.

Economy Extensive irrigation has made Eastern Neuquén and the valley of the Río Negro a major dairy farming and fruit-growing region. About 75% of all Argentine fruit are grown in this area, about 60% of it for export. Apples are the principal crop but pears and table grapes are also grown and there are many wine *bodegas* nearby. The province is a major producer of petroleum and natural gas, meeting about 15% of Argentina's energy needs. Historically oil extraction has been centred on Cultral-Có and nearby Plaza Huincul, though the discovery of new oil fields in the extreme south of the province has move the centre of production to the town of Rincón de los Sauces. Marble and cement are mined further west around Zapala.

Neuquén

Phone code: 0299
Colour map 5, grid A3
Population: 200,000
538 km W of Bahía Blanca; 1,147 km W of Buenos Aires

Neuquén, lies at the extreme eastern tip of the province at the confluence of the Ríos Limay and Neuquén, which form the Río Negro. On the opposite side of the Río Neuquén and connected by bridge is Cipolletti, a prosperous centre of the Río Negro fruit-growing region. A pleasant provincial capital and industrial city, Neuquén was founded in 1904, just after the arrival of the railway; its origins are reflected in the central location of the railway station. The city's main industries are food processing, but it also benefits from serving the oilfields to the west and north with heavy equipment and construction materials.

Sights The former railway station, at Olascoaga y Pasaje Obligado, has been converted into a cultural centre and exhibition centre. On the northern outskirts of the city at the Parque Centenario there is a *mirador* with panoramic views over the city and the confluence of the rivers (be sure *not* to take the bus to Centenario industrial suburb). South of the centre there is also a pleasant walk along the Río Limay. Museums include **Museo Histórico Dr Gregorio Alvarez**, General San Martín 280. Housed in 1899 railway company building, includes old photos and section on dinosaurs. ■ *Mon-Fri 0800-2000, Sun 1700-2100*. **Museo de Ciencias Naturales**, Argentina 1400, includes exhibitions of dinosaur fossils found in the region.

Excursions **Lago Pellegrini**, 36 km north, is an artificial lake where watersports are held. **Embalse Cerro Colorado** is another artificial lake 40 km northwest where there artificial and natural swimming pools (take bus marked 'Banda del Medio' from terminal). North of the lake is **Añelo**, where there is an archaeological museum.

Sleeping **Centre** L *Del Comahue*, Argentina 377, T4422440, F4473331. Reservations at 0810

Do not confuse the streets Félix San Martín & General San Martín

3333506 or at reservas@hoteldelcomahue.com.ar Very good, with sauna, gym and swimming pool, restaurant '1900 cuatro'. **A** *Apolo*, Olascoaga 361, T4422334, F4422335. Good, but overpriced, discounts if paying with cash. **AB** *Suizo*, Rodríguez 167, T/F4422602. Discounts if paying with cash, new wing, restaurant. **AB** *Amucán*, Tucumán 114, T4425209. Good. **AB** *Crystal*, Olascoaga 268, T4422414, F4424147. Large, overpriced. **B** *Neuquén*, Roca 109, T4422403. Overpriced. *Huemul*, Tierra del Fuego 334, T4422344. Clean, small rooms, good value. **C** *Alcorta*, Alcorta 84, T4422652. New section good value, also **D** per person without bath. **C** *Inglés*, Félix San Martín 534, T4422252. Convenient, without breakfast. Recommended. **D** per person *Hosp Pani*, Felix San Martín 238, with bath, **E** per person without, run down, near bus terminal.

Elsewhere L *Holiday Inn Express*, Goya y Costa Rica (just off Route 22, west of centre), T4490100, 3-star, with restaurant. **AL** *Hostal del Caminante*, Route 22 13 km west, T4440118. Good rooms, pool, popular in summer, restaurant, recommended for visiting nearby *chacras* and their fruit crops. **A** *Arrayán*, Route 22, T4440128. With pool. *ACA Cipolletti*, Ruta Nacional 22 y Av Luis Toschi, eastern outskirts, T471827.

Camping Municipal site near the Río Limay, free, packed with locals during weekends.

Eating *Tutto al Dente*, Alberdi 49, pasta, *ñoquis con salsa de camarones* recommended. *Le Primoule*, in barrio los Nogales, *trucha al limón*. Recommended. *1900 Cuatro*, at *Hotel del Comahue; Barracuda*, Rivadavia 265, for basic and fast meals; also try in *Tía* supermarket 1st floor, Olascoaga y Félix San Martín.

Festivals All the towns in the Río Negro valley celebrate the *Fiesta Nacional de la Manzana* in the second half of Mar.

Shopping **Bookshops** *Libracos*, Perito Moreno y Corrientes, many books on Patagonia in Spanish, few books in English. Recommended. *Siringa*, Argentina y Alberdi (in Galería Española, beside Cine Español), books of local and regional interests; chocolates and cakes. **Supermarkets** *La Anónima*,*Tía* and *Wal Mart*, all on route 22, east of Olascoaga.

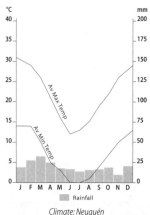

Climate: Neuquén

The Lake District

Local Taxis *Confluencia*, T4438880. *Radio Taxi*, T4422502. **Mechanic** Normando **Transport**
Toselli, Mitre 801 (Former South American superbike champion), for cars or motor-
bikes, highly recommended.

Long distance Air Airport 7 km west of centre. Buses: *Indalo* (US$1.50) getting on
at Sarmiento, near bus terminal, or *Turismo Lanín* (US$1.50) from the bus terminal to
Plottier, getting off at the access road to the airport. Taxi US$8. To **Buenos Aires**, *Aus-
tral* and *Lapa*. To **Bahía Blanca**, *Lapa*. The regional airline *TAN* flies to many Argentine
cities including **Bahía Blanca**, **Comodoro Rivadavia**, **Córdoba**, **Mendoza**, **Bariloche**,
San Martín de los Andes and, in **Chile**, Puerto Montt and Temuco. *Southern Winds* to
Córdoba, **Rosario**, **Tucumán** and **Salta**.

Bus Terminal at Mitre 147. Left luggage: US$2 a day per item. To **Buenos Aires**, 15-16
hrs, US$43-55, many companies. To **Mendoza**, 12-13 hrs, US$37-41, *Andesmar*, *TAC*, *El
Rápido*, *Alto Valle*. To **Córdoba**, 15-16 hrs, US$48-59, TUS, TAC. To **Bariloche**, 5-6 hrs,
US$20-30, many companies. To **Esquel**, 10-11 hrs, US$39-48, *TAC*, *Andesmar*, *Vía
Bariloche*. To **Mar del Plata**, 14 hrs, US$51, *El Rápido*, *La Unión del Sud*. To **San Martín de
los Andes**, 6-7 hrs, US$22-26, many companies. To **Junín de los Andes**, 5 hrs,

Neuquén centre

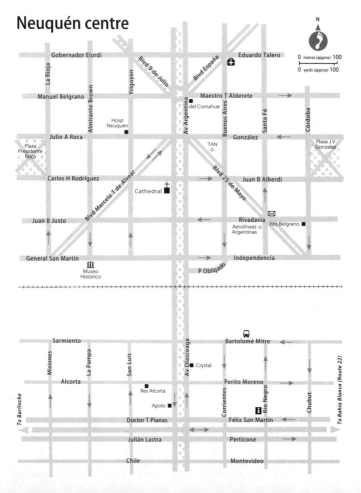

The Lake District

US$20-24, many companies. To **Aluminé**, 6 hrs, US$15-20, *Pehuenche, Albus, La Estrella, Del Sur y Media Agua*. To **Zapala**, 2-3 hrs, US$10, *Albus, El Petróleo, Cono Sur, Centenario*. To **Plaza Huincul**, 1½ hrs, US$6, *El Petróleo, Albus, Centenario, Cono Sur*. To **Caviahue** (6 hrs, US$24) and Copahue, 6½ hrs, US$27, *El Petróleo, Centenario*. To **Chos Malal**, 6 hrs, US$24, *El Petróleo, Cono Sur*. To **Villa La Angostura**, 10 hrs, US$26-38, *Albus, Del Sur y Media Agua*. To **Las Lajas**, 4 hrs, US$15, *Cono Sur, El Petróleo, Centenario*.

To Chile To **Temuco** via Zapala and Paso Pino Hachado, 12-14 hrs, US$45, seven companies, all 1 to 3 times a week. To **Valdivia**, US$45-52, *Andesmar, Centenario*, several times a week. To **Osorno**, US$43, *Andesmar*, daily. To **Frutillar** (US$48) and **Puerto Montt** (US$53), *Andesmar*, several times a week. To **Santiago**, 20 hrs, US$45, *El Rápido, Andesmar*, several times a week.

Directory **Airline offices** *Aerolíneas Argentinas/Austral*, Santa Fe 52, T4422409/4440736. *Lapa*, Argentina 30, T4488335/4440662. *TAN*, 25 de Mayo 180, T4424834/4440605. *LADE*, Brown 163, T4431153, 4440817. *Southern Winds*, Argentina 237, T4420124. *TAPSA*, T4440690, *American Jet*, T4441085. **Banks** *HSBC*, Justo 75. *Lloyds Bank*, Justo e Yrigoyen, for TC's. *Pullman*, Alcorta 144. **Consulates** *Chile*, La Rioja 241, T4422727. **Communications** Post office Rivadavia y Santa Fe. **Phones** Telecom, 25 de Mayo 20. Many *locutorios* in the centre. **Internet** Paseo del Sol, Perito Moreno y Río Negro. **Laundry** Felix San Martín 518. Roca y Yrigoyen. Salta y Justo. **Tour operators** *ASATEJ*, Brown 360, T/F4430860, neuquen@asatej.com.ar **Tourist offices** Félix San Martín 182, T4424089, F4432438, turismo@neuquen.gov.ar Mon-Fri 0700-20300, Sat/Sun 0800-1500.

Routes from Neuquén to Bariloche

The most direct road from Neuquén to Bariloche (426 km) is by Route 237, which branches off Route 22 at a point 50 km east of Neuquén and runs south-west along the Embalse Ezequiel Ramos Mexía (816 sq km). At the northern end of the lake, near the dam, is the small town of **El Chocón**, built for construction workers on the nearby power station. This area is famous for the wealth of dino-saur fossils found in recent years from the Cretacic period (100 mn years ago). Some of these can be seen in the Museo Paleontológico Ernesto Bachmann (0900-1900 daily) including fossils of *Gigantosaurus Carolinii*, a carnivorous dinosaur larger than the more famous Tyrannosaurus Rex. Guided visits to the area are offered by *Aventura Jurásica* in El Chocón, T4901243. **Sleeping** at **AL** *La Posada del Dinosaurio*, in El Chocón, T0299-4901118, F4901161, posadadino@infovia.com.ar With breakfast, good.

Beyond the small town of **Piedra del Aguila** there are views of the Lanín vol-cano to the west, then the road drops over an escarpment to cross the Río Collón Curá, where it joins Route 40 for 20 km, before branching off onto Route 237 which runs through the impressive valley of the Río Limay to Confluencia (see page 373) and through the Valle Encantado to Lago Nahuel Huapi where there are fine views over Cerros Catedral and Tronador. This route is fast but misses Junín de los Andes and San Martín de los Andes. The most attractive route is to follow Route 237 (as above) to the Río Collón Curá, then take Route 40 (and later Route 234) northwest to Junín de los Andes.

Northern Neuquén

Route 22 runs west from Neuquén through fruit-growing region of the Río Limay and the oil-producing zone around Plaza Huincul and Cultral-Có.

Plaza Huincul Situated 107 km west of Neuquén, Plaza Huincul was the site of the first oil
Population: 11,000 find in 1918. The Museo Municipal Carmen Funes includes the vertebrae of

Dinosaurs in Argentina

Few countries can equal Argentina in importance for students of dinosaurs; the relative abundance of fossils near the surface has made the country one of the most significant for the study of dinosaur evolution. The main Argentine examples of dinosaurs from the Triassic period (225-180 million years ago) can be found in the Ischigualasto and Talampaya National Parks in San Juan and La Rioja respectively. Among them is the small Eoraptor lunensis, 220 million years old, considered one of the oldest discovered anywhere in the world.

Outstanding examples of Jurassic dinosaurs (180-135 million years old) have been discovered in Patagonia. Cerro Cóndor, in Chubut, is the only site of Middle Jurassic dinosaurs found in the Americas, and is therefore of great importance for understanding the evolutionary stages between the Upper and Lower Jurassic periods. At least 5 examples of patagosaurus fariasi have been found here, indicating that these dinosaurs at least were social creatures, possibly for purposes of mutual defence. In Santa Cruz traces of dinosaurs from the Upper Jurassic period have been found in rocks which indicate that at that time the climate was arid and desert-like. This also demonstrates that dinosaurs could live and reproduce in such adverse conditions.

Important discoveries of dinosaurs from the Cretacic period (135 to 70 million years ago) have been made in Neuquén and Chubut. Dating from the period of the separation of the continents of South America and Africa, these provide evidence of the way in which dinosaurs began to evolve in different ways due to their geographical isolation. One example of this is carnotaurus sastrei, which has horns and very small hands. One of the interesting features is the greater size of Patagonian dinosaurs: the Argentinosaurus huiculensis is one of the largest herbivorous dinosaurs found on earth while the carnivorous Gigantosaurus carolinii was larger than the better known Tyranosaurus Rex discovered in North America.

Carnotaurus Sastrei

argentinossaurus huinclulensis, believed to have weighed over 100 tons and to have been one of the largest herbivorous dinosaurs ever to have lived on Earth as well as a nest of fossilised dinosaur eggs. **Sleeping** at Hostería Tunquelén, T463423.

Zapala lies in a vast dry plain with views of snow capped mountains to the west. Formerly the western terminus of a railway line originally planned to extend across the Andes to Chile, it is situated at the junction of Route 22 with Route 40. A convenient stopping point en route to Chile, it is also a base for visiting the Parque Nacional Laguna Blanca. There is an airport and an ACA service station. **Museo Mineralógico Dr Juan Olsacher**, Etcheluz 52 (next to the bus terminal), neumin@zapala.com.ar is one of the best museums of its type in South America, it contains over 2,000 types of mineral and has the finest collection of fossils of marine reptiles and marine fauna in the country. On display are the largest turtle shell from the Jurassic period ever found and an ophthalmosaur. ■ Mon-Fri 0900-1300, free, closed weekends.

Zapala
Phone code: 02942
Colour map 5, grid A2
Population: 35,000
Altitude: 1,012 m
185 km W of Neuquén

Sleeping AB *Hue Melén*, Brown 929, T4422391, F442407. Good value, expensive restaurant. **B** *Huincul*, Roca 311, T431422. Large, quiet, overpriced restaurant. **B** *Coliqueo*, Etcheluz 159, T421308, convenient. **B** *Pehuén*, Vega y Etcheluz, T423135. Comfortable, interesting display of local maps. **C/D** *Res Odetto Grill*, Ejército Argentino 455, T422176, cheapest option, modest, friendly. **Camping** Municipal site.

Transport Local Taxi T430290/430050. **Bus** Terminal at Etcheluz y Uriburu, T431311. To **Neuquén**, 2-3 hrs, US$10, *Albus, Centenario, Cono Sur, El Petróleo*. To **San Martín de los Andes**, 3-4 hrs, US$18-20, *Albus, Centenario, El Petróleo, TAC*. To **Junín de los Andes**, 2½-3½ hrs, US$17-18, *Albus, El Petróleo, Centenario, TAC*. To **Villa La Angostura**, 5-6 hrs, US$30-35, *Albus*. To **Aluminé**, US$10, *Albus, Yumbel, Aluminé Viajes*. To **Chos Malal**, 3 hrs and other northern destinations, *El Petróleo, Cono Sur*. To **Las Lajas**, 1 hr, US$4-5, *Centenario, El Petróleo, Cono Sur*. To **Caviahue**, (3 hrs, US$15) and **Copahue** (3½-4 hrs, US$17) daily with *Centenario, El Petróleo*. To **Bariloche**, *Albus, TAC, Vía Bariloche*. To **Buenos Aires**, 18 hrs, US$50-60, many companies. To **Temuco** (Chile), US$43, Mon/Wed/Fri, *Centenario* (buy Chilean currency before leaving).

Directory Banks Three banks including*Banco de la Nación Argentina* but difficult to change TC's. **Internet** Instituto Moreno, Moreno y López y Planes. CPI, Chaneton y Garayta. **Tourist office** San Martín y Mayor Torres, T421132, open (summer) Mon-Fri 0700-1930, Sat/Sun 0800-1300, 1600-1900, closes earlier off season.

Parque Nacional Laguna Blanca
35 km SW of Zapala

Covering 11,250 ha at altitudes between 1,200 m and 1,800 m, this park is one of only two reserves in the Americas created to protect swans and it is a RAMSAR site. The laguna, 1,700 ha, is one of the most important nesting-areas of the black-necked swan in Argentina. Other bird-life includes the

Zapala

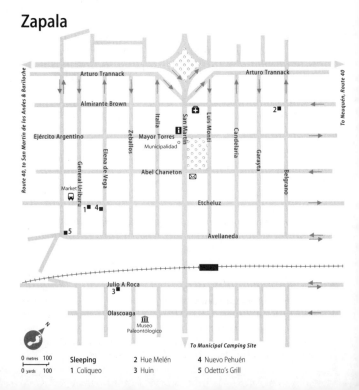

| Sleeping | 2 Hue Melén | 4 Nuevo Pehuén |
| 1 Coliqueo | 3 Huin | 5 Odetto's Grill |

several duck species, among them the Andean ruddy duck, plovers, sandpipers, grebes and Chilean flamingos. The steep slopes of the laguna are nesting sites for birds of prey such as the red-backed hawk and the peregrine falcon. The surrounding area, covered with scrub and bushes, provides a habitat for mountain cats, foxes and rodents. A rough track runs round the lake, suitable for four-wheel drive vehicles only. Nearby the Arroyo Ñireco has eroded the volcanic rock to form a deep gorge. Southwest of the park Route 46 continues through the spectacular *Bajada de Rahue*, dropping 800 m in under 20 km before reaching the town of Rahue, 120 km southwest of Zapala.

Climate Temperatures rise to 40°C in summer, but drop below 0°C in winter, when drizzle and snow are common. Annual rainfall is around 200 mm. Spring is the best time to visit, though it can be very windy.

Access Route 46, which runs across the park, branches off Route 40, 10 km south of Zapala. The park entrance is 10 km from this turning, and the lagoon lies 4-5 km beyond this. No public transport and little traffic makes hitchhiking difficult.

Essentials *Guardaparque* post near southeast corner of the laguna. Small visitors centre and restaurant. Entry US$2. Free camping. *Guardaparque's* office on Vidal, next to *Hotel Pehuén*, in Zapala.

From Zapala Route 13 runs west to the Chilean frontier at Paso de Icalma, **West of Zapala** through a vast mountainous region where forests of *pehuén* are the main feature. Some 50 km west of Zapala, there is a small ski resort called Primeros Pinos, referring to the place where the first trees can be seen. From here the road (*ripio*) continues to the eastern shores of **Lago Aluminé**, 107 km west of Zapala. The small town of **Villa Pehuenia**, on the northern shore, offers accommodation and basic services during the tourist season in summer, while there are campsites all along the lakeshore. There are two small natural reserves in the area, Batea Mahuida and Chañy, created to protect areas of pehuén trees and volcanic environments. Excursions can be made to the nearby mountains and volcanoes and to **Lago Moquehue**, further west. This lake lies in a more humid area with more diverse tree species than the surrounding forests. At the extreme southern tip of the lake there is a village where accommodation is offered. Good camping sites can be found on the lake shores. South from Lago Moquehue and reached by Route 11 are the smaller Lagos Pilhué and Ñorquinco (which lie within the Parque Nacional Lanín) and lago Pulmarí. Route 11 meets Route 23: this runs north to the east of Lago Aluminé and south to the town of **Aluminé**, which lies in the valley of the beautiful Río Aluminé. From Aluminé there is access to **Lago Rucachoroi**, 23 km west inside the national park and surrounded by old pehuen forests. The town of **Rahue**, 16 km south of Aluminé, gives access to the valley of the Río Quillén and the beautiful Lago Quillén, from where there are fine views of the nearby Lanín volcano. This area, where the largest annual rainfall in Argentina (over 4 m) was ever registered, has a very diverse native flora which is, in shady places, as dense as tropical jungle.

The Lake District

Sleeping at Lagos Aluminé and Moquehue (phone code 02942) *Lago Aluminé*, T498019. *La Bella Durmiente*, T496172. *Camping Trenel*, on southern shore of Lago Moquehue, T431550, hot showers, restaurant, information and excursions. **Aluminé Pehuenia**, Crouzeilles 100, T496340. *Aluminé*, Joubert 336, T496174. *Nid Car*, Joubert y Benigar, T496131.

Directory Tour operators *Amuyén*, Villegas 348, T496368, for rafting, horseriding, trekking, cycle hire. **Tourist office** T496154.

Frontier crossings with Chile

Paso Pino Hachado (1,864 m) lies 115 km west of Zapala via Route 22, almost completely paved. On the Chilean side a *ripio* road run northwest to Lonquimáy, 65 km west of the frontier. Temuco lies 145 km southwest of Lonquimáy.

Argentine immigration and customs 9 km east of the frontier, open 0700-1300, 1400-1900. **Chilean immigration and customs**, in Liucura, 22 km west of the frontier, open Dec-Mar 0800-2100, Apr-Nov 0800-1900. Very thorough searches and 2-3 hr delays reported. **Transport** Buses from Zapala and Neuquén to Temuco use this crossing.

Paso de Icalma (1,303 m) lies 132 km west of Zapala and is reached by Route 13 (*ripio*). On the Chilean side this road continues to Melipeuco, 30 km west of the frontier, and thence to Temuco.

Argentine immigration and customs Open 0700-1300, 1400-1900. **Chilean immigration and customs** Open Dec-Mar 0800-2100, Apr-Nov 0800-1900.

North of Zapala

Route

Route 22 continues northwest from Zapala to **Las Lajas**, Km 55, which is the base for visiting the nearby cave system of **Cuchillo Cura** and the **Cueva del Léon**, one of the most spectacular in Patagonia. For guided tours ask in the tourist office in Las Lajas or contact Roberto Amarilla, T02942-499122. From Las Lajas Route 40 runs north via Chos Malal and Malargüe to Mendoza. Unpaved in sections between Chos Malal and Malargüe, this route to Mendoza is more scenic, but slower, than the main Neuquén-Mendoza route (Nos 151 and 143 via Santa Isabel and San Rafael). Route 22 goes southwest to the Chilean frontier at Paso Pino Hachado, 59 km west of Las Lajas. Route 21 branches off Route 22 about 10 km noth of Las Ljas and runs northwest to Longcopue (handicrafts market on Sat and Sun). In Longcopue Route 26 branches off northwest towards Caviahue and Copahue via the Chico gorge, while Route 21 runs north to the remote countryside of the far north of the province.

Reserva Provincial Copahue-Caviahue

170 km NW of Zapala

Covering 28,300 ha of mountainous terrain, this park includes the still-active Copahue volcano (2,953 m) and protects the northernmost *pehuén* or monkey-puzzle trees in Argentina. The park includes the **Termas de Copahue** (altitude 1,980 m), a thermal resort enclosed in a gigantic amphitheatre formed by mountain walls and considered to have some of the best thermal waters in South America. The *termas* are open from December to April only; in winter Copahue is deserted and covered by thick snows (resort information T495050).

Caviahue (altitude: 1,600 m), 18 km southeast, is a small village in beautiful scenery on Lago Agrio. Suitable for horseriding and trekking in summer, it is a winter sports resort between Jul and Sep; there are three ski lifts, excellent for cross country skiing, snow-shoing and snowmobiling (and cheaper than Bariloche). A bus service connects the two resorts.

Excursions can be made to **Laguna Escondida**, a 30-minute walk at the top of the hill behind the town. There are great views of the lake, volcano and forests; good for ice-skating in winter. About 3 km west of Caviahue is the Cascada Escondida, 15 m high and is situated in a gorge covered with dense native forest of pehuén and nothofagus. Another waterfall is Salto del Agrio, 18 km east of Caviahue (2 km off route 27), a large waterfall in a basaltic area. Rec- ommended. At Las Maquinitas, southeast of Copahue and reached by Route 26, there are thermal waters (free access, no services).

Another good walk is to Siete Cascadas and the Chilean frontier at Paso Pucón Mahuida (four hours round trip from Caviahue), reached by crossing bridge over the Río Agrio and following a dirt road west along the river passing seven different waterfalls. At first the road climbs steeply through a forest of pehuén. From the edge of the forest the road becomes impassable for vehicles; from here it is an hour's walk, mostly over a field of huge rocks to the pass, where there is a small lagoon with ducks. There are fine views over the Copahue volcano. Recommended only in good weather and preferably not alone. Do not enter Chile without first obtaining an exit stamp in Caviahue.

To climb Copahue volcano (half day excursion) from Copahue follow the Río Blanco past Lagunas Las Mellizas. Inside the crater, there is a small lake with warm acidic water, which drains into the arroyo Agrio. Panoramic views of the lower valleys and active volcán Villarrica in Chile. It is necessary to hire a guide.

Sleeping Copahue (phone code 02948): *Valle del Volcán*, T495048, 3-star. *Termas*, T495045, 3-star. *Pino Azul*, T495071. *Hualcupén*, T495049, decesco@satlink.com **D** per person *Res Codihue*, T495031, with poor breakfast. Several others. **Caviahue B** *Lago Caviahue*, T/495110, very clean, apartments with kitchen, restaurant, great views. *La Cabaña de Tito*, T495093, cabañas near lake, excellent meals. Highly recommended. *Farallon*, T495062, apartments with kitchens. *Caviahue Sky*, T495064. **D** per person *Caniche Lodge*, **E** per person in summer, kitchen facilities, run by Caniche and Gerard, ski instructors and guides. **Camping** 3 km out of town, summer only.

Tour operators *Caviahue Tours*, San Martín 623, Buenos Aires, T43141556, for information on the region.

Transport Air Charter flights from Buenos Aires in winter to Caviahue. **Buses** To/from **Neuquén**, El Petroleo and Centenario, both daily, 6 hrs, US$25, via Zapala (US$13).

Chos Malal was founded as a fortress in 1879 and became a mining centre. The restored fortress houses the **Museo Histórico Olascoaga**, which contains artefacts of the 'Conquest of the Wilderness'. **Sleeping** at **AB** *Chos Malal*, San Martín 89, T422472. Faded grandeur but clean, a couple of hostels and a municipal campsite on the Río Curi Leuvú. ■ *Getting there: To Neuquén, 6 hrs, US$25, Cono Sur and El Petróleo, 1 bus each daily.*

Chos Malal
Phone code: 02948
Population: 8,600
Altitude: 862 m
211 km N of Zapala

From Chos Malal Route 43 runs north across mountain ranges to **Andacollo** (altitude 1,415 m) where there is basic accommodation. At **Huinganco**, 7 km east of Andacollo (two campsites) remains of gold mines can be seen and visits can be made to the **Reserva Cañada Molina**, which protects an old forest of cypresses and other native species. From Andacollo Route 43 continues north, following the Río Nahueve, which drains the remote Lagunas de Epulafquen, a group of small lakes amid mountain scenery and *nothofagus* forests close to the Chilean frontier. ■ *Getting there: To Neuquén via Chos Malal, Cono Sur 1 a day, 8 hrs, US35.*

North of Chos Malal

The Lake District

Parque
Provincial
Tromen
37 km NE of Chos Malal
covering 24,000 ha

This park surrounds Lago Tromen, a nesting site for migratory birds flamingoes, black-necked swans, ducks. East of the lake is the **Tromen** volcano (4,114 m). Another peak, Cerro Waile (3,182 m) has a flat summit, where skiing is possible though there are no services. ■ *Getting there: By ripio road which runs north from Chos Malal along the west bank of the lake and then (unpaved) northeast to meet Route 40. For transport from Chos Malal contact Viajes Wayle, Gral Paz 385, T/F422003.*

Junín de
los Andes
Phone code: 02972
Colour map 5, grid A2
Population: 9,000
Altitude: 773 m
204 km S of Zapala;
218 km N of Bariloche

Situated on the Río Chimehuin, Junín de los Andes is known as the trout capital of Argentina (the fishing season runs from mid November to the end of April). Less touristy than San Martín de los Andes, it is quieter and cheaper and offers a good base for visiting the northern part of Parque Nacional Lanín (see page 368). Excursions may also be made to Mapuche communities between Junín and Aluminé, further north along Route 23. For information on Mapuche culture contact Mirta Cañicul at the national park office in Junín, T491160. There is a small **Museo Salesiano** in the centre at Ginés Ponte y Nogueira.

Sleeping AB/B *Hostería Chimehuín*, Suárez y 25 de Mayo, T491132, F491319, rucahueney@jandes.com.ar, near river, classic fishing hostel, good breakfasts, open all year. **B** *Alejandro I*, Route 234, on northern edge of town, T491182. Open fishing season only, restaurant. **B/C** *Res Marisa*, Rosas 360, T491175, cheapest. **B** *Res El Cedro*, Lamadrid 409 (main plaza), T492044. Gloomy. **C** *Posada Pehuén*, Coronel Suárez 560, T491569, F491587. Good value, restaurant, charming owners, Rosi and Oscar Marconi, also offers excursions. Recommended. **C** *El Montañés*, San Martín 555, T491155, convenient, also offers fishing tours. **D** per person *San Jorge*, Antártida Argentina, T/F491147, hotelsanjorge@smandes.com.ar Open Nov-Apr, beautifully located with lovely views, good value, with restaurant, English spoken. Recommended. **E** per person *Marita & Aldo*, 25 de Mayo y Olavarría, T491042. Open summer only, shared rooms and floor space with bathroom and kitchen facilities, 'the best place for socialise in a funny atmosphere', highly recommended for backpackers, good meals. **Estancia L** *Estancia Huechahue*, southeast of town (reached from the Junín-Bariloche bus), T491303. English run, comfortable, farmhouse accommodation, horseriding, fishing, river trips.

Camping *Mallín Beata Laura Vicuña*, Ginés Ponte 861, T491149, F491808, campinglv@jandes.com.arOn the river, hot showers, electricity, small shop, discounts for stays over two days, also cabañas *La Isla*, on opposite band of the river, quieter.

Junín de los Andes: centre

Eating *Ruca Hueney*, Colonel Suárez y Milanesio (main plaza). Good trout and pasta dishes, friendly service. Recommended. *Ravese's II*, San Martín 539, *minutas* and pizzas. *La Aldea del Pescador* Route 234 y Necochea, pasta and *parrilla*. *Roble*, Ginés Ponte y Milanesio, popular bar, sandwiches and pizzas, open late.

Tour operators *Tromen*, Lonquimay 195 (also at Paseo Artesanal, near main plaza in summer), T491022, tromen@jandes.com.ar (Buenos Aires T42870256).

Transport   Local Taxi *El Rápido*, T491666. *Los Puesteros*, T491176. **Long distance Air** Chapelco airport, 19 km southwest on the road to San Martín de los Andes (can be reached by taking any bus to San Martín). Taxi US$20. Flights to **Buenos Aires**, *Austral*. To **Neuquén** and **Bariloche**, *TAN*, T427872. **Bus** Terminal at Olavarría y Félix San Martín (do not confuse with Gral San Martín). To **San Martín de los Andes**, 45 mins, US$4, several a day, *El Petróleo, Centenario, Ko Ko, Airén*. To **Neuquén**, 7 hrs, US23, several companies. To **Bariloche**, US$16, Ko Ko. To **Buenos Aires**, 21 hrs, US$65-75, several companies. To **Chile**: Service to Pucón (4 hrs), Villarrica (4½ hrs), Temuco (5 hrs) and Valdivia (6 hrs) via Paso Tromen, *Empresa San Martín* Tue/Thu/Sat, Igi Llaima, Mon/Wed/Fri/Sun.

Directory Banks *Western Union*, Milanesio 570, for cash and TC's. **Communications** Post office, Suárez y Don Bosco. **Telephones**, locutorio at Milanesio 540. **Internet** *Chab*, Don Bosco 532 (in Galería de la Montaña). **Laundry** Laverap, Ginés Ponte 340. Aqualav, Milanesio 683. **Tourist offices** Milanesio y Coronel Suárez, T/F491160, turismo@jandes.com.ar Daily 0800-2200 (fishing season), closes 2100 off season. **Parques Nacionales** office for information on Parque Nacional Lanín in same building, T491160, very helpful.

Paso Tromen, known in Chile as Paso Mamuil Malal, is situated 64 km north-west of Junín de los Andes and reached by a unpaved road (Route 60) which runs through Parque Nacional Lanín. Some 3 km east of the pass a turning leads to Lago Tromen. South of the pass is the graceful cone of the Lanín volcano: this is the normal departure point for climbing to the summit (see below). This crossing is less developed than the Huahum and Puyehue routes further south; it is unsuitable for cycles and definitely not usable during heavy rain or snow (June to mid-November). Parts are narrow and steep. From the *guardaparque* centre footpaths lead to a mirador (1½ hours round trip) and to the point where Lago Tromen drains into Río Malleo (4 km). **Frontier with Chile**

Argentine immigration and customs At Puesto Tromen, 3 km east of the pass.

Transport For Igi-Llaima and Empresa San Martín buses between Junín de los Andes and Pucón see above. Officially these only picks up passengers at the pass. Hitchhiking over the pass is not difficult in summer.

Camping Campsite at Puesto Tromen; take food as there are no shops at the pass. There is a CONAFcampsite at Puesco (Chile) free, no facilities.

Chilean immigration and customs At Puesco, 8 km west of the pass, open Dec-Mar 0800-2100, Apr-Nov 0800-1900.

On the Chilean side the road continues through glorious scenery, with views of the volcanoes of Villarrica and Quetrupillán to the south, to Pucón, 69 km west of the pass, on Lago Villarrica. **Into Chile**

The Lake District

Parque Nacional Lanín One of the largest parks in Argentina, Lanín is dominated by the snow capped **Lanín Volcano** which lies in the north of the park on the Chilean frontier. Stretching along the frontier with Chile for some 200 km, the park covers 379,000 ha and includes 24 glacial lakes, one of which (Lago Lacar) drains into the Pacific. The northern parts of the park (between Lagos Ñorquinco and Tromen) are dominated by the *pehuén* tree, in some parts mixed with *lengas* and *ñires*. Further south there are large stretches of other southern beech species, including *roble, rauli* and *coihue*. These forests increase in diversity further west where rainfall is heaviest. The wildlife is typical of the Andean-Patagonian region, including cougars, wildcats and foxes those these are rarely seen. The park is also home to the rare and endangered *pudu*. Another attraction are the large numbers of red deer, introduced into the park from Europe and Asia, which have degraded the vegetation and are hunted.

Parque Nacional Lanín

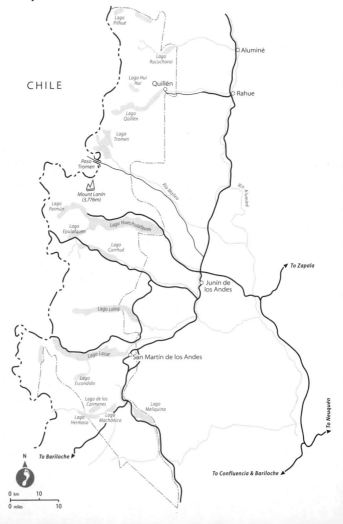

Access There are several entrances to the park, most of them reached from Route 23 which runs south from Lago Aluminé to Junín de los Andes. Easiest access points are from Junín and San Martín de los Andes. Park entry US$3. Park Administration is in San Martín de los Andes.

A popular attraction is **Lago Huechulafquen**, a very beautiful lake 15 km northwest of Junín, offering fishing, beautiful scenery and superb views of the nearby Lanín volcano. ■ *Ko Ko bus daily, US$6.* On the north shore, there are campsites which offer a base for trekking to the top of Cerro Chivo (2,064 m), a seven hour round trip from Bahía Cañicul, through a forest. At the western end of the lake is another lake, Lago Paimún, the point where Lago Paimún drains into Lago Huechulafquen is also a good base (with campsites and trekking or bike trails) for exploring the surroundings. Treks from here include: to the **base of Lanín** volcano (a seven hour round trip) through a *pehuén* forest, climbing to 1,400 m and to **Termas de Epulafquen**, a 10 to 12 hour walk, two days advised. The termas can also be reached by a road which branches off route 234, 4 km south of town and then runs west 25 km.

To Lanín from Junín de los Andes

Another possibility is by taking Route 62 from San Martín de los Andes, which runs north to Lago Lolog, reaching then the smaller Lago Currhue 40 km from the diversion. Route 62 then runs through old *pehuén* forests along the south shore of the larger Lago Currhue, then past Lago Verde and Laguna Escorial, where an impressive lava field (El Escorial) covers an area of 7.5 km long. There is a path going up from Lago Verde to the base of an inactive volcano Achen Niyeu and Cerro Huanquihue (a three hour walk, two hours more to the top of the volcano).

To Lanín from San Martín de los Andes

Climbing Lanín One of the world's most beautiful mountains, Lanín (3,768 m) is geologically one of the youngest volcanoes of the Andes; it is now extinct. There are two *refugios* at about 2,400 m which are free and sleep 14 to 20 people. The volcano is climbed from the Argentine frontier at Paso Tromen, starting out from the *guardaparque* post. After a walk through a *lenga* forest to the base of the volcano, follow a path over arroyo Turbio. From here there are three paths to the *refugios*: the shortest but steepest (four hours), follows the *espina de pescado*, the easiest, the *camino de mulas* is the longest (seven hours) and is marked (the third, *canaleta*) should be used only for descent). From the *refugios* it is six to seven hours over ice fields to the summit.

Equipment Because of its relative accessibility, the risks are often underestimated: crampons and ice-axe are essential. An authorised guide is essential for beginners. Equipment is checked by the *guardaparques*. The *Club Andino* in Junín, can arrange guides and equipment hire.

Sleeping Near Lagos Huechulafquen and Paimún LL *Huechulafquen*, T426075, half-board. **LL** *Refugio del Pescador*, T491319, full-board, golf course. **LL** *Paimún*, T491201, full-board. **Camping** Several sites including *Bahía Cañicul*, US$5 per person, hot showers, restaurant, shop. *Bahía II*, free, beautiful scenery but packed in summer. *Piedra Mala*, US$4 per person, hot showers, expensive shop.

The Lake District

San Martín de los Andes

Population: 20,000
Colour map 5, grid A2
Phone code: 02972
158 km N of Bariloche

San Martín de los Andes is a lovely but expensive little town at the eastern end of Lago Lacar. Founded in 1898, it is the best centre for exploring southern parts of the Parque Nacional Lanín.

There are fine views over the town and lake from Mirador Bandurrias, 6 km west on the north shore of the lake. There is excellent skiing on Cerro Chapelco, 10 km south, and facilities for water skiing, windsurfing and sailing on Lago Lacar. There is a small museum of local history, the Museo Primeros Pobladores.

Excursions The *ripio* road (Route 48) to the Chilean frontier at Paso Hua Hum runs along the northern shore of **Lago Lacar** offerings fine views. There is a boat service (T4427380) to Huahum from San Martín (daily from December to March, July to August, Tuesday/Thursday/Saturday, off season) at 1000, returning 1800, US$35 plus US$5 park entry) stopping at Cachín waterfalls (about 2 km from Hua Hum in dense forest) Hua Hum and Quila Quina. There is also a road along the southern shore to Quila Quina, 18 km west, where there are Indian engravings, a lovely waterfall and a guided nature trail along the lake shore. Quila Quina can also be reached by boat, several times a day, December to March US$10 return (T428427).

San Martín de los Andes

■ **Sleeping**	6 Intermonti	12 Los Pinos
1 Anay	7 La Cheminee	13 Peumayén
2 Colonos del Sur	8 La Masía	14 Posta del Cazador
3 Crismallu	9 La Raclette	15 Puma
4 Cumelén	10 Las Lengas	16 Turismo
5 El Viejo Esquiador	11 Las Lucarnas	

The Lake District

Cerro Chapelco (2,394 m), 20 km south, offers superb views over Lanín and many Chilean peaks. There is a ski resort with 29 pistes, 11 lifts, a ski-school, three places to eat but no accommodation (daily lift pass US$25); in summer this is a good destination for cycling, trekking, archery, horseriding or swimming.

The most popular trips by car are to **Lagos Lolog**, **Aluminé**, **Huechulafquen** and **Paimún** (bus from San Martín via Huechulafquen to Paimún, 0800, US$2, last return 1800, *Empresa San Martín*). This area is described above under **Parque Nacional Lanín**. To **lagos Traful**, **Meliquina**, **Filo Hua Hum**, **Hermoso**, **Falkner and Villarino**, (see page 372).

The streets of San Martín might have been deliberately named to confuse the unwary traveller. Perito Moreno runs east-west, crossing Mariano Moreno which runs north-south. Beware also Rudecindo Roca which is two blocks north of General Roca. **Street names**

Tourist office supplies private addresses only when the hotels are full. *Alihuen Lodge*, Route 62 km 5 (road to Lago Lolog), T426588, lovely location and grounds, good restaurant, highly recommended. **L** *La Cheminèe*, General Roca y Mariano Moreno, T/F427617, lachimenee@smandes.com.ar Cosy, very good but expensive, English spoken. **AL** *La Masía*, Obeid 811, T/F427879, good, garden and playroom. **A** *Viejo Esquiador*, San Martín 1242, T427690, F428283, viejoesquiador@smandes.com.ar Warm, family run. Recommended. **A** *Las Lengas*, Pérez 1175, T427659, T/F427938, laslengas@smandes.com.ar Good rooms, pool, sauna (extra charge). **A** *La Posta del Cazador*, San Martín 175, T/F427501, laposta@satlink.com English and French spoken. Highly recommended. **A** *La Raclette*, Pérez 1170, T/F427664, small but charming rooms, restaurant only in winter. **AB** *Colonos del Sur*, Rivadavia 686, T427224, F427106, colonoshotel@smandes.com.ar Refurbished, good value. English, German spoken. Confitería. **AB** *Anay*, Drury 841, T/F427514, anay@smandes.com.ar Central, family run, English spoken, good. **AB/B** *Crismalu*, Rudecindo Roca 975, T/F427283, Good. **AB/B** *Turismo*, Mascardi 517, T/F427592, restaurant (menu: US$8 per person). **AB** *Peumayén*, San Martín 851, T/F427232, central, friendly, good. **AB** *Cumelén*, Elordi 931, T/F427304, rooms in varied styles, good value off season. **AB** *Los Pinos*, Brown 420, T427207, small chalets, good value off season. Recommended. **AB** *Intermonti*, Villegas 717, T/F427454, hotelintermonti@smandes.com.ar Good rooms in new wing, **D** per person in old wing. **AB** *Las Lucarnas*, Pérez 632, T427085, F427985, small, good rooms, English and French spoken. **E** per person *Hostel Puma*, Fosbery 535 (take Rivadavia to the north, two blocks after crossing the bridge), T422443, F428544, puma@smandes.com.ar Hostelling International discounts, rooms for 4 with private bathroom, also double rooms **B**, kitchen facilities, laundry, information on local trails, internet, cycle hire (US$10 a day). Highly recommended. **E** per person *La Casa del Trabun*, Elordi 186, T442775. Sleeping bags essential, kitchen facilities. **E** per person *Hosp Turístico Caritas*, Cap Drury 774, T4427313. Run by church, floor space for sleeping bags in summer. *Albergue Universitario Técnico Forestal*, Pasaje de la Paz s/n, T4427618. Youth hostel style

Sleeping

Lots of accommodation, though it is expensive in season & single rooms are scarce. Prices given are for high season; low season is much cheaper

Camping *ACA*, Koessler 2176 (on the access road), T427332, hot water, laundering facilities. Recommended. On the southern shore of the lake: *Catritre*, Route 234 km 4, T428820, good. *Quila Quina*, T426919, pleasant, with beaches.

Pionieri, General Roca 1108, excellent Italian meals, also local specialities, very good service, English and Italian spoken. Recommended; same owners run *Los Patos* next door for take-away food, T428459. *La Chacha*, Rivadavia y San Martín, local specialites (trout & venison), very good. *El Amanecer de Carlitos*, San Martín 1374, pancakes, sandwiches & omelettes cheap. Recommended. *Ku*, San Martín 1053, local **Eating**

The Lake District

dishes. *Piscis*, Villegas 598, local dishes, also pasta and *parrilla*. *La Tasca*, Moreno 866, excellent *picadas regionales*. Recommended. *Costanera*, on the waterfront, varied menu, nice atmosphere with lakeviews. *Pura Vida*, Villegas 745, the only vegetarian restaurant in town, small, also fish and chicken dishes. *La Iguana Azul*], San Martín y Mariano Moreno, nice atmosphere, eat in the garden (if sunny). also bikes for hire (US$5 per hr). *Dely*, Villegas y M.A.Camino (waterfront), *confitería* with beautiful views of the lake.

Shopping Handicraft market in summer in Plaza San Martín. Nearby mapuche handicrafts are sold through an government agency. *Rozenburg's*, Mascardi 546, wide variety of home-made jams. Good chocolates at *Mamusia*, San Martín y Mariano Moreno, but Tolkien fans should visit *El Hobbit*, San Martín 416 for chocolates and more; for woollen clothes, *Lucana*, San Martín 960. *El Regional*, Villegas 953, local jams and trout, deer and boar products; good ceramics at Las Araucarias 33, Barrio Jardín, T426598. *Travesía*, San Martín y Drury, outdoor and ski equipment. Supermarket: Cumepén, Villegas 950, large variety, good prices.

Sport **Fishing** Season runs from mid Nov to the end of Apr; for fishing guides, contact the tourist office or the national park office. *Jorge Cardillo fly shop*, General Roca 626, T/F428372, cardillo@smandes.com.ar, sells fishing equipment and offers guided fishing excursions. Fishing guide service also from *Travesía*, San Martín y Drury. **Skiing** Cerro Chapelco is said to have some of the best slopes in Argentina with very good snow conditions. There are several chair-lifts of varying capacity and a ski-tow higher up. There are restaurants but no accommodation. Bus from San Martín to slopes: Ko Ko (US$7 return), or a van from San Martín y Elordi, twice a day (US$8 in summer; US$10-14 in winter, both return). For prices and more information www.chapelco.com.ar

Tour operators Many including *Tiempo Patagónico*, San Martín 950, T/F427113, 10% discount to ISIC card holders, offers rafting excursion on Río Hua Hum for US$55 per person (including ticket to Hua Hum), also horseriding and conventional tours round the region; *Chapelco Aventura*, Elordi y San Martín, T/F427845, chapelco@interar.com.ar, T/F427157 (in Chapelco), manages all the activities run in cerro Chapelco. Erik Sweet (*The Patagonia Experience*), T428480, mundovertical@smandes.com.ar, is a mountain guide in the Parque Nacional Lanín.

Transport **Local Car hire** *AVIS*, San Martín 998, T427704. *ICI rent a car*, Villegas 590, T427800. *Localiza*, Villegas 977, T428876. *El Sol*, San Martín 461, T421870. **Cycle hire** *HG Rodados*, San Martín 1061, US$5 per hr or US$12 per day. *El Rayo*, San Martín 960, US$5 per hr or US$15 per day; same prices at *La Iguana Azul* at San Martín y Mariano Moreno. **Mechanic** *Taller Futbol 5*, on San Martín. Recommended. Also at ACA station.

Long distance **Air** Chapelco Airport, 23 km east of centre, 1 km off route 234. Taxi US$18. Also van service operated by *Caleuche*, T422115, cheaper. Cheapest option is to take any bus for Junín de los Andes and alight at the access road. **Bus** Terminal at Villegas y Coronel Díaz. To **Buenos Aires**, 22 hrs. US$66-90, many companies. To **Neuquén**, 7 hrs. US$24, many companies. To **Villa La Angostura** via the Seven Lakes Drive, 3 hrs. US$12, daily, *Ko Ko, Albus*. To **Bariloche**, 4 hrs; US$17, daily, *Ko Ko*, (via the Seven Lakes drive in summer; otherwise via La Rinconada) and *Albus*. To **Junín de los Andes**, 45 mins; US$3-4, several companies. To **Villa Traful**, US$12, *La Araucana*. To **Cerro Chapelco**, 40 mins; US$3.50, 3 times a day, *Ko Ko*. To **Quila Quina**, 45 minutes; US$3.50, *Airén*, 4 a day. To **Lago Lolog**, 45 minutes; US$2.50, *Airén*, 4 a day. To **Lago Paimún**, 2½ hrs; US$10, twice a day, *Airén*. To **Paso Tromen**, US$15, daily, *Centenario*. **To Chile**: to Temuco, 6 hrs; US$25, *Empresa San Martín*, Mon/Wed/Fri, *Igi Llaima*,

Tue/Thu/Sat. To Puerto Montt, 10 hrs; US$25, Tue/Thu, *Empresa San Martín*. Reduced services from Jun to mid-Nov. When Paso Tromen is closed buses go via Hua Hum and do not pass through Pucón *en route* to Temuco: in that case change to JAC bus in Villarrica for Pucón. When Paso Hua Hum is closed there are no buses.

Airline offices *Aerolíneas Argentinas/Austral*, Drury 876, T427003/427636; *TAN/LAPA*, San Martín 941, T429357/428206; *LADE*, San Martín 915, T427672. **Banks** *Banco de la Nación*, San Martín 687, cash only. *American Express*, San Martín 1141, T4428453. *Andina*, Drury 868, (Western Union) for cash and TC's, 3% commission. **Communications** Post office General Roca y Pérez, Mon-Fri 0800-1300, 1700-2000, Sat 0900-1300. **Telephones** *Cooperativa Telefónica*, Drury 761. Internet *El Living.com]* Drury 610, US$9 per hr (including coffee), friendly place. **Medical services** *Hospital* Ramón Carrillo, San Martín y Coronel Rodhe, T427211. **Laundry** *Laverap*, Drury 880, 0800-2200 daily. *Marva*, Drury y Villegas, 0900-1300, 1600-2130 Mon-Fri, 0900-1300 Sat. **Tourist offices** San Martín y Rosas (opposite plaza San Martín), T/F427347 or 427695, everyday 0800-2200 (in summer), 0800-2100 (in winter); www.7lagos.com **National Park office** Frey 749. — **Directory**

Paso Hua Hum is usually open all year round and is an alternative to the route via the Paso Tromen (see page 367). Paso Hua Hum (659 m) lies 47 km west of San Martín de los Andes along Route 48 (*ripio*) which runs along the north shore of Lago Lacar. For buses on this route see under San Martín. — **Frontier with Chile**

Argentine and Chilean immigration Open summer 0800-2100, winter 0900-2000.

The road continues on the Chilean side to Puerto Pirehuico at the southern end of Lago Pirehueico, a long, narrow and deep lake, totally unspoilt except for some logging activity. At its northern end lies Puerto Fuy. Accommodation is available in in private houses in Puerto Pirehueico and Puerto Fuy. Ferries cross the lake between the two ports (from January to February three daily, and from November to December and March to April two daily, from May to October they are daily except Sunday). Buses connect Puerto Pirehueico with Panguipulli, from where transport is available to other destinations in the Chilean Lake District. — **Into Chile**

From San Martin to Bariloche

This route, one of two, provides access to two beautiful peaceful lakes before crossing a mountain pass and entering the spectacular Valle Encantado. Route 63 (unpaved) turns southeast off Route 234, 26 km south from San Martín and then runs along Lago Meliquina. At Km 54 an unpaved track runs to isolated Lago Filo-Hua-Hum. Route 63 then climbs to the Paso de Córdoba, Km 77, (1,300 m) and enters Parque Nacional Nahuel Huapi. At **Confluencia**, Km 93, the road meets Route 237, the paved Neuquén-Bariloche highway, which runs southwest through the **Valle Encantado**, where there are fantastic rock formations including *El Dedo de Dios* (The Finger of God) and *El Centinela del Valle* (The Sentinel of the Valley), before reaching Bariloche, 157 km from San Martín de los Andes. — **The direct route**

Sleeping Confluencia *Hostería La Gruta de las Virgenes*, T426138, situated on a hill with views over the two rivers, very hospitable; also motel *El Rancho* just before Confluencia. ACA station.

This very beautiful route (Route 234), partially paved and closed after heavy rain or snowfall, runs through the Lanín and Nahuel Huapi National Parks. One of the most famous tourist routes in the Argentine Lake District, it offers — **The Seven Lakes Drive**

The Lake District

views of the southern beach forests and of seven main lakes (including Lagos Lacar and Nahuel Huapi). It is particularly attractive in April/May when the forested slopes turn red and yellow.

At Km 17 from a bridge you can see the **Arroyo Partido**, the watershed between the Pacific and Atlantic oceans: at this point the rivulet splits, one stream flowing west and the other east. The road passes **Lago Machónico** at Km 30 and **Lago Hermoso** at Km 36. At Km 48 it runs between **Lago Villarino** and **Lago Falkner** before passing the northwestern corner of **Lago Traful** at Km 58. At Km 77 Route 65 branches off to the east, running along the south shore of Lago Traful through Villa Trafull to meet the main Neuquén-Bariloche highway (Route 237) at Confluencia.

Situated on the southern shore of Lago Traful, **Villa Traful** is often described as a 'camper's paradise', there are marvellous views, waterfalls, attractive walks and excellent fishing (licence needed). All roads are dirt; drive carefully, avoiding wild cattle!

Sleeping Lago Villarino: *Hostería Lago Villarino*, good food, beautiful setting, camping. **Villa Traful** *Hostería Villa Traful. Hostería El Rincón del Pescador.* **Lago Hermoso** *Refugio Lago Hermoso*, T15556607. **Camping** At Vulcanche, T479061, vulcanche@infovia.com.ar

At Km 80 the road runs along the north side of **Lago Correntoso** before turning south. At Km 99 Route 234 meets Route 231, the road between Bariloche and the Chilean frontier at Paso Puyehue (see below). There is a particularly beautiful view from the bridge over the Río Correntoso, a few kilometres north of Villa La Angostura.

Villa La Angostura

Phone code: 02944
Colour map 5, grid B2
Population: 8,000
108 km S of San Martín
de los Andes;
90 km NW of Bariloche

Villa La Angostura is a rapidly growing town on the shore of Lago Nahuel Huapi. There are two distinct centres: El Cruce, on Route 234, and La Villa, the old centre, 3 km further south, where the port is. They are linked by a regular bus service, though the route between them is a pleasant walk. El Cruce, the commercial and administrative centre, offers the cheaper options for accommodation and eating, while the old centre provides access to the small Parque Nacional Los Arrayanes (see below) and to Laguna Verde, a lagoon surrounded by forests, within a small natural reserve, where two native species of fish are protected. About half-way between the two centres there is a chapel designed by Bustillo (1936); nearby is El Messidor, a luxury residence, also designed by Bustillo (1942) and owned by the state, formerly the summer resort of Argentine presidents. Although the surrounding forests offer excellent walking, in winter the focus is on the ski resort of Cerro Bayo, 9 km north of town.

Excursions There are fine views of Lagos Correntoso and Nahuel Huapi from **Mirador Belvedere**, northwest of El Cruce; from the *mirador* a path goes to Cascada Inacayal, a waterfall 50-m high situated in an area rich in native flora. Another beautiful waterfall, **Cascada Río Bonito**, lies 8 km east of El Cruce off Route 66. The foot of **Cerro Bayo** is 1 km further on, a ski lift takes you to the platform at 1,500 m, from which it is a short trek to the summit (1,782 m).

Ask in the tourist office for accommodation in private houses, cheaper than hotels

Sleeping LL *Las Balsas*, on Bahía Las Balsas (off Av.Arrayanes), T494308, small, exclusive, high standard, good location. **A** *Angostura*, in La Villa, T494224, traditional hotel built in 1938, very good location, restaurant. **AB** *Verena's Haus*, Los Taiques 268, T494467, no children, no smokers, German, English spoken, cosy house and garden, very good, recommended, also light meals. **AB/B** *Las Piedritas*, Huemul y Route 231, T/F494222, einstein@cybernet.com.ar Small, pleasant, good value off season, English spoken, excursions and transfers to/from Bariloche airport restaurant. **B/C** *Nahuel*, Route 231 y Huiliches, T494737, good rooms, restaurant (menu US$5-7). **B/C** *Río Bonito*, 2 blocks from bus terminal, T494110, English spoken, discounts for long stays.

Camping *El Cruce*, 500 m from terminal, US$4 per person, dirty toilets. *ACA Osa Mayor* (2 km along Bariloche road, pleasant, open late Dec to mid-May), *Municipal Lago Correntoso*.

Eating *Il Postino*, Las Fucsias 113, pasta. *Bianchi*, Las Retamas y Topa Topa. *Lado Sur*, Calle Los Taiques, local dishes. *La Recova*, Av Arrayanes 51, local specialities and *minutas*; *Los Troncos*, Av Arrayanes 67, local dishes and *minutas*.

Sport Climbing *Club Andino Villa La Angostura*, Cerro Bayo 295, for excursions and information. **Fishing** Season from mid Nov to the end of Apr. Permit US$50. A list of fishing guides can be consulted at the tourist office (eg *Marcelo Illodo*, T494800, US$110 a day per group; *Oscar Frangi*, T15558420, US$30 per hr or US$200 a day per group). **Horseriding** Rates are usually about US$15 per hr. *Cabalgatas Correntoso*, T15552950, cabalgatascorrentoso@cybersnet.com.ar Offers horseback excursions in the surrounding area and to Villa Traful. **Skiing** At Cerro Bayo, 9 km north of town, includes 20 km of pistes, 10 ski-lifts and ski school. There also 200 ha, where fields covered with deep snow allow snowboard activity. **Ski-passes** daily US$19-27; weekly US$116-162 (high season during the winter school holidays in the second half of Jul).

Tour operators There are a few local agencies including *Angostura Turismo*, Arrayanes 235, T494405. *Terpin Turismo*, Los Notros 41, T/F494551, offers bike excursions US$15 per person, half-day canoe trips US$50 per person, and other guided tours in the area.

Transport Local Bus Terminal on the main road. Empresa 15 de Mayo to Lago Correntoso and other places in the surrounding areas. **Car hire** *Relem rent a car*, Las Mutisias 146, T494336. *Angostura Turismo*, Arrayanes 235, T494405. **Cycle hire** US$3 per hr or US$15 a day. *Free Bike*, Las Retamas 159, T495047. *Ian*, Topa Topa y Las Fucsias, T495005. **Taxi** *Alén*, T495187. US$55 to Bariloche, US$60 to Villa Traful US$120 to San Martín de los Andes. **Long distance Bus** To San Martín de los Andes, hrs. US$11-13, *Ko Ko* and *Albus*. To Bariloche, 1 hr; US$5-8, *Algarrobal, Ko Ko, TAS-Choapa, Albus*. To Neuquén, US$26-30, *Andesmar* and *TEC*. To Buenos Aires, US$73, *Andesmar*. **Services to Chile** *Empresa San Martín* to Paso Puyehue, US$5 Tue/Thu. To Osorno, 4 hrs. US$12-14, and Puerto Montt, US$12-14 daily, *Andesmar, TAS-Choapa*, also *Empresa San Martín*, Tue/Thu.

Directory Banks *Andina*, Arrayanes 282, T494920, for cash and TC's. **Communications** Post office, Siete Lagos 26; Phones, Arrayanes y Cerro Bayo, also internet. **Medical services** *Hospital Rural Arraiz*, Copello 311 (at barrio Pinar), T494170. **Tourist office** opposite bus terminal at Siete Lagos 93, T/F494124, www.villalaangostura.net.ar Open daily 0800-2100.

This park, covering 1,000 ha on the Quetrihué Peninsula, within the Parque Nacional Nahuel Huapi, was created to protect a forest of Arrayán trees. The Quetrihué Peninsula is one of the few places where the Arrayán grows to full size of a tree; some of the specimens are 300 years old.

Parque Nacional Los Arrayanes

Access The park lies 15 km south of El Cruce, the modern part of Villa La Angostura, and can be reached by a 12 km path along the Quetrihué Peninsula from La Villa

The Arrayán

The Arrayán (Myerceugenella apiculata) is a myrtle-like tree, found on both sides of the Andes, growing near water in groves of 15-20 ha which have been declared national monuments. The twisted contorted trunks have pale orange bark which peels as the tree grows. It has pure white flowers in January and February and produces blue/black fruit in February/March. Its leaves have medicinal uses. Though it grows from Neuquén south to the Río Chubut, the two main arrayán forests in Argentina are on the Quetrihué peninsula (Quetrihué is myrtle in Mapuche) and Isla Victoria in Parque Nacional Nahuel Huapi and along the Río Arrayanes in the Parque Nacional Los Alerces.

(allow 3-4 hrs on foot or 3 hrs by bicycle). **Boat** Two companies offer boat trips (45 mins) from the pier at La Villa, US$12 one way, US$22 return. See page 381 for sailings from Bariloche. Out of season boats only sail if demand is sufficient.

Frontier with Chile
This route is liable to closure after snow

Officially known as Paso Samore, **Paso Puyehue** (1,280 m) lies 125 km north-west of Bariloche by Route 231, which runs west from the main San Marín-Bariloche highway along the northern side of Lago Nahuel Huapi. It is unpaved west of Villa La Angostura. Although less scenic than the ferry journey across Lake Todos Los Santos and Laguna Verde this crossing is cheaper, more reliable and still a beautiful trip.

Argentine customs and immigration Open winter 0900-2000, summer 0800-2100.

Crossing by private vehicle For vehicles entering Chile, formalities are quick (about 15 mins), but includes the spraying of tyres and shoes have to be wiped on a mat (pay US$2 to 'Sanidad'). Passage will be much quicker if you already have Chilean pesos and don't have to change at the border. A circular trip from Bariloche can be done by going first via Puyehue to Puerto Montt, returning via Tromen Pass (see the Villarrica volcano, good road), then Junín and San Martín de los Andes.

Into Chile On the Chilean side the road is paved via Entre Lagos and Lago Puyehue to **Osorno**. Chilean immigration is at Anticura, 22 km west of the border. Open the second Saturday in October and the second Saturday in March, 0800-2100, otherwise 0800-1900.

Essentials Sleeping Anticura *Hostería y Canañas Anticura. Camping Catrue.* **Transport** For bus services from Bariloche to Osorno, Puerto Montt and Valdivia. (See page 385).

Parque Nacional Nahuel Huapi
Contains the most diverse & spectacular natural phenomena

Covering some 750,000 ha and stretching along the Chilean frontier for over 130 km, this is the oldest national park in Argentina, created in 1934 but originating from a donation in 1903 by Francisco Perito Moreno of 7,500 ha of land around Puerto Blest to the state. Extending across a mountainous environment, the park contains lakes, rivers, glaciers, waterfalls, torrents, rapids, valleys, forest, bare mountains and snow-clad peaks. Among the peaks are Tronador (3,478 m), Catedral (2,388 m), Falkner (2,350 m), Cuyín Manzano (2,220 m), López (2,076 m), Otto (1,405 m) and Campanario (1,049 m).

There are several large lakes and dozens of smaller ones. The largest is **Lago Nahuel Huapi** (altitude 767 m), 96 km long, not more than 12 km wide and covering over 60,000 ha. Some 465 m deep at its deepest spot around Puerto

Blest, the lake is very irregular in shape; it has seven long arms or *brazos*, reminiscent of the Norwegian fjords. There are many islands: the largest is **Isla Victoria**, on which stands the forest research station where new species of vegetation are acclimatized. The **Quetrihué peninsula**, near Isla Victoria has been set aside as a separate park, the **Parque Nacional Los Arrayanes**. Trout and salmon have been introduced. The lake drains eastwards into the Río Limay which, below its junction with the Río Neuquén, becomes the Río Negro, Argentina's second largest river.

Parque Nacional Nahuel Huapi

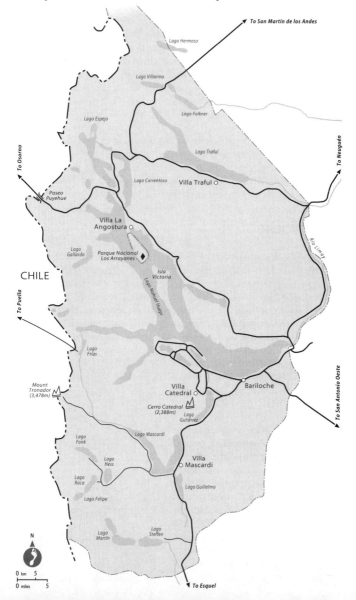

North of Lago Nahuel Huapi are other lakes: **Lago Correntoso**, separated from one of the northern *brazos* of Lago Nahuel Huapi by glacial morraine; **Lago Espejo** and **Lago Traful**. The three main lakes south of Lago Nahuel Huapi are **Lago Gutiérrez**, **Lago Mascardi** and **Lago Guillelmo**, can be reached by Route 258 from Bariloche to Esquel.

Vegetation varies with altitude but includes large expanses of southern beech forest and near the Chilean frontier, where rainfall is highest, there are areas of Valdivian rainforest. There are *coihues* (evergreen beeches) over 450 years old and *alerces* over 1,500 years old. Eastern parts of the park are more ste ppe-like with shrubs and bushes. Wildlife includes the *pudú*, the endangered *huemul* and river otter, as well as foxes, cougars and guanacos. Among the birds are magellan woodpeckers and austral parakeets as well as large flocks of swans, geese and ducks. Best times to visit are Aug for skiing and February for walking, avoiding the busy months of Jul and January.

Swimming in the larger lakes such as Nahuel Huapi and Huechulafquen is not recommended, for the water is cold. But swimming in smaller lakes such as Lolog, Lacar, Curruhué Chico, Hermoso, Meliquina, Espejo, Hess and Fonck is very pleasant and the water – especially where the bottom shelves to a shingly beach – can be positively warm.

Essentials Park information centre in Bariloche. Visitors centre at Puerto Pañuelo. Park entry US$5; 10-day 'green pass' permitting entry to Nahuel Huapi, Lanín and Lago Puelo national parks, US$10. Camping is permitted at specified sites but not along Lago Nahuel Huapi. Bariloche is the usual centre for visiting the park: details of accommodation, transport and tours are given in that section.

Bariloche

Phone code: 02944
Colour map 5, grid B2
Population: 100,000
Altitude: 770 m
436 km W of Neuquén

Sitting on the south shore of Lago Nahuel Huapi, the centre of Bariloche is beauti-fully situated upon a glacial moraine at the foot of Cerro Otto. It has been trans-formed in recent decades by the building of hotels which overshadow the civic buildings built in 'Bariloche Alpine' style. Around the centre steep streets climb the heights of Cerro Ventana, Cerro Negro and Cerro Carbón. Founded in 1903 and renowned for its chocolate industry, it is the best centre for exploring the national park. A major destination for groups of secondary school students, the city is very busy in school holidays (July and 15 December-10 January). The best times for a visit are out of season, either in the spring or autumn, although the weather is unpredictable. The forests around are particularly beautiful in May.

Sights At the heart of the city is the **Centro Cívico**, built in 'Bariloche Alpine style' and separated from the lake by Avenida Rosas. It includes the **Museo de La Patagonia** which has collections of stuffed animals, Indian artefacts and material from the lives of the first white settlers. ■ *Tue-Fri 1000-1230, 1400-1900, Mon/Sat 1000-1300, US$3.* The attached **Biblioteca Sarmiento**, a library and cultural cen-tre. ■ *Mon-Fri, 1000-2000.* The

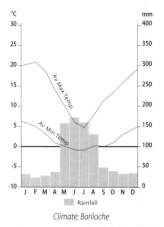

Climate: Bariloche

(left vertical margin) The Lake District

Alejandro Bustillo and the 'Estilo Bariloche'

Many of the public buildings of Bariloche owe their particular style to the architect Alejandro Bustillo and his colleague, Ernesto de Estrada. Though the so-called Estilo Bariloche (Bariloche style) of their designs drew its inspiration from the Alps, the materials employed were local: stone from Cerro Otto and timber from the forests.

Bustillo's opportunity came in 1935 when he won a public competition to design the Hotel Llao Llao, the first building to be commissioned by Parques Nacionales, the Argentine National Parks authority. In the following years he designed many other buildings in the national park, among them the Cathedral and the National Park Intendancy in Bariloche, the Hotel on Isla Victoria (sadly destroyed by fire), the Capilla La Asunción in Villa La Angostura and the refugio on Cerro Catedral. The Centro Civico in Bariloche and a number of other buildings were the work of Estrada.

Admirers of Bustillo's work may like to look out for his buildings elsewhere in Argentina, among them the Banco de la Nación in the Plaza de Mayo in Buenos Aires and the monumental buildings which have come to symbolize Mar del Plata: the Casino, Hotel Provincial and Rambla.

cathedral, built in 1946 (interior unfinished) lies six blocks east of here, with the main commercial area between. Opposite the main entrance to the cathedral there is a huge rock left in this spot by a glacier during the last glacial period. On the lakeshore at 12 de Octubre y Sarmientos is the **Museo Paleontológico**, which has displays fossils mainly from Patagonia including an ictiosaur and replicas of giant spider and shark's jaws.

Excursions

Llao-Llao, a resort 24 km west, can be reached by Avendia Bustillo which runs along Lago Nahuel Huapi (bus No 20, 45 minutes, US$2). For hotels on this road see page 383. The resort is dominated by the beautiful *Hotel Llao-Llao*, opened in 1937, burned down within a few months and rebuilt almost immediately. Superbly situated on a hill with chocolate box views, it overlooks the **Capilla San Eduardo**, like the hotel designed by Bustillo, and **Puerto Pañuelo**.

Llao-Llao

This peak is reached by a chairlift from Km 17.7 on the road to Llao-Llao (0900-1800 daily, extended opening in summer, US$10). From the summit there are fine views of the San Pedro Peninsula, Lago Moreno and the surrounding area. The closest hill from the centre is **Cerro Viejo**, reached by a cable car (US$6, daily 1000-1300, 1430-1900) from Avenida Bustillo Km 1; from here there are views of the town and the lake.

Cerro Campanario

The Circuito Chico, one of the 'classic' Bariloche tours, is a 61 km circular route along Avenida Bustillo around Lago Moreno Oeste, past Punto Panorámico and back through Puerto Pañuelo and Llao-Llao itself. Tour companies do the circuit and it can be driven in half a day (it can also be cycled, but beware bus drivers on Avenida Bustillo). It can be extended to a full day: Bariloche-Llao Llao-Bahía López-Colonia Suiza (on Lago Moreno Este)-Cerro Catedral-Bariloche; the reverse direction misses the sunsets and afternoon views from the higher roads, which are negotiable in winter (even when snow-covered).

Circuito Chico

The Lake District

Cerro Otto Cerro Otto, 5 km southeast, is the nearest ski resort (cable car US$20; 1000-1800; at the top is a revolving restaurant; (entry US$3.50) and a nice *confitería* belonging to Club Andino 20 minutes walk away at Regugio Berghof. By car by take Avenida de los Pioneros, then the signed dirt track 1 km out of town. To climb Cerro Otto on foot (two to three hours): turn off Avenida de los Pioneros at Km 4.6, then follow the trail past Refugio Berghof, splendid views. Recommended. ■ *Getting there: an hrly service from Mitre y Villegas, 0930-1800 high season, reduced service low season, US$7 return, no charge if buying ticket for cable car.*

Cerro Catedral At Cerro Catedral (2,338 m), 21 km southwest, there is one of the major ski-resorts in Argentina. Divided into two sectors, Robles Catedral to the south and Alta Patagonia to the north, there are a total of 67 km of ski-slopes and 32 ski-lifts. In summer it is popular with walkers: red and yellow markers painted on the rock mark a trail from the summit which leads to *Refugio Frey* (**E** per person, well equipped, blankets, meals) on the edge of a small mountain lake (allow six hours). A half-day excursion is possible taking a bus to Virgen de las Nieves on Cerro Catedral, walking 2 km to arrive at beautiful Lago Gutiérrez and then walking along the lake shore to Route 258 which takes you back into Bariloche (about four hours).

Bariloche

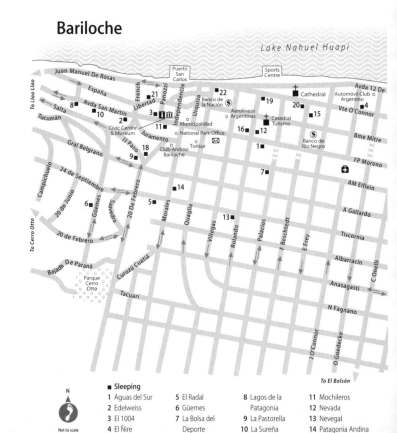

To El Bolsón

N

Not to scale

■ **Sleeping**

1 Aguas del Sur	5 El Radal	8 Lagos de la
2 Edelweiss	6 Güemes	Patagonia
3 El 1004	7 La Bolsa del	9 La Pastorella
4 El Ñire	Deporte	10 La Sureña

11 Mochileros	
12 Nevada	
13 Nevegal	
14 Patagonia Andina	

Sleeping LL *Catedral*, T460006, F460137, hcatedral@bariloche.com.ar Large, luxurious, pool, restaurant, sauna, gym, also apartments, discount for one week stay. *Pire Hue*, T460039, open high season only, 5-star, restaurant. *St Moritz*, T460014, F460084, mc@bariloche.com.ar Restaurant, gym, ski facilities, playroom.

Transport Bus *CODAO del Sur*, *Moreno* 470, T432830 daily service to/from Bariloche.

Ski facilities Alta Patagonia: lift passes daily US$40 (high ski season), US$22 (low ski season); weekly US$200 (high season), US$110 (low season); hrly lessons US$60 (high season), US$51 (low season); daily ski hire US$19 (high season), US$16 (low season). Check prices also at Robles Catedral.

The surrounding countryside offers beautiful walking, for example to Lago **Walking** Escondido on a 3 km trail which turns off the Circuito Chico near Bahía López (see above). A longer walk is to Cerro López (three hours, with a *refugio* after two). Take Colonia Suiza bus (from Moreno y Rolando) and alight at Picada. Longer still is the hike to *refugio Italia* (same bus, but alight at SAC); details of this and three to five day continuations from *Club Andino*. One-day excursions can also be made to San Martín de los Andes along the Seven Lakes Drive (see above). Before hiking buy moisturizing creams for exposed skin. In summer *tábanos* (horseflies) are common on the lake shores and at lower altitudes; lemon juice is a good deterrent but can cause skin irritation.

Isla Huemul, on Lago Nahuel Huapi, **Boating** was the site of Argentine scientific work on nuclear fusion in the 1950s. Boats sail from Puerto San Carlos, 30 minutes voyage, two hours on island, five sailings a day (reduced service off-season) US$16.

Isla Victoria, on Lago Nahuel Huapi, is reached by half-day excursion (1300-1830) from Puerto Pañuelo (with transport from Bariloche). There is also a full-day excursion (0900-1830, or 1300 till 2000 in season) which includes the **Parque Nacional Los Arrayanes** on the Quetrihué peninsula further north (see above) as well as Isla Victoria, picnic lunch advised, US$30 from Bariloche, US$22 from Puerto Pañuelo. These tours only visit part of Isla Victoria and you only spend one hour in the park which is often crowded. Some boats going to Arrayanes call first at Isla Victoria, early enough to avoid boat-loads of tourists. *Turisur* have four catamarans with a bar and cafetéria. All boats are very crowded in season, but operators have to provide seating for all passengers.

The Lake District

15	Piuké	**19**	Sunset
16	Premier	**20**	Sur
17	Puyehue	**21**	Tirol
18	San Francisco	**22**	Tres Reyes

The trip to **Puerto Blest**, at the western end of Lago Nahuel Huapi, and **Lago Frías**, visiting native forest and rainforest, is highly recommended. This is usually done as a nine-hour excursion, leaving at 0900 (afternoon departure also December to March), offered by *Turisur* and *Catedral*, US$35: bus to Puerto Pañuelo, boat to Puerto Blest, bus to Puerto Alegre and again by launch to Puerto Frías (excursion from Puerto Blest ot Lago Frías, US$9 extra). From Puerto Frías there is a beautiful but long walk through the Paso de las Nubes to Cerro Tronador (see page 388). A visit to the Cascada de los Cántaros is made (stay off the boat at the Cascada and walk around to Puerto Blest through beautiful forest, one hour. Recommended). Note that a cheaper alternative is to take 0700 bus to Puerto Pañuelo, then 0800 boat to Puerto Blest. **Sleeping** at **B** *Puerto Blest*, T425443, half pension, good, book through *Turismo Catedral*.

There are also boat excursions across **Lago Mascardi**, US$35.

Tours There are numerous tours: most travel agencies charge the same price. It is best to buy tours on the spot rather than in advance, although they get very booked up in season. Tours offered include:

Whole-day trip to Lagos Gutiérrez, Mascardi, Hess, the Cascada Los Alerces and Cerro Tronador and the Black Glacier, leaving at 0800, US$29, interesting but too much time spent on the bus.

Twelve-hour minibus excursions to San Martín de los Andes, US$34, via the Seven Lakes Drive and returning via Paso de Córdoba and the Valle Encantado but these involve 10 hours on the bus and few stops (taxi for this route US$30 per person).

There are also tours around the Circuito Chico (see above), US$13, half-day. To Cerro Catedral, half-day, US$13 plus ski-lift. To El Bolsón with a journey on *La Trochita*, full-day US$45. For tours to Peulla (Chile) see page 386.

If staying only one or two days in the area the best excursions are to Cerro Tronador on the first day, and on the second to Cerro Catedral in the morning and Isla Victoria in the afternoon (possible only December to March when there are afternoon departures for the island).

Essentials

Sleeping
Out of season, prices are reasonable, in all ranges, especially if you bargain; in season everything is very expensive

The most complete listing with map is published by the Oficina Municipal de Turismo, which you are advised to consult if you arrive in the high season without a reservation. It also has a booking service at Florida 520 (Galería), room 116, Buenos Aires. Most hotels outside the town include half-board, and those in the town include breakfast. Hotels with lake views normally charge US$5 extra per room per day, for the view in high season; the following selection gives lake-view high-season prices where applicable. The following specialise in school-trips in Jul and from 15 Dec to 15 Jan: Ayelén, Bariloche Ski, Interlaken, Millaray, Montana, Piedras and Pucón.

Centre LL *Panamericano Bariloche*, San Martín 532, T425846, F426789, hotel@panameri.com.ar 5-star, large, modern, casino, heated pool, gym, restaurant *La Rondine*. **L** *Nevada*, Rolando 250, T422778, large, good but ricey. *Edelweiss*, San Martín 202, T430462, F425655, www.edelweiss.com.ar 5-star, excellent food, enclosed pool, highly recommended. **L** *Sunset*, Rolando 132, T425137, reservas@hotelsunset.com.ar Half-board, turkish baths, sauna, restaurant with beautiful lake views. Recommended. **A** *Tirol*, Libertad 175, T426152, host_tirol@bariloche.com.ar Small, English, German spoken, good. **A** *Tres Reyes*, 12 de Octubre 135, T426121, F424230, hreyes@bariloche.com.ar 4-star, lakeside, splendid views, highly recommended. **AB** *La Pastorella*, Belgrano 127, T424656, F424212, www.bariloche.org/hosteria/pastorella Half-board, small, no children, French,

English spoken. Recommended. **AB** *Aguas del Sur*, Moreno 353, T424329. Half-board, large, central. **AB** *La Sureña*, San Martín 432, T422013, F424875, hosteria@ infovia.com.ar Small, English, Italian spoken. **AB** *Sur*, Beschtedt 101, T422677, bazzano@ infovia.com.ar **AB** *El Ñire*, O'Connor y O'Connor, T423041. Small, pleasant, English spoken. **B** *Premier*, Rolando 263, T426168. Small rooms, English, German spoken. **B** *Puyehue*, Elordi 243, T422196. Small, quiet. **B** *El Radal*, 24 de Septiembre 46, T422551. Small, very clean, comfortable, restaurant. **D** per person *Piuké*, Beschtedt 136, T423044. Small, German, Italian spoken. **C** *Guemes*, Guemes 715, T424785. Small. Recommended. **C** *Victoria*, Mitre 815, T427436. Basic, clean, negotiable rates. **C** per person *San Francisco*, 20 de Febrero 493, T426554. Half-board, convenient. **C** *Nevegal*, Rolando 615, T423307, quiet, clean.

Family accommodation **D** per person *Familia Baumann*, Pioneros 86, T429689, F424502, ingridb@arnet.com.ar Apartments, sleep 1-6, German, English spoken. Recommended. **E** per person *Rosán*, Guemes 691, T423109, beautiful garden, kitchen facilities, helpful, English, German spoken, also camping. Recommended. **E** per person *Señora Iris*, Quaglia 526, small, clean, kitchen facilities. **E** per person *Eloisa Lamunière*, Paso 145 ground floor), T422514. Modern apartment, small, pleasant, kitchen facilities. **E** per person *Nogarre*, Elflein 58, T422438. Comfortable, with bath; **E** per person *Familia Pirker*, 24 de Septiembre 230, T424873. Flats sleep 3, German, English spoken. **E** per person *La Casa de los Amigos*, Anasagasti 348, basic, small; **E** per person *Casa Nelly*, Beschtedt 658, T422295. Friendly, information, also camping. **E** per person *Familia Posaz*, Frey 635, kitchen facilities, basic, clean, small. **E** per person *No me olvide*, off Av Pioneros Km 1, T429140 (bus 50/51, to corner of calle Videla, then follow signs). Nice house in quiet surroundings.

Hostels **E** per person *Patagonia Andina*, Morales 564, T421861, www.bariloche. com.ar/patagoniaandina, breakfast extra, laundry, information, cycle hire US$10 per day, internet. Recommended. **E** per person *La Bolsa del Deporte*, Palacios y Elflein, T423529, bolsadep@bariloche.com.ar, without breakfast, English, German spoken, sports equipment rental, laundry, Internet access. Recommended. **E** per person *El 1004*, San Martín 127, piso 10, T432228, elalfabeta@cybersnet.com.ar Rooms for 3-4, also floor space **F** per person, kitchen facilities, great views, information, English spoken. **E** per person *Mochilero's*, San Martín 82, piso 1, T423187, cecilia@ bariloche.com.ar Rooms for 2 to 5, also floor space F per person, travel agency. **E** per person *Ruca Hueney*, Elflein 296, central, kitchen facilities, very hospitable. **E** per person *Consorcio Bariloche Center*, San Martín 127, T494422228, F494431584, alfabeta@cybersnet.com.ar, dormitories with kitchen facilities, English spoken, also floor space.

Road to Llao Llao (Av Bustillo) **LL** *Llao-Llao*, Bustillo Km 25.5, T448530, F445781, www.llaollao Deservedly famous, superb location, fine views from some rooms (check when booking), golf course, spa, water sports, restaurant. **L** *El Casco*, Bustillo Km 11.6, T461032. 4-star, lakeside, open high season only, restaurant. **L** *Tunquelén*, Bustillo Km 24.5, T/F448400, tunque@bariloche.com.ar 4-star, lakeside with spendid views, restaurant. **L** *La Cascada (Best Western)*, Bustillo Km 6, T441046, F441076, lacascada@infovia.com.ar 5-star, lakeside and situated in, 3 ha of beautiful park with waterfall, heated pool, sauna, restaurant. **C** per person *Piccolo Paradiso*, Panque 12521, (off Bustillo Km 12.5), T/F462009. Outdoor activities and Spanish courses; **C/B** per person *Katy*, Bustillo Km 24.3, T/F448023. Cosy, good value, beautiful park. Recommended. **B** *La Caleta*, Bustillo Km 1.9, T441837. Cabañas sleep 4, open fire, excellent value. Recommended. **E** per person *Hostel Alaska (Hostelling International)*, Av Bustillo Km 7.5, T461564, www.bariloche.com.ar/usuarios/alaska (Bus 10, 20, 21, getting off at La Florida, then 400 m up the hill, log cabin in nice surroundings, dormitories for 6 and 8, clean, without breakfast, kitchen facilites, Internet access, cycle hire US$10 a day.

The Lake District

List of sites from tourist office

Camping Several sites on Av Bustillo including: *Selva Negra*, Km 2.5, T444013. US$8 per person, highly recommended. *El Yeti*, Km 5.6, recommended, also cabañas. *Petunia*, Km 13.5. Well protected from winds by trees, hot showers, shop, recommended, also cabañas. For tent repairs: *Fraca*, Moreno 371.

Eating *Kandahar*, 20 de Febrero 698, evenings only, excellent, Argentine dishes, run by ski champion Marta Peirono de Barber, US$20. *La Marmite*, Mitre 329, cosy, mixed fondues recommended, US$16. *El Viejo Munich*, Mitre 102, good meat and fish, US$20. Recommended. *Caza Mayor*, Quaglia y Elflein, game and fish, good, US$22. *La Jirafa*, Palacios 288, good food, good value, US$10. *Simoca*, Palacios 264, Tucumán specialities, US$10. *Familia Weiss*, Palacios 170, also Palacios y V.A.O'Connor, excellent local specialities US$18, menu US$10. *La Rondine* in *Hotel Panamericano Bariloche*, very good, US$20. *Jauja*, Quaglia 366, good local dishes, friendly, recommended, US$15 (also take away round the corner). *La Andinita*, Mitre 56, a classic, small, good value, friendly atmosphere US$7. *Cocodrilo´s*, Mitre y Urquiza, good value, US$10, also take away. *Vegetariano*, Elflein y Morales, also fish, excellent food, very nice place, highly recommended, US$8. *La Alpina*, Moreno 98, good value, open fire, cheese fondue recommended, US$12. *Friends*, Mitre 302, good food, convenient, lively, open 24 hrs, pizza by the metre, US$12. *La Bohemia*, Moreno 48, seafood specialities, warm atmosphere, live piano music in season, US$14. *Rock Chicken*, Quaglia y Moreno, small, busy, good value (also take away). Recommended. *El Boliche de Alberto*, Villegas 347, very good steak.

Av Bustillo *La Casa del Bosque*, Km 4.6, restaurant and Welsh tea room. *El Patacón*, Km 7, excellent *parrilla*. *La Posta del Río*, Km 10, reasonable. *Blest*, Km 11.6, open till midnight, brews own beer (very good), local and German dishes, nice atmosphere. Recommended. *Kalinka*, Km 21, tea room. *21*, Rolando 245 (downstairs), open 2100, basic, cheap beer, table football, live rock music at weekends. Very good ice cream at *Helados de la Abuela Goye*, Quaglia 221.

Entertainment *Cine Arrayanes*, Moreno 39. *Biblioteca Sarmiento*, in the Centro Cívico, cineclub, theatre, concerts.

Shopping The main commercial centre is on Mitre between the *Centro cívico* and Beschtedt and includes lots of *galerías*. **Chocolate** The products of the local chocolate industry are excellent and are sold by several shops along Mitre including *El Turista*, No 231, where you can watch chocolate being made and *de la abuela Goye*, No 258, as well as at *Estrella Alpina*, Pioneros 4501, and *Benroth*, Beschtedt 569. Local chocolate specialities include 'Papas de Bariloche' and 'chocolate en rama'. Local wines from the Alto Río Negro are also good. Woollen goods are recommended. **Handicrafts** at *Feria Artesanal Municipal*, Moreno y Villegas, daily 0900-2100. Recommended. *Burton Cerámica*, Bustillo 4100, makes and sells Patagonian pottery. **Vegetarian** and health foods at *Feria Naturista*, Elflein 73, and at *La Esquina de las Flores*, 20 de Febrero 313. **Bookshops** *Cultura*, Elflein 78, has a good range of technical books, some in English and German; *La Barca*, Mitre 131; *Uppsala*, Rolando 265. **Supermarkets** *Todo*, Mitre 281 (also fast food), Moreno 319. *La Anónima*, Albarracín 651. *Tia*, Moreno 909. **Winter clothing and outdoor equipment** *Scandinavian*, San Martín 130. *½ caño*, Moreno 371. *Buenos Aires Ski*, Moreno 60.

Sport

Many activities (eg rafting, parachuting, horseriding, birdwatching) can be arranged through travel agencies

Climbing At higher levels, winter snow storms can begin as early as Apr, making climbing dangerous. Cerro Catedral offers a wide range of good peaks and there is something in the area for every kind of mountaineer. National park mountain guides are available but can be expensive. Best information from *Club Andino Bariloche* (CAB), 20 de Febrero 30, T/F422266, (T424531 in summer), www.clubandino.com.ar The Club gives information about hiking and climbing in the area (map of footpaths, US$7), and also about their *refugios* (about US$7 per person; take sleeping bag). In treks to *refugios* remember to add costs of ski lifts, buses and food. Tonchek Arko: *Excursiones, Andinismo y Refugios de Montaña en Bariloche*, check at local bookshops. **Cycling** *Dirty Bikes*, V.A.O'Connor 681, T/F425616, dirtybike@bariloche.com.ar. US$4 per hr, US$15 per day. **Fishing** excellent trout fishing Nov-Mar (permits required). *Baruzzi Deportes*, Urquiza 250, T424922, F428374, offers guided fishing excursions in the whole area (flycast, troll-ing, spinning) for experts and newcomers; US$150-300 (Trout Unlimited membership discounts). **Horseriding** for trekking by horse contact *Carol Jones* or *Hans Schulz*, through Tourist office, or at *Cumbres y Lagos Patagonia* (see under tour operators) or *Tom Wesley*, Mitre 385, T435040, US$18 per 1½ hrs. **Skiing** Between Jul and early Oct there is good skiing on Cerro Catedral and Cerro Otto but the snow is unreliable, except at the top. Skiing is best organised with a tour company, especially from Buenos Aires, through whom you can secure discounts as part of an inclusive deal. Ski hire fees depend on quality, dearer at Cerro Catedral than in town (for ski facilities and prices see under Excursions to Cerro Catedral); ski clothing can also be rented by the day. **Swimming** The pool on the lake shore is beautifully sited but somewhat run down. See under page 378 for swimming in the lakes.

Tour operators

Check what the cost of your tour includes: funicular rides, chair lift & national park entry are usually charged as extras.

Agencies charge same prices in general. *ASATEJ*, San Martín 127, T/F421314, asatej@bariloche.com.ar, for cheap plane fares and information. Recommended. *Catedral Turismo*, Mitre 399, T/F425444, cattur@bariloche.com.ar, recommended for local excursionsl and trip to Puerto Montt via lakes (see below). *Turisur*, Villegas 310, T426109, F426629, turisur@bariloche.com.ar, boat and overland local excursions. *San Carlos Travel*, Mitre 213 piso 2, T/F432999, sancartrav@bariloche.com.ar, birdwatching and other specialist tours. Recommended. *Cumbres y Lagos Patagonia*, Villegas 222, T423283, F431835, cumbres@bariloche.com.ar, for rafting, horseriding, trekking, fishing. recommended. *Tacul Viajes*, San Martín 430, T/F426321, tacul@bariloche.com.ar, ISIC discount. Recommended.

Transport

Local The centre of Bariloche can be negotiated on foot. **Taxi** *Auto Jet*, T08002222408, 422408; *Remises Bariloche*, T430222. See also car hire below.

Long distance Air Airport, 15 km east of town. Taxi: US$10; bus service run be Vía Bariloche, leaving 1½ hrs before any flight from Quaglia 238: US$3.

Bus Terminal 3 km east of centre. Taxi from/to centre; US$3-3.50; bus 20, 70, 71, 83, US$1. Left luggage: US$1/3 hrs, US$2 per day. To **Buenos Aires**, 22 hrs, US$60-75, many companies. To **Bahía Blanca**, 14 hrs, US$40, *El Valle, Vía Bariloche, Andesmar*. To **Comodoro Rivadavia**, 14 hrs, US$47, *Don Otto*. To **El Bolsón**, 2 hrs, US$7-10, *Charter, Vía Bariloche, Don Otto, Mar y Valle*. To **Esquel**, 4-5 hrs, US$8-18, *Don Otto, Andesmar, Mar y Valle, Vía Bariloche*. To **Puerto Madryn**, 14 hrs, US$46, *Mar y Valle, Don Otto*. To **San Martín de los Andes**, 4 hrs, US$17, *Ko Ko* via the Seven Lakes Drive only in summer, Albus. To **Villa La Angostura**, 1 hr, US$6, *Algarrrobal, Ko Ko* in summer only. To **Villa Traful**, 2 hrs, US$10, Sat/Sun, *Albus*. To **Mendoza**, 18 hrs, US$45-55, *TAC, Andesmar*. To **Neuquén**, 7 hrs; US$15-17, daily several companies. **Bus company details**: Vía Bariloche, T432444. El Valle, T431444. Andesmar/Albus, T430211. Mar y Valle, T432269. TAC, T432521. Chevallier/La Estrella/Ko Ko, T425914. Don Otto/Río de la Plata, T421699. Flechabus, T15610605. Charter, T421689. Algarrobal, T423081. CODAO del Sur/Bus Norte, T432830. Cruz del Sur, T422818. TAS Choapa, T432521. **To Chile** To **Osorno** (4-6 hrs) and **Puerto Montt**, 7-8 hrs US$18-20, daily, *Bus Norte, Río de la Plata, TAS Choapa, Cruz del Sur, Andesmar* (sit on left side for best views). For **Santiago** or **Valdivia** change at Osorno.

The Lake District

Car hire Fuel costs about 40% less than national price. *Hertz*, Rosas 673, T421244. *AVIS*, San Martín 130, T431648. *A Open Rent a Car*, Mitre 382, T426325. *Localiza*, San Martín 463, T424767, reliable, helpful, best km allowance. To enter Chile a permit is necessary; many companies include its cost in their rates, giving it immediately. **Mechanic** *Auquén*, VAO'Connor 1068, fast, reasonable, highly recommended.

Train Station 3 km east of centre, near bus terminal. T423172. See bus section for transport to the centre. Booking office closed 1200-1500 weekdays, Sat afternoon and all Sun. To **Viedma**, 16 hrs, US$18 *turista* ° 41.50 *pullman*, Thu/Sun. To **Jacobacci**, US$7 *turista*) Tue/Wed/Sat. Check for changes especially during summer. Scenery only interesting between Bariloche and Pilcaniyeu (first 3 hrs); if travelling in *turista* or *primera* expect a thick layer of dust on everything after few hrs.

Directory **Airline offices** *Aerolíneas Argentinas/Austral*, Quaglia 238, T423091/422144. *TAN*, Quaglia 238, T427889 /432969. *LADE*, Quaglia 238, T423282. *Kaikén*, Palacios 266, T420251/428181. *Southern Winds*, Villegas 147, T423704/428181. *LAPA*, Villegas 121, T423714/429183. *SAPSA*, Mitre 321, T429012. **Banks** ATMs at banks. *Banca Nazionale del Lavoro*, San Martín 192. *Banco Francés BBV*, San Martín 336. *Scotiabank Quilmes*, Mitre 433. *Casas de Cambio: Sudamérica*, Mitre 63. for TC's. **Consulates** *Austria*, 24 de Septiembre 230, T424873. *Brazil*, Moreno 126 piso 5, T425328. *Chile*, Rosas 180, T422842. *France*, T441960. *Germany*, Ruiz Moreno 65, T425695. *Italy*, Beschtedt 141, T422247. *Lebanon*, Quaglia 242 piso 3, T431471. *Switzerland*, Quaglia 342, T426111. **Communications** Post office Moreno 175, Mon-Fri 0800-2000, Sat 0830-1300. **Telephone** Telecom centre, Mitre y Rolando many *locutorios* in the centre. **Internet** Cyberclub, Mitre 340 piso 1 (*Galería del Sol*), US$5 per hr. **Telecom**, Mitre y Rolando, US$5 per hr, open until 2300. *Cybermac Café*, Rolando 217, US$6 per hr, check promotions. *Cybercafé*, Quaglia 220, US$6 per hr, open until midnight. *Puerto San Carlos*, at the pier, US$6 per hr (with coffee). **Medical services** *Hospital Zonal*, Moreno y Frey, T107 (for emergencies). *San Carlos*, Bustillo Km 1, T422533. **Immigration office** Libertad 191, T423043, Mon-Fri 0900-1300. **Laundry** *Lavematic*, San Martín 325 and Beschtedt 180. *Laverap*, Elordi 520 and Quaglia 321. **Tourist offices** At *Centro cívico*, Mon-Fri 0800-2100, Sat, Sun & Bank holidays 0900-2100, securismo@ bariloche.com.ar Very helpful. Local and provincial information is given also at 12 de Octubre 605, daily 0900-1900. **Parque Nacional Nahuel Huapi** office, San Martín 24, T423111, Mon-Fri 0900-1400. Park wardens are also useful sources of information. In Buenos Aires, some maps and information are given at the national park office, Santa Fe 690, or at the provincial offices.

The lakes route to Chile
No cars are carried on the ferries on this route

This popular route to **Puerto Montt**, involving ferries across Lago Nahuel Huapi, Lago Frías and Lago Todos Los Santos, is outstandingly beautiful whatever the season, though the mountains are often obscured by rain and heavy cloud. It is also however a long and tiring journey and has been criticized as very commercialized.

The route is as follows: from Bariloche to Puerto Pañuelo by bus, from Puerto Pañuelo to Puerto Blest by catamaran (2½ hours), from Puerto Blest to Lago Frías by bus, across the lake to Puerto Frías by boat (20 minutes), from Puerto Frías to Peulla by bus (one hour) via the frontier at Paso Pérez Rosales (978 m), from Peulla to Petrohué by boat (2½ hours) across Lago Todos Los Santos, passing the Osorno volcano, then by bus to Puerto Montt via Puerto Varas. This journey is not recommended in wet or foggy weather (check weather forecast on Chilean TV, available in many hotels).

Sleeping Peulla AL *Hotel Peulla*, PO Box 487, Puerto Montt, T44253253. Includes dinner and breakfast, cheaper out of season, beautiful setting by the lake and mountains, restaurant and bar, good but expensive meals, cold in winter, often full of tour groups (tiny shop at back of hotel). **D** per person *Res Palomita*, 50 m west of Hotel, half board, family-run, simple, comfortable but not spacious, separate shower, book ahead in season, lunches; accommodation is also available with local residents: Elmo and Ana Hernández Maldonado (only house with a balcony), **D** with breakfast, use of kitchen, helpful, clean. **Camping** Opposite Conaf office, US$1.50. Ask the commander of the military garrison at the beach nearest the hotel if you can camp on the beach; no facilities. Good campsite 1¾ hour walk east of Peulla, take food.

Transport In theory this route can only be followed by taking the package offered by *Turismo Catedral*: they own the exclusive rights, using their own boats and bus from Puerto Pañuelo to Puerto Frías and operating with Andina del Sud on the Chilean side. The journey can be done in 1 or 2 days: the 1-day crossing (operates 1 Sep-30 Apr) costs US$110 (to Peulla US$40). No student reductions. This excursion does not permit return to Bariloche next day. Lunch at Peulla is extra, US$18, take own food (but you will not be able to carry it over the frontier), buy ticket day in advance, departs 0700). For the 2-day crossing (operates all year round), there is an overnight stop in Peulla. Several tour companies sell this tour, includes transport, board and lodging. Book in advance during the high season. A cheaper alternative is to buy the trip in sections and take advantage of local bus services to Puerto Pañuelo (0700). You can also walk the 29 km section from Puerto Frías to Peulla, but you will need to do this quickly to catch the boat.

The journey into Chile is via the Paso Perez Rosales **Argentine immigration and customs** At Puerto Frías, open all year. **Chilean immigration and customs** At Peulla, open daily 0800-2100 summer, 0800-2000 winter. There is an absolute ban in Chile on importing any fresh food – meat, cheese, fruit – from Argentina. **Exchange** You are strongly advised to get rid of all your Argentine pesos before leaving Argentina; it is useful to have some Chilean pesos before you cross into Chile from Bariloche. Chilean currency can be bought at Peulla customs at a reasonable rate.

Frontier with Chile

Founded in 1853 as part of the German colonization of the area, Puerto Montt is a popular centre for excursions to the Chilean Lake District. Opportunities in and around the town abound for sailing, fishing, climbing, skiing, parachuting and numerous other sports. Good views over the city and bay are offered from outside the Intendencia Regional on Avenida X Region. A paved road runs 55 km southwest to Pargua, where there is a ferry service to the island of Chiloé. The port of **Angelmó**, 2 km west, is used by fishing boats and coastal vessels, and is the departure point for vessels to Puerto Chacabuco, Puerto Aisén, and Puerto Natales. Angelmó has become a tourist centre with many seafood restaurants and handicraft shops (reached by Costanera bus along Portales and by collective taxi Nos 2,3,20 from the centre, US$0.30 per person).

Into Chile: Puerto Montt
Population: 110,000

The Lake District

Essentials See the *South American Handbook* or the *Chile Handbook* for further details. Accommodation is expensive in season, much cheaper off season. Full listing available from tourist office. There are many tour operators including *Andina del Sud*, very close to central tourist kiosk, Varas 437, T44257797. Operate the Chilean part of the boat/bus trip via Lago Todos Los Santos between Puerto Montt and Bariloche as well as a range of other tours.*Travellers*, Av Angelmó 2456, T/F4258555, Casilla 854, close to 2nd port entrance. Open Mon-Fri 0900-1330,1500-1830, Sat 0900-1400 for booking for Navimag ferry *Puerto Edén* south to Puerto Natales, as well as trips to Osorno volcano and other excursions, money exchange, flights. Also sells imported camping equipment and runs computerized tourist information service, book swap, English-run. Recommended. A tourist office is Sernatur (Chilean tourist authority) in the Intendencia Regional, Av Décima Región 480 (3rd floor), Casilla 297, T44254580, F4254580. Open 0830-1300, 1330-1730 Mon-Fri. Also kiosk on Plaza de Armas run by the municipality, open till 1800 on Sat. Telefónica del Sur and Sernatur operate a phone information service (INTTUR), dial 142 (cost is the same as a local call). Dial 149 for chemist/pharmacy information, 148 for the weather, 143 for the news, etc. Automóvil Club de Chile: Esmeralda 70, T44252968.

Transport **Air** El Tepual Airport, 13 km northwest of town. *ETM* bus from terminal 1½ hrs before departure, US$2. To **Santiago** at least 2 daily flights by *LanChile*, *Ladeco* and *National* (cheaper). To **Punta Arenas**, *LanChile*, *Ladeco* and *National* (both cheaper) daily. *National* also flies to **Concepción** and **Temuco**. Flights to **Bariloche**, **San Martín de los Andes** and **Neuquén**, TAN, 2 a week. **Bus** Terminal on sea front at Portales y Lota, has telephones, restaurants, *casa de cambio* (left luggage, US$1 per item for 24 hrs). There are services to all parts of the country.

South of Bariloche

Route 258, the road from Bariloche to El Bolsón, runs through Parque Nacional Nahuel Huapi, passing three beautiful lakes in the first part of the journey, Lagos Gutiérrez, Mascardi and Guillelmo. On the shore of Lago Gutiérrez, in a grotto, is the Virgen de las Nieves (Virgin of the Snows).

Villa Mascardi
Colour map 5, grid B2
Km 35

At the southern end of Lago Mascardi, Villa Mascardi is a small village from where a *ripio* road with a one-way system (west only before 1400, east only after 1600) runs towards Cerro Tronador and Cascada Los Alerces. From **Pampa Linda**, 40 km west of Villa Mascardi at the foot of Cerro Tronador, there is easy access to the Black glacier of Tronador. Pampa Linda is also the starting point for a two-day walk over Paso de los Nubes to Laguna Frías and Puerto Frías on the Chilean frontier. Ask the rangers at Pampa Linda about conditions. The 22 km route to Paso de los Nubes (1,335 m) is not always well marked and should only be attempted if there is no snow on the pass (normally passable only between December and February). Allow at least six hours to reach Puerto Frías from the pass. From Puerto Frías a 30 km road leads to Peulla on the shore of Chilean Lago Todos Los Santos.

Climbing Tronador From Pampa Linda two other paths lead up Cerro Tronador (3,478 m): one, 15 km long, leads to *Refugio Otto Meiling*,(2,000 m), situated on the edge of the eastern glacier, another hour from the Refugio takes you to a view over Tronador and the lakes and mountains of Parque Nacional Nahuel Huapi; the other path leads to a *refugio* on the south side of the mountain.

Cascada Los Alerces Some 9 km west of Villa Mascardi, a road runs 18 km through the beautiful valley of the Río Manso to Lago Hess and the nearby Cascada Los Alerces. This is the starting point for trekking excursions in a more remote area of small lakes and forested mountains, including Lagos Fonck, Roca, Felipe and Cerros Granito and Fortaleza.

Lagos Steffen and Martín About 20 km south of Villa Mascardi, another one-way dirt road leads to Lagos Steffen and Martín, where a footpath runs along the southern shore of both lakes. Check with the ranger at Lago Steffen about conditions on the path towards Lago Felipe and Lago Roca.

Sleeping *Tronador* on Lago Mascardi 24 km northwest of Villa Mascardi, T468127/441062. Luxury, beautiful setting, highly recommended, also **camping**, *La Querencia* and *Las Carpitas*. *Hostería Pampa Linda* T442038, restaurant, horseriding, excursions. There is a campsite at the Ranger post in Pampa Linda.

C Posada Lago Hess, T462249, also half and full board. **D** *Hostería Río Villegas*, pleasant, friendly, restaurant. Rates at *refugios* are about US$7 per person (details from Club Andino Bariloche). For free campsites in the national park ask the rangers.

Transport Bus Buses from Bariloche to El Bolsón pass through Villa Mascardi. Daily bus to Pampa Linda from *Club Andino* in Bariloche, summer only.

El Bolsón

Dominated by Cerrol Piltriquitrón (2,284 m) El Bolsón is an attractive small town situated in beautiful countryside in an Andean valley. The town is famous for its soft fruit and hops. The surroundings are ideal for mountain walks with many streams and waterfalls.

Phone code: 02944
Colour map 5, grid B2
Population: 10,000
130 km S of Bariloche

Cascada de El Hoyo, 15 km south of town, **Cascada Escondida**, 10 km northwest of town (on the way you pass a botanical garden) and **Cascada Mallín Ahogado**, 10 km north of town (close to *Los 7 Suabos* where good local dairy products are offered) are some of the waterfalls to be seen. Panoramic views of the town can be seen from **Cerro Amigo** (round trip, one hour). There are also fine views from **Cerro Piltriquitrón** (six to seven hour round trip), food and shelter at refugio (1,400 m). Check at the tourist office or at *Club Andino Piltriquitrón*, Sarmiento y Roca, only Tuesdays and Fridays, 1730-1930, T492600.

Excursions

A walk to **Hielo Azul** has been recommended. Leave El Bolsón via San Martín, take Azcuénaga, and follow signs indicating Cabeza del Indio. Cross the bridge, turn left at shop, follow road around Loma del Medio for about 4 km. Then, turn left to the campsites on Río Azul, walk to the river, then follow the riverside path on right for another 4 km. Cross the wire-and-wood bridge over Río Azul, then follow red markers uphill through the forest for 15 km (1,000 m ascent). Stay at the log cabin near waterfalls, possible climb to the glacier (1½ hours) or ridge (about 3½ hours). The hut is normally occupied by Ramiro: US$6 per person, take sleeping bag, matches, food and water purifier. For the **Parque Nacional Lago Puelo**, see below.

AB *Cordillera*, San Martín 3220, T492235, cordillerahotel@elbolson.com Large, with breakfast, good. **AB** *Amancay*, San Martín 3217, T492222. Small, welcoming. **C** per person *La Casona de Odile*, 5 km north in Barrio Luján (2 km off Route 258, regular bus from main square), T492753, odile@red42.com.ar By reservation only, open Nov-Apr, farm with lavender and trout, French, English, German spoken. Recommended. *Kramer*, 20 km north at Rinconada del Mallín Ahogado (La Golondrina bus from main square Mon-Fri 745, 1215, 1800), warmly recommended, wholefood meals, sauna, pool, horseback and trekking excursions. **B** *Valle Nuevo*, 25 de Mayo y Belgrano, T15602325. Small, quiet, good value. **B** *La Posada de Hamelin*, Granollers 2179, T492030, gcapece@elbolson.com Open Nov -Apr, cosy, family ambience, good value. Recommended. **C** *Luz de Luna*, Dorrego y Brown, T492881, small, quiet, good value, large garden. **D** per person *Steiner*, San Martín 670, T492224, old farm, pool, German spoken. Recommended. **D** per person *Las Margaritas*, Guemes y Moreno, T493620, in good conditions. **D** per person *La Paz*, Sarmiento y Hernández, T492252, basic, clean, small, friendly. **E** per person *Salinas*, Roca 641 (50 m from ornithological museum), T492396, without breakfast, basic, cooking facilities. Recommended. **E** per person *El Pueblito* (Hostelling International), 4 km north in Barrio Luján (1 km off route 258, regular bus from main square), T493560, pueblito@hostels.org.ar Large cabin in quiet surroundings, information, English, French spoken, very friendly, small dormitories, meals on request. **E** per person *Sol del Valle*, 25 de Mayo y Pellegrini, T15602325,

Sleeping
Book in advance in Jan & Feb

The Lake District

clean. Recommended. **F** per person *Ecológico*, Pagano y Costa del Río, T491293, hot water, cooking facilities. Accommodation is also available in the nearby villages of Villa Turismo and Golondrinas.

Camping *Aldea Suiza*, 4 km north on Route 258, T492736, recommended, tennis courts, good restaurant, US$6 per person. *El Bolsón*, 1 km north on Route 258, T492595, clean, recommended, small brewery, US$5 per person. *La Chacra*, Route 258 (15 min walk), T492111, hot showers, kiosk, meals, US$5 per person. *Ecológico*, Pagano y Costa del Río, T491293, US$4 per person.

Eating *Calabaza*, San Martín y Hube, nice atmosphere, very good food, also vegetarian dishes, recommended, ISIC discount. *Don Diego*, San Martín 3217. Good, open summer only. *El Viejo Maitén*, Roca y San Martín, good. *Parrilla Las Brasas*, Sarmiento y Hube, good. *Jauja*, San Martín 2867. Great pasta, very friendly. *La Paz*, Sarmiento y Hernández, good and convenient. *La Tosca*, San Martín y Roca, café, warm atmosphere, restaurant summer only. *La Posada del Alquimista*, Belgrano y Berutti, lively bar with pool tables and access to Internet. *EG3* service station, Belgrano y Moreno. Simple meals and cheap sandwiches. Good *facturas* and other bakery products at *Los Cordobeses*, Moreno 3053, run by Argentinean-Greek family.

Festivals *Fiesta del Lúpulo* (Hop Festival), end of Feb and *Fiesta de la Fruta Fina* (Berry Festival) at El Hoyo, Jan.

Shopping *La Huella*, Sarmiento y Dorrego, T491210. For tent hire and outdoor equipment. Handicraft and food market, worth to see, Tue, Thu, and Sat from 1000 on the main square.

Tour operators *Quen Quen Turismo*, Belgrano y Berutti, T493522, quenquen@red42.com.ar 4 hrs horseriding to río Azul or to Cerro Piltriquitrón, US$45 per person, rafting in Río Manso, US$60 per person, parachuting US$70 per person; *Transitando lo Natural*, Dorrego y San Martín, T492495 F492028, transitando@elbolson.com. Birdwatching tours from US$15 per person, flights from US$19 per person, canyoning US$70 per person.

Transport **Air** *LADE* (San Martín 3170) flies weekly to **Bariloche**, **El Maitén**, **Esquel** and **Comodoro Rivadavia**. **Bus** To **Esquel**, 2-3 hrs; US$6-7, direct, *Andesmar, Mar y Valle, Vía Bariloche, Don Otto, TAC* or via Parque Nacional Los Alerces (highly recommended route), *Transportes Esquel* (from ACA service station), Sat/Sun out of season, more frequencies in summer, to El Maitén (connecting with Old Patagonian Express) ask at TAC (Belgrano y San Martín, T493124), to **Bariloche**, 1½-2 hrs, US$8 many companies. To **Trelew**, **Puerto Madryn** or **Comodoro Rivadavia** check with the companies going to Esquel for onward connections. To **Buenos Aires** (usually with connection at Bariloche Charter). Companies: Andesmar, Belgrano y Moreno, T492178; Don Otto, Belgrano y Berutti, T493910. Mar y Valle and Vía Bariloche, Moreno 2871, T493093. Charter, Sarmiento y Roca, T492333. **Car hire** Try *Quen Quen Turismo*, details above. **Cycle hire** *La Rueda*, Sarmiento 2972, T/F492465, US$3 per hr or US$14 per day. **Taxi** *Tour*, T491341. *Cordillera*, T492727.

Directory **Banks** Exchange facilities for US$ at banks (open Mon-Fri, until 1300) *Banco Nación*, San Martín y Pellegrini. *Banco Río Negro*, San Martín y Roca. **Communications** Post Office San Martín 1940. **Internet** *La Posada del Alquimista*, Belgrano y Berutti (US$6 per hr), Biblioteca Sarmiento, San Martín y Roca (US$6 per hr). **Tourist Office** San Martín y Roca, T492604, Mon-Fri 900-2000, Sat & Sun 1000-2000, very helpful, free maps.

This park, covering 23,700 ha, protects an area of southern beechforest around Lago Puelo which drains into Chile. As a result of the warm temperatures resulting from low altitude (200 m) and the high rainfall, the forest is rich in species, among them the *arrayán* and the *pitra*, as well as *coihues* (evergreen beech) and cypresses. Wildlife includes huemul, pudu and foxes. There is fishing for trout and salmon. Canoes can be rented for US$3 per hour. The park is best visited between November and April, though the northern shore of the lake is crowded in January February.

Parque Nacional Lago Puelo
16 km SE of El Bolsón on the Chilean frontier

There are short explanatory trails from the Administration Centre, eg 'Bosque de las Sombras' or Forest of the Shadows, worthwhile to see a small Tolkien-style forest on the way to 'La Playita'. A longer walk may be made to the Chilean border (nine hours round trip), compulsory to follow fast immigration procedures at Gendarmería on the way from the pier; possible to go on to Puerto Montt (four to five days journey). A four-day walk may be made to El Turbio and Cerro Plataforma. Take the boat at the pier, or walk five hours from El Desemboque, then 12 hours from El Turbio to Cerro Plataforma (check with Leandro, local ranger at 'La Costa' in El Turbio); horses to hire at El Turbio, US$25 each horse per day. No services provided at El Turbio, other than basic food from locals.

Access No entry fee. The main entrance is along a road south from El Bolsón, unpaved from Villa Lago Puelo, 3 km north of the park, where there are shops and fuel. Entrance is also possible from El Desemboque, on the eastern side of the park, take the bus from El Bolsón to Esquel, alight at El Hoyo, then walk 14 km to El Desemboque.

Services Administration Centre is 500 m north of the lake (all year round Mon-Fri 800-1500). Information Office opened only in summer at 'el muelle' or the pier.

Sleeping Outside the park **D** per person *Enebros*, in Villa Lago Puelo, T15557331. Small, cosy. **D** per person *Hostal del Lago*, 1 km north of the lake, T499199. Basic, restaurant. There are also cabañas. In the park there are two campsites near the pier, the one to the left, US$5 with some services provided. To the right, US$2, no services provided; other camp sites at the Gendarmería, free, and in more remote areas (ask rangers).

Transport Regular bus service, Quimey Quipán, from San Martín y Dorrego in El Bolsón, US$2. Horses may be hired at the pier, and in more remote areas possibly (ask locals). Boats crossing to El Turbio or Arroyo Aguja, expensive, check at the pier.

The Lake District

South of El Bolsón

Route 258 continues southeast. At Epuyén, Km 165, a village famous for its hops and fruit, there are waterfalls; a side road runs west to Lago Epuyén. **Sleeping** at **D** per person *Refugio del Lago*, 8 km off Route 258 on the lake T02945-499025, F499050. French owned, restaurant, also cabins and camping, horseriding, boats, organised excursions. Recommended.

Epuyén

Famous for the ranch where Butch Cassidy, the Sundance Kid and Etta Place lived between 1901 and 1905, Cholila lies 76 km south of El Bolsón on Route 71, which branches off Route 258 at Km 179. The ranch lies 13 km north of town but a US$10 fee is charged for visiting. A dirt road runs west 12 km from the town to Lago Cholila. There are superb views of the lake, crowned by the Matterhorn-like mountains of Cerros Dos and Tres Picos. From Cholila Route 71 continues southwest into the Parque Nacional Los Alerces (see below).

Cholila
Phone code 02945
Colour map 5, grid B2

Excursions There is a good walk around Lago Mosquito: continue down the road from *El Trébol* past the lake then take a path to the left, following the river. Cross the river on the farm bridge and continue to the base of the hills to a second bridge. Follow the path to the lake and walk between the lake and the hills, crossing the exit river via a suspension bridge just past *El Trébol* – six hours.

Sleeping and eating C per person *El Trébol*, at Lago Los Mosquistos, T/F498055, eltrebol@teletel.com.ar Comfortable rooms with stoves, meals and half board also available, popular with fishing expeditions, reservations advised, bus stops in village 4 km away. **AB** per person *Hostería La Rinconada*, T498091, larinconada@interlink.com.ar, also **AL** full board, excursions, riding, kayaking. *Hostería El Pedregoso*, at Lago Cholila, 8 km west, T498319. *Las Piedras*, Route 71 outside village, Welsh tea room, chocolate cake recommended. **Camping F** per person *Autocamping Carlos Pelligrini*, next to El Trébol; free camping in El Morro park. *Camping El Abuelo*, 13 km south.

Festivals *Fiesta del Asado*, (Barbecue Festival) end of Jan.

Esquel

Population: 28,000
Colour map 5, grid B2
Phone code: 02945
290 km S of Bariloche

Esquel is a modern town in a fertile valley. Originally an offshoot of the Welsh colony in the Chubut valley, nearly 650 km to the east, Esquel is known for its tulips, chocolate, jellies and jams. A centre for visiting the Parque Nacional Los Alerces, it is also famous for La Trochita.

There are two small musems, the **Museo Indigenista y de Ciencias Naturales**, Belgrano y Chacabuco that opens daily except Tuesday, 1600-2000 and the **Museo de Arte Naíf**, Rivadavia near 25 de Mayo. Some 15 km north is the ski-resort of **La Hoya**, which has 20 pistes and nine ski-lifts. The surrounding area is good walking country and there are good views from the mountains surrounding the town: Cerros La Cruz, Nahuel Pan, La Hoya and Leónidas Alemán can all be rreached in half a day or a day. Other good walks are to Laguna La Zeta, 4 km west, and to the valley of río Percey, 15 km west (check at the tourist office for entering the national park, across this valley, and for other trekking excursions).

Sleeping **L** *Cumbres Blancas*, Ameghino 1683, T/F455100, cumbres@teletel.com.ar New, small, luxurious, playroom, sauna and massages, restaurant with local specialities. **L** *Tehuelche*, 9 de Julio 831, T/F452420, tehuelche@teletel.com.ar Good, restaurant. **AB** *Sol del Sur*, 9 de Julio 1086, T452189/2427, soldelsur@teletel.com.ar Central, modern, large rooms, English spoken. **AB** *La Posada*, Chacabuco 905, T/F454095, laposada@teletel.com.ar Very good, though small rooms, cosy, English spoken. **AB/B** *La Tour d'Argent*, San Martín 1063, T/F454612, www.cpatagonia.com/esq/latour Small, good value, central, nice patio, restaurant. **B** *Esquel*, San Martín 1044, T452534, central, helpful. Recommended. **B** *Angelina*, Alvear 758, T452763. Good value, excellent breakfast, Italian spoken. Recommended. **D** per person *La Casona*

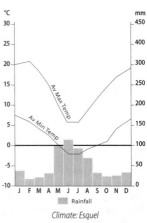

Climate: Esquel

Butch and Sundance

The tale of the most famous twosome in the history of the American West has been retold countless times and become the source of almost as many myths. Though the 1969 movie starring Paul Newman and Robert Redford showed them being gunned down by half the Bolivian army, rumours have persisted that, having faked their deaths, they returned to the United States. While painstaking research by Dan Buck and Ann Meadows discounts stories of their escape from Bolivia, the mystery continues. The exhumation in 1991 of the unmarked graves in Bolivia in which they were supposedly buried failed to provide conclusive evidence.

There is little mystery about the events which led the two outlaws along with Etta Place, Sundance's girlfriend, to move to Cholila between 1901 and 1905. Both Cassidy (real name Robert LeRoy Parker) and the Kid (born Harry Longabaugh) had pursued careers in which periods of legal employment had been mixed with distinctly illegal activity. In the late 1890s the two were part of a loosely-organized gang known as the Train Robbers' Syndicate, the Hole in the Wall Gang and the Wild Bunch, which operated out of Brown's Park, a high valley on the borders of Utah, Colorado and Wyoming. Gang members specialized in hold-ups on railway payrolls and banks. In 1900 they celebrated the wedding of one of their colleagues by having their photo taken. This was their big mistake: the photo was recognized by a Wells Fargo detective. With their faces decorating wanted posters across the land, Cassidy, Sundance and Etta left for Argentina in February 1901.

Using the names Santiago Ryan and Harry Place, the outlaws settled on government land near Cholila and applied to buy it. Pinkerton detectives soon tracked them down and informed the Argentine authorities. By 1905 it was time to move on before either the Pinkertons or the locals could make further moves. Needing money to start up elsewhere they raided banks in Río Gallegos and Villa Mercedes. The Río Gallegos job was particularly audacious: posing as ranching company agents, they opened a bank account with US$7,000, spent two weeks at one of the best hotels, socialized with the city's high society and then entered the bank to close their accounts and empty the safe before escaping to Chile. Shortly afterwards Etta returned to the United States and disappeared from the history books.

No longer welcome in Argentina, Butch and Sundance moved to Bolivia, finding work at the Concordia tin mine. Though scrupulously honest in their dealings with the mine, their occasional disappearances for a few days sometimes coincided with hold-ups. Lack of capital to settle as respectable ranchers was, however, to be their undoing. In 1908 near Tupiza in southern Bolivia they seized an Aramayo mining company payroll, gaining only a fraction of the loot they expected. With military patrols in pursuit and the Argentine and Chilean authorities alerted, they rode into the village of San Vicente but were recognised. Besieged, they did not, as in the film, run into the awaiting gunfire: with Sundance fatally wounded, Butch shot his partner and then committed suicide. Curiously their deaths were not widely reported in the United States until the 1930s. Ironically while wild stories of their deaths had circulated long before 1908, one of them featuring Butch face down in a Paris slum with a 'crooked knife fast between his shoulders', they were now reported as having secretly returned to the States: Butch was said to have become a businessman, a rancher, a trapper and a Hollywood movie extra, while Sundance had run guns in the Mexican Revolution, migrated to Europe, fought for the Arabs against the Turks in the First World War, sold mineral water, founded a religious cult and still found time to marry Etta.

(Adapted from Digging Up Butch and Sundance by Ann Meadows, London, 1996)

de Olgbrun, San Martín 1137, T453841. Good apartments, central, also cabañas on the road to Trevelin. **B** *La Hoya*, Ameghino 2296, T451694, 1 km on road to airport. **C** *Lihuen*, San Martín 820, T452589, ejarque@teletel.com.ar Small, good value, English spoken. **C** *Maika*, 25 de Mayo y San Martín, T/F452457. Central, overpriced. **C** *El Cisne*, Chacabuco 777, T452256. Very clean, good, recently refurbished, good cooking facilities. **C** *Huemul*, Alvear 1015, T450817. **D/C** *Los Tulipanes*, Fontana 365, T452748. Good rooms and service. Recommended. **C** *Huentru Niyeu*, Chacabuco 606, T452576. Good, modern. **E** per person *Rowlands*, Rivadavia 330, T452578, Welsh spoken, basic. Recommended. **E** per person *Argentino*, 25 de Mayo 862, T452237. Old fashioned hotel, clean, basic, great bar worth seeing. **On outskirts AB** *Canela*, Los Notros y Los Radales (off road to Trevelin, 1 km from town), T453890. Apartments, sleep 4, tea room. **AB** *La Chacra*, 4 km south, T45802, .peaceful, huge breakfast, English spoken. *Lago Verde* (Hostelling International), Volta 1081 (near railway station), T/F452251, esquel@hostels.org.ar Small, garden, comfortable, private bathrooms, no cooking facilities, English spoken, campsite, also travel agency. Recommended. *Millalen*, Ameghino 2063, T456164, gmartin@unpate.edu.ar Run by tourist guides, clean, good, recommended, also, camping, good cabins and basic huts for rent. *El Hogar del Mochilero*, Roca 1028 (in low season ask at Roca 1023), T452166. Camping with free firewood, hot water, also basic and large dormitories, access to internet.

Camping *La Colina*, Darwin 1400 (on hill overlooking town), T454962, US$3.50 per person. Hot showers, kitchen facilities, lounge with log fire, highly recommended. *La Rural*, Route 259 km 1 (on southwestern outskirts), T15681429, full facilities.

Esquel centre

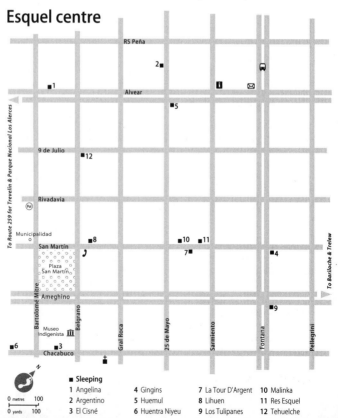

■ Sleeping

1 Angelina	4 Gingins	7 La Tour D'Argent	10 Malinka
2 Argentino	5 Huemul	8 Lihuen	11 Res Esquel
3 El Cisné	6 Huentra Niyeu	9 Los Tulipanes	12 Tehuelche

•••

La Trochita (The Old Patagonian Express)

Esquel is the terminus of a 402 km branch-line from Ingeniero Jacobacci, a junction, 194 km east of Bariloche, on the old Buenos Aires-Bariloche mainline. This narrow-guage line (0.75-m wide) took 23 years to build, being finally opened in 1945. It was made famous outside Argentina by Paul Therroux who desribed it in his book The Old Patagonian Express. The 1922 Henschel and Baldwin steam locomotives (from Germany and USA respectively) are powered by fuel oil and use 100 litres of water every kilometre. Water has to be taken on at least every 40 km along the route. Most of the coaches are Belgian-built and also date from 1922.

If you want to see the engines you need to go to El Maitén where the workshops are.

Until the Argentine government handed responsibility for railways over to the provincial governments in 1994, regular services ran the length of the line. Since then services have been maintained between Esquel and El Maitén by the provincial government of Chubut. For timetable see below.

*In El Maitén there are two hotels, same owner, both overpriced: Accomazzo, with good restaurant; **A3** La Vasconia, near station, basic. On Thursday a bus for Esquel meets the train in El Maitén, check details first in Esquel.*

•••

Cassis, Sarmiento 120, cosy, German and English spoken, try lamb or trout, *De María*, Rivadavia 1024, parrilla. *Don Chiquino*, 9 de Julio 970, pasta. *Galo*, Ameghino 880, check for special events. *La Trochita*, 25 de Mayo 633, basic meals. *Palio*, Ameghino 1140, pasta and parrilla. *Pizza Don Pipo*, Fontana 649, good pizzas, also take away. *La Española*, Rivadavia 740, excellent beef, some Arab dishes. *Vascongada*, 9 de Julio y Mitre, trout specialities. *La Tour d'Argent*, San Martín 1063, local dishes. *Cumbres Blancas*, Ameghino 1683, local dishes. *Tehuelche*, 9 de Julio 831. Take away at *Doña Chefa*, 25 de Mayo 920, T454348. **Tea rooms** *Vestry*, Rivadavia 1065 (behind the Welsh chapel), Welsh corner in Esquel, with music, books, information, and the famous teas, ask here for visits to the chapel. *Melys*, Miguens 346 (off Ameghino 2000), also good breakfast, US$5. *Canela*, Los Notros y Los Radales (off road to Trevelin, 1 km from town), English specialities. **Eating**

Tango lessons in a warm atmosphere at *Hotel Argentino*, 25 de Mayo 862, worth seeing, Tue, Thu and Sat evenings, dancing later on Fri and Sat. **Welsh choir** rehearsals at the chapel (built in 1915), Rivadavia 1065, check dates at *Vestry* tea room (behind the chapel); Casino, Ameghino 1024; bowling at Ruderico, Sarmiento 647. **Entertainment**

Casa de Esquel, 25 de Mayo 415, wide range of rare books on Patagonia, also souvenirs, and hats; also books at *Leonardo*, Ameghino 872; *La Casona de Olgbrun*, San Martín 1137, a variety of handicrafts and souvenirs; more handicrafts at *Shunam*, 9 de Julio 1034; *Esquel Crem*, Ameghino 1605, local dairy products made with sheep's milk; home made chocolate and the famous local mazard berry liquor is sold at *Braese*, 9 de Julio 1059; *Benroth*, from Bariloche, offers home made chocolate at 9 de Julio 1027. **Shopping**

Fishing Few opportunites to hire fishing gear; best to take your own; ask for fishing guides at the tourist office (eg Sebastián Ferrer, T452292, English spoken, offers a 1-day guided excursion for fly casting and spinning for 2 people in the national park, including boat and meals (licence extra US$50 per person) for US$150. **Skiing** La Hoya, 15 km north, has 20 km of pistes and 9 ski-lifts, season Jul-Oct, cheaper than Bariloche: ski pass US$10-18 depending on season, gear hire US$7 a day. Accommodation at *Hostería La Hoya*, open only in ski season. For skiing information ask at tourist office, or at *Club Andino Esquel*, Volta 649, T453248. **Sport**

The Lake District

Tour operators *Esquel Tours*, Fontana 754, T452704. Good for tours to Lagos Menéndez and Cisne. *Patagonia Verde*, (run by owners of Lago Verde Hostel), 9 de Julio 926, T454396, offers non conventional circuits (eg to Piedra Parada in the Chubut valley), agents for *Rotativo Patagónico*, offering guided journeys with minibuses to Bariloche (US$73), to Perito Moreno (US$73), to El Calafate (US$156); *Trekways*, Roca 687, T/F453380, T451000, trekways@cybersnet.com.ar, for trekking, canoeing, canyoning, estancias, horseriding, knowledgeable guides, ask for excursions to Chile. Recommended.

Transport **Local** The city centre can be negotiated on foot. **Long distance** **Air** Airport, 20 km east, US$14 by taxi, US$4 by *Esquel Tours*, Fontana 754, T452704.To **Comodoro Rivadavia** and **Bariloche**, *LADE*, 2 a week, to **El Bolsón**, **Puerto Madryn** and **Trelew**, *LADE*, once a week.

Bus Terminal, Alvear y Fontana, left luggage US$1 per item per day. To **El Bolsón** (2-3 hrs; US$6-8.50), direct, *Andesmar, Don Otto, Mar y Valle, TA.C, Vía Bariloche* or via Parque Nacional Los Alerces (beautiful route), *Transportes Esquel*, US$14, out of season Sat and Sun only, more services in summer. Recommended. To **Bariloche** (4-5 hrs; US$12-18), *Andesmar, Don Otto, Mar y Valle, TAC, Vía Bariloche*. To **Trevelin** (1 hr; US$1.50, every hr on weekdays, every 2 hrs weekends), *CODAO*. To **Trelew** (8 hrs; US$25-28) and **Puerto Madryn** (9 hrs; US$30), *Mar y Valle, Empresa Chubut, Don Otto* (only to Trelew). To **Comodoro Rivadavia** (8 hrs; US$29), *ETAP, Don Otto*. To **Buenos Aires** (US$90), *TAC* direct or *Vía Bariloche* with onward connection from Bariloche. To **El Maitén**, 2½ hrs daily except Wed & Sun, *Jacobsen*. To **Río Pico**, 4½ hrs, Mon/Wed/Sat, *Jacobsen*. To **Alto Río Senguer**, Mon and Thu, *ETAP*. **To Chile**: to Coyhaique, Wed and Sun, *ETAP*. To Osorno and northern destinations with *Andesmar*, connecting in Bariloche. **Companies**: Andesmar, T450143; Don Otto and Empresa Chubut, T453012; Mar y Valle, T453712; Jacobsen and Vía Bariloche, T453528; TAC, T451110; ETAP, T454756; Transportes Esquel, T453529; CODAO, Ameghino 1045, T455222.

Taxi *Unión*, Roca 477, T0800 333 2806 or 454370. **Cycle hire** *Tierra*, Rivadavia 873, T454366, US$3 per hr. **Car hire** *Localiza*, Rivadavia 1168, T453276; *Avis*, 15683333; Mechanic, Brown y 9 de Julio, beside 'Claudia' hairdressers.

Train 'La Trochita' to El Maitén, 6 hrs; US$25 weekly (usually Thu but check in advance); also short trips to Nahuel Pan, 2½ hrs return; US$15, almost everyday; timetables change in summer adding services, check at station, off Alvear 1800 and 300 m up the hill, T451403, or at latrochita@elbolson.org

Directory **Airline offices** *LADE*, Alvear 1085, T452124. **Banks** (open mornings only) *Banco Nación*, Alvear y Roca, *Bansud*, 25 de Mayo 737, *Banco del Chubut*, Alvear 1131, ATM. *Viajes Sol del Sur*, 9 de Julio 1086, accept TCs, open Mon-Fri, 1000-1300. *Viasur*, 9 de Julio 1027, Amex TCs only accepted. **Communications** Post office, Alvear y Fontana, Mon-Fri 0830-1300 and 1600-1930, Sat 0900-1300. Telephone *Terminal de Comunicaciones*, public phones at the bus terminal. **Internet** *Cyberclub Esquel*, San Martín y 25 de Mayo, US$8 per hr (US$3 minimum), Mon-Fri until 2100. *PCMaster Computación*, Rivadavia 701, US$6 per hr, Mon-Fri 900-1300 and 1600-2030, Sat 900-1300. **Laundry** *Laverap*, Mitre 543. *Marva*, San Martín 941, Mon-Sat 0800-2200 (Sun until 1500). **Tourist office** Alvear y Sarmiento, T/F451927, www.esquelonline.com.ar Very friendly and helpful, Mon-Fri 0730-2000, Sat 0900-1200 and 1500-1900, Sun mornings only.

Trevelin Another offshoot of the Welsh colony in the Chubut valley, Trevelin has a Welsh chapel (built in 1910 and now closed) and there are several tea rooms. **Museo Regional** in the old mill (1918) includes artefacts from the Welsh colony and, upstairs, a model of the Futaleufú hydro-electric dam. ■ *1100-1900, entry US$2.* **El Malacara**, 200 m from main plaza, is John Evans' house, one of the first settlers, kept with all his belongings. Outside is the grave of his horse,

Population: 5,000
Colour map 5, grid B2
Phone code: 02945
23 km SW of Esquel

Malacara, who once saved his life. Guided tours to both sites, US$2. Also horseriding around the farm, now run by Evans'grandaughter (mentioned by Chatwin´s in *In Patagonia*.

Molino Nant Fach, Route 259, 22 km southwest towards the frontier, a former flour mill, now a museum with a display of farming implements, carriages, and artefacts used by the first Welsh settlers, in beautiful surroundings. Entry US$3. The **Nant-y-fall Falls**, 17 km southwest on Route 259 to the frontier, are four waterfalls in a natural reserve surrounded by beautiful forest, entrance US$0.50.

Sleeping C *Estefanía*, Perito Moreno, T480148. Clean, good value. **D** per person *Pezzi*, Sarmiento 351, T480146, marianapezzi@hotmail.com Dec-Mar, English spoken, very friendly, garden, highly recommended. *Trevelin*, San Martín 327. **D** per person *Casaverde* (Hostelling International), T/F480091, trevelin@hostels.com.ar Attractive house with fine views over valley, cooking facilities, sheets and towels supplied, rooms sleep 3-6, highly recommended, kayaks for hire. **B** *La Granja Trevelin*, 4 km north towards Esquel, T480096. Cabins, camping, hot water, macrobiotic meals, good Italian cooking, excellent horses for hire. *Granja La Colina*, 24 km south on Route 259 to Chile, T480548. Also camping, shop, cafeteria, fishing, horseriding. **C** *Aikén Leufú*, on the road to Futaleufú dam, T451317. Cabins sleep 2, also camping, full services. *Autocamping La Paz* (see under Parque Nacional Los Alerces). *Camping Adventure*, on the Río Percey, T480267. **E** per person *Refugio Wilson*, 7 km northwest on sloppes of Cordón Situación' run by *Gales al Sur* travel agency (see below).

Eating *El Rancho de Mario*, main plaza, parrilla and home made pasta. *Clery Fondue*, near El Malacara, regional meals and fondue. *Ruca Laufquen*, San Martín y Libertad, parrilla. *Patagonia Celta*, Molino Viejo y 25 de Mayo. *Nain Maggie*, Perito Moreno 179, Welsh tea room, recommended (there is a custom of giving a newly-married couple a *torta negra* – black cake – on their wedding day, to be eaten on their first anniversary).

Tour operators *Gales al Sur*, Patagonia 186, T/F480427, galesalsur.com.ar. Tours to Chilean border, national park and Futaleufú dam; also Old Patagonian Express and rafting, trekking, bike and horseriding excursions in 4WD vehicle (US$20-120 per person); internet access, cycle hire (US$3 per hr; US$18 per day).

Transport Bus *CODAO* to Esquel, 1 hr; US$1.40, every hr on weekdays, every 2 hrs at weekends. To Chilean border, US$4.30, Mon and Fri, adding services on Tue-Wed-Thu in summer, connecting at the border with bus to Futaleufú (Chile). To Lago Rosario, Corcovado, Carrenleufú.

Directory Tourist office main plaza, open in daylight hrs, very helpful. Fishing guides.

This park covers 263,000 ha, taking its name from the *alerces* (*Fitzroya cupressoides*) which it was established to protect. Some of them are over 2,000 years old. There are four large lakes and several smaller ones; the northern lakes, **Lagos Rivadavia** and **Menéndez**, drain into **Lago Futalaufquén** and from there into the southernmost **Lago Amutui Quimei**, an artificial lake which empties into the Río Futaleufú which flows west into Chile.

Parque Nacional Los Alerces
60 km W of Esquel

The western side of the park, where rainfall is highest, has areas of Valdivian forest. The eastern side has similar natural attractions to those in the Nahuel Huapi and Lanín parks, including forests of *coihue*, *lenga* and *alerce*, but is much less developed for tourism. The most accessible part of the park is the east bank of Lago Futalaufquén, reached by Route 71 which runs through the park. The west side of the lake less accessible and relatively untouched by tourism. Lago Futalaufquén has some of the best fishing in this part of Argentina (season 15 November-Easter): local guides offer fishing trips on motor boats. A recommended journey for motorists is to spend the night at El Bolsón, enter the Los Alerces park via Cholila and drive right through it to Esquel, travelling the whole length of Lagos Rivadavia and Futalaufquén.

There are good short explanatory **trails** (no more than an hour long) seeing native flora or **aboriginal paintings** on rocks from Villa Futalaufquen. From the road along the west coast of Lago Futalaufquen to Puerto Limonao and Hotel Futalaufquen, there are good walk to **Cerro Alto El Dedal** (1,900 m), six hours to summit, with great views of the lakes and the cordillera. **Cinco Saltos** is three hours away where there are five waterfalls. Cross the mountains to **Lago Krugger** takes 12 hours.

Boat excursions Regular full day launch trip from Puerto Limonao (reached by early morning minibus) across Lago Futalaufquen, (a sheer delight), along Río Arrayanes to windless Lago Verde, where there are two campsites (see below). From here you can walk out to Lago Rivadavia (8 km), and Lago

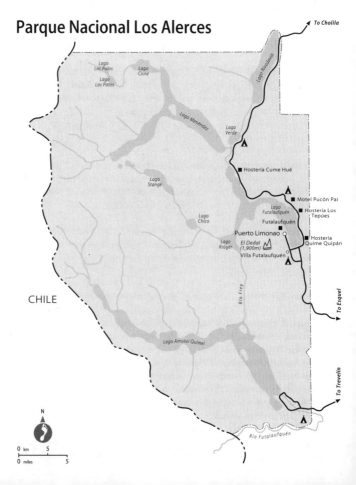

Parque Nacional Los Alerces

Cholila (50 km). There is also a boat service from Puerto Chucao (reached after a 30 min walk across the bridge over Río Arrayanes), across Lago Menéndez to its western side (1½ hours) to visit the old *alerce* forest and remote Lago Cisne; book in advance through travel agent in Esquel or Trevelin and arrive early to claim your space (boat departures daily in high season from Puerto Limonao, nine hours round trip, US$40-50 per person high season; low season, few services, US$28 per person); ask for boat excursions to Lago Krugger.

The southern part of the park can be reached from a separate entrance from Trevelin following the Río Futaleufú to reach the Futaleufú hydroelectric dam, behind which is Lago Amutui Quimei; the dam supplies power to the alumina plant at Puerto Madryn, 500 km to the east. Guided tours to the dam itself, hourly in season, small fee. There is no public transport to the dam.

Services The park administration is at Villa Futalaufquén, at the southern end of Lago Futalaufquén, where there is a small Visitors' Centre with displays on the flora and fauna of the park. Nearby are a service station, a kiosk where fishing licences are sold and 2 expensive supermarkets.

Sleeping East side of Lago Futalaufquen *Quime Quipán*, 5 km from Villa Futalaufquen, T454134. Recommended for fishing, closed in winter, with restaurant, also one cabin to hire. *Pucon Pai*, 10 km from Villa Futalaufquen, T451425, recommended for fishing (holds a fishing festival to open the season), good restaurant, open out of season for large groups only, also campsite: *Cume Hue*, 27 km from Villa Futalaufquen, T453639, also, restaurant. Cabins at *Los Tepúes*, 10 km from Villa Futalaufquen, T471013, simple, rustic, open all year. *Tejas Negras*, 13 km from Villa Futalaufquen, T471046, tea room. *Bahía Rosales*, 14 km from Villa Futalaufquen, also campsite. **West side of Lago Futalaufquen** *Hotel Futalaufquen*, 4 km from Villa Futalaufquen, T471008, cleaona@teletel.com.ar Recommended, especially rooms 2/3 and 4/5 which have balconies overlooking the lake, open Nov-Apr, good walking near the hotel. Camping at *Los Maitenes*, on the south side of the lake, T451003. **Lago Krugger** Refugio Lago Krugger, also campsite, fishing, ask for ISIC and youth card holders discounts. **Near the Futaleufú dam** *Autocamping La Paz*, T452829 or 15681604, campsite with full services, also cabins, watersports, horseriding, fishing. Several campsites at Lago Rivadavia, Lago Verde, and Río Arrayanes (free-US$6 per person, according to facilities, some charge a fee per tent).

Tours Agencies in Esquel or Trevelin for trip to El Alerzal (alerce forest). Other tours offered are less interesting because they only involve short stops at points of interest. For short guided excursions, ask at visitors centre in Villa Futalaufquen (eg José Alarcón offers excursion with horseriding in Lago Rivadavia for US$8 per hr; Julio Rosales, T453622, goes to Cerro La Torta charging US$10 per hr). Contact Telluride Flyfishers, PO Box 1634, Telluride, Colorado, T800-828-7547. *Trevelin Lodge*, specialises in fishing, run by O'Farrell Safaris, organises tours, white-water rafting and horseriding.

Transport Bus From Esquel, 1 daily, *Transportes Esquel* (T453529), more frequent in summer (Villa Futalaufquen: US$4; Lago Verde: US$8; Lago Rivadavia: US$9).

There are two frontier crossings just south of Esquel, at **Paso Futaleufú** and **Paso Palena**. On the Chilean side roads from these crossings link up to provide a route to Chaitén. **Paso Futaleufú** lies 70 km southwest of Esquel via Trevelin and is reached by Route 259 (*ripio* from Trevelin). The frontier is crossed by a bridge over the Río Futaleufú. This is an easy crossing: one hour for all formalities. **Frontier with Chile**

The Lake District

Not Butch and Sundance

In 1911 the North American bandits, William Wilson and Robert Evans, whom Bruce Chatwin confused, in In Patagonia with Butch Cassidy and the Sundance Kid, (see page 393), were killed in Río Pico by the *Argentine Frontier Police. Their bodies were buried near the old Hahn store, 4 km east of Río Pico on Route 19, 3 km up a very bad road. The grave is marked with an iron cross (1912 date on cross is incorrect).*

Argentine immigration and customs On the Argentine side of the bridge. Travellers entering Argentina should note that Argentine border officials only give transit visas: you must legalize your stay within 10 days either by leaving the country or by renewing your entry stamp at an immigration office. **Chilean immigration and customs** In Futaleufú, 9 km west of the frontier.

Camping Several campsites along Route 259 between Trevelin and the international bridge.

Transport Bus From Esquel to Paso Futaleufú, Codao Mon/ Fri, US$4.50, 2 hrs, with extra departures on Tue/Wed/Thu in summer, connecting at the frontier with a minibus to Futaleufú (Chile) US$3. Very little traffic for hitching.

Into Chile The road continues on the Chilean side towards Chaitén. Outside Puerto Ramírez take the right turn to Chaitén (left goes to Palena).

Paso Palena lies 120 km southeast of Esquel and is reached by Route 17 from Trevelín which runs to Corcovado, 75 km east of Tecka (reached by *ripio* road). From Corcovado it is 26 km west to the frontier.

Argentine immigration and customs At the frontier, open daily 0900-1800. Only transit visas are issued (see above under Futaleufú crossing). **Chilean immigration** At Palena, 11 km west of frontier.

Sleeping Cabañas in Corcovado and several *pensiones* in Palena.

Transport Bus From Esquel and Trevelin *CODAO* goes to Lago Rosario, Corcovado, and Carrenleufú. On the Chilean side *Expreso Yelcho* bus runs to Chaitén, 5½ hrs, US$12, 2 a week.

South of Esquel

Route Route 40 continues (paved) south from Esquel. There are few settlements or services along this road. At **Tecka** (population 1,000; altitude 710 m; phone code 02945), Km 101, Route 62 (paved) branches off east and follows the valley of the Río Chubut to Trelew. Route 40 continues south to **Gobernador Costa** (population: 1,700; altitude: 640 m; phone code; 02945), a small service centre for the *estancias* in this area on the Río Genoa at Km 183.

Sleeping Tecka *Hotel Tecka. Res Josene.* **Gobernador Costa D** *Res Jair*, San Martín y Sarmiento, clean, friendly. **D** *Hotel Vega.* **Camping** Municipal site in Gobernador Costa US$2.

Río Pico lies in a wide green valley close to the Andes and is best visited from December to February. It is the site of an early 20th-century German settlement and some old houses remain from that period. At Estancia Hahn, 4 km east of town, you can see the old store and pioneer's houses, and the grave of Wilson and Evans (see box). Nearby are several lakes, good for fishing and free camping, ask locals for hitching; the northern shore of Lago Tres, 23 km west of town, is a peaceful and remote place, with a rich birdlife and wild strawberries at the end of January. Some 30 km north of Río Pico lies the huge **Lago Vintter**, reached by Route 44. There are also smaller lakes good for trout fishing. Permits from the *Municipalidad* in Gobernador Costa.

Río Pico
Phone code: 02945
Colour map 5, grid C2
Population: 1,000
80 km W of
Gobernador Costa

Sleeping *Hospedaje Solís*, basic. **E** per person *El Pollo Dorado*, breakfast extra, restaurant. camping at Municipal Campsite. *Laurín*, cabins at Lago Vintter, T492017.

Transport **Bus** From Esquel to Río Pico, 4½ hrs, Mon/Wed/Sat, *Jacobsen*, T453528.

At Km 221, Route 40 (poor *ripio*) forks southwest through the town of **Alto Río Senguer** from which visits can be made to the relatively unexplored Lago Fontana and Lago La Plata. Provincial Route 20 (paved) heads almost directly south for 81, before turning east towards Sarmiento and Comodoro Rivadavia. At La Puerta del Diablo, in the valley of the lower Río Senguer, Route 20 intersects provincial Route 22, which joins with Route 40 at the town of Río Mayo (see page 428). This latter route is completely paved and preferable to Route 40 for long-distance motorists.

South of Gobernador Costa

Sleeping **Alto Río Senguer** *Bety Jay*. *Hosp Fogón Criollo*. **Camping** Good informal sites on the west side of the bridge across the Río Senguer; *hosterias* for fishing at Lagos Fontana and La Plata (details from tourist offices in Esquel or Comodoro Rivadavia).

Transport **Bus** From Esquel to Alto Río Senguer, *ETAP*, Mon, Thu.

The Lake District

Patagonia

10

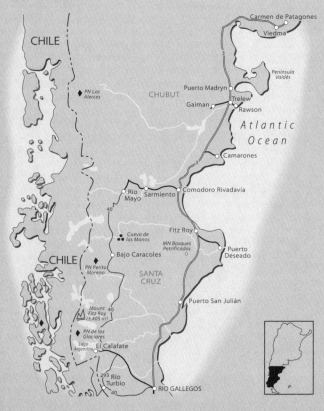

Almost everything in Patagonia is on a large scale including its physical features and the distances between human settlements. The traveller will also notice the enormous skies and the views over long distances which are often particularly beautiful in the early morning and at dusk as the light reflects off the Andean range.

Most of Argentine Patagonia is a vast treeless plateau stretching south of the Rio Colorado towards the Magallan Straits which separate South America from Tierra del Fuego. The Atlantic coast is rich in marine life, most easily seen on the Peninsula Valdés, near the city of Puerto Madryn. Nearby, inland from Trelew, is the Chubut Valley, the centre of the Welsh settlement in Argentina in the nineteenth century. Further south, centred on the little town of Calafate, is one of the most popular destinations for travellers to Argentina, the Parque Nacional Los Glaciares; here are several glaciers including the famous Perito Moreno Glacier and the Fitzroy massif, an increasingly popular centre for climbing and walking.

Although geographically Argentine Patagonia consists of the provinces of Neuquén, Río Negro, Chubut and Santa Cruz, this section describes only the latter two provinces and eastern parts of Río Negro: for Neuquén and western Río Negro see The Lake District.

Background

Geography

Most of Argentine Patagonia is dry steppe stretching west from the Atlantic coast to the foothills of the Andes. Though the steppes appear flat, they rise steadily to over 1,000 m in the foothills of the Andes: they appear flat because of the lack of features such as trees, hedges or buildings. The Andean range is much lower than further north, with peaks between 2,000 and 2,500 m and a few above 3,000 m. Between the mountains are U-shaped glacial valleys, some filled by lakes. A large part of the southern Andes are covered by two ice fields (*campos de hielo*) from the edges of which glaciers drop eastwards into the lakes and rivers of Argentine Patagonia and westwards into the fiords along the Chilean coast.

Several rivers flow eastwards from the Andean foothills. In the north are the Río Colorado, which marks the northern boundary of Patagonia, and the Río Negro, which drains much of the Argentine Lake District. Further south is the Río Chubut, 500 km long, which takes the waters of the Southern Lake District; its major tributary, the Río Chico, receives the waters of the Río Senguer and drains Lagos Musters and Colhué Huapi, two large lakes near Colonia Sarmiento. The two main rivers of Santa Cruz province are the Río Deseado, which takes the waters of Lago Buenos Aires, and the Río Santa Cruz, which drains Lago Argentino and Lago Viedma, both of which are fed by the great glaciers of the Parque Nacional Los Glaciares. Further south are two smaller rivers, the Ríos Coyle and Gallegos.

Climate There are marked differences between the seasons; spring and autumn are short, summer and winter are long. Temperature ranges are high, especially in western inland areas, though the highest absolute temperatures, rising to 45°C occur in the eastern parts of the valleys of the Río Negro and Río Colorado. Strong westerly winds are common especially in spring and summer. Annual rainfall levels are high in the watershed of the Andes, but drop rapidly as you go east. Large parts of eastern Patagonia receive little rainfall.

Wildlife and flora

Eastern and central areas, which receive little rainfall, are virtually desert, though, during a brief period in spring, after the melting of the snows, there is grass on the steppe. Further west, in the foothills of the Andes, the high rainfall supports a line of beech forests. Here there are two fine national parks, the Parque Nacional Los Glaciares, which attracts large numbers of visitors, and the little known Parque Nacional Perito Moreno.

Lesser Rhea   *Magellan Geese*

The wilds of the Atlantic coast

One of the great attractions of the Atlantic coast is provided by the breeding seasons of bird species and marine mammals, mainly in spring and summer.

The most impressive birds are, perhaps, the magellan penguins, which nest in huge colonies on the Valdés Peninsula, at Cabo Dos Bahías, Ría Deseado, Cabo Vírgenes, Monte León and on the Isla de los Estados. Other sea-birds include four species of cormorants, among them the beautiful red-legged cormorant (found only in Ría Deseado and Bahía San Julián in Santa Cruz), several species of gulls including the kelp gull and the black-headed gull, and terns including the South American tern. Look out particularly for the Antarctic giant petrel, the black-browed albatross, the snowy sheathbill and several species of oystercatcher.

Marine mammals include the southern elephant seal, southern sea lion, southern furry seal, southern right whale and commerson's dolphin. The killer whale is difficult to see, though the best place to spot them is in waters near colonies of southern sea lions in March and April.

Southern Elephant Seal

The most impressive mammals on the steppe are the herds of guanacos. Other mammal species include the *mara* (Patagonian hare) and the Patagonian Piche (the southernmost armadillo in the world). Predators include red and grey foxes as well as the elusive puma.

Along the Patagonian coast there are sea lion and penguin colonies; some protected waters are breeding grounds for the Commerson's dolphin and the grey dolphin. Elephant seals and southern right whales breed along the coast of Valdés peninsula and the nearby gulfs.

Many bird species migrate northwards to avoid the harsh Patagonian winter. Bird species which may be seen include the lesser rhea, the common diuca-finch, the austral negrito (found mainly near water), the Patagonian mockingbird, the rufous-collared sparrow (found nearly everywhere), the Patagonian yellow-finch and the red-breasted long-tailed meadowlark. There are also mimetic species such as the elegant-crested tinamou, the lesser seedsnipe and burrowing owl. The lakes are inhabited by ducks such as the crested duck and the red shoveller, as well as Chilean flamingoes and grebes.

Mara or Patagonian hare

Magellan geese and ashy-headed geese can be found on grasslands and wetlands, though the ruddy-headed goose is an endangered species. Birds of prey include the red-backed hawk, the black-breasted buzzard-eagle, the peregrine falcon as well as the very common crested caracara. For further details of bird-species see *Aves de Argentina y Uruguay*, available, in English, from main bookshops in Buenos Aires as well as major tourist centres in Patagonia.

Patagonia

Sheep farming

As you travel around Patagonia you will probably see few sheep; they are hard at work grazing around the small streams which are usually hidden from the road. Some idea, however, of the importance of sheep to the rural economy is given by the way in which land values and incomes from estancias are calculated.

In many societies land is valued for status and security rather than its productivity. In Patagonia, however, with its vast expanses of unoccupied and poor quality land, the value of an estancia is calculated in terms of the area of land required to support one sheep: this ranges from 1 ha in the cordillera to 2 ha in the central meseta and 3 ha on the costa. For the purpose of pricing land, one sheep is valued at US$60, a figure which has not changed for decades and which is well above the real market price of sheep. Thus a hectare of land which can support one sheep is valued at US$60.

In recent years many Patagonian estancias have looked to tourism as an additional (or even their major) source of income. Without such extra income, it is reckoned that the minimum viable size for an estancia is 5,000 sheep, which should produce an annual income of US$40,000. The calculations on which this is based are as follows. With raw wool priced at US$1.50 (the average sheep produces 4 kg of wool a year) 5,000 sheep produce an income of US$30,000. Another US$10,000 can be earned through the sale of animals: about 10% of the flock is sold every year for an average price of US$20 per animal.

Not surprisingly the most popular breed of sheep is the one which works hardest converting the sparse grasslands into wool and meat. This is the Corriedale, originally from Scotland; it produces more wool than the Merino, but its wool is coarse, which, naturally, helps explain its low value. This, perhaps more than anything else, explains the economics of Patagonian estancias: sheep are grazed because the land is too poor for other uses.

Economy

Most of the land is devoted to sheep raising. The great sheep *estancias* are situated in the shelter provided by the canyons which intersect the land from east to west and in the depression which runs north from the Strait of Magellan to Lagos Argentino and Buenos Aires and beyond. Over-grazing has led to soil erosion. Wild dogs, pumas and red foxes are the sole predators of the sheep. Because of the high winds and insufficient rainfall there is little arable farming except in the north, in the valleys of the Colorado and Negro rivers. Some cattle are raised in both these valleys where irrigation permits the growing of alfalfa.

Patagonia is rich in extractive resources: the oil of Comodoro Rivadavia and Tierra del Fuego, the little exploited iron ore of Sierra Grande, the coal of Río Turbio, the hydro-electric capacity of El Chocón, plentiful deposits of minerals (particularly bauxite) and marine resources. The exploitation of some of these has been slow.

The largest city in Argentine Patagonia is Comodoro Rivadavia, the only centre with a population over 100,000. Most of the towns are small ports, which used only to work during the wool-shipping season but have livened up since the local economy began to diversify. The high tidal range makes it impossible in most of them for ships to tie up at docks (except at Puerto Madryn, Puerto Deseado and Punta Quilla, near Santa Cruz.

'A little Wales beyond Wales'

The Welsh settlement in Patagonia dates from the arrival of 165 settlers in July 1865. Landing on the bay where Puerto Madryn now stands, they were forced by lack of water to walk south across the parched land to the Chubut valley, where they found flat cultivable land and settled. The first 10 years of the settlement were hard indeed and they were forced to rely on trade with the Tehuelches, supplies delivered by the British navy and support from the Argentine government which was eager to populate its territory.

The settlement was partly inspired by Michael D Jones, a non-conformist minister who provided much of the early finance and recruited settlers through the Welsh language press and through the chapels. Jones, whose aim was to create a 'little Wales beyond Wales' far from the intruding influence of the English, took particular care to recruit people with useful skills, particularly farmers and craftsmen. Between 1865 and 1915 the colony was reinforced by about 3,000 settlers from Wales and the United States. Finding that the land was barren unless irrigated, they began work on the network of irrigation channels which can still be seen. Early settlers were allocated 100 hectares of land, but by 1885 all irrigable land had been allocated and the settlement began to

expand westwards along the valley.

The success of the colony was partly due to the creation of their own Cooperative Society, which sold their produce and bought necessities in Buenos Aires. By 1900 the Society, which also acted as a bank, had 14 branches. Early settlers were organised into chapel-based communities of 200-300 people, which were largely self-governing and which organised social and cultural activities as well as operating an insurance scheme. Relations with the Tehueulches were initially very poor; in the early days the settlers agreed to kill any approaching Tehuelche to prevent news of the colony spreading, but this was not done and gradually relations improved.

Though the colony prospered after 1880, it was badly weakened by the Great Depression of the 1930s in which the Cooperative Society collapsed and many farmers lost their savings. While the aim of creating a 'little Wales beyond Wales' succeeded in that the Welsh language was kept alive for four generations, it is now dying out. Nevertheless, it is interesting that this desert land gave the Welsh language one of its most enduring classics, Dringo't Andes ('Climbing the Andes'), written by one of the earliest women settlers.

History

The Portuguese Fernão Magalhães (Magellan), then in the service of Spain, was the first to visit the coast of Patagonia in 1519. The first European to traverse Patagonia from south to north was the English sailor, Carder, who saved his life in a 1578 shipwreck in the Strait of Magellan, crossed the Strait, walked to the Río de la Plata and arrived in London nine years later.

For several centuries European attempts to settle along the coast were deterred by isolation, lack of food and water and the harsh climate as well as the fierce resistance of the indigenous peoples, but these were almost entirely wiped out in the 'Campaign of the Wilderness' 1879-1883. Before this there had been a long established European colony at Carmen de Patagones; it shipped salt to Buenos Aires during the colonial period. There had also been a settlement of Welsh people in the Chubut Valley since 1865. After the Campaign of the Wilderness colonization was rapid, the Welsh, Scots and English taking a great part. Chilean sheep farmers from Punta Arenas moved north along the depression at the foot of the Andes, eastwards into Santa Cruz.

The Battle of Carmen de Patagones

The church in Carmen de Patagones displays two Brazilian flags, seized in 1827 in one of the more unusual skirmishes of the early independence period. During the 1820s the Río Negro was used as a base by privateers who attacked shipping along the Brazilian coast. A Brazilian fleet of four ships entered the port to attack two privateers sheltering there. Fired on from above by guns on Punta Redondo, two Brazilian vessels foundered on the sandbanks of the Río Negro. The attackers landed 400 men to seize the guns but local forces, led by Captain Bynon, a Welshman, seized the Brazilian ships, preventing the attackers' escape. A total of 627 Brazilians were taken prisoner. A monument on Cerro Caballada, a hill east of the town, commemorates the 'victory'.

Services

In summer hotel prices are very high especially in Calafate. During Argentine summer holidays (January to February) getting a hotel room in Calafate can be very difficult. Note that ACA establishments, which charge the same prices all over Argentina, are a bargain in Patagonia, where all other accommodation is expensive. As very few hotels and restaurants have air conditioning or even fans, it can get uncomfortably hot in January. Camping is increasingly popular. Many hotels are closed between early April and mid November and many bus services do not operate in this period. Travellers' cheques are hard to change throughout Patagonia.

Routes

The main road south, Route 3, runs near the coast to Río Gallegos and then enters Chile and crosses the Magellan Straits to Tierra del Fuego by the car ferry at Primera Angostura: it has fairly regular traffic and adequate services. The alternative route, Route 40, runs further west, zigzagging across the moors; it is lonely and is good in parts, poor in others (more details given below). There is hardly any traffic even between December and February, the tourist season. However, it is by far the more interesting road, with fine views of the Andes and plenty of wildlife; it also provides access to two national parks, the Parque Nacional Perito Moreno and the Parque Nacional Los Glaciares. Camping along this route is no problem, and there are good hotels at Perito Moreno and Calafate as well as more basic accommodation at Gobernador Gregores, Río Mayo and Río Turbio. Some of the best accommodation along Route 40 is in *estancias*.

Hitchhiking is generally difficult except on Route 3 in spring and summer; camping equipment is useful as long delays can be expected even in the tourist season.

Driving in Patagonia

Many of the roads are gravelled (*ripio*). The price of a good windscreen protector varies according to make of car, but can be US$50 in Buenos Aires. For a VW Kombi they are hard to find at a reasonable price. More primitive versions can be bought for much less – for example US$5 in San Julián, and probably elsewhere – or made from wire mesh, wood and string. The best types are the grid-type, or inflatable plastic ones which are made for some standard-type vehicles, the only disadvantage being some loss of visibility.

Drivers should look out for ruts and holes in the road: particularly bad sections are sometimes marked by signs warning '*zona de baches*'. Also look out for *guardaganados* (cattle grids) even on main highways. They are signed; cross them very slowly. Always carry plenty of fuel, as service stations may be as much as 300 km apart. Make sure you have plenty of warm clothing, and anti-freeze in your car. Fuel prices are much lower in Patagonia than in the rest of the country because no taxes are imposed (US$0.60 per litre *super*; US$0.50 per litre *normal*).

Northern Patagonia

Two major rivers, the Ríos Colorado and Negro, empty into the Atlantic. The northernmost of these, the Río Colorado, is the northern limit of Patagonia.

Carmen de Patagones and Viedma

These two towns lie opposite each other on the Río Negro, 30 km inland from the sea and some 250 km south of Bahía Blanca. They are connected by two bridges and a passenger ferry. Viedma, on the south bank, was founded as Mercedes de Patagonia in 1779, but was destroyed almost immediately by floods, after which Carmen de Patagones was founded on higher ground on the north bank. Capital of Río Negro province, Viedma was destroyed again by floods in 1899.

Colour map 5, grid A5
Viedma:
population 40,000;
phone code 02920
Carmen de Patagones:
population 16,000;
phone code 02920

Viedma To the west of the main square, Plaza Alsina, is the **cathedral**, built by the Salesians in 1912. The former convent, next door, dating from 1887 is now a cultural centre housing the **Museo del Agua y del Suelo** and the **Museo Cardenal Cagliero**, which has ecclesiastical artefacts. Two blocks east, on the Plaza San Martín, are the French-style **Casa de Gobierno** (1926) and, opposite, the **Museo Gobernador Tello**, with displays on local history. The **Mercado Artesenal**, at Sarmiento 347, is worth a visit and there is an attractive treelined **Costanera** (riverside walk) with sailing clubs. Catamaran trips can be taken along the river.

Sights
Swimming is recommended on the southern side, where the shore is shady

Carmen de Patagones The town centre, just east of the river, lies around the Plaza 7 de Mayo. West of the plaza is the **Iglesia del Carmen**, built by the Salesians in 1880. Behind it is the **Torre del Fuerte**, the tower of the stone fortress built in 1780 against Indian attacks. The **Casa de la Tahona**, one block south of the Plaza, is a disused 18th-century flour mill, now housing the Casa de la Cultura. Another late colonial building, **La Carlota**, stands one block east of La Tahona. Near the river bank at Viema y Baraja, is the **Museo Histórico Regional**, containing displays on the town's history. ■ *Mon-Fri 0900-1200, 1900-2100, Sun 1900-2100*. Nearby are the **Cuevas Maragatas**, the caves in which the first colonists lived.

At **El Cóndor**, 30 km south, there is a beautiful beach. The *faro* (lighthouse) is the oldest in the country, dating from 1887. Facilities include hotel which opens from January to February, restaurants and shops, free camping on beach 2 km south. ■ *3 buses a day in summer*. At **Playa Bonita**, 12 km further south, there is good fishing. **Punta Bermeja**, 60 km south, is the site of a sealion colony covering 200 ha and visited by some 2,500 sealions in summer. ■ *Daily bus in summer; hitching easy in summer*.

Excursions

Patagonia

Sleeping & eating

Unless otherwise stated all services are in Viedma

B *Austral*, Villarino 292, T422019. Recommended, modern. *Viedma*, Zatti y Urquiza, T425481. **C** *Peumayen*, Buenos Aires 334, T425243. *Nigar*, Mitre 490, T422833. *Res Río Mar*, Rivadavia y Santa Rosa, T424188. **Carmen de Patagones** *Patagones*, Yrigoyen y Comodoro Rivadavia, T461495. *Reggiani*, Bynnon 420, T461389. **Camping** Good municipal campsite near the river, US$14 per tent plus US$4 per person, all facilities including hot showers, but can be noisy at weekends. *Restaurant Munich*, Buenos Aires 150, open late.

Transport

Air Aeropuerto Gobernador Castelo, 5 km south. To Comodoro Rivadavia, *Austral* (the city is also served by *LADE*). **Bus** Terminal at C A Zatti y Lavalle about 6 blocks from main plaza. To/from **Buenos Aires** US$45, *La Estrella*r air conditioning, *Cóndor*. To **San Antonio Oeste**, US$7.50. **Train** To Bariloche, Wed and Sat, 16 hrs, US$41 pullman, via San Antonio Oeste.

Directory

Banks Travel agency at Namuncurá 78, exchanges Amex cheques. **Tourist offices** Belgrano 544, 9th floor.

San Antonio Oeste

Phone code: 02934
Colour map 5, grid A5
Population: 11,000

Situated almost 180 km further west, San Antonio Oeste lies on a peninsula in the Bahía San Antonio. **San Antonio Este**, a modern port on the eastern side, is the most important fruit exporting port in the country. The Bahía San Antonio is a nature reserve, protecting large numbers of migratory birds.

Excursions include a trip to **Las Grutas**, 17 km south, which is a small, popular seaside resort, developed in the 1960s with good safe beach and seafood restaurants. The caves themselves are not really worth visiting. The whole resort closes down in mid-March and retires to Buenos Aires.

Sleeping **B** *Kandava*, Sarmiento 240, T421430, hot water, good. **C** *Golfo Azul*, simple. **C** *Iberia*, Sarmiento 241, without breakfast, small rooms, but recommended. **D** *Betty*, Islas Malvinas 1410, T422370. *ACA* has a **Unidad Turística**, T497095. With 6-bedrooms, no restaurant. **C** *Tour du Golfe*, Bariloche y Sierra Grande, 3 bedrooms, cooking facilities. **Camping** Many good camping sites, eg *La Entrada*, US$5 per tent, on edge of town above beach, *AMVI*, clean, near beach.

Viedma & Carmen de Patagones centre

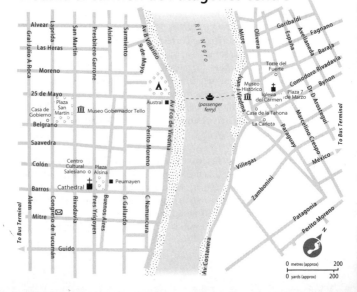

Transport Bus From San Antonio hrly US$1.30. North to **Bahía Blanca** and south to **Río Gallegos** and **Punta Arenas** by *Transportes Patagónicos*; to **Viedma** 0700 daily, US$7.50; to **Puerto Madryn** and **Trelew**, Don Otto, 0200 and 1530, 4 hrs, US$20; to **Buenos Aires**, US$46 via Bahía Blanca, frequent. **Train** Lines east to **Viedma** and west to **Bariloche**. Services: Wed and Sat evening to Bariloche, Wed and Sat 0600 to Viedma.

North From San Antonio Oeste a road runs north 91 km through bush country providing fodder for a few cattle, with a view to the west of the Salinas del Gualicho (salt flats), before joining Route 250 which runs northwest to meet the Zapala-Bahía Blanca highway (Route 22) at Choele Choel, 178 km north of San Antonio Oeste (see page 162). **Routes**

South Route 3 runs south to Puerto Madryn. At Km 123 is **Sierra Grande**, a former iron ore mining town; the mines can be visited with local guides. Drivers should note that Sierra Grande is the northernmost location where cheap fuel can be found.

Sleeping In Sierra Grande *La Posada*, Calle 2, No 170, T481068. *La Terminal*, Calle 2, No 240, T481250. **Camping** Behind ACA garage which has café, no facilities but free hot showers at YPF garage.

Puerto Madryn and Peninsula Valdés

Puerto Madryn

Puerto Madryn is a port on a wide bay known as Golfo Nuevo. A popular tourist centre, the town is a centre for visits to coastal nature reserves at Punta Loma and Península Valdés. Skin-diving and other outdoor activities are popular.

Phone code: 02965
Colour map 5, grid B5
Population: 60,000
250 km S of San Antonio Oeste

The site of the first Welsh landing in 1865, Puerto Madryn was founded in 1886 and named after the Welsh home of the colonist, Jones Parry. The town has a giant alumina plant. ■ *Visits, Mon 1430, arranged at the tourist office.* It also has fish processing plants. The **Museo de Ciencias Naturales y Oceanográfico**, Domecq García y J Menéndez, has displays on local flora and wildlife. Informative and worth a visit. ■ *Tue-Fri 0900-1200, 1630-2030, Sat/Sun 1630-2030 entry US$2.*

There are various excursions. **Punta Loma** is a sealion reserve, 15 km southeast it is open during daylight hours and best visited at low tide. December and January are the best months. ■ *Information and video. US$5 (free with ticket to Península Valdés). Access is via the coastal road from town; allow 1½ hrs by bike; taxi US$20.* **Playa El Doradillo**, 16 km northeast, is a long beach, excellent during the season for whale-watching. ■ *Getting there: Taxi US$20.* For the nature reserves on the **Peninsula Valdés**, see below.

L *Península Valdés*, Roca 155, T471292, F452584, www.hotel-peninsula-valdes.com, modern, very good, highly recommended. Sauna, gym. **AL** *Playa*, Roca 187, T451446, playahotel@playahotel.com.ar Large, modern, many rooms are small and overpriced, ask for recently refurbished rooms. **AL** *Villa Pirén*, Roca 439, T/F456272, piren@internet.siscotel.com New, very good rooms and apartments, gym, sauna, ask for room with a view. **AB** *Costanera*, Brown 759, T453000, modern, good. **A** *Bahía Nueva*, Roca 67, T/F451677, www.bahianueva.com.ar Very comfortable, bar, gardens, English spoken, recommended. **A** *Hostal del Rey*, Brown 681, T/F471093. Run down. **B** *La Posta*, Roca 33, T472422. Small, good value. **AL** *Tolosa*, Roque Sáenz Peña 253, **Sleeping**
Often full in summer, when prices rise; make bookings early; apartments are a convenient option (see below)

T471850, F451141, tolosa@hoteltolosa.com.ar Large, modern, standard rooms are small. **A** *Aguas Mansas*, José Hernández 51, T456626, T/F473103, amansas@hotel net.com.ar Modern, pool. **AB** *El Cid*, 25 de Mayo 850, T/F471416, hotelcid@info via.com.ar Recently refurbished, good rooms. **B** *La Posada de Madryn*, Mathews 2951, T/F474087, hotel@la-posada.com.ar On the southern outskirts, small, quiet, good value, English and French spoken. Recommended. **B** *Muelle Viejo*, Yrigoyen 38, T471284, good room. *Del Centro*, 28 de Julio 149, T473742, old fashioned, recently refurbished, beautiful patio. **C** *Anclamar*, 25 de Mayo 874, T451509, clean, basic. **B** *Hipocampo*, Vesta 33, T472766, T/F473605, small, helpful, near the beach. **B** *Manolo´s*, Roca 763, T472390, small. **C** *Vaskonia*, 25 de Mayo 43, T472581, old fashioned, central, basic, clean. **B** *Petit*, Alvear 845, T451460, F456428, respetit@info via.com.ar Small, good value. **AB** Sra Fernández Duque, Roberts 78, T/F451643,duquealq@infovia.com.ar Apartments and small houses for day rental, in southern residential area, sleep 4, fully equipped, English spoken, highly recommended. **B** *Marina*, Roca 7, T/F454915, teokou@infovia.com.ar; small, good apartments for up to 5 people. **B/C** *Santa Rita*, Gob Maiz 370, T471050, kitchen facilities, helpful, often recommended. **D/E** per person *Puerto Madryn Hostel*, 25 de Mayo 1136, T/F474426, hi-pm@satlink.com.ar/madryn@ hostels.org.ar Hostelling International, modern house with nice garden, laundry and kitchen facilities, rooms for 2 and 4 people, good, bike rental, English and French spoken, information. **E** per person *Huefur*, Mitre 798, T453224, huefur@ssdnet.com.ar, dormitories for 12 people, small rooms for 2, 4, 6 people, laundry and kitchen facilities, English spoken, access to internet.

Camping out can be interesting as you can watch foxes, armadillos, skunks & rheas roaming around in the evening

Camping *ACA*, 3.5 km south of town centre (at Punta Cuevas), T452952, open Sept-Apr, hot showers, café, restaurant (not expensive), shop, no kitchen facilities, shady trees, close to the sea. Many people camp on the beach. 2 municipal sites: 1 at Ribera Sur, 1 km before ACA site on same road along beach (gives student discount). All facilities, very crowded, US$3 per person and US$2 per tent for 1st day. Also room with bunkbeds, **F** per person. Bus from town stops 100 m before entrance. The other is north of town at Barrio Brown.

Eating *Don Jorge*, Roque Sáenz Peña y Mitre, parrilla, pasta. Recommended. *El Náutico*, Roca 790, good food, especially fish. *Paris*, Roca 672, good. *Roselli*, Roca y Roque Sáenz Peña, good pizzas. *El Chalet*, Humphreys 123, European cuisine, small, cosy, English, German and Italian spoken; *El Barco*, at Punta Cuevas, south of town, seafood, splendid seaview. *Plácido*, Roca 506, seafood, nice. *Adesso*, 25 de Mayo y 9 de Julio, pizza and pasta. *Yoaquina*, on the beach, south of centre, nice atmosphere. *Nola*, Roca 485. *Como en Casa*, España 187, T455850, take away. *Halloween*, Roca 1355, T450909, take away, pizza and empanadas. *Havanna*, Roca y 9 de Julio, café and *alfajores*. *Café de la Ciudad*, 25 de Mayo y 28 de Julio, café, very popular. *Barbarians*, 25 de Mayo y 28 de Julio, good coffee.

Entertainment **Nightclubs** *El Jardín*, Mitre y Sarmiento. *Salsa Discobar*, Brown y 3° Rotonda. *El Rancho*, Brown y 4° Rotonda, American music, small, entry US$10. **Cinema** Auditorium 28 de Julio 129. **Pool** at Zar y 28 de Julio, old bar; **Casino,** Roca 636.

Sport Puerto Madryn is a **diving centre**. Tours for beginners about US$50 per person, ask at *Safari Submarino*, Mitre 80, T474110; *Abismo*, Roca 550, T451483; *Ocean Divers*, Brown (second roundabout); advanced courses (PADI) US$300, and courses on video, photography and underwater communication; windsurf boards, kayaks, jet ski, sailing boats for hire, ask at *Na Praia*, *Golfo Azul*, or *Cucamonga* (on the beach, south of centre); **fishing** at Golfo San José (from US$60 per person), Jorge Schmidt, T451511; Peke Sosa, T471291; sandboard, on the nearby dunes, Pablo Neme, T471475. **Horseriding**: *El Moro*, T474188; *El Recuerdo*, T471126.

MAG, Roca 1082, handicrafts, souvenirs, 10% discount for Hostelling International **Shopping**
card holders; *Re Creo*, Roque Sáenz Peña 101, maps and books of regional interest in
Spanish, also Internet access; chocolates and Welsh cakes, at *Tia Beryl*, 28 de Julio 149;
for sailors, *Nautifot*, Roca 249.

Several agencies do tours to the Valdés Peninsula, all are for 12 hrs, see below. Prices **Tour operators**
are usually similar but shop around. Note that some agencies run larger buses than
others and that return distances of some tour destinations are high: Peninsula Valdés
380 km, Punta Tombo 400 km, Ameghino Dam 400 km. The last 2 are better from
Trelew as they often involve 'sight-seeing' in the Chubut valley and a lot of time is
spent travelling.Excursions to Península Valdés: *Argentina Visión*, Roca 536, T451427,
F451108, arvision@arvisión.com.ar offers a tour (including boat trip and entrance fee
to reserve) for US$60 per person; *Mar y Valle*, Roca 297, T450872, US$35 per person
for a day excursion including whale watching; try also at *Cuyun Co*, Roca 165,
T451845, cuyunco@satlink For whale watching (only from Puerto Pirámide), *Tito
Botazzi*, Mitre 80, T/F474110. *Jorge Schmidt*, T451511. Other excursions: for walks, led
by biologists, to nearby coast, associated with 4x4 circuits, *Argentina Visión*, address
above. *Pablo Neme*, Humphreys 85, T471475 offers bike and tour to Cerro Avanzado
for US$15 per person. *XTMountain Bike*, Roca 742, T472232, offers tour to Península
Valdés for US$35 per person (group of 6). 4x4 vehicles. *Hydrosport*, Muelle Viejo,
T495065 offers short boat trips for US$20 per person. *Ibarra*, T451991, offers a half an
hour flight over the bay on an ultralight plane (US$50); for a flight on a Cessna 172, call
Karina Kees, T15671790. For a day at a Patagonian estancia, contact *Estancia San
Guillermo*, T473535 (US$20 per person, lunch included). *Estancia Rincón Chico*,
T471386/471733; *Agroturismo El Deseado*, T456030, cuyunco@satlink.com

Puerto Madryn

■ Sleeping	4 Hostal del Rey	8 Península Valdés
1 Bahía Nueva	5 La Posta	9 Tolosa
2 Costanera	6 Marina	10 Vaskonia
3 Del Centro	7 Muelle Viejo	11 Villa Pirén

N
Not to scale

Patagonia

Transport **Local Car hire** *MAG*, Roca 1082, T473491, from US$44 a day; *Localiza*, Roca 536, T456300; *Rent a Car*, Roca 277, T450295. **Cycle hire** *Future Bike*, 25 de Mayo y Belgrano, T15665108, US$10 per day; *Na praia*, on the beach, US$6 per hr, US$10 per 3 hrs; also try Hostelling International, 25 de Mayo 1136, US$8 per half a day, for Hostelling members; US$10 per half a day for non members. **Taxi** outside bus terminal, T452966/474177 charges US$20 to Punta Loma Reserve, or Playa El Doradillo; US$50 to Puerto Pirámide, US$140 to Península Valdés or Punta Tombo, and US$45 to Trelew airport.

Long distance Air Puerto Madryn Airport, 10 km west of centre, reached by taxi or check at *Dinar*. Only *LADE* and Dinar operate from here. Daily flights to Buenos Aires and Comodoro Rivadavia with Dinar. More flights from Trelew airport, 7 km north of Trelew. Buses to Trelew stop at entrance to airport if asked. *Aerolíneas Argentinas* and *LAPA* operate from Trelew airport and run buses there. Taxi US$45.

Bus New terminal at Irigoyen y San Martín (behind the old railway station). To **Buenos Aires**, US$40-56, several companies. To **Comodoro Rivadavia**, 6-7 hrs, US$16-21, *El Pingüino, TUS, Andesmar, TAC, El Cóndor, Don Otto*. To **Río Gallegos**, 18 hrs; US$40-55, *El Pingüino* (connecting to El Calafate, Río Turbio, Punta Arenas, Puerto Natales), *Andesmar, TAC, Don Otto*. To **Córdoba**, 18-20 hrs, US$39-67, *TUS, El Pingüino, Andesmar*; to **Trelew**, 1 hr, every hr, US$3.70 with *28 de Julio*, US$4.30 with *Mar y Valle*. To **Puerto Pirámide**, 1 hr, US$6.50, on Thu and Sun, *Mar y Valle*; to **Esquel**, 9 hrs; US$31 daily except Wed, *Mar y Valle*; to **Bariloche**, 15 hrs, US$46, daily, except Weds, *Mar y Valle*. **Companies** *Andesmar*, T473764. *El Cóndor*, T471125. *Don Otto*, T451675. *El Pingüino*, T456256. *TUS*, T451962. *28 de Julio/Mar y Valle*, T472056. *Que Bus*, T455805.

Hitching For hitching north, try on the industrial estate road, or take a Trelew bus to the main highway then walk 3 km to the service station/truck stop. With luck it is possible to get to Bahía Blanca in 1 day. To hitch south try at petrol stations on Calle Gales. To hitch to Península Valdés (very difficult), try at the petrol station on route 1 (take Domecq García northwards).

Directory **Airline offices** *Dinar*, Roca 165, T451845. *LADE*, Roca 117, T451256. *Aerolíneas Argentinas* and *LAPA*, Roca 303, T451048. **Banks** *Banco Nación*, 9 de Julio 117. For TC's and US dollars, *Banco del Chubut*, 25 de Mayo 154 and *Banco Almafuerte*, Roque Sáenz Peña 25 y 25 de Mayo, both accept cash only. **Communications** Post Office, Belgrano y Maiz, 0900-1200, 1500-1900. **Telephone**, many *locutorios* in the centre. **Internet** *Madryn Computación*, Roca 31, Mon-Sat 0800-2200

Northeast Chubut

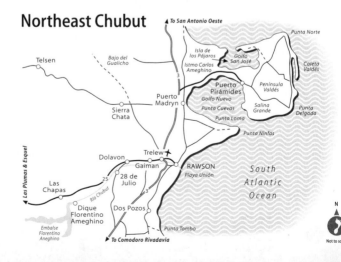

▲ *To San Antonio Oeste*

Punta Norte

Telsen

Bajo del Gualicho

Isla de los Pájaros

Golfo San José

Istmo Carlos Ameghino

Caleta Valdés

Sierra Chata

Puerto Madryn

Puerto Pirámides

Golfo Nuevo

Península Valdés

Salina Grande

Punta Delgada

Punta Cuevas

Punta Loma

Punta Ninfas

S o u t h

A t l a n t i c

O c e a n

Las Plumas & Esquel

Dolavon

Trelew

Gaiman

RAWSON

Playa Unión

28 de Julio

Las Chapas

Río Chubut

Dique Florentino Ameghino

Dos Pozos

Embalse Florentino Aneghino

Punta Tombo

▲ *To Comodoro Rivadavia*

N

Not to scale

(US$6 per hr). *Telecom*, 28 de Julio 293 (opposite main square). *Arnet*, Marcos Zar 125, Mon-Sat 0900-2100. *Re Creo*, Roque Sáenz Peña 101. **Laundry** *Laverap*, 25 de Mayo 529, 0800-2000. Recommended. **Medical services** For emergencies call 107 or 451240. **Tourist office** Roca 223, T452148, T/F453504, sectur@madryn.gov.ar Mon-Fri 0700-2100, Sat, Sun & Bank Holidays 0830-2030 (everyday 0700-0100, in summer); has a book for messages, very friendly.

Peninsula Valdés

The Peninsula Valdés, declared a World Heritage Site by UNESCO in 1999, is connected to the mainland by a narrow isthmus, the Istmo Carlos Ameghino. This separates the Golfo San José to the north from the Golfo Nuevo to the south. At the heart of the peninsula are large saltflats, one of which, Salina Grande, is 42 m below sea level. Though the peninsula is private property, it is a nature reserve and its coastline is one of the main centres of marine life in Argentina. The beach along the entire coast is out of bounds and this is strictly enforced.

There is an interesting visitor centre at the entrance to the reserve on the isthmus, some 79 km east of Puerto Madryn. A conservation officer is stationed here. ■ *Entry: foreigners US$10, Argentines US$45, check for reductions with ISIC card; tickets are also valid for Punta Loma.*

Isla de los Pájaros, in the Golfo San José, 5 km from the entrace. Its seabirds can only be viewed through fixed telescopes (at 400 m distance), except for recognized ornithologists who can get permission to visit. The best time to visit is between September and April.

These are the main marine wildlife colonies

Punta Norte, at the northern end of the peninsula, 97 km from the entrance, has elephant seals. The breeding season is late September to early October but during the first half of August the bull-seals arrive to claim their territory. They are best seen at low tide. There are also sea lions.

Caleta Valdés is 45 km south of Punta Norte. There are colonies of Magallanic penguins and elephant seals which can be seen at close quarters. The breeding season is from September to October. Killer whales have also been seen here.

Punta Delgada, at the southeastern end of the peninsula, 91 km from the entrance, is where elephant seals and other wildlife can be seen, though not penguins, from the high cliffs.

■ *Getting there: The peninsula is easily reached if you have your own transport, in fact the best way to see the wildlife is by car. See above for car hire; taking a taxi is worth considering if you can get a group together (taxi US$30 per person for the day). Hitching is very difficult, even at weekends in season. Peninsula roads are all gravel except the road from Puerto Madryn to Puerto Pirámide.*

Puerto Pirámide is the centre for visits to the peninsula. It is from here that whale-watching boat trips depart. Sailings are controlled by the Prefectura, according to weather and sea conditions. Some 5 km southwest of Puerto Pirámide there is a sea lion colony that is best visited from December to April.

Puerto Pirámide
Colour map 5, grid B5
107 km E of Puerto Madryn

Sleeping Puerto Pirámides A *The Paradise*, T495030, F495003, paradise@satlink.com, with restaurant. **AB** *ACA*, T495004. With restaurant and a service station with good café and shop. **AB** *Agua Marina*, T495008, orca@satlink.com Old school building, also excursions. **C** per person *Estancia El Sol*, T495007, with restaurant.

Patagonia

A Peninsula of penguins

Distinctive for their dark upper and white underparts, penguins are flightless but highly aquatic birds. Their wings have become reduced to short hard flippers which can propel them up to 40 km per hour when they porpoise through the water (leaping quickly over the surface to take breath). Their feet are webbed with strongly developed claws. They are essentially marine animals, which come ashore only to breed or moult. On land they are clumsy birds which walk with a distinctive slow waddle; when on snow or ice they can move much faster by tobogganing using their feet and flippers.

There are 17 species, recognised in six genera, found throughout the southern hemisphere from the Galapagos Islands to Antarctica. Fossil evidence from Antarctica indicates that early penguins included a species which stood almost 2 m high. Seven species breed in the Southern Ocean; these have particularly adapted feathers and a layer of blubber for insulation. The sexes are alike; they breed in large rookeries on land near the sea, or, in the case of Emperor Penguins, on pack-ice. Most species, except the larger ones, lay two eggs and both sexes share incubation. The chicks are fed by regurgitation of partly digested food from the parents. Penguins eat krill, fish, squid, and smaller organisms, which they capture by diving, for some species, to great depths. They are preyed upon at sea by Leopard seals and Killer whales; on land skuas, fulmars and mammals such as dogs take their eggs and chicks and sometimes seize the occasional adult.

The Magellan Penguin (Spheniscus magellanicus) is a medium sized (75 cm high) temperate penguin with conspicuous black and white bands on the face, neck and upper breast. Its range covers southern South America but vagrants have been found on South Georgia. In Argentina there are large rookeries on Peninsula Valdés and at Punta Tombo, Cabo Dos Bahías, Ría Deseado, Cabo Virgenes, Monte Leon and on the Isla de los Estados. Occasionally a vagrant of another species can be found at these sites. Magellan penguins excavate burrows, up to a metre long, where they nest. The young are paler and greyer blue with only a single indistinct breast-band and dirty grey cheeks. During summer parades of adults may be seen going to sea and returning with food for the chicks.

Magellan Penguins

C *El Médano*, T495032. **E** per person *El Español*, T495031, basic but pleasant, with restaurant. **Camping** Municipal site, T495000. Near the black sand beach, hot showers in evening only, dirty, busy, get there early to secure a place, shop; do not camp on the beach, people have been swept away by the incoming tide. Several cabins and apartments for hire (convenient for a group staying more than one night): eg **B** *El Cristal*, T495033, 4 bed cabañas, confitería, recommended. **Punta Delgada AL** *Faro*, T471910, in a lighthouse, half and full board, comfortable, excellent food, recommended. In **estancias** on the peninsula: *Bella Vista*, T471463, full board, excursions; *La Elena*, T424400, situated at Salinas Grandes, old Spanish settlement, full board, excursions.

Eating *Posada del Mar* for pastas. *The Paradise*, fish, seafood, helpful, recommended, good value food and beer, good atmosphere. *El Español*, bar (1904). Reasonably priced restaurant at Punta Norte for meals and snacks. Restaurant at Faro in Punta Delgada.

Shopping In summer there are several well-stocked shops, but if staying take sun and wind protection and drinking water. There is a shop which sells original Patagonian Indian work.

Tour operators Excursions are organized by tourist agencies in Puerto Madryn (addresses above). Full-day tours take in Puerto Pirámides (with whale-watching in season), plus some, but not necessarily all, of the other wildlife viewing points. Prices are US$25-30 per person plus the entry to the national park; boat trip to see whales US$20 extra. Most tour companies stay 50-60 mins on location. *Tito Bottazzi*, T495050, recommended. *Hydrosport* T495065, rents scuba equipment and boats, has a small restaurant, and organizes land and sea wildlife tours. Off season tours run when demand is sufficient, usually on Thu and Sun, departing at 0955 and returning at 1730. To avoid disappointment check all excursion dates and opening times in advance if possible. Tours do not run after wet weather in the low season.

Take drink with you, food too if you don't want to eat in the expensive restaurants. Binoculars are also a good idea

Tourist offices There is a small tourist office on the edge of Puerto Pirámide, useful information for hikes and driving tours.

Transport Bus Mar y Valle from Puerto Madryn, Thu, Sun, US$6.50 one way.

The Chubut Valley

The Río Chubut, 820 km long and one of the most important rivers in Patagonia, rises in the eastern foothills of the Andes and flows into the Atlantic at Bahía Engaño. The river has been dammed upstream from Trelew to form the Embalse Florentino Amenghino, which irrigates the lower valley and provides electricity. A paved road (Route 25) runs west through the valley to Esquel (see page 392).

The capital of Chubut Province, Rawson lies on the Río Chubut 7 km inland from its mouth. Founded in 1865, the first Welsh settlement in the valley, it is a town of official buildings. There are three small musuems: the **Museo de la Ciudad**, above the cinema on Jardín de las Americas, containing a collection of historical objects and old photos; the **Museo Regional Don Bosco**, Don Bosco y Sarmiento, with a varied collection including artefacts from Welsh settlement, free entrance; and the **Museo Policial**, Avenida Antártida, entry free. In the **Parque San Martín**, on the outskirts, there is a zoo and a reconstruction of important artefacts of local history including the vessel *Mimosa* which brought the first Welsh settlers in 1865. There is a small port, Puerto Rawson, 5 km down river, where, at the end of the day, a small but colourful fishing fleet arrives with the day's catch, worth seeing. There are boat trips to see **dolphins**, T15672002, US$20; nearby is **Playa Unión**, a beach with casino and many restaurants, busy in summer.

Rawson
Phone code: 02965
Colour map 5, grid B5
Population: 25,000

Patagonia

Sleeping and eating AB *Provincial*, Mitre 551, T/F481300. Renovated, comfortable, restaurant. **AB** *Punta León*, José Hernández y Juan de la Piedra (Playa Unión), T498041, with breakfast. Restaurants include *La Plaza*, Moreno y Maiz; *Provincial*, Mitre 551; and *Marcelino*, opposite the port at Puerto Rawson, seafood.

Transport Bus From main square: to **Trelew**, US$1, 28 de Julio or Rawson; to Playa Unión and Puerto Rawson, US$1.

Directory Tourist office 9 de Julio280, T481113/485272, www.patagoniachubutur.com.ar

Trelew

Phone code: 02965
Population: 90,000 *Pronounced 'TrelAYoo', and situated some 20 km west of Rawson, Trelew is the largest town in the valley. Founded in 1884, it was named in honour of Lewis Jones, an early settler. The town has a modern centre, but there are a few older buildings.*

Sights Here are some of the older buildings worth looking at. The beautifully decorated bar at the **Hotel Touring Club**, Fontana 240, dates from the early 20th century. The **Capilla Tabernacle** on Belgrano between San Martín and 25 de Mayo, is a red brick chapel dating from 1889. Nearby is another brick building from the same period, the San David Welsh Hall. On the road to Rawson, 3 km south is **Chapel Moriah**, the oldest standing Welsh chapel. Built in 1880, it has a simple interior and a cemetery with the graves of many original settlers, including the first white woman born in the Welsh colony. The **Museo Paleontológico Egidio Feruglio**, Fontana 140, is one of the best museums in Argentina. It houses a wide range of fossils and other items of paleontological and anthropological interest from Patagonia; book in advance for guided tours in English, German and Italian. ■ *Mon-Fri 1000-1800, Sat/Sun 1000-2000, US$6, students US$4 (ask for leaflet in English)*. The **Museo Regional**, Fontana y 9 de Julio, has displays on indigenous societies and on failed Spanish attempts at settlement and on Welsh colonization. Its interesting. ■ *Mon-Fri 0700-1300, 1400-2000, US$2.*

Excursions There is a lovely rock and sand beach with birds and other wildlife at **Playa Isla Escondida**, 70 km south with secluded camping but no facilities.

The **Embalse Florentino Ameghino** is an oasis of cool green trees which lies west along the Chubut valley. Recommended for a change of landscape and to the towns of the Chubut valley, see below.

The **Reserva Natural Punta Tombo** is a wildlife reserve 107 km south covering 210 ha. This is the largest breeding ground for Magallenic penguins in Patagonia: over 180,000 couples nest here every year. The wildlife is very varied: guanacos and rheas are visible on the way to the colony, where scavenger birds like chimangos, skuas and kelp gulls can be seen. Punta Tombo should be visited between September and March. In January and February the young take to the water while the reserve closes from late March. Check with the tourist office in Trelew that visits are permitted: when they are it is a fantastic experience. The best time to visit is early morning. ■ *Getting there: There are 2 routes to the reserve: 1 is by a well marked road which branches off Route 3, west of Dos Pozos (not shown on ACA map): driving time 2 hrs. The other is by a turning which branches off Route 1 (a ripio road between Trelew and Camarones). Park entrance US$5. Travel agencies in Trelew and Puerto Madryn run tours, spending 30 mins at the site. You can share a taxi from Trelew (US$110).*

Sleeping **L** *Rayentray*, San Martín 101, T434702, F435559, rcvtw@internet.siscotel.com With breakfast, large, modern, good value, some rooms small, heated pool and gym, sunbed and sauna (extra charge), restaurant, travel agency. **AL** *Libertador*, Rivadavia 31, T420220, hlibertador@infovia.com.ar With breakfast, well-located, modern, large, good rooms, restaurant only for guests. **A** *Centenario*, San Martín 150, T426111, T/F421524, centenario@infovia.com.ar With breakfast, modern, large, central, restaurant; **B** *Galicia*, 9 de Julio 214, T433802, castroab@infovia.com.ar With breakfast, recently refurbished, good, some rooms very small. **B** *Touring Club*, Fontana 240, T/F425790, htouring@internet.siscotel.com Breakfast extra, refurbished rooms in modern style, English spoken, large halls and recommended bar. **B** *City*, Rivadavia 254, T/F433951, With breakfast, central, good, overpriced. **B** *Provincia*, Fontana 625, T420944, breakfast extra, large, old fashioned, refurbished, some rooms small. **D** per person *Rivadavia*, Rivadavia 55, T434472, with breakfast, well-located. Recommended. **D** per person *Argentino*, Matthews 186, T436134, without breakfast, clean, basic, with private bathrooms, close to terminal. **C** *San Carlos*, Sarmiento 758, T421038, without breakfast, small, basic, clean, no kitchen facilities. **C/D** *Avenida*, Lewis Jones 49 (opposite museums), T434172, breakfast extra, run down, basic, dirty. **F** per person *Gimnasio Municipal* (Municipal Sports Centre), Mitre 37, T420160, only for groups of 4 or more people, showers.

Camping   Raul G Lema, Rucalhue 964, T430208, offers free camping space in garden and local information, speaks English (taxi US$5 or ask at Estrella del Sur Turismo).

Eating

Casa Tia supermarket, Soberanía Nacional y Belgrano 1st floor, open until midnight, good food, cheap, big portions, recommended; *Sugar*, 25 de Mayo 247, main square, nice atmosphere; *Centenario*, San Martín 150, basic meals, cheap; *Lo de Halda*, Belgrano 455, small, warm atmosphere; *Rancho Aparte*, Fontana 236, lunch: *tenedor libre*; *El Quijote*, 25 de Mayo 90; *La Casona*, Sarmiento 331; *La Casa de Juan*, Moreno 360, cosy, good pizzas; on the outskirts, try *La Quesería*, Chacra 85 N (off route 7 to Rawson), local dairy products, variety of cheeses, open lunchtime only; *El Viejo Molino*, Gales y Mitre, café, nicely refurbished old mill. Café at *Hotel Touring Club*, popular, good coffee.

Local holidays

28 Jul, *Founding of Chubut*; 13 Dec, *Petroleum Day*.

Shopping

Souvenirs at *El Rincón del Pingüino*, San Martín 127; chocolates at Belgrano 247, and at Don Bosco 23; for camping equipment, *Camping Sur*, Pellegrini 389.

Tour operators

Agencies run tours to Punta Tombo US$30 (plus US$10 entry), Chubut Valley half-day US$15, Embalse Florentino Ameghino US$30. Tours to Península Valdés are best done from Puerto Madryn. *Patagonia Grandes Espacios* (Sur Turismo), Belgrano 330, T434081, surrel@internet.siscotel.com Good excursions; *Nievemar Tours*, Italia 20, T434114, nievemar@internet.siscotel. com and others.

Transport

Local Car hire   Rent a Car San Martín 129, T420898; *AVIS*, Paraguay 105, T434634; *Localiza*, San Martín 88, T435344; *Dollar*, at the airport.

Long distance Air   Airport, on Route 3, 5 km north of centre, taxi US$6-8. Local buses to/from Puerto Madryn stop at the airport entrance if asked, (US$3.70-4.30); turning is 10 mins walk (not recommended at night). *Lapa* and *Aerolíneas Argentinas* have flights to/from **Buenos Aires**, **Río Gallegos** and **Ushuaia**. *Aerolíneas Argentinas* also to **Río Grande**; *Lapa* (and *TAN*) also to **Comodoro Rivadavia**. **Bus** Terminal 1 km north of centre (opposite Plaza Centenario), bus US$0.70, taxi US$2. To **Buenos Aires**, 19-21 hrs; US$42-65, *TAC, El Pingüino, Que Bus, Don Otto, El Cóndor*; to **Comodoro Rivadavia**, 4-5 hrs, US$16, *TAC, El Pingüino, Andesmar, TUS, Transportadora Patagónica, Don Otto, El Cóndor*; to **Río Gallegos**, 15-17 hrs; US$48-53, *TAC, El Pingüino* (connecting

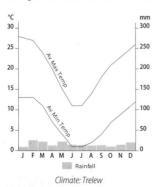

°C / mm scale chart

Av Max Temp

Av Min Temp

J F M A M J J A S O N D
Rainfall

Climate: Trelew

to El Calafate, Río Turbio, Puerto Natales, Punta Arenas), *Andesmar, Transportadora Patagónica*; to **Rawson**, 30 mins; US$1, hrly; to **Gaiman**, (30 mins; US$1.40) and **Dolavon** (1 hr; US$2.60) hrly, *28 de Julio*; to **Puerto Madryn**, 1 hr, *28 de Julio*, hrly US$3.70, also *Mar y Valle*, US$4.30; to **Esquel**, 8 hrs; US$25-28, *Mar y Valle, Empresa Chubut, Don Otto*; to **Puerto Pirámide**, 2½ hrs; US$10. Thu and Sun, *Mar y Valle*. **Companies** Andesmar, T433535; TUS, T421343; El Pingüino, T427400; Don Otto, T432434; TAC, T431452; El Cóndor, T433748; 28 de Julio/Mar y Valle, T432429; Que Bus, T422760; El Ñandú, T427499. **Hitching** South: take the Rawson bus to the fly-over 5 km out of town; there is a junction north of town for Puerto Madryn traffic.

Directory **Airline offices** *Aerolíneas Argentinas*, 25 de Mayo 33, T420170, 420060; *LADE*, Fontana 227, T435740; *LAPA*, Belgrano 285, T423438, 421459; *TAN*, Urquiza 824, T428662. **Banks** open Mon-Fri 0830-1300. *Lloyds Bank*, 9 de Julio 102; *Banco Nación*, Fontana y 25 de Mayo; *Banco Francés*, Belgrano 272; *Banca Nazionale del Lavoro*, Belgrano 271; *La Caja*, Fontana y San Martín; *Sur Turismo*, Belgrano 326 for TC's. **Communications** Post Office 25 de Mayo y Mitre. **Telephone** *Telefónica* Roca y Tucumán, and several *locutorios* in the centre. **Internet** *Telefónica*] 25 de Mayo 219 (0730-0100); San Martín y Rivadavia, (both charge US$5 per hr). **Tourist office** San Martín y Mitre, T420139, eturismotw@arnet.com.ar Mon-Sat 0800-2000 (0730-2100 in summer), friendly.

Trelew

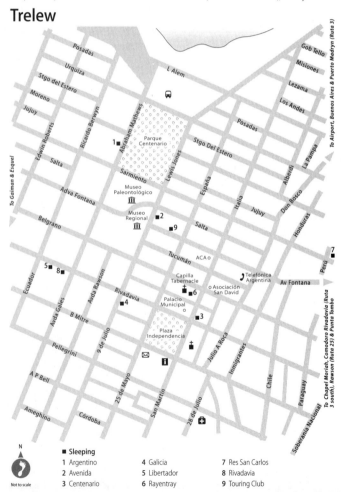

N Not to scale

■ Sleeping

1 Argentino	4 Galicia	7 Res San Carlos
2 Avenida	5 Libertador	8 Rivadavia
3 Centenario	6 Rayentray	9 Touring Club

Patagonia

Welsh chapels in the Chubut

One of the main remnants of the Welsh influence in this area are the 15 chapels which scatter the lower Chubut. The largest, in Gaiman, holds about 450 people, a large congregation for what was then a very small town. The Salón San

David in Trelew was intended as a replica of the church in the town of St David's in South Wales. Almost all are of brick though one, Capilla Salem, 5 km south of Gaiman, was built of wood covered entirely with corrugated zinc.

West of Trelew

Route 25 runs west along the northern edge of the irrigated floodplain of the Río Chubut, past Gaiman and Dolavon, before continuing through attractive scenery to Esquel and Trevelin.

Gaiman is a pretty town of well-built brick houses. Among the older buildings in the town are the first house (1874), Tello y Evans, open daily 1400-1900, US$1; the **old railway station** (1909), which houses the regional museum (see below); the **old Hotel** (1899), Tello y 9 de Julio and the **Ty Nain tea room** (1890), Yrigoyen 283 (see below). On the south side of the river there are two old chapels, the **Capilla Bethel** (1913) and the **Capilla Vieja** (1888). **El Desafío**, two blocks west of plaza, is a private theme-park, started in 1980 by Joaquín Alonso. Made entirely of rubbish (drinks cans, bottles, piping and wire), it is a labyrinth of coloured plastic, glass and aluminium with mottos at every turn. ■ *Daily until 1800, US$5.*

Gaiman
Phone code: 02965
Colour map 5, grid B4
Population: 5,000
18 km W of Trelew

    Museo Histórico Regional Galés, Sarmiento y 28 de Julio, in the old railway station, (US$1), Tue-Sun 1500-1900, displays artefacts from the period of Welsh settlement; the curator Mrs Roberts is 'full of stories'.

    Parque Paleontológico Bryn Gwyn, on the Chubut river, 8 km south of town, entrance US$4, 1000-1800, to experience some fieldwork in paleonthology, associated with the Museo Paleontológico Feruglio in Trelew.

Sleeping **C** per person *Gwesty Tywi*, Jones 342, T491292, gwestywi@infovia.com.ar, **B** *Unelem*, Tello y 9 de Julio, T491663, unelem@arnet.com.ar, restaurant and tea room. **B** *Plas Y Coed*, Jones 123, T491133, with breakfast, also tea room; **Camping** *Los Doce Nogales*, close to Ty Te Caerdydd tea room, T15518030, showers.

Eating *Unelem*, Tello y 9 de Julio. *El Angel*, Jones 850. *Na Petko*, Brown 100, basic meals in an old house, beergarden. Welsh teas are served from about 1500 (US$10-12) by several Tea Rooms, including *Plas Y Coed*, Jones 123, oldest excellent tea 'and enough food for a week'. Marta Rees, the owner speaks English and is very knowledgeable about the area. Highly recommended. *Ty Gwyn*, 9 de Julio 111. Recommended. *Ty Nain*, Yrigoyen 283, frequented by tour buses, display of historical items. *Ty Te Caerdydd*, Finca 202, 2 km from town, very good. Most facilities are closed out of season.

Transport **Bus** To/from Trelew, 1/2 hrs; US$1.40, 28 de Julio, hrly.

Founded in 1919, Dolavon is the most westerly Welsh settlement in the valley. The main street runs parallel to the irrigation canal built by the settlers; there is a chapel over the canal. The old flour mill at Maipú y Roca dates from 1927 and can be visited, US$1. The key is kept in the Municipalidad, Roca 188 (next to Banco Provincial del Chubut). **Sleeping** at the municipal campsite, 2 blocks

Dolavon
Phone code: 02965
Colour map 5, grid B4
Population: 2,700
38 km W of Trelew

Patagonia

Valley of the Martyrs

West of Las Plumas, Route 25 runs through the Valle de los Martires, named after three Welsh settlers, captured here in 1884 by the Indians and killed, while prospecting for gold. A fourth, John Evans, escaped thanks to the speed of his horse. Evans later settled in Trevelin, where there is a grave to the horse to which he owed his life.

north of the river, good facilities, free. Tea room, *Drayg Goch*, 28 de Julio 345.
■ *Getting there: Buses to/from Trelew, 1 hr, US$2.60, 28 de Julio, several a day.*

West of Dolavon At Km 113 a road branches south to the **Embalse Florentino Ameghino**. This reservoir stretches along some 80 km of the Chubut valley, covers 7,000 ha and irrigates 20,000 ha in the lower Chubut valley. Black-necked swans can be seen and there are watersports facilities and campsites. Excursions are organised by travel agencies in Trelew. ■ *Getting there: Buses from Trelew, 2 hrs, US$7, El Ñandu, Suns only.*

Route 25 continues west, crossing the Río Chubut at Las Plumas (Km 184) before running alongside it. There are towering rock formations in varied colours, particularly at **Los Altares**, Km 288, where there is an ACA Motel and bar. Some 5 km east of the small town of **Paso de Indios** a *ripio* road branches north, providing an alternative route to Esquel via **Paso del Sapo**. At **Tecka**, Km 508 (see page 400), Route 25 (later Route 62) meets Route 40, the Esquel-Gobernador Costa road.

Central Patagonia

Camarones
Phone code: 0297
Population: 800

Situated 275 km south of Trelew and 300 km north of Comodoro Rivadavia, Camarones is a fishing port on Bahía Camarones, reached by a 72 km paved road branching off Route 3. **Sleeping** at B *Kau I Keu Kenk*, Sarmiento y Roca, good food, recommended, owner runs trips to penguin colony. Two others, **C**, the one by the power station is not recommended. Campsite. ■ *Getting there: Buses, Don Otto, from Trelew, Mon and Fri, 2½ hrs, returns to Trelew same day 1600.*

Reserva Natural Cabo Dos Bahías
This reserve, 35 km southeast at the southern end of the bay and reached by a dirt road, covers 160 ha and protects a penguin colony of some 12,000 couples; there are also sea lions and guanacos. ■ *Entry US$5, open all year. Ask the park ranger in Camarones for a lift on Monday or Friday. Hitchhiking is difficult, but possible at weekends. No taxis available (private cars charge US$50-60, ask at Busca Vida).*

Comodoro Rivadavia

Phone code: 02967
Colour map 5, grid C4
Population: 158,000

The largest city in the province of Chubut, Comodoro Rivadavia is 387 km south of Trelew. Little visited by travellers, it is an important centre for the Argentine oil industry.

Sights
Comodoro Rivadavia was founded in 1901 as a port for the agricultural communities inland around Colonia Sarmiento, but its early development was limited by lack of water. Early settlers included Boer immigrants fleeing British rule in southern Africa. **Rada Tilly**, 12 km south, is a resort with a very good beach and restaurants. Sealions can be seen at low tide. ■ *Getting there: Buses Expreso Rada Tilly every 30 mins.* Excursions may be made to **Colonia Sarmiento** and the **Bosques Petrificados** (see below).

Patagonia

A *Austral*, Rivadavia 190, T472200, F472444. Noise from traffic but otherwise comfortable, reasonable restaurant. **AB** *Comodoro*, 9 de Julio 770, T472300. Overpriced, restaurant, nightclubs, car rental. **AB** *Res Azul*, Sarmiento 724, T467539. Comfortable, spotless. Recommended. **C** *Colón*, San Martín 341, T462283. Run down, but quiet and safe. **C** *Comercio*, Rivadavia 341, T4622341. Old fashioned, dirty, near bus terminal, hot showers. **C** *Hosp Belgrano*, Belgrano 546, T478439. Gloomy, clean, quiet. **C** *Hosp Praga*, España y Sarmiento, shower. **C** *Rada Tilly*, Piedrabuena, in Rada Tilly, T451032, modern. *Motel Astra*, southern access of Route 3, T425394. **Camping** Municipal site at Rada Tilly, hot and cold water. There is another, free, campsite at north end of beach, cold water only (watch out for clayslides when it rains).

Sleeping

La Rastra, Rivadavia 348, very good for *churrasco*, but not much else. *Pizzería El Nazareño*, San Martín y España, good. *Bom-Bife*, España 832, good food, inexpensive. Several *rotiserías*, much cheaper, on 400 block of Rivadavia, in municipal market.

Eating

28 Jul, *Founding of Chubut*; 13 Dec, *Petroleum Day*.

Local holidays

From here southward, prices begin to rise very rapidly, so stock up before reaching Río Gallegos (although bear in mind you are not allowed to take food into Chile).

Shopping

Puelche EVT, Rivadavia 527. *Richard Pentreath*, Mitre 952. *San Gabriel* and *Atlas* at San Martín 488 and 263, respectively. *Monitur*, 9 de Julio 948.*Aonikenk Viajes*, Rawson 1190, T4466768, offer tours to the petrified forests, US$75 per person, with 2 hrs at the site.

Tour operators

Local VW dealer Comercial Automotor, Rivadavia 380, recommended. VW concession: Av Irigoyen in Barrio Industrial, also recommended. **Car rental** Avis, 9 de Julio 687, T/F496382.

Transport

Long distance Air Airport, 9 km north. Bus No 6 to airport from bus terminal, hrly (45 mins), US$0.40. Taxi to airport, US$7. To **Buenos Aires**, *Lapa*, *Dinar* and *Aerolíneas Argentinas/Austral*. Major cities south of Córdoba and Mendoza are served by *Austral*, *Lapa*, *TAN*, *TAPSA* and *Andesmar*. *LADE* flies once a week (Wed) to Perito Moreno, Gobernador Gregores, Calafate, Río Gallegos, Río Grande, Ushuaia, and on Mon to Puerto Deseado, San Julián, Gob Gregores, Calafate, Río Turbio, Río Gallegos, Santa Cruz; once a week to Bariloche via Trelew and Viedma, or Trelew and Esquel, or via Esquel, El Maitén and El Bolsón; other services to Neuquén via the Lake District and to Trelew.

Patagonia

Comodoro Rivadavia centre

Only oil

Since the first discoveries of oil in the region, Comodoro Rivadavia's prosperity and growth have fluctuated with the prospects of the oil industry. The first major oil find in Argentina occurred just north of the town while drilling for water in 1907. Although in 1910 the government established an agency to drill for oil elsewhere in the region, international oil companies only became interested in Argentina after the First World War. Between 1919 and 1923 over 30 oil companies were registered in the country, most of them with capital from Europe or the United States. In 1922, in response to

this, President Hipólito Yrigoyen created Yacimientos Petroleros Fiscales, destined to become the most important company in oil exploration and extraction. Much of its success is usually attributed to its first director, Col Enrique Mosconi, who is remembered by the name given to the neighbourhood of Comodoro Rivadavia where the 1907 find occurred.

Today most of Argentina's oil production occurs in Patagonia, about 33% of it from wells in south and west of the Comodoro Rivadavia. A 1,770-km pipeline carries natural gas to Buenos Aires, and there is a petrochemical plant.

Bus Terminal conveniently located in centre; has luggage store, good *confitería* upstairs, lousy toilets, *remise* taxi booth, some kiosks. Services to **Buenos Aires** daily at 1200 and 2115, 32 hrs, US$108; to **Bariloche**, US$55 (*Don Otto* at 2150, Sun, Tue, Thu, stops at Sarmiento midnight, Esquel at 0600 and for 30 mins at El Bolsón at 0900, arrives 0600 at Bariloche); to **Esquel** (paved road) 8 hrs direct with *ETAP* and *Don Otto*. direct, Fri 1230, 10 hrs, via Río Mayo, Mon, Thu, 0100, 15½ hrs, to Río Mayo Tue, Thu, Sun, 1700 and 1900, 5½ hrs. In summer buses heading south usually arrive full; to **Río Gallegos**, *Don Otto* 2345 daily, *Pingüino*, 2100, and *Transportadores Patagónica* 2200 daily, 11 hrs, US$30; to **Puerto Madryn**, US$16-21 and **Trelew**, US$26, several compa-nies; to **Caleta Olivia**, *La Unión*, hrly, US$3.50; to **Sarmiento**, US$7, 2½ hrs at 0700, 1300, 1900; to **Mendoza**, daily at 0130, 20 hrs; to **Córdoba**, Tue, Fri, Sun, 1200, 33 hrs. **To Chile** To **Coyhaique**, *Angel Giobbi*, US$30, 12 hrs, 2 a week (Mon and Thu) 0100, Jun-Sep and 3 a week (Mon, Wed, Fri), 0100, Oct-May (weather permitting), also Turibus, Tue and Sat 0800.

Hitchhiking There is a truck stop at Astra, 20 km north on Route 3, where you can contact drivers whether heading north or south. Hitch out of the centre or take any bus going north. Expensive truckdrivers' restaurants along the road; buy food in supermarkets.

Directory **Airline offices** *Aerolíneas Argentinas/Austral*, 9 de Julio 870, T462191/462605. *Lapa* and *LADE*, Rivadavia 396, T472400. *TAN*, T477268. **Banks** *Lloyds Bank*, Rivadavia 266, Oct-Mar 0700-1300. Apr-Sept 1200-1800. No exchange transactions after 1000 in summer, 6% commission on TCs, pays US$ cash on TCs but minimum US$300. The *Banco de la Nación*, San Martín 108, has the best rates on US$ but does not change TCs. Amex agent is *Orbe Turismo Show*, San Martín 488, T429699, 5% commission for US$, does not change TCs. Several travel agencies also change money including *Roqueta Travel*, Rivadavia y Pellegrini, *Ceferino*, 9 de Julio 852, and *CRD Travel*, Moreno 844 (TCs accepted). **Communications** Post office San Martín y Moreno. **Consulates** *Belgium*, Rivadavia 283. *Chile*, Sarmiento 936. *Italy*, Belgrano 1053. **Tourist offices** Rivadavia y Pellegrini.

From Comodoro Rivadavia to Chile

Route 26 runs west, amid oil wells, from Comodoro Rivadavia towards the Chilean frontier and the Chilean towns of Coyhaique and Puerto Aisén.

Sarmiento lies on the Río Senguer just south of two great lakes, **Lago Musters** and **Lago Colhué Huapi**, both of which offer good fishing in summer. Founded in 1897 and formally known as Colonia Sarmiento, its early settlers were Welsh, Lithuanians and Boers. On the north side of the plaza is the **Museo Desiderio Torres**, with displays of Indian artefacts. ■ *Mon-Fri 0900-1400, Sat/Sun 1000-1400 summer, Mon-Fri 1330-1930 winter.* Excursions can be made to two areas of **petrified forest**: the **Bosque Petrificado José Ormachea**, 32 km south along a gravel road, entry US$10, and the **Bosque Petrificado Víctor Szlapelis**, some 40 km further southwest along the same road (follow signposts, road from Sarmiento in good condition). These forests, 60 million years old, of fallen araucaria trees nearly 3 m round and 15-20 m long, are a remarkable sight. There are rangers at both sites. The forests should be visited in summer as the winters are very cold. Taxi from Sarmiento US$39 (three passengers), including a one hour wait, for each extra hour, US$9. Hitching is difficult except in summer. Contact Sr Juan José Valero, the park ranger, Uruguay 43, T097-4898407 for guided tours, ask him about camping at the entrance(see also the *Monumento Natural Bosques Petrificados* below, page 434).

Colonia Sarmiento
Phone code: 0297
Colour map 5, grid C3
Population: 7,000
156 km W of Comodoro Rivadavia

Sleeping **B** *Hostería Los Lagos*, Roca y Alberdi, T493046. Good, heating, restaurant. **E** *Colón*, P Moreno 645, restaurant, cheap. **B** *Lago Musters*, P Moreno y Coronel, T493046. *San Martín*, San Martín y P Moreno, cheap, good restaurant. **D** *Ismar*, Patagonia 248, restaurant. In Dec-Mar you may be permitted to sleep in the Agricultural School (take sleeping bag) on the road to petrified forest, opposite the ACA petrol station. **Camping** Municipal site near Río Senguer, 2 km north of centre on Route 243, basic, no shower, US$3 for tent, US$1 per person.

Tourist office Av San Martín, casi Alberdi, T4898220, friendly, has map of town.

Around Comodoro Rivadavia

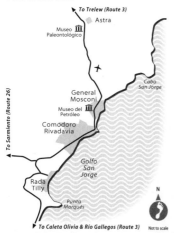

Transport Bus Overnight services to **Esquel** on Sun, Tue and Thu, take food for journey as cafés are expensive. To **Comodoro Rivadavia**, 0700, 1300, 1900. To **Chile**, Giobbi buses leave at 0200.

West and south of Colonia Sarmiento

Route 20 continues west and then northwest along the valley of the Río Senguer, before joining Route 40 which runs north to Esquel, 448 km, at the southern edge of the Lake District (see page 392). Hitching along this road is very difficult, even in summer. Route 22, branching off 72 km west of Sarmiento runs southwest, 54 km, to meet route 40 at Río Mayo.

Patagonia

Río Mayo
Phone code: 0297
Colour map 5, grid C2
Population: 2,600
Fuel available

Although Río Mayo is little more than a route centre, each November it is the site of the *Fiesta Nacional dela Esquila* (the National Sheep-shearing Competition). The area is so windy that windmills have been built to generate electricity. The small **Museo Escalada** is just off the plaza. If travelling south buy food here as it gets more expensive.

Sleeping C *Covadonga*, San Martín 575, T420014, very good. C *Hotel Pingüino*. C *A'Ayones*, T420044, modern, heating. **D** per person *San Martín*, San Martín y Perito Moreno, T420066, comedor. *Res Aka Ta*, San Martín 400, T420054. **Camping** Free site on northern outskirts near river.

Transport Bus *Giobbi* buses from Comodoro Rivadavia to Coyhaique, Chile, pass through Río Mayo at 0600 on Mon, Wed and Fri (Mon and Thu, Jun to Sep), US$14, 6 hrs, seats are scarce. To Esquel, Giobbi, 0600.

Frontier with Chile
There are 2 crossings W of Río Mayo

Coyhaique Alto is reached by a 133 km road (87 km *ripio*, then dirt) which branches off Route 40 about 7 km north of Río Mayo. On the Chilean side this road continues to Coyhaique, 50 km west of the frontier. See above under Comodoro Rivadavia for bus services on this route.

Chilean immigration At Coyhaique Alto, 6 km west of the frontier, open May-Aug 0800-2100, Sep-Apr 0700-2300.

It is wild but beautiful place (this route is better than that via Coyhaique Alto)

Paso Huemules is reached by a road which branches off Route 40, some 31 km south of Río Mayo and runs west 105 km via **Lago Blanco** (fuel), where there is a small *estancia* community, 30 km from the frontier. There is no hotel but the police are friendly and may permit camping at the police post. This road continues from **Balmaceda** on the Chilean side of the frontier to Coyhaique.

Chilean immigration Open May-Jul 0800-2100, Sep-Apr 0700-2100.

Route 40 from Río Mayo to Calafate

This stretch of Route 40 crosses one of the most uninhabited parts of Patagonia. Road conditions vary, depending on how recently each stretch was repaired. It is paved as far as Perito Moreno; south of there it is *ripio*, though it improves considerably after Las Horquetas. There is no public transport and very few other vehicles even in mid summer. Hitching along this road is virtually impossible. Super grade fuel is available in most places: it is important to carry extra, especially between Bajo Caracoles and Tres Lagos since the only source of fuel between them involves a 72-km detour to Gobernador Gregores (see page 431).

Perito Moreno
Phone code: 02963
Colour map 5, grid C2
Population: 3,000
137 km S of Río Mayo

Not to be confused with the famous glacier of the same name near El Calafate, nor with Parque Nacional Perito Moreno

Perito Moreno lies near the source of the Río Deseado. Southwest of the centre is the Laguna De Los Cisnes, where varied birdlife can be seen including flamingos and black-necked swans. The second largest lake in South America, **Lago Buenos Aires**, lies 25 km west, extending into Chile as Lago General Carrera and draining westwards into the Río Baker, one of the biggest rivers in Chile.

South of Perito Moreno is the crater of **Cerro Volcán**; after passing the Gendarmería on your right, take the first left (dirt road) at the three-road junction with Route 40. It is 12 km to the path to the crater – ask permission at the Estancia to continue. Hitching may be possible in summer. For the **Cueva de las Manos**, see below.

Patagonian Estancias

Estancias offer some of the best accommodation along Route 40 as well as a variety of activities. The architecture of Patagonian estancias is adpated to the climate and surroundings and is usually less luxurious than that of estancias on the pampas. Due to the climate most estancias receive guests only between October and April. Estancias in Santa Cruz province, including those along Route 40, maintain an information office in Buenos Aires which also arranges reservations (see page 118). Even in season booking ahead is advisable because of the long distances involved.

Sleeping **C** *Argentino*, San Martín 1386, dirty, no showers. **C** *Belgrano*, San Martín 1001, T42019. With shower, no heating, restaurant. Recommended. **D** *Austral*, San Martín 1327, T42042. **C** *Santa Cruz*, on Belgrano, heating, shared bath and hot water. **Estancia A** per person *Telken*, 30 km south on Route 40, T02963-432079, F02963-432373 (Buenos Aires 4797-7216), accommodation Oct-Apr, discounts for families with 2 children, breakfast included, other meals extra, horseriding, fishing, English and Dutch spoken, transport from Perito Moreno, camping. Recommended. **Camping** Good site 200 m east on road out of town, clean, hot showers. Parque Julio Roca near Laguna De Los Cisnes, T432121, sheltered, but dirty, US$5 per person, also cabañas, **D** per person sleep 6, basic, no sheets, clean. *Juan Carlos Ramos*, T432049, US$3 per person.

Eating *Pipach III*, next to *Hotel Austral*, good pizzas and *empanadas*.

Transport **Air** Airport 7 km east of town, try to hitch as there is only 1 taxi; *LADE* flies from Perito Moreno to **Río Gallegos** on Tue, check in well in advance. **Bus** To **Los Antiguos**, 2 a day, US$3; to **Comodoro Rivadavia**, 6 hrs, 1730, US$18. **Hitchhikers** To the south are warned that, especially outside the tourist season (Jan to mid-Feb), it is usually quicker to head for the coast at Caleta Olivia and go south from there than to take Route 40 via Gobernador Gregores and Piedrabuena.

Directory **Banks** US$ cash can be exchanged at **Banco de la Provincia de Santa Cruz**. No ATM. Better rates from Plácido Treffinger, San Martín opposite Municipalida. Difficult to change TC's, though the *Hotel Belgrano* may do so. **Tourist offices** San Martín 1222, T432222.

Frontier with Chile
Though there are two crossings west of Perito Moreno, the easiest and most commonly used is via **Los Antiguos**, which lies 67 west of Perito Moreno and 2 km east of the frontier. The town is reached by Route 43 which runs along the southern edge of Lago Buenos Aires. Enjoying a favourable microclimate, it is a fruit-growing area with an annual cherry festival in early January. Salmon fishing is also available as is fuel.

Sleeping **B** *Argentino*, comfortable, restaurant. **Camping** outstanding municipal site, hot showers, 2 km from centre, US$3 per person, also *cabañas* **D** per person. At Km 29 **AB** *Hostería La Serena* offers accommodation in *cabinas*, 10% reduction to *South American Handbook* readers, good restaurant and organizes trips in both the Chilean and Argentine Lake Districts, open Oct-Jun; further details from Geraldine des Cressonières, Estancia La Serena, Casilla 87, 9040 Perito Moreno, Santa Cruz, T0963-432340, cellular068246549. Nearby is Los Chilcas where Indian remains can be found (trout fishing).

Phone code: 02963

Tourist office 11 de Julio 432, T491036.

Patagonia

Route 40

"To see the real Patagonia, with its immense desert-like plains and mountains, rent a car and travel along Route 40 between Perito Moreno and Calafate. The road has been improved in recent years so you so not need four-wheel drive (in summer); the only bad bit is a 5 km section north of Tres Lagos, where there are big stones on the road, but drive slowly if you are not used to gravel. This region is the most isolated in Patagonia; because of low wool prices a lot of estancias have been abandoned and most of the hotels marked on the maps have been closed. The landscape is of mesetas, mountains and valleys, mostly covered with yellow grass; in the evening light you have the impression of endless, shimmering golden plains and hills. Stay overnight at estancias in the middle of nature and allow yourself at least ten days, with excursions off the road to the Cueva de las Manos, Lago Posadas, Parque Nacional Perito Moreno and Chaltén."

Transport Bus To **El Calafate**, *Chaltén Travel*, US$68, via Perito Moreno (and with possible connections for La Cueva de Las Manos), daily in Dec-Feb, subject to demand (minimum 6 passengers) in Nov and Mar. To **El Chaltén**, minibus service by ***Itinerarios y Travesias***, (details under El Chaltén) once a week 1 Nov-15 Mar with additional service 15 Dec-15 Feb, US$93, minimum 3 passengers.

Into Chile *Transportes VH* buses cross the border by new bridge to Chile Chico, 8 km west, US$2, 45 mins. If hitching to Chile Chico look for lift on Argentine side of frontier to avoid problems returning to Los Antiguos if you can't get a lift.

North of Lago Buenos Aires The other route is via the roads which go around the north side of Lago Buenos Aires to Puerto Ibáñez. At the roundabout, north edge of town, go straight, on the biggest road; at the police checkpoint, turn right onto a small road. Follow this 75 km and then turn left along north side of Lago Buenos Aires.

Bajo Caracoles and around

Bajo Caracoles
Phone code: 0297
Colour map 6, grid A2
Population: 100
Km 264

Bajo Caracoles is a tiny, forlorn pit stop, with very expensive grocery store and is the nearest stepping off point for visiting the **Cueva de las Manos** (see below). West of Bajo Caracoles, 72 km along Route 39 are **Lago Posadas** and **Lago Pueyrredón**, two beautiful lakes with contrasting blue and turquoise waters and separated by a narrow isthmus. Guanacos and rheas can be seen and there are sites of archaeological interest.

Sleeping and eating Bajo Caracoles C *Hotel Bajo Caracoles*, T434963. decent, meals. **Lago Posadas** *Hostería Lagos del Furioso*, T/FBuenos Aires 48120959, open Nov-Apr, comfortable, horse-riding, trekking and excursions in vehicles offered. ***Lago Posadas***, cabañas, meals.

Cueva de las Manos
Colour map 6, grid A2

Situated 47 km northeast of Bajo Caracoles in the canyon of the Río Pinturas, contains outstanding examples of prehistoric cave paintings, the oldest of which are estimated to be 10,000 years old. In the cave's four galleries are over 800 paintings of human hands, all but 31 of which are of left hands, as well as images of guanacos and cameloids. Painted in red, orange, black, white and green, they are interesting even for those not interested in rock art. The canyon itself, 270 m deep and 480 m wide, is worth seeing: its rock walls are hues of red and green and are especially beautiful in the evening light. A ranger lives at the

site; he looks after the caves and is helpful with information. ■ *Getting there: access is via an unpaved road which branches east off Route 40 3 km north of Bajo Caracoles. US$3. No public transport goes anywhere near the caves.*

Sleeping A *Hostería Cueva de Las Manos*, 20 km from the cave, T02963-432085, open 1 Nov-5 Apr, with hostel (**D** per person) from 10 Dec, closed Christmas and New Year, includes breakfast, other meals US$20, runs tours to the caves, US$20 with guide (15 without), horseriding, transport to Perito Moreno US$30. *Estancia Turística Casa de Piedra*, 75 km south of Perito Moreno on Ruta 40, camping **F**, also has rooms **E** per person, hot showers, breakfafst extra, homemade bread, use of kitchen, excursions to Cueva de las Manos, 10 km by vehicle then 1½-2 hrs' walk, and volcanoes by car or horse, in Perito Moreno ask for Sr Sabella, Av Perón 941, T432199. If it is not busy the ranger may let you sleep inside the park building. *Camping Casa de Piedra*, on Route 40, 9 km from the caves. US$3 per tent.

Tours From Perito Moreno, US$200 for groups of up to 10; ask at tourist office. Hector Yerio, T432127, takes up to 7 people in a pickup, US$100, 2 hrs journey, 5 hrs at site. A cheaper alternative is to ask at the only hotel in Bajo Caracoles. No transport at all off season.

Paso Roballos is 99 km northwest of Bajo Caracoles via (unpaved) Route 41, which runs past Lago Ghio and Lago Columna. On the Chilean side this road continues to Cochrane, Km 177. Though passable in summer, it is often flooded in spring. No public transport. If hitching, allow a week.

Frontier with Chile

There is no food between Bajo Caracoles and Tres Lagos though water can be obtained from streams and *estancias* are about every 25 km, except between Río Chico and Lago Cardiel (90 km). South of Bajo Caracoles Route 40 crosses the Pampa del Asador and then, near **Las Horquetas**, Km 371, swings southeast to follow the Río Chico. At **Tamel Aike**, Km 393, there is a police station and water but little else. At Km 464 Route 25 branches off to San Julian via **Gobernador Gregores**, 72 km southeast, where there is fuel and a good mechanic, while Route 40 continues southwest towards Tres Lagos. At Km 531 a road heads west to **Lago Cardiel**, a very saline lake with no outlet and good salmon fishing. **Tres Lagos**, at Km 645, is a solitary village with a supermarket and fuel at the junction with Route 288. A road also turns off northwest to **Lago San Martín**, which straddles the frontier (the Chilean part is Lago O'Higgins).

Bajo Caracoles to Calafate

Sleeping Las Horquetas *Hotel Las Horquetas*. **Gobernador Gregores AB** *San Francisco*, T491039. **B** *Cañadon Leon*, T491082. Also municipal campsite, T491398. **Tres Lagos E** per person *Restaurant Ahoniken*. Municipal campsite, T495031, dirty showers, US$3 per person. Camping also at *Estancia La Lucila*, 52 km north of Tres Lagos off Route 40, basic, US$3, water, barbeque, "a little, green paradise". **Estancias A** per person *La Angostura*, T452010, F454318, also horseriding, trekking, fishing, recommended. **Lago San Martín AB** per person *Estancia La Maipú*, T02966-422613, F011-49034967, the Leyenda family offer accommodation, meals, horse riding, trekking and boat excursions on the lake, "real atmosphere of a sheep farming *estancia*" (Santiago de la Vega), recommended.

From Tres Lagos Route 40 (in poor condition) runs west towards **Lago Viedma**. At Km 680 a road runs west to the Fitz Roy sector of Parque Nacional Los Glaciares (see below). At Km 701 there is a bridge over Río La Leona. Nearby is a hotel which has a bar/café. From here it is 73 km further to Route 11, the main (paved) highway from Río Gallegos to Calafate.

Patagonia

Parque
Nacional Perito
Moreno
Colour map 6, grid A2

Situated southwest of Bajo Caracoles on the Chilean frontier, this is one of the wildest and most remote parks in Argentina. Extending over 115,000 ha at altitudes above 800 m, the park includes eight large lakes, seven of which drain into Chile, while the eighth, Lago Burmeister, empties into the Río Chico which flows towards the Atlantic. There are also numerous smaller lakes and ponds. Outside the park, but towering over it to the north is **Cerro San Lorenzo** (3,706), the highest peak in southern Patagonia. Between the lakes are other peaks, permanently snow-covered, the highest of which is Cerro Herros (2,770 m). The Sierra Colorada, its rocks a mass of differing colours runs across the northeast of the park: erosion of these coloured rocks has given the lakes differing colours. At the foot of Cerro Casa de Piedra are a network of caves which contain cave paintings, accessible only with a guide. Ammonite fossils can be found in many parts of the park.

Lower parts of the park are steppe, covered with dense *coiron* grasses and shrubs. Higher up are areas of southern beech forest especially *lenga* and *coihue*. Wildlife includes guanacos, foxes and one of the most important surviving populations of the rare huemul. Birds include flamingos, ñandus, steamer ducks, grebes, black-necked swans, Patagonian woodpeckers, eagles and condors. The lakes and rivers are unusual for Argentina in that only native species of fish are found.

Much of the park is closed to visitors. The most accessible part is around Lago Belgrano, 12 km from the entrance. Several good hikes are possible from here: to the peninsula of Lago Belgrano, 8 km, where there are fine views of Cerro Herros; to the Río Lacteo, 20 km; to Lago Burmeister, via Cerro Casa de Piedra, 16 km. There are also longer walks of up to five days. You should inform rangers before setting out on a hike.

Parque Nacional Perito Moreno

Francisco Moreno, 'El Perito'

Travellers to Patagonia will find it hard to miss the name of Francisco Pascasio Moreno (1852-1919). Commemorated by a national park, a town and a world famous glacier, Moreno, a naturalist and geographer, travelled ceaselessly in Patagonia, exploring areas previously unknown to the authorities in Buenos Aires. At the age of 20 he paid his first visit to Patagonia, travelling up the Río Negro to Lago Nahuel Huapi, along the Río Chubut and then up the Río Santa Cruz to reach the giant lake which he named 'Lago Argentino'. Expeditions such as this were dangerous: apart from the physical hardships encountered, relations between whites and Indians were

frequently poor. On a later expedition, Moreno was seized as a hostage but escaped on a raft which carried him for 8 days down the Río Limay to safety.

His fame established, Moreno was elected to congress and was appointed Director of the Museo de Ciencias Naturales in La Plata. In 1901 he became an expert (perito) adviser to the Argentine team in the negotiations to draw the frontier with Chile. His reward was a grant of lands near Bariloche, which he handed over to the state to manage, an act which can be seen as the initial step in the creation of the national parks system. Fittingly his remains are buried in a mausoleum on Isla Centinela in Lago Nahuel Huapi.

■ *Getting there: There is no public transport into the park but it may be possible to arrange a lift with estancia workers from Hotel Las Horquetas. Access is via an unpaved road, 75 km, which branches off Route 40 near Las Horquetas. Visitor centre near Lago Belgrano, open 0800-2200. Rangers have maps and information leaflets. Entry free. There is a national park office in Gobernador Gregores, T/F4966-491477.*

Sleeping AB per person *Estancia La Oriental*, T02962-452196, F02962-452235, 1 km from Lago Belgrano. Full board, clean, horseriding, trekking, camping site **D** per person, recommended. **Camping** four free sites inside the park: Lago Burmeister, Mirador Lago Belgrano, Cerro de Vasco, Alberto de Agostini, no facilities.

From Comodoro Rivadavia to Rio Gallegos

Caleta Olivia lies on the Bahía San Jorge. Founded in 1901, it became the centre for exporting wool from the *estancias* of Santa Cruz. Since the discovery of oil in 1944, it has become an important oil town: Pico Truncado, the gas field which feeds the pipeline to Buenos Aires, is some 50 km southwest. On the central roundabout in front of the bus terminal is *El Gorosito*, a huge granite monument of an oil driller with the tools of his trade. Local holiday 20 Nov (founding of the city).

Caleta Olivia
Phone code: 0297
Colour map 5, grid C4
Population: 28,000
74 km S of Comodoro Rivadavia

Sleeping B per person *Robert*, San Martín 2151, T461452. **AB** *Grand*, Mosconi y Chubut, T461393. **B** *Capri*, Hernández 1145, T461132. Municipal campsite with hot showers near beach, T4850999, US$3 per person.

Transport Bus To **Río Gallegos**, Pingüino, US$27, 2230, TAC US$32, 12 hrs. To **Comodoro Rivadavia**, many buses, 1 hr, US$4. To **Calafate**, 5 hrs. To **Perito Moreno** and **Los Antiguos**, 5 hrs, 2 daily.

Directory Banks ATM at **Banco del Chubut**, on San Martín.

Patagonia

Fitz Roy
Km 144

Situated at the junction with Route 43, which runs west via Pico Truncado and Perito Moreno to Lago Buenos Aires and the Chilean frontier at Los Antiguos. Named the captain of Darwin's ship, *Beagle*, Fitzroy is the easiest base for visiting the **Monumento Natural Bosques Petrificados**. Fuel is available. **Sleeping** at **B** *Fitzroy*, good, cheap food, camping sometimes possible.

Monumento Natural Bosques Petrificados

Extending over 10,000 ha in a bizarre landscape surrounding the Laguna Grande, this park contains much older petrified trees than the forests further north around Sarmiento. The trunks, mainly of *araucaria* trees, are up to 35 m long and 150 cm in diameter. There is a small visitor centre and a well documented 1-km nature walk. ■ *1000-2000, no charge but donations accepted; please do not remove 'souvenirs'. Getting there: 2 access roads branch off from Route 3 south of Fitzroy: at Km 22 provincial route 93 (dirt) runs southwest for 70 km where it joins the other road, provincial route 49 (bad ripio) which turns off at Km 86 and runs west 48 km to the entrance.* There is a campsite at *Estancia la Paloma*, T02974-43503, some 25 km east of the entrance.

Puerto Deseado

Phone code: 02967; Colour map 6, grid A4 Population: 7,100 Airport

Puerto Deseado lies on the northern shore of the estuary of the Río Deseado which drains Lago Buenos Aires. It is reached by Route 281 which branches off Route 3, 10 km south of Fitzroy. Founded in 1884, it is the most important fishing port in Patagonia and a centre for visiting a number of nature reserves along this part of the coast.

Outside the former railway station is the **Vagón Histórico**, a carriage now used as the tourist office. There are few sights within the town, the attractions being around and about, but the **Museo Regional Patagónico**, in the Colegio Salesiano, Colón y Almirante Brown may be visited.

The **Reserva Natural Ría Deseado**, the submerged estuary (*ría*) of the Río Deseado, 42 km long, is an important nature reserve. Extending over some 10,000 ha, it protects a colony of Magellanic penguins, the nesting areas of four species of cormorants including the unique red legged cormorant, and breeding grounds of Commerson's dolphin, which, with its black and white pattern, is considered one of the most beautiful in the world.

The **Gruta de Lourdes**, 24 km west, is a huge cave which attracts pilgrims to see the Virgen de Lourdes. Further south along the same road is the **Cañadon del Puerto**, a *mirador* offering fine views over the estuary.

Cabo Blanco is a nature reserve 88 km north, the site of the largest fur seal colony in Patagonia. The breeding season is December to January. The lighthouse (1916) is one of the oldest along this coast.

The **Reserva Natural Bahía Laura**, an uninhabited bay 155 km south along *ripio* and dirt roads, is black-necked cormorants, ducks and other seabirds can be found in abundance.

Isla Pinguinos is an offshore island where there is a colony of Magallanic penguins, as well as cormorants and steamer ducks.

Sleeping

AB *Los Acantilados*, Pueyrredón y España, T470167. Beautifully located, ACA discount, poor breakfast. **AB** *Colón*, Almirante Brown 450, T470304. **AB** *Isla Schaffers*, San Martín y Moreno, T472246, modern, central. *Oneto*, Fernández y Oneto, T470455. *Res Sur*, Ameghino 1640, T470522. *Res Alvares*, Pueyrredón 367, T470053. *Hosp Los Olmos*, Gob Gregores 849, T470077. *Albergue Municipal*, Colón y Belgrano, T470260, dormitory style. **Estancia** *La Madrugada*, accommodation, excursions to sea lion colony and cormorant nesting area, English spoken, highly recommended, T434963

A railway carriage with a history

Built in 1898, the Vagon Histórico, now operating as a tourist office, has a grimly appropriate name: in 1921 it was the headquarters of Colonel Hector Benigno Varela, a cavalry officer despatched by Argentine President Hipolito Yrigoyen to end a strike by shepherds in an episode little known outside Patagonia until the publication of Bruce Chatwin's In Patagonia.

Although the strike of 1920-1921 began as a protest movement in Río Gallegos led by anarchists, it spread rapidly across the sparsely populated countryside. Living in barracks on estancias and employed by owners who, whether British or Argentine, lived elsewhere, the shepherds, mostly Chileans, were badly hit by wage cuts which followed the collapse of world wool prices at the end of the First World War. The

isolation of Patagonia made it impossible for estancia owners to bring in workers from elsewhere to break the strike. Facing armed groups riding across Patagonia to enforce the strike, the owners appealed for government help.

Under pressure from the army and ultra right-wing groups who used the fact that most of the shepherds were Chileans to claim that the strike was really a Chilean plot to seize the territory, Yrigoyen ordered Varela to pacify Santa Cruz at all costs. Varela seems to have had no qualms about obeying his orders: offering the strikers an amnesty in return for surrender, he had many of them shot. The final showdown came at the Estancia La Anita, near Calafate, one of the largest in the province: some 300 men surrendered of whom 120 were shot after being forced to dig a mass-grave.

---

or in Puerto Deseado: Almirante Zar 570, T470204, F72298. **Camping** Municipal site, Av Costanera, T4870579, dirty.

Eating *El Viejo Marino*, Pueyrredón 224, considered best by locals. *La Casa de Don Ernesto*, San Martín 1245, seafood and *parrilla*. *El Pinguino*, Piedrabuena 958, *parrilla*.

Local holidays 31 Jan, *San Juan Bosco*; 9 Oct, *Coat of Arms day*.

Directory **Tour operators** *Gipsy Tours*, T472155, F472142, run by Ricardo Pérez, excursions by boat to Ría Deseado reserve, 2 hrs, US$25, knowledgeable, honest. **Tourist office** San Martín y Almirante Brown, in the *vagón histórico*, T470220.

Puerto San Julián

Lying on the Bahía San Julian, 268 km south of Fitzroy, this is the best place for breaking the 834 km run from Comodoro Rivadavia to Río Gallegos. Founded in 1901 on a peninsula overlooking a fine natural harbour, the town grew up to serve the sheep estancias of this part of Santa Cruz.

Phone code: 02962
Colour map 6, grid A4
Population: 5,300

Sights North of town the ruins of the *Frigorifico Swift*, a meat-packing plant opened in 1910, can be seen. Today it is an important fishing port. Clay grinding can be seen at Molienda Santa Cruz and ceramics are made at the Escuela de Cerámica. There is a good handicraft centre at Moreno y San Martín. Just north of the town is Punta Caldera, a popular summer beach. The first mass in Argentina was held here after Magellan had executed a member of his crew. Francis Drake also put in here to behead Thomas Doughty, after amiably dining with him. A couple of museums are here. **Museo Regional**, at the southern end of San Martín, mainly archaeology and **Museo de Arte Marino**, 9 de Julio y Mitre, Mon-Fri 0900-1400, local paintings.

Patagonia

Excursions The **Reserva San Julian**, on the shores of Bahía San Julian, covers 10,400 ha. This reserve includes the islands, Banco Cormorán and Banco Justicia, where there is a colony of Magallanic penguins and where there are nesting areas for these species of cormorants and other birds. Boat hire US$10. **Cabo Curiosa**, 15 km north, has fine beaches. The ruins of **Florida Blanca** ca be found 10 km west, a colony founded in 1870 by Antonio Viedma. **Estancia La María**, 150 km west, offers transport, accommodation **C** per person with bath, **D** per person without, meals and trekking. The estancia covers one of the main archaeological areas of Patagona, including a huge canyon with 87 caves with paintings including human hands and guanacos 4,000-12,000 years old, less visited than the Cueva de las Manos. Contact Fernando Behm, Saavedra 1168, T42328, F42269, guided tours US$36 per person, six hours walk.

Sleeping **AB** *Municipal*, 25 de Mayo 917, T42300/1. Very nice, well-run, good value, no restaurant. **AB** *Bahía*, San Martín 1075, T43144. Modern, comfortable, good value. Recommended. **AB** *Res Sada*, San Martín 1112, T42013. Good rooms, poor breakfast, on busy main road. **B** *Colón*, San Martín 301, older. **C** *Aguila*, San Martín 500 block, sleazy, cheapest in town. **Camping** Good municipal site on the waterfront at Magallanes y Mariano Moreno, T452806, US$5 per site plus US$3 per person, repeatedly recommended, all facilities.

Southern Santa Cruz & Parque Nacional Los Glaciares

▲ Parque Nacional Los Glaciares		
1 Ventisquero Perito Moreno	2 Canal de los Témpanos	4 Lago Onelli	6 Spegazzini Glacier
	3 Brazo Rico	5 Upsala Glacier	7 Punta Gualichó

Sportsman, Mitre y 25 de Mayo, excellent value. *Rural*, Ameghino y Vieytes, good, but not before 2100. A number of others. Also bars and tearooms. **Eating**

Air Weekly services (Mon) with *LADE* to Santa Cruz, Río Gallegos, Puerto Deseado, Gob Gregores, Comodoro Rivadavia, Calafate/Lago Argentino and Río Turbio. **Bus** To **Buenos Aires**, *Transportadora Patagónica*, *Pingüino*. To **Río Gallegos**, *Pingüino*, 6 hrs, US$14. **Hitching** Walk 5 km to petrol station on Ruta 3. **Transport**

Banks *Banco de la Nación*, Mitre y Belgrano, and *Banco de la Provincia de Santa Cruz*, San Martín y Moreno. **Communications** Post office Belgrano y San Martín. **Medical services** Hospital: Av Costanera entre Roca y Magallanes. **Pharmacy:** *Del Pueblo* on San Martín 570. **Tourist offices** San Martín 581, T42871. **Directory**

Route 521 (*ripio*) runs inland northwest from San Julián to Route 40. The only settlement along this road is **Gobernador Gregores** (see above) 215 km west of San Julián. **Route**

Known officially as Comandante Luís Piedrabuena, the town is named after the first Argentine citizen to settle in Patagonia (1859), who lived on Isla Pavón, an island in the river. A small museum marks the spot and there is a campsite (T497187). Piedrabuena lies on the Río Santa Cruz which drains Lago Argentino and is one of the most important rivers in Patagonia. **Piedrabuena**
Phone code: 02962
Colour map 6, grid B3
Population: 3,300
146 km S of San Julián

Excursions can be made to **Santa Cruz**, 36 km east on the estuary of the Río Santa Cruz. Founded in 1878, Santa Cruz was capital of Santa Cruz province until 1904. There is a small museum, the **Museo Regional de História** at Avenida Piedrabuena y Moreno. Southeast of town, near the mouth of the Río Santa Cruz is **Punta Quilla**, a major deep water port.

Monte León is a provincial nature reserve 56 km south of Piedrabuena, which includes the Isla Monte León, an important breeding area for cormorants and terns, where there is also a penguin colony and sea lions. There are impressive rock formations and wide isolated beaches at low tide. It is reached by a 22 km dirt road which branches off Route 3 36 km south of Piedrabuena.

Sleeping Piedrabuena AB *ACA Motel*, T47145. Simple, functional but good, warm and nice food. **AB** *Hostería El Alamo*, Lavalle 08, T47249. Quiet, breakfast extra. Recommended. *Andalucia*, Belgrano 170, restaurant (good pasta). **C** *Res Internacional*, Ibáñez 99, T47197. Recommended. **C** per person *Hotel Vani*. **Camping** Sites south of town on Route 3; also on Isla Pavón. **Santa Cruz AB** *Hostal de la Ría*, 25 de Mayo 645, T48038. *Hostería Turística*; *Anel Aike*, both **C**. *Posada de Pinky*, Balestra y 25 de Mayo. **Camping** A free muncipal site.

Inland Provincial Route 9 (1603 on some maps, unpaved, no petrol) branches off Route 3, 43 km south of Piedrabuena and runs west to Calafate along the edge of a plateau with occasional panoramic views across the valley of the Río Santa Cruz below. Then at about Km 170 it drops down into the valley itself to follow the river into the hills and to Lago Argentino. Route 288 runs direct from Piedrabuena to Tres Lagos on Route 40, thence west and south to Lagos Viedma and Argentino. Most traffic to El Calafate goes via Río Gallegos. **Routes**

Patagonia

Río Gallegos

Phone code: 02966
Colour map 6, grid B3
Population: 75,000
235 km S of
Piedrabuena

Río Gallegos lies on the estuary of the Río Gallegos, 18 km from its mouth. Founded in 1885, Río Gallegos is capital of Santa Cruz province and has a large military base. It grew rapidly after 1945 as the port for transporting coal from the mines of El Turbio and as a centre for trade in wool and meat from the estancias of the province. It is drab, but has a good shopping centre on the main street, Avenida Roca.

Sights The small Plaza San Martín, one block from the post office is well tended, with flower beds and statues. Outside the post office is a balcony, preserved from a demolished house, commemorating the meeting of Presidents Errázuriz and Roca to end Chile and Argentina's 1883 Magellan Strait dispute. There is a deep-water port at Punta Loyola at the mouth of the estuary.

Museums **Museo Regional**, San Martín y Ramón y Cajal 51, has collections of local history, flora, fauna, rock samples. ■ *Mon-Fri 1000-1800, Sat/Sun 1100-1900*. **Museo de los Pioneros**, Alberdi y Elcano in the former house of a Arthur Fenton, a British physician who was one of the early pioneers, free. ■ *1300-2000*. **Museo Malvinas Argentinas,** Pasteur 48. Arms and equipment used in the 1982 Falklands/Malvinas War. ■ *Mon-Thu 0800-1200, Tue/Fri 1300-1730, 3rd Sun of month 1530-1800*. **Museo de Arte**, Maipú 13. Collection of works by local artists. ■ *Tue-Fri 0830-1900, Sat/Sun 1400-1800*. **Museo Casa de Gregores,** Alcorta 473. Collection of artefacts from the life of a former governor of Santa Cruz province. ■ *Mon-Fri 1000-1200, 1500-1800*.

Excursions **Laguna Azul**, 62 km south near the Monte Aymond frontier crossing, is a lagoon in the crater of an extinct volcano. ■ *Reached by Route 3*. **Cabo Vírgenes**, 134 km south, has a provincial nature reserve protecting the second largest colony of Magellanic penguins in Patagonia, entry US$5. The Navy allows visitors to climb up Cabo Vírgenes lighthouse for a superb view. ■ *Branch off Route 3 onto Route 1 (unpaved), 15 km south of Río Gallegos, from where it is 119 km. You can hitch from this junction with oil workers going to the lighthouse at the Cape. Take a taxi at the turn off by 0700. Take drinking water. It is possible to arrange return with day trippers from Río Gallegos, or ask at the lighthouse or naval station.* South of Cabo Virgenes are the ruins of **Nombre de Jesús**, one of the two settlements founded by Pedro Sarmiento de Gamboa in 1584. The other was south of Punta Arenas in Chile. There are several **estancias** including **Hill Station**, 63 km north of Río Gallegos and **Monte Dinero**, T0966-26900, 13 km north of Cabo Virgenes, where the Fenton family offers accommodation **L** per person, food and excursions to penguins, horseriding, English spoken, expensive, excellent. Recommended.

Sleeping **L** *Costa Río*, San Martín 673, T/F423412, costario@internet.siscotel.com Comfortable,
Do not confuse discounts for ACA members. **A** *Comercio*, Roca 1302, T422458, F422172,
the street Comodoro hotelcom@internet.siscotel.com.ar With breakfast, good beds, comfortable, restau-
Rivadavia with (nearby) rant with good fixed-price menu. **AB** *Santa Cruz*, Roca 701, T420601. With heating,
Bernardino Rivadavia good coffee bar, breakfast. **AB** *Punta Arenas*, Sphur 55, T422743. In new wing, very comfortable, also **B** in old wing, without breakfast. **AB** *Covadonga*, Roca 1214, T420190. Without breakfast, comfortable, recommended. **AB** *Nevada*, Zapiola 480, T425990. English spoken, good beds, parking, no breakfast. **B** *Cabo Virgenes*, Comodoro Rivadavia 252, T422141. Recommended. **B** *Oviedo*, Libertad 746, T/F420118, comfortable, kitchen facilities. Recommended. **B** *Alonso*, Corrientes 33, T422414, F421237. Without breakfast, good beds. **B** *París*, Roca 1040, T420111, **C** without bath, old fashioned, poor beds.

C *Colonial*, Urquiza y Rivadavia, T422329. Cheaper without bath, poor, dirty bathrooms. C *Central*, Roca 1127, central, quiet, cold shower, no heating. C *Pensión Belgrano*, Belgrano 123, dirty, basic but friendly, good restaurant. D *Res Internacional*, Sphur 78, without bath, with heating, kitchen and laundry facilities, helpful, but insecure. D per person *Res Betty*, Alberdi 458, meals, recommended. D per person *Piscis* (no sign), Avellaneda y Magallanes, T/F420329. Owned by army officers' club, without breakfast, good beds, excellent value. Recommended. **Private house** Barrio Codepro ll, Casa 71, T423789, **E** per person, recommended.

Camping *Camping ATSA* Route 3, behind YPFstation and west of bus terminal, T420301, US$6 per person plus US$1 for tent, poor. Also try the YPFservice station. Also *Club de Pesca* site at Guer Aike, 30 km away, T425215.

Eating Plenty and good, some specializing in seafood. Evening meals are hard to find before 2000. *Restaurant Díaz*, Roca 1173, cheap. *Bifería La Vasca*, Roca 1084, snack bar, good value, young crowd, rock music, open till 0300. *El Horneo*, bar of *Club Español*, Roca 862, good meals, cosy, reasonably priced, internet access. *Jardín*, Roca 1315,

Río Gallegos

Sleeping

1 Alonso
2 Cabo Vírgenes
3 Central
4 Comercio
5 Costa Río
6 Covadonga
7 Internacional
8 Nevada
9 Paris
10 Piscis
11 Punta Arenas
12 Santa Cruz

To Punta Arenas & Tierra del Fuego

good, cheap, popular. *Club Británico*, Roca 935, good, reasonably priced. *El Palenque*, Corrientes 73, *parrilla*, recommended. *Cosa Nostra*, 9 de Julio 230, fresh pasta, good, reasonably priced. *Monaco*, Roca y San Martín, good café. *Le Croissant*, Zapiola y Estrada, good bakery.

Local holidays   31 Jan; 19 Dec, *Foundation of Río Gallegos*.

Shopping   *Artesanías Koekén*, San Martín 336, leatherwork, woollen goods, local produce. *Artesanías Santacruceñas*, Roca 658. *Tia* department store, Roca 740, good supermarket section. Supermarket *La Anónima*, Roca y España. Most places take a 2-3-hr lunch break.

Sport   **Fishing** The southern fishing zone including the Ríos Gallegos, Grande, Fuego, Ewan, San Pablo and Lago Fagnano, near Ushuaia. It is famous for runs of sea trout. See page 58.

Tour operators *Interlagos*, *Pingüino* and *Quebek* at bus terminal and airport offer tours to Calafate and Perito Moreno glacier, US$70, without accommodation.

Transport   **Local Car rental** *Localiza*, Sarmiento 237, T424417; *Eduardo Riestra*, San Martín 1508, T421321. Essential to book rental in advance in season. **Car parts and repairs** *Turbisur*, Corrientes 177, cheapest; *Repuestos Sarmiento*, on Sarmiento, owner very friendly and helpful. **Motorcycle mechanic** Juan Carlos Topcic, Costa Rica 25, friendly and helpful. **Taxi** *Radio taxi*, V Sarsfield y Roca, T422369. Hiring a taxi for group excursions may be no more expensive than taking a tour bus. *AL*, Entre Ríos 350, T422453, for taxis and car rental, not cheap.

Long distance Air Airport 6 km west of town. Bus No 1 to Barrio Consejo Agraria takes you most of the way there. Minibus service US$3. Taxi (*remise*) to/from town US$6; hitching from car park is easy. You can spend the night at the airport prior to early morning flights. In summer make your bookings in advance. *Aerolíneas Argentinas's* Buenos Aires-Auckland-Sydney flight (2 a week) stops at Río Gallegos, but the return journey does not. To/from **Buenos Aires**: *Aerolíneas Argentinas* (direct or via Trelew), *Austral* (via Bahía Blanca and Comodoro Rivadavia), *Lapa* (via Trelew or Comodoro Rivadavia), *Dinar* (via Comodoro Rivadavia). Several flights to **Ushuaia** and **Río Grande**, direct (*Aerolíneas Argentinas*, always booked, but standby seats available), *Austral* or *Lapa*. *TAPSA* to Río Grande, Ushuaia and Comodoro Rivadavia. *LADE* to **Río Turbio** and Calafate, twice a week, to Ushuaia and **Comodoro Rivadavia** once a week. *LADE* flights should be booked as far in advance as possible. The Ladeco service from Punta Arenas to **Port Stanley** on the Falkland Islands/Islas Malvinas stops once a month in either direction. Both *Pingüino* and *Interlagos* can arrange packages to Calafate including accommodation and trip to Moreno glacier from their offices at the airport.

Bus Terminal at corner of Route 3 and Av Parque, 3 km from centre (crowded, no left luggage, *confitería*, few toilets, kiosks); taxi to centre US$3, bus US$1 (Nos 1 and 12 from posted stops on Roca). To **Calafate**, via airport, 4-5 hrs, US$20-25, *Pingüino* and *Quebek*, sometimes with double-deckers offering great views, very crowded in season; turn up with ticket 30 mins before departure: in winter both companies operate 3 times a week; *Pingüino* offers 2-night excursion to Calafate, sold at airport only, US$93 in single room, credit cards accepted. *Pingüino* daily at 2100 to **Caleta Olivia**, US$30, 11 hrs. To **Trelew** and **Puerto Madryn** daily (18 hrs), US$55. To **Comodoro Rivadavia**, *Pingüino*, *Don Otto* and *TAC*, 10 hrs, US$30. For **Bariloche**, take this bus to Comodoro Rivadavia, then the 2150 *Don Otto* bus to Bariloche (fare to Bariloche US$88). *Andesmar* to **Mendoza**, leaves Fri 1300, arrives 0900 Sun, via Comodoro Rivadavia,

Puerto Madryn and Neuquén. To **Buenos Aires**, 36 hrs, *Pingüino, Don Otto, TAC,* US$70-100. To **Río Turbio**, 4 hrs, US$15. *Pingüino,* daily 1400, *Quebek/Tacsa* daily 1300 (hitching practically impossible). No buses to/from Río Grande. **Hitchhiking**   To **Buenos Aires** is possible in about 5-7 days; appearance important; hitching to **Tierra del Fuego** possible from service station in front of bus terminal, be there at 0600. To **Calafate**, from police control outside town.

To Chile Bus to Puerto Natales, *Pingüino,* Tue/Sat, 1100, 7½ hrs, US$22. Alternatively take a bus to **Río Turbio** and change. To **Punta Arenas**, *Pingüino,* 1300, US$20 daily. **Car**   Make sure your car papers are in order (go first to tourist office for necessary documents, then to the customs office at the port, at the end of San Martín, very uncomplicated).

Airline offices   *Aerolíneas Argentinas*, San Martín 545, T420181. *Austral*, Roca 917, T422038. *Dinar*, San Martín 695. *LADE*, Fagnano 53, T422316. *Lapa*, Estrada 71, T428382. *TAN*, T425259. **Banks**   Lots of ATMs. *Lloyds Bank*, Sarmiento 47, open 1000-1600, cash advance on Visa and Mastercard, high commission. Many banks on Roca including *Banco de Santa Cruz*, Roca y Errázuriz, fair rates, Mastercard. *Banco Almafuerte*, Roca 990, changes cash. Change TCs here if going to Calafate, where it is even more difficult. *Banco Tierra del Fuego*, changes TCs with 2.5% commission. *Banco de Crédito Argentino*, Roca 936, quick cash advance on Visa upstairs. *Cambio El Pingüino*, Zapiola 469, may also change European and South American currencies, 7% commission. *Cambio Sur*, San Martín y Roca, often has good rates. ATMs at *La Caja*, Roca y San Martín, and at *La Anónima* supermarket. **Communications**   **Post office** Roca 893, *poste restante* service unreliable, and at the airport. **Telephone** Roca 613. **Consulates**   *Chile*, Mariano Moreno 136, Mon-Fri, 0900-1300; tourist cards issued at border. **Laundry**   *El Tumbaito* Alberdi y Rawson. *Laverap*, Corrientes 277. **Tourist offices**   Provincial office, Roca 863, T/F422702, tur@spse.com.ar Mon-Fri, 0900-2000, Sat/Sun (summer only) 1000-2000, helpful, English spoken, has list of *estancias*. They will phone round hotels for you. Also at airport 0830-1830 daily and bus terminal.

Directory

Argentina's longest road, Route 40, ends at **Río Gallegos**, or more precisely, Punta Loyola. It runs from Bolivia for over 4,667 km. Its last section has been rerouted south of Lago Argentino to follow the Chilean border and go through Río Turbio. The original route, via La Esperanza, forms the main part of the Río Gallegos-El Calafate route (see below). This road (323 km, all paved) is worth while for the number of animals and birds which can be seen; however, it is flat and subject to strong winds.

Routes

The **Monte Aymond** crossing, 68 km south of Río Gallegos and reached by Route 3, provides the only direct route from Río Gallegos to Tierra del Fuego. For bus passengers the border crossing is very easy; similarly for car drivers if papers are in order. On the Chilean side the road continues to Punta Delgada, Km 30, and Kimiri Aike, where a road turns off for the crossing to Tierra del Fuego via the Primera Angostura (see page 488).

Frontier crossing

Patagonia

El Calafate and the Parque Nacional Los Glaciares

Phone code: 02902
Colour map 6, grid B2
Population: 3,000
312 km NW of Río
Gallegos

This little town lies on the southern shore of Lago Argentino, one of the largest lakes in the country. Though El Calafate was founded in 1927, it grew very slowly until the opening of the road to the Perito Moreno glacier in the 1960s. It exists almost entirely as a tourist centre for the Parque Nacional los Glaciares, which is 50 km further west.

Sights Just west of the town centre is Bahía Redonda, a shallow part of the lake. In winter when it freezes, ice-skating and skiing are possible. At the eastern edge of Bahía Redonda is **Laguna Nimes**, a bird reserve where there are flamingos, black necked swans and ducks, recommended. There is scope for good hill-walking to the south of the town, while Cerro Elefante, west of Calafate on the road to the Moreno glacier is good for rock climbing.

Excursions For excursions to the Moreno glacier, Upsala Glacier and Fitz Roy, see below.
Travel by road to the most interesting spots is limited & may require expensive taxis. Tours can be arranged at travel agencies, or with taxi drivers at the airport Walk to the top of the Cerro Calafate, 2½-3 hrs, for views of the silhouette of the southern end of the Andes, Bahía Redonda and Isla Solitaria on Lago Argentino.

At **Punta Gualichó**, on the shores of Lago Argentino 15 km east of town, there are painted caves (badly deteriorated). Several agencies run tours. ■ *2 hrs, US$16.* Some 12 km east of Calafate on the edge of the lake there are fascinating geological formations caused by erosion.

El Galpón, 21 km west, is an *estancia* offering evening visits (from 1730) which feature walks through a bird sanctuary where 43 species of birds have been identified, displays of sheep shearing and a barbecue as well as horseriding (visits at other times on request). ■ *Transport arranged, English spoken, US$40 per person with dinner, US$20 per person without, US$5 per person transport; in Calafate T/F491793; Buenos Aires, Paseo Colón 221, piso 7, T4343-8185, F4334-2669.*

Lago Roca, 40 km south, has trout and salmon fishing, climbing, walking, and branding of cattle in summer. There is good camping in wooded area and a restaurant. A daily excursion is operated by *Tursimo Leutz* (see below for details). ■ *US$35 pp plus US$22 for lunch at Estancía Nibepo Aike.*

Essentials Calafate is very popular in January-February, when booking all transport in advance is recommended and accommodation can be difficult to find. Many hotels are open only from October to April/May. Credit cards are accepted by most hotels, though often 10% commissions is charged. Most shops accept credit cards.

Sleeping **L** *Los Alamos*, Moyano y Bustillo, T491145, F491186, posadalosalamos@cotecal.com.ar Best, comfortable, very good food and service, extensive gardens, recommended. **L** *Kau-Yatún*, Estancia 25 de

El Calafate detail

N

Not to scale

■ **Sleeping**
1 Amado
2 Cerro Cristal
3 El Quijote
4 Hospedaje Alejandra
5 Kapenke
6 Paso Verlika
7 Upsala

● **Eating**
1 Casablanca
2 La Estancia
3 La Vaca Atada
4 Mi Viejo
5 O'Nelli
6 Pietro's Café
7 Ricks Café

Patagonia

The Calafate

Whoever eats the fruits of the Calafate will return to Patagonia (Berberis buxifolia) or so the story goes: whether they do or not, they are likely to have purple stained lips and fingers! This spiny, shiny leaved, hardy shrub grows to 2 m in height and has single bright yellow/orange flowers dotted along its arching branches in Spring. The deep purple grape-like edible berries are also found singly or in pairs. Also known as the Magellan barberry, its wood is used for making red dye.

Mayo, (10 blocks east of town centre), T491259, F491260, kauyatun@cotecal.com.ar Old *estancia*, comfortable, restaurant and barbecues, horseriding and other tours with guides. **L** *El Mirador del Lago*, Libertador 2047, T/F491213, miradordellago@cotecal.com.ar Good accommodation, acceptable restaurant. **L** *El Quijote*, Gob Gregores 1191, T491017, F491103, elquijote@cotecal.com.ar Recommended.

AL *Frai Toluca*, Perón 1016, T/F491773, fraitolucahotel@cotecal.com.ar Good views, comfortable, restaurant. **AL** *Kalken*, V Feilberg 119, T491073, F491036, hotelkalken@cotecal.com.ar With breakfast, spacious. **AL** *Michelangelo*, Espora y Gob Moyano, T491045, F491058, michelangelohotel@cotecal.com.ar With breakfast, modern, good restaurant, accepts TC's (poor rates). **AB** *Amado*, Libertador 1072, T491134, familiagomez@cotecal.com.ar Without breakfast, restaurant, good. **A** *ACA Hostería El Calafate*, 1° de Mayo 50, T491004, F491027. Modern, good views, open all year, **AB** to members. **AB** *Hostería Schilling*, Paradelo 141, T/F491453. With breakfast,

El Calafate

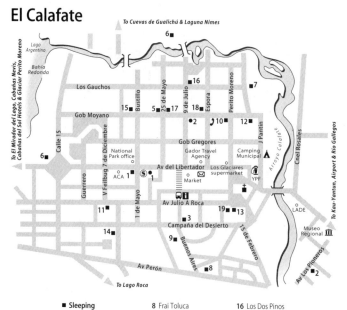

Not to scale

■ **Sleeping**
1 ACA Hostería
2 Albergue del Glaciar
3 Albergue Lago Argentino
4 Cabañas Nevis
5 Calafate Hostel
6 Cayupe Albergue Patagonico
7 Del Norte
8 Frai Toluca
9 Hospedaje Buenos Aires
10 Jorgito
11 Kalken
12 La Cueva de Jorge Lemus
13 La Loma
14 Las Cabañitas
15 Los Alamos
16 Los Dos Pinos
17 Los Lagos
18 Michelangelo
19 Schilling

● **Eating**
1 El Rancho
2 La Cocina

Related map
A El Calfate centre detail, page 442

casino, nice rooms, poor beds. **AB-B** *La Loma*, Roca 849, T/F491016 (Buenos Aires: Callao 433, 8a 'P', T/F371-9123), lalomahotel@cotecal.com.ar With breakfast, modern (poor beds) highly recommended, multilingual, restaurant, tea room, spacious rooms, attractive gardens, also cheaper rooms. **AB** *Paso Verlika*, Libertador 1108, T491009, F491279, with breakfast, restaurant. **AB** *Kapenke*, 9 de Julio y Gob Gregores, T491093. Includes breakfast, good beds. Recommended. About 1 km west of town are: **AB** *Cabañas Nevis*, Libertador 1696, T493180, F491193. Sleep 4, lake view, full board good value. **B** *Cabañas Del Sol*, Libertador 1956, T491439, good meals, highly recommended.

B *Upsala*, Espora 139, T491166 F91075, with breakfast, good beds. Recommended. **B** *del Norte*, Los Gauchos 813, T/F491117. Cheaper without bath, open all year, kitchen facilities, comfortable, owner organizes tours. Highly recommended. **B** *Las Cabañitas*, V Feilberg 218, T491118, lascabanitas@cotecal.com.ar Cabins, hot water, kitchen and laundry facilities, helpful. Recommended. **B** *Los Lagos*, 25 de Mayo 220, T491170, F491348. Very comfortable, good value. Recommended. **B** *Cerro Cristal*, Gob Gregores 989, T491088. Helpful, recommended.

D/E per person *Calafate Hostel*, Gob Moyano y 25 de Mayo, T/F492212, chaltentravel@cotecal.com.ar, small dormitories, also **B** double, Hostelling International discounts, kitchen and laundry facilities, internet, new. **D/E** per person **Albergue & Hostal del Glaciar**, Los Pioneros 251, T/F491243, www.glaciar.com info@glaciar.com Discounts for ISIC and Hostelling International members, open mid-Sep-30 Apr, internet access, good kitchen facilities and lounge, English German and Italian spoken, also rooms with bath (**B**) and sleeping bag space (**E** per person), restaurant with good value fixed menu, repeatedly recommended, runs tour agency *Patagonia Packpackers*, runs tours to Moreno glacier (US$40, repeatedly recommended) and elsewhere, free shuttle service from bus terminal, *poste restant*. **E** per person *Lago Azul*, Perito Moreno 83, T491419. Only 2 double rooms. Highly recommended. **C** *Hosp Belén*, Los Gauchos 300 y Perito Moreno, T491028. Warm, hot water, cooking facilities, family welcome. Highly recommended. **D/E** per person *Hosp Jorgito*, Gob Moyano 943, T491323. Without bath, basic, cooking facilities, heating, breakfast extra, often full, also camping. Recommended. **E** per person *Hosp Los Dos Pinos*, 9 de Julio 358, T/F491271. Dormitory accommodation, cooking and laundry facilities, also cabins **AL**, and camping **F** per person, arranges tours to glacier, popular. **E** per person *Hosp Buenos Aires*, Buenos Aires 296, 200 m from terminal, T491399, hospbuenosaires@cotecal.com.ar Kitchen facilities, helpful, good hot showers, luggage store.

D per person *Cayupe Albergue Patagonico*, on north side of river towards Laguna Nimes, T491125. Small

albergue & hostal del glaciar & PRIVATE SUITES

YOUTH HOSTEL & PRIVATE SUITES
cooking facilities
internet access
lockers in rooms
restaurant
alternative tour
to moreno glacier

los pioneros 251
el calafate, santa cruz
argentina
tel: +54 2902 491243
info@glaciar.com
www.glaciar.com

Hotel La Leona

If you take a bus from Calafate to El Chaltén there is a good chance that it will stop for refreshments at the Hotel La Leona, a single storey building some 100 km north of Calafate near the bridge which takes Route 40 across the Río La Leona. Sheltered by a poplar grove and described by the sign outside as a "Hotel de Campaña, Bar, Confitería", the hotel owes its existence to a much earlier age before the arrival of modern roads and motor vehicles. Transport across the great expanses of Patagonia was very slow; wool, the main product of the early settler economy, was transported by wagons which covered 20 km a day. Long delays were often caused by rivers, especially in spring, the main sheep shearing season, when the rivers were often flooded. Although the larger rivers, such as the Río La Leona, were crossed by balsas (rafts), smaller rivers were forded, the large wagon wheels being designed for this purpose.

At regular intervals along these trails postas were established, usually consisting of a general store and a simple hotel; though many postas are still marked on local maps only a few still offer services to the traveller. One which does is La Esperanza and another is La Leona.

Today the Hotel La Leona fills up several times a day with busloads of thirsty travellers. Famous for its home-made cakes ("the best cakes in the whole of Patagonia" according to Danny Feldman of the Albergue del Glaciar), the hotel is still run by members of the Westerlund family who have owned it since it was built around 1910. As there is no electricity, the cakes are still baked in the original oven, fuelled by coal from Río Turbio. Photos of earlier generations of the family can be seen on the walls and visitors can also try their hand at la argolla, a traditional Patagonian game which involves placing a ring which hangs from the ceiling onto a hook on the wall. Give it a try: its more difficult than it looks.

Apart from the cakes and refreshments, the family offer simple but very clean accommodation and can organise excursions to some petrified forests on a nearby estancia. Visitors should, however, note that it is closed between the end of April and the beginning of October.

dormitories, kitchen facilities, breakfast US$3 extra. **D/E** per person *Hosp Alejandra*, Espora 60, T491328. Without bath, good value. Recommended. **E** per person *Albergue Lago Argentino*, Campaña del Desierto 1050, T491423, F491139. Near bus terminal, dormitory accommodation, limited bathrooms, kitchen facilities, English spoken, helpful. Some private houses offer accommodation: these include Enrique Barragán, Barrio Bahía Redonda, Casa 10, T491325, **E**, recommended. **F** per person *Apartamentos Lago Viedma*, Paralelo 158, T491159, F491158. Hostel, 4 bunks to a room, cooking facilities. **F** per person *La Cueva de Jorge Lemos*, Gob Moyano 839, behind YPFstation, dormitories, kitchen facilities, popular and cheap, tours offered. If in difficulty, ask at tourist office from which caravans, tents (sleep 4) and 4-berth *cabañas* may be hired, showers extra.

Parque Nacional los Glaciares L *Hostería Los Notros*, 80 km west of Calafate on the road to the Moreno glacier, T/F491437, www.lastland.com Half-board, spacious, rooms with glacier views, recommended. **AB** per person *Estancia Nibepo Aike*, in the far south of the park on the shores of Brazo Sur, T420180. Horseriding, expeditions, fishing, boat tours to glacier, recommended. **LL** per person *Estancia Helsingfors*, on the southern shore of Lago Viedma. With breakfast, all other meals available, many treks, boat trips and flights over glaciers available, also riding, sheep-shearing. Recommended. **E** per person *La Leona*, T491418, 106 km north of Calafate near east end of Lago Viedma. Without bath, camping. For accommodation in El Chaltén in the northern part of the park see below.

Camping Municipal campsite behind YPF service station, T491344, reservations off season 491829 US$4 per person, hot water, security, parillada, open 1 Oct-30 Apr. Also at *AMSA*, Olavarriía 65, T492247, US$5 per person. *Camping Vialidad*, 5 de Octubre, T492277 and at *Hosp Jorgito* and *Hosp Los Dos Pinos* (details above). 3 campsites in the park *en route* to the glacier: *Río Mitre*, near the park entrance, 52 km west of Calafate, 26 km east of the glacier, US$3 per person. *Bahía Escondida*, 7 km east of the glacier, no toilets or showers, free, popular in summer. Site at Arroyo Correntoso, 10 km east of the glacier, no facilities but nice location and lots of firewood. Take food to all 3O. On Lago Roca, *Camping Lago Roca*, T499500, US$4 per person restaurant/ confitería. Another campsite is *Camping Río Bote*, 35 km east of Calafate on road to Río Gallegos, T02966-428753, US$3 per person.

Eating Excellent restaurant at *Hotel Los Alamos*. *Hostería Kau-Yatun* has show with dinner, US$30. *Onelli*, Libertador 1197, reasonable *pizzería*, open out of season. *El Rancho*, 9 de Julio y Gob Moyano, selection of 32 pizzas. *Casablanca*, Libertador y 25 de Mayo, good breakfasts. *Michelangelo*, Espora y Gob Moyano, very expensive but magnificent steaks. Recommended. *Paso Verlika*, Libertador 1108, small, 2 courses with wine US$16, credit cards 10% extra, good value. *La Tablita*, Libertador y Rosales just east of the bridge, large and good *parrillada*. *Don Raul*, Libertador 1472, cosy, *tenedor libre*. *Mi Viejo*, Libertador 1111, *parrilla*. *El Rancho*, 9 de Julio y Gob Moyano, large, cheap and good pizzas, popular, free video shows of the glacier. Highly recommended. *La Loma* (address above), friendly, home food. *Maktub*, Libertador 905, excellent pastries and snacks, pricey. *Bar Don Diego de la Noche*, Libertador 1603, lamb and seafood, live music, good atmosphere. *The Family House* , Espora 18, *La Estancia*, 9 de Julio 29, *parrillada*, very good value. *Rick's Café*, Libertador 1105, *tenedor libre* US$11. *La Vaca Atada*, Libertador y 25 de Mayo, wide menu. *La Cocina*, Libertador 1245, *pizzería*, pancakes, pasta. *Acuarela*, Libertador 1177, good ice-cream, wide selection. Several cafés along Libertador including *Pietro's Café*, Libertador y Espora.

Festivals People flock to the rural show on 15 Feb, *Lago Argentino Day*, and camp out with much revelry; dances and *asados*. There are also barbecues and rodeo et cetera on *Día de la Tradición*, 10 Nov.

Sport **Ballooning** *Hotel Kau Yatun* (details above) organises balloon trips over Calafate and Lago Argentino, US$38 for 2½ hrs, US$65 for 5 hrs. **Cycle hire** *Bike Way*, Espora 20, T492180, US$6 per hr, US$25 per day. **Fishing** *Fishing & Adventure*, Roca 2192, T/F493050/491345, offer fishing excursions, half-day US$95 per 1 person to US$220 per 4 persons, full-day US$270 per 1 person to US$570 per 4 persons. Also 3 day expeditions. **Horseriding** *Cabalgata en Patagonia*, Roca 2063, T493203, cabalgataen patagonia@cotecal.com.ar Treks offered to Bahía Redonda (US$30) Gualicho (US$50); also 5 day excursion in Parque Nacional Los Glaciares. **Ice trekking** Walking excursions on the Perito Moreno glacier (known as *mini-trekking*), usually finishing with champagne or whisky with ice chipped from the glacier are run by *Hielo y Aventura*, 1½ hrs, US$65 Jan-Feb and Holy Week, US$50 other times between 15 Oct and Mar 15, plus US$15 for transport to the glacier, book ahead (this trip is sold by most agencies in Calafate). **Rafting** *Nonthue Aventura*, Libertador 1177, T491179, offer rafting on the Río Santa Cruz, 0800 and 1500, 4-5 hrs, US$30 without transport, US$40 with transport. **Offroading** *Mil Outdoor Adventure*, Paredelo 253, T491437, F491816, gxpress@cotecal.com.ar Variety of excursions in 4WD vehicles, offering excellent opportunities to visit otherwise inaccessible parts of the Patagonian steppe, short-trip US$40 per person, long-trip US$75 per person, recommended.

Shopping **Supermarkets** *Alas* , 9 de Julio 59, wide selection. *Los Glaciares*, Libertador y Perito Moreno, accepts US$ cash and Visa. *Ferretería Chuar*, Libertador 1242, is the only place selling white gas for camping.

Many agencies, most of them along Libertador, including *Interlagos*, No 1175, T492195, F491241. *Los Glaciares*, No 924, T/F491159, recommended, good value. *Hielo y Aventura*, No 935, T491053. *Turismo Leutz*, 25 de Mayo 43, T492316. *Albergue del Glaciar*, *Calafate Hostel* (*Chaltén Travel*) and *Hotel del Norte* (details above) run their own agencies which offer tours. Most agencies charge the same rates for excursions: to the Moreno Glacier US$30 for a trip leaving 0830, returning 1800, without lunch, 3 hrs at glacier; *Albergue del Glaciar* and *Calafate Hostel* tours are more expensive but offer extra services or alternative routes. To Lago Roca, at 0930 return 1700, US$25; to Cerro Fitz Roy, at 0600 return 1900, US$50, Gualichó caves, 2 hrs, US$16 (see excursions, above).

Tour operators

Local Car hire *Freelander*, Paradelo 253, T491446, F491816, freelander@cotecal. com.ar, US$50-100 per day.

Transport

Long distance Air New airport 20 km east (with a longer runway than Aeroparque). Airport charge for departing passengers US$18. In the baggage claim area there is a toll-free telephone with direct connection for reservations at 8 hotels (including *Albergue del Glaciar*). *Aerobus* bus service, US$6 one way, US$10 return, connects with all arrivals and departures and calls at hotels in Calafate (details from *Albergue del Glaciar*). Services: *Aerolíneas Argentinas* and *Lapa* to/from Buenos Aires and Ushuaia; *Southern Winds* to/from Bariloche and Ushuaia. *LADE* twice a week to Río Turbio, US$20, 3 a week in summer to connect with buses to Puerto Natales and Torres del Paine. *LADE* once a week to Perito Moreno (Thu high season, Fri low season, US$42; *LADE* also to Río Gallegos 3 times a week and to Comodoro Rivadavia. Air fares can be cheaper than buses especially on *LADE*.

Bus Terminal on Roca, 1 block from Libertador. Bus schedules change annually. To **Río Gallegos**, US$25, 4 hrs, *Interlagos* daily at 0900 (summer) or 0915 Tue, Thu, Sat (winter), *Tacsa/Quebek* daily 0300, 0915 and Mon, Fri, Sat, Sun 1600, *El Pingüino* daily 1600, all via Río Gallegos airport. To **Comodoro Rivadavia**, **Puerto Madryn** and all destinations north to **Buenos Aires**, go to Río Gallegos and change (most services are overnight). Note that there are no buses from Río Gallegos to Ushuaia (the only overland bus route to Tierra del Fuego is via Chile). To **Río Turbio**, *Cootra* daily, 4 hrs, US$23. Taxi to Río Gallegos, 4 hrs, US$200 irrespective of number of passengers, up to 5 people.

Along Route 40 Minibus service to Los Antiguos (for Chile), US$68, via Perito Moreno, US$65, (and with possible connections for La Cueva de los Manos) departing daily Dec-Feb and subject to demand (6 passengers minimum) in Nov and Mar. Book in advance through *Chaltén Travel* (address below).

To El Chaltén Daily services in summer, 4 hrs, US$25 one way, are run by *Chaltén Travel*, Libertador 1177 and in terminal, T/F492212, rancho@cotecal.com.ar Depart 0800 and Caltur, Libertador 1080 and terminal, T/F491368, caltur@cotecal. com.ar, depart 0700. Best to book return before departure during high season. Day trips from Calafate involve too much travelling and too little time to see the area. Some agencies offer excursions eg return travel by regular bus and 1 night accommodation US$79. Off season, travel can be difficult: little transport for hitching. Agencies charge US$200 one way for up to 8 people, US$300 return.

To Chile *Cootra* to **Puerto Natales** via Río Turbio, daily, US$25, 6 hrs. Also direct services (in summer), US$25, 5 hrs, Bus Sur, Tue, Sat 0800 and Zaahj, Wed, Fri, Sun 0800, book in advance.

Directory **Airline offices** *LADE*, Libertador 1080, T491262. **Banks** Take cash as there are no *Casas de Cambio*, and high commission is charged on TCs. *Banco de la Provincia de Santa Cruz*, Libertador, ATM, 3% commission on TCs, 20%! commission on Visa and Mastercard advances, *Banco de Tierra del Fuego*, 25 de Mayo, ATM. Travel agencies such as Interlagos change notes; *YPFgarage* and *Chocolate El Calafate* and some other shops give good rates for cash; *Albergue del Glaciar*, 5% commission on TCs. *El Pingüino* bus company, 6% commission. The *Scorpio* snack bar on Libertador is reported to give best rates; try also Dos Glaciares supermarket. **Communications** **Post Office** on Libertador. Postal rates much lower from Puerto Natales (Chile) and delivery times much quicker. **Telephones** run by Cooperativa Telefónica de Calafate (Cotecal), office at Espora y Gob Moyano, 0700-0100. Fax US$6.50 per page, cheaper from Puerto Natales, expensive internet access. All services expensive, collect call impossible. **Laundry** *El Lavadero*, Libertador 1118, US$6 a load. **Tourist offices** Tourist office in bus terminal, T/F491090/492884, secturelcalafate@cotecal.com.ar Hotel prices detailed on large chart at tourist office; has a list of taxis but undertakes no arrangements. Helpful staff. Oct-Apr 0700-2200 daily. For information on the Parque Nacional los Glaciares National Parks office at Libertador 1302, T491005, Mon-Fri 0800-1500.

Parque Nacional Los Glaciares

This park, the second-largest in Argentina, extends along the Chilean frontier for over 170 km and covers more than 660,000 ha. Some 40% of the park is covered by the hielos continentales, *giant ice fields which straddle the frontier. Of the 47 major glaciers which flow from the icefields, 13 run east descending into the park to feed two great lakes: Lago Argentino and, further north, Lago Viedma. There are also about 190 smaller glaciers not connected to the ice fields.*

East of the ice fields are areas of southern beech forest, especially lenga, ñire and guindo. Further east are areas of Patagonian steppe, with shrub vegetation. Bird life is prolific with some 100 species such as the patagonian woodpecker, the austral parakeet, the green-backed firecrown, black-necked swans, Andean ruddy ducks and torrent ducks. Guanacos, grey foxes, skunks and rheas can be seen on the steppe while the rare huemul inhabits the forest.

Climate Generally cold, depending on altitude and season. Rainfall ranges from 2,000 mm in the far west to 100-150 mm in the east, falling mainly between Mar and late May. The best time to visit is between Oct and Mar. Many facilities are closed off-season. Lighting fires is prohibited throughout the park.

Two sectors of the park are popular with travellers: the southern area around Lago Argentino and the northern area around Mount Fitz Roy. Access to the central sector, north of Lago Argentino and south of Lago Viedma, is difficult and there are few tourist facilities though *estancias* such as *Helsingfors*, *Nibepo Aike* and *La Cristina* offer accommodation and excursions.

Lago Argentino This lake, the source of the Río Santa Cruz, one of the most important rivers in Patagonia, covers 1,560 sq km and lies 187 m above sea level. Fed by glaciers which flow from the Campo de Hielo Sur, its waters are very cold (3-8°C) and are milky white due to mineral particles. At its western end there are two networks of fiords (*brazos*), fed by glaciers (*ventisqueros*). The major attraction in the park is the Perito Moreno glacier; excursions also run to a group of four other glaciers further north, including the Upsala glacier.

Ventisquero Moreno Spectacular especially at sunset, the Moreno glacier is constantly moving and never silent. The ice, with its vivid blue hues, is riven by cravasses; in the middle it moves at about 1.7 m a day compared with 0.45 m a day at the sides. The noise as it cracks and strains can be heard at some distance. As pieces break off

•••

The Advance of the Moreno Glacier

The Moreno Glacier is frequently said to be in retreat as a result of global warming. Though the glacier no longer blocks Brazo Rico on a three-yearly cycle as it last did in 1988, such statements must be treated with caution.

Glaciers are usually described by glaciologists as advancing, retreating or stable. This can cause confusion since even a retreating glacier will continue moving slowly forward; its frontage or snout retreats because it melts or breaks up at a faster rate than its forward movement. Though the Moreno glacier no longer behaves as it did until 1988, it is considered by glaciologists to be stable: its rates of forward movement and break-up are in a rough equilibrium.

One of the most puzzling things about glaciers is the way they change their behaviour. As far as is known, the Moreno glacier did not block Brazo Rico until 1917; according to early scientific studies its snout was 750 m away from the Magallanes Peninsula in 1900, a distance that had dropped to 350 m by 1908. In 1917 the small dam formed by the ice broke after a few weeks; the next time the glacier blocked the fiord was in 1934-5. Between this date and 1988 the glacier moved forward more vigorously: in 1939 when it reached the Magallanes Peninsula again, the water in Brazo Rico rose 9 m and flooded coastal areas, leading to attempts by the Argentine navy to bomb it from the air. These failed but the waters eventually broke through. After 1939 the glacier reached the Peninsula about every three years until 1988. Its changed behaviour since then may be related to global warming, but perhaps we also need to know why the glacier started advancing so vigorously in the first place.

•••

and collapse into the water, there is a dull roar. The glacier can be viewed from wooden catwalks (there is a fine of up to US$500 for leaving the catwalks) and by boat. It was until recently one of the few in the world still advancing. Some 30 km long (covering an area larger than the Federal District of Buenos Aires), it reaches the water at a narrow point in one of the fiords, Brazo Rico, opposite Peninsula Magallanes: 5 km across and 60 m high, it used to advance across Brazo Rico, blocking the fiord roughly every three years; as the water pressure built up behind it, the ice would break, reopening the channel and sending giant icebergs (*témpanos*) rushing down the appropriately named Canal de los Témpanos. This last occurred in Feb 1988.

Tours From Calafate there are buses by Interlagos, US$40. Many agencies also run minibus tours, US$25-28 return (plus US$3.50 park entry) leaving 0800 returning 1800, giving 3 hrs at glacier, book through any agency in Calafate, return ticket valid if you come back next day (student discount available). *Albergue del Glaciar* trips (US$40) go out by different route passing the *Estancia Anita* and have been repeatedly recommended. Walking tours, 2 hrs, on the glacier (known as *minitrekking*) are run by *Hielo y Aventura* and sold by several agencies in Calafate (addresses above), US$67, recommended, but not for the fainthearted, take your own lunch. Taxis, US$80 for 4 passengers round trip. Out of season, trips to the glacier are difficult to arrange, but you can gather a party and hire a taxi (remise taxis T491745/91044); take warm clothes, and food and drink. (camping near ranger post, very popular, good views of glacier, showers at confiteria, US$2). Ask rangers where you can camp out of season, no facilities except a decrepit toilet block.

Boats Trips on the lake (known as *Safari Nautico*) are organized by *Hielo y Aventura*, with large boats for up to 60 passengers, US$20 per person, 1 hr offering the best views of the glacier.

Patagonia

The Upsala Glacier

The surface of the glacier is so smooth, it was used by the Argentine army for training units sent to Antarctica

The fiords at the northwestern end of Lago Argentino are fed by four other glaciers. The largest is the **Upsala** glacier, named after the Swedish university which commissioned the first survey of this area in 1908. With a surface area of 870 sq km, it covers three times the area of the Perito Moreno glacier. Some 60 km in length it is the longest glacier flowing off the Southern Patagonian icefields. Unusually it ends in two separate frontages, each about 4 km wide and 60 m high; only the western frontage can be seen from the lake excursion.

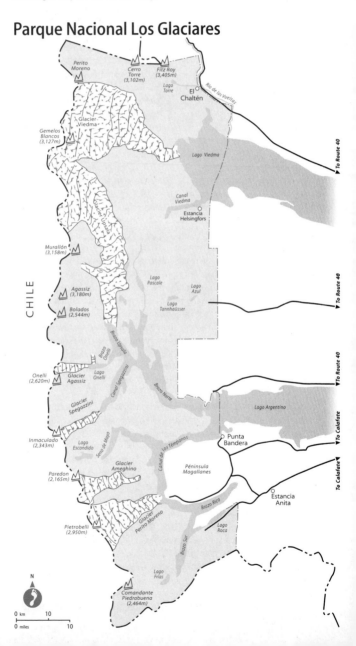

Parque Nacional Los Glaciares

The other glaciers are much smaller: **Spegazzini**, further south, has a front-age 1½ km wide and 130 m high. In between are **Agassiz** and **Onelli**, both of which feed **Lago Onelli**, a quiet and very beautiful lake, full of icebergs of every size and sculpted shape, surrounded by beech forests on one side and ice-covered mountains on the other.

Tours Tour boats from Punta Bandera, 50 km west of Calafate, visit the Upsala glacier, Lago Onelli and glacier (restaurant) and the Spegazzini glacier, (check before going that access to the face of the Upsala glacier is possible). This service is daily in season, alternating between the catamaran *Serac*, US$89, or the motor boat *Nunatak* US$79. These prices do not include bus fares from Calafate (US$20), park entry fee (US$5) or food (US$14 optional: take your own). Bus departs 0730 from Calafate for Punta Bandera, returns to Calafate at 1930; a tiring day, it is often cold and wet, but memorable. Out of season it is extremely difficult to get to the glacier. Many travel agencies make reservations.

Clearly visible from a distance, Cerro Fitz Roy (3,405 m) towers above the nearby peaks, its sides normally too steep for snow to settle. Named after the captain of the *Beagle* who saw it from afar in 1833 (its Tehuelche name was El Chaltén), it was first climbed by a French expedition in 1952. It stands in the far north of the park, 230 km north of Calafate at the western end of Lago Viedma and is part of a granite massif. Other peaks include Cerro Torre (3,128 m), Poincenot (3,076 m), Egger (2,673 m), Guillaumet (2,503 m), Saint-Exupery (2,600 m), Aguja Bífida (2,394 m) and Cordón Adela (2,938 m). Occasionally at sunrise the mountains are briefly lit up bright red for a few seconds. This phenomenon is known as the *amanecer de fuego* ('sunrise of fire').

Fitz Roy
Colour map 6, grid B2

The area around the base of the massif offers fine walking opportunities (see below) and there are stupendous views. The best months for a visit are usually March to April when the weather is generally stable and not very cold and the autumn colours are stunning. Mid-summer, December and January, and spring, September to October, are generally very windy.

Hiking Trails around the base of the Fitzroy massif are: **1** Northwest from El Chaltén via a good campsite at Lago Capri, wonderful views, to Campamento Río Blanco, and, nearby Campamento Poincenot, two to three hours, from where a path leads up to Laguna de los Tres (blue) and Laguna Sucia (green), two to three hours return from the camps; **2** From Campamento Río Blanco a trail runs north along the Río Blanco and west along the Río Eléctrico via Piedra del Fraile (four hours) to Lago Eléctrico. At Piedra del Fraile, just outside the park, there are cabanas (**E** per person with hot showers) and campsite, US$5 per person, plus expensive shop; from here a path leads south up Cerro Eléctrico Oeste (1,882 m) towards the north face of Fitz Roy, two hours, tough

A map is essential, even on short walks. Full information can be obtained from the national park office

Patagonia

Peaks in the Fitz Roy Range

Fitz Roy (Chaltén)
(3,405m)

Poincenot
(3,076m)

Cerro
Torre
(3,128m)

Egger
(2,673m)

Saint
Exupéry
(2,600m)

Rafael
(2,482m)

Val de
Vois
(2,653m)

Mermoz
(2,754m)

Guillaumet
(2,503m)

Standhardt
(2,730m)

Techado
Negro

Bífida

Mocho

but spectacular views. This route passes through private property: the owner allows you to walk through only; **3** West from El Chaltén along the Río Fitz Roy to Laguna Torre, beautifully situated at Cerro Torre and fed by Glaciar Torre, three hours; and **4** Southwest from El Chaltén along a badly marked path to Laguna Toro (6 hours), the southern entrance to the icefields. Do not stray from the paths.

El Chaltén
Phone code: 02962
Colour map 6, grid B2

Situated 230 km northwest of Calafate, El Chaltén lies at the foot of Cerro Fitz Roy and at the mouth of the valley of the Río de las Vueltas. Though the village was founded in 1985 for military reasons (to settle the area and preempt Chilean territorial claims), it has grown rapidly as a centre for trekking and climbing, it also offers cross-country skiing opportunities in winter.

There is a small chapel, the **Capilla Tomás Eger**, named after an Austrian climber killed on Fitz Roy and built entirely from materials brought from Austria. There are fine views of the Fitz Roy range from the national park office and also from Estancia Madsen which can be reached by crossing the footbridge over the Río de las Vueltas. The *Día de la Tradición* (10 November) is celebrated with gaucho events, riding and barbecue.

The Fitz Roy area

Sleeping **LL** *La Aldea*, T493040, laldearg@internet.siscotel.com 5 bed apartments. **AB** *La Casa de Piedra*, T/F493015, with bath, restaurant, guided tours. **AB** *Cabañas Cerro Torre*, T493061, built for the Herzog film 'El Grito de la Piedra', cabins sleep 4/6, kitchenette. **AB** *Hostería Los Ñires*, T493009. Restaurant. Also small dormitories **D/E** per person with kitchen facilites and camping US$5 per person. **L** *Hostería El Puma*, T493017, fitzroyexpediciones@infovia.com.ar Owned by *Fitz Roy Expeditions*, with breakfast, very comfortable rooms, lounge with log fire. Highly recommended. **AB** *Fitz Roy Inn*, T493062 or Calafate 491368, caltur@cotecal.com.ar With breakfast, restaurant, also **D** per person in shared cabins. **D/E** per person *Albergue Patagonia*, T/F493019, alpatagonia@infovia.com.ar Hostelling International discounts. Dormitory accommodation, kitchen and laundry facilities, book exchange, cycle hire, English, Dutch spoken, accepts TC's, open all year, comfortable. Recommended. **A** *Lago del Desierto*, T493010, F493016, alessandra@arnet.com.ar Good beds, Italian spoken, restaurant, camping US$5 per person. **AB/B** *La Base*, T493031, with kitchen facilities. **AB** *Posada Poincenot*, T493022. With breakfast, meals served. **D/E** per person *Albergue Rancho Grande*, T493005, rancho@cotecal.com.ar Hostelling International discounts. Small dormitories and family rooms, large lounge, restaurant, good bathrooms, laundry and kitchen facilities, English, Italian, French, German spoken, highly recommended, reservations in Chaltén Travel, Calafate, T491833. **B** per person *Estancia La Quinta*, 3 km from Chaltén, T493012, half-board, no heating, prepares lunch for trekkers. Recommended.

Credit cards & TCs are not generally accepted: take cash

Camping *Camping Madsen*, at the foot of the main trails, free. *Ruca Mahuida*, T493018, altamont@infovia.com.ar Best, good services, clean, very helpful, showers, stores gear, US$6 per person. Recommended. *El Relincho*, T493007, US$3 per person plus US$2 for shower.A stove is essential for camping as firewood is scarce and lighting fires is prohibited in campsites in the National Park. Take plenty of warm clothes and a good sleeping bag. It is possible to rent equipment in El Chaltén, ask at park entrance. Equipment and cycles for hire at *Viento Oeste* artesania shop. All campsites in National Park free, no toilets, please bury your waste. Hot showers available at Albergue Patagonia and Confiteria La Senyera, US$2.

Eating Apart from hotels: *La Senyera del Torre*. Recommended. *Ruca Mahuida*, excellent. *Josh Aike*, excellent *confitería*, good pizzas, chocolate, homemade food, beautiful building, recommended. *Josh Aike*, for chocolate and pizzas. *Zafa Rancho*, bar with piano and cinema screen. There is also a bar near *Albergue Rancho Grande* which brews its own beer.

Shopping *Despensa 2 de Abril* is said to be cheapest but has very little fresh food. *El Charito* has a good range of fruit and vegetables. The best bread is baked by Sra Isolina and can be bought from her house (where Rodolfo Guerra rants horses; see below) or from *El Charito*. *El Volcán*, hardware store, sells camping gas. Fuel is available. For handicrafts try *Viento Oeste*.

Several small shops but there is a wider selection of goods in Calafate

Sport **Climbing** Base camp for climbing Fitz Roy is Campamento Río Blanco (see above). Most of the peaks in the Fitzroy massif are for very experienced climbers as is the *Campo de Hielo Continental* (Ice Fields) which mark the frontier with Chile (no access from Chile). For details on hiring horses to carry equipment see under trekking below. *Fitzroy Expediciones*, T493017, F491364, owned by experienced guide Alberto del Castillo, organize rock climbing courses and adventure excursions including two-day ascents of Cerro Eléctrico and Cerro Solo, one day trekking expeditions on the *Campo de Hielo Continental*, 8 hrs, US$75 including equipment. Ten-day crossings of the *Campo de Hielo* are also offered, US$1,150 per person, group size 4 to 8 persons. Highly recommended, English and Italian spoken. For the icefields guides are

Patagonia

essential; necessary gear is double boots, crampons, pickaxe, ropes, winter clothing; the type of terrain is ice and rock. The best time is mid-Feb to end-Mar; Nov-Dec is very windy; Jan is fair; winter is extremely cold. Permits for climbing are available at the national park information office. Equipment hire from *Viento Oeste* handicrafts shop. **Trekking** The park information centre provides photocopied maps of treks but the best is *Trekking En Chaltén y Lago Del Desierto* published by Zagier and Urruty, 1992, US$10 (Casilla 94, Sucursal 19, 1419 Buenos Aires, T45721050, F45725766, zagier@warn.com.ar) and is available in shops in Calafate and Chaltén. For trekking by horseback with guides: Rodolfo Guerra, T493020, best horses; *El Relincho*, T493007, for packhorses. Prices: Laguna Capri US$20; Laguna Torre, US$25, Río Blanco US$30, Piedra del Fraile US$30, Laguna Toro US$30. **Fishing** Licences from *Viento Oeste*. Season runs from mid-Nov to mid-Apr.

Transport Local Mechanic Tico Hermanos, T493028. **Long distance Bus** For services from Calafate see above. In summer services to Calafate, US$25, 4 hrs, are operated by *Chaltén Travel* (book through *Albergue Rancho Grande*), depart daily 1800, and Caltur (book through *Fitzroy Inn*), depart 1700. To **Los Antiguos** via **Perito Moreno**, minibus service run by *Itinerarios y Travesías*, Herrera 2451, (1273) Buenos Aires, T/F43029533, 1 a week 1 Nov-15 Mar, with additional service 15 Dec-15 Feb, minimum 3 passengers, US$93, book through *Albergue Patagonia*. **Boat** Across Lago Viedma to *Estancia Helsingfors* leaving from Bahía Túnel, 5 km from El Chaltén, daily service in Jan/Feb, 0930 (with bus pick-up from hotels), service subject to weather conditions. Details from *Estancia Helsinfors* or *Nova Terra* agency (details under Calafate).

**Lago del
Desierto**

37 km N of El Chaltén

Surrounded by forests, this lake is reached by an unpaved road which leads along the Río de las Vueltas via Laguna Condor, where flamingos can be seen. A path runs along the east side of the lake to its northern tip, from where a trail leads west along the valley of the Río Diablo to Laguna Diablo. There is a campsite at the southern end of the lake and *refugios* at its northern end and at Laguna Diablo.

Sleeping L *Cabañas Lago del Desierto*, sleep 5, kitchen, also camping US$6 per person, bookings through Hotel *Lago del Desierto* in Chaltén.

Transport Excursions from El Chaltén by *Chaltén Travel* daily in summer; daily boat trips on the lake on *La Mariana II*, 1030, 1330, 1630, 2 hrs, US$30 (details and booking, *Hotel El Quijote*, Calafate).

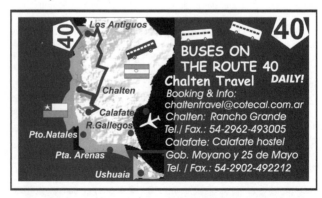

From Calafate to Chile

There are two alternative routes, the longest but easiest of which is via the main Calafate-Río Gallegos road as far as La Esperanza, Km 161, where Provincial Route 7 (*ripio*), branches off west along the valley of the Río Coyle. The alternative is to take Route 40 (*ripio*) which branches off at El Cerrito, Km 91 and runs 70 km southwest to join Route 7 at Estancia Tepi Aike, 78 km west of La Esperanza (where there is fuel and a café). This shorter route is closed in winter. From here the road continues to the border crossing at Cancha Carrera (see below) and then runs south towards Río Turbio. Guanacos and condors can be seen at intervals along this route and on clear days there are fantastic views of Torres del Paine to the west.

For public transport on this route see under Calafate

Sleeping La Esperanza D per person *Restaurant La Esperanza*, bunk beds, with bath. Also *cabañas* at the YPF service station, **AB**, sleep 6; campsite. **Fuentes del Coyle**, 31 km east of Cancha Carrera, there is an unnamed Hotel, **D** per person, cold, dirty.

The **Paso Cacha Carrera**, 129 km west of La Esperanza and 42 km north of Río Turbio, is the most convenient crossing for Parque Nacional Torres del Paine. Open all year. On the Chilean side the road continues to Cerro Castillo, 7 km west of the frontier, where it meets the road from Puerto Natales, 65 km south, to Parque Nacional Torres del Paine.

Frontier with Chile

Argentine customs and immigration At Cancha Carrera, 2 km east of the frontier, fast and friendly. **Chilean customs and immigration** At Cerro Castillo, open 0800-2200. **Sleeping** At Cerro Castillo there are *Hosp Loreto Belén* and *El Pionero*.

Some 257 km west of Río Gallegos to which it is linked by railway line (no passengers) and only 30 km northeast of the Chilean town of Puerto Natales, Río Turbio is the site of Argentina's largest coalfield. Little visited by travellers, it is a good centre for trekking and horse riding. The tourist office is in the Municipalidad. Visits can be made to **Mina Uno**, the first mine to the south of the town, and to the present mining and industrial area, on the eastern outskirts where there is a museum, the **Museo del Carbón**. ■ *Mon-Fri 0700-1200*. About 4 km south of town is **Valdelén**, a ski resort, situated just inside the frontier on the slopes of Sierra La Dorotea.

Río Turbio

Phone code: 02902
Colour map 6, grid B2
Population: 8,000

Sleeping and eating AB/B *Hostería Capipe*, at Dufour, 9 km west, T482935, F482930, restaurant. **AB** *Gato Negro*, T421226, also dormitory accommodation **E** per person. **AB** *Hostería De La Frontera*, T421979. **AB** *Nazo*, Gob Moyano 464, T421800, F421334, nazo@oyikil.com.ar **D** per person *Albergue Municipal* at Mina Uno. *Restaurant El Ringo*, near bus terminal, will shelter you from the wind.

Hotels almost always full

Sport Skiing Valdelén, with 6 *pistes*, is ideal for beginners. There is also scope for cross-country skiing nearby. Season runs from early Jun to late Sep, the *pistes* enjoying electric lighting to extend the short winter afternoons.

Transport Air Airport 15 km southeast near 28 de Noviembre; taxi US$10 per person. *LADE* flights to Río Gallegos. **Bus** To **Puerto Natales**, 2 companies, US$4, regular. To **Río Gallegos**, 4 hrs, US$15, *Quebek/Tacsa* daily 0100, *El Pengüino* daily 0200. To **Calafate**, *Cootra* daily, 5 hrs.

Paso Mina Uno, 5 km south of Río Turbio and 25 km north of Puerto Natales, this crossing is open all year in the daytime only. On the Chilean side the road

Frontiers with Chile

Patagonia

runs south to join the main Puerto Natales-Punta Arenas road. **Argentine immigration** is open 0800-2200.

Paso Casas Viejas crossing, 33 km south of Río Turbio, is reached by Route 40 via 28 de Noviembre. On the Chilean side this runs east to join the main Puerto Natales-Punta Arenas road, 3 km west of the frontier. **Argentine and Chilean immigration** is open all year 0800-2200.

Chilean Patagonia

11

Chilean Patagonia

A land of fjords, glaciers, lakes and mountains, Chilean southern Patagonia is a very popular destination. The great attraction is the Parque Nacional Torres del Paine; justly famous for its glaciers, its glacial lakes and three distinctive columns (the 'towers' after which the park is named) which point vertically like fingers from the Paine massif. Torres del Paine should not be missed, but this region has other attractions including the glaciers which descend from Monte Balmaceda at the southern end of the Parque Nacional Bernardo O'Higgins. The base for visiting both parks is Puerto Natales, which is often reached on the ferry Puerto Eden from Puerto Montt. Most other visits to this area begin in Punta Arenas, the most southerly city in Chile.

Background

Geography

This chapter covers the Chilean part of southern Patagonia, stretchings south from the icefields of the *Campo de Hielo Sur* to the *Estrecho de Magallanes* (Straits of Magellan) which separate South America from Tierra del Fuego. The coastline is heavily indented by fiords; offshore are numerous islands, few of which are inhabited. The remnants of the Andes stretch along the coast, seldom rising above 1,500 m. Mountains above this altitude include the Cordillera del Paine (several peaks over 2,600 m) and Cerro Balmaceda (2,035 m). Most of the western coast is covered by thick rainforest, but further east is grassland.

Together with the Chilean part of Tierra del Fuego and Isla Navarino, this part of Chile is adminstered as Región XII (Magallanes). The whole region is sparsely populated. Although Región XII covers 17.5% of Chilean territory, its population is around 171,000, under 1% of the Chilean total. This population is overwhelmingly urban: 160,000 live in towns, most of them in Punta Arenas, the main settlement.

Climate

When travelling in this region, protection against the ultraviolet rays of the sun is essential

Strong, cold, piercing winds blow, particularly during the spring, when they may exceed 100 km an hour. These bring heavy rain to coastal areas, over 4,000 mm a year on the offshore islands. Further east the winds are much drier; annual rainfall at Punta Dungeness at the east end of the Straits of Magellan is only 250 mm. Along the coast temperatures are moderated by the sea: summer temperatures are more variable, though seldom rising above 15°C. In winter snow covers the country, except those parts near the sea, making many roads more or less impassable, except on horseback. The winds parch the ground and prevent the growth of crops, except in sheltered spots and greenhouses.

History

Although southern Patagonia was inhabited from the end of the ice ages, the first Europeans did not visit until the 16th century. In 1519 Hernando de Magallanes, a Portuguese sailor serving the Spanish crown, sailed through the Straits that bear his name. The strategic importance of the Straits, connecting Europe with the Pacific, was quickly recognized: soon Spanish naval and merchant ships were using the route, as were mariners from other countries including Francis Drake on his world voyage (1578). However the route became less important after 1616 when the Dutch sailors Jacob le Marie and Cornelius van Schouten discovered a quicker route round Cape Horn.

Guanaco

Although at independence Chile claimed the far southern territories along the Pacific coast, little was done to carry out this claim until 1843 when, concerned at British activities in the area and at rumours of French plans to start a colony, President Bulnes ordered the preparation of a secret mission. The expedition, on board the vessel *Ancud*, established Fuerte Bulnes on a rocky point; the fort was abandoned in 1848 in favour of the new settlement of Punta Arenas.

Economy

Sheep farming is still important to the local economy; much of the meat is exported to Islamic countries, whereas locally produced beef is mainly sold domestically. Potatoes are an important crop, but owing to the climate most other vegetables are grown under cover. Although fishing is perhaps the oldest economic activity in the region, it has been transformed by the growth of salmon farming. Forestry has become more important but also controversial as a result of the use of native forests for woodchips for export to Japan, Taiwan and Brazil. Although oil production has declined as reserves have become depleted, large quantities of natural gas are now produced. About 33% of Chilean coal comes from large open cast coal mines on the Brunswick Peninsula, northwest of Punta Arenas; most of it is shipped to the thermal power stations of northern Chile. Tourism is growing rapidly, making an increasingly important contribution to the local economy.

Punta Arenas

The most southerly city in Chile, and capital of Región XII, Punta Arenas lies 2,140 km south of Santiago. It is situated on the eastern shore of the Brunswick Peninsula facing the Straits of Magellan at almost equal distance from the Pacific and Atlantic oceans. The city is a centre for the local sheep farming and fishing industries and exports wool, skins, and frozen meat. It is also the home of La Polar, the most southerly brewery in the world. Although it has expanded rapidly, particularly in recent years, it remains tranquil and pleasant.

Phone code: 061
Population: 110,000

Good roads connect the city with Puerto Natales, 247 km north, and with Río Gallegos in Argentina. Punta Arenas has certain free-port facilities; the Zona Franca is 3½ km north of the centre, on the righthand side of the road to the airport.

Ins & outs

Chilean Patagonia

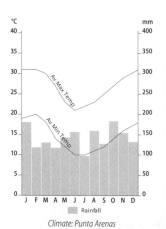

°C / mm
40 / 400
35 / 350
30 / 300
25 / 250
20 / 200
15 / 150
10 / 100
5 / 50
0 / 0
J F M A M J J A S O N D

Av Max Temp
Av Min Temp

▨ Rainfall

Climate: Punta Arenas

After its foundation in 1848, Punta Arenas became a penal colony modelled on Australia. In 1867 it was opened to foreign settlers and given free port status. From the 1880s it prospered as a refuelling and provisioning centre for steam ships and whaling vessels. It also became a centre for the new sheep *estancias* since it afforded the best harbour facilities.

History
The city's importance was reduced overnight by the opening of the Panama Canal in 1914

Around the **Plaza Muñoz Gamero** are a number of former mansions of the great sheep ranching families of the late 19th century. See the **Palacio Sara Braun**, which dates from 1895

Sights
C Pedro Montt runs E-W, while C Jorge Montt runs N-S

and which now houses the *Hotel José Nogueira*, see below. In the centre of the plaza is a statue of Magellan with a mermaid and two Fuegian Indians at his feet. According to local wisdom those who rub the big toe of one of the Indians will return to Punta Arenas. Just north of the plaza on Calle Magallanes are the **Palacio Braun Menéndez** (see below) and the **Teatro Cervantes**, which is now a cinema: the interiors of both are worth a visit. Further north, at Av Bulnes 929, is the **cemetery**, well laid out with avenues of cypresses and containing the family tombs of settler families, most of them arranged by nationality. Just inside the fate is the enormous tomb of the Menendez family; the tomb

Punta Arenas

To Patagonian Institute, Free Port, Airport & Ferry to Porvenir, Puerto Natales

To Fuerte Bulnes & Puerto del Hambre

N

Not to scale

Chilean Patagonia

La Anónima

The centre ol Punta Arenas bears witness to the influence of the people who benfitted most from the Chilean government's distribution of lands in the area after 1881. José Menéndez, whose Estancia San Gregorio covered 90,000 ha; his neighbours Sara and Maunco Braun at the Pecket Harbour Estancia; their associate Juan Blanchard; and José Noguiera, who married Sara Braun. After Noguiera's death in 1893, his holdings were merged into Braul & Blanchard, which became the largest commercial landowner in Chile; their factory at Puerto Bories, north of Puerto Natales, processed and exported meat from all over southern Argentina and Chile

Further opportunities came the way of Menéndez and Braun & Blanchard after 1899. Following the meeting between the Argentine and Chilean Presidents in Punta Arenas, the Argentine government allowed Chilean entrepreneurs to invest in Argentine Tierra del Fuego. José Menéndez founded two estancias in the Río Grande area, which

were named after himself and after his wife, Maria Behety, while Braun & Blanchard established the Estancia Sara, near San Sebastián.

Although the two companies were linked by the marraige of Maurico Braun to José Menéndez's daughter Josefina, rivalry between them was intense until both were hit by an economic crisis in 1907. In the following year they merged their holdings into the Sociedad Anónima Importadora y Exportado de la Patagonia, usually known simply as La Anónima, and in 1910 they moved their headquarters to Buenos Aires. In the following years the company extended its influence over southern Argentina; apart from its extensive landholdings, it established a chain of general stores in 45 cities and towns, built slaughter houses, meat-processing plants and port facilities, and operated shipping services, newspapers and radio stations. Its continued existence can be seen in Argentina in the form of the supermarket chain known simply as La Anónima.

of Sarah Braun is set apart in its own gardens. On the northwest side of the cemetary is the statue of **Indicito**, the little Indian,now an object of reverence, bedecked with flowers, the left knee well-rubbed. ■ *0800-1800 daily*.

West of the Plaza Muñoz Gamero on Calle Fagnano is the **Mirador Cerro de La Cruz** offering a view over the city. Nearby on Waldo Seguel are two reminders of the British influence: the **British School** and **St James Church** next door. The **Parque María Behety**, south of town along 21 de Mayo, features a scale model of Fuerte Bulnes and a campsite, popular for Sunday picnics.

Museo Regional Salesiano Mayorino Borgatello has extensive displays on indigenous peoples, the work of the missionaries and the impact of European settlement, as well as a section on oil exploration upstairs which are excellent. ■ *Tue-Sat 1000-1300 and 1500-1800, Sun 1500-1800, hrs change frequently, US$2.50. In the Colegio Salesiano, Av Bulnes 374, entrance next to church.*

Museo de Historia Regional Braun Menéndez is located in the former mansion of Mauricio Braun, built in 1905. Recommended. Part is set out as room-by-room regional history, the rest of the house is furnished. ■ *Closed Mon. Open (summer) Tue-Sat 1100-1600, Sun 1100-1400 and (winter) 1100-1300, entry US$2. Guided tours are in Spanish only. Magallanes 949, off Plaza de Armas, T244216.*

The **Instituto de la Patagonia** houses the **Museo del Recuerdo**, an open-air museum with artefacts used by the early settlers, pioneer homes, and botanical gardens. ■ *Outdoor exhibits open Mon-Fri 0800-1800, indoor pavillions 0830-1115, 1500-1800. Av Bulnes Km 4 north (opposite the university), T244216.*

Museums

Chilean Patagonia

Excursions **Reserva Forestal Magallanes**, 7 km west of town and known locally as the Parque Japonés, this reserve extends over 13,500 ha and rises to 600 m. Follow Independencia up the hill; 3 km from the edge of town take the right turning for Río de las Minas. The entrance to the reserve is 2 km beyond, there you will find a self-guided nature trail, 1 km long, free leaflet. The road continues through the woods for 14 km, passing by several picnic sites. From the top end of the road a short path leads to a lookout over the Garganta del Diablo (Devil's Throat), a gorge formed by the Río de las Minas, with views over Punta Arenas and Tierra del Fuego. From here a slippery path leads down to the Río de las Minas valley and thence back to Punta Arenas. ■ *Administration at Conaf in Punta Arenas. Turismo Pali Aike offers tours to the park, US$3.75 per person.*

Situated 56 km south of Punta Arenas, **Fuerte Bulnes** is a replica of the wooden fort erected in 1843 by the crew of the Chilean vessel *Ancud*. Nearby is Puerto Hambre. Tours by several agencies, US$12. At the intersection of the roads to Puerto del Hambre and Fuerte Bulnes, 51 km south of Punta Arenas, is a small marker with a plaque of the Centro Geográfico de Chile, ie the mid-way point between Arica and the South Pole.

Reserva Forestal Laguna Parrillar, 53 km south, covering 18,814 has older forest than the Magallanes Reserve and sphagnum bogs. There is a three hour walk to the tree-line along poorly marked paths. There are fine views from the Mirador. There is no public transport, radio taxi US$60.

Seno Otway is the site of a colony of Magellanic penguins 70 km north of Punta Arenas. It can be visited from November to March only. Rheas and skunks can also be seen. ■ *Tours by several agencies, US$12, entry US$4; taxi US$35 return.*

A small island 25 km northeast, **Isla Magdalena** is the location of the Monumento Natural Los Pingüinos, a colony of 150,000 penguins. Deserted apart from the breeding season (Nov-Jan), the island is administered by Conaf. Magdalena is one of a group of three islands, the others are Marta and Isabel, visited by Drake, whose men killed 3,000 penguins for food. It can be visited by boat trips run by Comapa.Recommended. ■ *Tue, Thu, Sat, 1530 (Dec-Feb), 2 hrs each way, with 2 hrs on the island, return 2100, coffee and biscuits served, US$30, subject to cancellation if windy; full refund given. Boat sails from Terminal Tres Puentes (reached by colectivo 15).*

Sleeping
■ *on map, page 462*
Price codes:
see inside front cover
Prices are substantially lower during the winter months (Apr-Sep). Most hotels include breakfast in the room price

LL *José Nogueira*, Bories 959, in former Palacio Sara Braun, T248840, F248832. Beautiful loggia, poor food, excellent service, lovely atmosphere. Recommended. **LL** *Finis Terrae*, Colón 766, T228200, F248124. Modern, some rooms small, safe in room, rooftop café/bar with lovely views, English spoken, parking, good value lunches, US$14. **L** *Isla Rey Jorge*, 21 de Mayo 1243, T222681, F248220. Modern, pleasant, pub downstairs, excursions, car hire. **L** *Tierra del Fuego*, Colón 716, T/F226200. Good breakfast, parking. Recommended. *Café 1900* downstairs.

AL-A *Apart Hotel Colonizadores*, Colón 1106, T244144, F226587. Clean, fully furnished apartments (2 bedrooms **AL**, 1 bedroom **A**) discounts for long stay. **A** *Hostería Yaganes*, Camino Antiguo Norte Km 7.5, T211600, F211948. *Cabañas* on the shores of the Straits of Magellan, nice setting. **A** *Hostal Patagonia*, Croacia 970, T249970, F223670, good breakfast, excellent. **AB** *Hostal Carpa Manzano*, Lautaro Navarro 336, T242296, F248864. Recommended. **AB** *Cóndor del Plata*, Colón 556, T247987, F241149. Small rooms, poor breakfast. **A** *Mercurio*, Fagnano 595, T/F242300. TV and phone, good restaurant and service. Recommended. **A** *Plaza*, Nogueira 1116, piso 2,

Wildlife spotting

A good place to photograph rheas (ñandúes) and guanacos is a few kilometres north of the checkpoint at Kon Aiken, the turnoff for Otway. Antarctic cormorants can be seen sitting on offshore rocks from the road to Fuerte Bulnes. The local skunk (chingüe) is apparently very docile and rarely sprays. Also look out for foxes and the Great Horned Owl.

T241300, F248613. (**B** without bath), pleasant, good breakfast. **AB** *Hostal de la Avenida*, Colón 534, T247532. Good breakfast, friendly, safe. Recommended. **AB** *Hostal Del Estrecho*, Menéndez 1048, T/F241011. With breakfast and bath. **AB** *Savoy*, Menéndez 1073, T241951, F247979. Pleasant rooms but some lack windows, good place to eat.

B *Hostal del Sur*, Mejicana 151, T227249, F222282. Large rooms, excellent breakfast. Highly recommended. **B** *Monte Carlo*, Colón 605, T222120, F243438, also **D** per person without bath, traditional, charming, good food. **B** *Ritz*, Pedro Montt 1102, T224422. Old, clean and cosy. Recommended (Bruce Chatwin stayed here: see his name in the guest book). **B** *Hotel El Pionero*, Chiloé 1210, T248851, F248263. With bath. **B** *Res Central*, No 1, España 247, T222315, No 2 Sanhueza 185, T222845. With bath (**D** without). Comfortable.

C *Albatros,* Colón 1195, T223131. Without bath, good. **C** *Hosp Lodging*, Sanhueza 933, T221035. With bath, **E** per person without, good value, heating, modern. **C** *Hostal Sonia Kuscevic*, Pasaje Darwin 175 (Angamos altura 550), T248543. Popular, Hostelling International discounts, with bath, breakfast, hot water, heating, parking. *El Bosque*, O'Higgins 424, T221764 (Santiago 3215012), elbosque@patagonian.com, breakfafst, use of kitchen, hot water, English spoken, internet, video, washing machine, associated projects at Yendegaia and Caleta María, hiking. **C** *Pink House*, Caupolicán 99, T222436. With breakfast, clean. **C** *Hostal Calafate*, Lautaro Navarro 850, T/F248415. Large breakfast. **C** *Hostal Calafate II*, Magallanes 922, T/F241281, calafate@entelchile.net, with bath, also **D** per person without bath, with breakfast, cable TV. **C** per person *Res Roca*, Magallanes 888, T243903. With bath, also **D** per person without bath, good.

D *Hostal Dinka's House,* Caupolicán 169, T226056. With breakfast, use of kitchen, noisy. **D** per person *Hostal Rubio*, España 640, T226458. With bath, helpful. Accommodation available in many private houses, usually **E** per person, ask at tourist office. **D** *Hosp Carlina*, Paraguaya 150, T247687. Motorcycle parking, meals, safe, quiet. Recommended. **D** *Hostal O'Higgins*, O'Higgins 1205, T225205, F243438. With breakfast, very clean. **D** *Hostal Paradiso*, Angamos 1073, T/F224212. With bath, also **C** without bath, breakfast, parking, use of kitchen. Recommended. **E** *Hosp Nena*, Boliviana 366, T242411. Friendly, with large breakfast. **E** per person, España y Boliviana, T247422. Without bath, clean, friendly, use of kitchen. **E** Sanhueza 750. Homely. Recommended. **E** per person *Hosp Independencia*, Independencia 374, T227572, with breakfast, kitchen facilities, camping. **E** per person *Alojamiento Golondrina*, Lautaro Navarro 182, T229708, kitchen facilities, meals served, English spoken. Recommended.

F per person *Backpackers Paradise*, Ignacio Carrera Pinto 1022, T222554, dormitories, with breakfast, repeatedly recommended. **E** per person *Hosp Miramar*, Errázurriz y Señoret, lovely views, good value. **F** per person *Alojamiento Prat*, Sgto Aldea 0520. Clean. Recommended. **F** per person *Backpackers Lodging*, O'Higgins 646, T220567, without breakfast, helpful. Dormitory accommodation may also be available at the

Not short on sheep

Although Bernardo Philippi, Governor of Punta Arenas, imported a few sheep from Chiloé in 1852, sheep farming did not become big business until the 1880s. In 1877 Governor Diego Almeyda brought 300 sheep from the Falkland Islands/Islas Malvinas; they were sold to a British merchant who left them on Isla Isabel in the Magellan Straits. Other merchants established sheep on other islands, where they could not stray and could be easily protected from Tehuelche hunters.

Sheep-farming was not without risks: up to 50% of the sheep died on the voyage from the Falklands/Malvinas, while fencing and other equipment were expensive. However the high price of wool made it worth while especially once the settlement of frontier disputes with Argentina in 1881 enabled the Chilean government to distribute land around Punta Arenas and on Tierra del Fuego. In 1884 alone 570,000 hectares were handed out in 90 lots in the Punta Arenas area. The main beneficiaries were a few local families, whose names are recalled in the street names of Punta Arenas. Their newly acquired lands were converted into sheep estancias, the equipment and many of the shepherds and other workers being brought from the Falklands/Malvinas, New Zealand and Britain.

Salvation Army hostel, Bellavista 577. Kitchen, hot showers, clean. Dormitory accommodation, **F** per person, also at the Colegio Pierre Fauré, Bellavista 697, in Jan/Feb.

Camping   There are no campsites in or near the city. Camping gas canisters from *Danilo Jordán*, O'Higgins 1120.

Eating
● *on map*
Many eating places close on Sun

Lobster has become more expensive because of a law allowing only lobster pots. *Centolla* (king crab) is caught illegally by some fishermen using dolphin, porpoise and penguin as live bait. There are seasonal bans on *centolla* fishing to protect dwindling stocks, do not purchase *centolla* out of season. At times *centolla* fishing is banned because the crabs can be infected with a disease which is fatal to humans. If this ban refers to the *marea roja* (red tide), it does not affect crabs, only bivalve shellfish. Mussels should not be picked along the shore owing to pollution and the *marea roja*.

Hotels   Good value set lunches and dinners at the *Cabo de Hornos*, excellent restaurants at *Los Navegantes* and *José Nogueira* which has a lovely dining room.

El Mercado, Mejicana 617, open 24 hrs, reasonably priced set lunch, expensive à la carte. *Centro Español*, Plaza Muñoz Gamero 771, above Teatro Cervantes. Large helpings, limited selection, reasonably priced. *El Mesón del Calvo*, Jorge Montt 687. Excellent, seafood, lamb, small portions, pricey. Recommended. *Sotitos*, O'Higgins 1138. Good service and cuisine, excellent. Recommended. *Lucerna*, Bories 624. Excellent meat, reasonably priced, good. *Calypso*, Bories 817. Open Sun evening, busy at night, smoky, cheap. *Bianco's Pizza*, Bulnes 01306. Excellent pizzas. Recommended. *El Quijote*, Lautaro Navarro 1087. Good sandwiches and fish dishes. Highly recommended. *Asturias*, Lautaro Navarro 967. Good food and atmosphere. *La Casa de Don Juan*, O'Higgins 1021. Spanish food. *El Estribo*, Carrera Pinto 762. Good grill, also fish. *Yaganes*, Camino Antiguo Norte Km 7.5. Beautiful setting, weekend buffet. *Golden Dragon*, Colón 529. Chinese, expensive. *Las Leyendas del Remezón*, 21 de Mayo 1469, local dishes, seafood and fish specialities. *La Terraza*, 21 de Mayo 1288. Sandwiches, *empanadas* and beer, cheap and good. *La Taberna del Club de la Unión*, Plaza Muñoz Gamero y Seguel. For drinks. For economic set lunches several along Chiloé: *Restaurant de Turismo Punta Arenas*, No 1280. Good, friendly. Recommended. *Los Años 60 The Mitchel*, No 1231. Also serves beer and 26 varieties of sandwiches,

Chilean Patagonia

Dar-es-Salaam and Aberdeen?

Today the wooden huts in Punta Arenas have given way to a mishmash of sandstone, concrete and brick. In characteristic New World fashion the town's grid layout pays no attention to topography, and streets continue straight up the hill behind the main square, giving way to steps where the gradient becomes too steep. On the stylish Avenida España, houses of the well-to-do sit smugly behind privet hedges: mock Luytens 'Bayko' styles cheek by jowl with Spanish haciendas, mid-European chalets, modernist Bauhaus blocks and Californian picture-house ranches. In the square itself more solemn Edwardian styles prevail, their dignity preserved in lemon-tinged stonework as yet unsullied by pigeon droppings. The feeling somehow combines the exotic promise of Dar-es-Salaam with the dourness of Aberdeen.

John Pilkington, An Englishman In Patagonia, Century, 1991.

open 24 hrs. *Parrilla Apocalipsis*, Chiloé esq Balmaceda. *Carioca*, Menéndez 600 y Chiloé. *Parrilla*, cheap lunches, snacks and beer, very friendly. *Lomit's*, Menéndez 722. Cheap snacks and drinks, open when the others are closed. *Kiosco Roca* (no sign), Roca 875. Early morning coffee. Cheap fish meals available at stalls in the *Cocinerías*, Lautaro Navarro south of the port entrance. Excellent *empanadas*, bread and pastries at *Pancal*, 21 de Mayo 1280. Also at *La Espiga*, Errázuriz 632. Excellent pastries at *Casa del Pastel*, Carrera Pinto y O'Higgins.

Entertainment

Bars and nightclubs *The Queen's Club*, 21 de Mayo 1455. *Sexywoman*, Av España. *Tentación*, Av Colón. Recommended. **Discos** *Abracadabra*, Bories 655. *Cuervo*, Menéndez 756. On the southern outskirts is *Torreones*, Km 5.5, T261985 and to the north is *Drive-In Los Brujos*, Km 7.5, T212600.

Sport

Golf 9-hole golf course 5 km south of town on road to Fuerte Bulnes. **Skiing** Cerro Mirador, only 9 km west from Punta Arenas in the Reserva Nacional Magallanes, is one of the few places where you can ski with a sea view. Transtur buses 0900 and 1400 from in front of *Hotel Cabo de Hornos*, US$3 return, taxi US$7. Daily lift-ticket, US$7; equipment rental, US$6 per adult. Mid-way lodge with food, drink and equipment. Season Jun to Sep, weather permitting. Contact the Club Andino, T241479, about crosscountry skiing facilities. Also skiing at Tres Morros.

Shopping
Many shops close 1230-1500

Handicrafts For leather goods and sheepskin try the Zona Franca; quality of other goods is low and prices little better than elsewhere; Mon-Sat 1030-2000 (bus E or A from Plaza Muñoz Gamero; many *colectivos*; taxi US$3). Handicrafts at *Pingüi*, Bories 404, (also stocks books on Tierra del Fuego, Patagonia and Antarctica). *Artesanía Ramas*, Independencia 799, *Chile Típico*, Carrera Pinto 1015, *Indoamérica*, Colón y Magallanes and outdoor stalls at the bottom of Independencia, by the port entrance. **Cameras** Wide range of cameras but limited range of film, from Zona Franca. *Foto Sánchez*, Bories 768, for Fuji film and *Fotocentro*, Bories 789, for Agfa: all have same day print-processing service. **Chocolate** Hand made chocolate from *Chocolatería Tres Arroyos*, Bories 448, T241522. *Chocolatería Regional Norweisser*, José Miguel Carrera 663. Both good. **Supermarkets** *Listo*, 21 de Mayo 1133. *Cofrima*, Lautaro Navarro 1293 y Balmaceda. *Cofrima 2*, España 01375. *Marisol*, Zenteno 0164.

Tour operators

Aventour, Nogueira 1255, T241197, F243354, aventour@entelchile.net English spoken, specializes in fishing trips, organize tours to Tierra del Fuego. *Yamana*, Colón 568, T221130, F240056, yamana@chileaustral.com Fishing expeditions, sea-kayaking, cycle hire, equipment hire. *Comapa*, Independencia 840, T241437, F247514, tcomapa@entelchile.net Tours to Torres del Paine, Tierra del Fuego, also trips to the Falklands/Malvinas, charter boats to Cape Horn and Isla Magdalena. *Turismo Runner*, Lautaro Navarro 1065, T247050, F241042. Adventure tours. *Arka Patagonia*, Magallanes 345, T248167, F241504. All types of tours, rafting, fishing, etc. *Turismo Pehoé*, Menéndez 918, T241373, F248052, pehoe@ctcreuna.cl Organizes tours and hotels, enquire here about catamaran services. *Turismo Aonikenk*, Magallanes 619, T/F228332. Recommended. *Maga Tour*, Ignacio Carrera Pinto 822, T/F227716, magatour@entelchile.net Specialists in rural tourism, including to *Estancia San Fernando*, on the road to Fuerte Bulnes, trekking, fishing, riding. *Turismo Pali Aike*, Lautaro Navarro 1129, T/F223301. *Turismo Viento Sur*, Fagnano 565, T226930, T225167, www.chileaustral.com/vientosur For camping equipment, fishing excursions, English spoken, good tours. Recommended. *Columbus Travel*, Sra Nadica Skármeta, T221994, knowledgeable, helpful with travel arrangements to Patagonia and the Falklands/Malvinas, booking agent for Russian planes to Antarctica. Most organize tours to Torres del Paine, Fuerte Bulnes and *pingüineras* on Otway sound: shop around as prices vary. Sr Mateo Quesada, Chiloé 1375, T222662, offers local tours in his car, up to 4 passengers.

Transport **Local Car hire** You need a hire company's authorization to take a car into Argentina, allow 24 hrs to arrange this. Damage to windscreens in very common so ask about the company's policy on this before hiring. *America Rent a Car*, Menéndez 631, T/F240852, try bargaining, friendly. *Hertz*, O'Higgins 987, T248742, F244729, English spoken. *Autómovil Club*, O'Higgins 931, T243675, F243097, and at airport. *Budget*, O'Higgins 964, T241696, F225983. *Internacional*, Waldo Sequel 443, T228323, F226334. Recommended. *Lubag*, Magallanes 970, T/F242023. *Todoauto*, España 0480, T212492, F212627. **Car repair** *Automotores del Sur*, O'Higgins 850, T224153. **Cycle parts** *José Aguila Quezada*, Arauco 2675, T265399. **Motorcycle parts** *Violic*, Sanhueza 285, T241606, also in the Zona Franca. **Taxi** Ordinary taxis have yellow roofs. *Colectivos* (all black) run on fixed routes, US$0.50 for anywhere on route. Reliable service from *Radio Taxi Austral*, T247710/244409.

Long distance Long distance transport is heavily booked from mid December to early february: advance booking is essential. **Air** Carlos Ibáñez de Campo Airport, 20 km north of town (served by Punta Arenas-Puerto Natales buses). Bus service by *Buses Transfer* (from office at Pedro Montt 966) scheduled to meet flights, US$2. *LanChile*, *DAP* and *Ladeco* have their own bus services from town, US$2.50; taxi US$12. The airport restaurant is good. To **Santiago**, *LanChile*, *Ladeco* and *Avant* daily US$220, via Puerto Montt (sit on right for views). When no tickets are available, go to the airport and get on the standby waiting list. To **Porvenir**, *Aerovías DAP* daily at 0815 and 1730, return 0830 and 1750 (US$20), plus other charter flights (eg to Puerto Natales with overflight of Torres del Paine, Antarctica), with Twin-Otter and Cessna aircraft. Heavily booked with long waiting list so make sure you have your return reservation confirmed. Military (FACh) flights approx 2 a month to Puerto Montt US$30, information and tickets from airforce base at the airport, Spanish essential, T213559; need to book well in advance. It is very difficult to get space during the summer as all armed forces personel and their families have priority over civilians. For flights to Puerto Williams see page 468. **International services** To Falkland Islands/Islas Malvinas, *Ladeco*, at least 2 a week (flies via Río Gallegos, Argentina, once a month). There are no flights to Ushuaia (Argentina).

Bus timetables are printed daily in La Prensa Austral **Bus** Buses leave from company offices. To **Puerto Natales**, 3 hrs, *Fernández, Bus Sur*, and *Buses Transfer* several every day, last departure 2000, US$7, with pick-up at the airport, book in advance. *In-Tur* (see tour companies above) runs a 2 daily circuit Punta Arenas-Puerto Natales-Torres del Paine in minibuses with snack, English-speaking guide and including national park entry; service runs mid-Oct to mid-Apr. *TurBus*, *Ghisoni* and *Austral* have services through Argentina to **Osorno** and **Puerto Montt**, *Queilén Bus* to **Castro**. Fares: to Puerto Montt or Osorno US$40 (53-70 depending on company in high season) 36 hrs; *TurBus* continues to **Santiago**, US$95 (US$60 in winter), 46 hrs. To **Castro**, US$60. To **Río Gallegos**, Argentina, via Route 255 through Punta Delgada, then Argentine Route 3: *Pingüino* daily 1200, return 1300; *Ghisoni*, daily except Fri, 1000; *Magallanes Tour*, Tue 1000; also *Bus Sur*. Fares US$20-22, officially 5 hrs, but can take up to 8, depending on customs, 15 mins on Chilean side, up to 3 hrs on Argentine side, including 30 mins lunch at Km 160. To **Río Grande**, *Hector Pacheco*, Mon, Wed, Fri 0730 via Punta Delgada, return Tue, Thu and Sat, 0730, 8-9 hrs, US$20, heavily booked. To **Ushuaia** via Punta Delgada, 12-14 hrs, *Tecni Austral* Tue, Thu, Sat 0800, US$48; *Tolkeyen*. **Companies** *Pingüino* and *Fernández*, Sanhueza 745, T242313, F225984; *Tecni Austral*, Lautaro Navarro 975, T223205; *Pacheco*, Colón 900, T242174; *Bus Sur*, Colón y Magallanes, T244464; *Bus Sur*, Menéndez 565, T244464; *Los Carlos*, Plaza Muñoz Gamero 1039, T241321; *Transfer*, Pedro Montt 966, T229613; *TurBus*, Errázuriz 932, T/F225315.

Overland to Argentina From Punta Arenas there are 3 routes to Calafate and Río Gallegos. **1** Northeast via Route 255 and Punta Delgada to the frontier at Kimiri Aike and then along Argentine Route 3 to Río Gallegos. **2** North along Route 9, turning 9 km before Puerto Natales for Dorotea (good road) and then northeast via La Esperanza (fuel, basic accommodation). **3** Via Puerto Natales and Cerro Castillo on the road to Torres del Paine joining the road to La Esperanza at Paso Cancha Carrera.

Sea Ferry For services to Porvenir, Tierra del Fuego, see page 455. **Ships** For *Navimag* services Puerto Montt – Puerto Natales, see under Puerto Montt (confirmation of reservations is advised). Visits to the beautiful fjords and glaciers of Tierra del Fuego are highly recommended. Comapa runs a once a fortnight 22-hr, 320-km round trip to the fjord d'Agostino, 30 km long, where many glaciers come down to the sea. The luxury cruiser, *Terra Australis*, sails from Punta Arenas on Sat via Ushuaia and Puerto Williams; details from Comapa. Advance booking (advisable) from *Cruceros Australis SA*, Miraflores 178, piso 12, Santiago, T6963211, F331871. Government supply ships are recommended for the young and hardy, but take sleeping bag and extra food, and travel pills. For transport on navy supply ships to Puerto Williams, enquire at Tercera Zona Naval, Lautaro Navarro 1150, or ask the captain direct, but be prepared to be frustrated by irregular sailings and inaccurate information. All tickets on ships must be booked in advance Jan-Feb. **To Antarctica** Most cruise ships leave from Ushuaia, though some call at Punta Arenas once or twice a season and agencies sell any spare berths on these. Some agencies eg *Comapa* (details above) sell berths on vessels leaving from Ushuaia. The only other possibility is with the Chilean navy. The navy itself does not encourage passengers, so you must approach the captain of the vessel in the port. Spanish is essential. The two naval vessels, the *Galvarino* and the *Lautaro*, charge US$80 per person per day. There is no accurate schedule. Accommodation includes 4 meals a day (2 with meat), laundry facilities. Take twice as much film as you think you'll need. During the voyage across the Drake Passage albatrosses, petrels, cormorants, penguins, elephant seals, fur seals, whales and dolphins can be sighted.

Airline offices *LanChile*, Lautaro Navarro 999, T241232, F222366. *Avant*, Roca 924, T228312.*Aerovías DAP*, O'Higgins 891, T223340, F221693, aeroviasdap@ctcinternet.cl Open 0900-1230, 1430-1930. **Banks** *Banco BCI*, 21 de Mayo 1199. *Banco Santiago*, on Plaza Muñoz Gamero, Visa. *Banco Santander*, Magallanes 997. *Corp Banca*, Magallanes 944. Most have ATMs. *Casas de cambio* open Mon-Fri 0900-1230, 1500-1900, Sat 0900-1230. Outside business hrs try *Buses Sur*, Colón y Magallanes, kiosk at *Calypso Café*, Bories 817 and the major hotels (lower rates).

Directory

Banks open Mon-Fri 0830-1400

Chilean Patagonia

Corp Banca, Magallanes y Menéndez. Argentine pesos can be bought at *casas de cambio*. Good rates at *Cambio Gasic*, Roca 915, Oficina 8, T242396. German spoken. *La Hermandad*, Lautaro Navarro 1099, T243991. Excellent rates, US$ cash for Amex TCs and credit cards. *Sur Cambios*, Lautaro Navarro 1001, T225656. Accepts TCs. *Kiosco Redondito*, Mejicana 613, in the shopping centre, T247369. **Communications** Post Office Bories 911 y Menéndez. Mon-Fri 0830-1930, Sat 0900-1400. **Telecommunications** for international and national calls and faxes (shop around as prices vary). *CTC*, Plaza Muñoz Gamero. Daily 0800-2200. *CTC*, Roca 886, local 23. Daily 0900-2030. *Entel*, Lautaro Navarro 957. Mon-Fri 0830-2200, Sat-Sun 0900-2200. *Telex-Chile/Chile-Sat*, Bories 911 and Errázuriz 856. Daily 0830-2200. *VTR*, Bories 801. Closed Sat afternoon and Sun. For international calls and faxes at any hr *Hotel Cabo de Hornos*, credit cards accepted, open to non-residents. **Internet** *Austrointernet Services*, Bories 687, piso 2, T/F229279/227971, US$6 per hr.*Canadian Language Institute*, O'Higgins y Carrera Pinto, US$5 per hr. *AustralInternet*, Croacia 690 and Bories 687, p 2, T/F229279, US$6 per hr. Also at *Backpacker's Paradise*, see sleeping, above. **Consulates** *Argentina*, 21 de Mayo 1878, T261912. Open 1000-1400, visas take 24 hrs, US$25. *Brazil*, Arauco 769, T241093. *Belgium*, Roca 817, Oficina 61, T241472. *Denmark*, Colón 819, Depto 301, T221488. *Finland*, Independencia 660, T247385. *Germany*, Pasaje Korner 1046, T241082, Casilla 229. *Italy*, 21 de Mayo 1569, T242497. *Netherlands*, Sarmiento 780, T248100. *Norway*, Independencia 830, T242171. *Spain*, Menéndez 910, T243566. *Sweden*, Errazúriz 891, T224107. **United Kingdom**, Roca 924, T247020. **Medical services** Dentists *Dr Hugo Vera Cárcamo*, España 1518, T227510. Recommended. *Rosemary Robertson Stipicic*, 21 de Mayo 1380, T22931. Speaks English. **Hospitals:** *Hospital Regional Lautaro Navarro*, Angamos 180, T244040. Public hospital, for emergency room ask for *La Posta*. *Clínica Magallanes*, Bulnes 01448, T211527. Private clinic, medical staff is the same as in the hospital but fancier surroundings and more expensive. **Laundry** *Lavasol*, the only self-service, O'Higgins 969, T243067. Mon-Sat 0900-2030, Sun (summer only) 1000-1800, US$6 per machine, wash and dry, good but busy. *Lavaseco Josseau*, Carrera Pinto 766, T228413. **Library** *Biblioteca Patrimonio Austral*, J Menéndez 741, specializing in culture and geography of the region. **Shipping offices** Navimag, Independencia 830, p 2, T241437, F225804, www.australis.com; Comapa (Compañía Marítima de Punta Arenas), Independencia 830, T244400, F247514. **Tourist offices** *Sernatur*, Waldo Seguel 689, Casilla 106-D, T241330. At the corner with Plaza Muñoz Gamero, 0830-1745, closed Sat and Sun. Helpful, English spoken. Kiosk on Colón between Bories and Magallanes Mon-Fri 0900-1300, 1500-1900, Sat 0900-1200, 1430-1730, Sun (in the summer only) 1000-1230. Turistel Guide available from kiosk belonging to *Café Garogha* at Bories 831. *Conaf*, Menéndez 1147, piso 2, T223841. Open Mon-Fri.

North from Punta Arenas From Punta Arenas a road runs to Puerto Natales, 247 km north. Around Villa Tehuelches, 100 km north of Punta Arenas, a sign invites you to see 'Panchito', a tame condor, US$0.25. Fuel is available in Villa Tehuelches.

Sleeping Along this road are several hotels, including **C** per person *Hostería Río Verde*, Km 90, east off the highway on Seno Skyring, T311122, F241008 rioverde@chileaustral.com With bath, heating, also offers *asados* and lunches. **B** *Hostal Río Penitente*, Km 138, T331694. In an old *estancia*. Recommended. **C** *Hotel Rubens*, Km 183, T226916. Popular for fishing. *Hostería Llanuras de Diana*, Km 215 (30 km south of Puerto Natales), T248742, F244729 (Punta Arenas), T411540 (Puerto Natales). Hidden from road, beautifully situated, restaurant. Highly recommended.

Puerto Natales

Phone code: 061
Population: 15,000
247 km N of
Punta Arenas

Puerto Natales lies on the eastern shore of the Seno Ultima Esperanza (Last Hope Sound) amid spectacular scenery and is the jumping-off place for the magnificent Balmaceda and Torres del Paine national parks. There are fine views over the Seno Ultima Esperanza to the Peninsula Antonio Varas.

Founded in 1911, Puerto Natales grew as an industrial centre: the biggest meatpacking factory in Patagonia was situated at Puerto Bories, 6 km north. Though much of the old plant was destroyed by fire, the administration buildings and housing can be visited. Until recent years the town's prosperity was based upon employment in the coal mines of Río Turbio, nearby in Argentina; with the decline of the mines tourism and fishing have become more important.

A recommended walk is up to **Cerro Dorotea** which overlooks the town and offers superb views of the Seno Ultima Esperanza and across into Argentina. The base of the Cero can be reached by any bus for Río Turbio or Punta Arenas.

Monumento Natural Cueva Milodón (50-m wide, 200-m deep, 30-m high), 25 km north, contains a plastic model of the prehistoric ground-sloth whose bones were found there in 1895. Evidence has also been found here of occupation by early Patagonian humans some 11,000 years ago. Nearby there is a visitor's centre with good displays on the mylodon and on local geology, summaries in English. There is free camping once the US$4 entrance fee has been paid. ■ *Buses J and B regular service US$7.50; taxi US$18 return or check if you can get a ride with a tour; both Adventur and Fernández tour buses to Torres del Paine stop at the cave.*

Estancia Rosario, on the Peninsula Antonio Varas on the western side of the Seno Ultima Esperanza, offers lunches, horseriding, US$22 per person for three hours, and other activities, transport across the sound included. Contact T410836 (or via Ganaustral, Eberhard 318, Puerto Natales T411475, F412117, ganasa@ctcinternet.cl).

Excursions

For excursions to the Torres del Paine & the Monte Balmaceda national parks, see below

Sleeping

■ *on map, page 472 Price codes: see inside front cover Most prices include breakfast. In season cheaper accommodation fills up quickly after the arrival of the 'Puerto Edén' from Puerto Montt*

LL *Costa Australis*, Pedro Montt 262, T412000, F411881. Modern, wonderful views over Seno Ultima Esperanza, popular cafetería. Recommended. **L** *Eberhard*, Pedro Montt 58, T411208, F411209. Excellent views, restaurant. **AL** *Alberto De Agostini*, O'Higgins 632-646, T410060, F410070, hotel.Agostini@entelchile.net, with bath, TV, good restaurant, helpful, **A** in winter. **L** *Martín Guisinde*, Bories 278, T412770, F412820. Pub, restaurant, modern. Recommended. **AL** *Palace*, Ladrilleros 209, T411134. Good food, overpriced. **A** *Juan Ladrilleros*, Pedro Montt 161, T411652, F412109. Modern, with bath, good restaurant, clean. Recommended. **A** *Glaciares*, Eberhard 104, T/F411452. Modern, snack bar. **A** *Hostal Sir Francis Drake*, Phillipi 383, T/F411553. Good views, snack bar. Recommended. **AB** *Hostal Lady Florence Dixie*, Bulnes 659, T411158, F411943. Modern, friendly. Recommended. **AB** *Lukoviek*, Ramirez 324, T411120, F412580. With breakfast, restaurant, helpful. **AB** *Lago Sarmiento*, Bulnes 90, T411542. With bath, comfortable living room with good view, well-run, recommended. **AB** *Saltos del Paine*, Bulnes 156, T410261. With breakfast, excellent.

B *Blanquita*, Carrera Pinto 409. Quiet. Recommended. **B** *Hostal Melissa*, Blanco Encalada 258, T411944. With bath, confitería. **B** *Natalino*, Eberhard 371, T411968. Clean and very friendly (tours to Milodón Cave arranged), **C** without bath, parking. **B** *Hostal Reymar*, Baquedano 414, T/F411434, with breakfast, good restaurant. **B** *Concepto Indigo*, Bories y Costanera, also **E** per person dormitory accommodation, lovely views, rock climbing courses and tours, good meeting place, slide shows, vegetarian restaurant. Recommended. **C** *Hostal Los Antiguos*, Ladrilleros 195 y Bulnes, T/F411488. Without bath, pleasant. **C** *Res Carahue*, Bulnes 370, T411339. With breakfast, laundry facilities, pleasant. **C** *Bulnes*, Calle Bulnes 407, T411307. With breakfast, good, stores luggage. **C** *Hostal Puerto Natales*, Eberhard 250, T411098. With bath. **D** *Res Centro*, Magallanes 258A, T411996. With bath. **D** *Res Sutherland*, Barros Arana 155. With bath, welcoming, clean, kitchen facilities. **D** *Res Asturias*, Prat 426, T412105, with breakfast, kitchen facilities, cosy.

E per person *Hosp Niko's*, Ramirez 669, T412810, with breakfast, good meals, English spoken, also dormitory accommodation, **F** per person, recommended. **E** per person *Hosp La Chila*, Carrera Pinto 442. Use of kitchen, welcoming, luggage store, bakes bread. Recommended. **E** per person *Hosp María José*, Magallanes 646, T413069,

Chilean Patagonia

F412218. Cooking facilities, internet, helpful. **E** per person *Hosp Gamma/Milodón*, El Roble 650, T411420. Cooking and laundry facilities, evening meals, tours. **E** per person *Los Inmigrantes*, Carrera Pinto 480. Good breakfast, clean, kitchen facilities, equipment rental, luggage store. Recommended. **E** per person *Res El Mundial*, Bories 315, T412476. Use of kitchen, good value meals, luggage stored. Recommended. **E** per person *Res Tierra del Fuego*, Bulnes 29. Clean, stores luggage, restaurant, good. **E** per person *Hosp Gabriella*, Bulnes 317, T411061. Clean, good breakfast, helpful, luggage store. Recommended. **E** per person *Hosp Elsa Millán*, Elcano 588. Good breakfast, homemade bread, dormitory-style, popular, hot water, warm, friendly, cooking facilities. Recommended. **E** per person *Res Dickson*, Bulnes 307, T411218. Good breakfast, clean, helpful, cooking and laundry facilities. Recommended. **E** per person *Pensión Ritz*, Carrera Pinto 439. Full pension available, friendly. **E** per person *Res Temuco*, Ramírez 310, T411120. Friendly, reasonable, good food, clean. **E** per person *Hosp Laury*, Bulnes 222. With breakfast, cooking and laundry facilities, clean, warm, friendly. **E** per person *Almirante Nieto*, Bories 206. Use of kitchen, dormitory accommodation, sleeping bag necessary, good meeting place, friendly. **D** per person *Casa Cecilia*, Tomás Rogers 60, T/F411797, redcecilia@entelchile.net. With bath, also **E** per person without bath, with breakfast, clean, cooking facilities, English, French and German spoken, kitchen facilities, heating, good camping equipment rental, information on Torres del Paine, tours organized, credit cards accepted, internet access, airline tickets sold, email access. Warmly recommended **E** per person *Hosp Patagonia Adventure*, Tomás Rogers 179, T411028. Dormitory style, and private rooms, friendly, clean, use of kitchen, breakfast, English spoken, camping equipment

Puerto Natales

Chilean Patagonia

for hire, book exchange. Recommended. **E** per person Sra Bruna Mardones, Pasaje Don Bosco 41 (off Philippi). Friendly, meals on request. **E** per person *Casa de familia Alicia*, M Rodríguez 283. With breakfast, clean, spacious, luggage stored, helpful. Recommended. **E** per person *Don Bosco*, Padre Rossa 1430. Good meals, pancakes for breakfast, use of kitchen, helpful. Recommended. Motorcycle parking, luggage store. **E** *Res Nataly*, O'Higgins 657. Dormitornies. **E-F** per person *Casa Teresa*, Esmeralda 463. Good value, warm, cheap meals, quiet, friendly. Recommended. Tours to Torres del Paine arranged. **F** per person *Res Lago Pingo*, Bulnes 808, T411026. Basic, with breakfast, laundry, use of kitchen, luggage stored, English spoken; similar at O'Higgins 70, 431 and Perito 443. **F** per person *Hosp Nancy*, Barros Arana 104, T411028, with breakfast, shared bath, large rooms, use of kitchen, TV and reading room, excursions and buses booked, lots of information, recommended. **F** per person Tomás Rogers 43, with breakfasft, use of kitchen, recommended.

North of Puerto Natales are **A** *Cabañas Kotenk Aike*, 2 km north of town, T412581, F225935, sleep 4, very comfortable. **L-A** *Cisne de Cuello Negro*, a former guest house for meat buyers at the disused meat packing plant, 5 km from town at Km 275 near Puerto Bories, T411498 (Av Colón 782, Punta Arenas, T244506, F248052). Friendly, clean, reasonable, excellent cooking. Recommended. **C** *Hotel 3 Pasos*, 40 km north, T228113. Simple, beautiful. In Villa Cerro Castillo, 63 km north. **B** *Hostería El Pionero*, T/F411646/691932 anexo 722. With bath, country house ambience, good service, horses available for hire for Torres del Paine.

Hotels in the countryside open only in summer months: dates vary For accommodation in the Torres del Paine area, see below

Don Alvarito, Blanco Encalada 915. Hospitable. *El Marítimo*, Pedro Montt 214. Seafood and salmon, good views, popular, slow service. *Mari Loli*, Baquedano 615. Excellent food, good value. *La Ultima Esperanza*, Eberhard 354. Recommended for salmon, seafood, enormous portions, not cheap but worth the experience. *Andrés*, Ladrilleros 381. Excellent, good fish dishes, good service. *Tierra del Fuego*, Bulnes 29. Cheap, good, slow service. *Café Midás*, Tomas Rogers 169, has book swap. *Melissa*, Blanco Encalada. Good coffee and sandwiches. *Centro Español*, Magallanes 247. Reasonable. *La Frontera*, Bulnes 819. Set meals, good value. [Evasion], Eberhard 595, café/*parrillada* with internet, pool tables. Cheap meals at *Club Deportivo Natales*, Eberhard 332. *Cristal*, Bulnes 439. Good sandwiches and salmon, good value. *La Repizza*, Blanco Encalada 294. Good value. *La Esquina*, Magallanes y Eberhard. Good bar.

Eating
● *on map*

Discos *El Cielo*, Esmeralda y Ramírez. *Milodón*, Blanco Encalada.

Entertainment

Camping equipment *Patagonia Adventure*, Tomás Rogers 179. *Casa Cecilia*, Tomás Rogers 54. German, French and English spoken, imported gear, also for sale. Recommended. Check all equipment and prices carefully. Average charges, per day: tent US$6, sleeping bag US$3, mat US$1, raincoat US$0.60, also cooking gear, US$1. **(Deposits required: tent US$200, sleeping bag US$100.)** It is often difficult to hire walking boots. Camping gas is widely available in hardware stores, eg *Soquina*, Baquedano y O'Higgins and at Baquedano y Esmeralda. **Fishing** Tackle for hire at *Andes Patagónicos*, Blanco Encalada 226, T411594, US$3.50 per day for rod, reel and spinners; if you prefer fishing with floats, hooks, split shot, etc, take your own. Other companies up to 5 times as expensive.

Sport

Chilean Patagonia

Handicrafts *Ñandu*, Eberhard 586. Popular. Also at Baquedano y Chorillos. Supermarket: *La Bombonera*, Bulnes 646. **Shoe repairs** *París*, Miraflores between Blanco Encalada and Baquedano. **Supermarket** *El Favorito*, Bulnes 1008. 24-hr supermarket Bulnes 300 block, markets good, food prices variable so shop around. Cheaper in Punta Arenas.

Shopping

Tour companies & travel agents   *Michay*, Baquedano 388, T411149. *Knudsen Tours*, Blanco Encalada 284, T411531. Recommended. *Path@gone*, Eberhard y Blanco Encalada, joint office for **Andescape**, T412877, F412592, andescape@chileaustral.com, and *Onas*, T414349, F412707, onas@chileaustral.com Handle most bookings for Torres del Paine, including *Andescape* and *Fantástico Sur refugios* and boat trips into the park. *Servitur*, Pratt 353, T411028. *Turismo Zaahj*, Prat 236. T412260, F411355. Recommended. *Turismo Cabo de Hornos*, Pedro Montt 380. *Turismo Tzonka*, Carrera Pinto 626, T411214. *Turismo Luis Díaz*, Blanco Encalada 189, T411654, for tours to Perito Moreno glacier (Argentina). Reports of the reliability of agencies, especially for their trips to Torres del Paine National Park, are very mixed. It is better to book tours direct with operators in Puerto Natales than through agents in Punta Arenas. Several agencies offer tours to the Perito Moreno glacier in Argentina, 1 day, US$40 without food or park entry fee, 14 hr trip, 2 hrs at the glacier (Take US$ cash or Argentine pesos as Chilean pesos not accepted); agencies will allow travellers to leave the tour in Calafate **Tourist offices**   Kiosk on waterfront, Av Pedro Montt y Phillipi; maps for US$1 from Eberhard 547. *Conaf*, O'Higgins 584.

Transport   **Local Bicycle hire**   *Casa Cecilia*, (see under sleeping). **Bicycle repairs**   *El Rey de la Bicicleta*, Ramírez 540, good, helpful. **Car hire**   *Andes Patagónicos*, Blanco Encalada 226, T411728, US$85 per day including insurance and 350 km free. *Avis*, Bulnes 632, T411775. *Todoauto*, Bulnes 20, T412837. US$110 per day for high clearance vehicle, others US$80 per day, or US$85 with driver. Hire agents can arrange permission to drive into Argentina, but this is expensive and takes 24 hrs to arrange. **Mechanic** Carlos González, Ladrilleros entre Bories y Eberhard. Recommended.

Long distance Bus   To Punta Arenas, several daily, 3½ hrs, US$6. Book in advance. To **Coyhaique** via Calafate, *Urbina Tours*, 4 days, US$120 (Nov-Mar). Out of season the only service to rest of Chile is with *Austral Bus*, Tue to Puerto Montt, US$150, book days in advance. **To Argentina**: to **Río Gallegos** direct, *Bus Sur*, US$22, Tue and Thu 1830 and *El Pingüino*, Wed and Sat 1100, US$13; hrly to **Río Turbio**, *Lagoper*, (Baquedano y Valdivia), *Turisur*, *Bus Sur*, *Cootra*, US$3, 2 hrs (depending on customs – change bus at border). To **Calafate**, *Cootra* via Río Turbio daily, US$23, 6 hrs, or *Bus Sur* (Mon/Fri 0900) and *Zaahj* (Tue/Thu 0900) more direct service via Cerro Castillo, 4-5 hrs, US$25, reserve 1 day ahead. **Companies**: Bus Fernández, Eberhard 555, T411111, *Bus Sur*, Baquedano 534, T411325 and *Bus Transfer*, Baquedano 414, T421616.

Ferry   The *Navimag* ferry Puerto Edén sails every Fri in summer to Puerto Montt, less frequently off season. Navimag office: Pedro Montt 262 Local B, Terminal Marítimo, T414300, F414361.

Directory   **Airline offices**   *LanChile/Ladeco*, Tomás Roger 78. **Banks**   *Banco Santiago*, Bulnes y Blanco

Poor rates for TCs, which cannot be changed into US$ cash   Encalada. Mastercard and Visa, ATM. **Casas de cambio** *Enio America*, Blanco Encalada 266 where Argentine pesos can be changed. *Cambio Stop*, Baquedano 380. Good for cash (also arranges tours). Another 2 at Bulnes 683 and 1087 (good rates; also Argentine pesos). Others on Prat. Shop around as some offer very poor rates. **Communications**   Post office Eberhard 417. Open Mon-Fri 0830-1230, 1430-1745, Sat 0900-1230. **Telephones** *CTC*, Blanco Encalada 23 y Bulnes. Phones and fax. *Entel*, Baquedano y Bulnes. **Internet Email** *CTC*, Baquedano 383, US$5.75 per hr. *El Rincón de Tata*, Prat 236, *Evasion*, Eberhard 595; also at *Casa Cecilia, Concepto Indigo, Hosp María José* (see under sleeping). **Laundry**   *Servilaundry*, Bulnes 513. *Lavandería Catch*, Bories 218, friendly service. *Servilaundry*, Bulnes 513. *Milodón*, Baquedano 462. **Shipping**   Navimag: Pedro Montt 262 Loc B, Terminal Marítimo, T/F411421.

Parque Nacional Bernardo O'Higgins   Often referred to as the **Parque Nacional Monte Balmaceda**, this park covers large expanses of the icefields of the Campo de Hielo Sur and the fjords and offshore islands further west, including Isla Wellington. The park is uninhabited; the small community of Puerto Edén on Isla Wellington is outside the park limits. Though the park is inaccessible except by air and sea, the south-ernmost section of the park, around Monte Balmaceda (2,035 m) lies at the northern end of the Seno Ultima Esperanza and can be reached by boat from Puerto Natales. Two boats *21 de Mayo* and *Alberto de Agostini* sail daily from Puerto Natales in summer and on Sunday only in winter (minimum 10 pas-sengers), when weather conditions may be better with less cloud and rain, US$55 (or US$50 cash). After a three hour journey up the Sound, the boat passes the Balmaceda Glacier which drops from the eastern slopes of Monte Balmaceda (2,035 m). The glacier is retreating; in 1986 its foot was at sea level. The boat docks one hour further north at Puerto Toro, from where it is a 1 km walk to the base of the Serrano Glacier on the north slope of Monte Balmaceda. On the trip dolphins, sea lions (in season), black-necked swans, flightless steamer ducks and cormorants can be seen.

■ *Getting there Bookings direct through Turismo 21 de Mayo, Ladrilleros 171, T/F411478 or from Eberhard 554, T411978 or through travel agencies, expensive lunch extra, take own food, drinks available on board. Take warm clothes, hat and gloves. This trip can also be used as a way of visiting Torres del Paine, either on foot by dingy. Walkers can follow a path along the Río Serrano to the Torres del Paine administration centre, 35 km, guided tours along this are available, permits may be needed from Conaf. The boat trip, operated by Onas (details under Puerto Natales) is described below under Torres del Paine.*

Parque Nacional Torres del Paine

This national park, a UNESCO Biosphere Reserve, is a must for its wildlife and spectacular scenery. With constantly changing views of fantastic peaks, ice-fields, vividly coloured lakes of turquoise, ultramarine and grey, and quiet green valleys, it is stunning. In the centre of the park is a granite massif from which rise the Torres (Towers) and Cuernos (Horns) of Paine, oddly shaped peaks of over 2,600 m. The valleys are filled by beautiful lakes drained by the Río Serrano, the most impor-tant river in the region, which flows south into the Seno Ultima Esperanza near Monte Balmaceda. Though most visitors enter and leave the park by road, it is also possible to do this journey by boat along the Río Serrano.

Situated 145 km NW of Puerto Natales; Covers 181,414 ha

The park is open all year round, although snow may prevent access in the winter how-ever during this season there are good, stable conditions and well-equipped hikers can do some good walking. Weather conditions are often stable in autumn (Mar- Apr) also. The warmest time is Dec-Mar, although it can be wet and windy. The spring months of Oct-Nov are recommended for the wild flowers. It is most visited during the summer months of Jan and Feb which should be avoided if possible. It is vital not to underestimate the unpredictability of the weather (which can change in a few mins), nor the arduousness of some of the stretches on the long hikes. Rain and snow-fall are heavier the further west you go, and bad weather sweeps off the *Campo de Hielo Sur* without warning. It is essential to be properly equipped against cold, wind and rain. The only means of rescue are on horseback or by boat; the nearest helicopter is in Punta Arenas and high winds usually prevent its operation in the park.

Climate

There are 15 peaks above 2,000 m, of which the highest is Cerro Paine Grande (3,050 m). On the western edge of the park is the enormous *Campo de Hielo Sur icecap*; four main glaciers (*ventisqueros*), Grey, Dickson, Zapata and Tyn-dall, branch off this and drop to the lakes formed by their meltwater. Two other glaciers, *Francés* and *Los Perros*, descend on the western side of the central *massif*. The park enjoys a micro-climate especially favourable to wildlife and

Allow a week to 10 days to see the park properly

Chilean Patagonia

Look under your feet

Few of the 60,000 people a year who visit Torres del Paine look closely at what they are treading on; a blanket of orchids, orange and yellow slipper plants, lathyrus (mauve sweet pea like flowers) and mauve Oxalis. In spring the hill slopes are a blaze of embothrim, with its brilliant red flowers, pernettya with its copious ruby-like fruits and calafate, a low shrub with bright yeloow single flowers and delicious red/mauve berries. In damper shady areas are clumps of gunnera magellancia as well as the copihue, the Chilean national flower.

Calceolaria

plants. There are 105 species of birds including 18 species of waterfowl and 11 birds of prey. Particularly noteworthy are condors, black-necked swans, rheas, kelp geese, ibis, flamingos and austral parakeets. The park is one of the best places on the continent for viewing large numbers of guanacos and rheas. Apart from guanacos 24 other species of mammals can be seen including hares, foxes, *huemules* (a species of deer), pumas and skunks. Over 200 species of plants have been identified.

Torres del Paine has become increasingly popular with foreigners and Chileans alike: in 1998 it received 60,000 visitors. Despite the best efforts to manage this large influx of visitors rationally, their impact is starting to show. Litter has become a problem especially around the *refugios* and camping areas. Please take all your rubbish out of the park and remember that toilet paper is also garbage.

Park information The park is administered by Conaf: the administration centre is in the south of the park at the northern end of Lago del Toro. ■ *0830-2000 in summer, 0830-1230, 1400-1830 off season*. The centre provides a good slide show at 2000 on Saturday and Sunday and there are also excellent exhibitions on the wildlife and flora of the park (Spanish with brief summaries in English), but no maps or written information to take away. For information in Spanish on weather conditions phone the administration centre (T691931). There are six ranger stations (*guarderías*) staffed by rangers (*guardaparques*) who give help and advice and will also store luggage (except at Laguna Amarga where they have no room). Rangers keep a check on the whereabouts of all visitors: you are required to register and show your passport when entering the park. You are also requested to register at a ranger station before setting off on any hike. **Access** There are entrances at Laguna Amarga, Lago Sarmiento and Laguna Azul. Entry: foreigners: US$15, Chileans US$6 (proceeds are shared between all Chilean national parks), climbing fees US$800.

Hikes

There are about 250 km of well marked trails. Visitors must keep to the trails: cross-country trekking is not permitted. The times indicated should be treated with caution: allow for personal fitness and weather conditions.

An impression of Torres del Paine

Torres del Paine is one of the most impressive mountain areas on Earth. There are few comparable sites with almost 1,000 m vertical shafts of basalt with conical caps atop steep forested talus slopes. These are the remains of frozen magma in ancient volcanic throats, everything else having been eroded; the highest is 3,243 m and may be seen from near sea-level. As well as these spectacular mountains the surrounding forest, with lakes, glaciers and open country is truly magnificent. Although outposts of civilization exist near the edges of the park it is quite easy to escape its influences in a few hours trekking.

Wildlife abounds; guanacos and condors are common, and other mammals and birds quite abundant. I recall a very peculiar scratching sound on the corrugated iron roof of a hut one morning, and emerged to find a large condor was roosting on the ridge but having difficulty securing a good grip with its claws. The region is sufficiently far south for the worst of the biting invertebrates to be only a minor problem.

Vegetation is typical South Andean. Although few trees reach great size, several valleys are thickly forested and little light penetrates. The grassland is distinct from the monotony of the pampa and dispersed sclerophyl forest. A complex series of lakes and streams leads into fjords extending sinuous distances from the sea. These are another attraction; many are glacial fed (and thus very cold); fortunately some strategic footbridges exist.

Much of the park was once a cattle ranch. This explains some of the older refugios which were huts where gauchos lived during round-up. Most cattle have now gone leaving the few hotels as the only commerce.

El Circuito The most popular hike is a circuit round the Torres and Cuernos del Paine: usually it is done anticlockwise starting from the Laguna Amarga *guardería*. From Laguna Amarga the route is north along the western side of the Río Paine to Lago Paine, before turning west to follow the Río Paine to the southern end of Lago Dickson. From here the path runs along the wooded valley of the Río de los Perros before climbing steeply to Paso John Gardner (1,241 m, the highest point on the route), then dropping to follow the Grey Glacier southeast to Lago Grey, continuing to Lago Pehoé and the administration centre. There are superb views, particularly from the top of Paso John Gardner.

Although some people complete the route in less time, it normally takes five to six days. In theory, lone walkers are not allowed on this route; camping gear must be carried. The circuit is often closed in winter because of snow. The longest lap is 30 km, between Refugio Laguna Amarga and Refugio Dickson (10 hours in good weather), but the most difficult section is the very steep slippery slope between Paso John Gardner and *Campamento* Paso. Although most people go anti-clockwise round the circuit, some advise doing it clockwise so that you climb to Paso John Gardner with the wind behind. The major rivers are crossed by footbridges, but these are occasionally washed away.

The W This route combines several of the hikes described separately below. From *Refugio Laguna Amarga* the first stage runs west via *Hostería Las Torres* and up the valley of the Río Ascensio via *Refugio Chileno* to the base of the Torres del Paine (see below). From here return to the *Hostería Las Torres* and then walk along the northern shore of Lago Nordenskjold via *Refugio Los Cuernos* to *Campamento Italiano*. From here climb the Valley of the Río del Francés (see below) before continuing to *Refugio Pehoé*. From here you can complete the third part of the 'W' by walking west along the northern shore of Lago Grey to *Refugio Grey* and Glaciar Grey before returning to *Refugio Pehoé*. A popular

Torres del Paine

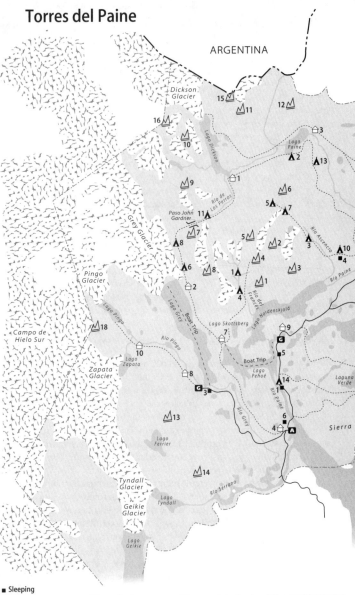

ARGENTINA

Dickson Glacier

Lago Dickson

Río de Los Perros

Grey Glacier

Paso John Gardner

Pingo Glacier

Campo de Hielo Sur

Lago Pingo

Río Pingo

Lago Zapata

Zapata Glacier

Lago Ferrier

Río del Francés

Lago Skottsberg

Lago Nordenskjöld

Boat Trip

Lago Pehoé

Laguna Verde

Río Paine

Sierra

Tyndall Glacier

Lago Tyndall

Geikie Glacier

Lago Geikie

Río Serrano

Río Grey

Río Ascencio

Lago Paine

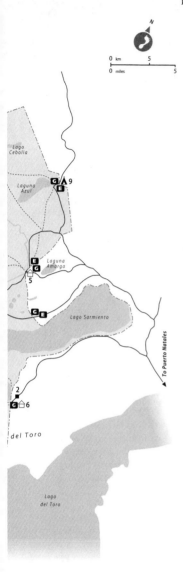

alternative to *El Ciruito*, this route can be completed without camping equipment as there is adequate accommodation in *refugios*. Allow four to five days.

From *Refugio Pehoé* this route leads **Valley of the** north across undulating country **Río del Francés** along the western edge of Lago Skottberg to *Campamento Italiano* and then follows the valley of the Río del Francés which climbs between (to the west) Cerro Paine Grande and the Ventisquero del Francés and (to the east) the Cuernos del Paine to *Campamento Británico*. Allow 2½ hours from Refugio Pehoé to *Campamento Italiano*, 2½ hours further to *Campamento Británico*. The views from the *mirador* above *Campamento Británico* are superb.

From *Guardería Grey* (18 km west by **To Lago Pingo** road from the administration centre) follow the Río Pingo, via *Refugio Pingo* and *Refugio Zapata* (4 hours), with views south over Ventisquero Zapata (plenty of wildlife, icebergs in the lake) to reach the lake (five hours from *Guardería Grey*). Ventisquero Pingo can be seen 3 km away over the lake. Two short signposted walks from Guardería Grey have also been suggested: one is a steep climb up the hill behind the ranger post to **Mirador Ferrier** from where there are fine views; the other is via a suspension bridge across the Río Pingo to the peninsula at the southern end of Lago Grey, from where there are good views of the icebergs on the lakes.

From *Refugio Laguna Amarga* the **To the base of** route follows the road west to **Torres del Paine** *Hostería Las Torres* before climbing along the western side of the Río Ascensio via *Refugio Chileno* and *Campamento Chileno* to *Campamento Las Torres*, close to the base of the Torres and near a small lake. Allow 1½ hours to *Hostería Las Torres*, then two hours to *Refugio Chileno*, two hours further to *Campamento Torres* where there is a

Chilean Patagonia

River running deep

> The voyage up the Río Serrano in a dingy offers a dramatic entry to the park. This wide and fast-flowing river drains the park into the Seno Ultima Esperanza, flowing through areas of thick evergreen forest. Above are mountain peaks and glimpses of the Paine massif can be seen away in the distance. At points along the river the wind sweeps down from the ice cap, whipping up the water which soaks passengers in the boat; at other points the river is sheltered and, if the weather is fine, you will want to take off your waterproofs and enjoy the sunshine.

lake: the path is well-marked, but the last 30 minutes is up the morraine; to see the towers lit by sunrise (spectacular but you must have good weather), it's well worth humping camping gear up to *Campamento Torres* and spending the night. One hour beyond *Campamento Torres* is *Campamento Japonés*, a good camping site.

To Laguna Verde From the administation centre follow the road north 2 km, before taking the path east over the Sierra del Toro and then along the southern side of Laguna Verde to the *Guardería Laguna* Verde. Allow four hours. This is one of the easiest walks in the park and may be a good first hike.

To Laguna Azul & Lago Paine This route runs north from Laguna Amarga to the western tip of Laguna Azul, from where it continues across the sheltered Río Paine valley past Laguna Cebolla to the *Refugio Lago Paine* at the western end of the lake. Allow 8½ hours.

The Río Serrano Although most visitors enter the park by road, it is also possible to do this by boat by taking one of the cruises from Puerto Natales up the Seno Ultima Esperanza to the Parque Nacional Bernardo O'Higgins and then transferring to a dingy for the trip up the Río Serrano to the Administration Centre. This trip can also be done in reverse to leave the park. It is also possible to sail down the Río Serrano from the Administration Centre to the Glacier Serrano and return, US$65. The voyage into the park can be combined with a short minibus tour of Torres del Paine and return trip by minibus to Puerto Natales, US$119. Advance booking through *Onas* in Puerto Natales, US$80 per person, highly recommended.

Equipment A strong, streamlined, waterproof tent is essential if doing *El Circuito*. Also essential are protective clothing against wind and rain, strong waterproof footwear, compass, good sleeping bag, sleeping mat, camping stove and cooking equipment. In summer take shorts and sunscreen also. You are strongly advised to take all necessary equipment from Puerto Natales and not rely on availability at the Andescape and Fantastico Sur *refugios*. Take your own food: the small shops at the Andescape and Fantastico Sur *refugios* (see below) and at the *Posada Río Serrano* are expensive and have a limited selection. Note that rats and mice have become a major problem around camping sites and the free *refugios*. Do not leave food in your pack (which will be chewed through): the safest solution is to hang food in a bag on wire. Maps (US$3), are obtainable at Conaf offices in Punta Arenas or Puerto Natales. Most maps are unreliable but the one produced by Cartographia Digital, US$5, has been recommended as more accurate.

Boat trips From *Hostería Lago Grey* at the southern end of Lago Grey to the Grey Glacier is a stunning trip recommended but often cancelled due to high winds. ■ *US$30 including refreshments, 2-3 hrs, min 8 passengers.* A voyage by catamaran can be taken from *Refugio Lago Pehoé* to *Refugio Pudeto.* ■ *US$15 one* way, 40 mins; summer schedule, from Pudeto 0900, 1200, 1700 and from Pehoé 1000, 1300, 1800, service operated by Fantástico Sur (details above under *Hostería Las Torres*), *off-season enquire in advance*.

Essentials

Hotels LL *Explora*, at Salto Chico on edge of Lago Pehoé, T411247. Ugly building but luxurious and comfortable, offering spectacular views, pool, gym, tours and transfer from Punta Arenas. Reservations: Av Américo Vespucci 80, piso 7, Santiago, T2066060, F2085479. **L** *Hostería Pehoé*, T411390 (closed Apr-Oct). 5 km south of Pehoé ranger station, 11 km north of park administration, on an island with spectacular view across the Lake to Cerro Paine Grande and Cuernos del Paine, "a stunning location which is wasted", run down, overpriced. Reservations *Turismo Pehoé* in Punta Arenas or Antonio Bellet 77, office 605, T2350252, F2360917, Santiago. **L** *Hostería Las Torres*, head office Magallanes 960, Punta Arenas, T226054, F222641, lastorres@chileaustral.com Good rooms and service, good restaurant with home-produced ingredients, English spoken, horse-riding, transport from Laguna Amarga ranger station. Highly recommended. **L** *Hostería Lago Grey*, T/F227528, or Punta Arenas T/F241042. Good food, small rooms, on edge of Lago Grey. **L** *Hostería Mirador del Payne*, on the eastern edge of the park, transport essential, (poor access road). Beautifully situated on Laguna Verde with spectacular views and good fishing, riding, hiking, birdwatching very friendly, comfortable, excellent food. Very highly recommended but an inconvenient base for visiting the park. Reservations: *Turismo Viento Sur* in Punta Arenas. **L** *Posada Río Serrano*, **AL** off season. Also **B/C** per person without bath. An old *estancia*, very run down and overpriced, some rooms with bath, some with shared facilities, breakfast extra, near park administration, with expensive restaurant and a shop (reservations advisable: run by *Turismo Río Serrano*, Prat 258, Puerto Natales, T410684).

Refugios These offer dormitory accommodation (sleeping bag may be hired, towel essential). **F** *Refugio Lago Toro*. Near administration centre, run by Conaf, hot showers, cooking facilities, good meeting place, sleeping bag and mattress essential, no camping, open summer only – in the winter months another more basic (free) *refugio* is open near administration centre. The following are run by *Andescape* (for address in Puerto Natales see page 428; also office in Santiago): *Refugio Lago Pehoé*, on the northeast arm of Lago Pehoé. *Refugio Grey*, on the eastern shore of Lago Grey. *Refugio Lago Dickson*. All modern, open all year, limited cooking and laundry facilities, meals served, kiosk with basic food and other supplies, rental of camping equipment. The following are owned by *Fantastico Sur* who also own *Hostería Las Torres* (address above): **D** *Refugio Las Torres*, near *Hostería Las Torres*; *Refugio Los Chilenas*, in the valley of the Río Ascensio; *Refugio Los Cuernos*, on the northern shore of Lago Nordenskjold. These are larger than the Andescape *refugios*, with better kitchen and bathroom facilities. Prices at Andescape and Fantástico Sur *refugios*: accommodation US$18, lunch US$8, dinner US$10, breakfast US$5, full board US$40, camping US$4.

Accommodation and meals in the *Andescape* and *Fantástico Sur refugios* should be booked in advance through *Path@gone* in Puerto Natales (reservations can also be made, if space allows, by asking staff in one *refugio* to radio another).

In addition there are 6 free *refugios*: *Zapata*, *Pingo*, *Laguna Verde*, *Laguna Amarga*, **Lago Paine** and **Pudeto**. Most have cooking areas (wood stove or fireplace) but *Laguna Verde* and *Pingo* do not. These are in very poor condition.

Camping In addition to sites at the Andescape and Fantástico Sur *refugios* there are the following sites: *Camping Serón* and *Camping Las Torres* (at *Hostería Las Torres*)

Chilean Patagonia

both run by Fantástico Sur. US$4, hot showers. **Camping Los Perros**, run by Andescape. US$4, shop and hot showers. **Camping Lago Pehoé** and **Camping Serrano**, US$20 per site at former (maximum 6 persons, hot showers) and US$15 per site at latter (maximum 6 persons, cold showers, more basic). **Camping Laguna Azul**, hot showers, **D** per site. Free camping is permitted in 7 other locations in the park: these sites are known as *campamentos*. The wind tends to increase in the evening so it is a good idea to pitch tents early (by1600). Fires may only be lit at organised *camping sites*, not at *campamentos*. The *guardaparques* expect people to have a stove if camping. (**NB** These restrictions should be observed as forest fires are a serious hazard.) *Guardaparques* also require campers to have a trowel to bury their waste. Beware mice, which eat through tents. Equipment hire in Puerto Natales (see above).

Tour operators Several agencies in Puerto Natales including *Servitur, Knudsen, Zaahj*, and *Luis Díaz* offer 1-day tours by minibus, US$37.50 plus park entry; these give a good impression of the lower parts of the park, though you spend most of the day in the vehicle and many travellers would argue that you need to stay overnight to appreciate the park fully. José Torres of *Sastrería Arbiter* in Calle Bulnes 731 (T411637) recommended as guide. *Enap* weekend tours in summer cost US$45 including accommodation and meals. *Buses Fernández* offer 2-day tours, US$132 and 3-day tours (which includes trip to the Balmaceda Glacier) US$177. Before booking a tour check carefully on details and get them in writing: increasingly mixed reports of tours. Many companies who claim to visit the Grey Glacier only visit Lago Grey (you see the Glacier in the distance). After mid-Mar there is little public transport and trucks are irregular. *Onas Turismo* (address under Puerto Natales tour companies) runs trips from the park down the Río Serrano in dinghies to the Serrano glacier and from there, on the *21 de Mayo* or *Alberto de Agostini* tour boats to Puerto Natales, US$90 each all inclusive. Book in advance.

Transport **Bus** From Puerto Natales *Gomez, Servitur, JB Buses* (addresses above) run daily bus services to the park leaving between 0630 and 0800, return departures 1500 from administration centre, 1600 from Laguna Amarga, 2½ hrs journey to Laguna Amarga, 3 hrs to the administration centre, US$10 one way, US$14 open return (return tickets are not interchangeable between all different companies), from early Nov to mid-Apr. In high season book in advance. **From Punta Arenas** For the daily *In-Tur* minibus service (in high season the buses fill quickly so it is best to board at the Administration): all buses wait at *Refugio Pudeto* until the 1430 boat from *Refugio Lago Pehoé* arrives. Travel between 2 points within the park (eg Pudeto-Laguna Amarga) US$3. At other times services by travel agencies are dependent on demand: arrange return date with driver and try to arrange your return date to coincide with other groups to keep costs down. Luis Díaz has been recommended, about $12 per person, minimum 3 persons. In season there are minibus connections from Laguna Amarga to the *Hostería Los Torres* and from the administration centre to *Hostería Lago Grey*. **From Torres del Paine to Calafate** (Argentina) either return to Puerto Natales and go to Río Turbio for bus to La Esperanza, or take a bus or hitch from the park to Villa Cerro Castillo border point (106 km south of the administration), cross to Paso Cancha de Carreras and try to link with the Río Turbio-La Esperanza-Río Gallegos bus schedule, or hitch.

Car hire Hiring a pick-up from *Budget* in Punta Arenas is an economical proposition for a group (up to 9 people): US$415 for 4 days. If driving there yourself, the road from Punto Natales is being improved: inside the park, the roads are narrow, bendy with blind corners; it takes about 3½ hrs from Puerto Natales to the administration, 3 to Laguna Amarga. Petrol available at Río Serrano, but fill up in case.

Horse hire *Baquedano Zamora*, Blanco Encalada 226, Puerto Natales, T/F412911 (or contact via the *Hostería El Pionero*, Cerro Castillo, T691932 anexo 722, via *Hostería Las Torres* or via *refugios*). US$35 per 3 hrs, US$70 per 8 hrs.

Tierra del Fuego

12

The largest island at the extreme south of South America, Tierra del Fuego is divided between Argentina and Chile. Both parts are covered in this section which also includes the Chilean island of Isla Navarino, situated to the south of Tierra del Fuego. Although northern Tierra del Fuego is flat windswept steppe, the south is a land of mountains, forests and lakes, usually visited from the Argentine city of Ushuaia, which is also a base for boat trips along the Beagle Channel. In winter Ushuaia also offers winter sports. On the southern shore of Isla Navarino is Puerto Williams, the only settlement on Isla Navarino.

Background

Geography

Tierra del Fuego is separated from the South American mainland by the Magellan Strait to the north. To the east is Atlantic Ocean; the Beagle Channel to the south separates it from the southern islands; a complex network of straits including the Whiteside, Gabriel, Magdalena and Cockburn channels divide it from the islands situated to the west.

The north of Tierra del Fuego is steppe but further south the island is crossed from east to west by the continuation of the Andes; in the Argentine sector these rise to around 1,500 m but in the Chilean part in the far southwest there are peaks of well over 2,000 m. The main rivers drain into the Beagle Channel and into Lago Fagnano, the largest lake on the island, which flows west to the sea via the Río Azopardo. There are a number of other lakes including Lagos Yehuin and Chapelmuth, just north of Lago Fagnano, and Lagos Blanco, Chico and Lynch in Chilean territory.

The northern and southern parts of the island have contrasting vegetation: the steppe is covered with grassland, while further south subantarctic forests grow on hills up to about 600 m. Poorly-drained low-lying areas in the south are covered with spagnum moss. Native wildlife includes guanacos and red foxes; musk rats, beaver and rabbits have been imported. In summer wild geese and ducks can be seen and some 150 other bird species have been identified; the Bahía San Sebastian is an important area for migratory birds. Trout and salmon inhabit nearly all the lakes and rivers.

Climate The island's climate is cold sub-Antarctic, though extremes of temperature are moderated by the sea and there are significant differences between north and south of the island. In Ushuaia southwesterly winds prevail, ranging in force from 15 km per hour to 100 km per hour. September to March are the windy months, while winter is normally calmer. In winter average daily temperatures hover around zero but in summer range from 13°C during the day to 5°C at night. Further north in Río Grande, where strong westerly winds blow up to 200 km per hour almost all year round, average temperatures range from -3°C to 2°C in winter and from 5°C to 15°C in summer. Rainfall is higher in Ushuaia than further north, with slight seasonal variations; in Río Grande most rain falls in summer and autumn.

History

Human habitation of Tierra del Fuego dates back some 10,000 years; four indigenous groups, all now extinct, inhabited the island until the early 20th century. The most numerous, the Onas (also known as the Selk'nam), lived in the north as hunter-gatherers living mainly on guanaco and several species of rodents. The southeastern corner of the island was inhabited by the Haus or Hausch, also hunter-gatherers, of whom very little is known. The same cannot be said for the Yaganes or Yámanas, who lived along the Beagle Channel and on the islands further south. A seafaring people who lived mainly on seafood, fish and seabirds, they were physically smaller than the Onas, but with a strongly developed upper body for rowing long distances. The fourth group, the Alacaluf, lived in the west of Tierra del Fuego as well as on the islands along the Chilean coast, surviving in these inhospitable conditions by fishing and hunting seals.

Thomas and Lucas Bridges

An orphan from Bristol, Bridges was so named because he was found as a child under a bridge with the letter T on his clothing. Bridges arrived in Tierra del Fuego in 1871 with his wife, young daughter and his adoptive father, Rev Despard, an early Christian missionary; he remained when Despard left after a massacre of Christians by the Indians. Until his death in 1898 Bridges lived near the shores of the Beagle Channel, first at Ushuaia and then Harberton, devoting his life to his work with the Yámanas (Yaghanes) and compiling a dictionary of their language. Of his six children the most famous was Lucas (1874-1949), who, after spending his early life among the Yámanas and Onas and learning their languages, became an outspoken defender of their rights and an opponent of the early sheepfarmers. His memoirs, The Uttermost Part of the Earth (1947), trace the tragic fate of the native population with whom he grew up.

The first Europeans to visit the island were members of an expedition led by the Portuguese Fernão Magalhães, who, in 1520, sailed through the channel that bears his name. As a result of the extreme dangers of such a voyage and the failure of Sarmiento de Gamboa's attempt to found settlements along the Straits in 1584, the indigenous population were left undisturbed until after South American independence.

Though Fitz Roy and Darwin visited in 1832, European settlement only occurred much later in the 19th century. In 1851 the South American Missionary Society, an Anglican society with missions on the Falkland Islands/Islas Malvinas sent seven missionaries to Picton Island to establish a mission, but they were driven off by the Yaganes and the first successful mission was only established 18 years later, at Ushuaia. The work of the missionaries was, however, disturbed by two developments, the discovery of gold and the growth of sheep-farming. As in southern Patagonia, the settlement of the frontier disputes between Argentina and Chile was followed by a desire by both governments to settle the area by allocating large expanses of land for sheepfarming. The main beneficiaries of this policy on Tierra del Fuego were the Menéndez and Braun families, already established in Punta Arenas.

Government and economy

Chilean Tierra del Fuego forms part of Region XII (Magallanes), the capital of which is Punta Arenas. The Argentine section of the island is part of the Province of Tierra del Fuego, Antartida y Las Islas del Atlántico Sur, the capital of which is Ushuaia. The population of the Argentine sector is around 70,000, most of whom live in the two towns of Río Grande and Ushuaia. Chilean Tierra del Fuego has a population of some 7,000, the majority of whom live in Porvenir.

For many years the main economic activity of the northern part of the island was sheepfarming, but Argentine government tax incentives to companies in the 1970s led to the establishment of new industries in Río Grande and Ushuaia and a rapid growth in the population of both cities; the subsequent withdrawal of incentives has produced increasing unemployment and emigration. The island is the site of the smallest and most southerly oil refinery in the world in Argentine San Sebastian. Tourism is increasingly important in Ushuaia.

Tierra del Fuego

Gold fever

The Tierra del Fuego Gold Rush is closely linked to the name of Julio Popper who settled in San Sebastián in 1887 where he founded the El Paramó mine. Popper died young in 1893, by which time his company had extracted 600 kg of gold from El Paramó and from along the Beagle Channel. After his death gold mining became a much larger scale business until, in 1909, the gold suddenly ran out. Despite its short life the gold rush had lasting consequences: among the prospectors from North America and Europe who arrived hoping to get rich, the largest group were Croats from Dalmatia, then part of the Austrian Empire; many of their descendents still live in the area.

Routes to Tierra del Fuego

Flights to and from the island are heavily booked in summer, especially in Jan and bus and ferry services are subject to cancellation due to weather conditions. There are no road/ferry crossings between the Argentine mainland and Argentine Tierra del Fuego: you have to go through Chilean territory. It is not always possible to cross the Chilean part in one day because of the irregularity of the ferry. There are two routes.

Via Punta Delgada The easternmost crossing, across the Primera Angostura (First Narrows), is 127 km south of Río Gallegos, 59 km south of the frontier at Monte Aymond. From **Punta Espora** on Tierra del Fuego, the road runs a further 128 km south through Cerro Sombrero to the frontier at San Sebastian (see below). **Sleeping E** per person *Hotel El Faro* in Punta Delgada and **C** *Hostería Tehuelche*, T061-694433 at Kamiri Aike, 17 km from port, with restaurant. There are several ferry crossings a day; schedules vary with the tides and are subject to delay due to weather conditions. Fares: foot passengers US$1, cycles free, cars US$14, one way. The ferry takes about 4 trucks and 20 cars; before 1000 most space is taken by trucks. There is no bus service to or from this crossing. If hitching, this route is preferable as there is more traffic.

Via Punta Arenas The alternative ferry crossing is between Punta Arenas and Porvenir. The road from Río Gallegos continues southwest from Punta Delgada 103 km to the intersection with the Punta Arenas-Puerto Natales road, 54 km north of Punta Arenas. From Porvenir, on Tierra del Fuego, a 225-km road runs east to Río Grande via the frontier at San Sebastián. From Tres Puentes, 5 km north of Punta Arenas (Bus A or E from Av Magallanes, US$1; taxi US$3) the *Melinka* sails Tue-Sat 0900, 0930 Sun in season, less frequently off season, depending on tides, 2½ hrs crossing (can be rough and cold). Fares: foot passengers US$6, cycles US$5, vehicles US$30. Reservations essential especially in summer, obtainable from Agencia Broom, Bulnes 05075, Punta Arenas, T218100, F212126, tabsa@entelchile.net (or T580089 in Porvenir). Timetable subject to change: check in advance. Return from Porvenir Tue/Thu/Sat 1230, Wed/Fri 1600, Sun 1700. The ferry company accepts no responsibility for damage to vehicles on the crossing. The best way to hitch from Río Gallegos to Punta Arenas is to take any lorry as far as the turn-off for Punta Delgada ferry. Then there is plenty of Chilean traffic from Punta Delgada to Punta Arenas.

Getting around Tierra del Fuego Throughout Tierra del Fuego the main roads are narrow and gravelled. The exceptions are San Sebastián (Argentina)-Ushuaia, which is paved, and the road for about 50 km out of Porvenir (Chile), which is being widened. Fuel is available in Porvenir, Cerro Sombrero and Cullen (Chile), and Río Grande, Ushuaia and San Sebastian (Argentina).

Shipwrecked in the Magellan Straits

The Estrecho de Magallanes, 534 km long, was and still is a treacherous passage and over the centuries it has claimed a long succession of victims. The hostile conditions which can prevail are perhaps best summed up in the words of Sir John Narborough: 'horrible like the ruins of a world destroyed by terrific earthquakes.'

From the Atlantic end the first navigational problem facing sailors is simply the difficulty of entering the Straits in the face of the fierce westerly gales which prevail, numerous sailing vessels having been forced back out to sea to wallow for weeks on end. Once in the straits the dangers are far from over: many ships have fallen victim to the notorious Williwaws, winds with the ferocity of tornados which spring up from nowhere, or the vicious Pamperos, which blow off the land with enough force to capsize a vessel.

Though in 1520 Magellan succeeded in passing through the straits which bear his name, few others managed to do so in the years which followed: of 17 ships which attempted the passage in the early 16th-century only one, the Victoria, succeeded in reaching the Pacific and returning to Europe. Twelve were lost near the eastern entrance and four returned in failure. The great attraction which drove these early navigators was the lure of a short route between Europe and the spices of the East. Once it was clear that there was no short route it was still a useful way for Europeans to reach the rich Pacific ports of Peru and Chile without disembarking and crossing Mexico or Panama on foot or by mule.

Although by the 19th century the replacement of sail by steam and the development of advanced navigation techniques lessened the dangers, losses continued: in 1869, for instance, the Santiago, an iron paddle steamer built in Glasgow and owned by the Pacific Mail line, went down off Isla Desolación at the western end with a cargo of gold and silver; there are no records of any salvage operation having taken place. While the opening of the Panama Canal in 1914 provided an alternative route between the Atlantic and Pacific Oceans, increases in ships' size mean that the Straits are still a busy shipping route, though today the cargo is more commonly oil than gold and silver. Casualties still occur, with, of course, the added risk of environmental disaster from oil spillage.

Chilean Tierra Del Fuego

Founded in 1894 as a port serving the sheep *estancias* of the island and inhabited mainly by the descendents of Croat immigrants , Porvenir is the only town in Chilean Tierra del Fuego. There is a small museum, the **Museo Fernando Cordero Rusque**, Samuel Valdivieso 402, mainly Indian culture.

Porvenir
Population: 4,500
Phone code: 061

Tierra del Fuego

Sleeping A *Los Flamencos*, Teniente Merino, T580049, best. C *Central*, Phillippi 298, T580077, hot water. C *Rosas*, Phillippi, T580088. With bath, hot water, heating, restaurant and bar. Recommended. E per person *Res Colón*, Damián Riobó 198, T580108, also full board. C *España*, Santos Mardones y Croacia, good restaurant with fixed price lunch. *Res Los Cisnes*, Soto Salas 702, T580227. E per person *Res* at Santos Mardones 366 (D with full board). Clean, friendly, heaters in rooms, hot water, good. E per person *Res Cameron*, Croacia, for shared room, 'friendly folk', good meals. D full board, sleep on dining-room floor for US$1. There is a hotel at the Transportes Senkovic office, Croacia y Almeyda; many good D *pensiones*, with full board, but they are often fully occupied by construction workers. At Cerro Sombrero, 46 km south of Primera Angostura: E per person *Hosteria Tunkelen*, recommended. F *Pensión del Señor*

For accommodation at San Sebastián see below

Alarcón, good, friendly. *Posada Las Flores*, Km 127, on the road to San Sebastián, reservations via *Hostal de la Patagonia* in Punta Arenas.

Eating *Club Croacia*, does wholesome and reasonable lunch (about US$5), also *Restaurante Puerto Montt*, Croacia 1169, for seafood, recommended. Many lobster fishing camps where fishermen will prepare lobster on the spot.

Transport Air From Punta Arenas – weather and bookings permitting, *Aerovías DAP*, Oficina Foretic, T80089, *Porvenir*, fly daily except Sun at 0815 and 1730, return at 1000 and 1930, US$20. Heavily booked so make sure you have your return reservation confirmed. **Bus** To **Río Grande**, Tue and Sat 1400, Gesell, US$20 heavily booked, buy ticket in advance, or phone. **Ferries** Terminal at Bahía Chilota, 7 km west, see above for details. From bus terminal to ferry, taxi US$6, bus (if running) US$1.50. **Hitchhiking** Police may help with lifts on trucks from Porvenir to Río Grande; elsewhere in Chilean territory hitching is difficult as there is so little traffic.

Directory Banks At *Estrella del Sur* shop, Santos Mardones.

Cameron
It is impossible to get permission to cross unmanned border from here to Ushuaia or to get a Chilean exit stamp

Cameron lies 149 km southeast of Porvenir on the opposite side of Bahía Inútil. From here a road runs southeast to Estancia Vicuña. Before Vicuña is a scenic fishing-ground and beyond a trail leads south to the Río Azopardo, which offers fine trout fishing (sleeping at *Estancia Almirantazgo*). South of here trails run across the Darwin Range to the *Estancia Yendegaia* near the Beagle Channel. For information on accommodation and flights to *Estancias Almirantazgo* and *Yendegaia* contact *Hostal El Bosque* in Punta Arenas.

Transport Bus To Cameron from Porvenir, from Calle Manuel Señor, Mon and Fri, 1700, US$10.

Frontier between Chile & Argentina

The only legal frontier crossing between the Chilean and Argentine parts of Tierra del Fuego is at **San Sebastián**, 142 km east of Porvenir. There are two settlements called San Sebastián, one on each side of the frontier but they are 14 km apart; taxis are not allowed to cross. Argentine time is one hour ahead of Chilean time, March to October.

Entry When entering Argentina make sure you get an entry stamp for as long as you require. When entering Chile remember that fruit, vegetables, dairy produce or meat are not permitted.

Sleeping In Chilean San Sebastian **E** per person *Hostería de la Frontera*, in the annex which is 1 km away from the more expensive main building. In Argentine San Sebastian **AB** *ACA* motel (service station open 0700-2300).

Transport Hitching Hitching south of San Sebastián is relatively easy: border police will sometimes arrange lifts to Ushuaia or Río Grande.

Argentine Tierra del Fuego

Río Grande

Río Grande is situated on the southern edge of the Bahía San Sebastian, an important area in summer for migratory birds. The largest settlement in Tierra del Fuego, it is a sprawling modern town in windy, dust-laden sheep-grazing and oil-bearing plains.

Phone code: 02964
Colour map 6, grid C4
Population: 35,000
87 km S of San Sebastian

The *frigorífico* (frozen meat) plant and sheep-shearing shed are among the largest in South America. There is a small museum, the **Museo de Ciencias Naturales y História**, at El Cano 225, ■ *Tue-Fri 0900-1700, Sat/Sun 1500-2000*.

Sights

At the Salesian Mission of **La Candelaria**, 11 km north along Route 3, is where there is a historical museum housing a collection Indian artefacts. There is also a natural history section. ■ *Mon-Sat 1000-1230, 1500-1900, Sun 1500-1900, US$1.50. Afternoon teas, US$3.* Nearby is the first parish church of Río Grande. **Estancia María Behety** lies 18 km southwest where horses can be hired. The **Refugio Dicky** is a private bird sanctuary covering 1,900 ha on Bahía San Sebastian.

Excursions

A *Atlántida*, Belgrano 582, T/F431914. Said to be best, without breakfast, restaurant, parking. **A** *Posada de los Sauces*, El Cano 839, T/F430868/432895. With breakfast, good beds, comfortable, good restaurant, bar. Recommended. **AB** *Los Yaganes ACA*, Belgrano 319, T430823, F433897. Comfortable, good expensive restaurant. **AB** *Federico Ibarra*, Rosales y Fagnano, T432485. With breakfast, good beds, large rooms, excellent restaurant. **AB** *Isla del Mar*, Güemes 963, T/F422883, next to bus terminal, with breakfast. **B** *Res Rawson*, Estrada 750, T425503, F30352. Cable TV, clean,

Sleeping
Accommodation can be difficult to find if arriving at night

No campsite. The gym has free hot showers for men, as has the ACA garage on the seafront

Río Grande centre

■ **Sleeping**
1 Antares
2 Atlántida
3 Avenida
4 Federico Ibarra
5 Hosp Noal
6 Isla del Mar
7 Los Yaghanes
8 Posada de los Sauces
9 Rawson
10 Villa

Not to scale

Tierra del Fuego

The Salesian Missions

Founded in 1893 by José Fagnano, La Candelaria was one of two missions set up by the Salesians to try to protect the Onas of Tierra del Fuego from the gold prospectors and estancieros (sheepfarmers). The first was established in Punta Arenas in 1886, the second, on Isla Dawson two years later. The latter quickly attracted over 1,000 Onas, shipped there by the estancieros. It was finally closed in 1920, by which time the anthropologist Martín Gusinde, counted only 276 surviving Onas, most of them on an estancia owned by the Bridges family.

poor beds. **B** *Villa*, San Martín 277, T422312, without breakfast, very warm. **B** *Hosp Noal*, Rafael Obligado 557, lots of bread and coffee for breakfast, cosy, recommended. **C** *Hostería Antares*, Echeverría 49, T421853. **C** *Avenida*, Belgrano 1001, T422561.

Eating *Don Rico*, Belgrano y Perito Moreno, in ultra-modern building in centre, interesting, closed Mon. *La Nueva Colonial*, Rosales 640, pizzeria, friendly. *Club de Pesca*, El Cano. *Rotisería CAI*, on Moreno, cheap, fixed price, popular with locals.

Festivals *Trout Festival*, third Sun in Feb; *Snow Festival*, third Sun in Jul; *Woodsman Festival*, first week of Dec.

Shopping *La Nueva Piedmontesa*, Belgrano y Laserre, 24-hr food store; *Tia* supermarket, San Martín y Piedrabuena, good selection. Food is cheaper than in Ushuaia.

Tour operators *Yaganes*, San Martín 641, friendly and helpful

Transport **Local Car hire** Ai Rent-a-Car, Belgrano y Ameghino, T432820, F430757. *Avis*, El Cano 799, T/F422571 and airport; *Localiza*, at airport, T430482. **Mechanic** and VW dealer *Viaval SRL*, Perito Moreno 927.

Long distance Air Airport 4 km west of town. Bus US$0.50. Taxi US$5. To **Buenos Aires**, *Aerolíneas Argentinas*, daily, 3½ hrs direct. *Austral* daily (except Sunday) and *Lapa* daily (except Sat) via Bahía Blanca, Comodoro Rivadavia and Río Gallegos. To **Ushuaia**, *Aerolíneas Argentinas* and *TAPSA*, daily. *TAPSA* also to Río Gallegos and Comodoro Rivadavia. *LADE* also to **Río Gallegos**, (book early in summer, 1 a week, Thu), continuing to **Comodoro Rivadavia** via Calafate, Gob Gregores and Perito Moreno. **Bus** All buses leave from terminal, El Cano y Güemes. To **Porvenir**, Chile, to connect with ferry to **Punta Arenas** 4 hrs, US$20, Pacheco, Wed, Fri, Sun, 1115, *Tecni Austral*, Tue, Thu, Sat 0800, meticulous passport and luggage control at San Sebastián; to **Punta Arenas**, Chile, via Punta Delgada, 10 hrs, US$30, *Pacheco*, Tue, Thu, Sat 1130, *Tecni Austral*, Mon, Fri, 1100; To **Ushuaia**, 4 hrs, *Tecni Austral* 2 daily, US$15, Tolkeyen, 4 a day, US$20 with meal, *Lider*, 4 a day, US$15 , sit on right for better views. There are no buses to Río Gallegos. **Hitching** Very difficult to hitch to Porvenir or north into Argentina (try the truck stop opposite the bus terminal or the police post 7 km out of town). Hitching to Ushuaia is relatively easy in summer.

Directory **Airline offices** *Aerolíneas Argentinas*, San Martín 607, T422711. *Lapa*, 9 de Julio 747, T432620. *LADE*, Laserre 425, T422968. *DAP*, 9 de Julio 597, T430249. *TAN*, Moyano 516, T422885. [TAPSA], San Martín 627, T431300/301, mariani@netcombbs.com.ar **Banks** *Banco de la Nación Argentina*, San Martín 200. *Banco del Sud*, Rosales 241, cash advance on Visa. *Superkiosko*, Piedrabuena y Rosales, cash only. Exchange is difficult: if coming from Chile, buy Argentine pesos there. **Communications** Post office Piedrabuena y Ameghino. **Laundry** *El Lavadero*, P Moreno y 9 de Julio. **Tourist offices** Tourist information at the Municipalidad, on Elano, Mon-Fri.

Ushuaia

Situated on the southern shore of Tierra del Fuego, Ushuaia is the most southerly town in the world. The location is stunning. From the centre there are views south over the green waters of the Beagle Channel and beyond to the Chilean island of Isla Navarino. Away from the main street, Avenida San Martín, the streets climb steeply towards the jagged snow-covered peak of Cerro Martial. In recent years the town has expanded beyond this central location, sprawling untidily along the coast. Despite Ushuaia's age, it retains the feel of the frontier town, with its jumble of architectural styles and its isolated location. Founded in 1884, the town functioned as a penal colony until 1947. Since the latter date it has been important as a naval base and more recently as the capital of Argentina's most southerly province. Though fishing still plays a key role in the local economy, Ushuaia has become an important tourist centre, particularly as the departure point for voyages to Antarctica. As in many remote island destinations, prices are high and Ushuaia is probably the most expensive town in Argentina.

Phone code: 02901
Colour map 6, grid C4
Population: 30,000
234 km SW of Río Grande

The **Presidio** or old prison, at the back of the Naval Base, houses the **Museo Marítimo**, with models and artefacts from seafaring days, the **Museo Antártico** and, in the cells, the **Museo Penitenciario**, which details the history of the prison. ■ *1000-1200, 1600-2300, US$7, students US$4. Yaganes y Gob Paz.* **Museo del Fin del Mundo**, Maipú y Rivadavia, T421863, has a small but interesting display of early photos and artefacts of the local Indian tribes, the missionaries and first settlers, as well as natural history section. Known as the 'museum at the end of the world' (you can get a stamp in your passport). Highly recommended. The building also contains an excellent library with helpful staff and a post office, open afternoons when the main one is closed. ■ *1000-1300, 1500-1930, US$5*

Museums

Cerro Martial offers fine views down the Beagle Channel and to the north, about 7 km behind the town. To reach it take the chairlift (*Aerosilla*, US$5) follow Magallanes out of town allowing 1½ hours. Several companies, *Pasarela, Kaupen, Eben Ezer* and *Body* run minibus services from the Muelle Turistico, Maipú y Lasserre, several departures daily in summer, US$5 return. There is skiing on the glacier in winter.

Excursions

Harberton lies 85 km east of Ushuaia and is the oldest *estancia* on the island, see box on page 496. Run by descendents of its founder, the British missionary Thomas Bridges, it offers guided walks through protected forest and refreshments are sold in the *Manacatush confitería*. Camping is possible. ■ *T22742. Getting there: Access is from a dirt road which branches off Route 3, 40 km east of Ushuaia and runs past Lago Victoria, then 25 km through forest before the open country around Harberton. Some parts of the road are bad; tiring driving, 5 hrs there and back. Bus services are operated by Body, US$30 return (details from the tourist office).* Tours are offered by agencies in Ushuaia. By land these cost US$55; take your own food if not wishing to buy meals at the *estancia*. For excursions to Harberton by boat see below.

Other excursions include: to the **Parque Nacional Tierra del Fuego** (see below); to the **Río Olivia** falls; and to **Lagos Fagnano** and **Escondido** which can be reached by bus services operated by several companies from the Muelle Turistico, Maipú y Lasserre.

Some tour agencies imply that their excursions to Harberton go to the *estancia* though in fact they only go to the bay; others go by inflatable launch from main boat to shore. Check thoroughly in advance. Food and drink on all boats is

Boat trips
Can be booked through most agencies

Wildlife of the Beagle Channel

Many bird-species can be viewed from the shore or on a boat-trip along the Channel. These include the Black-browed Albatross (whose long wings enable it to glide effectively over large distances), the Antarctic Giant Petrel, the Southern Fulmar, the Great Glebe, the Kelp Goose (the male of which is an unmistakeable white), Imperial and Rock Cormorants, Steamer ducks, Kelp gulls, the South American tern, the Black Oystercatcher, the Snowy Sheathbill and the Antarctic Skua. The shores of the Beagle Channel are also breeding grounds for several sea mammals, including the Southern Sea Lion and the Southern Fur Seal.

expensive, best to take your own. Note that the Beagle Channel can be very rough. Here are the main trips. The sealion colony at Isla de los Lobos, two hours on the *Ana B*, US$35, four hours on the *Tres Marías* US$45. Lapataia Bay and Isla de los Lobos, five hours on the *Ezequiel MB*, US$40. Isla de los Lobos and Estancia Harberton is six hours on the *Luciano Beta*, US$75,

Ushuaia

Not to scale

■ **Sleeping**

1 Albatros	4 Canal Beagle	7 Hostería Alakaluf	10 Malvinas
2 Antártida	5 César	8 Hostería América	11 Mustapic
3 Cabo de Hornos	6 Fernández	9 Maitén	12 Refugio del Mochilero

Tierra del Fuego

Tuesday, Thursday, Saturday. Isla de los Lobos and the Isla Martillo Penguin colony takes four hours on the *Luciano Beta*, US$60.

Prices double on 12 Dec and accommodation may occasionally be hard to find Dec-Mar – the tourist office will help with rooms in private homes and with campsites. Accommodation, food and drink are all expensive. **Sleeping**

On the road to the Martial Glaciar overlooking the city are: **LL** *Las Hayas*, Km 3, T430710, F430719, lashayas@overnet.com.ar Colourful large rooms, pool; and **LL** *del Glacier*, Km 3.5, T430640, F430636, glaciar@infovia.com.ar Modern, casino, pool rooms, shuttle to/from *Hotel Albatros*. **L** *Tolkeyen*, at Estancia Río Pipo 5 km from town, T445315, F445318, tolkeyen@tierradelfuego.org.ar With recommended restaurant (see below).

LL/L *Albatros*, Lasserre y Maipú, T430003, F430666, glaciar@infovia.com.ar Modern, includes breakfast, good views. **L** *Ushuaia*, Lasserre 933, 1 km north of town, T430671/F424217. With breakfast, restaurant, sauna. **L/AL** *Las Lengas*, Florencia

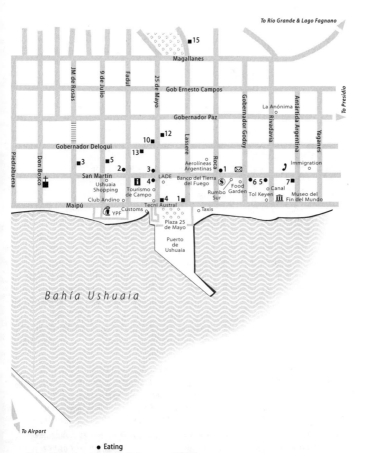

● **Eating**		
13 Saint Christopher	**1** Barcibo Ideal	**4** El Galeon
14 Torres al Sur	**2** Barcleit 1912	**5** La Casa de los Mariscos
15 Ushuaia	**3** Cafe del Esquiná	**6** Moustacchio

Tierra del Fuego

● ●

☞ *Estancia Harberton*

In a land of extremes and superlatives, Harberton still stands out as special. The oldest estancia on Tierra del Fuego and the oldest house on the island, it was built in 1886 on a narrow peninsula overlooking the Beagle channel. Its founder, the missionary Thomas Bridges, was given the land by President Roca for his work among the local Indians and for his help in rescuing the victims of the numerous shipwrecks in the channel. Harberton is named after the Devonshire village where his wife Mary was born. The farmhouse was prefabricated by her carpenter father and then assembled on a spot chosen by the Yamana Indians as the most sheltered. The English connection is still evident in the neat garden of lawns, shrubs and trees between the jetty and the farmhouse. Behind the buildings is a large vegetable garden, a real rarity on the island. Visitors will notice that there is much more

wildlife around the estancia than in the Tierra del Fuego National Park, probably owing to the remoteness of Harberton.

Still operating as a working farm, mainly with cattle and sheep, Harberton is run by Thomas Goodall, great-grandson of the founder. Visitors receive a conducted tour of the farm buildings and immediate surroundings: though there are guides, Thomas in his dungarees and horn-rimmed glasses, and his wife, Natalie, are usually also on hand.

Natalie is an internationally recognized expert on whates and dolphins, which accounts for the whale jawbone arch over the garden entrance. There is also a "house of bones" where dolphin, whale and seal carcasses are cleaned and labelled for research, and entire skeletons displayed. Harberton is well worth the visit, particularly by sea as the voyage up the Beagle Channel is equally memorable.

● ●

1722, T423366, F424599, laslengas@tierradelfuego.org.ar Superb setting, heating, good dining room. **A** *Canal Beagle*, Maipú y 25 de Mayo, T421117, F421120, restaurant. **A** *Malvinas*, Deloqui 615, T422626, F424482. Without breakfast, comfortable, helpful, heating, good views. Recommended. **A** *Cabo de Hornos*, San Martín y Rosas, T422187, F422313, cabohornos@tierradelfuego.org.ar Comfortable, often full, good value, restaurant not open to non-residents. **A** *César*, San Martín 753, T421460, F432721, cesarhostal@infovia.com.ar Comfortable, with breakfast, recommended. **A** *La Posada*, San Martín 1299, T433330, laposada@tierradelfuego.org.ar, with breakfast, good. **B** *Res Fernández*, Onachaga y Fitzroy, T421192. With breakfast, good beds. **AB** *Posada Fin del Mundo*, Valdez 281, T422530. Family atmosphere, with breakfast, recommended. **AB** *Mustapic*, Piedrabuena 238, T421718, F423557. Also **B** without bath, multi-lingual owner, small rooms, poor beds, great views. **AB** *Maitén*, 12 de Octubre 140, T422745, F422733. Good value, 1 km from centre, no singles, 10% discount for ISIC and youth card holders. **AB** *Hostería América*, Gob Paz 1665, T423358, F431362, without breakfast, modern. **B** *Capri*, San Martín 720, T421833, without breakfast. **AB** *Hostería Alakaluf*, San Martín 146, T436705, F431603 with breakfast, quiet, warm, highly recommended.

D per person *Hosp Torres al Sur*, Gob Paz 1437, T430745, torrealsur@impsat1.com.ar Hostelling International discounts. Dormitories, heating, good atmosphere, kitchen facilities, highly recommended. **D** per person *Home*, Kayen 565, comfortable, quiet. **D** per person *Albergue Bouchar*, Bouchard 490, T435102. Dormitories, laundry facilities, without breakfast. **D** per person *Hostal Kaisken*, Gob Paz 7, T436756, kaisken@infovia.com.ar, with kitchen and internet facilites. **D/E** per person *Albergue Saint Cristopher*, Deloqui 636, T422945, without breakfast. **E** per person *Casa Azul*, Las Primulas 283, Barrio Ecológico, T434769, floor space. **E** per person *Refugio del Mochilero*, 25 de Mayo 241, T436129, F 431190, refmoch@satlink.com Small dormitories with kitchen facilities. **E** per person *Casa del Turista*, Belgrano 236, T421884, large kitchen, clean rooms helpful. **E** per person *Casa de Alba*, Belakamain 247, T430473, guiad@infovia.com.ar, friendly, good beds.

Private homes AB/B *Hostería Linares*, Deloqui 1522, T423594, **B** without bath. **AB** *Miguel Zapruscky*, Deloqui 271, T421316. **B** without bath, parking, TV, kitchen, English spoken. Recommended. **E** per person *Silvia Casalaga*, Gob Paz 1380, T423202. Dormitories, comfortable, heating, breakfast extra, no sign, recommended. **B** *María Navarrete*, 25 de Mayo 440, T423068. Without bath or breakfast, cooking facilities. **B** *Familia Cárdenas*, 25 de Mayo 345, T421954. Without bath or breakfast, quiet. **B** *Zulema Saltzmann*, Roca 392 y Campos. **E** per person *Posada de los Angeles*, Gob Paz 1410, basement, good kitchen. **D** per person *Adrienne Grinberg*, Bouchard y Rivadavia, T423148. With breakfast, warm, English, French spoken. *Familia Galeazzi*, Gdor Valdez 323, T423213, F432605, in pleasant suburb close to town, rooms, also 5-bed cabaña, excellent food, highly recommended. An up to date list of private accommodation is available from the tourist office. Many people offer rooms in private houses at the airport. There is no youth hostel. Hostel for sporting groups only at Haruwen Sports Complex.

Lago Escondido A *Hostería Petrel*, 54 km from Ushuaia after a spectacular climb through Garibaldi Pass, on the road to Río Grande (bus departs 0900, returns 1500, US$17 return, minimum 4 people), T433569, trout fishing possible, boat rides, friendly staff.

Lago Fagnano B *Hostería El Kaiken*, 100 km north of Ushuaia on a promontory, T492208, also **C** cheaper rooms and bungalows, nice site. Facilities at *Kaiken* and *Petrel* are open all year round. These inns are recommended for peace and quiet.

Camping None in town. West of Ushuaia are: *Ushuaia Rugby Club Camping* (Km 4) US$15 per tent, restaurant and good facilities; *Ushuaia Camping Municipal* (Km 8) US$15 per tent, toilets, cold showers. East of town on Route 3 are: *Camping del Solar del Bosque* (Km 14) US$5 per person, hot showers; *Camping Río Tristen*, in the Haruwen Winter Sports complex (Km 36), T/F424058, US$5 per tent, electricity, bar, restaurant. Inside the Parque Nacional Tierra del Fuego (entry fee US$5) is *Camping Lago Roca*, 18 km from Ushuaia, at Lapataia, by forested shore of Lago Roca, with good facilities, dirty, showers (US$3), noisy, reached by bus January-February, small shop, cafetéria. There are also 4 free sites with no facilities: *Camping Río Pipo*, 10 km from Ushuaia; *Ensenada Camping* 14 km from Ushuaia; *Camping Las Bandurrias* and *Camping Laguna Verde*, both 21 km from Ushuaia. Hot showers, free, at YPF on main road.

Barcleit 1912, Fadul 148 Cordon bleu cooking at reasonable prices. *Kaupé*, Roca 470, English spoken, excellent food and wine, recommended, expensive. Best place to eat lamb is at *Tolkeyen*, Estancia Río Pipo, 5 km from town, meal US$15, taxi US$7. *Barcito Ideal*, San Martín 393, good, cheap, *tenedor libre* US$14, very popular with travellers. *Moustacchio*, San Martín 298, good fish, good *tenedor libre* US$14. *Volver*, Maipú 37, interesting decor, sea view, good food and service, not cheap. *La Casa de los Mariscos*, San Martín 234, fish, seafood. Two cafés: *Café de la Esquina*, San Martín y 25 de Mayo, recommended, and opposite, *El Galeón*. Good value set price lunches at the restaurant in *Ushuaia Shopping*, San Martín 788. *Bidu Bar*, San Martín 898, good music, lunches, good meeting place; excellent homemade chocolate sold at a shop at San Martín 785. *Massera*, San Martín 270-72, good ice cream.

Eating

The coffee bar at the airport is very expensive

Discos include *Barny's*, Antártida Argentina 196 and *Ozono*, San Martín 45; *Cronos*, Perito Moreno 3 km east of town.

Entertainment

Tierra del Fuego

Festival 12 Oct, *Founding of Ushuaia*.

Shopping Most things are more expensive than elsewhere but some cheap imported goods, eg
Camera film is electrical equipment and cigarettes. Good boots at *Stella Maris*, San Martín 443.
cheaper in Chile *Bookshop Libros*, San Martín y 9 de Julio (Ushuaia Shopping). Supermarkets: *La Anónima*, Perito Moreno 1600, also Rivadavia y Gob Paz; *Tía*, 12 de Octubre y Karukinka; *La Victoria*, Kuanip y Tolhuin; *Suma*, San Martín y Onas, clean toilets.

Sport There is a sports centre on Malvinas Argentinas on west side of town (close to seafront).
Beachcombing can Ice skating rink at Ushuaia, gym in winter (when lagoon is frozen). **Fishing** Trout season
produce discoveries of is 1 Nov-31 Mar, licences US$20 per week, US$10 per day. Contact Asociación de Caza y
whale bones Pesca at Maipú y 9 de Julio, which has a small museum. **Fly Casting**, Del Michay 667, T435769, fishing@infovia.com.ar Offer a range of fishing excursions, provide equipment. Fishing enthusiasts may be interested in visiting the fish hatchery 7 km east of Ushuaia, visiting hrs daily 1400-1700. There are brook, rainbow and brown trout and land-locked salmon. Take No 1 bus east-bound on Maipú to the end of the line and continue 2½ km on foot to the hatchery. Birdwatchers will also find this ride rewarding. Fishing excursions to Lago Fagnano are organized by *Yishka*, Gob Godoy 115, T431535, F431230. For **Skiing, hiking, climbing** contact *Club Andino*, Fadul 5. **Skiing** a downhill ski run (beginner standard) on Cerro Martial. There is another ski run, Wallner, 3 km from Ushuaia, open Jun-Aug, has lights for night-skiing and is run by Club Andino. The area is excellent for cross country skiing; *Caminante* organizes excursions 'off road'. 20 km north east of Ushuaia is Valle Tierra Mayor, a large flat valley with high standard facilities for cross country skiing, snow shoeing and snowmobiling; ski-school, rentals and a cafetéria; bus in the morning and 1400 from *Antartur*, San Martín 638. The Haruwen Winter Sports complex is 36 km east on Route 3 (Km 36).

Tour operators All agencies charge the same fees for excursions: Tierra del Fuego National Park, 4 hrs, US$25. Lago Escondido, 5 hrs, US$30. Lagos Escondido and Fagnano, 8 hrs, US$45. With 3 or 4 people it is often little more expensive to hire a *remise* taxi. The 2 largest agencies are: *Rumbo Sur*, San Martín 342, T422441, F430699, rumbosur@satlink.com Runs a range of tours on water and on land and offers a 2-day package to Calafate, US$150 including transport and hotel, good value, also organizes bus to ski slope, very helpful; and *Tolkeyen/Pretour*, Maipú 237, T437073, pretoushu@arnet.com.ar Recommended. Others include *Antartur*, Gob Paz 1569, T423240, F424108, antartur@tierradelfuego.org.ar *All Patagonia*, Fadul 26, T433622, F430707, allpat@satlink.com Amex agent. *Canal*, Rivadavia 82, T437395, canal@satlink.com Offer a range of activities including horseriding and excursions to otherwise inaccessible destinations in 4WD vehicles. Recommended. *Turismo de Campo*, 25 de Mayo 76, T437351, F432419, infor@turismodecampo.com *Estancia* tourism, horseriding and trekking. Recommended guide: Domingo Galussio, Intervú 15, Casa 211, 9410 Ushuaia, bilingual, not cheap (US$120). Recommended.

Transport **Local Air** At the airport ask around for a pilot willing to take you on a 30-min flight around Ushuaia, US$38 per person (best to go in afternoon when wind has dropped). Alternatively ask about flights at the tourist office in town. Aerial excursions over the Beagle Channel with local flying club, hangar at airport, 3-5 seater planes, 30 mins: Lago Fagnano, Lapataia and Ushuaia Bay. **Car hire** *Tagle (Avis)*, San Martín y Belgrano, T422744 and airport, good. *Río Grande*, El Cano 799, T422571. *Localiza*, San Martín 1222, T432136, and at airport. Recommended. *Seven*, San Martín 802, T437604. *Rastro*, Maipú 13, T422021. *Cardos*, San Martín 845, T436388, F435222. *Dollar*, Maipú y Sarmiento, T432134. **Cycle hire** DDT Cycles Sport, San Martín 1258. **Seven Deportes**, San Martín y 9 de Julio.

Long distance Air Aeropuerto Internacional Malvinas Argentinas, 4 km from town, taxi, US$5 (no bus). Departure tax: to Río Grande US44; for all other destinations US$13. Services are more frequent in high season; in winter weather often impedes flights. In the summer tourist season it is sometimes difficult to get a flight out: it may be worth trying Río Grande. *Aerolíneas Argentinas* and *Lapa* to Buenos Aires via Río Gallegos and/or Trelew, all year round, 5 hrs. To **Río Grande**, *TAPSA*, also *LADE*, US$14. Kaiken's services to/from Ushuaia are as for Río Grande. To **Río Gallegos**, *LADE* 2 a week US$35, also *TAPSA, Lapa, Aerolíneas Argentinas* and *Austral* US$50-63. *LADE* to **Comodoro Rivadavia** via Río Grande, Río Gallegos, and Calafate (US$55), Gobernador Gregores and Perito Moreno on Wed (to Calafate only in summer).

There are no flights to Punta Arenas or Puerto Natales in Chile

Bus To **Río Grande** 4 hrs, *Tolkeyen*, 4 daily, US$20 with meal, *Tecni Austral*, 2 daily, US$15, and *Lider*, 4 daily, US$15. To **Punta Arenas** via Punta Delgada, 14 hrs, *Tecni Austral/Ghisoni* joint service, Mon, Wed, Fri, 0700, US$45, *Tolkeyen/Pacheco* joint service, Tue, Thu, Sat 0800, US$50 with meal. To **Punta Arenas** via Porvenir, 12 hrs, *Tecni Austral*, Tue, Thu, Sat 0500, US$45, *Tokeyen/Pacheco* joint service, Wed, Fri, Sun 0800, US$50 with meal. **Companeis** *Tecni Austral, Tolkar, 25 de Mayo 50*, T/F423396; *Tolkeyen*, Maipú 237, T/F437073; *Lider*, Gob Paz 921, T436421.

Hitching Trucks leave Ushuaia for the refinery at San Sebastián Mon-Fri; a good place to hitch from is the police control on Route 3.

Train A Decauville gauge train for tourists runs along the shore of the Beagle Channel between the Fin del Mundo station, west of Ushuaia and the boundary of the Tierra del Fuego National Park, 4.5 km, 3 daily, US$26 (tourist), US$30 (1st class), plus US$5 park entrance and US$3 for bus to the station. Run by *Ferrocarril Austral Fueguino* with new locomotives and carriages, it uses track first laid by prisoners to carry wood to Ushuaia; tickets from Tranex kiosk in the port, T430709, www.trendelfindelmundo.com.ar Sit on left outbound.

To Puerto Williams (Chile) No regular sailings. Yachts based at the *Club Náutico* carry charter passengers in summer, returning the same day; enquire at the Club, most possibilities in Dec because boats visit Antarctica in January. Luxury cruises around Cape Horn via Puerto Williams are operated by the Chilean company, *Tierra Austral*, 7/8 days, US$1,260 and by **Ushuaia Marina**, San Martín 788, T/F424058, www.ushuaiamarina.com.ar US$300 per person per day.

To Antarctica most tourist vessels to Antarctica call at Ushuaia and, space permitting, take on passengers. Enquire at *Rumbo Sur* or *All Patagonia* for last minute offers. All agencies charge similar price, US$2,200 per person for 8/9 day trip, though prices may be lower for late availability, which are posted in window of *Rumbo Sur*.

Airline offices *LADE*, San Martín 552, T21123, airport T21700. **Aerolíneas Argentinas**, Roca 116, T21218, airport 21265. *Lapa*, 25 de Mayo 64, T32112, F30532. *Alta*, San Martín 788, T32963, or at airport, T22620/23049. *DAP*, San Martín 626, T31373. *Lan Chile*, Gob Godoy 169, T31110. *TAPSA* agents: *Rumbo Sur*. **Banks** Banks open 1000-1500 (in summer). Useful to have credit cards here as difficult to change TCs and very high commission (up to 10%), but *Banco del Sud*, Maipú 600 block. *Banco de la Nación Argentina*, Rivadavia y San Martín, only bank which accepts Chilean pesos. Cash advance on Mastercard at *Banco de Tierra del Fuego*, San Martín 1044, accepts Amex TCs, 3% commission. *Casas de Cambio* include *Gredi Sol*, 25 de Mayo 50 and *Thaler*, San Martín 877. Tourist agencies and the *Hotel Albatros* give poorer rates. *Listus* record shop, San Martín 973, sweet shop next door, or *Caminante* travel agency for better rates for cash. **Communications** Post office San Martín y Godoy, Mon-Fri 0900-1300 and 1700-2000, Sat 0830-1200. **Telecom** Rivadavia 163, also fax and internet services. Internet*Food Garden*, San Martín 312, also snacks. *Don Guido Cybercafe*, Godoy 45, surf the net for US$10 per hr, also offers

Directory

Tierra del Fuego

• •

Isla de Los Estados (Staten Island)

"This long (75 km) and guarded island lies east of Tierra del Fuego. Except for the caretakers of the lighthouse and an occasional scientist few people ever set foot on this cloud-shrouded reserve of Fuegian flora and fauna that no longer

exist on the main island. During the 18th and 19th centuries large numbers of ships were wrecked or lost in the treacherous waters surrounding this island. Much gold, silver and relics await salvage."
Robert T Cook

• •

mailbox facilities for e-mail, 0800-2400. **Consulates** *Chile*, Malvinas Argentinas y Jainen, Casilla 21, T421279. *Finland*, Paz y Deloqui. *Germany*, Rosas 516. *Italy*, Yaganes 75. **Laundry** Rosas 139, between San Martín and Deloqui, open weekdays 0900-2100, US$8. **Tourist offices** San Martín 674, T432000/1, F424550, 'best in Argentina', literature in English, German and Dutch, helpful, English spoken. Large chart of hotels and prices and information on travel and staying at Estancia Harberton. Has noticeboard for messages. Open Mon-Fri 0800-1000, Sat/Sun 0900-2000. *National Park Office*, San Martín 1395, has small map but not much information. The *ACA* office on Maipú also has maps and information.

Parque Nacional Tierra del Fuego

Covering 63,000 ha of mountains, lakes, rivers and deep valleys, the park stretches west to the Chilean frontier and north to Lago Fagnano, though large areas have been closed to tourists to protect the environment. The lower parts are forested; tree species include lenga, ñire and coihue. Wildlife includes several species of geese including kelp geese, ducks among them the beautiful torrent duck, magellanic woodpeckers and austral parakeets. Introduced species like rabbits, beavers and muskrats, have done serious environmental damage. Near the Chilean frontier beaver dams can be seen and with much luck and patience the beavers themselves. Stand still and down-wind of them: their sense of smell and hearing are good, but not their eyesight.

There are several beautiful walks: the most popular ones are an interpreted trail along Lapataia Bay which is good for birdwatching; a 5 km walk along Lago Roca to the Chilean frontier at Hito XXIV; and a 2½ km climb to Cerro Pampa Alta which offers fine views. Good climbing on Cerro Cóndor, recommended. There are no recognized crossing points to Chile. In winter the temperature drops to as low as -12°C, in summer it goes up to 25°C. Even in the summer the climate can often be cold, damp and

Parque Nacional Tierra del Fuego

Sierra de Beauvoir
Lago Fagnano
CHILE
Sierra de Vinciguerra
Lago Alto
Sierra de Valdivieso
Río Pipo
Cascada del Río Pipo
Cerro Martial
Laguna Roca
Camping Lago Roca
Camping Río Pipo
Ushuaia
Cerro Cóndor
Laguna Negra
Bahía Lapataia
Canal Beagle
To Río Grande (Route 3)

Tierra del Fuego

Shackleton, 'Yelcho' and the rescue from Elephant Island

Shackleton's 1914-16 expedition to cross the Antarctic is one of the epics of polar exploration. Shackleton's vessel, Endurance, which left England in August 1914 with 28 men aboard, became trapped in pack-ice in January 1915. After drifting northwards with the ice for eight months, the ship was crushed by the floes and sank. With three boats, supplies and the dogs, the group set up camp on an ice floe which continued to drift north for eight months. In April 1916, after surviving on a diet largely of seals and penguins, the party took to the boats as the ice broke up. After seven days at sea they reached Elephant Island. From there Shackleton and five other men sailed 1,300 kilometres in one of the boats on a 17 day voyage to South Georgia, where there were whaling stations. On reaching the south shore of South Georgia, Shackleton and two men crossed the island (the first such crossing and achieved without skis or snowshoes) to find help. Shackleton, from whom nothing had been heard by the outside world (Endurance had no radio) since leaving the island 18 months before, was not at first recognized.

Though the British government was sending a rescue vessel to Elephant Island, the delays involved led Shackleton to seek help locally. After ice had prevented two rescue attempts, the first from South Georgia and the second from the Falkland Islands/Islas Malvinas, Shackleton went to Punta Arenas, where the British community raised £1,500 to buy Emma, a small schooner with a wooden hull (best for the pack-ice) which was towed towards Elephant Island by the tug Yelcho but, after continuing alone, Emma was threatened by ice and the attempt was abandoned. Shackleton pursuaded the Chilean authorities to permit a fourth attempt using Yelcho after meteorological conditions had changed. Leaving Punta Arenas on 25 August 1916, the vessel encountered thick fog, but, unusually for the time of year, little ice and it quickly reached Elephant Island where the men, who had endured an Antarctic winter under upturned boats, were down to four days of supplies.

Though the expedition failed to cross Antarctica, Shackleton's achievement was outstanding: despite the loss of Endurance, the party had survived two Antarctic winters in extreme conditions without loss of life. Shackleton himself returned to the region in 1921 to lead another expedition, but in January 1922, though aged only 47, he suffered a fatal heart attack while in South Georgia.

---

unpredictable. The *Club Andino* in Ushuaia has a booklet explaining routes in the park (in Spanish) and poor map.

Access The park entrance is 12 km west of Ushuaia. Park administration is at Lapataia Bay. Entry US$5. In summer buses and minibuses, US$5 one way, to the park are run by several companies including: *Pasarela*, Fadul 5, T421735; *Kaupen*, T434015; *Eben-Ezer*, T431133 and *Alvear*, all leaving from the Muelle Turistico at Maipúe y Lasserre. Timetables vary with demand, tourist office has details. *Caminante* also runs a 1 day excursion to the park, including trek, canoeing, *asado* lunch, US$70 inclusive (small groups, book early). Ask at the tourist office about cycling tours in the park, US$65 full day, also 'Eco Treks' available and cultural events. It is possible to hitchhike, as far as Lapataia.

For sleeping details see page 497, camping

Tierra del Fuego

Isla Navarino (Chile)

Situated on the southern shore of the Beagle Channel, Isla Navarino is totally unspoilt and beautiful, with a chain of rugged snowy peaks, magnificent woods and many animals, including large numbers of beaver which were introduced to the island and have done a lot of damage. The only settlement on the island is

Puerto Williams
phone code: 061
Population: 1,500

Puerto Williams, a Chilean naval base. Situated about 50 km east of Ushuaia, this is the most southerly place in the world with a permanent population. It is small, friendly and remote.

Sights The **'Museo del fin del Mundo'** ('End of the World Museum') is full of infor-
Further information & mation about vanished Indian tribes, local wildlife, and voyages including
tours: Rumbo Sur, San Charles Darwin and Fitzroy of the *Beagle*, a must. ■ *1000-1300, 1500-1800*
Martín 342, Ushuaia *(Mon-Thu); 1500-1800 (Sat-Sun), Fri closed (subject to change). US$1.*

Excursions Sights include beaver dams, cascades, the Villa Ukika, 2 km east of town, the place where the last descendants of the Yaghan people live, and the local *media luna* where rodeos are held. For superb views, climb Cerro Bandera (three to four hours round trip, steep, take warm clothes).

Sleeping **AB** *Hostería Walla*, on the edge of Lauta bay, T223571. 2 km out of town (splendid walks), very hospitable, good food. **D** per person *Pensión Temuco*, Piloto Pardo 224, also half board, comfortable, hospitable, good food, hot showers, recommended. You can also stay at private houses. **D** per person *Coiron*, owned by *Sim Ltda*, is a *refugio* with shared bath and kitchen, 4 beds per room, info, contact Jeanette Talavera, T621150, F621227, coiron@simltd.com Her husband, Wolf Kloss, www.simltd.com, runs sailing trips, trekking tours and many other adventure activities. **Camping** You can camp near the *Hostería*: collect drinking water from the kitchen. No equipment rental on island; buy food in Punta Arenas.

Transport **Air** From Punta Arenas, *DAP* on Mon and Fri 1400, Wed 0830, return Mon and Fri 1800, Wed 1000, US$64 single. Book well in advance; 20 seater aircraft and long wait-ing lists (be persistent). The flight is beautiful, with superb views of Tierra del Fuego, the Cordillera Darwin, the Beagle Channel, and the islands stretching south to Cape Horn. Also army flights available (they are cheaper), but the ticket has to be bought through *DAP*. *Aeropetrel* will charter a plane to Cape Horn (US$2,600 for 8-10 people).

Boat No regular sailings to/from Ushuaia (see above). From Punta Arenas, the *Ñandú* or *Ultragas* leaves on a fixed schedule every 10 days, about midnight, arrives 1700 each way, reclining chairs, no food, US$45 one way. Enquire at the office, Independencia 865, next to service station. The *Navarino* sails from Punta Arenas in 3rd week of every month, 12 passengers, US$150 per person one way; contact the owner, Carlos Aguilera, 21 de Mayo 1460, Punta Arenas, T228066, F248848 or via Turismo Pehoé. A small cargo vessel, the *Beaulieu*, sails from Punta Arenas once a month and carries a few passengers, US$300 return, 6 days. Navy and port authorities may deny any knowledge, but every-one else in Puerto Williams knows when a boat is due.

Boat trips Ask at the yacht club on the off chance of hitching a ride on a private yacht. Luxury cruises around Cape Horn are run by *Tierra Austral* for US$800, 6 days. Captain Ben Garrett offers adventure sailing in his schooner *Victory*, from special trips to Ushuaia to cruises in the canals, Cape Horn, glaciers, Puerto Montt, Antarctica in Dec and Jan. Write to *Victory Cruises*, Puerto Williams (slow mail service); Fax No 1, Cable 3, Puerto Williams; phone (call collect) asking for Punta Arenas (Annex No 1 Puerto Williams) and leave message with the Puerto Williams operator.

Directory **Airline offices** *Aerovías DAP*, *LanChile*, *Ladeco* in the centre of town. **Communications** Post office: closes 1900. **Telephone:** CTC, Mon-Sat 0930-2230, Sun 1000-1300, 1600-2200). **Tourist offices** Near the museum (Closed in winter). Ask for details on hiking. Maps available.

Background

13

Background

History

Archaeology and prehistory

Some 30,000 years ago the first peoples crossed the temporary land bridge spanning Asia and America and the Bering Strait, and began a long migration southwards, reaching South America about 20,000 BC and Tierra del Fuego by 9,000 BC. Hunters and foragers, they followed in the path of huge herds of now extinct animals such as mammoths, giant ground sloths, mastodons and wild horses which became extinct due to climate change. In some areas, as along the Chilean coasts, these early inhabitants switched to fishing; in others they began to plant crops and domesticate animals, adopting in the process a more sedentary lifestyle.

The most important archaeological sites in Argentina are situated in the Northwest and West which were the areas of the most highly developed cultures south of the Central Andes. This region became a meeting place for people already settled there with peoples and influences from northern Chile, the Central Andes, the Chaco and the hunter-gatherers of the south. Three distinct periods can be identified in the cultural development of the region: the Early period (500 BC to AD 650), the Middle period (AD 650-850) and the Later period (AD 850-1480). The early period witnessed the beginnings of agriculture as well as pottery and metalworking. The Middle period was marked by the influence of the great culture of Tiahuanaco in present-day Bolivia. Fine metal objects, some of them of gold and silver, were made and new plant varieties were introduced. The later period featured the influence of the cultures of Santa María and Belén, notable for their giant, polychrome funerary urns.

In general the peoples of the northwest lived in chiefdoms led by one or more leaders. Practicing intensive agriculture and successfully domesticating animals, they produced food surpluses. A special house was used as a temple, but they left little architecture. Two of the most important of these cultures were the Tafí or Tafí del Valle and the Condorhuasi in the western valleys of La Rioja and San Juan. Both produced fine metal objects from gold, copper and copper alloy. Ceramics and stone sculptures produced by both show feline-related figures, while Condorhuasi artefacts often show males and females as crawling figures. The Tafi are famous for their stone pillars and monoliths, often used to form enclosures or placed as the focus of a stone enclosure. A third centre of cultural development occurred further north, in the Humahuaca valley, where the Middle and Later periods saw the building of small villages of rectangular stone houses, which gradually, as at Tilcara, grew into small urban settlements in good defensive sites and with fortifications. Metal working was fully developed and tools made of bones were also used. Unlike the Tafi and Condorhuasi, the Humahuaca cultures also used hallucinogenic substances characteristic of San Pedro de Atacama (Chile) and the Central Andes. Later sites in the valley have the bodies of adults placed face down inside houses or in stone-lined tombs. Ceramics imported from Bolivian cultures and Pacific shells have been found in these tombs.

By the end of the Later period, the peoples of the Northwest had been drawn into informal links with the Inca Empire: highways linking their communities with the empire were built and trade with the Incas is indicated by their clothing, music, handicrafts and fortifications.

Town planning in the 16th century

Perhaps the most obvious influence of Spanish settlement for the traveller is the characteristic street plan of towns and cities. Colonial cities were founded by means of an official ceremony which included the tracing of the central square and the holding of a mass. A series of Royal Ordinances issued in Madrid in 1573 laid down the rules of town planning. The four corners of the main plaza were to face the four points of the compass "because thus the streets diverging from the plaza will not be directly exposed to the four principal winds, which would cause much inconvenience." The plaza and the main streets were to have arcades which were seen as "a great convenience for those who resort thither for trade." Away from the plaza the streets were to be traced out "by means of measuring by cord and ruler" in the now-familiar grid-pattern. Once this was done building lots were to be distributed, those near the plaza being allocated by "lottery to those of the settlers who are entitled to build around the main plaza".

The Ordinances specified the principles underlying the distribution of the major public buildings: "In inland towns the church is not to be in the centre of the plaza but at a distance from it in a situation where it can stand by itself, separate from other buildings so that it can be seen from all sides. It can thus be made more beautiful and it will inspire more respect. It should be built on high ground so that in order to reach its entrance people will have to ascend a flight of steps. Nearby the cabildo and the customs house are to be erected in order to increase its impressiveness but without instructing it in any way. The hospital of the poor who are ill with non-contagious diseases shall be built facing the north and so planned that it will enjoy a southern exposure."

The Ordinances also advised settlers on how to deal with hostility from the indigenous population: "If the natives should wish to oppose the establishment of a settlement they are to be given to understand that the settlers desire to build a town there not in order to deprive them of their property but for the purpose of being on friendly terms with them; of teaching them to live in a civilized way; of teaching them to know God and His Law ... While the new town is being built the settlers ... shall try to avoid communication and intercourse with the Indians. Nor are the Indians to enter the circuit of the settlement until the latter is complete and in condition for defence and the houses built, so that when the Indians see them they will be filled with wonder and will realize that the Spaniards are settling there permanently and not temporarily."

"Royal Ordinances Governing the Laying Out of New Towns" by Zelia Nuttall, Hispanic American Historical Review, May 1922, pages 249-254.

Central & Southern Argentina

Away from the northwestern highlands were other peoples who have left less archaeological evidence. Among them were the Comechingones, who inhabited what are now the provinces of Córdoba and San Luis. Living in settlements of pit-dwellings, the bottom half of which were built underground, they used irrigation to produce a range of crops. In the far northeast on the eastern edge of the Chaco were the Guaraní; organized into loose confederations, they lived in rudimentary villages and practised slash-and-burn agriculture to grow maize, sweet potatoes, manioc and beans. They also produced textiles and ceramics.

Further south the Pampas and Patagonia were much more sparsely populated than the Northwest and most groups were nomadic until long after the arrival of the Spanish. One of the most important of these were the Querandí, who eked out a living by hunting guanaco and rheas. Patagonia was inhabited by scattered nomadic groups, including the Pampa, the Chonik and the Kaingang. Most of these managed to avoid contact with white settlers until the 19th century. In the steppes of Patagonia the Tehuelche and Puelche lived as nomadic hunters living off guanaco, foxes and game.

In the far south, in southern Patagonia and Tierra del Fuego, there were four indigenous peoples, two of them land-based and two sea-based. All lived as hunter-gatherers. Considering the inhospitable climate all wore very little clothing: capes, waterproof moccasins, feather headdresses and jewellry. The sea based peoples, Yaghanes and Alacaluf, had canoes, paddles, bailers and mooring rope, but lacked fishhooks, catching fish with spears or by hand. Seals were their main food, but they also ate sea-birds and fish. The land-based Ona and Haush gathered plants and hunted guanaco and foxes for food and for their hides. They also hunted sea-mammals from the shore.

European exploration and settlement

At the time of the arrival of the first Europeans the territories which today make up Argentina were sparsely populated. About two-thirds of the indigenous population lived in the northwest of the territory, the present-day provinces of Córdoba, Santiago del Estero, Tucumán, Catamarca, La Rioja, Salta and Jujuy. European exploration began in the Plata estuary. In 1516 Juan de Solís, a Portuguese navigator employed by the Spanish crown, landed on the shore of the estuary, but his men were killed by Querandí Indians. Four years later he was followed by Magellan who explored the Plata, before turning south to make his way into the Pacific. In 1527 both Sebastian Cabot and his rival Diego García sailed into the estuary and up the Ríos Paraná and the Paraguay. Cabot founded a small fort, Sancti Spiritus, not far from the modern city of Rosario, but it was wiped out by the Indians about two years later. Despite these difficulties Cabot took back to Spain stories of a great Indian kingdom beyond the Plata estuary, rich in precious metals. A Portuguese expedition to the estuary, led by Affonso de Souza, returned with similar tales and this led to a race between the two Iberian powers. In 1535, Pedro de Mendoza, set out with 16 ships and a well-equipped force of 1,600 men and founded a settlement at Buenos Aires. The natives soon made life too difficult; the settlement was abandoned and Mendoza returned home, but not before sending Juan de Ayolas with a small force up the Río Paraná in search of the fabled Indian kingdom. In 1537 this force founded Asunción, in Paraguay, where the natives were friendly.

After 1535 the attention of the Spanish crown switched to Peru, where Pizarro was engaged on the conquest of the Inca Empire, and the small settlement at Asunción remained an isolated outpost. It was not until 1573 that a force from Asunción travelled south to establish Santa Fe. Seven years later Juan de Garay refounded Buenos Aires but it was only under his successor, Hernando Arias de Saavedra (1592-1614), that the new settlement became secure.

By the time of Mendoza's expedition to the Plata estuary, Spanish expeditions were already exploring northern parts of present-day Argentina. In 1535 Diego de Almagro led a party from Peru which crossed the northwest. In the latter half of the 16th-century expeditions from Chile and Peru led to the foundation at the eastern foot of the Andes of the oldest towns in Argentina: Santiago del Estero, Tucumán, Córdoba, Salta, La Rioja, Jujuy, San Juan, Mendoza, and San Luis. The aims of the Spanish was to create better trading links between the Chilean heartland and Peru (avoiding the Atacama desert) and to find new sources of Indian labour. A total of 25 cities were founded in present-day Argentina in the 16th century, 15 of which survived, at a time when the total Spanish population was under 2,000.

Colonial rule Throughout the colonial period the Argentine territories were an outlying part of the Spanish empire and of minor importance. Spanish colonial settlement and government was based in Peru, which was endowed with the vast mineral wealth of Potosí in Alto Peru (present-day Bolivia) and large supplies of Indian labour. In the Argentine lands, by contrast, there were no great mineral deposits and the Indian population was sparse. The nomadic nature of many Indian groups made any attempt at control difficult, again in contrast to Peru where Spanish rule could be superimposed on the centralized administration of the defeated Incas.

From 1543 all the Spanish territories in South America were governed from Lima, the Vice-Regal capital and trade with Spain was routed via Lima, Panama and the Caribbean, thus preventing Buenos Aires from becoming an important port. Its slow growth after 1680 was partly due to the establishment of a Portuguese base at Colonia del Sacramento on the opposite bank of the estuary in 1683: the need to confront the Portuguese led Spain to strengthen her presence, while the Paraná delta north of the city near Tigre provided ample opportunities for smuggling British and Portuguese goods into Buenos Aires. By 1776 the city's population was only 24,000, though this was double the size of any of the cities of the interior. Although in that year when Spain reorganized its colonial administration and created the Viceroyalty of Río de la Plata, with Buenos Aires as capital, the city's control of the *cabildos* (town councils) in distant towns was very tenuous.

The Wars of Independence As in the rest of Spanish America, independence was partly a response to events in Europe, where Spain was initially allied to Napoleonic France. In 1806 and 1807 the British, at war with Napoleon, made two attempts to seize Buenos Aires but were defeated. In 1808 Napoleon invaded Spain, deposing King Ferdinand VII, and provoking widespread resistance from Spanish guerrilla armies. Throughout Spanish America the colonial elites debated where their loyalties lay: to Napoleon's brother Joseph, now officially King? to Ferdinand, now in a French prison? to the Viceroy? to the Spanish resistance parliament in Cadiz?

On 25 May 1810, the *cabildo* of Buenos Aires deposed the viceroy and established a *junta* to govern on behalf of King Ferdinand VII. This move provoked resistance in outlying areas of the viceroyalty, Paraguay, Uruguay and Upper Peru (Bolivia) breaking away from the rule of Buenos Aires. Factional rivalry within the *junta* between supporters of independence and their opponents added to the confusion and instability. Six years later, in July 1816, when Buenos Aires was threatened by invasion from Peru and blockaded by a Spanish fleet in the Río de la Plata, a national congress held at Tucumán declared independence. The declaration was given reality by the genius and devotion of José de San Martín, who boldly marched an Argentine army across the Andes to free Chile, and (with the help of Lord Cochrane, commander of the Chilean Navy), embarked his forces for Peru, where he captured Lima, the first step in the liberation of Peru.

Since independence

The 19th century The achievement of independence brought neither stability nor unity. For over 40 years conflict centred around disputes between Unitarists and Federalists. The former, found mainly in the city of Buenos Aires, looked to Europe for their inspiration and advocated free trade, education, white immigration and strong central government. The Federalists, backed by the provincial elites and many of the great *estancieros* of Buenos Aires province, resisted, defending local autonomy and traditional values. Behind the struggle were also economic interests: Buenos Aires and the coastal areas benefitted from trade with Europe; the interior provinces did not. As the conflict raged the territory, known officially as the United Provinces of the Río de la Plata, had none of the features of a modern state: there was neither central government, army, capital city nor constitution.

The British invasions of Buenos Aires, 1806-7

The history of southern Latin America would be very different if British attempts to displace Spain as the dominant power in the region in 1806 and 1807 had succeeded. These attacks, at a time when Spain was France's ally in the Napoleonic Wars against Britain, involved 25,000 men, including over 14,000 troops. The first invasion was the brainchild of naval captain Sir Home Popham. Having captured Cape Town from the Dutch early in 1806, Popham decided, without British government authorisation, to launch an attack on Buenos Aires, anticipating support from London in the event of success. On 25 June 1806 Popham's force of 1,571 men, under the command of General Beresford, landed near Buenos Aires, forcing the city of 50,000 inhabitants to surrender within a few days and seizing nearly US$1.5 million in bullion and specie.

Once the porteños realized that Beresford's occupation was unauthorised and that he could not guarantee British support against Spain if they opted for independence, they began to plan to drive the invaders out. After 47 days of British rule Beresford's small army was attacked in the centre of the city by a larger force and, on 12 August, he was forced to surrender, he and his men being interned in the interior. Meanwhile the British government had decided to send troops under General Whitelocke to reinforce the British toe-hold in South America. After a short seige, Montevideo surrendered to the British in February 1807 and became the forward base for the attack on Buenos Aires. On the morning of 5 July 1807 6,000 British troops stormed the city, but as they advanced through the narrow streets they were raked with artillery and musket fire and assaulted by missiles hurled from the rooftops. With British casualties reaching 50%, Whitelocke surrendered and agreed to evacuate the Río de la Plata altogether on condition that all British prisoners would be released. The dream of establishing a British presence in Spanish Southern America had received a major setback.

Order, of a sort, was established after 1829 by Juan Manuel de Rosas, Governor of Buenos Aires. His overthrow in 1852 unleashed another round in the battles between Unitarists and Federalists and between Buenos Aires and the provinces. In 1853 a constitution establishing a federal system of government was finally drafted. Buenos Aires province refused to join the new Argentine Confederation, which had its capital at Paraná. Conflict between the two states erupted over the attempt by Buenos Aires to control and tax commerce on the Río Paraná. The victory of Buenos Aires at Pavón (1861) opened the way to a solution: the city became the seat of the federal government; Bartolomé Mitre, former governor of Buenos Aires became the first president of Argentina. There was another political flare-up of the old quarrel in 1880, ending in the humiliation of the city of Buenos Aires, which was separated from its province and made into a special federal territory.

Although there was resistance to the new constitution from some of the western provinces, the institutions of a modern state were created in the two decades after 1861: a national bank, bureaucracy, postal service and army were all established, but perhaps it was the building of railways across the pampas which did most to create national unity, breaking the power of the provincial leaders (caudillos) by enabling the federal government to send in troops quickly. The new army was quickly employed to defeat Francisco Solano López of Paraguay in the War of the Triple Alliance (1865-1870) and then to conquer all the Indian tribes of the pampas and the south in the 'Conquest of the Wilderness' (1879-1880).

In the last quarter of the 19th century Argentina was transformed: the newly acquired stability encouraged foreign investment; the pampas were fenced, ploughed up and turned over to commercial export agriculture; railways and port facilities were built; and widespread immigration from Europe transformed the

Background

'The Caligula of the River Plate'

Juan Manuel de Rosas is the most controversial figure in 19th-century Argentine history. Born in 1793 into a landholding family, Rosas rose to dominate Buenos Aires province and the Río de la Plata for over two decades. After building a fortune in the meat-salting business and acquiring large estates in the south of the province, he allied with the Federalists against the Unitarists, defeating the Unitarist leader Lavalle and becoming provincial governor in 1829. Though he gave up office in 1832, he returned in 1835 and remained governor until his defeat at the battle of Caseros in 1852.

Though Rosas opposed the Unitarists and claimed to be a Federalist, he was no supporter of the rights of the other provinces. He opposed the Unitarists because they stood for European ideas and 'progress'; he used his control over Buenos Aires to dominate the other provinces, but resisted plans to link them formally under a constitution. Arguing for territorial expansion at the expense of the Indians, he based his power on the support of other estancieros, who were rewarded with sales and gifts of conquered land, and on the gauchos whose following he cultivated and to whom he appealed as a proven military leader and horseman. Arguing, on becoming governor, that the only alternative was chaos, he demanded and received 'extraordinary powers' which simply legalised his brutal methods. Ruling by decree, he replaced the bureaucracy with his own supporters and built a standing army of 20,000 men, paid from the proceeds of estancias confiscated from his opponents. In many cases 'justice' was administered personally, Rosas reading the police reports and simply writing the sentence on the files.

In government Rosas's reliance on propaganda, conformity and terror draw parallels with 20th-century dictatorships: terror was in the hands of the Mazorca, death squads which answered directly to the Dictator; all citizens were forced to wear red, the Federalist colour; newspapers, official documents and even private correspondence had to begin with

character of Buenos Aires and other cities around the Plata estuary. Political power, however, remained in the hands of a small group of large landowners and their urban allies. Few Argentines had the vote and the opposition Unión Cívica Radical, excluded from power, conspired with dissidents in the army in attempts to overthrow the government.

The 20th century One of the landmarks of modern Argentine history was the 1912 Sáenz Peña law which established universal manhood suffrage. Sáenz Peña, president between 1910 and 1916, sought to bring the middle and working classes into politics, gambling that the Conservatives could reorganize themselves and attract their votes. The gamble failed: the Conservatives failed to gain a mass following and the Radicals came to power. Radical presidents Hipólito Yrigoyen (1916-1922 and 1928-1930) and Marcelo T de Alvear (1922-1928) found themselves trapped between the demands of an increasingly militant urban labour movement and the opposition of the Conservatives, still powerful in the provinces and with allies in the armed forces.

The military coup which overthrew Yrigoyen in 1930 was a turning point: the armed forces returned to government for the first time in over 50 years and were to continue to play a major political role until 1983. Through the 1930s a series of military backed governments, dominated by the Conservatives, held power; the Radicals were outlawed and elections were so fraudulent that in Avellaneda in 1938 more people voted than were on the register. Yet the armed forces themselves were disunited: while most officers supported the Conservatives and the landholding elites, a minority of ultra-nationalist officers, inspired by developments in Europe,

the slogan 'Long live the Federation and Death to the Unitarist Savages'. Opponents fled to Montevideo from where they plotted his overthrown and Rosas responded by blockading the Uruguayan capital.

Controlling the other provinces was more difficult. Allying himself to provincial caudillos such as Quiroga in La Rioja, Rosas overthrew opponents or weakened them by blockading the Río Paraná. It was this that led to his downfall. His treatment of French merchants led to a French blockade of Buenos Aires in 1838-40 and a dispute over access to the Río Paraná led to an Anglo-French blockade in 1845-1848. His policy over the Paraná also annoyed the Brazilian government, which wanted access to Mato Grosso, and provoked unrest in the Argentine province of Entre Ríos, governed by his ally Urquiza. In 1852 Urquiza challenged Rosas and, supported by Brazilian and Uruguayan forces as well as Unitarists from Montevideo and British and French finance, defeated the dictator at Caseros, just outside Buenos Aires. Rosas rode from the battlefield to the house of the British Consul, took refuge on a British ship and left to spend the remaining 25 years of his life farming quietly in Hampshire, where, according to John Lynch, he treated the farm workers in much the same way as he had treated the gauchos of the pampas.

Controversy still surrounds Rosas's career. Sarmiento and others saw him as the epitome of barbarism, opposing their mission to 'civilize' the pampas by bringing education, European ideas and European settlers. Later generations have sometimes portrayed him as a nationalist hero, focussing on his imposition of unity and his resistance to British and French pressure. Before his election as president Carlos Menem praised Rosas and grew long sideburns in imitation of the dictator. The recent use of his portrait on the 20 peso note is just one of the latest moves in the continuing debate over the man labelled by his opponents the 'Caligula of the River Plate'.

supported industrialization and the creation of a one-party dictatorship along fascist lines. The outbreak of war in Europe increased these tensions and a series of military coups in 1943-1944 led to the rise of Colonel Juan Domingo Perón. When the military allowed a return to civilian rule in 1946 Perón swept into power winning Presidential elections. His government is chiefly remembered by many Argentines for improving the living conditions of the workers, through the introduction of paid holidays and welfare measures. Especially in its early years the government was strongly nationalistic, taking control over the British-owned railways in 1948. Opposition parties were harassed and independent newspapers taken over. Although Perón was easily re-elected in 1951, his government soon ran into trouble: economic problems led to the introduction of a wage freeze which upset the labour unions which were the heart of Peronist support; the death of Evita in 1952 was another blow; a dispute with the church in 1954-1955 added to Perón's problems. In September 1955 a military coup unseated Perón who went into exile, in Paraguay, Panama, Venezuela, the Dominican Republic and, from 1961 to 1973, in Spain.

Perón's legacy dominated Argentina for the next two decades. No attempt was made to destroy his social and economic reforms, but the armed forces determined to exclude the Peronists from power. Argentine society was bitterly divided between Peronists and anti-Peronists and the economy struggled, partly as a result of Perón's measures against the economic elite and in favour of the workers. Between 1955 and 1966 there was an uneasy alternation of military and civilian régimes. The military officers who seized power in 1966 announced their intention to carry out a Nationalist Revolution, but were quickly discredited by a deteriorating economic

Background

Juan Domingo and Evita

The casting of Madonna as Evita in the Alan Parker film of the same name showed yet again how divisive a figure Eva Perón remains in Argentina: the Peronistas were outraged at what they saw as an insult to 'Santa Evita' while anti-Peronists were delighted by their opponents outrage. Evita, who died tragically of cancer at the age of 33, is undoubtedly better known to foreigners than her former husband, Juan Domingo, though it is he who made more of an impact on the lives of Argentines than she.

The story of Evita's early life is well known. Born in 1919 near Los Toldos in Buenos Aires province, the fifth illegitimate child of Juana Ibarguren and Juan Duarte, she was brought up in Junín, before moving at the age of 15 to Buenos Aires. Despite failing to make it as a film or theatre star, she was successful in radio soap operas. Her relationship with Perón began in 1944 and they married in October 1945. As first lady in a society in which women were denied the vote, she offended the elite by the key role she played in government. As president of the Eva Perón Foundation, a social welfare organization, she distributed help to the needy who queued for hours to see her. The Foundation, funded by 'voluntary' donations from the trade unions and taxes on lottery tickets and entry to casinos and horseracing, built hospitals, low-income housing and schools. In 1948 she toured France, Italy and Spain, receiving film star attention in weary post-war Europe. In 1951, when Perón ran for re-election, her nomination as his vice-presidential running mate aroused so much hostility among the armed forces that she was forced to withdraw. Her death in 1952 transformed her into a myth so powerful that after Perón's overthrow, the military had her embalmed corpse smuggled from the country and buried in a secret grave in Italy to prevent it falling into the hands of the Peronist masses.

Although he was to dominate Argentine politics for 30 years, Perón was unknown to most Argentines until 1943 when he was aged 48. Brought up on a Patagonian estancia where his father was manager, he was sent to a boarding school before attending the military academy. He rose slowly in the army, becoming, in 1931, an instructor at the military academy, where he wrote books advocating the need for strong political leadership and a state-regulated economy. After periods as military attaché in Chile and Italy, he was one of the organizers of the Grupo de Oficiales Unidos, a secret society of junior officers which sympathized with the Axis cause in the Second World War. After a military coup in June 1943, Perón, though initially only a junior minister, soon emerged as the leading member of the government: as Under-Secretary of War, he put his supporters into key positions; as Secretary of Labour he encouraged the formation of trade unions, winning the support of their

situation. The Cordobazo, a student and workers insurrection in Córdoba in 1969, was followed by the emergence of several guerrilla groups and the growth of political violence. As Argentina became more ungovernable Perón, from his exile, refused to denounce those guerrilla groups which called themselves Peronist.

In 1971 General Alejandro Lanusse seized power, promising a return to civilian rule and calculating that the only way to control the situation was to allow Perón to return. When the military bowed out in 1973, elections were won by the Peronist candidate, Hector Campora. Perón returned from exile in Madrid to resume as President in October 1973, but died on 1 July 1974, leaving the Presidency to his widow, Vice-President María Estela Martínez de Perón, his third wife, known as 'Isabelita'. Perón's death unleashed chaos: hyper-inflation, resumed guerrilla warfare and the operation of right wing death squads who abducted people suspected of left-wing sympathies. In March 1976, to nobody's surprise, the military overthrew

members by approving pay increases and benefits. His rise provoked hostility among fellow officers and the Argentine elite; in October 1945 he was dismissed and arrested, but massive workers demonstrations on 17 October led to his release and historic appearance on the balcony of the Casa Rosada.

Elected president in February 1946, he was re-elected in 1951 after altering the constitution to permit his candidacy. Perón aimed to create what he called the 'organized community': all important social and economic groups were forced to join an organization linked to the Peronist party. The regime's power-base was the labour movement which Perón, hailed as 'Argentina's No 1 Worker', had organized; workers received increased wages and a range of welfare benefits. An attempt was made to force industrialization, financed by a state monopoly over foreign trade.

After his overthrow in 1955 Perón spent 17 years in exile in Paraguay, Panama, Venezuela, the Dominican Republic and Spain. From exile he controlled the Peronist party and its trade unions through a network of agents. His return, in 1973 was dramatic, his plane being diverted from Ezeiza airport after rival left and right wing Peronists opened fire on each other. This incident heralded the final showdown of his career. Elected president in October 1973, he was faced by hyperinflation and the struggle between incompatible groups of left and right wing supporters in the Peronist movement. The young revolutionary Peronists, whose support he had encouraged in exile, were soon disillusioned and resumed their violence. By the time of his death, in July 1974, Argentina was on the threshold of a new and more terrifying round of conflict.

The continuing controversy over Perón's place in Argentine history mirrors the contradictory nature of his regime. An army officer for over 30 years, he was ejected by the army in 1955, an institution which then prevented his return until 1973. Descendent of a bourgeois family, he drew his support from the urban workers and rural poor and was hated by the Buenos Aires middle classes. In recent years, his role after 1945 in the sale of passports to escaping war criminals from the Fascist powers has been the subject of considerable discussion, both in Argentina and abroad.

Isabelita and replaced her with a *junta* led by Gen Jorge Videla.

The new government closed Congress, outlawed political parties, placed trade unions and universities under military control and unleashed the so-called 'dirty war', a brutal assault on the guerrilla groups and other displays of opposition. Gen Videla was appointed President in 1978 by the military; his nominated successor, Gen Roberto Viola took over for three years in March 1981 but was overthrown by Gen Leopoldo Galtieri in December 1981. The latter was in turn replaced in June 1982 by Gen Reynaldo Bignone, following military defeat in the Falklands/Malvinas.

Confidence in the military ebbed when their economic policies began to go sour in 1980. In 1982-1983 pressure for a return to civilian rule grew, particularly after the Falklands/Malvinas War with Great Britain in 1982. Discredited by the stories of returning conscripts, the armed forces withdrew to barracks. Elections in October

From Guerrilla War to 'Dirty War'

The 'Dirty War', unleashed by the armed forces after 1976 in response to the guerrilla attacks of the early 1970s, is one of the most violent incidents in modern South American history. While Argentine society is understandably chastened by the experience, hardly a month goes by without this grim episode provoking further controversy.

Guerrilla groups began operating in most Latin American countries in the 1960s, usually with little success. From 1969 several groups emerged in Argentina, among them the Montoneros and the People's Revolutionary Army (Ejército Revolucionario del Pueblo or ERP). The former, inspired by a curious mixture of Peronism, Catholicism and Marxism, proclaimed allegiance to the exiled Perón. Often middle and upper-middle class by background and wanting to liberate the working classes from the evils of capitalism, they idealized Perón and the 'social justice' of his government of 1946-1955, a period which most of them were too young to remember. Since the urban working classes were mainly Peronist, these youthful idealists assumed that Perón was a revolutionary leader and that his return would be the prelude to revolution. The ERP, by contrast drawing their inspiration from Trotsky and Che Guevara, argued that political violence would push the military government towards increased repression which would ignite working class opposition and lead to civil war and socialist revolution.

If Peronists and non-Peronists disagreed over their aims, their methods were similar: kidnappings and bank robberies raised money and gained publicity; army and police officers were assassinated along with right wing Peronists. Wealthy Argentine families and multinational companies were forced to distribute food and other goods to the poor to obtain the release of kidnap victims. Perhaps the most spectacular of these episodes was carried out by the Montoneros: in 1970 they kidnapped and later `executed' General Pedro Aramburu, a former president.

Called upon to denounce the

1983 were won by Raúl Alfonsín and his Unión Cívica Radical (UCR). During 1985 Generals Videla, Viola and Galtieri were sentenced to long terms of imprisonment for their parts in the 'dirty war'. While Alfonsín's government struggled to deal with the legacy of the past, it was overwhelmed by continuing economic problems, the most obvious of which was hyperinflation. When the Radicals were defeated by Carlos Menem, the Peronist (*Justicialist*) presidential candidate, Alfonsín stepped down early because of economic instability. Strained relations between the Peronist Government and the military led to several rebellions, which Menem attempted to appease by pardoning the imprisoned Generals. His popularity among civilians declined, but in 1991-92 the Economy Minister, Domingo Cavallo, succeeded in restoring confidence in the economy and the Government as a whole. The symbol of this stability was the introduction of a new currency pegged to the United States dollar. After triumphing in the October 1993 congressional elections at the expense of the UCR, the Peronists themselves lost some ground in April 1994 elections to a constituent assembly. The party to gain most, especially in Buenos Aires, was Frente Grande, a broad coalition of left wing groups and disaffected Peronists. Behind the loss of confidence of these dissident Peronists were unrestrained corruption and a pact in December 1993 between Menem and Alfonsín pledging UCR support for constitutional changes which included re-election of the president for a second term of four years.

By the 1995 elections, the majority of the electorate favoured stability over constitutional concerns and returned President Menem. The Peronists also increased their majority in the Chamber of Deputies and gained a majority in the Senate.

guerrillas which operated in his name, Perón from his exile in Madrid, refused. With the return to civilian rule the Montoneros ended their violence and worked to elect their hero. Now operating semi-openly, the movement gained many supporters, especially students and young people. In May 1974, months before his death, Perón, denounced his leftist supporters and after his death they resumed their violence, this time under the slogan "If Evita were alive, she would be a Montonera". In 1974 they kidnapped Jorge and Juan Born, heirs and managers of the giant Bunge y Born grain exporting company, and ransomed them for US$64 million.

Long before Perón's return, right wing groups linked to the army and police had begun to take action against suspected guerrillas. By 1974 suspected leftists were regularly disappearing at the hands of the Argentine Anticommunist Alliance (known as the 'Triple A') which was linked to José López Rega, Minister of Social Welfare and closest advisor to Isabel Perón who became president after her husband's death. The 'Dirty War', launched by the military government which seized power in 1976 was, in a sense, a continuation of this: all three armed services operated their own death squads and camps in a campaign of indiscriminate violence. By 1978/79 both the ERP and the Montoneros had ceased to function. In the process thousands of people disappeared: although an official report produced after the return to civilian rule put their number at 8,960, some 15,000 cases have now been documented and human rights groups now estimate the total at some 30,000. They are remembered still by the Mothers of the Plaza de Mayo, a human rights group made up of relatives, who march anti-clockwise around the Plaza de Mayo in central Buenos Aires every Thursday at 1530 with photos of their 'disappeared' loved ones pinned to their chests. Their continued protests highlight one of the most controversial aspects of the restoration of civilian rule: the laws passed in 1986/7 which shielded junior officers

Menem's renewed popularity was short-lived: joblessness remained high and corruption unrestrained. Concurrent with changes at the Finance Ministry and measures to take the economy beyond the 1995 recession (see page 517), labour legislation reform was highly unpopular as it contravened some of Peronism's founding tenets. In July 1996, the Radicals won the first direct elections for mayor of Buenos Aires and in mid-term congressional elections in October 1997 the Peronist Party lost its ruling majority. Most votes went to the Alianza Democrática, formed by the Radicals and the Frepaso coalition. The latter's candidate for Buenos Aires province, Graciela Fernández Meijide, defeated Hilda Duhalde of the Peronists, whose husband, Eduardo, was provincial governor. In addition to the Peronists' poor showing, several senior members were embarrassed by alleged involvement with millionaire Alfredo Yabrán. Many suspected Yabrán of criminal activities, not least of ordering the murder of journalist José Luis Cabezas (January 1997). The case fuelled the rivalry between Duhalde and Menem but in May 1998 Yabrán, who was being sought by the police, committed suicide.

In November 1998 Alianza Democrática chose the Radical Fernando de la Rua as its candidate for the October 1999 presidential election. Moves from Menem supporters to put forward Menem for a further (constitutionally dubious) term of office helped delay the Peronist choice of candidate until July 1999 when Eduardo Duhalde received the backing of Menem. Although Alianza Democrática offered little change in economic policy, the Peronists were harmed by the corruption scandals surrounding the Menem administration and the continuing rivalry between Menem and Duhalde, enabling De la Rua to win the presidency and take

The Anglo-Argentine War of 1982

Though the dispute between Britain and Argentina over the Falkland Islands/Islas Malvinas led to armed conflict in 1982, its historical roots can be traced to before Argentine independence. Records of early European voyages in the area are ambiguous but the Dutch sailor Sebald de Weert made the first generally acknowledged sighting of the islands in 1598. When the English navigator John Strong landed in 1690 he named the Falkland Sound after Lord Falkland; this name was later applied to the island group. The Spanish name Islas Malvinas *is derived from the French* Iles Malouines, *the appellation given by sailors from the French port of St Malo who also visited in the 17th century.*

In 1764 France established a small colony on the islands at Port Louis. At about the same time the British built an outpost at Saunders Island. In 1766 the French government sold Port Louis to Spain which turned it into a military garrison and penal colony and, in 1770, expelled the British from Saunders Island. Although Madrid, under threat of war, permitted the reestablishment of the British post the following year, it was withdrawn in 1774.

In 1811, following the outbreak of the Wars of Independence in South America, Spain also withdrew her forces from the

islands. In 1820 they were claimed by an expedition from Buenos Aires, which raised a flag at Port Louis (renamed Soledad). In 1831 a United States warship destroyed a promising colonisation project under the auspices of a German-born merchant from Buenos Aires who had arrested United States sealers operating in the area. After British warships expelled a force from Buenos Aires in 1833, the islands came under British rule.

During his first administration (1946-1955) Perón focussed on the disputed status of the islands as part of an appeal to Argentine nationalism and linked the issue to Argentina's claim over parts of the Antarctic and his plan to create a 'Greater Argentina'. In 1965 the United Nations called on the two states to resolve their differences peacefully. Talks over the islands took place but were complicated by the hostility of the islanders themselves towards any change in their status.

Though contingency plans for an Argentine invasion had existed for many years, in 1982 the Argentine military regime calculated that the opportune moment had arrived. The decision by the British government to reduce its military commitment in the area and withdraw the patrol ship HMS Endurance *suggested London was losing interest. Severe*

office in December 1999. Prospects for the new administration are mixed: there is potential for conflict over economic and social policy, particularly between the conservative wing of the Radicals (led by De la Rua) and the more leftist Frepaso. Moreover, although Alianza Democrática is the largest grouping in the lower chamber, the Peronists still control the Senate (where elections are due in December 2001) as well as two thirds of the provinces including the three key provinces of Buenos Aires, Córdoba and Santa Fe.

economic problems in Argentina threatened the military's hold on power and the regime calculated that a successful invasion would unite the population behind it. An incident on the island of South Georgia, also claimed by Argentina though not part of the Falklands/Malvinas group, provided the opportunity.

The Argentine force of 5,000 men which landed on 2 April 1982 quickly overwhelmed the small British garrison without loss of life. The British military and civilian authorities were expelled and the 1,700 inhabitants placed under an Argentine military governor. Though most Latin American states sympathized with Buenos Aires over the sovereignty issue, many were unhappy with the use of force. Backed by a United Nations resolution and the crucial logistical support of the United States, the British government launched a naval force to regain the islands. On 25 April, as this fleet approached the area, a British force recaptured South Georgia. Over the following three weeks the war was fought in the air and on the seas around the Falklands/Malvinas: the Argentines lost numerous aircraft, the cruiser General Belgrano, and several other vessels. The British lost two destroyers, two frigates and a landing vessel. After the sinking of the General Belgrano, the Argentine navy stayed in port or close to shore, leaving the airforce and army to carry on the battle.

The British reoccupation of the islands began with an amphibious landing under heavy fire at San Carlos on 21 May. From here British troops marched across the island and attacked ineffective Argentine defensive positions around the capital. Though some Argentine army and marine units resisted, most of the Argentine troops were poorly trained and equipped conscripts who were no match for British regular forces. On 14 June Argentine forces surrendered.

Casualties in the war outnumbered the small island population. Argentine losses were 746 killed, over 300 on the General Belgrano, and 1,336 wounded; the British lost 256 killed and 777 wounded. Three islanders were killed on the final assault on the capital.

The consequences of the war for Argentina were wide-ranging. The military government was, perhaps, discredited less by defeat than by its obvious misjudgement of the situation, by its blatant misleading of the public during the conflict and by the accounts given by returning troops of incompetent leadership and lack of supplies. General Galtieri was replaced as President and preparations were made for a return to civilian rule.

The economy and government

Structure of production

Argentina is one of the more highly developed countries of the region. It has the third largest gdp in Latin America, but by far the highest per capita income. Wealth traditionally came from farming although agriculture, forestry and fishing now account for only 6% of gdp. Nevertheless, over half of export earnings are generated by farming and food processing. There has been a shift from livestock to crop production since the 1960s. The area sown to oilseeds has risen steeply, now exceeding that of wheat. Although the fertility of the pampas was once so high that fertilizers were unnecessary, overexploitation and soil erosion have made its use essential, increasing the costs of farmers also hit by rising costs, falling commodity prices and lack of cheap credit to invest in modernization. In the 1990s, 150,000-200,000 small and medium sized farms were under severe financial pressure and many faced bankruptcy, leading to a consolidation of land holdings. Cresud, the only landholding company traded on the stock market, increased its holdings from 20,000 to 348,000 ha in 1994-96. Cattle and sheep herds have been reduced because of stiff competition abroad, low wool prices and outbreaks of foot and mouth disease. A vaccination drive started in 1989 has been successful and no further outbreaks have been recorded since 1994, leading farmers to hope that beef import bans imposed by the USA, Japan and Southeast Asian countries might be lifted. Exports of about 450,000 tonnes a year, earning some US$900 mn, could double if the bans are lifted. Fishing received a boost in 1993 from an agreement with Britain to share fish resources in the South Atlantic, thereby increasing by 70% Argentina's share of the illex squid catch.

Manufacturing was developed behind high import protection barriers, but these have now been swept aside. The sector accounts for 26% of gdp and is closely linked with agricultural activity, with food processing and beverages accounting for a quarter of manufacturing output. The regional customs union, Mercosur, opened up a huge market for companies established in Argentina and many food companies have been bought by multinationals. Trade with Brazil has traditionally been biased towards foodstuffs but enterprises in other areas are now growing. Several multinational motor vehicle companies are investing in new plant, many around Córdoba. All plan to sell vehicles to other Mercosur countries as well as within Argentina.

Argentina is self-sufficient in energy and has an exportable surplus of oil, natural gas and hydroelectricity. Hydroelectric potential lies on 10 main rivers: the rivers Paraná and Uruguay in the north where huge joint projects have been built with Paraguay (Yacyretá, Corpus) and Uruguay (Salto Grande), and on rivers in Río Negro and Neuquén provinces. The Government is divesting its stake in electricity generating and will offer its participation to private investors once ratification is secured from the Paraguayan and Uruguayan parliaments. More hydroelectricity generating plants are planned which will be built under concession by private contractors. Argentina has had nuclear power since 1974 when the first stage of the Atucha power station was opened using German technology. Crude oil output is around 785,000 b/d (domestic consumption 485,000 b/d, exports 300,000 b/d) and reserves are to be kept at 10 years' production with more exploration in a US$3bn, 10-year investment programme. The country has more natural gas than oil and reserves are about 560 billion cubic metres, equivalent to about 30 years' consumption at present rates.

Mining was discouraged by previous administrations, who declared the border region a security zone and closed to foreign investment, but there are substantial mineral deposits in the foothills of the Andes. Investment is now being encouraged by new legislation introduced in 1993. The first major project will be the Bajo de la Alumbrera porphyry copper and gold deposit in Catamarca which is believed to have 752 million tonnes of ore. Mining operations will start in 1997 and production should reach 180,000 tonnes of copper and 640,000 ozs of gold a year. Another copper-gold deposit in Catamarca is Agua Rica, which could be developed into an open pit mine to rival Alumbrera. Both are being developed by Australian and Canadian companies. Lithium deposits at the Salar del Hombre Muerto dry lake bed also in Catamarca are believed to be sufficient for 70 years' production.

Recent trends

In the 1980s large fiscal deficits, monetary expansion and a high velocity of circulation caused very high inflation, which was difficult to curb because of structural imbalances in the economy, inadequate levels of investment and inefficiencies and corruption in both the public and private sectors. The Government introduced several stabilization programmes, the first of which was the Austral Plan, named after the currency it introduced, but none was successful. Output and investment contracted as confidence was eroded and the economy became increasingly dollarized. The external debt rose sharply but rescheduling agreements with commercial bank creditors backed by IMF financing facilities all collapsed as policy commitments were not met and payment arrears mounted.

The Menem administration tackled structural economic reform, which initially brought further recession and unemployment. In 1991 it passed a Convertibility Law, fixing the peso at par with the US dollar and permitting the Central Bank to print local currency only if it is fully backed by gold or hard currency. This was the key to achieving price stability; the annual average growth of consumer prices fell from 3,080% in 1989 to 3.9% in 1994 and remained in single figures thereafter. Dozens of state companies were privatized, many using debt reduction techniques. Fiscal surpluses were recorded in 1992-93 and gdp growth rates averaging 7.7% a year were recorded in 1991-94. After a current account surplus in 1990, increasing deficits were recorded in following years, reaching nearly US$10bn in 1994, but these were amply financed by capital inflows and international reserves increased. Imports soared from US$3.7 bn in 1990 to US$19.9 bn in 1994, while gross domestic investment in the same years rose by 22% to 23% of gdp. In 1993 an agreement was signed with international banks to restructure bank debt by securitizing it into bonds, following the Mexican model of debt or debt service reduction.

Cracks began to appear in the model in the second half of 1994 when a fiscal deficit became apparent. Tax collections fell and current spending rose. The tax structure concentrates on consumption with a high rate of VAT, but the demand side of the economy had been growing only slowly, partly because of rising unemployment as a result of privatizations and streamlined payrolls. The devaluation of the Mexican peso in December 1994 created what became known as the 'tequila effect'. Loss of confidence in Mexico spread to other Latin American countries and Argentina suffered a sharp liquidity squeeze as US$8bn in bank deposits, 15% of the total, fled the country. Many banks were merged, yet at 130, there were still too many for the country's deposit base. Unemployment soared to over 18% by May 1995, consumer demand fell sharply, tax collections dwindled and a recession loomed. Riots broke out in parts of the country as provincial governments failed to pay wages for several months.

The Government turned to the IMF, which negotiated a US$7 bn rescue package with multilateral lenders. In 1995 exports rose by 33%, as goods were diverted from the weak domestic market, encouraged by high commodity prices and a consumer boom in Brazil, but gdp declined by 2.5%. The recession appeared to be over by the end of the year, though, with industrial production, imports and demand picking up, and unemployment declining, while 90% of bank deposits had returned. A private pension scheme was launched to ease pressure on the bankrupt state scheme as well as raise the savings ratio, reduce dependence on foreign capital and increase investment funds for industry.

In the first half of 1996 the slow rate of recovery had a negative impact on fiscal revenues and the target for the deficit was exceeded. The introduction of new and unpopular austerity measures led to the dismissal of Finance Minister Domingo Cavallo, the architect of the 1990s economic restructuring and liberalization programme, for political reasons. His successor, Roque Fernández, formerly president

Mad about wine

Argentina has been making wine since the first Spanish settlers planted the first vines in 1554. During the present century it has consistently figured amongst the major world producers, occupying fourth or fifth ranking according to the annual harvest. Yet its wines have never, until the last two or three years, been recognized abroad, mainly because Argentines have devoted themselves to drinking what they produce. Per capita consumption of wine, up to the start of the 1950s, was third in the world.

Argentina's wine country extends along the length of the Andean foothills, from Salta in the north, to the Rio Negro valley in the province of the same name, in the south. Scattered vineyards can be found in the provinces of La Pampa, Neuquen, Cordoba and even Buenos Aires (exclusively a home industry). However, the heart of the winelands and capital of wine is Mendoza province, with over 70% of production.

It is a surprise for the first-time vistor to this part of the country to see the lush vineyards and vegetation in general emerge as if by magic out of the semi-arid desert which is a feature of most of western Argentina, which suffers from the Andean rain-shadow. Only south of San Rafael, in the southernmost part of Mendoza, does the desert begin to give way to the lush natural vegetation which is typical of western Patagonia. The answer is, of course, irrigation, the eternally snow-capped Andean range providing some of the purest and most mineral-rich water available anywhere. This system of irrigation – rainfall seldom surpasses 200 mm per year, and mostly falls in the summer when it is little needed – is one of the reasons for Argentina's rather special and characteristic wines.

Reflecting its strongly European character, with Spanish and Italian influence predominating, but with strong minor inputs, Argentine wine and drinking habits are strongly European in character. The main grape varietals are mostly of French origin. Cabernet Sauvignon, Merlot, Malbec and Syrah for red wines; Chardonnay, Chenin, Sauvignon Blanc, Riesling and Torrontés for whites.

If one can select two grapes which can be called truly Argentine, Malbec and Torrontés are they. In Argentina the Malbec grape has found climates and soils which allow it to

of the central bank, pursued similar economic policies, which provoked strikes. Nevertheless, gdp expanded by 4.3% in 1996 and by a further 8.4% in 1997. Strong growth could not mask serious problems which threatened to deter foreign investors: the trade deficit rose steeply as commodity prices fell, the Brazilian economy slowed and the dollar remained strong. The stock exchange suffered severe knock-on effects from the southeast Asian financial crisis of 1997-98. Tax revenues continued to be insufficient to lower the fiscal deficit. In April 1998 the IMF recommended that growth be slowed and that trade and current account deficits be brought in line with previously agreed targets. President Menem was unlikely, though, to embark on a course of limiting spending in the run-up to the 1999 elections.

Government

The country's official name is La República Argentina (RA), the Argentine Republic. The form of government has traditionally been a representative, republican federal system. Of the two legislative houses, the Senate has 72 seats, and the Chamber of Deputies 257. Under the 1853 Constitution (amended most recently in 1994) the country is divided into a Federal Capital (the city of Buenos Aires) and 23 Provinces. The Federal government is headed by the President, who is elected by universal suffrage for a four-year term and who may serve two consecutive terms (until 1994 the presidential term was six years with no immediate reelection). Each Province has

develop to far greater heights than it can reach in France. Argentina's finest red wines, in the opinion of such experts as Hugh Johnson and Jancis Robinson, are her Malbec varietals; superior – and different – to the far better known Cabernet Sauvignon. If Argentina is finally becoming known abroad, it is as much due to her Malbec wines as to any other.

If Malbec can be considered almost Argentine in character and nationality, Torrontés has no such limits. Its origin is somewhat doubtful, but most experts agree that it is probably a descendant of a vine originally brought over from Galicia (Spain). It is only found as a noble grape in Argentina, where it produces, according to where it is cultivated, a strongly perfumed, sweet-smelling wine which when tasted is incredibly dry but fruity. The strongest and most marked characteristics are found in the provinces of Salta and La Rioja. Those that are made in San Juan and Mendoza are of lesser interest and generally less perfumed, while that which comes from Rio Negro is a light, more delicate and extremely easy wine to drink. For first timers, it is probably best to begin with a Rio Negro Torrontés before graduating to a Salta or La Rioja version. The best brands are Canale (Rio Negro), Nacari (La Rioja) and Etchart (Salta).

With a per capita consumption of 40 litres of wine per annum, Argentines are amongst the world's leading wine consumers (third in the global league), but are now far off the all time record of nearly 91 litres registered in 1970. More than 90% of that wine was common table or jug wine. Today, while drinking less Argentines are drinking better. The drop in consumption has been all in the jug wine sector, while noble wines have increased at their expense, particularly the sparkling wine sector, which is booming. Apart from local concerns, sparkling wines are made by local affiliates of Möet & Chandon, C H Mumm and Piper-Heidsieck. By far the most popular is that made by Chandon, who also make generic and varietal wines. Top noble wines range between the $7 and $12 per bottle range at good wine stores, while excellent medium range wines can be had from between $3 and $5. Restaurants tend to double and even triple these prices.

its own Governor, Senate and Chamber of Deputies. The Constitution grants the Federal Capital self government under a Mayor who is directly elected.

The location of power within this system is complex. Though the Federal government is usually seen as very powerful, this power partly depends on the President's own party having control over Congress. Moreover the Federal Capital and the provinces of Buenos Aires, Santa Fé and Córdoba, which between them contain 70% of the total population, can exercise a powerful counterweight, especially if they are controlled by the opposition.

People

The population at latest estimate (1995) was 34,600,000, the third largest population in South America after Brazil and Colombia, making Argentina one of the least densely populated countries in the continent. In the Federal Capital and Province of Buenos Aires, where almost 40% of the population lives, the people are mainly of European origin. In the far northern provinces, at least half the people are *mestizos* though they form about 15% of the population of the whole country.

Though Argentina is a largely white society there are 13 different indigenous minorities, totaling about 500,000 people, 3% of the total population. Most live in

Indigenous peoples

Blacks in Argentina

Though Argentina is usually seen as a nation of white, predominantly European immigrants, Africans played an important role in its history. While slavery was by no means as important as in Brazil or the Caribbean, by the 18th century it was common in many parts of the colony, especially in towns, as most slaves were domestic servants or artisans; slavery was also important on the sugar estates of Tucumán, in the textile workshops of Catamarca and in rural areas of Mendoza and Córdoba. In Buenos Aires there were black cofradías (Catholic lay organizations) open to slaves and free blacks alike. One aspect of black community life which particularly disturbed the authorities was dancing: in the 1760s it was banned, but later it was tolerated within limits. In 1769 one priest complained that Africans dancing outside his church to celebrate Easter had made so much noise that he had been unable to perform the service. At independence there were probably 30,000 slaves in a total population of 400,000, while in the city of Buenos Aires 29% of the population were black or mulatto.

The creole leaders of the independence movement were ambivalent towards slavery: the slave trade was banned in 1812, though illegal trading continued for many years. Although no moves were made to abolish slavery, the new government's desperate need for troops to fight the Spanish led it to buy slaves from masters; such soldiers were promised freedom after 5 years if they survived. Black troops played an important role in the struggle for independence. Some 1,500 of the 5,000 troops in San Martín's Army of the Andes were black and San Martín regarded them as his best infantry.

Slavery was finally abolished 1853 when the Constitution formally outlawed it, but the decline in numbers of blacks and mulattoes in the 19th century is rarely explained by historians: massive European migration is part of the answer as well as the high mortality rate of black soldiers who formed an important part of the Argentine forces in the War of the Triple Alliance against Paraguay. However, another explanation is that as Argentine society became more self-consciously white, writers and historians ignored the black contribution, while blacks themselves dyed their hair and tried to hide their origins.

communities in the north, bordering Bolivia and Paraguay. The largest group, about 30% of the total, are the *Colla* in the northwest, who speak Quechua and are closely related to indigenous groups in Bolivia. The other large minorities are the *Toba* (20%), the *Wichi* or *Mataco* (10%), the *Mapuche* (10%) and the *Guarani* (10%). Several of the smaller groups are in danger of extinction: in 1987 the Minority Rights Group reported the death of the last *Ona* in Tierra del Fuego and noted that the 100 remaining *Tehuelches* were living on a reservation in southern Patagonia. A number of organizations represent indigenous interests, but any legislation, under federal law, has to be enacted separately by each province.

Immigration The transformation of the Humid Pampa through immigration, began a process which has made Argentina into a society of predominantly European origin. White immigration was encouraged by the 1853 Constitution and the new political stablity after 1862 encouraged a great wave of settlers from Europe. Between 1857 and 1930 total immigration was over 6,000,000, almost all from Europe. About 55% of these were Italians, followed by Spaniards (26%), and then, far behind, groups of other Europeans and Latin Americans. British and North Americans normally came as stockbreeders, technicians and business executives. By 1895 25% of the population of 4,000,000 were immigrants. There were also large numbers of migrant workers, known as *golondrinas* (swallows) who crossed the Atlantic each year to work on the harvest.

The gaucho in history and legend

The gaucho, the cowboy of the Pampas, played an important role in Argentine history though, unlike his North American counterpart, he has long since become a cultural and political symbol. Gauchos emerged as a distinct social group in the early 18th century, hunting wild cattle on the pampas and adopting aspects of the lifestyle of the Indians. The classic gaucho lived on horseback, dressing in a poncho, a chirpá (baggy trousers), which were held up by a tirador or broad leather belt, and homemade boots with iron spurs. Armed with boleadoras (three stones linked with leather which when expertly thrown would wrap around the legs of animals) and a facón or large knife, he roamed the pampas in a period before fencing and private property, when the herds of wild cattle and horses seemed inexhaustible. Understandably his way of life gave little time for officials who tried to extend government control over the pampas. The urban population in turn regarded the gaucho as a savage, almost on a par with the Indians, and governments tried to tame him with anti-vagrancy laws and military conscription.

Inevitably perhaps this lifestyle was doomed, brought to an end in the 19th century by fencing, railways, the campaigns against the Indians and the redistribution of land which followed. Increasingly the term gaucho came to mean a ranch worker who made a living on horseback tending cattle. However, as real gauchos disappeared from the pampas, they became a major subject of Argentine folklore and literature.

Over 1,300,000 Italians settled in Argentina between 1876 and 1914, a majority of them from the north. Their influence can be seen in the country's food, its urban architecture and its language, especially in Buenos Aires where the local vocabulary has incorporated *Lunfardo*. Though this started out as the language of thieves, many of its expressions have become part of the city's slang. Today it is estimated that 12.8% of the population are foreign born. Although most immigrants are of European origin, there are also important communities of Syrians, Lebanese, Armenians, Japanese and Koreans.

Culture

Arts and crafts

Modern South American handicrafts represent either the transformation of utilitarian objects into works of art or the continued manufacture of pieces which retain symbolic value. Some traditional handicrafts are threatened by factors such as urbanization, the loss of types of wood and plant fibres through the destruction of forests and the replacement of the horse by farm machinery. At the same time, the survival of handicrafts has been helped by new demands from city dwellers and tourists. The most important areas for arts and crafts in Argentina are in the north of the country, regions where the indigenous minorities and pre-hispanic traditions are strongest.

As the Inca Empire grew in the years before the arrival of the Spanish, it inherited many of the skills and traditions of pre-Inca cultures. Although northwestern Argentina had not been brought within the Inca Empire, it had developed strong links with modern Peru and Bolivia. After the conquest Spanish trade routes which ran through the northwest towards Lima contributed towards maintaining these influences. Two of the major areas of craftwork today are in the valleys of Catamarca and western Salta.

Background

The Buenos Aires Herald

Founded in 1876, the Herald's finest hour occurred during the dark days of the 1976-1983 military government; despite death threats, the Herald was the only Argentine paper to cover human rights' abuses and its news editor, Andrew Graham-Youll, was forced to leave for Britain. The newspaper's courageous stand received international recognition in 1978 when it was awarded the Moors-Cabot prize seen by some as the 'Oscar of journalism' for being a "still, small voice of calm" in a climate of fear and violence.

Since the return to civilian rule the paper's fortunes have fluctuated. But it still offers "a universal view of what the world looks like as seen from Buenos Aires" as its former co-editor, Nicholas Tozer, explains – an eclectic mix of international news, insights into Argentine life and the particular interests of the English-speaking community. The Sunday edition features a review of local political developments and Dereck Foster's justly famous food column.

Woodcarving In colonial times the most important area for woodcarving was the northeast. Though woodcarving dated back beyond the Spanish conquest, a major influence on its development was the Catholic church, and particularly the Jesuit missions or *reducciones*. In Misiones, as in Paraguay, the indigenous Guaraní were set to work to build churches and produce woodcarvings and other handicrafts to decorate them. Although the Indians were left to fend for themselves after the expulsion of the Jesuits, some of the traditional techniques survive today in the woodcarvings of this area.

Further north *palo santo* (Bulnesia sarmiento), a greenish scented wood, is used extensively in wood carving by communities who live along the Río Pilcomayo which forms the frontier with Paraguay. At Campo Durán, north of Tartagal in the lowland area of northeastern Salta, the hollow trunk of the *palo santo* tree is adapted for making wooden masks, used in traditional agricultural ceremonies. Isolated groups of Toba, Chané and Mataco Indians in this part of the province produce exquisite carvings of birds and animals, using a variety of local woods including *palo santo*, the reddish *quebracho* (Schinopsis balansae), the brown or black *guayacan* (Caesalpina Paraguariensis) and a yellow wood known locally as *mora* (Chorophora Tinctoria). Cowbones are used to make the beaks and feet, as well as an inlay to decorate spoons and other utilitarian items. *Palo santo* vessels for drinking *mate* are made, replacing the traditional gourd.

In the valleys of Catamarca and Salta in the northwest wood from the cardoon cactus is used for carving small objects and furniture, though overexploitation of the cardoon has led to restrictions on its use.

Textiles & weaving Woven cloth was the most highly prized possession and trading commodity in the Andes in pre-Columbian times. Some of that tradition survives in the valleys of Catamarca and Salta, where ponchos, blankets, wallhangings and rugs are woven from alpaca and lambs wool. Ponchos are produced in most of these valleys including the beautiful red and black *poncho de Güemes*, named after the local independence leader Martín Güemes. Hand-made ponchos represent at least a week's work and often much more. Perhaps the most important centre is the village of Santa María in Catamarca province but just south of Cafayate.

Further south on the pampas from colonial times through to the 19th century the most readily available source of clothing was animal hides, which were cut into strips of different widths and then used to plait clothing, saddlery and stirrups. Fine leatherwork is still produced in many parts of the pampas.

Jewellery & metalwork While the Spanish were dazzled by the Incas' use of gold, it was the pre-Inca cultures who had mastered the art of working with metal. In the colonial period the Spanish preferred to work in silver rather than gold and great quantities of silver were mined at Potosí in Alto Peru. In Argentina silverwork is particularly associated with the gauchos of the pampas. Here as in neighbouring Uruguay all the trappings of riding: stirrups, bits, rings, halters and spurs, were often made from silver, as well as costume accessories such as engraved buttons and belts. *Mate* drinking is another tradition associated with the *gauchos*; the traditional gourd, used for drinking *mate* was also often replaced with a vessel made of silver; the *bombilla* or pipe through which it is drunk is still frequently made of silver.

Handicrafts can be purchased in Buenos Aires and in northern Argentina. For further information see *Arts and Crafts of South America* by Lucy Davies and Mo Fini (Tumi, 1994).

Cinema

'To enter a cinema in Calle Lavalle and find myself (not without surprise) in the Gulf of Bengal or Wabash Avenue seems preferable to entering the same cinema and finding myself (not without surprise) in Calle Lavalle.' (Jorge Luis Borges).

Borges, Argentina's greatest writer and sometime film critic, had a lifetime attachment to the movies, even when his eyesight failed him later in life. In the 1920s and 1930s, however, he could go regularly to the cinemas clustered in Calle Lavalle or in Av Corrientes, in central Buenos Aires. In 1922, the city had some 27,000,000 film goers each year and 128 movie theatres, the largest, the Grand Splendid seating 1,350 people. By 1933 there were 1,608 cinemas throughout Argentina, with 199 in the capital. However, as Borges points out, the taste of the cinema going public was for Hollywood movies. Hollywood has dominated the screens in Latin America for the first hundred years of film history, averaging some 90% of viewing time in Argentina. The history of a national cinema in Latin America is, therefore, the story of men and women working under the influence of the power of Hollywood, with its control of production, distribution and exhibition.

The question of whether to reject or accept the Hollywood model is not a simple one, certainly not as simple as the radical theorists of cultural imperialism in the 1960s (such as the film maker Fernando Solanas, see ???) would have us believe. It is not just a matter of rejecting the dominant model and asserting a utopian free space of national cinema. Hollywood created a universal way of seeing cinema which was strongly influenced by the advanced technology itself, technology with which poorer competitors could not compete. However Hollywood also offered communities access to modernity and ways of understanding modern, urban life. Argentine culture has always developed through dialogue between cultures; receiving and understanding the lessons of Hollywood as well as its powerful limitations is an integral part of the cultural process. Hollywood stimulates debates and adds a dynamic element in the development of artistic creation. Argentine cinema must therefore be seen within this broader global framework.

The earliest pioneers of Argentine cinema concentrated on documentaries because this was a niche in which international competitors were not greatly concerned. Documentaries on regional topics, football competitions, civic ceremonies and military parades reflected society's self image, especially that of Argentina's ruling elite: its fashions, its power, its ease and comfort in modern cities and in a spectacular rural landscape. The most successful fictional film maker of the silent era (and beyond), José ('*El negro*') Ferreyra (1889-1943) used the structures of melodrama, embodied in the lyrics of tango, to express a society in transition. The tango protagonist is often stranded in the world of modernity ('*Anclado en París*' or anchored in Paris) dreaming and singing nostalgically of his mother, friends, the lovers' nest (*bulín*) and the neighbourhood (*barrio*). In contrast, an *ingenu(e)* is propelled into the world of modernity, prostitutes have hearts of gold and the *barrio* offers the site for homespun

Fernando Solanas

After an early career working in different facets of the culture industry, from advertising to journalism, Solanas began working on documentary shorts from the early sixties and became a founder member of the radical group of film makers, Cine Liberación, together with Octavio Getino, Gerardo Vallejo and others. Between 1966 and 1968 this group directed La hora de los hornos (The Hour of the Furnaces), a colossal four-hour documentary divided into three parts which traced the nature of Argentina's neo-colonial dependency on Europe and postulated revolutionary Peronism as the liberating future for Argentina. Formally complex, ideologically black and white, the film was screened in a clandestine manner throughout the military regimes of the late sixties and early seventies and went on general release with the return of Perón in 1973. It became one of the touchstones of the 'new' Latin American cinema. The film was accompanied by a seminal essay, 'Towards a Third Cinema', which looked to revolutionary Latin American cinema as an alternative to the dominance of both Hollywood and 'author' cinema.

Solanas's first work of fiction 'Los hijos de Fierro' (The Sons of Martin Fierro) was started in 1972 but was not completed until 1977, by which time he had been forced into exile by the military government. This attempt to link the mythology of Peronism to the nationalist, liberationist myths surrounding the 19th-century epic poem Martín Fierro was condemned to a circuit of international film festivals outside Argentina where its symbolism was largely misunderstood.

Solanas's exile in France was difficult: he produced only one documentary and later examined the complexities of the exile experience in Tangos, el exilio de Gardel (Tangos, the Exile of Gardel, 1985), a film part financed under the new democratic regime of Alfonsín in Argentina. The tone of this was very different to the earlier films, seeking to explore dreams and desires through music and choreography and hauntingly beautiful imagery. His next film, Sur (South, 1988) explored Argentina under dictatorship and finding its path in the new democracy in the same evocative blend of music, theatre, dream narrative and strong political concern. El viaje (The Journey, 1992), a search of a son for his father, who personifies Argentine (and Latin American) identity, drew on the strong Argentine theatrical tradition of the grotesque: it is in part a grotesque farce levelled at corrupt politicians. Solanas's uncompromising political engagement has brought him death threats and exile and has disrupted his career, but he remains irrepressibly committed to politics and to new ways of making movies that break conventions and ask us to look afresh at the world around us.

wisdom. The trauma of the new in these early movies is both desire and threat. Ferreyra could sometimes count on Argentine band leaders such as Roberto Firpo to give his silent films live backing. Remarkably, in a world of solitary small-scale production, the first animated feature film in the world was produced in Argentina – El apóstol (The Apostle, 1917), animated by Quirino Cristiani and produced by Federico Valle. Most films, however, did not reveal such technical virtuosity and Argentine movies could only be seen sporadically among the foreign imports.

The coming of sound in the late 1920s created a new, complex situation in Latin America. Many shared the optimism that talkies would call a halt to the dominance of Hollywood: if the image could be understood everywhere, surely language and music were particular to specific cultures. These optimists could surely have been right, but they were wrong: for a number of years, the expense and complexity of the new technologies were too daunting for poorer countries, while Hollywood soon got over its hesitancies about dubbing and subtitling to remain the world market leader. But sound did give an opportunity for certain countries – in particular Argentina, Brazil and Mexico – to develop national industries. In Argentina two major studios were opened, Lumitón and Argentina Sono Film, which began production in 1933 to exploit the potential of tango-led national cinema. Ferreyra continued his work from the silent era, while a new director, Manuel Romero (1891-1954) made formulaic movies in rapid succession and to great popular acclaim: titles such as *Mujeres que trabajan* (Working Women, 1938) and *Los muchachos de antes no usaban gomina* (Back Then, Boys Didn't Use Hair Cream, 1937), which starred Mireya, the tart with the heart, oblivious to the advances of rich men about town. The great tango singer Carlos Gardel (1890-1935) made his movies as part of Hollywood's Hispanic film drive in the early 1930s, when the studios were afraid of losing regional markets and remade versions of Hollywood films in different languages. But the question of whether he might have stayed in the Hollywood system as a singing star in English, or return to Argentina to help develop the national industry, remained unanswered with his early death in a plane crash in 1935. Other stars, but with nothing like the national or indeed international resonance of Gardel, Latin America's first cultural superstar, were actress Niní Marshall (1913-1997), the comic Luis Sandrini (1905-1980) and the singer Libertad Lamarque (1908-).

Other directors began to learn the language as well as the successful formulae of film making. A growing sophistication can be seen in the work of Leopoldo Torres Ríos (1899-1960) in his realist urban dramas, Mario Soffici (1900-1977), in particular the memorable *Prisioneros de la tierra* (Prisoners of the Land, 1939), which had a favourable review even from Borges, and Luis Savlavsky (1908-1995). A fleeting attempt was made to create an epic Argentine western (a southern?) with Lucas Demare's (1910-1981) *La guerra gaucha* (The Gaucho War, 1942) and *Pampa bárbara* (Barbarous Pampa, 1945), but the gauchesque tradition, outlined in the section on literature, never achieved even a fraction of the same mythic significance in film as the cowboy in the western.

By the late 1940s the formulae were becoming somewhat weary and repetitive and state protection for national cinema, introduced by the Peronist régime, could not halt this decline. International companies could soon bully the government into lifting credit restrictions, exhibitors could flaunt the screen quotas and production money tended to be channelled into safe, non innovative productions. It was time for a change. From the mid to late fifties, the changes could be perceived in several different countries and were given the name, by critics and the film makers themselves, of 'new cinema'.

New cinema had both aesthetic and highly charged political meanings. Film clubs and journals created a climate of awareness of film as an art form and the tenets of Italian neo-realism and the '*politique des auteurs*' of *Cahiers du Cinema* provided alternatives to the studio based Hollywood system. In Argentina, Leopoldo Torre Nilsson (1924-1978) and Fernando Birri (1925-) showed the different tendencies within new cinema. Torre Nilsson was an 'author' who explored aristocratic decadence and his early film *La casa del ángel* (The House of the Angel, 1957) was greeted with praise all over the world. Influenced by Bergman, French New Wave and its British contemporaries, Karel Reiss and Lindsay Anderson and in close collaboration with his wife, the writer Beatriz Guido, he explored the contradictions and decline of Argentine upper class and genteel bourgeois society. Birri, a student of Zavattini and neo realism, sought to use neo realist principles to explore the hidden realities of Argentina. His film school in Santa Fé made an important documentary about young shanty town children, *Tire dié* (Throw us a dime, 1957) and helped pioneer a more flexible, socially committed, cinema, 'with a camera in hand and an idea in the head' in the famous phase of Brazilian director Glauber Rocha.

Younger film makers of the sixties like Manuel Antín (1926-), David Kohon (1929-) and Leonardo Favio (1938-) initially followed Torre Nilsson's and their Parisian counterparts' example in exploring, often through literary adaptations, middle-class anomie and alienation or the sexual rites of passage of the young, set in the cafés and streets of Buenos Aires. Meanwhile, the growing climate of revolutionary sentiment of the late 1960s was reflected in Solanas's *La hora de los hornos* (The Hour of the Furnaces, 1966-8), a key text of populist radicalism.

After a brief spell of radical optimism in the late 1960s and early 1970s, reflected in a number of other nationalist-populist movies, the dream of the second coming of Perón turned into the nightmare that led to the brutal military take-over in March 1976. Strict censorship was imposed on cinema, with only the lightest comedies and thrillers escaping total ban or cuts. Film makers such as Solanas, who went into exile, found it difficult to adapt to the new conditions and remained in a cultural wilderness, unlike the Chilean refugee Diaspora, which made many important films in exile. Within Argentina, the tight military control began to slacken in the early 1980s and some important films were made, including María Luisa Bemberg's (1922-1995) *Señora de nadie* (Nobody's Woman, 1982) which was premiered the day before the invasion of the Falklands/Malvinas.

With the return to civilian rule in 1983, the Radical government abolished censorship and put two well known film makers in charge of the National Film Institute, Manuel Antín and Ricardo Wullicher (1948-). Antín's granting of credits to young and established directors and his internationalist strategy had an immediate effect. For several years there was a great flowering of talent, a development that would only be halted temporarily by the economic difficulties of the late 1980s. The trade paper *Variety* (25 March 1987) commented on this new effervescence: 'Never before has there been such a mass of tangible approval as in the years since democratic rule returned at the end of 1983. In 1986, the Hollywood Academy sealed the trend with its first Oscar for an Argentine picture, "The Official Version".' The first massive box office success of these years was Bemberg's *Camila*, which commented by analogy on the recent traumas of Argentine society, a topic taken up directly in Luis Puenzo's (1946-) *La historia oficial* (The Official Version, 1986) and Solanas's two films about exile and the return to democracy: *Tangos, el exilio de Gardel* (Tangos the Exile of Gardel, 1985) and *Sur* (South, 1988). Puenzo, Bemberg and Solanas remained the most visible directors in the 1980s and 1990s, but dozens of other directors made movies in a range of different styles. Eliseo Subiela (1944-) directed several poetic, highly personal, movies, while Lita Stantic, made perhaps the most complex film about the 'dirty war' of the military régime, *Un muro de silencio* (A Wall of Silence, 1993). This was a success with the critics, but was ignored by the public, which preferred to view politics and repression through a gauze of melodrama and rock music, as in Marcelo Piñeyro's *Tango feroz* (1993).

After 1989 the Menem government introduced credits and a percentage of box office and video sales to the film industry and there is currently buoyancy and optimism in the industry. How this will be sustained in times of economic decline and with the increasing globalization of cinema remains the open question for the next century.

Fine art and sculpture

Pre-columbian art The earliest expressions of indigenous art in Argentina are **cave paintings** inhabited by hunter-gatherers some 10,000 years ago. There are many of these in Patagonia, though in most cases access is difficult and there are no tourist facilities. The most famous site is La Cueva de las Manos, in Santa Cruz province, recognised as a World Heritage Site by UNESCO; here the images of hundreds of hands can be seen, created by applying paint around the hand itself. There are also paintings further south in the caves at Punta Gualicho, on the edge of Lago Argentino, near Calafate. Ancient indigenous artists also left their mark in northwestern Argentina. At Inca Cueva, near Humahuaca, painting simple geometric motifs with a small brush or directly with the hands, in red, black and white; these were executed by hunter-gatherers who lived here some 4,000 to 5,000 years ago. In the main cave, archaeologists have been able to reconstruct a large pictorial sequence lasting some 10,000 years and stretching from the first geometric paintings to those which record the encounter of the indigenous with the Spanish *conquistadores,* images of strangely dressed armed horsemen which contrast with the simple representations of men with feathers in their hands, bows and arrows in their hands and leading llamas and alpacas. This site is constantly being damaged as it is unprotected and not equipped for tourism. One of the most important collections of cave paintings in the country is Cerro Colorado in the north of the province of Córdoba. There are hundreds of sites with more than 30,000 motifs distributed on the walls and roofs. Among the great variety of figures are battle scenes between indigenous peoples, dressed in feathers and armed with bows and arrows, and Spaniards, represented by horsemen with lances, swords and boots. This is one of the few places in the country where the indigenous peoples' view of the *conquistadores* can be seen. These images, dating from the middle of the 16th century, were made by the ancestors of the Comechingones.

In Northwestern Argentina the sedentary agricultural cultures have left numerous archaeological remains of artistic value: stone sculptures, ceramics, metal work, mainly in bronze and gold, and, after the Inca conquest, textiles, leather masks, wood, feathers, and work with *chaquiras* (small pieces of shells) and glass beads.

During the first centuries AD the early planters in the western valleys of the provinces of Tucumán and Catamarca were experts in working granite. The most complex of these works were made by the Alamito culture and were known as 'supplicants', a reference to the position of the figures with their arms and faces looking up and imploring or pleading. These carvings, heavily polished, are schematic representations of humans with some zoomorphological traces. Their originality lies in the high level of abstraction, found both in the lines and the spaces which make them resemble modern sculptures. Very few of these survive. The best known can be seen in the Museo de Ciencias Naturales in La Plata where authorised replicas are sold, as well as in the Museo Adán Quiroga in Catamarca and the Museo Arquelogico Ambato in La Falda. Other important examples of early works in stone include: masks in the form of the human faces, probably used as funeral offerings; mortars or ceremonial vessels, decorated with human and feline motifs, which were used to prepare psycheactive substances; and the *menhires* or standing stones, originally found in circles and ceremonial sites, but relocated into the Parque de los Menhires in Tafi del Valle; now in a poor condition, these were originally painted and carved on one of their faces.

The most common expression of indigenous art in the northwest is, without doubt, **ceramic work**, which is found in numerous forms, techniques and styles throughout the 2,000 years of cultural development, from the origins of the agricultural societies (BC 550) right up to the Spanish conquest. In the early or formative period we can find numerous styles, outstanding among which are La Candelaria and Condorhuasi, both of which produced vessels representing hybrids of humans and animals. Those of La Candelaria are in the form of globes, grey or black in colour, while those of Condorhuasi are red with a complex geometric decoration painted in black and white.

From the first millenium onwards the indigenous societies of the northwest became much more militarised, experiencing first Inca domination and annexation to the Inca state in 1490, and then, from the beginning of the 16th century, the Spanish invasion and conquest. Although the making of weapons and defensive constructions dominated, some of these societies, notably that of the valley of Santa María, north of Catamarca, are best remembered for their artistic work, the famous Santa Maria urns. It is clear, from their abundance and their high artistic quality that these were commercialised. These urns, originally used for the burial of children, may be found in museums throughout the world: richly painted with a variety of geometric and natural motifs in black, white and red. One of the treasures of the Museo Etnográfico in Buenos Aires is a 'Quiroga urn', made in the same style, which has, along with the customary twisted neck, an image of a person playing the panpipes. The metal work of this period is also outstanding: discs, axes, bells and other pieces finely decorated with human faces outlined with very simple lines, people with shields and serpents with two heads, all decorated in red.

Southwest, in the province of Neuquén, is the territory of the Mapuche, who crossed the Andes from Chile during the 18th century. Experts in various arts, they are noted particularly for their textiles, with its complex and coloured geometric motifs, for their silver-work including breastplates, earrings and brooches worn by women during fiestas and ceremonies, and for the wooden carvings which generally imitate the severe faces which can be found on the *rehues*, (trunks which form part of the altars used in shamanic rituals). Contemporary expressions of these artistic traditions can be found in good handicraft shops, both in the region and in Buenos Aires.

Colonial Art Argentina (along with neighbouring Uruguay) is arguably the most European of Latin American cultures. Mass immigration and the 19th century extermination of the few remaining Indians have made a culture which defines itself largely in relation to Europe. The partial exception to this is in the north of the country, where proximity to the great Andean civilizations had some effect on local production, but on a much smaller scale than in neighbouring countries.

As the region which is now Argentina was of little importance to the Spanish, there is very little colonial art or architecture in most of Argentina. In the Northern regions of Salta, Jujuy and Misiones, there are some impressive colonial buildings, and some good examples of colonial painting, especially the remarkable portraits of archangels in military uniform in the churches at Uquía and Casabindo, but nothing on the scale of neighbouring Peru or Bolivia.

The 19th century In the 19th century, as Argentina gained Independence and consolidated itself as a modern nation, the ruling elite of the country were determined to make Argentine culture as close to Europe as possible, against what they saw as the 'barbarism' of native customs. The prosperous Buenos Aires bourgeoisie commissioned European architects to build their mansions and collected European fine and decorative arts to decorate them. Rich Argentines travelled to Europe to buy paintings, and gradually began to demand that European painters come to Argentina to depict the wealth and elegance of the ruling class through portraits and landscapes. The most famous of these foreign artists was Carlos Enrique Pellegrini, whose fine society portraits can be seen in the Museo Nacional de Bellas Artes in Buenos Aires. While painters like Pellegrini came to work in Buenos Aires, another type of artist came to South America on scientific expeditions to register topography or flora and fauna. Many of these 'traveller artists' provided an image of the country which was to influence local artists: a familiar case of Europeans providing Argentina with an image of itself rather than vice-versa. Most famous of these traveller artists were the Englishman Emeric Essex Vidal and the German Johann Moritz Rugendas.

By the middle of the century, as Argentina became more politically stable, a new generation of Argentine-trained artists appeared in Buenos Aires. They absorbed some of the techniques and interests of the European artists who were the first to depict their country, but they also discovered a new interest in Romanticism and

Realism. Most famous in this period was Prilidiano Pueyrredón (1823-70), who Argentines consider to be their first national painter. Of more obvious appeal is the rather eccentric Cándido López (1839-1902) whose work has only recently been reevaluated. López followed the Argentine army to the north of the country during the wars with Paraguay and Uruguay. There he began to depict the great battles in a characteristic naive style. López left behind a remarkable series of paintings, which are often displayed in their own room in the Museo Nacional de Bellas Artes in Buenos Aires.

By the end of the century, there were a considerable number of artists working in Argentina, many of whom had been through the National Art School. Generally speaking, they absorbed European movements such as Impressionism, Realism or Expressionism several decades after they appeared in their original forms. Some, such as Martin Malharro, Fernando Fader or Benito Quinquela Martin, were quite talented. Their often melancholic works can be seen in the Bellas Artes Museum or the Municipal 'Eduardo Sivori' Museum in Buenos Aires.

It is in the 20th century that Argentina really found its artistic expression, becoming for many decades an artistic 'superpower' in Latin America and beyond. The dynamism, size and mix of nationalities in the capital created a complex urban society in which artists and intellectuals have prospered. Some of the bohemian attraction of Buenos Aires can still be felt in its more intellectual cafés and districts. This cultural effervescence has been at the expense of the regions; the capital totally dominates the country, and most artists are forced to move there to have any chance of success. **The 20th century**

The first avant-garde artistic movement in Buenos Aires emerged in 1924 with the formation of a groups which called itself 'Martin Fierro', in homage to the national epic poem of the same name. This group brought together a small number of high class intellectuals, the most famous of which was the writer Jorge Luis Borges. The most important visual artist was Xul Solar (1887-1963), who illustrated many of Borges's texts. Solar was one of the 20th century's most eccentric and engaging artists. He had a great interest in mysticism and the occult, and tried to create an artistic system to express his complex beliefs. Solar's works are mostly small scale water-colours in which a sometimes bizarre visionary world is depicted. Many of them are covered in inscriptions in one of the languages he created: Neo-Creole or Pan-Lengua. During the final decades of his life Solar lived in a house on the Paraná Delta near Tigre, where he created a total environment in accordance with his fantastic world, even inventing a new game of chess with rules based on astrology. There is now a Xul Solar Museum in the house where he was born in Buenos Aires and where many of his water-colours and objects are displayed.

Intellectual life in the 1920s was divided into two factions, each named after districts in the city. The elegant Calle Florida gave its name to the sophisticated Martin Fierro set, who belonged to the elite. Several blocks away, the working class Boedo district gave its name to a school of working class socialist artists who rejected the rarefied atmosphere of Florida in favour of socially critical paintings in a grim realistic style. Possibly the most important artist associated with this group was Antonio Berni (1905-81). Some of Berni's murals, together with those of his colleagues, can be seen on the roof of the Galerias Pacifico in Calle Florida.

It was not until the 1940s, with the political crisis provoked by the Second World War, that a new avant-garde movement emerged to overtake the Martin Fierro group. In the mid 1940s, a group of young artists founded an abstract art movement called 'Madí' (a nonsense word) which attempted to combine sophisticated abstract art inspired by Russian Constructivism with a more chaotic sense of fun. Madí works are characterized by blocks of bright colours within an irregular frame, often incorporating physical movement within the structure of the work. As such, they are somewhere between painting and sculpture. For the first time in Argentina, Madí developed artistic principles (such as the irregular frame, or the use of neon gas) before the rest of the world.

Madí was a short-lived adventure, plagued by infighting amongst its members and political divisions. The cultural climate under Perón (1946-55) rejected this type of 'decadent' art in favour of a form of watered-down populism. It was not until the 1960s that cultural life regained its momentum.

The 1960s were a golden age for the arts in Argentina. As in many countries, the decade brought new freedoms and questions to young people, and the art scene responded vigorously. Artistic activity was focused around the centre of Buenos Aires between Plaza San Martin and Av Cordoba, an area known as the *'manzana loca'* (crazy block). This area contained a huge number of galleries and cafés, and most importantly the Di Tella Institute, a privately-funded art centre which was at the cutting edge of the visual arts. Artistic movements of the time ranged from a raw expressionism called 'Nueva figuración' to very sophisticated conceptual art. The most provocative form of art during this period took the form of 'happenings', one of the most famous of which (by Marta Minujin) consisted of a replica of the Buenos Aires obelisk made in sweet bread, which was then eaten by passers-by.

After the military coup of 1966 the authorities began to question the activities of these young artists, and even tried to censor some exhibitions. The Di Tella Institute closed, leaving the 'manzana loca' without a heart, and making it more dangerous for alternative young artists to live without harassment (often for little more than having long hair). During the 'leaden years' of the military government during the 1970s, there was little space for alternative art, and many left-wing artists abandoned art in favour of direct political action. However, one space in Buenos Aires continued to show politically challenging art: the Centro de Arte y Comunicación (or CAYC), often through works which were so heavily coded that the authorities would not pick up the message.

Since the restoration of democracy in 1983, Argentina has been coming to terms with the destruction or inefficiency of many of its cultural institutions over recent decades. The last few years have seen a rebirth of activity, with improvements in the National Museum of Fine Arts and the creation of the important Centro Cultural Recoleta and more recently the Centro Cultural Borges (in the Galerias Pacifico). There are important alternative art centres, especially the Ricardo Rojas Centre and the Klemm Foundation which show some of the most interesting young artists. The art scene in Buenos Aires is now very vibrant, if somewhat confusing, with myriad conflicting and apparently contradictory styles and tendencies.

Literature

'Hard to imagine that Buenos Aires had any beginning/ I consider it as eternal as air and water', wrote Jorge Luis Borges in a homage to the city of his birth in 1923. By the 1920s, Buenos Aires was a thriving metropolitan centre, but its beginnings were altogether more modest.

The isolation of the Río de la Plata region and the low priority attributed to it by the Spanish during the colonial period were reflected in the underdevelopment of intellectual life: in 1776 there were only four primary schools and two secondary schools in Buenos Aires, all church run, to serve a city of some 25,000 people. Yet Enlightenment ideas, Romanticism and the economic tenets of free trade were introduced into this ever more complex society from Europe and North America. The works of Smith, Locke, Voltaire, Rousseau amongst others influenced the small literate elite of young intellectuals such as Mariano Moreno (1778-1811), one of the architects of the Independence movement. The way in which European forms could be adapted to American realities became one of the constant themes of Argentine

Jorge Luis Borges, 1899-1986

Borges always talked of the two lineages that made up his family history: the Argentine and the British. Born in Buenos Aires, he observed a tension between the world 'outside', the city in the process of great demographic change, and the world 'inside' his father's library 'of unlimited English books'. Throughout his life he was obsessed by both the myths and realities of Argentina and its culture and also by the heterodox space of readings from universal literature. His original blending of these different concerns and sources has made him the most widely cited and influential figure in Argentine literature, with a world-wide reputation that transcends national boundaries.

In 1914, at the age of 15, Borges travelled with his family to Europe, only returning to Buenos Aires in 1921. He lived in Switzerland and Spain, he learned Latin, French and German, became acquainted with the modernist movements in Europe and began to write. He was thus well equipped to become an active member of the literary avant garde which emerged in Buenos Aires in the 1920s: a decade in which he was frantically busy, contributing to every little magazine and publishing seven books of poetry and essays. Although in later life he called these works naive, they reveal his dominant obsessions: a sideways view of life and literature, perceived from 'las orillas' (the outskirts, the margins) and a philosophical and literary reappraisal of authorship and individual consciousness.

From the 1930s he worked as a librarian and a literary journalist, producing his first book of short stories, Historia universal de la infamia' (A Universal History of Infamy) in 1935. From the late 1930s, he moved quietly onto the offensive, publishing in quick succession a series of significant essays, book prologues and short stories, the latter comprising what is arguably the most important collection of stories in the history of Latin American literature, the magisterial Ficciones' (Fictions, 1944). In this volume, he turned inside out the received conventions of literary nationalism, realism and authorship, in stories that explored the nature of literature itself, philosophy and metaphysics. Ficciones was followed by El Aleph in 1949 and his most important book of essays, Otras inquisiciones (Other Inquisitions, 1952). A masterful story-teller, he never wrote more than a few pages and was never tempted by the novel form, insisting that more could be explored in a few elliptical, highly suggestive and poetic lines than in hundred of pages of dull realist prose.

The late forties brought almost total blindness and a running dispute with the demagoguery of Perón, who, for Borges, was the embodiment of a populist nationalism that he considered the worst aspect of Argentine identity. Borges's opposition to a figure who, in the forties and from the late sixties, embodied the hopes of so many, led a whole generation of Argentine critics to ignore the truly radical propositions of his own writing. His rise to international prominence occurred in the sixties in Europe and the United States, at a time when his own work was mainly confined to poetry, a form which, with the onset of blindness, he could compose and restructure in his head. But it was perhaps the world-wide attention to his fictions which brought him, late in life, to publish two further books of stories, 'El informe de Brodie' (Dr Brodie's Report, 1970) and 'El libro de arena' (The Book of Sand, 1975), works that he claimed to be 'realist' but which are just as ironic and subversive as his earlier work. In his final years he kept up publishing essays and poems, and travelled the world with his constant companion María Kodama, whom he married. He died in Geneva in June 1986, the city where, as an adolescent, he had learned new languages and developed his heterodox readings.

intellectual and literary production, first in the form of political tracts and later in early nationalist poetry. Outside the cities, popular culture did not rest on strong cultural survival among the scattered and impoverished indigenous groups or in any developed African Argentine presence, but rather in the oral tradition of storytelling and music of the gauchos, Argentina's cowboys, the itinerant inhabitants of the pampas. Gaucho poets, like Medieval troubadours, would travel from settlement to settlement, to country fairs and cattle roundups, singing of the events of the day and of the encroaching political constraints that would soon bring restrictions to their traditional way of life.

The 19th century The earliest literary forms of Argentina in its struggle for independence between 1810 and 1820 were patriotic poems written by Bartolomé Hidalgo (1788-1822) and Hilario Ascasubi (1807-71), amongst others, which gave an urban, stylized form to the oral culture of the gaucho and put literature at the service of political struggle. As the attempt to consolidate the nation state in the aftermath of independence would be fought out for a further 30 years, writers such as Esteban Echeverría (1805-51) would play a leading role in these debates through literary salons, in poetry and in short fiction. Perhaps the most important tract of the generation, which was to become one of the vertebral texts of Argentine cultural history, was published in 1845 by an exile politician, Domingo Faustino Sarmiento (1811-88): *Facundo: Civilization and Barbarism*. Other memorable protest literature against the Rosas régime included Echeverría's 'El matadero' ('The Slaughterhouse', published posthumously in 1871) and José Mármol's melodramatic novel of star crossed lovers battling against the cut-throat hordes of Rosas: *Amalia* (1855).

The consolidation of Argentina along the lines advocated by Sarmiento and the growth of the export economy in alliance with British capital and technology may have benefitted the great landowners of the Littoral provinces, but those who did not fit into this dream of modernity- in particular the gaucho groups, turned off the land and forced to work as rural labourers- found their protest articulated by a provincial landowner, José Hernández (1834-1886), who wrote the famous gaucho epic poems *El gaucho Martín Fierro* (1872) and its sequel, *La vuelta de Martín Fierro* (The Return of Martín Fierro), 1879. The first part of *Martín Fierro* (the second part was an accommodation to political power interests) is a genuine shout of rage against the march of progress and modernity that disrupts local communities and traditional ways of life. Framed as a gauchesque song, chanted by the dispossessed outlaw, it became one of the most popular works of literature and Martín Fierro came to symbolize the spirit of the Argentine nation.

Yet this was an isolated cry of protest. As a small group of families led the great export boom, the 'gentleman' politicians of the 'Generation of 1880' wrote their memoirs, none better than Sarmiento's *Recuerdos de Provincia* (Memoirs of Provincial Life, 1850.). Also among this group are Lucio Victorio Mansilla (1831-1913) and Miguel Cané (1852-1905). But, as Buenos Aires grew into a dynamic modern city, the gentleman memorialist soon gave way to the professional writer: professional not in the sense of the possibility of writers making a living through writing – difficult today, impossible then – but rather in the writers' perceptions of themselves as writers. The key poet in this respect was the Nicaraguan Rubén Darío (1867-1916), who lived for an important period of his creative life in Buenos Aires and led a movement called *modernismo* which asserted the separateness of poetry as a craft, removed from the dictates of national panegyric or political necessity. It was Darío who would give inspiration to the poet Leopoldo Lugones (1874-1938), famous also for his prose writings on nationalist, gauchesque themes. Lugones's evocation of the gaucho as a national symbol would be developed in the novel *Don Segundo Sombra*, by Ricardo Güiraldes (1886-1927), the story of a boy taught the skills for life by a gaucho mentor.

The complex urban societies evolving in Argentina by the turn of the century created a rich cultural life. In the 1920s a strong vanguard movement developed which questioned the dominant literary orthodoxies of the day. Little magazines such as *Martín Fierro* (another appropriation of the ubiquitous national symbol) proclaimed novelty in poetry and attacked the dull social realist writings of their rivals the Boedo group. Argentina's most famous writer, Jorge Luis Borges (1899-1986) began his literary life as an avant garde poet, in the company of writers such as Oliverio Girondo (1891-1967) and Norah Lange (1906-1972). Many of these poets were interested in expressing the dynamism and changing shape of their urban landscape, Buenos Aires, this Paris on the periphery. Roberto Arlt also caught the dreams and nightmares of the urban underclasses in novels such as *El juguete rabioso* (The Rabid Toy, 1926) and *Los siete locos* (The Seven Madmen, 1929).

    Much of the most interesting literature of the 1930 and 1940s was first published in the literary journal *Sur*, founded by the aristocratic writer, Victoria Ocampo. By far the most important group to publish in its pages were Borges and his close friends Silvina Ocampo (1903?-1993), Victoria's sister, and Silvina's husband, Adolfo Bioy Casares (1914-) who, from the late 1930s, in a series of short fictions and essays, transformed the literary world. They had recurrent concerns: an indirect style, a rejection of realism and nationalist symbols, the use of the purified motifs and techniques of detective fiction and fantastic literature, the quest for knowledge to be found in elusive books, the acknowledgement of literary criticism as the purest form of detective fiction and the emphasis on the importance of the reader rather than the writer.

**The early
20th century**

The 10-year period of Perón's first two presidencies, 1946-1955, can be seen as a deliberate assault on the aristocratic, liberal values which had guided Argentina since the Generation of 1880. Claiming to be a new synthesis of democracy, nationalism, anti-imperialism and industrial development, Peronism attacked the undemocratic, dependent Argentine oligarchy (personified in such literary figures as Victoria Ocampo and Adolfo Bioy Casares). The period 1946-1955 was seen by most intellectuals and writers as an era of cultural obscurantism and some writers such as Julio Cortázar (1914-1984) – in the 1940s and 1950s a writer of elegant fantastic and realist stories- chose voluntary exile to remaining in Perón's Argentina. The novelist, Ernesto Sábato (1911-) set his best novel *Sobre héroes y tumbas* (On Heroes and Tombs, 1961) partly in the final moments of the Peronist régime, when the tensions of the populist alliance were beginning to become manifest. But Perón was not much interested in the small circulation of literature and concentrated his attention on mass forms of communication such as radio and cinema. This period saw further mature work from the poets Enrique Molina (1910-), Olga Orozco (1922-) and Alberto Girri (1919-1991), whose austere, introspective verse was an antidote to the populist abuse of language in the public sphere. The literary field was to be further stimulated, after the downfall of Perón, with the development of publishing houses and the 'boom' of Latin American literature of the 1960s.

**Peronism &
Literature**

In Argentina the sixties was a decade of great literary and cultural effervescence. The novel to capture this mood was Cortázar's *Rayuela* (Hopscotch, 1963), which served as a Baedeker of the new, with its comments on literature, philosophy, new sexual freedoms and its open, experimental structure. It was promoted in a weekly journal *Primera Plana*, which also acted as a guide to expansive modernity. Thousands of copies of *Rayuela* were sold to an expanded middle class readership in Argentina and throughout Latin America. Other novelists and writers benefited from these conditions, the most significant being the Colombian Gabriel García Márquez who published what would later become one of the best selling novels of the 20th century, *Cien años de soledad* (One Hundred Years of Solitude, 1967) with an

The 1960s

Manuel Puig, 1932-1990

Argentina's most talented postmodernist writer, Puig was brought up in a small town in the Argentine pampas, some fourteen hours by train from the capital. A survival instinct, he often said, made him construct another point of reference to that of everyday provincial life: the town cinema, which, from early childhood, became a daily pilgrimage. He tried to pursue this abiding love of the movies in professional terms, leaving Argentina in the mid fifties for Italy to study in the heart of Cinecittà at the famous Centro Sperimentale di Cinema. However, he was not impressed by its dominant orthodoxy of neo-realist social protest, which did not conform to what he called his 'hybrid pampa-MGM' view of the world.

He began writing film scripts but found his métier when a script based on his own personal experiences turned into a novel. He set the story in an Argentine laundry room, with his aunt gossiping about everyday life. She was supposed to have only a few lines of dialogue, but ended up talking for over thirty pages, the opening of Puig's first novel, La Traición de Rita Hayworth (Betrayed by Rita Hayworth, 1968).

It was Puig's particular genius to turn banality into a form of art, expressing the desires and hopes and frustrations of ordinary people: hopes which were structured, in the main, by the culture industry through serial novels, women's magazines and advertisements, radio soaps, the lyrics of tango, film melodrama, film stars. These cultural forms allowed one to dream alternative dreams for a while but made the awakening all the more difficult: in the end, living in a small town in Argentina in the thirties or forties, one would always be betrayed by Rita Hayworth. In his best novels, Rita Hayworth, Boquitas Pintadas (Heartbreak Tango, 1969) and the book (turned into a film) that brought him international recognition, El beso de la Mujer Araña (Kiss of the Spider Woman, 1976), he shows the attractions and entrapments of the spider woman's web of mass culture. These novels also reveal his abiding interest in the way that gender roles are constructed and reproduced in society (often through mass culture) and his sympathy for women and homosexual men.

It was the radical proposition of Kiss – a dialogue and a developing love affair in prison between a lower middle class homosexual and an upper middle class revolutionary – that caused some of Puig's novels to be banned in Argentina under the dictatorship and forced him into exile from the mid seventies in New York and later in Brazil. Four novels followed, together with several published plays and film scripts, all structurally complex but effortlessly fluid in their narration, exploring the gaps between illusion and reality and exploring the survival strategies, against the odds, of his sympathetically drawn characters. His early death from a treatable illness, at the age of 57, seemed, like his life, to be drawn from one of his novels: optimistic, futile and ultimately courageous.

Argentine publishing house. Significant numbers of women writers helped to break the male monopoly of literary production, including the novelists Beatriz Guido and Marta Lynch and the poet Alejandra Pizarnik (1936-1972), with her intense exploration of the inner self.

Literature under the Military Dictatorships The 'swinging' sixties were curtailed by a military coup in 1966. As, in the years which followed, Argentine political life descended into anarchy, violence and repression, virtually all forms of cultural activity were silenced and well known writers including Haroldo Conti and Rodolfo Walsh 'disappeared'. Many more had to seek exile including the poet Juan Gelman, whose son and daughter in law counted among the disappeared.

Understandably this nightmare world provided the dominant themes of the literary output of these years. The return in old age of Perón, claimed by all shades of the political spectrum, was savagely lampooned in Osvaldo Soriano's (1943-1998) novel *No habrá más penas ni olvido* (A Funny, Dirty Little War, 1982, but completed in 1975). The world of the sombre designs of the ultra right wing López Rega, Isabel Perón's Minister of Social Welfare, is portrayed in Luisa Valenzuela's (1938-) terrifying, grotesque novel *Cola de lagartija* (The Lizard's Tail, 1983). Of the narrative accounts of those black years, none is more harrowing than Miguel Bonasso's (1940-) fictional documentary of the treatment of the Montoneros guerrilla group in prison and in exile: *Recuerdo de la muerte* (Memory of Death, 1984). Other writers in exile chose more indirect ways of dealing with the terror and dislocation of those years. Daniel Moyano (1928-1992), in exile for many years in Spain, wrote elegant allegories such as *El vuelo del tigre* (The Flight of the Tiger, 1981), which tells of the military style takeover of an Andean village by a group of percussionists who bring cacophany.

Within Argentina critical discussion was kept alive in literary journals such as *Punto de Vista* (1978-) and certain novels alluded to the current political climate within densely structured narratives: Ricardo Piglia's (1941-) *Respiración artificial* (Artificial Respiration, 1980) has disappearance and exile as central themes, alongside bravura discussions of the links between fiction and history and between Argentina and Europe.

Following Alfonsín's election victory in 1983, the whole intellectual and cultural field responded to the new freedoms. Certain narratives depicted in harsh realism the brutalities of the 'dirty war' waged by the military and it was the novelist, Ernesto Sábato, who headed the Commission set up to investigate the disappearances. He wrote in the prologue to the Commission's report *Nunca más* (Never Again, 1984): "We are convinced that the recent military dictatorship brought about the greatest and most savage tragedy in the history of Argentina".

The Return to Civilian Rule

Current literature echoes the famous lines by Borges in the essay 'The Argentine Writer and Tradition': "I believe that we Argentines ... can handle all European themes, handle them without superstition, with an irreverence which can have, and already does have, fortunate consequences." While many of the writers that first brought modernity to Argentine letters have died – Borges, Victoria and Silvina Ocampo, Girri, Cortázar, Puig – the later generations have assimilated their lessons. Juan Carlos Martini writes stylish thrillers, blending high and low culture. Juan José Saer (1937-), from his self imposed exile in Paris, recreates his fictional world, Colastiné, in the city of Santa Fé, in narratives that are complex, poetic discussions on memory and language. The most successful novel of recent years is Tomás Eloy Martínez's (1934-) *Santa Evita* (1995) which tells/reinvents the macabre story of what happened to Evita's embalmed body between 1952 and the mid 1970s. The narrative skilfully discusses themes that are at the heart of all writing and critical activity. The critic, like the embalmer of Evita's body, 'seeks to fix a life or a body in the pose that eternity should remember it by'. But what this critic, like the narrator of Eloy Martínez's novel, realizes is that a corpus of literature cannot be fixed in that way, for literature escapes such neat pigeon holes. Instead, glossing Oscar Wilde, the narrator states that 'that the only duty that we have to history is to rewrite it'. The ending of the novel makes the point about the impossibility of endings: "Since then, I have rowed with words, carrying Santa Evita in my boat, from one shore of the blind world to the other. I don't know where in the story I am. In the middle, I believe. I've been here in the middle for a long time. Now I must write again". (*Santa Evita*, New York and London, 1996, page 369.)

Background

Carlos Gardel

Gardel, whose name is virtually synonymous with Tango, was born in 1890 in Toulouse, France, to Berthe Gardés and, according to his birth certificate, "an unknown father". To avoid the social stigma, his mother emigrated to Buenos Aires when her son was only two years old. Just as the exact origin of the Tango is itself something of a mystery, Gardel's formative years around the Abasto (or wholesale market) district of the city are obscure, at least until around 1912 when he began his artistic career in earnest, performing as one half of the Duo Gardel-Razzano, singing songs in the local traditional styles of the Estilo and Cifra. Only a year later he began his prolific career with Columbia, recording 15 traditional songs. It was not until 1917, however, that Gardel and Tango finally came together, but by the early 1920s he was singing entirely within this relatively new genre and achieving success as far

afield as Madrid. The Duo Gardel-Razzano dissolved in 1925 and Gardel became a solo artist and the very epitome of the Tango both in Argentina and, following his tours to Europe, around the world. Between 1933 and 1935 he was based in New York, where he played roles in four Spanish-speaking films and one English-speaking film for Paramount. On 24 June 1935, while on a tour of South America, his plane from Bogota to Cali crashed into another on the ground while taking off from Medellín, Colombia. Gardel was killed instantly, to the immense grief of his public. The brilliance of his voice and personality, the manner in which he represented the spirit of the Río de la Plata to his fans at home combined with the universality of his appeal, the sheer volume of his recordings and the untimely nature of his dramatic death to ensure the endurance of his name.

Music and dance

Buenos Aires contains a third of the country's population and its music is the Tango. Indeed to the outside world there is no other Argentine music. Although also sung and played, the Tango was born as a dance just before the turn of the 20th century. The exact moment of birth was not recorded by any contemporary observer and continues to be a matter of debate, though the roots can be traced. The name 'Tango' predates the dance and was given to the carnivals (and dances) of the black inhabitants of the Río de la Plata in the early 19th century, elements of the black tradition being taken over by whites as the black population declined. However, the name 'Tango Americano' was also given to the Habanera (a Cuban descendent of the English Country Dance) which became the rage in Spain and bounced back into the Río de la Plata in the middle of the 19th century, not only as a fashionable dance, together with the polka, mazurka, waltz and cuadrille, but also as a song form in the very popular 'Zarzuelas', or Spanish operettas. However, the Habanera led not a double, but a triple life, by also infiltrating the lowest levels of society directly from Cuba via sailors who arrived in the ports of Montevideo and Buenos Aires. Here it encountered the Milonga, originally a Gaucho song style, but by 1880 a dance, especially popular with the so-called 'Compadritos' and 'Orilleros', who frequented the port area and its brothels, whence the Argentine Tango emerged around the turn of the century to dazzle the populace with its brilliant, personalized footwork, which could not be accomplished without the partners staying glued together.

As a dance Tango became the rage and, as the infant recording industry grew by leaps and bounds, it also became popular as a song and an instrumental genre, with the original violins and flutes being eclipsed by the *bandoneón* button accordion, then being imported from Germany. In 1911 the new dance took Paris by storm and returned triumphant to Buenos Aires. It achieved both respectability and notoriety, becoming a global phenomenon after the First World War, with the golden voice of

The Zamba de Vargas

The stately and elegant Zamba, *directly descended from the colonial* Zamacueca *and thus a first cousin to the Chilean and Bolivian* Cueca *and the Peruvian* Marinera, *is the quintessential Argentine folk dance. Of the many zambas in the contemporary repertoire, none is finer than the justly famous* Zamba de Vargas. *Although first made famous by Andres Chazarreta, the words and melody are traditional and Chazarreta always claimed to have learned the song at his grandmother's knee. The words refer to an incident in the Battle of Pozo de Vargas (1867) between forces led by the rebel Felipe Varela from La Rioja and the government forces recruited in Santiago del Estero by General Antonio Taboada. According to the lyrics, Taboada's forces were at the point of being routed by Varela when their band struck up a popular zamba which so inspired them that they took new heart and crushed their foes. To my mind the most beautiful and stirring version on record is that of the Salta group, Los Chalchaleros.*

Carlos Gardel giving a wholly new dimension to the music of the Tango until his death in 1935. After losing some popularity in Argentina, it came to the forefront again in the 1940s (1920-50 is considered the real golden age). Its resurgence was assisted by Perón's decree that 50% of all music played on the radio must be Argentine, only to suffer a second, much more serious decline in the face of rock music over the following two decades. Fortunately, it has lately experienced a notable recovery, to the point where it is no longer difficult, as was the case until quite recently, to see the Tango and Milonga danced in Buenos Aires. Apart from Carlos Gardel, other great names connected with the Tango are Francisco Canaro (Uruguayan), Osvaldo Pugliese and Astor Piazzolla, who has modernized it by fusion with jazz styles (*nuevo tango*).

If the Tango represents the soul of Buenos Aires, this is not the case in the rest of the country. The provinces have a very rich and attractive heritage of folk dances, mainly for couples, with arms held out and fingers clicked or handkerchiefs waved, with the 'Paso Valseado' as the basic step. Descended from the Zamacueca, and therefore a cousin of the Chilean Cueca and Peruvian Marinera, is the slow and stately Zamba, where the handkerchief is used to greatest effect. Equally popular throughout most of the country are the faster Gato, Chacarera and Escondido. These were the dances of the Gaucho and their rhythm evokes that of a cantering horse. Guitar and the *bombo* drum provide the accompaniment. Particularly spectacular is the Malambo, where the Gaucho shows off his dextrous footwork, the spurs of his boots adding a steely note to the rhythm.

Different regions of the country have their own specialities. The music of Cuyo in the west is sentimental and very similar to that of neighbouring Chile, with its Cuecas for dance and Tonadas for song. The northwest on the other hand is Andean, with its musical culture closer to that of Bolivia, particularly on the Puna, where the Indians play the *quena* and *charango* and sound mournful notes on the great long *erke*. Here the dances are Bailecitos and Carnavalitos, while the songs are Vidalitas and the extraordinary high pitched Bagualas, the very essence of primeval pain. In the northeast provinces of Corrientes and Misiones, the music shares cultural similarities with Paraguay. The Polca and Galopa are danced and the local Chamamé is sung, to the accordion or the harp, the style being sentimental. Santiago del Estero has exerted the strongest influence on Argentine folk music as a result of the work of Andres Chazarreta: it is the heartland of the Chacarera and the lyrics are often part Spanish and part Quichua, a local dialect of the Andean Quechua language. Down in the Province of Buenos Aires you are more likely to hear the Gauchos singing their Milongas, Estilos and Cifras and challenging each other to a Payada or rhymed duel. Argentina experienced a great folk revival in the 50s and 60s and

The payadores

The payadores, *originally Gaucho troubadors, can still, with luck, be heard at the domas de potros (rodeos) in the pampas. Accompanying themselves on the guitar, the* payadores *engage in musical duels (payadas), alternating in improvising verses and aiming to outdo each other with clever rhyming and verbal wit. The verses develop a particular theme within a strictly regulated format, relating historical or contemporary events or expressing popular morality. Similar contests are held elsewhere in Latin America: in the Brazilian Northeast, the Venezuelan Llanos and the hill country of Puerto Rico.*

The most famous old-time payador *was Santos Vega, said to have lived in the early 19th century and to have been finally defeated in a payada by "Juan Sin Ropa" (Naked John), though it must be added that Vega's existence is wrapped in mystery. More recently Gabino Ezeiza (1858-1916), a black* payador, *achieved a fame that has lasted to this day as the last "natural" (ie unlettered)* payador. *Alas, I have not been able to find out anything about the Englishman, A MacCarthy, "El Inglesito de la Boca"! Among contemporary* payadores *who have been recorded are Angle Colovini, Catino Arias, José Curbelo, Roberto Ayrala and Miguel Franco.*

some of the most celebrated groups are still drawing enthusiastic audiences today. These groups include Los Chalchaleros and Los Fronterizos, the perennial virtuoso singer and guitarist, Eduardo Falú and, more recently, León Gieco from Santa Fe.

Sport

It is said that sport came to Argentina through the port of Buenos Aires, brought first by British sailors, who played football on vacant lots near the port watched by curious locals who would later make it their national passion, and later by immigrants who brought with them their own favourite sports.

Football is out on its own, both in terms of participation and as a spectator sport. Behind it in second place come two sports which attract far more fans than players: boxing and motor-racing. Although there are now few Argentine boxing champions and world title fights are rarely held here, there is a big TV audience for most title fights abroad. Despite the lack of local world class drivers, the legend of Juan Manuel Fangio is still very much alive and the Argentine Formula One Grand Prix in April is one of the events of the year in Buenos Aires, even if there are no Argentine drivers.

Though the best polo in the world is played in Argentina, it is not a major participation sport, due to its cost. Though it is played throughout the country and all year round, the top players who play all over the world return only for the high handicap season between September and November. This consists of three main tournaments, played on the outskirts of Buenos Aires, followed by the Argentine Open, which takes place in Palermo, the 'cathedral of polo'.

Golf is another popular sport which, thanks to the climate, can be played all year round in most of the country. While 33,311 players registered with the Argentine Golf Association at the last count, it is calculated that about 100,000 people play golf each weekend at the country's 200 plus courses. About half of these players and half the courses are in Gran Buenos Aires, with one right in the city at Palermo, as well as several driving ranges. Some clubs allow visitors to play in return for a green fee.

Other popular participation sports include rugby, hockey and tennis, although the latter's popularity, at its height in the 70s and 80s, has declined since the retirement of international stars like Guillermo Vilas and Gabriela Sabatini. There is, of course, nothing like international success to popularize a sport, and this has been the case with both rugby and hockey.

Football crazy?

Argentina's first World Cup victory in 1978 at the River Plate stadium is, for many people, a lasting memory: the streets of central Buenos Aires packed with crowds, jumping and dancing. Even today, whenever the national team wins a World Cup match, thousands dance around the obelisk in central Buenos Aires, while cars rush round them, sounding their horns as they did in 1978.

First played in an organized fashion by British residents in the late 19th century, football quickly became the passion of the people, the main talking point in bars, clubs and wherever people meet. It fills most of the sports pages in newspapers and can be seen on TV screens on most evenings. This popularity, more or less common to most of South America, has been put down to the 'Latin temperament' and the low living standards of the majority of people, who can afford little

enjoyment and find something to live for through following their favourite team: at the end of an often frustrating week they give vent to their feelings in a soccer stadium. Although Argentina is one of the great exporters of players, mostly to European clubs, as soon as a leading player is sold, another young star replaces him: they seem to spring up like weeds.

The season stretches from the end of August to the end of June, with a two-month break in the heat of the summer from Christmas to the end of February. Most matches are played on Sundays, with two games brought forward for TV screening, one to Friday evening and another to Saturday evening. Club members get into home games free. Although the Argentine Football Association has set a standard price of US$10 for standing room, clubs are free to set whatever price they wish for seating.

'The hand of God'

When Argentines travel abroad they are frequently asked about Diego Maradona, perhaps the only well-known Argentine in most countries. A national hero and arguably the best footballer ever (though Brazilians would counter this with the claims of Pele), Maradona's story is the kind of rags to riches tale typical of many South American football stars, more poignant, perhaps, because he reached such fame in Europe as well as in his homeland. After making his first division debut when barely 17 years old, Maradona played 91 times for his country and would have easily passed the century mark had his career not been interrupted by 15 month bans for drug-taking. Sadly, the man who, as a little boy, used to astound spectators at half time during matches and on TV with his unequalled ball juggling skills could never quite

handle fame. Moreover, many would say that he has made a habit of surrounding himself with the wrong people.

The high point of Maradona's career was undoubtedly the World Cup finals of 1986, when he led Argentina to the title, scored his famous 'hand of God' goal in the 2-1 victory over England and was judged best player in the tournament. His nadir came in his fourth World Cup in 1994, when he received his second suspension for drug-taking. Nevertheless, despite his unpredictable behaviour, the Argentine love affair with Maradona continues. When he made his fifth comeback at the age of 36, a delirious capacity crowd at the Boca Juniors stadium greeted him with smokebombs, fireworks and ticker-tape, even though he showed few signs of his former artistry.

One typical sport which is native to Argentina is *pato* (duck), a cross between polo and basketball. Originally played between large bands of *gauchos* on horseback using a duck in a basket as a ball, it was at one point prohibited for being dangerous. Today, with proper rules, teams of four horsemen and a football with

Background

Polo

Though the 20th century has seen great swings of fortune for many Argentines, one thing has remained constant: they rule the world at polo, a sport introduced by British railway and meatpacking entrepreneurs. These origins are evident in the Hurlingham Club, the centre of polo in Buenos Aires, which is so English it could have been transplanted from London.

Polo was ideally suited to the flat plains of the pampas and perhaps also to the people: naturally lightweight and brought up in a country founded on horses and cattle, Argentines took to polo like birds to the air. The availability of horses and the skill of the people meant that the sport had a much broader social base than elsewhere where it has remained a game for the rich.

Since 1924 when Argentina first sent a polo team to the Olympic Games and won the gold medal, they have dominated the polo world. Today most good polo teams (there are four in a team) in the world include an Argentine or two. Playing as professionals alongside the other players

who are usually amateurs, they are known colloquially in the polo world as "hired assassins". Though polo is a very social sport in England, Argentine professionals have tended not to learn English or to mix socially. Many of those who play in England are country boys who visit for the summer season, taking a string of perhaps a dozen polo ponies with them. Though paid for playing by the team's patron, they sell their ponies at the end of the season to increase their income, before returning home to train more ponies for the following English season. Argentine polo ponies, small thoroughbreds, specially bred for polo, are regarded as among the best in the world.

In a world where money plays an increasing role in sport, polo has been no exception and some Argentine professionals are now breaking into big money: in the 1997 the Heguy brothers, members of Argentina's best polo family, signed up to play for Prince Jefri of Brunei for a reported fee of US$5 million.

handles instead of a duck in a basket, it is one sport which is unique to Argentina.

In Buenos Aires, unlike most other cities in the country, there are numerous sports clubs where members can play a wide range of sports and, with ability and inclination, represent the club in national and international competitions. There are also large numbers of private clubs where, paying by the hour, you can rent a tennis court, play five-a-side football or practice a variety of other sports.

Religion

Throughout Spanish America the Catholic Church played an important role in the conquest. From the start of the colonial period Spanish control in South America was authorized by the Papacy; in return the colonial powers were to support the conversion of the indigenous population to Catholicism. This close identification of Church and State helps to explain why the main centres of Church power and activity were usually (though not always) close to the main centres of Spanish settlement. While present-day Argentina, a frontier territory on the outskirts of empire, was therefore of relatively minor importance to the Church hierarchy, it became a focus for work by missionary orders, particularly the Jesuits. Jesuit activity in Argentina was centred in two areas: around Córdoba, where they established a training college for the priesthood, and in Misiones and adjoining areas of present-day Paraguay and Brazil, where an extensive network of *reducciones* was set up to convert and protect the indigenous population.

Tricky truco

Similar in some respects to poker, truco *(meaning 'trick') is the most famous Argentine card game. A game for two, four or six players, it is commonly played in bars while drinking wine or in parks whilst consuming maté. The game's rules and the strategies involved are so complex that it is said that you need to watch others play for two months before*

you are dealt a hand. If you are tempted to try be warned that truco *is very competitive. When* truco *is played with more than two players, success depends partly on your ability to communicate the contents of your hand to your partners, usually by facial signals. As in poker it is also essential to be able to bluff your opponent.*

As in much of Spanish America, the Church lost most of its formal political power at independence. Although today over 90% of Argentines are officially Roman Catholics, the Church's political and social influence is much less significant than in neighbouring Chile or in most other South American countries. One reason for this is the introduction of a system of non-religious state schools in the 19th century. The great waves of immigration in the late 19th and early 20th centuries also affected the position of the Church; while the majority of immigrants were Catholics, significant minorities were not, including the large numbers of East European Jews and the Arab immigrants from Lebanon and Syria. Both of these communities have a strong presence especially in Buenos Aires; the largest mosque in South America was opened in the capital in September 2000 and there are estimated to be 800,000 moslems in the country.

Yet the Catholic Church's power and influence should not be underestimated. The support of the Church hierarchy was important in bringing Perón to power in 1946 and the rift with the Church played a key role in the overthrow of the latter in 1955. The strongly conservative nature of the Catholic hierarchy became particularly apparent during the 1976-1983 military dictatorship; unlike its Chilean counterpart, the Argentine hierarchy was silent on the issue of human rights violations and gave little support to relatives of the disappeared. According to *Nunca Más*, the official report on the disappeared, military chaplains attended some torture sessions and even assisted in the torture! Yet the Church was not untouched by the violence of the dictatorship: at least 15 priests who were working among the poor were victims of the military regime.

The lingering influence of the Church can be seen in several ways: in the continuing legal ban on abortion (divorce was finally legalised in 1986) and in the constitutional provision (removed in the 1994 amendments) which required the President to be a Catholic (and which necessitated Carlos Menem's conversion). The extent to which the Church relies on state support was revealed in a 1993 report which estimated that the Church received annual payments of US$400 million to help it maintain Catholic schools and universities and to fund the salaries of senior clergy.

As in some other parts of Latin America, this close identification of the Catholic Church with the state has, in recent years, provided opportunities for evangelical churches, including the Baptists and Mormons, to recruit followers, particularly among newcomers to the large cities.

The land

Argentina is the second largest country in South America in area, extending across the continent some 1,580 km from east to west and 3,460 km from north to south. Its northernmost point is at latitude 22°S, that is just within the tropics; at Tierra del Fuego and Isla de los Estados it extends south of 54°S, the latitude of Scotland or Labrador. The coast of this territory, extending over 2,000 km, runs wholly along the Atlantic apart from the north coast of the Beagle Channel which links the Atlantic and the Pacific. The western frontier with Chile follows the crest of the Andes, but below 46°S, the drainage is complex and border disputes have arisen ever since the Treaty of 1881 between the two countries established the principle that the frontier should follow the watershed.

Geology and landscape

Together with Brazil, Paraguay and Uruguay, Argentina is the visible part of the South American Plate which has been moving for the past 125 million years away from its former union with Africa. The submerged part of this plate forms a broad continental shelf under the Atlantic Ocean; in the south this extends over 1,000 km east and includes the Falkland Islands/Islas Malvinas. Since the 'break' between the plates, there have been numerous invasions and withdrawals of the sea over this part of the South American continent, but the Andean mountain building from the end of the Cretaceous (65 million years ago) to the present day dominates the surface geology. Of the many climatic fluctuations, the Pleistocene Ice Age up to 10000 BC has done most to mould the current landscape. At its maximum, ice covered all the land over 2,000 m and most of Patagonia. In the mountains, ice created virtually all the present day lakes and moraine deposits can be found everywhere. However, the special feature of the heartland of Argentina is the fine soil of the Pampas, the result of ice and water erosion and the unique wind systems of the southern cone of the continent.

The Northwest Northern and western Argentina are dominated by the satellite ranges of the Andes. Between the mountains of the far northwest is the *puna*, a high plateau rising to 3,400-4,000 m, on which are situated saltflats or *salares*, some of which are of interest for their wildlife. East of this is the *pre-puna*, the gorges and slopes ranging in altitude from 1,700 m to 3,400 m which connect the *puna* with the plains. On the fringe of the Andes are a string of important settlements, including Salta, Tucumán and Mendoza. Though the climate of this region is hot and dry, there is sufficient water to support maize and pasture and a thriving wine industry, mostly relying on irrigation. East of the Andes lie several ranges of hills, the most important of which are the Sierras de Córdoba and the Sierras de San Luis. These are mostly of ancient Pre-Cambrian rocks.

The Paraná Basin The vast Paraná basin stretches from the borders with Brazil and Paraguay to the Atlantic at Buenos Aires. In the northeast it mainly consists of geologically recent deposits. The easternmost part of this basin, between the Ríos Paraná and Uruguay, is the wettest part of the country. Known as Mesopotamia and consisting of the provinces of Entre Rios, Corrientes and Misiones, it is structurally part of the Brazilian plateau of old crystalline rocks, the 'heart' of the South American Plate. Here there are undulating grassy hills and marshy or forested lowlands, among them the Esteros del Iberá, an extensive area of flooded forest similar to the Pantanal in Brazil. The horizontal strata of the rocks in this area is dramatically evident in the river gorges to the north and the spectacular Iguazú falls shared with Brazil.

Northwest of Mesopotamia and stretching from the Paraná and Paraguay rivers west to the Andean foothills and north into Paraguay and Bolivia, lies the Gran Chaco, a vast plain which covers the provinces of Formosa, Chaco and Santiago del Estero, as well as parts of Santa Fe and Córdoba. It is crossed from west to east by three rivers, the Teuco-Bermejo, the Salado and the Pilcomayo. Annual rainfall ranges from 400 mm in the western or Dry Chaco, a semi-desert mainly used for cattle ranching, to 800-1,200 mm in the eastern or Wet Chaco, where periodic floods alternate with long periods of drought.

The Chaco

South of 33°S, the latitude of Mendoza and Rosario, is a great flat plain, known as the Pampas. Extending almost 1,000 km from north to south and a similar distance from east to west, the Pampas cover some 650,000 sq km, including most of Buenos Aires province, southern Córdoba, Santa Fe and Entre Ríos, northeastern La Pampa and a small part of San Luís. This area is crossed by meandering rivers and streams and there are many lakes, lagoons and marshes. Geologically the Pampas are similar to the Chaco, basic crystalline and granite rocks almost completely overlain with recent deposits, often hundreds of metres thick. Prevailing winds from the southeast and southwest help to create the fine loess type soils which make this one of the richest farming areas in the world, ideal for grasslands and cattle ranching. Being comparatively close to the ocean, extremes of temperature are rare, another favourable feature.

The Pampas

A distinction is often made between the 'wet' *Pampa* and the 'dry' *Pampa*. The former, inland from Rosario and Buenos Aires is the centre of wheat, maize and other cereal production and the latter, west of 64°W, is where cattle ranching predominates.

Patagonia extends from the Río Colorado (39°S) south to the Magellan Straits and covers some 780,000 sq km. Most of this area consists of a series of tablelands and terraces which drop in altitude from west to east. The basic rocks are ancient, some classified as Pre-Cambrian, but the surface has been subjected to endless erosion. Rainfall is lighter and the winds stronger than in the Pampas frequently stripping the surface of cover and filling the air with dust. Only where rivers have scored deep valleys in the rock base can soil accumulate, allowing more than extensive sheep farming.

The Patagonian Steppe

From the Straits of Magellan north to Lago Argentino (46°S) and beyond, a geological depression separates the edge of the South American Plate from the Andes. Most of Patagonia was under ice during the Quaternary Ice Age, and has been rising since the ice receded. This area was presumably the last to be uncovered. However, considerable volcanic activity associated with the uplift of the Andes has taken place along the depression which is transversely divided into basins by lava flows. Alluvial and glacial deposits have created relatively fertile soils in some areas, useful for sheep and producing attractive wooded landscapes in the lake regions in contrast to the general desolation of Patagonia.

Geographically the Isla de los Estados forms the southernmost extent of the Andes, which then swing north to become the border between Chile and Argentina just north of the Paine mountains. The 350 km section north of Paine is one of the most dramatic stretches of the Andes. The crest lies under the Southern Patagonian Icecap, with glaciers reaching down to the valleys on both the Argentine and Chilean sides. On the Argentine side this has created the spectacular range of glaciers found in the *Parque Nacional Los Glaciares*, the most famous of which, the Perito Moreno Glacier, is one of the highlights for many travellers to Argentina. The northern end of this section is Cerro Fitz Roy, which, along with the Torres del Paine (in Chile) at the southern end, is among the most spectacular hiking and climbing centres in South America.

The Andes

Background

• •

☞ *Fact file...*

Geographic

Land area	2,780,092 sq km
forested	18.6%
pastures	51.9%
cultivated	9.9%

Demographic

Population (1998) 36,125,000

annual growth rate (1995-2000)	1.2%
urban	86.9%
rural	13.1%
density	13 per sq km

Religious affiliation

Roman Catholic	87.7%

Birth rate per 1,000 (1995-2000)   19.9%
(world average 25.0)

Education and health

Life expectancy at birth

male	69.6
female	76.8

Infant mortality rate (per 1,000 love
births) (1995-2000)   22

Physicians	1 per 376 persons
Hospital beds	1 per 227 persons

Population age 25 and over with no
formal schooling   5.7%

Literate males(over 15)	96.2%
Literate females (over 15)	96.2%

Economic

GDP (1998)	US$298,130 mn
GDP per capita (1998)	US$8,255
Total external debt (1999)	US$140,500
Tourism receipts (1995)	US$4,306 mn
Inflation (1999-2000)	-0.74%
Radio	1 per 1.6 persons
Television	1 per 2.9 persons
Telephone	1 per 6.2 persons

Employment

Population economically active (1995)
14,345,101

Unemployment rate (2000)	15.4%

Percent of labour force in

agriculture	12.0
mining	0.5
manufacturing	19.9
construction	10.1
Military forces	73,000

Source Encyclopaedia Britannica and
Latin America Monitor

• •

Further north between 46°S and 47°S there is another icecap, the North Patagonian Icecap, centred on Monte San Valentín on the Chilean side of the frontier. North of this lie 1,500 km of mountain ranges rarely exceeding 4,000 m; on the east side of these are a series of attractive lakes, formed by a mixture of glacial and volcanic activity. The high section of the Andes begins at 35°S and includes Aconcagua, 6,960 m, the highest peak outside the Himalayas. For a further 1,000 km northwards, the ranges continue to the border with Bolivia with many peaks over 6,000 m, the Argentine side becoming progressively drier and more inhospitable.

Rivers

The most important river system in the country is the Río de la Plata; fed by the Paraná and Uruguay rivers. With their major tributaries, the Bermejo-Teuco, the Pilcomayo, the Paraguay and the Salado del Norte, the Ríos Paraná and Uruguay, drain the northeast and northwest of the country as well as Uruguay, Paraguay and large parts of southern Brazil. Western Argentina is drained by the Rios Mendoza and San Juan, which form the Desaguadero, which, in years of exceptional rainfall, flows into a network of lakes in the Pampas and thence via the Colorado into the Atlantic south of Bahía Blanca. The Río Negro, formed by the Ríos Neuquén and Limay, drains most of the Lake District, flowing into the Atlantic at Viedma. Further south the Chubut flows eastwards to reach the sea near Trelew.

Climate

Climate ranges from sub-tropical in the north east to cold temperate in Tierra del Fuego, but is temperate and quite healthy for much of the year in the densely populated central zone. Between December and the end of February Buenos Aires can be oppressively hot and humid. The Andes have a dramatic effect on the climate of the south: although on the Chilean side of the mountains there is adequate rainfall from Santiago southwards, very little of this moisture reaches the Argentine side. Furthermore, the prevailing winds in Patagonia are southwest to northeast from the Pacific. The result is a temperate climate with some mist and fog near the coast, but not much rain. Further inland, the westerlies, having deposited their moisture on the Andes, add strength to the southerly airstream, creating the strong dry wind (*El Pampero*) characteristic of the Pampas. Only when these systems meet humid maritime air in the northeast of the country does rainfall significantly increase, often through violent thunderstorms, with the heaviest precipitation in Mesopotamia where the summer months are particularly wet.

The highest temperatures are found in the northeast where the distance from the sea and the continuous daytime sunshine produce the only frequently recorded air temperatures over 45°C anywhere in South America. The northwest is cooler due to the effects of altitude, rainfall here occurring largely in the summer months. Further details are given in the text.

Vegetation

Few countries offer as wide a range of natural environments as Argentina; its varied vegetation supports equally diverse wildlife. The main types of vegetation are described below. Details of some of the animals to be seen are given where appropriate in the text; to avoid repetition they are not described here. The 10 main vegetation types are as follows:

Llanura Pampeana

Extensive cattle grazing and arable farming have altered the original vegetation of the Pampas, notably through the introduction of tree species, such as the eucalyptus for shelter. The least altered areas of the pampas are the coastal lowlands, the Paraná delta and the southern sierras. The sandy soils of the coastal lowlands, including marshes and estuaries, are home to pampas-grass or *cortadera*. In the marshy parts of the Paraná delta there are tall grasses, with *espinillo* and *ñandubay* (Prosopis) woods in the higher areas. Willows and alisos grow along the river banks while the ceibo, the national flower of Argentina, grows in the nearby woodlands.

Espinal

These are open woodlands and savannas which extend in an arc around the pampas covering southern Corrientes, northern Entre Ríos, central Santa Fe, large parts of Córdoba and San Luis and the centre-west of La Pampa. In these areas xerophitic and thorny woods of prosopis and acacia predominate. The major prosopis species are the *ñandubay*; the white algarrobo; the black algarrobo and the caldén. The *ñandubay* is found in Entre Ríos and parts of Corrientes, along with the white *quebracho*, *tala*, *espinillo* and, on sandy soils, *yatay* palms. The white algarrobo and black algarrobo are found in areas of Santa Fe, Córdoba and San Luis which have been heavily affected by farming. The caldén appears across large areas of La Pampa, southern San Luis and southern Buenos Aires, along with bushes such as the alpataco and the creosote bush (*Larrea*).

Monte

Bushy steppe with few patches of trees, in areas with rainfall from 80 mm to 250 mm. Covering large areas of San Juan, Mendoza, La Pampa and Río Negro, it can be found as far north as Salta and as far south as Chubut. Vegetation includes different species

The Ceibo

This (Erythrina cristagalli) is the national flower and national tree of both Argentina and Uruguay. Though it is the most common tree found in the Plata estuary, it rarely grows above 5 m in this area, whereas in the northern provinces it can reach twice this height. It is a member of the bean (Leguminosae) family and in Spring has racemes of deep scarlet waxy flowers which are the reason for its alternative names of Coral tree or Coxcomb tree. Its fruits are insignificant. Its grey/green leaves reach 10 cm in length and are trifoliate.

of the creosote bush, which have small resinous leaves and yellow flowers, as well as thorny bushes from the cacti family and bushes such as *brea*, *retamo* and *jume*. In the northern areas of *monte* the white algarrobo and sweet algarrobo can be found, while the native willow grows along the riverbanks as far south as the Río Chubut.

Puna & Prepuna Low rainfall, intense radiation and poor soils inhibit vegetation in the *puna*, the major species being adapted by having deep root systems and small leaves; many plants have thorny leaves to deter herbivors. These include species of cacti, which store water in their tissue, and the *yareta*, a cushion-shaped plant, which has been overexploited for firewood, as well as the *tolilla*, the *chijua* and the *tola*. The *queñoa*, which grows to over 5 m high in the sheltered gorges and valleys of the *prepuna*, is the highest growing tree in Argentina. These valleys also support bushes from the *Leguminosae* family such as the *churqui*, and species of cacti, such as the cardoon and the *airampu*, with its colourful blossom.

High Andean Grasslands Extending from Jujuy to Neuquén, and then in discontinuous fashion, south to Tierra del Fuego, these areas range in altitude from over 4,200 m in Jujuy to 500 m in Tierra del Fuego. Main grasses, adapted to the cold and winds include *iros*, *poa* and *stipa* as well as some endemic species.

Subtropical Cloudforest Often known as *yungas*, this extends into Argentina from Bolivia and covers parts of the sub-Andean sierras; it is found in eastern Jujuy, central Salta and Tucuman and eastern Catamarca. Its eastern sides receive the humidity of the winds which cross the Chaco from the Atlantic. Winters are dry but temperature, rainfall and humidity vary with changes in latitude and altitude. These forests are important regulators of the water cycle, preventing erosion and floods. It is best visited in three national parks: Baritú, Calilegua and El Rey.

Vegetation changes with altitude. Along the edge of the Chaco at the foot of the hills and rising to 500 m, where annual rainfall up to 1,000 m, is a transition zone with mainly deciduous trees such as the *palo blanco*, the *lapacho rosado* and *lapacho amarillo* (pink and yellow tabebuia); the *palo borracho* (Chorisia bottle tree), the *tipa blanca* and the huge *timbo colorado* or black eared tree. Higher and reaching from 500 to 800 m in altitude, where there is greater humidity, are montane or laurel forests. Predominant tree species here are the laurel, the jacaranda and the *tipa;* epiphytes (orchids, bromeliads, ferns, lichens, mosses) and climbers are abundant. Above 800 m and rising to 1,300-1,700 m annual rainfall reaches some 3,000 mm, concentrated between November and March. Here myrtle forest predominates, with a great diversity of species, including great trees such as the *horco molle*, a wide range of epiphytes, and, in some areas such as Baritu, tree ferns. Higher still the evergreen trees are replaced by deciduous species, including the mountain pine (Podocarpus), the only conifer native to the northwest, the walnut and the alder. Above these are clumps of *queñoa* and, higher still, mountain meadow grasslands.

The eastern or Wet Chaco is covered by marshlands and ponds with savanna and caranday palm groves, as well as the characteristic red *quebracho,* a hard-wood tree overexploited in the past for tannin. The dry Chaco, further west, is the land of the white *quebracho* as well as cacti such as the quimil (*opuntia*) and the *palo borracho* (*Chorisia*). Similar climatic conditions and vegetation to those in the Dry Chaco are also found in northern San Luis, Córdoba and Santa Fe and eastern Tucumán, Catamarca, Salta, Jujuy, La Rioja and San Juan.

The Chaco

This is found mainly in Misiones, extending southwards along the banks of the Ríos Paraná and Uruguay. The wet climate, with annual rainfall up to 2,000 mm, and high temperatures produce rapid decomposition of organic material. The red soils of this area contain a thin fertile soil layer which is easily eroded.

Subtropical Rainforest

This area offers the widest variety of flora in Argentina. There of over 2,000 known species of vascular plants, about 10% of which are trees. Forest vegetation rises to different strata: the giant trees such as the *palo rosa*, the Misiones cedar, *incienso* and the *guatambú* rise to over 30 m high. The forest canopy includes species such as strangler figs and the pindo palm, while the intermediate strata includes the fast growing *ambay* (*Cecropia*), tree-ferns, the *yerba mate* and bamboos. Llianas, vines and epiphytes such as orchids and bromeliads as well as ferns and even cacti compete in the struggle for sunlight.

In the hills of northwestern Misiones there are remnants of forests of Paraná pine (*Araucaria angustifolia*).

This grows along the eastern edges of the southern Andes, from Neuquén in the north to Tierra del Fuego and Isla de los Estados in the south. These are cool temperate forests including evergreen and deciduous trees. Species of *nothofagus* predominate, the most common being *lenga* (low deciduous beech), *ñire* (high deciduous beech), *coihue* and *guindo*. The *Pehuen* or Monkey puzzle tree (*Araucaria araucana*), is found in northwestern and northcentral Neuquén. The fungus *llao llao* and the hemiparasitic *Misodendron* are also frequent. Flowering bushes include the *notro* (firebush), the *calafate* (Burberis boxifolis) and the *chaura* (prickly heath).

Sub-Antarctic Forest

Areas of the lake district with annual rainfall of over 1,500 mm are covered by Valdivian forest, with a wider range of species. The *coihue* (southern beech) is the predominant species of *nothofagus*, reaching as far south as Lago Buenos Aires. Below colihue canes form a dense undergrowth; flowers include the *amancay* (alstromeria), mutisias, and near streams, the fuschia. Arrayán trees also grow near water, while the Andean Cypress and the *Maiten* grow in the transition zone with the Patagonian steppe.

In areas where annual rainfall reaches over 3,000 mm, there is a wider range of trees, as well as epyphites, climbers, ferns, and lichens such as Old Man's Beard. The *alerce* (larch) is the giant of these forests, rising to over 60 m and, in some cases over 3,000 years old.

Magallanic forest, found from Lago Buenos Aires south to Tierra del Fuego, is dominated by the *guindo* (evergreen beech) as well as the *lenga,* the *ñire* and the *canelo* (winter bark). There are also large areas of peatbog with sphagnum mosses, and even the carnivorous *Drosera uniflora*.

Plantlife in this area has adapted to severe climatic conditions: strong westerly winds, the heavy winter snowfall which occurs in some years, high evaporation in summer, low annual rainfall and sandy soils with a thin fertile layer on top. The northwest of this area is covered by bushy scrublands: species include the *quilembai, molle,* the *algarrobo patagónico,* the *colpiche,* as well as *coiron* grasses. Further south are shrubs such as the *mata negra* and species of *calafate*. Nearer the mountain

Patagonian Steppe

National parks & protected areas

♦ National parks	10 Lanín	20 Quebrada de los	26 Iberá
1 Baritú	11 Lihue Calel	Condoritos	27 Ischigualasto
2 Calilegua	12 Los Alerces	21 Sierra de las	28 Laguna Brava
3 Chaco	13 Los Arrayanes	Quijadas	29 Otamendi
4 Diamante	14 Los Cardones	22 Talampaya	30 Peninsula Valdés
5 El Palmar	15 Los Glaciares	23 Tierra del Fuego	31 San Antonio
6 El Rey	16 Mburucuyá		
7 Iguazú	17 Nahuel Huapi	♦ Nature reserves	♦ Natural Monuments
8 Lago Puelo	18 Perito Moreno	24 Colonia Benitez	32 Bosques Petrificados
9 Laguna Blanco	19 Pilcomayo	25 Formosa	33 Laguna de los Pozuelos

ranges the climate is less severe and the soil more fertile: here there is a herbaceous steppe which includes *coiron blanco* and shrubs such as the *neneo*. Overgrazing by sheep has produced serious desertification in many parts of the Patagonian steppe.

National parks

Argentina has an extensive network of parks and protected areas, the most important of which are designated as national parks. The history of Argentine national parks is a long one, dating from the donation by Francisco 'Perito' Moreno of 7,500 ha of land in the Lake District to the state. This grant formed the basis for the establishment of the first national park, Nahuel Huapi, in 1934.

There are 19 national parks, stretching from Parque Nacional Baritú, on the northern frontier with Bolivia to Parque Nacional Tierra del Fuego in the far south. Additional areas have been designated as natural monuments and natural reserves and there are also provincial parks and reserves. The largest national parks are all in western Argentina; these include a string of eight parks in the Andean foothills in the Lake District and Patagonia. The main national parks and other protected areas are shown on the map and further details of all of these are given in the text.

The main administration office of the Argentine National Parks authority is at Santa Fe 680, near the Plaza San Martín in central Buenos Aires. Leaflets are available on some of the parks. Further details are given under Buenos Aires.

Footnotes

14

Footnotes

Basic Spanish

General pronunciation

The stress in a Spanish word conforms to one of three rules: 1) if the word ends in a vowel, or in **n** or **s**, the accent falls on the penultimate syllable (*vent**a**na, vent**a**nas*). 2) if the word ends in a consonant other than **n** or **s**, the accent falls on the last syllable (*habl**a**r*); 3) if the word is to be stressed on a syllable contrary to either of the above rules, the acute accent on the relevant vowel indicates where the stress is to be placed (*pantal**ó**n, met**á**fora*). Note that adverbs such as *cuando*, 'when', take an accent when used interrogatively: *¿cuándo?*, 'when?'

Vowels
a	not quite as short as in English 'cat'
e	as in English 'pay', but shorter in a syllable ending in a consonant
i	as in English 'seek'
o	as in English 'shop', but more like 'pope' when the vowel ends a syllable
u	as in English 'food'; after 'q' and in 'gue', 'gui', **u** is unpronounced; in 'güe' and 'güi' it is pronounced
y	when a vowel, pronounced like 'i'; when a semiconsonant or consonant, it is pronounced like English 'yes'
ai, ay	as in English 'ride'
ei, ey	as in English 'they'
oi, oy	as in English 'toy'

Unless listed below **consonants** can be pronounced in Spanish as they are in English.

b, v	their sound is interchangeable and is a cross between the English 'b' and 'v', except at the beginning of a word or after 'm' or 'n' when it is like English 'b'
c	like English 'k', except before 'e' or 'i' when it is as the 's' in English 'sip'
g	before 'e' and 'i' it is the same as **j**
h	when on its own, never pronounced
j	as the 'ch' in the Scottish 'loch'
ll	as the 'g' in English 'beige'
ñ	as the 'ni' in English 'onion'
rr	trilled much more strongly than in English
x	depending on its location, pronounced as in English 'fox', or 'sip', or like 'gs'
z	as the 's' in English 'sip'

Greetings, Courtesies
hello	*hola*	pleased to meet you	*mucho gusto/encantado/ encantada*
good morning	*buenos días*		
good afternoon evening/ night	*buenas tardes noches*	please	*por favor*
		thank you (very much)	*(muchas) gracias*
goodbye	*adiós/chao*		
see you later	*hasta luego*	yes	*sí*
how are you?	*¿cómo está?/¿cómo estás?*	no	*no*
		excuse me/ I beg your pardon	*permiso*

Footnotes

I do not understand	*no entiendo*
please speak slowly	*hable despacio por favor*
what is your name	*¿cómo se llama?*
Go away!	*¡Váyase!*

Basic questions

where is_?	*¿dónde está_?*
how much does it cost?	*¿cuánto cuesta?*
how much is it?	*¿cuánto es?*
when?	*¿cuándo?*
when does the bus leave?	*¿a qué hora sale el autobús?*
arrive?	*llega -*
why?	*¿por qué?*
what for?	*¿para qué?*
what time is it?	*¿qué hora es?*
how do I get to_?	*¿cómo llegar a_?*
is this the way to the church?	*¿la iglesia está por aquí?*

Basics

bathroom/toilet	*el baño*
police (policeman)	*la policía (el policía)*
hotel	*el hotel (la pensión, el residencial, el alojamiento)*
restaurant	*el restaurante*
post office	*el correo*
telephone office	*el centro de llamadas*
supermarket	*el supermercado*
bank	*el banco*
exchange house	*la casa de cambio*
exchange rate	*la tasa de cambio*
notes/coins	*los billetes/las monedas*
travellers' cheques	*los travelers/los cheques de viajero*
cash	*el efectivo*
breakfast	*el desayuno*
lunch	*el almuerzo*
dinner/supper	*la cena*
meal	*la comida*
drink	*la bebida*
mineral water	*el agua mineral*
soft fizzy drink	*la gaseosa/cola*
beer	*la cerveza*
without sugar	*sin azúcar*
without meat	*sin carne*

Getting around

on the left right	*a la izquierda/ derecha*
straight on	*derecho*
second street on the left	*la segunda calle a la izquierda*
to walk	*caminar*
bus station	*la terminal (terrestre)*
train station	*la estación (de tren/ferrocarril)*
bus	*el bus/ el autobus/la flota/ el colectivo/ el micro etc*
train	*el tren*
airport	*el aeropuerto*
aeroplane/airplane	*el avión*
first/second class	*primera/segunda clase*
ticket	*el boleto*
ticket office	*la taquilla*
bus stop	*la parada*

Accommodation

room	*el cuarto/la habitación*
single/double	*sencillo/doble*
with two beds	*con dos camas*
with private bathroom	*con baño*
hot/cold water	*agua caliente/fría*
noisy	*ruidoso*
to make up/clean	*limpiar*
sheets	*las sábanas*
blankets	*las mantas*
pillows	*las almohadas*
clean/dirty towels	*toallas limpias/sucias*
toilet paper	*el papel higiénico*

Health

chemist	*farmacia*
(for) pain	*(para) dolor*
stomach	*el estómago*
head	*la cabeza*
fever/sweat	*la fiebre/el sudor*
diarrhoea	*la diarrea*
blood	*la sangre*
altitude sickness	*el soroche*
doctor	*el médico*
condoms	*los preservativos*

contraceptive (pill)	*anticonceptivo (la píldora anticonceptiva)*	eight	*ocho*
		nine	*nueve*
		ten	*diez*
period/towels	*la regla/las toallas*	eleven	*once*
		twelve	*doce*
contact lenses	*las lentes de contacto*	thirteen	*trece*
		fourteen	*catorce*
aspirin	*la aspirina*	fifteen	*quince*
		sixteen	*dieciseis*

Time

		seventeen	*diecisiete*
at one o'clock	*a la una*	eighteen	*dieciocho*
at half past two/ two thirty	*a las dos y media*	nineteen	*diecinueve*
		twenty	*veinte*
at a quarter to three	*a cuarto para las tres* or *a las tres menos quince*	twenty one	*veintiuno*
		thirty	*treinta*
		forty	*cuarenta*
it's one o'clock	*es la una*	fifty	*cincuenta*
it's seven o'clock	*son las siete*	sixty	*sesenta*
it's twenty past six/ six twenty	*son las seis y veinte*	seventy	*setenta*
		eighty	*ochenta*
it's five to nine	*son cinco para las nueve/son las nueve menos cinco*	ninety	*noventa*
		hundred	*cien* or *ciento*
		thousand	*mil*
in ten minutes	*en diez minutos*		

Key verbs

To Go *ir*

> I go *voy*; you go (familiar singular) *vas*; he, she, it goes, you (unfamiliar singular) go *va*; we go *vamos*; they, you (plural) go *van*.

five hours	*cinco horas*
does it take long?	*¿tarda mucho?*
Monday	*lunes*
Tuesday	*martes*
Wednesday	*miercoles*
Thursday	*jueves*
Friday	*viernes*
Saturday	*sábado*
Sunday	*domingo*
January	*enero*
February	*febrero*
March	*marzo*
April	*abril*
May	*mayo*
June	*junio*
July	*julio*
August	*agosto*
September	*septiembre*
October	*octubre*
November	*noviembre*
December	*diciembre*

To Have (possess) *tener*

> *tengo; tienes; tiene; tenemos; tienen* (also used as To Be, as in 'I am hungry' *tengo hambre*)
> (NB *haber* also means to have, but is used with other verbs, as in 'he has gone' *ha ido. he; has; ha; hemos; han. Hay* means 'there is'; perhaps more common is *No hay* meaning 'there isn't any')

To Be (in a permanent state) *ser*

> *soy* (profesor - I am a teacher); *eres; es; somos; son*

To Be (positional or temporary state) *estar*

> *estoy (en Londres* - I am in London*); estás; está (contenta* - she is happy); *estamos; están.*

Numbers

one	*uno/una*
two	*dos*
three	*tres*
four	*cuatro*
five	*cinco*
six	*seis*
seven	*siete*

This section has been compiled on the basis of glossaries compiled by André de Mendonça and David Gilmour of South American Experience, London, and the Latin American Travel Advisor, No 9, March 1996.

Index

Shorts

Map index

Footnotes

Sales & distribution

Footprint Handbooks
6 Riverside Court
Lower Bristol Road
Bath BA2 3DZ England
T 01225 469141
F 01225 469461
discover
@footprintbooks.com

Australia
Peribo Pty
58 Beaumont Road
Mt Kuring-Gai
NSW 2080
T 02 9457 0011
F 02 9457 0022

Austria
Freytag-Berndt Artaria
Kohlmarkt 9
A-1010 Wien
T 01533 2094
F 01533 8685

Freytag-Berndt
Sporgasse 29
A-8010 Graz
T 0316 818230
F 3016 818230-30

Belgium
Craenen BVBA
Mechelsesteenweg 633
B-3020 Herent
T 016 23 90 90
F 016 23 97 11

Waterstones
The English Bookshop
Blvd Adolphe Max 71-75
B-1000 Brussels
T 02 219 5034

Canada
Ulysses Travel Publications
4176 rue Saint-Denis
Montréal
Québec H2W 2M5
T 514 843 9882
F 514 843 9448

Europe
Bill Bailey
16 Devon Square
Newton Abbott
Devon TQ12 2HR. UK
T 01626 331079
F 01626 331080

Denmark
Nordisk Korthandel
Studiestraede 26-30 B
DK-1455 Copenhagen K
T 3338 2638
F 3338 2648

Scanvik Books
Esplanaden 8B
DK-1263 Copenhagen K
T 3312 7766
F 3391 2882

Finland
Akateeminen Kirjakauppa
Keskuskatu 1
FIN-00100 Helsinki
T 09 121 4151
F 09 121 4441

Suomalainen Kirjakauppa
Koivuvaarankuja 2
01640 Vantaa 64
F 09 852751

France
FNAC – major branches

L'Astrolabe
46 rue de Provence
F-75009 Paris 9e
T 01 42 85 42 95
F 01 45 75 92 51

VILO Diffusion
25 rue Ginoux
F-75015 Paris
T 01 45 77 08 05
F 01 45 79 97 15

Germany
GeoCenter ILH
Schockenriedstrasse 44
D-70565 Stuttgart
T 0711 781 94610
F 0711 781 94654

Brettschneider
Feldkirchnerstrasse 2
D-85551 Heimstetten
T 089 990 20330
F 089 990 20331

Geobuch
Rosental 6
D-80331 München
T 089 265030
F 089 263713

Gleumes
Hohenstaufenring 47-51
D-50674 Köln
T 0221 215650

Globetrotter Ausrustungen
Wiesendamm 1
D-22305 Hamburg
T040 679 66190
F 040 679 66183

Dr Götze
Bleichenbrücke 9
D-2000 Hamburg 1
T 040 3031 1009-0

Hugendubel Buchhandlung
Nymphenburgerstrasse 25
D-80335 München
T 089 238 9412
F 089 550 1853

Kiepert Buchhandlung
Hardenbergstrasse 4-5
D-10623 Berlin 12
T 030 311 880
F 030 311 88120

Greece
GC Eleftheroudakis
17 Panepistemiou
Athens 105 64
T 01 331 4180-83
F 01 323 9821

India
India Book Distributors
1007/1008 Arcadia
195 Nariman Point
Mumbai 400 021
T 91 22 282 5220
F 91 22 287 2531

Israel
Eco Trips
8 Tverya Street
Tel Aviv 63144
T 03 528 4113
F 03 528 8269

For a fuller list, see www.footprintbooks.com

Italy
Librimport
Via Biondelli 9
I-20141 Milano
T 02 8950 1422
F 02 8950 2811

Libreria del Viaggiatore
Via dell Pelegrino 78
I-00186 Roma
T/F 06 688 01048

Netherlands
Nilsson & Lamm bv
Postbus 195
Pampuslaan 212
N-1380 AD Weesp
T 0294 494949
F 0294 494455

Waterstones
Kalverstraat 152
1012 XE Amsterdam
T 020 638 3821

New Zealand
Auckland Map Centre
Dymocks

Norway
Schibsteds Forlag A/S
Akersgata 32 - 5th Floor
Postboks 1178 Sentrum
N-0107 Oslo
T 22 86 30 00
F 22 42 54 92

Tanum
Karl Johansgate 37-41
PO Box 1177 Sentrum
N-0107 Oslo 1
T 22 41 11 00
F 22 33 32 75

Olaf Norlis
Universitetsgt 24
N-1062 Oslo
T 22 00 43 00

Pakistan
Pak-American Commercial
Hamid Chambers
Zaib-un Nisa Street
Saddar, PO Box 7359
Karachi
T 21 566 0418
F 21 568 3611

South Africa
Faradawn CC
PO Box 1903
Saxonwold 2132
T 011 885 1787
F 011 885 1829

South America
Humphrys Roberts
Associates
Caixa Postal 801-0
Ag. Jardim da Gloria
06700-970 Cotia SP
Brazil
T 011 492 4496
F 011 492 6896

Southeast Asia
APA Publications
38 Joo Koon Road
Singapore 628990
T 865 1600
F 861 6438

In Hong Kong, Malaysia,
Singapore and Thailand:
MPH, Kinokuniya, Times

Spain
Altaïr
C/Balmes 69
08007 Barcelona
T 933 233062
F 934 512559

Altaïr
Gaztambide 31
28015 Madrid
T 0915 435300
F 0915 443498

Libros de Viaje
C/Serrano no 41
28001 Madrid
T 01 91 577 9899
F 01 91 577 5756

Il Corte Inglés – major
branches

Sweden
Hedengrens Bokhandel
PO Box 5509
S-11485 Stockholm
T 08 611 5132

Kart Centrum
Vasagatan 16
S-11120 Stockholm
T 08 411 1697

Kartforlaget
Skolgangen 10
S-80183 Gavle
T 026 633000
F 026 124204

Lantmateriet Kartbutiken
Kungsgatan 74
S-11122 Stockholm
T 08 202 303
F 08 202 711

Switzerland
Office du Livre OLF
ZI3, Corminboeuf
CH-1701 Fribourg
T 026 467 5111
F 026 467 5666

Schweizer Buchzentrum
Postfach
CH-4601 Olten
T 062 209 2525
F 062 209 2627

Travel Bookshop
Rindermarkt 20
Postfach 216
CH-8001 Zürich
T 01 252 3883
F 01 252 3832

Tanzania
A Novel Idea
The Slipway
PO Box 76513
Dar es Salaam
T/F 051 601088

USA
NTC/ Contemporary
4255 West Touhy Avenue
Lincolnwood
Illinois 60646-1975
T 847 679 5500
F 847 679 2494

Barnes & Noble, Borders,
specialist travel bookstores

Advertisers

Argentina

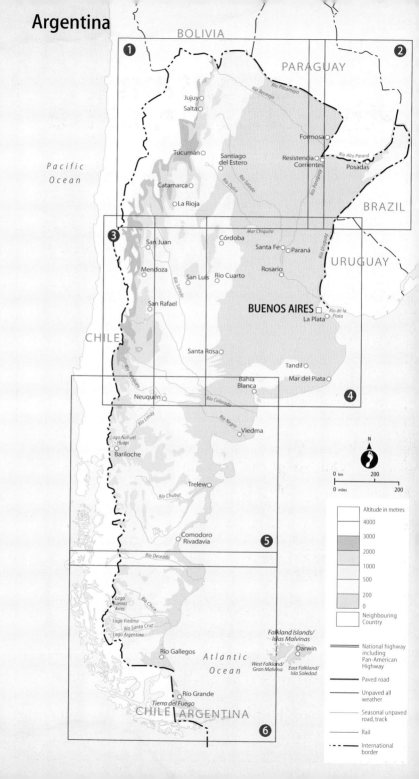

BOLIVIA

PARAGUAY

1

2

Jujuy
Salta

Río Bermejo
Río Pilcomayo

Formosa

Tucumán

Santiago del Estero

Resistencia
Corrientes

Río Alto Paraná

Posadas

Pacific Ocean

Catamarca

Río Dulce

Río Salado

Río Paraguay

La Rioja

BRAZIL

3

San Juan

Córdoba

Mar Chiquita

Santa Fe
Paraná

Río Uruguay

URUGUAY

Mendoza

San Luis

Río Cuarto

Rosario

Río Salado

San Rafael

BUENOS AIRES
La Plata

Río de la Plata

CHILE

Santa Rosa

Tandil

Mar del Plata

Bahía Blanca

4

Neuquén

Río Neuquén

Río Colorado

Río Limay

Río Negro

Viedma

Lago Nahuel Huapi

Bariloche

Trelew

Río Chubut

Altitude in metres

4000

3000

2000

1000

500

200

0

Neighbouring Country

Comodoro Rivadavia

5

Río Deseado

Lago Buenos Aires

Río Chico

Lago Viedma

Río Santa Cruz

Lago Argentino

Falkland Islands/
Islas Malvinas

Darwin

Atlantic Ocean

Río Gallegos

West Falkland/
Gran Malvina

East Falkland/
Isla Soledad

National highway including Pan-American Highway

Paved road

Río Grande

Tierra del Fuego

CHILE ARGENTINA

6

Unpaved all weather

Seasonal unpaved road, track

Rail

International border

N

0 km 200
0 miles 200

Map 2

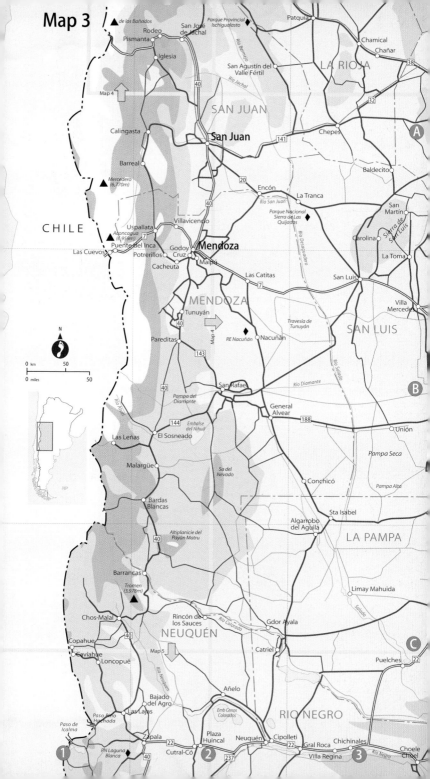

Map 4

Map 5

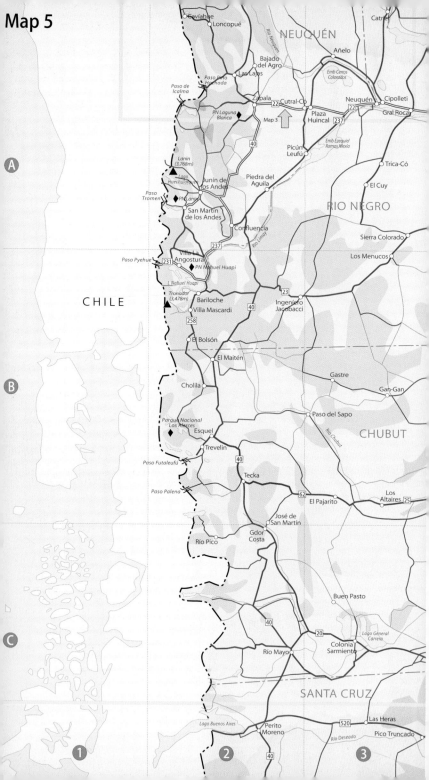

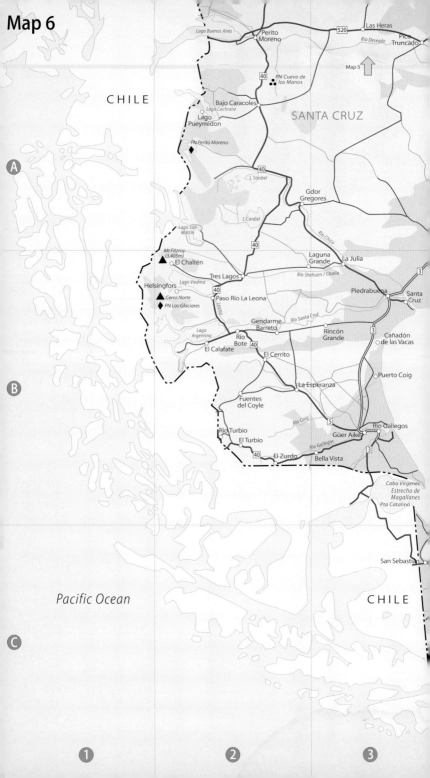

Map 6

Caleta Olivia

Fitz Roy
Jaramillo

Río Deseado

Puerto Deseado

*Reserva
Natural
Río Delgado*

SANTA CRUZ

Atlantic Ocean

3

San Julián
*Reserva Natural
Río Delgado*

N

0 km 50
0 miles 50

Pta de Arenas

3

Río Grande

TIERRA DEL
FUEGO

PN Tierra
del Fuego
*Sierra de Beauvoir
Lago Fagnano*

3

Sierra de Vinciguerra

Ushuaia

Harberton

Canal Beagle

*Estrecho de
La Maire*

C San Diego

I de los
Estados

A

B

C

4

5

6

Will you help us?

We try as hard as we can to make each Footprint Handbook as up-to-date and accurate as possible but, of course, things always change. Many people write to us - with corrections, new information, or simply comments.

If you want to let us know about an experience or adventure - hair-raising or mundane, good or bad, exciting or boring - we would be delighted to hear from you. Please give us as precise information as possible, quoting the edition number (you'll find it on the front cover) and page number of the Handbook you are using.

Your help will be greatly appreciated, especially by other travellers. In return we will send you details about our special guidebook offer.

email Footprint at:
arg2_online@footprintbooks.com

or write to:
Elizabeth Taylor
Footprint Handbooks
6 Riverside Court
Lower Bristol Road
Bath BA2 3DZ
UK